The

HORIZON
COOKBOOK

and Illustrated History of
Eating and Drinking
through the Ages

The

HORIZON
COOKBOOK

and Illustrated History of Eating and Drinking through the Ages

by

WILLIAM HARLAN HALE

and

THE EDITORS OF HORIZON MAGAZINE

EDITOR IN CHARGE
WENDY BUEHR

RECIPES EDITOR TATIANA McKENNA

HISTORICAL FOODS CONSULTANT MIMI SHERATON

PUBLISHED BY
AMERICAN HERITAGE PUBLISHING CO., INC.

BOOK TRADE DISTRIBUTION BY
DOUBLEDAY & COMPANY, INC.

TABLE OF CONTENTS

HORIZON
BOOK DIVISION

EDITORIAL DIRECTOR
Richard M. Ketchum

GENERAL EDITOR
Alvin M. Josephy, Jr.

Staff for this Book

EDITOR IN CHARGE
Wendy Buehr

ART DIRECTOR
Mary Ann Joulwan

FOOD EDITOR
Meryle R. Evans

COPY EDITOR
Brenda Savard Bennerup

ASSISTANT EDITORS
Nathan Adams
Margot Price Brill
Jane Hoover Polley

PICTURE RESEARCHER
Sara Hunter Hudson

TEXT RESEARCHER
Nancy Simon Kaufman

ART ASSISTANT
Carol Fogel

EDITORIAL ASSISTANTS
Pam Meacham Ross
Shelley Benoit

EUROPEAN BUREAU
Gertrudis Feliu, *Chief*
Mary Jenkins

AMERICAN HERITAGE
PUBLISHING CO., INC.

PRESIDENT
James Parton

EDITORIAL COMMITTEE
Joseph J. Thorndike, *Chairman*
Oliver Jensen
Richard M. Ketchum

SENIOR ART DIRECTOR
Irwin Glusker

PUBLISHER, HORIZON MAGAZINE
Paul Gottlieb

FRONTISPIECE: *For guidance in good party giving, hosts might do well to follow the example of the gods, as shown by the seventeenth-century Fleming, Hendrick van Balen the Elder.*
MUSEE DES BEAUX ARTS, ANGERS; GIRAUDON

PART ONE

Illustrated History
of Eating and Drinking
through the Ages

INTRODUCTION

"A clever cook," Erasmus observed, "can make . . . good meat of a whetstone." "A fine sauce will make even an elephant or a grandfather palatable," added the irreverent gourmet, Grimod de La Reynière.

Today, with quality meats, fresh vegetables, and succulent fruits available in most American and European markets, the cook is seldom called upon to practice such magical arts. But throughout history and in many less fortunate parts of the modern world, creative cooking has played a crucial role in making limited food resources the stuff of nourishment, ritual, and communal celebration.

The ancients, for whom eating and drinking were chief public divertisements, devoted a great deal of thought to the place of the cook in the cosmos. Cooks, they reasoned, were only slightly lower than the gods in divine gifts, for they had brought men from cannibalism to civilization with their sauces. A *Coquus Gloriosus*, it was said, was the first earthling to master the Promethean fire, the first to wear the victor's crown at the Olympian games; it was a cook from whom Bacchus was descended and a cook, one Cadmus of Phoenicia, who taught the West the alphabet. Is it any wonder that a fish, exquisitely prepared by one of that noble profession, was seen to smile with satisfaction as it simmered in the pan?

The Greeks were so enamored of the dinner hour that they could make it last for days on end (the dialogue of one symposium of enthusiastic eaters recorded by Athenaeus fills fifteen books). The Romans would as soon have read recipe books as odes. On the other side of the world, men no less than Confucius and Lao-tse turned their deepest thoughts to the kitchen. As

Brillat-Savarin, the ideological descendant of these classical gourmets observed in the eighteenth century, "the pleasures of the table are of all times and all ages, of every country and of every day."

The pursuit of these pleasures has changed the face of the earth. In search of better, more reliable food sources nomadic man matured into farmer and husbandman, history's first technologist; and his ventures to sea as fisherman emboldened him to set sail for exotic spices, turning once-legendary lands into familiar market places. In all this Europe has been both prime mover and principal beneficiary. Rice from the Orient and corn and potatoes from the Americas have long since become staples of the Western diet. Coffee, tea, sparkling wines, and distilled liquors have provided the *raison d'être* for new rituals of hospitality. New kinds of public eating and drinking establishments have evolved to serve a more sociable, leisured population. And as foods of better quality and more variety have become available, so, too, cooking techniques have become more sophisticated.

Much remains to be solved before all the world will share in these good things. Cockaigne, that secular Paradise where the rivers flow with wine and there is cake enough for everyone, is as much a dream as the ancient Greek Elysium. But as the Roman Persius wisely predicted some twenty centuries ago, the palate has truly been "the teacher of art and the giver of ingenuity," and for all anyone can guess in this year, new foods and flavors may lie still untapped in the laboratories. It is a thought which would have tantalized Erasmus and the good Grimod, who knew—and as this history will tell—a clever cook can conquer almost anything.   *The Editors*

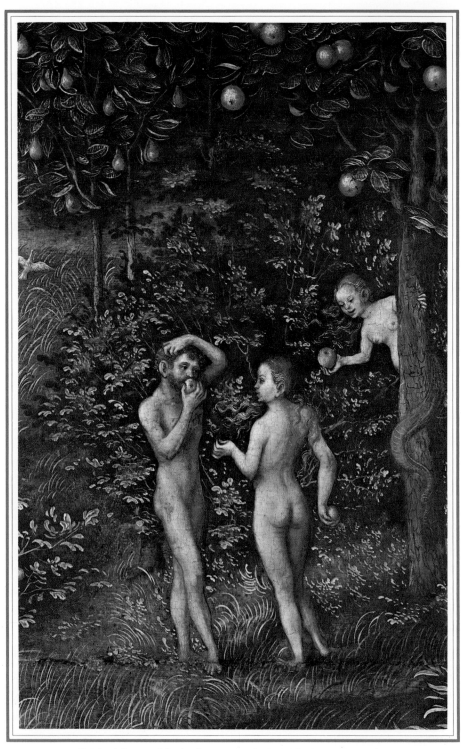

Original sin—and food—from a 1530 painting by Lucas Cranach

FIRST
THE
APPLE

Man lives by food and in great part by its festivities. Beasts forage or prey until they have a bellyful, but man very early invented that basic social rite, the meal. The meal gave rise to the feast, often shared with his gods, and the feast one day was to evolve into the massive nineteenth-century Sunday dinner of Western peoples.

Innumerable occasions, religious and secular, over the centuries have called for a ceremonial board—birthdays, harvest days, holy days, even death days. In the *Iliad* King Priam ends the funeral for his slain son Hector with a banquet—the first wake known to literature. The custom of the birthday party, the historian Herodotus tells us, was well established among ancient Persians of rank, who liked to observe their anniversaries "with a dinner of special magnificence," having "an ox or a horse or a camel or a donkey baked whole" for the event. Man's very calendar, with its survivals of seasonal celebrations, describes his ancestral absorption with the gathering of his crops and the rebirth of spring. At harvest time ancient man approached his deities with sacrifices or first fruits; we have Thanksgiving and recall, if we do not practice, the custom of grace before meat. The ancient Hebraic rite of the consumption of the paschal lamb along with unleavened bread at Passover stands in close relation to that most solemn observance of Christendom, Easter, and both suggest some elements of the ancient festivals that marked the beginning of the planting season. The Occidental New Year, which is widely celebrated today with tin horns and all-night cavorting, was (before Caesar's Romans reformed the calendar and declared wintry Januarius to be the first month) marked in many cultures by rites of atonement and purification followed by feasts for the encouragement of fertility and new crops. The Babylonians, the Western world's first astronomers, reckoned the year from either the seedtime moon of March or the harvest moon of September, and they observed the first days of their new year somewhat as earnest Christians keep the Lenten season.

In the beginning there was fire, and when primitive man learned to capture and use it rather than flee from it in terror like the other animals, a profound distinction arose between his way of life and theirs. Having provided himself with a source of warmth and light against the cold and dark, he learned before long to throw killed game upon the flame rather than devour it raw, and so laid the basis for an entirely new diet (and for the gradual recession of his huge jaws). Just when the hearth came into being remains a matter of conjecture; recent discoveries in the Durance valley in France date man-made fires back some 750,000 years. Probably it was the hearth, with the clan eating their cooked kill around it and protected by its glow against hostile beasts, that served to turn primeval man into a social animal.

Yet for aeons he remained only the most elementary sort of cook. Down

Paleolithic meat, by a Lascaux cave painter

through paleolithic times—that is, to some twelve thousand years ago—the only method of cooking was that of roasting over the open fire. (The pleasure so many urban and suburban men in our time find in staging a cookout or a barbecue may reflect a primordial instinct—besides which, there are few delights finer than a cut of beef raising its savor over a bed of charcoal and hickory.) A more varied diet was to arise only with the invention of indirect, or "off-the-fire," cooking, which involved utensils—a slab for frying, a pot for boiling, and an oven for baking.

Early man discovered that the hard kernel of wild grasses, all but indigestible to him in its raw form, could be made palatable if its husk were cracked open by fire. Experiments were no doubt made with "popping" hard grains by throwing them on the coals, but there was no way to retrieve them from the fire; a stone slab placed over the flame was a logical improvement. It would transmit heat to the kernels gradually and permit them to be recovered. This was the first frying pan. A related discovery, also originating with the use of stones as a heat-transmitting agent, involved water as the softener and cooking medium. Long before earthenware or iron vessels came into being, prehistoric man hit upon the scheme of lining a pit with stones preheated by prolonged direct contact with fire and filling the pit with water. When the water rose to a boil, he would immerse the kernels. To this day the cooking pit survives in the New England coastal ceremony of the clambake, with shellfish steamed by the juices of sea grasses tossed upon hot stones embedded in sand. For prehistoric man the pit was the vessel for his first crude gruels or mashes. What he had created was neither an efficient cookpot nor an oven, but it foreshadowed the principles of both. Along the way he may also have witnessed for the first time the chemical process of fermentation, since kernels when watered and heated and left to stand awhile under warm conditions become affected by the converting yeasts. Aeons later the yeasts were to make man both a baker and a brewer. Which came first is uncertain.

Yet cookery could not progress beyond its simplest stages without containers—above all, the vessel able to hold liquids and solid foods over continuing heat. Stewing, porridge- and soup-making, pickling in brine, controlled fermentation—all these processes involving extraction and preservation of

food flavors—required a pot. The rise of culinary art began, in effect, with the bowl of clay. Clay also went into that other major late-prehistoric invention, the oven—of all man's cooking containers perhaps the most valuable since it provided his daily bread. First constructed of packed clay, later of brick, it provided the dry, even heat that made baking possible.

Man's outburst of inventiveness in cooking techniques and utensils coincided with a period that saw fundamental change in his estate. Indeed, these innovations were a basic part of that change, often called the neolithic revolution. The era beginning some eight millennia before the time of Christ saw men gradually shifting from simple hunters and gatherers of food to shepherds, stockmen, and cultivators. The revolution—perhaps more accurately evolution—proceeded at different paces in various areas of the neolithic world, with herding an intermediate stage along the way to civilization. Man's nomadic ways would continue even after he had domesticated animals, but farming meant settlement and the creation of fixed communities. Grain, grown from seed, had to be sown on prepared soil at the proper season and harvested at the

Sumerian chafing dish with ornamental legs

The Gift of Fire

*F*rom his lofty vantage atop Mount Olympus, Zeus had been noting man's progress with jealous alarm. To keep the social climber in his place, he decided to withhold the precious element of fire, decreeing that raw meat should be man's diet. But Zeus had not figured on the meddlesome Prometheus. This self-appointed champion of mankind promptly lit a torch from the fiery chariot of the sun, hid its glowing ember in a fennel stalk, and brought the gift to earth. Having outwitted the tyrannical Zeus once, Prometheus was emboldened to test his strength further. He took man aside and showed him how to prepare his sacrifices so that the gods might be tricked into eating the tougher joints while leaving the most tender fillets for the cook. For this and other effronteries, so the Greek legend goes, Zeus finally had the young Titan bound to the highest peak in the Caucasus with a hungry vulture as his sole companion. Of small comfort to the beleaguered Prometheus, man has never ceased to be grateful. Fire festivals no less than harvest celebrations were among the first rituals of civilizing man, and many continue to this day in forms altered to suit the doctrines of religions that have superseded them.

From China, where the three-day "eating of cold food" was observed in April, to Peru, where the summer solstice was greeted by fasting, the custom of extinguishing the old flame and kindling the new has universally symbolized man's search for rebirth. The New Year, Easter, May Day, Midsummer Night, Halloween, Christmas—all can trace some part of their ritual to celebrations of fire which banished their enemies, purged their fields of blight, forged their metals, chased away the cold and damp, and baked their festive cakes. In Rome a temple was built to Vesta, goddess of the hearth (the goddess of the oven rated only a festival), and the ceremonial flame was maintained there by a sorority of patrician virgins, the only mortals deemed suitably pure to perform the sacred tasks of relighting the fire on the first day of the new year, March 1. Appointed for terms of thirty years and paid a small salary for their services, the vestal virgins were expected to remain chaste, under penalty of being buried alive should they stray from their appointed rounds—keeping the state's flame alive as their own fires dimmed.

proper time. Seed had to be preserved for the next season; against a hand-to-mouth existence, granaries, with a continuing capital of food, were needed. The possibilities for leisure and the crafts this increasing security afforded

Ornamented Iranian bowl

laid the basis for stable life and civilized societies. It replaced a haphazard existence with opportunities for ritual, religion, and social cooperation. It provided time to develop better agricultural tools and techniques. (The potter's art and a rudimentary calendar were among the first results. In observing the cycle of the year—floodtime, seedtime, harvest—for his own practical necessity, man learned to watch the movement of sun, moon, and stars.)

The wild upland grasses of regions such as Anatolia and western Persia were parents of the wheat, barley, and rye of early Mesopotamia, where man's first cities arose. In neolithic China the first crop was millet, to be followed by rice perhaps a long time after the cultivation of rice had begun in India; the first written Chinese mention of rice dates back to only 2800 B.C. The ancestral wild herds of the Middle East gave rise to that region's plentiful stock of domestic sheep, goats, and cattle, with the result that stock raising could be combined

with farming. A man's wealth might then be counted in kine. (Thus Job in his prosperity could boast of "seven thousand sheep, and three thousand camels, and five hundred yoke of oxen, and five hundred she asses," which made him "the greatest of all the men of the east.") Other areas remained poor in meat, and their cultures—those of China and Japan in particular—developed largely on a vegetarian basis. In the pre-Columbian civilizations of Central and South America, there were almost no domestic animals for meat, milk, wool, or burden (the Andean llama and alpaca coming closest in usefulness), but there was extremely varied domestication of plants: in addition to bringing corn to a high state of cultivation, the Indians raised the indigenous potato, numerous forms of beans, gourds, and squashes, and such other produce unknown in the Old World as the tomato, the peanut, the green pepper, chocolate, vanilla, chili, the guava, the avocado, and the pineapple. Indeed, as one leading scholar, Richard S. MacNeish, writes, by the time their European conquerors arrived in the sixteenth century A.D., Indians "had made agricultural advances far beyond those of the Old World."

Ultimately the New World's cornucopia of vegetables and fruits was to be brought to Europe to augment the diet of the Old World, one of the most notable contributions being the potato, which became the staple of the German and the Irish diets. At the same time, Europe was to introduce into the Americas its cattle and sheep, thereby providing (along with the horse) entirely new

15

bases for American existence. Yet this exchange, while particularly dramatic, was only one peak of a process of food migration and development that had been going on since neolithic times. Every food plant important to man was not only growing in that early era, but many were already spreading far from their places of origin, undergoing important genetic changes as they took root in new soils and climates.

Not only were wheat, barley, and rice on the move. A species of broad bean

Assurbanipal partying with his Assyrian queen

was spreading from western Asia over much of Europe and was used in Bronze Age Troy, Egypt, and even Spain. The lentil, possibly native to lands near the Himalayas, was known to Assyrians and early Egyptians and was brought to the neolithic Balkans and southern Germany by Danubian peoples. Cabbage, which may have originated in the Mediterranean area, appears to have been raised by Bronze Age lake dwellers beside Lake Zurich. A form of spinach, perhaps related to the types in distant Turkistan and Afghanistan, was consumed in central Europe at about the

same time. The peach spread from Persia; the plum perhaps from Russia or the Balkans. The Roman gastronome Lucullus is reported to have brought back the cherry tree from the Black Sea; meanwhile, the apple tree had long been flourishing north of the Alps, while the vine sacred to Dionysus had been transplanted from Asia Minor to lands as remote as Punjab and Kashmir.

The history of rising civilization is intertwined from the start with man's far-ranging pursuit of food and the usages, rituals, and pleasures he has derived from it. At the outset it might be remarked that man is omnivorous. He is also voracious. At the same time he tends to be ceremonious about eating. The story of his relationship to food is therefore complex. Other animals are highly selective in their diets, some being only red-meat eaters, others only plant eaters, still others partial to insects or spawn of the sea. But man—barring occasional food laws and taboos—will and does ingest almost every edible substance that nature provides. Included on man's menu are blubber of seal (among the Eskimos), sheep's eyes (an Arab specialty), frogs' legs (among the French), larks' tongues (favored by the Elizabethans), hippopotami (particularly in Uganda), water lilies (among the Chinese), animals' intestines cooked into a pudding with gruel (enjoyed by ancient Greeks), the organs of sheep mixed with suet, onions, and oatmeal (the Scotsmen's "haggis"), and domestic cats stewed in sherry (a favorite among the Basque workmen).

The intensity of man's quest for food has left its mark upon the entire globe, which he has scoured and often despoiled in the pursuit. In northwestern China, vast areas of the once-rich "yellow earth" that supported an advanced Bronze Age culture and gave rise to Chinese civilization have long since been eroded and reduced to rubble and wind-blown loess—the result of a process of overuse that may have begun some four thousand years ago. Ancient Sumerian tablets tell that the lords of Lagash garnered for their tables, and for those of their gods, such Mesopotamian bounty as goats, sheep, oxen, doves, chickens, ducks, fish, figs, dates, cucumbers, butter, oil, and grain; but the country around ruined Lagash today is largely barren wasteland. Only broken monuments survive in sandy Libya to testify that here once lay the most ample granary of imperial Rome, despoiled by human locusts.

Wars have been fought and whole subcontinents won not only for the sake of more meat or fish or grain, but for the very spices and condiments with which to preserve and flavor them. The Apocrypha of the Old Testament speaks of salt as "basic to all the needs of man's life." It had become an essential from the time man learned to cook and to try to preserve his foods, and it was accessible to many early peoples in the form of deposits such as those of Syrian oases, Dead Sea shores, Nile delta lakes, and Alpine outcrops. Early Iron Age men cut into the salt-bearing strata around Hallstatt high in the Austrian mountains; and the Roman historian Strabo writes that the salt mines of Spain's Sierra Nevada were being worked more than five centuries before Christ. But

the Western world's urge for more and finer spices helped set in motion adventures that were ultimately to encircle the globe. Saffron and myrrh could be had from Mesopotamia; ginger was sought from Arabia; the quest for pepper and cloves, nutmeg and cinnamon, led—once Arab and Ottoman interference with the trade had been broken—to the opening and colonizing of the Far East. The hunt for new fisheries in the Atlantic, particularly after the Hansa seaports had monopolized North Sea and Baltic grounds

A hurried meal at an Assyrian army kitchen

in the fourteenth century, had much to do with the exploration of the New World; the search for a Northwest Passage undoubtedly was bent as much on spices as it was on the rumored gold and rubies of Cathay.

At the same time, while lusting for his food, man has revered its sources. From the start he has seen it not only as the result of his hunt or toil, but as a gift bestowed (and sometimes withheld) by powers greater than himself. Man's gratitude to his gods for the fruits of the earth has taken many forms. The Indians of southwestern Yucatán,

17

Gold ewer from Mesopotamia

where maize ("Indian corn") had been developed from a wild pod-enclosed kernel into a cereal grain, demonstrated this humility well. Anthropologists Robert Redfield and Warner Lloyd have written of their agriculture:

"It is not simply a way of securing food. It is also a way of worshipping the gods. Before a man plants, he builds an altar in the field and prays there. He must not speak boisterously in the cornfield; it is a sort of temple. The cornfield is planted as an incident in a perpetual sacred contract between supernatural beings and man. By this agreement, the supernatural yield part of what is theirs—the riches of the natural environment, to man."

In other cultures the supernatural donors not only had to be propitiated but also fed—sometimes, as among the Aztecs, with human sacrifice, although usually an animal would do. Herodotus relates that among the Egyptians a bull was ceremonially slaughtered after libations of wine and invocations to the gods; it then was disemboweled, stuffed with bread, honey, raisins, figs, frankincense, myrrh, and finally was burned. The men who offered the sacrifice pre-

served a fast until the ceremony was completed, after which they dined on what was left of the carcass.

Among its basic beliefs, the ancient world abounds in stories of beneficent earth and fertility spirits, many of whom tend to disappear with the death of winter and are resurrected with the first shoots of spring. A generic myth is that of a primordial earth mother or grain goddess who has a child god or goddess of vegetation who comes and goes with the seasons. Innumerable changes were rung on this theme. In Egypt the deity Osiris, broadly the god of death and resurrection, but also the god of grain, vanishes with the Nile's annual decline, to be mourned by his consort Isis until the river rises once again, renewed by her tears. An old pyramid inscription speaks of him causing "the fields to flourish with golden corn" even though his handsome form remains in the realm of the dead.

The Greek Persephone, daughter of Demeter, the earth goddess who first bestowed grain to mankind, is doomed through her abduction by Hades to spend the fallow months of each year in the underworld, until the earth's reawakening restores her to her fields and hills. The Eastern civilizations cast their players similarly: Adonis, coupled in ancient Syrian cult with Astarte, and Attis joined Cybele in Phrygian mythology, to revive as a vegetation spirit with the vernal equinox. Dionysus, a god very likely of Thracian origin, whose worship entered Greece in connection with fertility rites and mystery cults, is the most famous of all the fruit-bringing deities as the provider of wine and the

Belshazzar

When Belshazzar gave a dinner party, nothing was too much trouble. The guest list was enormous—the "four hundred" then numbered many times over when all the warriors and priests essential to maintenance of domestic tranquillity were invited. The table service to accommodate the crowd could have bought a small kingdom. The din of laughter and music was such that a whole city might collapse unnoticed around the revelers. And that, according to Daniel's account in the Bible, is precisely what happened. As "Belshazzar the king made a great feast to a thousand of his lords and drank wine before the thousand," Darius and the Persian armies slipped into the capital and promptly ended Babylonian supremacy in Mesopotamia. One can imagine the luxury of the evening—the lords were seated on high chairs, their feet off the floor as was the custom, at rows of long tables ranged in the palace courtyard. The sweet perfume of blossoming fruit trees filtered down from the Hanging Gardens nearby, to join with the wailing of reed flutes, the clashing

of cymbals, the handclapping of dancing maidens, in a farrago of sensual delights. Eunuchs served dark red wines poetically labeled "Divine Liquid" and "Unguent of the Heart," brought from the palace of Nabonidus, Belshazzar's father, or from the far-off vineyards of Assyria. A heady brew of barley and a wine of date palms stiffened with honey were also offered, and at a signal from the king, the meal began in earnest. As a first course, they might have sampled a salted river perch garnished with locusts and seasoned with ginger and coriander, followed by roasted ducks and geese from royal farms, sauced with mint and mustard. A profusion of vegetables—turnips, leeks, carrots, and onions—and a salad of cress, lettuce, and endive were also brought round. So it must have gone until the profligate host, over a dessert of honeyed barley cakes, glanced up and saw a hand write upon the wall, "God hath numbered thy kingdom and finished it. . . . Thou are weighed in the balances, and are found wanting. Thy kingdom is divided, and given to the Medes and Persians." Belshazzar's life was ended, and with it a thousand years of sophistication, not only in the art of cooking but in man's ability to draw sustenance from a baked and parched land.

patron of its joyous, sometimes frenzied, festivals; he too is a seasonal god, doomed to die each autumn, when the vine must be cut back to bare stock after the harvest of the grapes. In his honor the Greeks erected numerous theaters where festivals were celebrated. The Athenians began with the *Oschophoria*, or vintage rites of October, followed in December with the *Rural Dionysia;* made sacrifices at the January *Lenaea*, or feast of the wine vats; observed a giddy three-day *Anthesteria* in February when the casks were opened; and with the com-

Joseph distributing grain to his brethren

ing of spring in March, held their splendid *Great Dionysia*, with its processions and the performance of new tragedies and comedies.

From Sumer of the third millennium before Christ, a frieze has survived that depicts priests milking, straining, possibly making butter, at a sacred dairy farm of the Sumerian mother goddess Ninhursaga. The first Mesopotamian farmers also built shrines that included granaries for the storing of produce (some of it set aside as offerings to the gods), the valuable agricultural surplus that would serve to sustain the people until their next harvest. Thus, the service of food and that of its divinities have gone hand in hand.

The Old Testament from the outset describes the Israelites as a people profoundly concerned with both, and with all the forms, laws, feasts, and restraints that should govern them. In Leviticus, Moses consecrates Aaron and his sons to the Lord and oversees the ritual consumption of the sacrificial calf and ram; there follows his pronouncement of those prohibitions against the use of "unclean" foods (particularly swine, animal blood, along with certain fish and birds) that have governed Jewish dietary laws ever since. Yet the well-provided table also offers great pleasure: we read of the Canaanites who at harvest "went out into the field and gathered their vineyards, and trode the grapes and made merry, and went into the house of their god, and did eat and drink." Moses commands the children of Israel to keep three great feasts a year, among them that of the Tabernacles, with the produce of threshing floor and wine press, in memory of the years spent wandering through the desert in search of the Promised Land: "Seven days shalt thou keep a solemn feast unto the Lord thy God . . . because the Lord thy God shall bless thee in all thine increase, and in all the works of thine hands, therefore thou shalt surely rejoice."

Food and food taboo, like feast and abstinence, have also been long interlinked. Many ancient kings and priests were required to limit their flesh diet to a few meats and to abstain from pork and goat in particular, perhaps on hygienic grounds. But there were other foods, especially the mushroom, on which they had a monopoly, deeming such delights too good for the common man. The Greek historian Herodotus describes a diet for Egyptian priests, which consisted of "bread made for them out of the sacred grain, and a plentiful daily supply of goose-meat and beef, with wine in addition. Fish they are forbidden to touch; and as for beans, they cannot even bear to look at them, because they imagine they are unclean (in point of fact the Egyptians never sow beans, and even if any happen to grow wild, they will not eat them, either raw or boiled)."

By contrast, the heroes of Homer are almost always feasting when not fighting or sulking. The *Iliad* describes a banquet given by the King of Lydia that lasted nine days and nights. We are told, too, that worshipers of the grain and fruit spirits Cybele and Attis were permitted the upper, "ascending," parts of vegetables but not the seeds, or "de-

Demeter blessing man and his harvest

scending" roots, at their festivals, while they could eat some meat—though not pork or fish. The art of making dough rise by the use of a yeast or other fermenting substance was known all over the Middle East by about 1500 B.C., but among the Israelites it became and remained the subject of religious restrictions under which the use of leaven was wholly forbidden during the Feast of the Passover and for most offerings at the altar—fermentation being to them a symbol of corruption. Jesus declared, "Beware of the leaven of the Pharisees," and Saint Paul urged the Corinthians, "Let us keep the feast . . . with the unleavened bread of sincerity and truth." The Roman *flamen Dialis*—the high priest who was regarded as the living embodiment of the chief god Jupiter—could eat neither leavened bread nor wheaten flour nor raw meat.

In India of the early Brahman period described in the *Rig-Veda* some fourteen hundred years before Christ, a pastoral society existed that counted its wealth in cattle and enjoyed nothing more than a great feast of beef. Yet later Hindu doctrines led to the prohibition of flesh food on the basis of ideas of transmigration. All animals might embody human or divine spirits; the cow, for example, was recognized as a direct descendant of Kamadhenu, a sacred spirit with the face of a beautiful woman. As a consequence, its milk was highly valued and its life protected. Dairy foods were, in fact, important in the diets of a large part of the ancient world—introduced by the Aryan Indians whose migrations in search of grazing lands for their herds took them westward. And because milk

21

soured very quickly in warm climates, butter and cheese were probably the most common forms in which dairy products were eaten. Agitated in a simple churn or carried in bags made of animal stomachs where the natural enzymes that cause milk to clot could work, the transformation was easily accomplished. Man thus discovered how to make dairy foods that stored better than milk and had a high nutritive value.

The people of China, on the other hand, have shown a traditional distaste for dairy products and particularly for cheese, apparently thought unclean. Unlike the Aryans, the agricultural Chinese could not support herds of milk cattle, while their long-standing foes, the nomadic herders of the steppes to the west of them, fed on milk and cheese. It has been thought by one authority that the Chinese disaffection for dairy products distantly reflects this ancient enmity. On a quite different level of taboo—"homeopathic," anthropologists call it —we learn of the avoidance of pork by Carib Indians for fear of acquiring "pigs' eyes," and of tortoises for fear of becoming as clumsy as they.

But while certain foods have been avoided in one or another place for reasons varying with time and culture, other foods have enjoyed special and joyous esteem wherever found. In the Near East and eastern Mediterranean area, a particular affection was bestowed on native honey and the olive, and above all, on the product of the vine.

Honey, ancient man's first and basic sweetener, was a gift of innumerable bees buzzing over flowering slopes long before man's first attempts at agriculture, and very early it acquired a special importance in his mind. Mesopotamian folklore saw it as a magical substance, with medicinal or purifying powers: gods drinking it were made immortal and immune to illness. Babylonians and Assyrians fermented it for the mead of their libations when they dedicated new shrines. The Promised Land of the Israelites was described as one "flowing with milk and honey." Dionysus the wine god is said to have found the streams of Mount Parnassus running with honey when he established himself there. In practice, mead-making may have arisen even earlier than neolithic times, and in Egypt honey was fermented with the juice of dates to produce a syrup of high alcoholic content. When mixed with flour and oil, it also produced the honey cake, an ambrosial treat offered to the gods of ancient Mesopotamia, and still a favorite sweetmeat of the Near East. The Romans are described as having consumed amounts of honey "out of snow-white jars" in observance of their New Year.

The evergreen olive tree, possibly native to southwestern Asia and cultivated in the Near East and eastern Mediterranean since the Neolithic Age—five

Sumerian priests at work in the temple creamery

Tributes of butter for the Persian Xerxes

thousand years ago or earlier—was also surrounded by a special aura. From time immemorial it was associated with ideas of peace and reward. Noah's ark brought back an olive branch from Mount Ararat, and the city of Athens received its name from Athena, who won a contest among the gods for the honor of naming the city by striking the ground and bringing forth the olive tree as the most valuable gift to man. Its fruit certainly was unique in value: thriving on lean and sandy soil, it yielded almost all the oil used in antiquity, for cooking, lighting, and cleansing; and the advancing diet as well as economy of the Mediterranean would have been inconceivable without it.

That particularly beloved growth, the grape-producing vine plant (*Vitis vinifera*), may have been cultivated before 4000 B.C. (or even, it has been suggested, well before 6000 B.C.) by tribesmen in Transcaucasia, to which it was indigenous. Either date takes us back to the very early days of agriculture, and testifies to man's ancestral predisposition toward alcoholic drinks. Fermenta-

tion of grain had already produced beer, probably no later than the production of bread itself, if not before. In Mesopotamia, the Oxford *History of Technology* estimates, at one time about 40 per cent of cereal production was for brewing. Fermented milk drinks, such as the *koumiss* of Asian plainsmen, probably followed in time the development of fermented honey and date juices. The South American Indians were to have their *paiwari*, converted from manioc, or cassava; the Aztecs, their *pulque*. But no crop was attended by more ritual and care than the grape and its yield. It was known in prehistoric Mesopotamia and was brought to Egypt before 3000 B.C.; a Sumerian record of 2400 B.C. describes a temple garden planted "like a mountain with vines." In Egypt irrigated vineyards produced as many as half a dozen varieties of grapes from white to deep red, and individual wines were named by origin and graded by inspectors. In Palestine cultivation of the grape was exceeded only by that of the olive and the fig. The Assyrian king Assurbanipal interested himself enough to make a wine list of the best growths.

Ancient mythology, poetry, and symbolism invest the fruit of this scraggly vine with vast generative and regenerative powers, in which the physical is coupled with the metaphysical. The product could be misused—or overused, as Noah, the Bible's first vineyardist, discovered to his grief. One day the forgiveness of God was to be pictured by the image of a flourishing vine. On a temporal level, meanwhile, the spreading use of wine did much to raise the standard of pleasure and taste at the tables of many Mediterranean peoples, even when it was mixed with honey, resin, or other substances that would make it almost unpalatable today.

Even by the time of ancient Sumer and Babylonia, there were ample agricultural resources and traditions of food and table. An Assyrian herbal of about the eighth century B.C. discusses some 250 plants both as to their dietetic and medicinal values. It speaks of lettuce as having "a narcotic principle"; of garlic as good "to chew and fumigate"; of leeks as having some value "against gray hairs"; of the cherry (*karšu*, or *cerasus* as it was to become in Latin) as having "a pleasant fragrance." The energy of Babylonians and Assyrians in irrigating and diking their lands greatly increased their yield. Herodotus remarks that "as a grain-bearing country Assyria is the richest in the world. . . . As for millet and sesame, I will not say to what an astonishing size they grow, though I know well enough . . . people who have not been to Babylonia have refused to believe even what I have said already about their fertility." Their diet ranged over a wide variety of cereals and fruits, some meat and river fish. From their resources and love of feasting one might construct a banquet menu somewhat as follows:

Garlic in Sour Cream
Barley Soup
Tigris Salmon
Roast Pig or Lamb
Goat Cheese
Honey Cakes
Dates and Pomegranates

But it remained for the Egyptians, blessed by the unique phenomenon of

Hieroglyphic seal motifs for Egyptian wine jars

the Nile floods that annually renewed their lands with fertile topsoil and enriched their vast delta in particular, to convert nature's food gifts into a cuisine. This astonishing people, as inventive as they were self-indulgent, made the most of everything edible within reach. From early, or Old Kingdom, times, they possessed a vigorous African strain of longhorn cattle; later they imported other strains from Asia. They grain-fed their steers to produce a good rib of beef, and force-fed their fowl to produce plump roasting birds, along with the makings of something resembling a *pâté de foie gras*. They relished pigeon, quail, and duck, and dined also on watermelon, artichokes, cucumber, lettuce, endives, leeks, radishes, beans, peas, dates, figs, apples, apricots, and cheese. An inscription of the Twentieth Dynasty mentions thirty different forms of breads and cakes in use. Another cites forty-eight varieties of baked meats and twenty-four of drinks. The basis of such amazing gastronomic totals remains obscure; evidently fine points of difference in preparation were being taken into account. In drink there appears to have been almost boundless choice: there were many grades of wines, along with five different types of beers—some of a strength equal to that of wine—along

The Ageless Olive

"*I*t is easier," the Talmud says, "to raise a legion of olive trees in Galilee than to bring up one child in the land of Israel." It probably was, for herein lay the secret of the olive's success in the harsh, arid lands of the ancient world—it flourished with a minimum of care where less hardy fruit trees would wither and die. The roots of the olive tree go far back in history and lie deep in the stony soil of Asia Minor. According to the Bible, the Hebrews found the olive growing wild in the land of Canaan, and there is evidence that the tree was first cultivated in neolithic Crete. Early records reveal that the Minoans carried on a prosperous trade in olive oil with Phoenicia and Egypt. By then the olive had become to the Mediterranean world what butter is to northern Europe today—the basis of all cooking. No other fruit was as versatile as the olive. In Palestine, where every kitchen was equipped with a press for extracting oil, the olive provided food and lamp fuel as well as cooking oil. Even the hard wood of the tree was of great value. All that was needed to make the olive orchard grow was patience and time. Ten years were required to produce the first harvest—thirty years to produce the best. The Greeks, who anointed not only their salads with olive oil but also their bodies, arrived at a mythical explanation for the tree, as they did for so many other wonders of

their world. It was a gift from Athena, they said; and they promptly installed a sacred olive tree at the Acropolis to honor the occasion. It was nearly as much a sacrilege as an economic disaster when, during the Peloponnesian War, the Spartans destroyed the olive groves in Attica. The Greeks worshiped the olive, but the Romans exploited it. In Cato's day, the average profit from an olive plantation was 6 per cent of the capital invested. In Spain and Portugal olive oil has been an important export since the time the Phoenicians introduced the tree there, as early as 1700 B.C. Unlike the world around it, the olive and its cultivation has remained unchanged throughout history. In the words of Lawrence Durrell: "The whole Mediterranean . . . the wine, the ideas . . . seems to ride in the sour pungent taste of those black olives. . . . A taste older than meat, older than wine. A taste as old as cold water."

with palm wine, date wine, a fermented pomegranate drink imported from Palestine and resembling hard cider, and many innocuous fruit juices.

The Egyptian feast, in length and elaborateness, became somewhat overwhelming. Garlands of lotus blossoms or other foliage were draped around the wine jars to keep away the flies. As course followed sumptuous course, dancing girls, harpists, and amorous singers moved among the guests, even at banquets supposedly in tribute to the dead. A typical aristocratic tomb, that of the architect Kha, a favorite of the Kings Amenhotep II and III, shows on its painted walls an array of provisions for the repose of his soul that includes butter, meat, oil, wine, milk, dates, and raisins, along with a complete set of kitchen utensils. Yet by the Eighteenth Dynasty—midway in ancient Egypt's history—celebration had reached a point where guests themselves consumed much of the funerary tribute and, moreover, drank too much. "Give me eighteen cups of wine, behold I should love drunkenness," reads an inscription attributed to a Seventeenth Dynasty Egyptian lady of position.

> *Sweet are the grapes of Horus,*
> *Sweeter the song-filled night.*
> *The lips of thy beloved*
> *Are washed with honey.*

So ran an old Egyptian chant, to the accompaniment of dinner instruments imported from the East. Rome in its time was to outdo Egypt in the amplitude and elegance of its table, in scents and revelry; and a later Western world was to exceed them all in the sheer scope of consumption. Neither a Pharaoh nor a Caesar could match the grandeur of King Edward I of England, who in 1274 was to order his sheriffs to provide 278 bacon hogs, 450 porkers, 440 fat oxen, 430 sheep, and 22,600 hens and capons for his coronation feast. Nor was Nefertiti the equal of Catherine de' Medici, the heiress who arrived in France in 1533 with her Florentine chefs to be married to the future King Henry II. She entertained in 1549 with a dinner for fifty that included 30 peacocks, 33 pheasants, 21 swans, 90 cranes, 66 guinea fowl, 30 capons, 90 pullets, 99 quail, in addition to a massive supply of hares, rabbits, and pigs. Neither the Pharaoh's guests nor those of King Edward or Catherine needed anything like the amount of food they ate festally, but ancestral memories of far hunts, lean years, and slender pickings may have lingered in their minds. Man's fare from the dawn of time has been determined not only by his sources of supply but by the means he has found to convert raw nature. The great fire, the ample feast, the noble libation, the glittering table, are all symbols of what he sees as his advancement. As late as 1939, in a part of the world that had supposedly overcome both scarcity and the temptations of gluttony, the President of the French Republic and Madame Lebrun were to be regaled during a state visit to the Court of St. James's by a three-day round of luncheons and dinners that overwhelmed them with dozens of courses (from *consommé quenelles aux trois couleurs* to *bombe glacée Victoria*) accompanied by twenty-one wines, not to mention after-dinner port and punch.

FOOD
OF
THE
PHARAOHS

Cakes, figs, and fowl for the goddess Isis—from a Nineteenth Dynasty relief

From sowing to reaping to the recording of the annual harvest on its way to government granaries,

The Staff of Life

While barbaric tribes of northern Europe were still subsisting on raw meat and wild plants, the Egyptians were enjoying no fewer than thirty varieties of breads and cakes. It was in the Nile valley that the oven was first invented and the process of leavening discovered. Housewife and royal baker alike daily performed (with full credit to their deities) the miracle of transforming soggy dough into fragrant, nourishing food. As staples in the Egyptian diet, bread—and the heady beer brewed by steeping spiced loaves in water

Bakers' tasks were well organized and highly specialized, beginning with the milling, left, and

the grain crops of the Nile valley were always under the watchful eye of the Pharaoh's lieutenants.

and allowing the broth to ferment—had their monetary value as well. The workers who built the pyramid of Cheops were paid a daily wage of three loaves and two jugs of beer, both probably consumed upon receipt. Taxes and tributes to officials rendered in loaves of bread were not so quickly digested. One can only guess how stale and unpalatable the nine hundred wheat loaves and the thirty-six thousand flat loaves distributed annually to one such officer must have been by the time they reached the tables of his dependents.

A Hebrew bread stamp

moving by gradual stages to the kneading board, the ovens, and, finally, the brewing vats, right.

The King's Pleasure

This duck-hunting scene, a panel taken from a gilt shrine dedicated to Tutankhamen and his queen, shows that the comforts of the home and table had not succeeded in completely destroying the royal zest for the more strenuous pursuits of the outdoors. In the Nile valley, the plains and marshes abounded with a great variety of wild game and fowl, and while hunting had become by then more a matter of sport than of sheer survival, it provided an important part of ancient man's diet.

Oasis in the Sun

A garden, c. 1400 B.C., from a Theban wall painting

Trained baboons gathering figs   *Force-feeding a goose*

The scented walks and shady groves that graced most private gardens in ancient Egypt must have been a source of inspiration to poet and cook alike, for it was there in their own back yards, a few steps from the kitchen, that fruits, vegetables, fish, and fowl—almost every food but red meat and cereals—were raised. In the garden at left, orchards of date palms, pomegranates, and vineyards grow along the borders; plots of vegetables and herbs grow within. Fish, as well as lotus, cress, and other water greens, share the pond which doubled as a reservoir for a complex irrigation system.

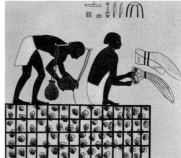

Beekeeper and hive   *Watering and weeding onions*

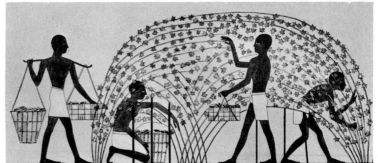

Slaves harvesting okra from trellises

Fruit
of
The Vine

Temperance was not a virtue in Egypt.
It was said of the Luxor vineyards that
production was "more plentiful than the
water of the Nile at its highest mark";
and there were few temple gardens or
private estates where scenes of the harvest and the trampling of the grapes—
often to music (opposite)—did not oc-
cur. Wines were stored in earthen jars
which were bedded on large pallets.
Each jar was carefully labeled by vintage.
Even dates were pressed and mixed with
honey to obtain a strong, syrupy drink.
Still, consumption outran supply, and
huge quantities of potent beer (sucked
through reeds by visiting Syrians above)
were needed to slake the national thirst.

The Brimming Cup

A good wine deserves better than an earthen cup, and throughout the ancient world, vessels were fashioned to honor the grape as well as the occasion. Most were made from silver or gold, but as early as 1600 B.C., the Egyptians had learned to make glass from quartz sand, tinting it with copper or iron. Tutankhamen drank from the calcite goblet shaped like a lotus flower, above.

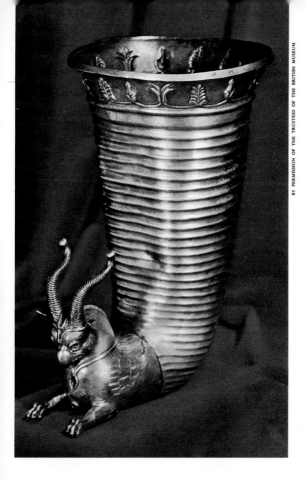

Dainty draughts and elixirs for an Eighteenth Dynasty queen of Egypt might have filled the blue, threaded glass vase, right. At lustier celebrations in the royal banquet halls of ancient Persia and Assyria, ringing toasts were likely raised in sturdier vessels: the griffin-handled rhyton of silver and copper above, and the lion-headed cup below.

37

A Matter of Tastes

The Egyptians either feasted or nibbled; there was no middle ground. Breakfast was an eat-as-you-go affair, a buffet of bread and meat washed down with a beer chaser. But a feast, whether it was the simple family celebration below or the boisterous, three-day marathon with dancing topless waitresses opposite, tested the endurance of everyone involved—cooks, servants, and guests alike.

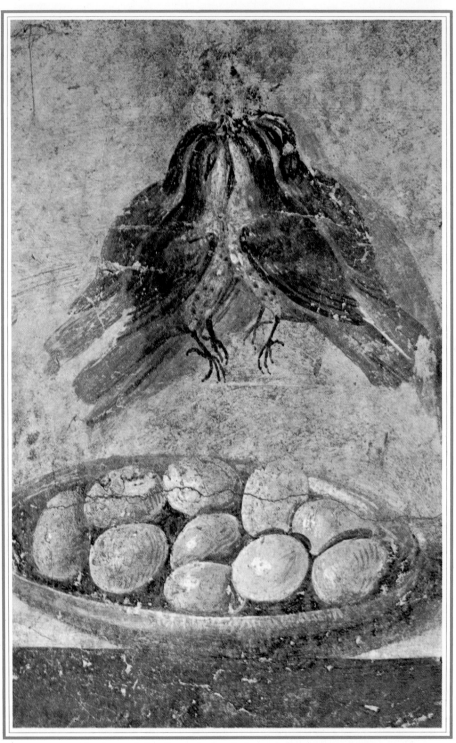

Two brace of thrushes and a bowl of eggs, from a Pompeian fresco

WHEN
EATING
BECAME
DINING

The chronicle of dining in classical antiquity begins with the robust aroma of Homeric oxen roasted on the outdoor spit and culminates in the perfumes and perversities of the banquets of Nero and of such even more outrageous Roman emperors as Domitian and Elagabalus. It embraces almost a thousand years of changing mores as well as sustenance. But along the way, from simplicity to decadence, the men of Greece and then of Rome raised the art of the table to the highest level of cultivation to be known in the West until that of eighteenth-century France. The West retains their legacy.

The primeval Homeric dinner, to be sure, did not always consist of red meat. Though the heroes preferred it, and the ancient commentator Eubulus rhetorically asks: "I pray you, where in Homer is the chief Who e'er eat fish, or anything but beef?" Homer himself tells of many occasions on which their fare was only a rudimentary mess of pottage. Such were the dishes of grated cheese and white barley mixed with wine prepared for Nestor by his captured Trojan girl slave; the comparable dish sweetened with honey and soporifics which Circe served to stupefy Odysseus and his sailors; and "the great pudding, stuffed with fat and blood," offered to the returning hero by King Antinous. Along with the feasting, the Homeric dinner was also a sociable affair. Thus when Odysseus is within a short sail of Ithaca after his ten years' wanderings he remarks, looking ahead to what may greet him, "There is no greater fulfilment of delight than when joy possesses a whole people, and banqueters in the halls listen to a minstrel as they sit in order due, and by them tables are laden with bread and meat, and the cup-bearer draws wine from the bowl and bears it round and pours it into the cups."

From that world of blood puddings, bards, and meals of friendship, a vast distance and several centuries take us to the most notorious table in all Rome —that of the boy emperor Elagabalus in the third century A.D. This painted wastrel liked to shower his guests with aromatic blossoms (a few unfortunate guests are said to have smothered) while they savored tongues of peacocks and nightingales and to arrange banquets according to a color sequence (one evening everything from the plates to the food itself was green, the next evening iridescent, the third blue). Once the brains of six hundred ostriches were provided as a delicacy. The chronicle known as the *Historia Augusta* relates that, on occasion, he would serve "twenty-two courses of extraordinary viands, and between each course he and

his guests would bathe and dally with women." After three rollicking years Elagabalus was murdered in a latrine and thrown into the Tiber.

Between these extremes lies a long evolution of tastes in food, drink, and manners of the table; and both early Greek and later Roman literature tell us much of a civilization evidently greatly taken up with them. One of the earliest of Greek lyric poets, Anacreon of sixth-century Asia Minor, wrote verses in praise of wine:

Water bring and bring me wine,
Bring the wreaths where flowers entwine;
Hasten, lad; our fists we try,
Matched together, Love and I.

Come, a wassail I would keep,
Drinking pledges flagon-deep.
Pour me wine, five measures, lad;
Measures ten of water add;
So good manners shall remain
In your Bacchant, foxed again.

Drink, good fellows, drink no more
With a clutter and uproar;
Thus, when Scythians hold a bout,
Wine goes in and tongues let out.
Gentlemen, observe a mean,
Tippling with good songs between.

Plato's famous dialogue, the *Symposium*, deals with a banquet at the house of the poet Agathon, made brilliant by the presence of a duly washed and brushed Socrates, and made memorable by the clamorous arrival of an inebriated Alcibiades who enters shouting, "Hail friends. . . . Will you have a very drunken man as companion to your revels?" Refusing the goblet of wine offered, he orders a wine cooler, "a vessel holding more than two quarts," which he promptly fills, empties, and refills. The intruder then launches into a diatribe against Socrates saying, "What follows I could hardly tell you if I were sober," excusing his candor with the Greek equivalent of *in vino veritas*. After the arrival of a second band of revelers, the drinking gets out of hand, and if Socrates' response was a discourse extolling the virtues of sobriety, not even

Faience cup from Cyprus

Aristodemus was in any condition to hear him. Upon awakening, Aristodemus notes, "There remained only Socrates, Aristophanes, and Agathon, who were drinking out of a large goblet which they passed around, and Socrates was discoursing to them."

Socrates' other disciple, Xenophon, in his own *Symposium*, provides a fanciful account of an even livelier banquet. When one of the guests orders an onion for his drink, his neighbor comments, "Niceratus is intent on going home smelling of onions to make his wife believe that no one would have even conceived the thought of kissing him." The master, who called the feast a perfect dinner, obliges with a song, after which

a clown, a girl acrobat, a citharist, and a flute player entertain. The banquet ends with a risqué skit about the wedding of Bacchus, the Roman Dionysus.

Plato himself, though disdainful of the pleasures of the table, pauses in another of his dialogues to mention his favorite food suppliers and advisers: Thearion the pastry cook, Mithaecus, who wrote a treatise on Sicilian cooking, and Saramus the wine dealer. The poet Aeschylus, usually concerned with bleak destiny, gives away a touch of his own humanity when he says:

But I will place this carefully fed pig
Within the crackling oven; and, I pray,
What nicer dish can e'er be given to man?

The loosening of restraints at a vinous spring festival is the subject of *The Frogs*, a sardonic tale by Aristophanes. Ever the critic of urbane Athenian ways, in a later work he lingers more approvingly over a simple countryman's luncheon—three olives, two onions, a loaf of bread, and a small goatskin of wine.

The Roman Horace dwells in his odes on the prandial pleasures of his Sabine farm, his tastes in wine, and his occasional surrender to its heady effects:

. . . Welcome, the sweet delight
Of danger! Lord of Wine
Lead on! I follow garlanded with vine.

And in a satire he relates the precise order of dishes and seating at the banquet of one miserly Nasidienus that overwhelmed the guests, particularly when a canopy over the table collapsed. And, in case the guests might fail to appreciate the supreme efforts to which their host has gone, he all but numbs them with copious commentary on the geographic origins of the foods set before them and the time of day and phase of the moon when the ingredients of each dish were found.

Much later Macrobius, a philosopher of sorts and chronicler of manners, described a formal dinner for high priests of state given in Julius Caesar's time that began with oysters and other shellfish in several forms and went through game pies, fillets of wild boar, sows' udders, pigs' heads, and ragouts of hare and fowl. He also took pleasure in recalling that at a banquet of the emperor Septimius Severus a splendid sturgeon (a fish then found chiefly in the Rhone and the Po) was borne in by crowned attendants to the sound of flutes. Martial, author of epigrams, delighted in giving out brief gastronomic hints, such as a recipe for cooked eggs ("If a white liquid surround the saffron-colored yolks, let the sauce of Spanish mackerel season the eggs."), and grew so enamored of truffles that he wrote of them in the first person: "We truffles that burst through the nurturing soil with our soft heads are of earth's apples second to mushrooms."

But for sustained and intensive interest in the subject of food, nothing in literature can approach the ambitious compendium written by Athenaeus, an Egyptian Greek of the third century A.D., under the name *The Deipnosophists,* or "The Banquet of the Learned." This unique work, cast at the outset in the form of a Platonic dialogue, purports to record the knowledge displayed on a multitude of subjects at a several-day symposium comprising philosophers,

grammarians, physicians, a prominent jurist, a poet, and a musician, most of them hailing from Hellenized and Romanized Egypt and Asia Minor. They discuss many matters of literature, law, music, and history, but it soon becomes apparent that their primary interest is the table, and for the greater part of the fifteen books of text that survive we are treated to a banquet of ancient gastronomic lore.

Some of the information is medicinal and at times cautionary. Of mushrooms: they "are good for the stomach and pass easily through the bowels, and are very nutritious." Of asparagus: "They are remedies for every kind of internal disorder." Of cabbage: "At Athens [it] used to be given to women who had just

Hoof-shaped mug depicting Greek farming

been delivered, as a sort of medicine." Of almonds: "There is nothing which is a greater provocative of drinking." Of carrots: "This vegetable is harsh, says Diphilus, but tolerably nutritious . . . it is indigestible, diuretic, and not without some influence in prompting men to amatory feelings." Of eggs, onions, et cetera: "One must set bounds to much eating, especially of such things as have anything glutinous or sticky about them; as, for instance, eggs, onions, calves' feet, snails . . . for they remain in the stomach a long time, and form a lump there, and check the natural moisture."

Much of the lore also falls into the category of helpful advice to the cook and marketer. Thus, of cabbage: "The finest and most delicious . . . is grown in Cyme; in Alexandria it is bitter; and the seed which is brought from Rhodes to Alexandria produces sweet cabbage for one year, after which time it degenerates again, from the nature of the soil." Of eggs: according to the food expert Heraclides of early Syracuse, "The best of all eggs are peacock's eggs; the next best are those of the fox-goose; and the third best are those of common poultry."

The speakers are particularly engrossed with sea food and its preparation, and they discourse at length on innumerable marine species, citing Aristotle for instance on the habitat and qualities of tuna and turning for practical guidance to the work of one Archestratus of Athens, a follower of Epicurus, who toward the end of the fourth century B.C. wrote a gastronomic tract under the title *The Luxurious Way of Living*. The fragments of this treatise that survive in *The Deipnosophists* include perhaps the first recipes set down in writing.

Thus Archestratus writes that "a boiled ray is good about midwinter. Eat it with cheese and assafoetida [a foul-smelling palm resin which was, unaccountably, favored as a condiment by the Romans]." When roasting a dogfish, strew it with cummin, be sparing of salt, and add nothing else but "some sea-green oil"; when boiling it, "add what fragrant herbs the garden gives," and be careful of the heat of the fire: stir frequently, "lest the meat should catch, and spoil your dinner so, before you know it." And further:

I counsel you always to boil a harp-fish
If he is white and full of firmish meat;
But if he's red and also no great size,
Then it were best, when you have
  prick'd him o'er
With a new sharpen'd knife, to roast
  him gently.
Sprinkle him then with oil and plente-
  ous cheese,
For he does like to see men liberal,
And is himself intemperate.

Such counsel, from so old a source, held the attention of Athenaeus and his learned table half a millennium after. The diners of course had ample experience of newer and more sophisticated cookery; thus one speaker tells of a whole pig being served one half roasted and the other half boiled ("[we] all marvelled at the cleverness of the cook") and moreover stuffed with such dainties as slices of sow's womb, the yolks of eggs, the entrails of birds with their ovaries, and fanciful seasonings. But while greatly respecting the genius of chefs, they sometimes wondered whether elaboration might not go too far. Again they looked to that older authority, Archestratus, who had stated with certitude, "Many are the ways and many the recipes for dressing hares; but this is the best of all, to place before a hungry set of guests a slice of roasted meat fresh from the spit, hot, season'd only with plain, simple salt. . . . All other ways are quite superfluous, such as when cooks pour a lot of sticky, clammy sauce upon it."

45

By the time the deipnosophists convened, the art of cookery in the Mediterranean world had progressed far beyond "sticky, clammy sauce." For detailed knowledge of its development, posterity is indebted to another author—a certain Apicius, believed to have been the writer of a compendium sometimes known as *De Re Coquinaria*, "The Art of Cooking."

Apicius' actual identity is uncertain; there were several Roman personalities by that name, one of them a rich courtier and epicure in the time of Augustus and Tiberius who wrote about food. Pliny called him *altissimus gurges*, or "sublime gullet," and it was said that when Apicius one day found that he had spent a hundred million sesterces of his fortune on food and had only ten million left with a prospect of starvation before him, he poisoned himself. This may well have been the Apicius who compiled what has come down as the Western world's oldest surviving cookbook.

More accurately, the recipes of Apicius comprise only a part of a fourth- or fifth-century-A.D. manuscript compiled by some anonymous editor from several Greco-Roman sources. *De Re Coquinaria* describes a culinary tradition based on the extraction and enhancement of flavors. It involved the basic art of preserving the best in meat, fish, and vegetables by cooking them in their own juices; of creating sauces to enrich these foods by the use of stock (or, as a modern chef would say, of making a court bouillon); of providing additives in the form of numerous spices, garnishes, and cooking wines. Thus the Romans developed a basic sauce called *garum*, or *liquamen*, from the entrails of fish cast into brine

and combined with condiments, water, wine, or vinegar. They boiled down wine or "must" for cooking purposes, creating *defrutum* and, when sweetened with honey, *mulsum*. These substances figure prominently in Apicius' recipes, which range from crayfish and mussels to venison, fried eggs, and a classic casserole of crane or duck with turnips, presented as follows:

"Wash and truss the bird and boil it in a large saucepan in water, salt, and dill, until half done. Cook the turnips so that they lose their pungency. Remove the duck from the pan, wash again, and put into another saucepan with oil, liquamen, and a bouquet of leek and coriander. Put over it one washed and finely chopped (uncooked) turnip, and braise. When it has been cooking for a while add *defrutum* to give it color. Then prepare the following sauce: pepper, cummin, coriander, assafoetida root, add vinegar, and some of the cooking-liquor; pour over the duck and bring to the boil. When it boils thicken with cornflour and add to the turnips. Sprinkle with pepper and serve."

But much of the pleasure of advanced cookery consisted in the game of intermixing flavors, textures, and even shapes with total disguise the goal. Apicius provides a recipe for a *"patina* [or mold] of anchovy without anchovy," in which other fish and jellyfish were used instead: "At table no one will know what he is eating." A leading comic dramatist of the Roman Republic, Plautus, mocked these trickster cooks as men "who serve you up whole pickled meadows in their patinae—men who make cows their messmates, who thrust herbs at you,

Lucullus

"*A*nd, indeed, Lucullus' life, like the Old Comedy, presents us at the commencement with acts of policy and war, at the end offering nothing but good eating and drinking, feastings and revellings, and mere play." History has all but forgotten the "acts" that earned Lucius Licinius Lucullus this grudging praise from Plutarch and the wherewithal to indulge his middle-aged appetites. As a general, Lucullus campaigned in Asia Minor, conquering the Persians and, more importantly, discovering the sophisticated cuisine of the East. Even then his strategy was aimed directly at the enemy's mid-section, stressing, as Plutarch observed, that "the seat of war [is] in the belly." The fabled Lucullan feasts that would forever link his name with high living began after his triumphal return to Rome; following a gigantic feed for the entire city, he gave up the public arena for the dining room. Tubero, the Stoic, possibly because he never made the guest list, was so scandalized by his extravagance that he called him, after the Persian potentate, "Xerxes  in a gown," but such political notables as Cato, Cicero, and Crassus were delighted to attend any banquet, large or small, that their friend might prepare. Leading poets, philosophers, and ranking foreign dignitaries also turned up regularly at the Lucullan table. At one such banquet, when the guests of honor protested their host's generosity, Lucullus replied self-indulgently, "Some of this, indeed my Grecian friends, is for your sakes, but more for that of Lucullus." According to Plutarch, even *en famille* this early gourmet demanded the best. Once when he was dining alone and was presented a simple supper, the general snapped at his cook, "What, did you not know, then, that to-day Lucullus dines with Lucullus?" He maintained several dining halls, from the sumptuous "Apollo," to more intimate chambers, and he had only to name the room to indicate to his chief steward how lavish the service should be. To keep his larder well stocked with delicacies befitting all occasions, he shopped the length and breadth of the Mediterranean world and kept wondrous gardens at his sprawling villa. Even the mighty Pompey, when he craved out-of-season or exotic fowl, was not above raiding the special fattening coops kept outside Rome by his former officer. When Lucullus died in 56 B.C., it was said in the senate that half of Rome suffered indigestion.

then proceed to season these herbs with other herbs." Later, the satirist Petronius remarks in praise of the ingenuity of his master chef, "he will make you a fish out of a sow's belly."

The chefs of Athens were never as artful nor as ambitious in the meals they prepared as were the Romans. The ten-hour banquet was unknown in Attica before the arrival of Alexander and the Macedonians sometime before 323 B.C. At this late period in Greek history, Attic dining customs resemble in extravagance those of the full-blown Empire. Witness the orgiastic feast once staged by the Macedonian conqueror, an alcoholic who enjoyed prancing about besotted and in costume. The party began with hors d'oeuvres of chickens, ducks, ring-doves, geese, hares, pigeons, turtledoves, partridges, and young goats. An intermission for entertainment by naked girl dancers was followed by a pig stuffed with "thrushes, ducks, warblers, peas purée poured over eggs, oysters and scallops. . . ." While the guests were digesting these entremets, a troupe of acrobats were brought in, some of whom "performed tumbling acts among swords, and blew fire from their mouths," so Athenaeus recounts. Then further rounds including skewered boars were served, and the drinking began in earnest, accompanied by more dancing girls decked out as nymphs and Nereids and staging erotic tableaus.

Obviously, the image of Greek simplicity contrasted with Roman self-indulgence is a gross oversimplification. For the two cultures, both setting forth from simple ways and diets, developed some strikingly similar customs of meals

and hospitality during their independent rises toward affluence. In the late stages of the Empire the Romans far surpassed their Greek mentors, becoming what the poet Vergil hoped they would be —*rerum dominos*, masters of the world. In fact, Rome was still a small and uncertain state beside the Tiber when a strong taste for luxury was first brought to southern Italy in the eighth century B.C. by the more sophisticated Greek colo-

Bronze pastry wheel from Gaul, c. 200 A.D.

nizers, many of them hailing from old cities in Asia Minor. Their settlement of Sybaris on the Adriatic coast became legendary for its pleasures, and one of the tyrants of Syracuse, Nysaeus by name, was notorious for his gluttony, drunkenness, and debauchery with boys and women alike.

Spartans, Athenians, and Romans all were very prone to look down on the self-indulgence of others. "The Attic race is quick and eloquent, and they eat little," wrote the Greek Eubulus; "but the Boeotians eat enormously." To "drink like a Scythian" was a term of obloquy in Athens. Anyone so foolish as to take his wine neat in Scythian fashion was, in the opinion of Herodotus, likely to go mad.

The Medes and Persians were viewed with particular disfavor. A typical story told was that of the Persian Cantibaris, who, whenever his jaws were weary with eating, had his slaves hold them open to pour more food into his mouth. It was also said that the Persians loved their wine so much that any important political decision that was made when their leaders were sober was reconsidered when they were drunk. Herodotus, at the climax of his history of the Persian Wars, relates that after the rout of Xerxes at Plataea the commander of the victorious Greeks, Pausanias of Sparta, entered a tent abandoned by one of Xerxes' Median officers to be astonished by the "gold and silver couches all beautifully draped, and gold and silver tables, and everything prepared for the feast with great magnificence." The Greek commander ordered that the feast be served to his officers, but ordered a simple Spartan meal to be served also, exclaiming as his men came to view the two boards, "Gentlemen, I asked you here in order to show you the folly of the Persians, who, living in this style, came to Greece to rob us of our poverty."

Republican Romans, for their part, held in contempt the ways of their neighbors to the north, the Etruscans, a race inordinately bent on the delights of table and sex. Surviving Etruscan figures on sarcophagi show their men to have been distinctly potbellied—indeed, the Roman nickname for an Etruscan was *obesus*. One Roman chronicler writes of their "unbridled luxury and indolence," adding with apparent envy that "twice a day they have tables sumptuously dressed and laid with everything that can contribute towards delicate living; they have coverings embroidered with flowers and are served wine in quantities of silver bowls." Another, Theopompus, writes that at the conclusion of Etruscan family parties of eating and drinking, servants bearing torches brought their masters female prostitutes, boys, or their own wives, and that multiple love-making went on in public.

On the side of virtue and restraint, there are equally impressive examples among the Greeks and Romans. Just as the Greeks had their Spartans, whose regimen included communal messes where the appetites of all male citizens were scrutinized, so there were Romans who prized nothing more highly than a virtuous and thrifty household. In the second century B.C., the Stoic philosopher Posidonius emphasized the frugality of meals as a particular quality of the Roman way of life before the state grew in size and wealth.

Sallust, who as one of Julius Caesar's tribunes must have shared in the new prosperity, thought the change came after the destruction of Carthage and Rome's other great adversaries. He added that the people were overcome by riches and leisure, and had become *dediti ventri* —slaves of their stomachs. Livy also emphasized that a love of luxury had entered Rome with Asiatic influences. No more vivid example of this trend exists than the emperor Claudius, a mighty drinker and feastgiver of the first century A.D. who often had as many as six hundred guests at his table and, according to Suetonius, rarely left it until utterly gorged and sozzled.

Yet not all late Roman emperors were excessive in their tastes either; the successor to Claudius and Nero, the middle-class Vespasian, was known for his frugal

49

tastes at board, and Tacitus writes that it became the fashion during his rule for high society to emulate him.

Sumptuary laws were passed at various times to enforce moderation. The cost of a meal, the number of guests, the variety of dishes, were legislated—and were consistently ignored by the aristocracy. Cato the Censor ordered that an *eques* (knight) be deprived of the public horse that was his perquisite, if he were too corpulent to ride it. Leading the conservative faction, he warned constantly against the incursion of Greek manners as a menace to the moral fiber of the Republic; and the struggle between Cato and his archenemies, the influential philhellenic tribe of the Scipios, convulsed the state and contributed to the rise of military dictators and to the end of the Republic.

In contrast to their banquet fare, the daily subsistence of both the post-Homeric Greeks and the Romans was largely a diet of grain dishes made more palatable by honey and wine and, whenever possible, supplemented by pork. Cretans long before them had raised sheep, goats, and hogs, had hunted hare and deer, had fished for tuna, lobster, crab, and had grown apples, quinces, and pears. The Mycenaeans, as we know from the decipherment of their tablets, had cultivated figs, olives, peas, and had raised coriander, celery, cummin, fennel, and mint. Later Greece and Rome continued to enjoy an adequate supply of cereals, fruits, and vegetables, but the plentiful cattle on which Homer's heroes feasted had declined to scattered herds on the meagre, eroded, and overgrazed grasslands of Attica. Red meat had be-

come a luxury. The Spartans had their black broth, a stew of pork, barley, salt, and vinegar. The Athenians consumed barley kneaded into a sort of porridge with water—"noble cakes," Plato called them—and griddlecakes. Hog puddings and sweetened sausages were very popular in Athens; "the stuffed paunch of an ass" was a delicacy. The early Romans boiled barley and wheat into a paste.

Though Rome had no commercial bakeries before the second century B.C., Athenaeus reports that there were at one point as many as seventy-two kinds of bread in Greece, and we can assume that the Romans must have known how to prepare many of these at home. The Romans also had their *placenta*, a honey-sweetened cake resembling that of Near Eastern cookery, and a traditional fruitcake was the *satura*, a mixture of barley mash, dried raisins, pine kernels, and pomegranate seeds laced with condiments and honeyed wine—a dish from whose name two interesting words derive. One is "satire," the Romans who invented and named this literary form looking upon it as a mixture or hodgepodge of many ingredients, sweet and sour; the other is "saturated."

The Greek peninsula—for the most part rugged and riverless, with its chains of mountains enclosing plains that lie sere during the long months of summer and autumn—was not hospitable to cultivation or cattle raising. Barely a fifth of it was (and is today) arable. The fisheries of the Aegean and eastern Mediterranean, too, were meagre, due to a lack of plankton in those transparent waters adequate to support large schools of fish. Many days, the small fishing boats returned to port with only a paltry catch of sardines, anchovies, squids, and octopi in their holds.

The Romans, however, were better favored, particularly as they expanded beyond their spare homeland in the Alban hills. They sought out the nearby plains of Etruria, finding the region "rich in [wheat], cattle and everything"—and it was from there, in the area between Fiesole and Arezzo, that the fine wheat came which was used as the basis of confectionery and what we know as pasta. Rome's greatest culinary advantage, as

Roman mosaic of a breadbasket

the state grew and prospered, lay in the very variety of the regions it incorporated and conquered, and in the efficient trade and transport network which fed back to the capital. There was game from the Laurentine forests, cheese from the herds of Tuscany, good wine from Campania (the best, that from Falernum); there were pickles and wine from Spain, pork from Gaul, apples and pears from Chios, lemons and pomegranates from Libya, plums from Damascus, apricots from Armenia, and peaches from Persia. And always important to the ancient world

was the oyster. To insure a constant supply, the Romans began seeding the salt ponds around Baia (Naples) about 100 B.C. Soon after, a richer supply of *ostreae* began coming in from faraway Britain, where the Roman invaders uncovered the great natural beds of Colchester and other estuaries of East Anglia. "Poor Britons," the historian Sallust remarked in 50 B.C., "there is some good in them after all—they produced an oyster."

Whatever the scarcity or abundance of foods, a remarkable similarity of customs of the table persisted between Greeks and Romans for many generations. Two meals a day, for instance, was the general rule, though some Romans did take a morning *jentaculum*—a piece of bread dipped in wine or eaten with honey or cheese or olives. A light meal (the *ariston* of the Athenians or the *prandium* of the Romans) consisting often of just a bowl of barley, perhaps a cut of cold meat, and a flask of wine, was eaten about midday and was frequently consumed standing up or *sine mensa*—without a set table, or cafeteria style. The main meal, the Greek *deipnon* or the Roman *cena*, took place in mid or late afternoon, preferably after exercise and a visit to the baths. (Nero was much criticized for sitting down to dinner as early as noon in his banquet halls "with fretted ceilings of ivory, whose panels could turn and shower down flowers and were fitted with pipes for sprinkling the guests with perfumes.") At dinner the practice among the gentry of both Greece and Rome was to recline on couches placed around the table. The couches were constructed with an incline at one end, so that the head of each diner rose

An Acquired Taste

*A*ll Gaul owes a huge debt to its ancient conquerors, for wine was most probably introduced into France by the Greeks, who left great stacks of *amphorae* about Marseilles as evidence. The Romans, too, found Gaul a ready market for their wines. Diodorus of Sicily wrote, "[The Gauls] have a real passion for wine . . . and, their greed leading them to drinking heavily, they get so drunk that they either fall asleep or become wild. This is why so many [Italian] merchants, impelled by their habitual cupidity, profit from [them]." When the natives discovered that they could cultivate the vine locally and even surpass Rome's production, the senate passed laws inhibiting competition, restricting foreign viticulture to the estates of wealthy colonists. The law seems to have had little effect, and by the end of the first century A.D., the grape was widely cultivated in Gaul, Sicily, and Etruria, where the *bucchero* or drinking horn, below, was used. Indeed, cereal production was so badly neglected that the Emperor Domitian decreed, again without much success, that no new vineyards should be planted in Italy and that half of those in the provinces should forthwith be uprooted and replaced by other crops. From contemporary writers, we know that classical wines were developed for a taste very different from that of today. They were rich in sugar, strong in alcohol, and concentrated in taste, due largely to the custom of leaving the grapes on the vine for several

 weeks after they had ripened—bringing about *la pourriture noble*, or "noble rot"—a practice still followed by the vintners of Sauternes. The wines were further adulterated with herbs, saffron, anise, flower scents, and (according to one writer who took a dim view of the practice and compared the vintners to pharmacists) sometimes colored with smoke. The wines of Vienne, among the most prized of modern growths, were resinated in Martial's day (and were called *vinum picatum*) as were those of Greece; and Pliny, whose oenological enthusiasms were second only to his interests as a naturalist, so admired the slow and careful processing of wines from the vineyards of the Ardèche region north of Avignon, that he studied the technique. He observed that after the vintagers had twisted the stem, "Some times they cut the entire branch and let it hang for a while, with the grapes still attached. Other farmers pick them when ripe, but before pressing them, they spread them out to dry in the sun or else dry them on hot bricks."

above the level of the board; the diner rested on his left arm and reached for food and drink with his right.

The Greeks, eating with their fingers, wiped their hands on morsels of bread that were then tossed to the dogs beneath the table; it remained for the Romans, who dipped their fingers in bowls of perfumed water between courses, to introduce the custom of the napkin. Often the guest would bring his own, using it to carry home what tidbits he could not finish at the table.

In Athens wives and children dined apart from their husbands and sat on straight chairs, often in another room; in Rome women were eventually admitted to the men's dining chamber, perhaps as a result of the influence of the more sociable Etruscans, who always considered feminine companionship essential to a good dinner. In either instance, the privilege of the dining couch was a mark of social distinction, and the lower orders of freedmen and educated slaves were not normally admitted to it.

Meticulous rules of precedence as to seating at a formal dinner were developed, particularly in Rome. There the practice was to group the couches around three sides of a rectangular table, leaving the fourth side open for service. To insure the liveliness of the conversation, the table was customarily set for no fewer than three—the number of the Graces—nor more than nine—for the nine Muses; the place of honor was the right-hand couch opposite the empty side of the table. A *nomenclator*, or usher, announced the names of the guests, who had duly washed hands and feet on entering, and assigned them to their places. Food

service then began—far more elaborate in later Rome, to be sure, than in Periclean Greece—the meal being divided into a series of courses beginning with a *gustatio*, or hors d'oeuvres of preliminary dishes, and going through one or more main engagements (*mensae primae*) to a climax of dessert.

Both Greek and Roman custom divided the formal dinner into two parts—the first in which one primarily ate, and the second in which one primarily drank, talked, and otherwise amused one's self and those assembled. In Greece the *symposium* (literally, drinking party) properly began with the end of eating and the offer of prayers and libations, particularly to Dionysus. So Xenophon writes of an exuberant evening with Socrates "when the tables had been cleared away, and the libations were made and a paean chanted." A *symposiarch*, or lord of the feast, might be appointed to lead a conversation on a given theme. Or he might oversee the bouts at wine: this happened for instance when Alcibiades, already well along in drink, invaded the famous symposium of Socrates with his revelers and made himself master of the evening. Had the group been able to stay awake, there might have been charades, parlor games, matches of wit and storytelling, throwing of knucklebones and dice, with tidbits of cake, dried fruit, grilled beans, and such to accompany the wine. In addition to the custom already established in Greece of bringing in entertainers ranging from jugglers to would-be Nereids, the Romans introduced the *commissatio*—a ceremonial drinking match at which a master of ceremonies dictated how many cups of wine each guest was to consume at one draught, and of what size and strength, and in what sequence around the table.

Such feasts, particularly as they took on ever greater length in Roman times, imposed considerable strain upon the digestive system. Vessels for self-relief were sometimes placed beneath the table. Belching, as a sign of satisfaction, was accepted and approved (as it is among certain Arab tribes to this day). Many rude jokes were made about breaking wind. In some circles there was resort to a *vomitorium* to purge the system and ready it for another round of food and drink. The poet-philosopher Seneca, himself on a strict diet, spoke with distaste of Romans who *"vomunt ut edant, edunt ut vomant,"* referring to a cycle of gorging and disgorging. But in general, vomiting appears to have been reviled by men of good taste, who preferred a bath and a massage, if need be, between stages of their banquet.

Perhaps the sharpest critique of overindulgence in later Rome, and certainly the liveliest, appears in the famed *Satyricon* by the first-century-A.D. author Petronius. Only portions survive of this work, sometimes called the first novel— a picaresque tale of the exploits of a band of wastrels taking their pleasure with new money. The ringleader, a Syrian freedman named Trimalchio, decided to stage a blowout of colossal proportions. At this boisterous affair, heralded by stewards and assisted by servants who first administered a pedicure to the guests, proceedings began with appetizers of fantastic design, including dormice (small rodents) rolled in honey and poppy seeds, and hot sausages laid on a

silver grill under which "black damsons and red pomegranates had been sliced up and arranged so as to give the effect of flames playing over charcoal." A donkey cast in Corinthian bronze stood on a side table; on its back were two panniers, one holding green olives, the other

Distributing the public grain supply in Ostia

black. While the guests were sampling these, a fanfare of trumpets announced the arrival of the host, "carried in propped up on piles of miniature pillows," as the American translator William Arrowsmith renders the scene, "in such a comic way that some of us couldn't resist impolitely smiling." A platter was borne in containing a peahen made of wood, with wings outspread as when setting. "Warbling waiters" thereupon plucked from the straw around her a pastry egg for each guest; inside were fat orioles seasoned with pepper. Jars of Falernian wine were passed around accompanied by dishes related to the guests' individual signs of the zodiac— chick-peas for Aries, a slice of beef for Taurus, a pair of testicles and kidneys for Gemini, the belly of a virgin pig for Virgo, a crawfish for Scorpio, and so on —followed by a flourish from the musicians and the entry of slaves bearing "fat capons and sowbellies and a hare tricked out with wings to look like a little Pegasus" accompanied by "four little gravy boats, all shaped like the satyr Marsyas, with phalluses for spouts."

Next was the presentation of "a wild sow of absolutely enormous size. . . . Perched rakishly on the sow's head was the cap of freedom which newly freed slaves wear in token of their liberty, and from her tusks hung two baskets woven from palm leaves: one was filled with dry Egyptian dates, the other held sweet Syrian dates. Clustered around her teats were little suckling pigs made of hard pastry, gifts for the guests to take home. . . . The slave who stepped up to carve . . . whipped out his knife and gave a savage slash at the sow's flanks. Under the blow the flesh parted, the wound burst open and dozens of thrushes came whirring out." This was followed by the presentation of a boiled calf with a helmet on its head, which was attacked and carved by a slave brandishing a sword and dressed up as Ajax. After this came a dessert designed by the confectioner in a large priapic shape surrounded by every kind of fruit. But this was not the end: Trimalchio invited all his guests to take a hot bath, after which a second service of courses began in another dining room, while those who felt they had better shift entirely to wine could drink in accordance with the rites of the *commissatio*.

Although this was written as burlesque, Petronius was not wildly exaggerating. Immense wealth was spreading among the newly rich. Favored by a corrupt court with all manner of supply contracts and trading monopolies, many of these men could and did emulate emperors in their magnificence. Rich *novi homines* had ice and snow, embedded in straw, transported all the way from the Alpine Ticino to their country estates around Rome in order to provide refrigeration. Fish ponds, or *vivaria*, were laid out amid their gardens to insure a constant and private supply of fresh trout, sturgeon, and carp. A single farm in the Sabine hills, so the historian Varro writes, brought in as much as sixty thousand sesterces in one year alone from the sale of thrushes raised in its aviaries for the luxury trade. Meanwhile, chefs skilled in handling the proliferating banquets became increasingly prized and costly. Livy recalls that while in early times a cook was considered "the lowest and least useful of slaves," a good one had since become "of prohibitive price." Only a very rich man could afford a first-class chef; Pliny remarks that "today . . . a cook costs as much as a triumph" (meaning the great public celebration honoring a returning military victor).

Almost all classical antiquity drank wine both at meals and at other festivities, and this fact has caused later censorious writers, particularly of Protestant and prohibitionist persuasion, to relate the eventual decline of the ancient, pagan world to its overuse. Actually, the wine consumed then, of a heavy, rather sweetish quality that would be unpalatable to most diners today, was almost universally diluted with water, the proportions leaning to five of water to three of wine. The Minoan Cretans drank wine in astonishing quantities, as their ruined cellars attest, though the studies of Sir Arthur Evans, the great archaeologist of Crete, leave some questions as to when. The Mycenaeans definitely savored it—we read in the *Iliad* of "Arne rich in vineyards," of "Epidauros full of vines"; and the recently discovered wine cellar thought to be that of the Homeric Nestor at Pylos could have accommodated six thousand liters. The Greeks especially enjoyed their wine at the annual festivals of Dionysus—the Haloa and Lenaea celebrations of winter, and the Eleusinian mysteries of the fall—and the Romans were partial to it at all times, first raising the grape in their own Alban hills and later also cultivating it in Spain, Syria, the Rhine valley, and especially France. Martial speaks of the excellent wine from *vitifera Vienna*—not, to be sure, the great Vienna of European history, where the Romans had an outpost too, but little Vienne along the banks of the Rhone (celebrated in our time by the presence there of one of the most hallowed restaurants of France, La Pyramide, and by the vineyards of Côte Rôtie and Hermitage).

It was surely not an abuse of wine that undid classical taste after it had reached its height. It was sheer gluttony and the lavish expenditure of men and money in its service. One Roman emperor, Vitellius, is said to have sent out a whole fleet to scour Mediterranean coasts for the makings of a single dish compounded of flamingo tongues, pike livers, pheasant brains, and lamprey milt. Great estates were converted for the production of peacocks, cranes, and pheasants for rich tables, leaving the emperors of Rome to provide handouts to the poor in the form of daily doles of grain.

Innumerable causes have been offered, particularly from the writings of Edward Gibbon on, for the decline and fall of Roman leadership and estate. One of the most curious causes, recently suggested by the American sociologist Seabury Colum Gilfillan, is that Roman aristocracy died off in large part from lead poisoning, induced by the use in wealthy circles of leaden cooking vessels. Wine or "must" that was boiled down to a syrup to make sauces and to sweeten wine, seems to have absorbed an especially heavy dose of lead, with a high frequency of sterility among this class the result. The poor, meanwhile, using ordinary earthenware that lacked a comparable chemical reaction, were spared. If this be true, the *defrutum* and *mulsum* prized by Apicius as elements of fine cuisine may have played some part in the dissolution of the Empire.

As the Roman Empire declined, so too did the influence of its cuisine, apparently throughout the Mediterranean. Enter the Visigoths, the Ostrogoths, the Vandals—peoples far removed from the cult or culture of the oyster, the sauceboat, and the pastry cook. Enter also the Christian converts, men and women from eastern Tarsus to the Appenines and Alps and beyond, who in many cases cast off all association with the pleasures of the pagan table. To them a meal, reflecting that holiest meal of their faith, was a ceremony of brotherhood—recalling Hebraic origins. The church father Tertullian of Carthage said that a man should eat only to the measure of his hunger. And amid the disarray of the world of A.D. 400 and after, great hunger lay ahead.

SALAD DAYS
OF
THE CAESARS

A cargo of Cyrenaic herbs readied for export, from a vase painting c. 550 B.C.

A shrine dedicated to lares, *gods of the Roman household*

Luxury Begins at Home

Dining at home, as depicted in a tomb relief

The *triclinium* was the favored room of the Roman household, and much time and care was lavished on its decoration. The extraordinary mosaic opposite was uncovered in the ruins of Pompeii, where it had once served as a dining room floor. It illustrates the wide range of sea food common to the classical diet: lobster, skate, eel, octopus. A *lararium* like the corniced shrine above was common to houses of every class. In return for offerings of wheat, salt, and wine, the gods blessed kitchen and table.

Behind the scenes at a Roman dinner, a small army of cooks and assistants was needed to prepare a meal

The Cook's Domain

A good cook was a household status symbol and could be worth his weight in sesterces. Most cooks considered themselves artists rather than galley slaves and had inflammable temperaments to match. The mistress who meddled in the kitchen risked having dinner sabotaged.

suitable to gracious living. In the next room, stewards kept the wine and the conversation flowing.

The Roman kitchen was crowded, simple, and smoky. Wood or charcoal burned on a raised brick hearth which was seldom equipped with a chimney. Many a cook toiling over his fire must have cursed Fornax, the goddess of the oven, and anyone else in earshot, every *jentaculum*, *prandium*, and *cena*. His pots and pans, which rested on grates above the fire, were usually of earthenware or iron. Implements like the Etruscan ladle, far left, and the strainer whose punctures form a Bacchic face, above, were also heavy, requiring a firm hand to manage them.

Homemaking was a skill acquired with time, patience, and energy. A mother and her daughter perform the age-old rite of the cooking lesson, as shown in the sixth-century-B.C. Boeotian terra cotta above.

Caveat Emptor

Imperial Rome was the supermarket of the Mediterranean world. Into the city's shops and stalls flowed the bounty of an empire: grains from Africa and Egypt, venison from Gaul, the cured meats of Andalusia, and rare spices from the East. One market, which was built by the Emperor Trajan, housed 150 shops; and more than 250 mills throughout the capital supplied flour to countless bakeries similar to the Pompeian shop shown in the wall painting opposite. The baker, perched atop his open-air stand to watch for prospective customers, makes a sale.

Vendors sell cutlery from open stalls.

A matron shops for a plump goose destined perhaps for the evening's meal.

63

In Vino Veritas

 The deceptively innocent but glassy-eyed mask in the insert at left belongs to Dionysus. He was not only the Greek god of wine but an entire religion unto himself. Intoxication was thought to wrest the human spirit from the mind's control. Wine, then, became everywhere in the classical world a medium of religious experience. The bronze sculpture above shows one true believer, minus spirit, sagging on the arms of two servants who are attempting to guide him homeward after a hard night's worship. Even the noble Socrates, himself a sometimes bibber, was moved to say, "So far as drinking is concerned, you have my hearty approval; for wine does of a truth 'moisten the soul' and lull our griefs to sleep." But he warned, "If we pour ourselves immense draughts, it will be no long time before both our bodies and our minds reel, and we shall not be able even to draw breath, much less to speak sensibly." These parting words of fatherly advice, though well meant, were seldom heeded.

The footed wine jar above—which was designed to stand inside a cooler—shows Satyrs during an orgy. For the Greek on the kylix below, the party is over.

OVERLEAF: *A detail from a vase painting, c. 400 B.C., depicts revelers lounging on couches. The krater resting at their feet was used for mixing the wine.*

Trade and Table

Aelius Aristides, in his impressions of second-century Rome, wrote: "So many merchantmen arrive here with cargoes from everywhere, at every season and with each return of the harvest, that the city seems like a common warehouse of the world." Undoubtedly, this was an accurate description, for the state of Rome's stomach relied, in great part, on the wealth of her colonies. Nearly half a million tons of wheat annually passed through Rome's great port of Ostia which was located only a short, two-day sail from the granaries of North Africa. Roman colonists who had settled and farmed the conquered lands provided the Empire with a steady flow of food-stuffs. Opposite, an early mosaic shows sailors carrying a menagerie of live game —an ostrich, a gazelle, and a trussed-up boar—aboard a ship which is about to sail for Rome and her hunting preserves.

Half the wines served in Rome were produced in Spain. But many came from Gaul, where boats filled to the gunwales with wine casks, top, plied the rivers of the fertile Moselle valley. The last leg of the long trip to Roman tables was accomplished by carts, above.

69

The War on Hunger

The imported wines and exotic birds of peaceful commerce were
for the rich. It took enormous tributes of cattle and wheat, received annually from captive lands, to fill the tables of the public
at large; and as the population swelled past a million, even these
food sources were insufficient. Under the Empire, Rome's armies
not only waged war but were responsible for shipping food back
to the home front. Trajan sought to increase local productivity,
too: veterans were forbidden to emigrate, and under a plan called
the *alimenta*, they were settled on tenant farms around the capital.
A program of public assistance, the *annona*, provided monthly
doles of grain to the urban proletariat; and *tesserae*, or ration cards,
were issued. By Trajan's time a third of Rome was on welfare.

As the Roman armies reaped victories, so too did they reap grain in the fields of their enemies. Above and at left, engravings after bas-reliefs on a column celebrating Trajan's campaigns show troops plundering fields of the Dacians of eastern Europe and returning to camp with the spoils.

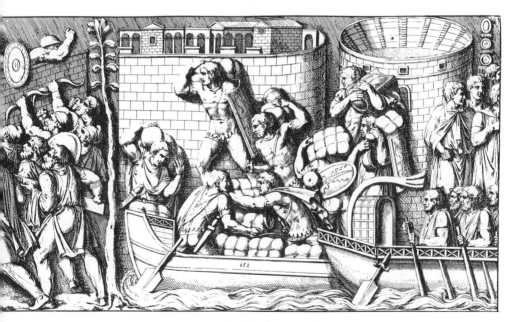

As Rome's supply routes reached farther into the interior of the continent, they were increasingly exposed to attack by marauding barbarians. The scene above shows a fortified city on the northeast frontier under siege. While troops repel the enemy at the wall, cohorts bring food to the fortress.

It was a glutted world that faced the lean times of the Christian era. The centuries of banqueting were drawing to a close. While pagan Rome had feasted horizontally from couches, the early Christian meal was eaten upright and with solemn dignity—at least in the retrospective version of the Biblical "Marriage at Cana," below.

Lord and serf arguing a fine point of horticulture in the well-tended herb garden of the manor

MEDIEVAL
FEAST
AND
FAMINE

A millennium is a long time to wait between first-class dinners. Yet even more time was to separate the last great tables of antiquity from those of the Renaissance, whose influence began spreading from Italian cities to France and beyond soon after A.D. 1500. The vast intervening epoch was by no means one of little taste. The medieval centuries presented a profusion and confusion of tastes—some advanced, some rudimentary, some ample, some ascetic—and these reflected the turbulence of the age, its new ethnic mixtures, and its insecurity. It was a time in which feast alternated with famine; plenty with scarcity; the king's peace with baronial anarchy; crusader with brigand (often united in the same person); a Saint Francis with Gargantua. It saw a return to mud huts and near savagery in areas where proud Roman cities had flourished along the Rhine and the Danube; in Spain it also saw the incursion of a Moorish culture of great refinement. The age suffered depopulation through barbarian invasions, plagues, and chronic famines, of which some of the earliest were so terrible that sporadic instances of cannibalism are recorded. France endured ten famines during the tenth century and twenty-six in the eleventh and twelfth; and England, it has been estimated, averaged one famine every fourteen years in the same period. The bubonic plague decimated the Eastern Roman Empire in the sixth century and spread to Sicily and southern Italy in the eighth, reaching its most virulent stage in the "Black Death" of fourteenth-century Europe. The age was also one of mighty influx of new blood, as Teutons and Slavs mixed theirs with that of older

Wine rations for William the Conqueror's men

Western stock. It saw Europeans almost constantly at war, fighting off Saracens in the south, viking raiders in the north, Huns, Avars, Bulgars, and Slavs in the east. Crusades and the recurrent struggles between partisans of emperors and partisans of popes also disturbed the Continent. Peaceable Christian life was preserved chiefly by the monasteries, those great refuges of both learning and practical craft for a Western world fallen into ignorance and disarray.

The first to suffer under such conditions was the poor peasant, subsisting

in bitter seasons on a diet of groats if he were lucky, and making a "feast" (so the fourteenth-century poem *Piers the Ploughman* by William Langland has it) of "a farthing's worth of mussels or a farthing's worth of cockles." There were better days for him, too:

> *"I have no penny," quoth Piers*
> *"Pullets for to buy*
> *Nor neither geese nor piglets*
> *but two green cheeses*
> *A few curds and cream*
> *and an oaten cake*
> *And two loaves of beans and bran*
> *to bake for my little ones*
> *And besides I say by my soul*
> *I have no salt bacon*
> *Nor no little eggs, by Christ*
> *collops for to make*
> *But I have parsley and leeks*
> *and many cabbages*
> *And besides a cow and a half. . . ."*

At the same time, the age found barons surfeiting themselves on tankards of mead and trenchers of spitted game in the smoky Great Halls of their castles, entertained by jongleurs, or minstrels, somewhat after the fashion of Homer's heroes. It was an era of hearty and often gross sexuality, culminating most visibly in the exhibitionist codpieces of the fifteenth century. It was also an age of tender romances—of Abelard and Héloïse, of Dante and his Beatrice, and the exquisite "courts of love," presided over by Eleanor of Aquitaine, with their cult of adoration and physical restraint.

Beginning with rawness and ruin, and only a shattered remembrance of things past, the age evolved a social system, based on feudal ownership of land, that for a time, roughly the twelfth century, brought relative stability and moderation to much of Europe. This tempered life was, however, short-lived. In the centuries that followed, the Lucullan dinners of abbots and other high clergy were judged particularly scandalous. The enthronement in 1467 of George Neville, the Archbishop of York and Chancellor of England, was celebrated by a feast that included (according to a kitchen list that has survived) 300 huge loaves of bread, 300 tuns of ale (about 75,000 gallons), 100 tuns of wine, 105 oxen, 6 wild bulls, 1,000 sheep, 304 pigs, 304 calves, and 400 swans. It took sixty-two cooks to prepare the meal. This kind of clerical indulgence caused much social unrest and led the reforming Archbishop Cranmer, in the next century, to inveigh against clerical extravagance. He ruled that an archbishop must not consume at one sitting more than six flesh dishes, and not more than four "second" dishes; a bishop could have only five of the first and three of the second; archdeacons and deacons were to be allowed only four and two respectively; and so on down. When Cranmer was condemned to be burned at the stake for his heretical beliefs, there were few friends to come to his defense.

Feast, famine, gluttony, temperance —there were correspondences between the cycles of life of the Middle Ages and those of Rome. Yet the contrasts were profound. The Roman Empire, even when overrun by invaders from the northeast and east in the fifth century A.D., still occupied about one fourth of the entire European continent, including almost all its most fertile areas. The Romans had cleared vast forest lands, drained marshes, built a network of over ninety thousand miles of roads, developed advanced techniques of stock-breeding and crop management, and brought together peoples from Britain to Asia Minor and from Gaul to Africa under the aegis of Roman law, language, and trade. Rome had also exported its civilized ways at table. We read of fifth-century festivities at which Romanized Gauls reclined on cushioned divans (though a few Gauls, disdainful of Roman indolence, preferred chairs, benches, stools, or wooden seats, covered with rugs). The guests ceremoniously wash their hands before and after the first course, don special robes and slippers, spread napkins which they have brought, and embark upon a repast that begins with a drink of heated wine mixed with honey, to be followed by fresh eggs, quarters of beef, mutton, and pork, all highly seasoned with pepper, pickles, caraway, and poppy seeds, saffron, aromatic balsam, honey, and salt. For the serious eaters there was also boar meat with a garniture of cooked apples, deer, roebuck, hare, and even the urus, "that wild buffalo whose horns become at once a cup and a trophy."

But gradually such scenes of dining extravagance disappeared as the peoples Rome had conquered and assimilated were in turn overwhelmed by rough tribes of Goths in Spain, Franks in Gaul, Angles and Saxons in England, and Norsemen along the northern seacoasts. Under these barbarian successors to the Roman proconsuls, such imperial centers as Arles, Reims, Trier, London, Cologne, Aix-la-Chapelle, Utrecht, Mérida, Cartagena, Vienna, and great Rome itself sank into oblivion. Wealth, splendor, and power survived for another six hundred years in Byzantium, the eastern part of the Empire; but in central and western Europe, almost all semblance of social order vanished, and civilization halted. The new barbarian kings were little more than local tribal chieftains; bands of brigands roamed the countryside; roads fell into disrepair, bridges collapsed and were not rebuilt, trade and communications almost came to a standstill; the successors to many productive estates were primitive communes whose peasants worked strips of land with crude plows. One traveler speaks of the desolation of the once-rich Danubian plain, where "not a laborer is to be seen." Vast areas cultivated by Romans and their *coloni*, or tenants, reverted to forest, marsh, and wasteland—the haunt of bears, boars, deer, and aurochs. By the tenth century, woodland had recovered a third of England, much of Spain, Italy, and the greater parts of fertile Gaul and the Low Countries.

Amid this decay, communities were economically isolated, their life one of sheer subsistence. In the event of crop failure or shortages of cattle, draft animals, or manpower, outside help was rarely available. Moreover, lack of enough fodder to tide animals over the winter (in turn the result of poor governance of soil) made it necessary to kill off most of the livestock in the fall. A great slaughter usually occurred at about Martinmas (November 11), with some of the unseasoned meat being served immediately and the rest salted or dried. This practice, which continued through

A yeoman's feast in slaughter season

most of the Middle Ages, resulted in a dismal winter diet made palatable only by resort to many herbs and spices. In addition, the livestock tended to be stunted and lean, since the art of selective breeding had been lost, and sick and healthy animals interbred. Then, if the meagre supply of winter meat ran out, even the few remaining brood cattle might have to be slaughtered—assuring more shortages of animals for plowing, breeding, and eating in the future.

Despite the disorder we associate with the term "Dark Ages," forces were stirring to restore a modicum of good life to western Europe. The feudal idea— that of the banding together of lords and tenants, masters and workers, for mutual protection and with mutual social and economic obligations—began to emerge even before the reign of Charlemagne. After having been crowned Holy Roman Emperor in the year 800, the Frankish king became through the power of his personality and his office one of the great unifying forces of European history. An inspired organizer, he brought local chieftains to order. He sought to turn the barbarian from the sword to the plowshare. He promoted efforts to reclaim lands become barren, and in 812 he issued *De*

Villis, a remarkable ordinance concerning the management of the royal domains of Aquitaine. It set forth a model scheme of imperial workshops and agricultural enterprises, listing everything from the number of millers, bakers, butchers, weavers, smiths, and fullers needed to an inventory of the specific vegetables and herbs he wished to see raised. In this, he was acting in concert with the power that had crowned him—the church of Rome, possessed now of more than a third of western Europe's land holdings under the stewardships of its bishoprics, abbeys, and monasteries.

Monasticism, with its ideals of asceticism and withdrawal, had come from the Christianized East to Italy in the fourth century. There it met with initial hostility, but by the seventh and eighth centuries, monasteries had established themselves as centers of stability in the European countryside. Major houses arose in places as distant as Jumièges in Normandy, Malmédy in Belgium, Bury St. Edmunds in England, St-Gall in Switzerland, Kempten and Fulda in Germany, Santiago de Compostela in Spain, and along the Scottish borderlands and Baltic marches. In France King Clovis founded the abbey of Ste. Geneviève; Dagobert endowed St-Denis; and Sigismund established St-Germain-des-Prés.

Peasants reaping and binding sheaves of grain

Many barons, thinking of prestige and heavenly reward, also provided lands and money for monastic communities. "From the seventh century," writes the modern historian Ferdinand Lot, "there was not a single nobleman or bishop who did not wish to ensure the salvation of his soul by a foundation of this kind." At the end of the tenth century, there were 543 abbeys with monastic enclosures in France alone.

Far more than retreats, these institutions became communities of advanced farming and industry. The church, through such voices as the reforming Benedict of Nursia, founder in A.D. 528 of the first monastic order in western Europe, took exception to the earlier ideal of the withdrawn and contemplative hermit. To the Benedictines of Monte Cassino, he proclaimed a gospel of manual labor as a Christian duty. Hard work (besides subduing the weaknesses of the flesh) would lead to the productivity Europe so desperately needed. Wide areas of wasteland were reclaimed by tonsured men working under their abbots. Bogs were drained, new fields seeded, gardens and orchards re-created, vineyards revived. (The wines of the Côte d'Or of Burgundy, well known in Roman times, became prized again in the seventh century.)

The monastery, as a model farm capable of surviving hard times, emerged as a storehouse of food to feed the surrounding populace. It was also the wayfarer's perennial inn, offering him lodging and a good meal by the refectory fire. Monks, some of whom may have heard of Apicius, were among the very few who had some notion of Roman cuisine. Indeed,

79

until the Renaissance the monastery appears to have been the chief transmitter of higher forms of cookery. It was also the center of communal life and culture, providing miracle plays and rough games that diverted the peasants of neighboring manors.

The Benedictine monastery of St-Gall on Lake Constance, for example, was a town unto itself—a self-contained center of civilized living even in A.D. 830. Enclosed by walls, it possessed in addition to the all-important abbey thirty-two buildings, several gardens for herbs and vegetables, a central fountain, and a courtyard surrounded by cloistered ambulatories reminiscent of a Roman villa. There were rooms for baking, brewing, drying fruit, and preserving; sheds for various breeds of animals; and quarters for the craft of cooper, wood carver, shoemaker, saddler, and smith. St-Gall had a herb, or "physic," garden that yielded roses, water cress, sage, rue, pennyroyal, peppermint, cumin, lovage, savory, rosemary, and fennel; a kitchen garden that grew such staples as cabbage, beets, parsnips, carrots, leeks, shallots, celery, parsley, and garlic; and an orchard that produced apples, pears, plums, quinces, peaches, and even figs. As its wealth increased, St-Gall extended its holdings to broad tracts in Swabia, Neustria, Alsace, and even Italy, with as many as four thousand "manors" of greater and lesser lands bound to it as fiefs. Each was obliged to supply an annual quitrent in the form of produce—another stimulus to agriculture.

But far greater than the enterprise of the Benedictines was the mighty colonizing work of the Cistercian order,

founded in 1098. Expanding rapidly from its mother abbey in Cîteaux south of Dijon, it settled on the northern moors of England, along the sandy wastes of the Bay of Biscay, amid the bogs and forests of Germany, and in the gorges of the high Vosges. In the Bordeaux country, and along the Rhine and Neckar rivers, Cistercians grew grapes for wine; in Normandy, they grew apples for cider; in Germany, Flanders, and England, they farmed the staple cereals for malt and ale. East of the Elbe, they raised horses. They mined large salt deposits. They successfully bred cattle, pickled the meat, and tanned the hides. They constructed dikes against the northern seas and drained the swamps to reclaim areas usable for meadow and pasture, for sheep runs and goose farms, and for the grazing of the Low Countries' scanty herds of cattle.

From such industry Europe was to acquire productive skills again. There remained severe limitations on the commerce of food, as of all other products. Apart from the half-ruined road system and the constant threat of marauders and pirates, there were tolls and local customs duties that impeded the passage of goods. There was a jumble of local laws and local currencies (even abbots at times minted their own money) that made business beyond the barter level difficult. There was virtually no investment capital. There was a language barrier—one part of Europe spoke in tongues descended from Latin, the other in German dialects. Yet travel, production, and trade gradually revived. The Celts of Wales and Ireland had long fared out to sea in their small boats to

In Praise of Folly

*I*n an era that idealized courtly love, swallowed whole the heroic *chansons de geste*, and listened patiently to somber admonitions to prepare for the afterlife, poetry celebrating the joys of wenching and wining was something of an anomaly. The poets of this uncommon verse came from the ranks of defrocked monks, itinerant scholars, and medieval equivalents of beatniks, and their verses were often audacious Latin parodies of the rhyme, rhythm, and melody of church liturgy: "Paternoster of the Wine," "Gospel According to the Silver Marks." Dubbed "goliards," a term derived from the Latin *gula* for "gullet," or perhaps from the Biblical Goliath, these merry mendicants hicced and hiked around the European countryside, with only their ribald songs for baggage. In exchange for bed, bread, and beverage (preferably alcoholic), the goliards would provide their host with an evening's entertainment. Not surprisingly, ecclesiastical authorities soon moved to suppress these "low strollers," and by the beginning of the fourteenth century they had all but silenced them. Their bawdy zest for living is heard in the song below, from a collection of *cantiones profanes* known as the *Carmina Burana*. The ballads, translated by the medieval authority George Whicher, were hidden under cloak and key in the Bavarian cloister of Benedictbeuern until their discovery in the nineteenth century.

Hircus quando bibit,	*When he drinks the lewd clodhopper*
que non sunt debita dicit,	*Uses language most improper;*
cum bene potatur,	*When he's altogether pickled,*
que non sunt debita fatur.	*Then by uncouth deeds he's tickled.*
Cum bene sum potus,	*When I'm in my cups my curse is*
tunc versibus effluo totus.	*That I simply slobber verses;*
Cum sicco siccor,	*But I'm quickly sick of* hic *or*
nec in hic, nec in hec, nec in hoc cor.	Haec *or* hoc *when lacking liquor.*

transport their salted meat and hides to the Continent in exchange for its salt, oil, wines, and cloth. By the eleventh century a modest international market was centered in Lombardy (particularly in Pavia and in Florence), the future seat of Italian banking. In the Low Countries, as new towns developed, a cloth industry based on sheepherding came into being. Soon Europe was to see great annual fairs, especially those of the Champagne region at Troyes (origin of troy weight standards), and of Provins and other centers near Paris, at which the goods of Flanders were exchanged for those of Italy, and the wines of France for spices from the East.

As they grew, such fairs and lesser local markets stimulated a formidable interchange of produce, and therewith an enhancement of the medieval diet. Normandy and Picardy exported apples. The south of France and eastern Spain again abounded in orchards. Oils, chestnuts, plums of southern Italy, were widely sold. Roquefort cheese was mentioned in 1070 in the records of Conques, a monastery on the pilgrimage route to Santiago de Compostela. Cheese from Gorgonzola was part of a bequest made to the school of St. Ambrogio by the Bishop of Milan in 879. As early as 1200 the hard cheese of Parma was also cured. Rice from Spain appeared on the market, as did Spanish saffron, ginger, sesame, figs, quinces, the first cultivated strawberries, and the lemons raised by its Moorish masters—though north of the Pyrenees citrus fruits remained a luxury for all but the richest men.

The fisheries of the Atlantic, too, expanded enormously under the stimulus

of trade and profit. Coastal peoples of far northern waters had long risked their lives in pursuit of seal, porpoise, and whale. Now herring, one of the cheapest and most nutritious fishes, traveling in schools of millions from the Shetland Islands in the spring to Yarmouth in the fall, made that port into a great trade

A French cheese merchant

center. There and in other North Sea ports huge catches of herring were brought in, salted down, barreled, and shipped to markets all over the Continent. Fishing fleets of several realms also pursued cod and haddock off the Dogger Bank, Iceland, and Norway. The Hanseatic League, a powerful mercantile confederation that originated among several free coastal cities including Germanic Lübeck, Hamburg, and Bremen, built much of its trade with the Baltic on the exchange of East Prussian wheat and Russian furs for fish and Scandinavian dairy products.

The Thames, still unpolluted, was itself a major source of supply for a people that strictly observed fifty-two weekly "fysshe dayes" in the year and moreover relied heavily on fish during Lent, which came providentially at a time when supplies of winter meat were running low. As Thomas Tusser put it neatly in his description of the "fermers dailie diet":

A Plot set downe, for fermers quiet,
*   as time requires, to frame his diet;*
With sometimes fish, and sometimes fast,
*   that household store, may longer last.*

Let Lent well kept, offend not thee,
*   for March and April breeders be.*
Spend herring first, save saltfish last:
*   for saltfish is good, when Lent is past.*

The Seine also had a profitable fish trade, and numerous breeding enclosures were built along its banks. Fish such as salmon and trout were especially prized; monasteries and noblemen's manors had their own "stews," or fish ponds, recalling Roman vivaria, to provide fresh carp, eel, and tench; and a noble sturgeon, wherever caught, became—like the whale—royal property subject to the disposition of the king.

In this agricultural revival, great prosperity came to the monastic foundations that had done so much to inspire systematic food production. While the rules of some orders—the Cistercian in particular—forbade them to sell produce in secular markets or to participate in fairs, large quantities were sold at the monastery doors. One critic suspicious of all this trafficking declared, "Flocks and fleeces, crops and granaries, leeks and potherbs, drinks and goblets are nowadays the reading and study of monks."

Gradually, actual labor on the land passed from the monks to serfs, acquired as the monasteries won more and more estates. Since the orders were in later centuries largely populated by sons of the feudal aristocracy, for whom manual labor could hardly have been an article of faith, the church proclaimed that "vicarious" labor, of monk supervising serf, was a suitable substitute. The Cistercian Caesar of Heisterbach wrote that the richest houses of his order were equipped to feed five thousand persons every day if need be. His Welsh brother in the church, Giraldus Cambrensis, known for his caustic criticism, explained with unusual tolerance, "this greed of theirs . . . arises from the hospitality which the members of this order, although in themselves the most abstemious of all others, indefatigably exercise, in their unbounded charity to the poor and to strangers." The thirteenth-century abbot of Leubus complained, "Scarcely a month passes by, nay, scarcely a day in which it is not necessary for the abbot to give away something. . . . One demands money . . . another grain, the one bread, the other hay, and he takes at the same time 100 head of sheep . . . the seventh would like to have his jug filled; the eighth demands fish; the ninth requests a measure of large cheese; the tenth, seed-cake; the eleventh, apples . . . but it is far worse when the huntsmen come with their servants and dogs. . . . They are as hungry as wolves and a loaf of bread for one of them is too small."

The outcome in any case led to a vast improvement in the daily board, though dishes tended to be heavy and robust rather than accomplished in any Roman sense, save on occasion at the high table of a leading abbot or great lord. The peasant's daily bread was coarse-grained and dark, made most commonly from barley, rye, or bean flour. The wealthy townsman or squire bought fine wheaten flour for the making of white loaves, cakes, or pastry; and as a treat for the tenant on a feast day or when he had finished some "boon-work," the lord might contribute one of his own white loaves, along with a joint of meat. Bakers and millers were licensed and were considered so essential to the economy as a whole that at one point Louis IX, the sainted king of thirteenth-century France, ordered that they be relieved of the military watch duties expected of his other subjects in Paris, in order not to interrupt their work.

It was an age of stews, thick broths, pies, and soups. Long-stored, salty, stringy meats were, as we would say, "tenderized" by hashing, mincing, and pounding, and were then served up with an admixture of wine or honey. A fish stew known as *chaudemer* was the ancestor of chowder. There was herring pie, a stew composed of pickled fish, raisins, currants, dates, and cinnamon placed in a "coffin"—that is, a pastry blanket—and baked. A truly royal pie is described by a chaplain in the fourteenth century court of Charles VI of France. It consisted of three partridges, six quails, a dozen skylarks, thrushes, and diced bacon mixed with *verjus*, a kind of vinegar made of green grapes or apples. There was a dish called venison frumenty, popular in fifteenth-century England, in which strips of deer meat were put into a soup made of wheat boiled in milk, to which the yolks of eggs, sugar, and salt were added. Sometimes several different stews or soups were served and consumed at one meal.

Amid Europe's forests, there had always been game in plenty, though hunting and venery became the prerogative of landlords who enclosed their demesnes as private parks; and poaching became a capital—but very prevalent—crime. The right to fish rivers and streams also belonged to the lord, though the peasant devised ways of trapping and spearing that readily escaped the keeper's eye. Hogs, which foraged for acorns in the woods, were particularly valued when cattle and fodder were scarce. The best flesh went into pickled "souse"; the trimmings, including parts of the head, feet, ears, tongue, tail, bones, and gristle, were set to simmer with an accompaniment of vegetables, sage, and other herbs to become "brawn"—a great favorite of people of moderate means.

Hawking for game birds was the pleasure of those who could afford falcons and hounds, but a great deal of "fowling," involving the use of nets and snares, was done by the peasants, who also became the custodians of flocks of poultry as barnyard domestication increased. Pheasants' eggs were a delicacy, but ordinary hens' eggs were commonly eaten fried or poached. A thirteenth-century Englishman counseled, "A fried egg does not need instruction, but dig not at it with your thumb turned down—move it about with the point of your knife." Advanced cooks managed to produce that challenge, the omelette.

Despite the growing variety of the fare, the common diet—except for those seasons and places in which absolutely fresh produce could be obtained—continued to be based on preserved meat and fish, and this led to a heavy impo-

Taillevent

When Guillaume Tirel was a mere scullion, scrubbing pots and tending fires, French cooking was still a relatively brutish, almost hazardous affair. The huge open kitchen hearth was better designed for warming drafty halls than for cooking dinners; and the chef's battery consisted of a few iron and copper pots suspended by chains, a turnspit or two, and a pair of andirons, occasionally fitted with crude braziers. Foods were either mercilessly boiled over a high flame or skewered for roasting, and the cook who approached his steaming pots to stir or add that certain something did so at his own peril. Tirel, or Taillevent as he called himself, had the good fortune to be born just as kitchens and the cook's estate were improving: oval-shaped ovens were built into the wall, and damping devices to control the heat were developed. He used his opportunities well. After several years of service to Philip VI of Valois and the Dauphin, he was summoned to the court of Charles V where he became "first squire and master of the kitchen garrisons." Around 1375 Tail-

levent put off his aprons long enough to write *Le Viandier*, the oldest French cookbook on record. The manuscript, which gives a detailed picture of the tastes and manners of the medieval court, enjoyed a phenomenal reputation not only in Taillevent's lifetime but in succeeding centuries, when it became one of the first books to be printed. Like all French chefs after him, Taillevent was much occupied with the secrets of making a fine sauce, a culinary innovation which was now literally within the reach of the clever cook. In the seventeen sauces described, including such classics as *cameline* and *sauce Robert*, the master recommends as thickening agents plain and grilled breads—flour as a binder was still unknown. Bread also figured in the popular "sops," etymologically and gastronomically the fore-runner of puréed soups. Sops were made of milk flavored  with wine, saffron, honey or other sweeteners. Slow-cooked *ragoûts, galimafrées, mortreux*, and *hochepots*, all newly fashionable, were explained; Taillevent even offered recipes for vegetables. (The very fact that he coaxed the king to eat his first cabbage was recorded as a matter of historical interest.) When Taillevent died in 1395, at the age of sixty-nine, he was buried beneath a tombstone portraying him in the honorary dress of a sergeant at arms, complete with helmet and mace. Fittingly, his shield was emblazoned with three cooking pots.

sition of sauces and seasonings to cover up the briny, stale flavors. Royal sauces relied on exotic flavors—Edward I of England ran up a spice bill of £1600 in one year—the equivalent of $100,000 today. But every household boasted an herb garden—even the peasant usually had a small plot of his own.

Salt, fundamental in the curing of meats and fish and in the disguising if not improving of flavors, was honored by a special place on the board. Often it was contained in a monumental salt-cellar placed just a little below the center of a lord's high table—whence comes the pejorative reference to guests seated "below the salt." The London Guild of Salters, aware of their importance, early coined their own motto: *"sal sapit omnia"* ("salt savors everything").

Hardly less prestigious were the Pepperers, who organized themselves as a guild in England in the eleventh century, when this common condiment was most widely imported. It had been brought to Europe by Arabs, though many Englishmen who traded for it were unaware of its origin. Cinnamon, and cloves as well, had begun to enter France as early as the eighth century, transported from China, India, and Indochina along the few tenuous trade routes then surviving in the Middle East. All but cinnamon were very expensive.

Crusaders who encountered sugar cane growing in Tripoli, where it had spread from Syria, delighted in sucking on the stalks and encouraged its 'importation as an improvement over the traditional sweetener, honey. But in large part Europe still relied on its own condiments. There was anise for meat jellies and

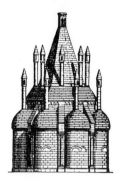

Abbey kitchen wing

liqueurs, and bay for soups, omelettes, and fowl stuffing. Caraway for bread and cakes also had medicinal value, along with dill, which "assuageth the rumbling in a man's womb," and sage, "also . . . good for venom or poison."

What came out of the pot was sometimes a mixture that to us would seem as foreign as anything in Homer: for example, *maumenye ryalle*, a stew of strong wine, cinnamon, soft pine cones, cloves, almonds, ale, and pulped hog's brawn. Saffron, ginger, salt, and more sweet wine completed the stupefying concoction. The English then as now were partial to a strong sauce of mustard. Chaucer's Frankeleyn, a rich freeholder in the *Canterbury Tales* and "Epicurus' owne sone," kept a year-round open house of food and drink:

> *With-oute beke mete was never his hous,*
> *Of fish and flesh, and that so plentyous,*
> *It snewed in his hous of mete and drinke,*
> *Of alle dayntees that men coude thinke.*

His cook was charged with all manner of hearty dishes, varying in particulars "after sondry seasons of the year"; and "he coude roste, and sethe, and broille, and frye, Maken mortreux, and wel bake a pye"—but woe unto him if the mustard sauce was not "poynaunt and sharp."

Herbs and condiments, in addition to being thrown into stewpots, medical preparations, and witches' brews, also played a major part in the medieval salad. A recipe for "salat" from *The Forme of Cury*, an important early cooking manual compiled by the master cooks of Richard II of England around 1390, advises, "Take parsel, sawge, garlec, chibollas [young onions], oynons, leek, borage, myntes, porrectes [a kind of leek], fenel, and ton tressis [cresses], rew, rosemarye, purslarye [purslane]; lave, and woisshe hem clene; pike hem, pluk hem small with thyn [thine] honde, and myng [mix] hem ind raw oile. Lay on vynegar and salt, and serve it forth."

Generally, customs and manners of the table were as bluff as the fare. Before the twelfth century, kitchens as such were a rarity. Food was prepared either at the hearth of the "hall" that served as the household's one meeting and dining space, or on the floor below, or in a separate building. By the fourteenth century, manors and castles were equipped with kitchens sometimes as spacious as the halls themselves, with high-domed roofs to let the steam and smoke escape. Large ovens bearing iron doors were built into the thickness of the wall. There were pantries, butteries (after *boutelle* for the bottles stored there), and pits for disposal of wastes. Occasionally, small dining rooms were built separate from the hall, but in great houses the custom of large numbers of people eating together persisted. The head of the household sat on a dais often under a canopy of embroidered

silk or wool; he was surrounded by his family and guests, who were ranged along the cloth-covered head table in order of precedence, while retainers sat at lower, trestle tables, food being sent down to them after those at the high table had taken their choice of the best cuts presented. In the twelfth century, typically, every two diners shared one large bowl or wooden trencher (so named for the *tranche*, or slice of stale bread, which had still earlier served as the dish) for their stews or meats. Everyone also was given a cup or mug for his wine or ale, though in poorer houses

Mother and child at work

and on ceremonial occasions everywhere, a single cup was passed around. Etiquette demanded that hands be washed before eating, that weapons be left at the door, and that hands remain above the board (except when tossing scraps to the dogs) as evidence that the guest carried no concealed dagger. Grace was said either before or after meals.

In royal and other great houses, a marshal was in charge of the arrangements. He supervised the airing of the hall, the freshening of the rush-strewn floor, the cleaning of the tables. He was protocol officer, too, designating the order of seating and the planning of entertainments. He was assisted by a butler who saw to the distribution of wine and bread—just the proper quality for each rank of diner, from fresh loaves for the master to four-day-old bread for the lowest table. The butler in a royal household also performed the rites of assay, tasting everything for possible poison before serving. A sewer (steward), a cupbearer, squires, pages, and various other assistants brought the dishes into the hall for presentation by squires and pages on bended knee. To carve before one's lord or noble father was part of a knight's education. Even great lords did table service to their liege: when Rudolf of Hapsburg was crowned Holy Roman Emperor at Aachen in 1273, the seven electors waited upon him as recalled in an ode of Friedrich Schiller: . . . *Die Speisen trug der Pfalzgraf des Rheins, Es schenkte der Böhme des perlenden Weins* . . . ("The Palatine duke proffered the dishes, The lord of Bohemia served sparkling wine").

In the Middle Ages one ate with a knife, a spoon, and with one's fingers, and numerous directives were offered on the proper use of each:

Let not thy spoone stand in the dysche
Whether thou be served with fleshe or fishe
Also eschewe, withouten stryfe
To foule the borde clothe with thy knyfe. . . .

Thus, do not leave your spoon in the bowl or wipe your knife on the tablecloth. Another: "With mete ne bere thy knyfe to mouthe," evidently meaning

that the food-bearing knife should not touch the tongue. One person who mastered the art of dainty consumption was Chaucer's aging Prioresse, the provincial Madame Eglentyne, whose painstaking table manners are described in one of the poet's most famous tongue-in-cheek passages:

At mete wel y-taught was she with-alle;
She leet no morsel from hir lippes falle,
Ne wette hir fingres in hir sauce depe.
Wel coude she carie a morsel, and wel kepe,
That no drope ne fille up-on hir brest.
In curteisye was set ful muche hir lest.
Hir over lippe wyped she so clene,
That in hir coppe was no ferthing sene
Of grece, whan she dronken hadde hir
* draughte.*

England in Chaucer's time was regarded by Continentals as an unsophisticated region, at the outskirts of trade

Stewards at a lord's table

and taste, and unfamiliar with what remained of the light of antiquity. Yet England shared with the Continent, among other things, a quite new fashion in mealtimes. Throughout western Europe the main meal of the day, once reserved for afternoon or evening, was advanced to the morning, the hour varying with place and period. We learn of

Frenchmen rising before dawn, dining at nine A.M., and supping at five:

> *Lever à cinq, diner à neuf,*
> *Souper à cinq, coucher à neuf,*
> *Fait vivre d'ans nonante et neuf.*

For an Englishman during the Yorkist age, however, this early dinner was only an epilogue to his traditional hearty breakfast, often taken at six. We read of Edward IV breaking his fast after very early Mass with ale, bread, and boiled beef, mutton, and herring.

While many ancients had contented themselves with two meals a day, only one of them substantial, now there were often four, the English in particular favoring a post-supper "livery" at about eight in the evening—or what we would consider a late buffet or formidable bedtime snack. A Venetian traveler visiting England during the disordered period of the Wars of the Roses commented on the huge amounts of food and drink Englishmen consumed, adding that even "when war is raging most furiously, they will still seek for good eating and all their other comforts. . . ." He noticed, also, a predilection among the English for drinking in public taverns—institutions new or strange to a proper Continental, more accustomed at that time to the abbot's table or the prior's garden if he went forth to dine and wine.

The pleasures of the medieval board were united with the observance of religious feast days, of which there were many, some carried over with new meanings from the pagan calendar. There was the solstitial Christmas, with its boar's head borne in on a garlanded platter and its mince pie, all enjoyed to the accom-

Jolly transactions at an English mill

paniment of carols; there was New Year's Eve and Twelfth Night, or the Feast of the Three Kings, with its proverbial "cakes and ale"—actually a "wassail bowl" (a concoction of ale and roasted apples spiced with cloves, ginger, nutmeg, and cinnamon) and spicecakes. Another ceremony connected with the Twelfth Night was the election of the King and Queen of the Bean. A cake containing a pea and a bean was portioned out and the happy recipients of the prizes crowned. To the frugal Spaniards, the *Fiesta de los Tres Rejes* was the day of greatest feasting.

There was Easter and Hocktide (the second Monday and Tuesday after Easter), observed with the first harvest of winter fields, duly blessed; and there was Michaelmas with its geese. Whitsuntide was marked with morris dances, cakes, and Whitsun ale, brewed from malt contributed by the parishoners and sold to raise money for the church. The summer solstice festival known as Saint John's Eve, or Midsummer Night, was celebrated with fires on hilltops (to symbolize the height the grain would reach) and much carousing; and so around to Sheepshearing Supper and Harvest Home. Yet almost any occasion, sacred or secular, provided an excuse for conspicuous consumption if the makings were available. Betrothals, burials, enthronements, or just visits among clans —any event would do.

A twelfth-century visitor to the high table of the Prior of Canterbury recorded that he had often seen sixteen or more very costly dishes presented there. An account of Saint Louis' dinner on a *maigre* or "fast day" in 1248 lists fresh fish, crayfish, crabs, new beans cooked in milk, eel pies, rice with almonds and powdered cinnamon, and finally junket, tarts, and fruits. A formal dinner in the following century (according to the royal chef Taillevent) might begin with a first course of capons with cinnamon broth, chickens with herbs, and venison, followed by a second course of roast beef, peacocks, capon pies, et cetera, with a third course of partridges, stewed pigeons, venison pâté, sugared tarts, and so on. The banquet celebrating the marriage of Henry IV of England and Joan of Navarre in 1403 was of a still higher order, and was served in successive courses—three of meat followed by three of fish, including also young pigs, woodcocks, plover, rabbits, quails, snipe, sturgeon, shellfish, lampreys, and pike. Each course concluded with a "soteltie" of sugar and pastry, the final dessert fashioned in the form of a crowned eagle.

The "soteltie"—literally, a subtlety—was the showpiece of the medieval chef, and several might appear during the meal as distant reminders of Rome.

There were intricate sweetmeat confections representing such subjects as Saint George slaying the dragon, a stag at bay, the Trinity watching over the Virgin Mary, or a royal panther. There were also trick pies that opened to release flocks of birds ("four and twenty blackbirds, baked in a pie"). A peacock with

Public censure for a drunkard

gilded beak, symbol of nobility and incorruptibility of soul, or a swan, a symbol of satisfaction of desire, might also appear on the table, though both must have promised more delights than they delivered, the peacock being rather stringy and the swan oily.

At one of the most spectacular banquets toward the end of the Middle Ages, the "Feast of the Pheasant" given by Philip, the Duke of Burgundy, in Lille in 1454, the Knights of the Golden Fleece in their red velvet robes were treated to an immense pie which opened to the festive strains of twenty-eight musicians playing inside. The climax came when a giant in Saracen dress led in an elephant carrying a beauteous girl, who symbolized in her person the captivity of the church in the East. The girl implored the knights at their glittering tables to rise and rescue Constantinople, seized the year before by the Turkish infidels. Next, a pheasant decked out with jewels was borne in, and Philip and his knights vowed in its name, if not in the name of the "captive" girl, to take up the sword on a new crusade—which, however, they never did. The Renaissance, and the social and political changes it brought, saw to that.

Usually, at a high lord's table, there were not only "sotelties" between courses but also *entremets*—a word signifying in that day not lesser dishes but the jugglers, jesters, acrobats, dancers, and minstrels who entertained the company at intermissions. Important dishes—they might be *fylettys en galentyne* (an elaborate meat loaf) or roast swan in full plumage —were often announced by a flourish of trumpets, as in antiquity. And like Martial and Petronius long before, there was Rabelais, the satirist, to poke fun at excessive gormandizing, presenting on one occasion in *Gargantua and Pantagruel* a mock dinner to whose "regular menu" were added 16 oxen, 32 calves, 63 young kids, 300 milch cows soaked in sweet wine, 700 woodcocks, 6,000 pullets, and so on and on—all in the hands of the ravenous chefs Wolfsauce, Hotchpot, and Lickjuice, along with the stewards Jockbottle, Clearglass, and Guzzlctun, who kept their own tankards "brimful with wine."

Indeed, the well-filled cup was ubiquitous in the age. While the early heroes had quaffed their viscous brew of mead made of fermented and spiced honey, and the English and Germans had vastly improved upon this with their superior malt ales, the culture and enjoyment of the grape survived the darkest days. Cultivators of the vine in England were especially protected by King Alfred, and the economic census known as the *Domesday Book*, assembled twenty years after William the Conqueror's arrival, lists thirty-nine productive vineyards there—several of them evidently pre-Norman. Some wine may have been made in Ireland in the earliest missionary days, and vineyards were established along the Moselle, Rhine, and Danube rivers in the eighth century, so successfully that German wine merchants were traveling to London in the early twelfth century and probably before. German grapes, however, were limited in that successful cultivation resulted almost exclusively in white wines, a rich and robust red growth eluding the vintners then as it has ever since. The wine of English vineyards, perhaps for reasons of climate, remained pale and thin; and with the shortage of labor due to the great fourteenth-century plague, and the consequent import of higher quality wines, its production eventually ceased.

The taste of the time ran to sweet and what we would call syrupy, or dessert, wines, among them the growths surreptitiously exported from the vineyards of Xeres (Jerez) where the Moslems were supposed to grow them, in accordance with the prohibitions of the Koran, for food rather than for wine. Also marketed abroad was the Portuguese wine known as Algarbe (an ancestor of port); such sweet types as the Trebbiano of Tuscany; and above all, what was known in England as Malmsey, a heavy drink which took its name from the Greek village Malmasia and was produced at its best in Crete.

It remained for France to build very gradually that culture of noble growths and vintages that one day were to be the accompaniment of the cuisine of a Vatel or a Brillat-Savarin; meanwhile, during the Middle Ages French wines were often drunk heavily sweetened and spiced, too. The monastery, again, played a part in improving and refining quality. Not only was a considerable amount of wine needed for sacramental purposes, as well as for refreshment at table for thirsty monks and those whom they entertained, but viticulture was a "cash crop," essential to the economy of their community. Large vineyards in Burgundy passed into the hands of clerical foundations. Several vineyards in Beaune, Vosne, and Gévrey were entrusted to the Abbey of Bèze by the Duke of Amalgaire in 630. Later, in 1275, the Gévrey vineyard was taken over by the Cluniacs; and shortly after, an enterprising peasant planted an adjacent vineyard, Le Champ de Bertin or Bertin's Field—source of Chambertin, the favored wine of Napoleon III. Pommard and Meursault wines in the Beaune district of the Côte d'Or can also be traced from the eleventh century and Cistercian husbandry. In the coastal valleys of the Gironde around Bordeaux, a somewhat lighter wine was developed (called *clairet*, or claret, for its clear color). Many of the estates there passed under English dominance following the accession of the duchy of Guyenne as part of Eleanor of Aquitaine's dowry in her marriage to Henry II. Perhaps one of the first Englishmen who had what we

might consider an advanced taste in wine was King John Lackland, for in 1212 he had his bursar import eight casks of Anjou wine along with twenty-six of Auxerre for his table. Before the fifteenth century, a semiannual convoy of English ships was setting out for the Gironde, to bring home cargoes of the newest growths—fresh wines being generally preferred to those of a preceding year, until the craft and value of aging wine were understood. There were also vineyards in what is now the heart of Paris, a city today far more concerned with the consumption of wine than its growth: the vineyard of Clos Bruneau thrived on the site now occupied by the Théâtre de l'Odéon.

In A.D. 1234 we first hear of a vineyard in the Pauillac district in the Bordeaux region owned by one Gombaud de Lafite. What his wine tasted like, especially when drunk green and possibly sugared and spiced, we can only surmise. But it was one of the fifty or more wines of note—some Cyprian, some Spanish, some from the Moselle, but mostly French—cited in a thirteenth-century poem entitled the *Bataille des Vins*. One day it was to become the renowned Château Lafite, ultimately crowned at a summit meeting of wine experts at the Paris Exposition Universelle of 1855 as the first of the *grands crus classés*, or great classified properties, of Bordeaux, and thus in the judgment of many experts, the finest wine in all the world. Soon after, its 173 acres, at a price equivalent to $1,500,000 today, were to become the property of the Rothschild family of bankers, geniuses at imaginative and first-class investment.

THE
GROANING
BOARD

King Arthur and his knights at the fabled Round Table

Pigs and peasant gathering acorns in November

A warm hearth in February

Readying the fields in March

The Four Seasons

These early-fifteenth-century illuminations from the *Très Riches Heures* of the Duc de Berry depict the seasonal rhythms of life on a feudal estate. The first plowing and seeding took place in spring; vegetables were farmed in summer. With the arrival of fall, the peasant looked to his livestock and filled his larder for the approaching winter months. A minimum of thirty-six bushels of wheat was required to support the average peasant's family through one year on the manor, but according to Langland's *Piers the Ploughman*, "in winter they suffer much hunger and woe."

Grape harvest in September

The Common Market

Fairs and markets were the lighter side of the Dark Ages and focal points of the burgeoning international economy. Caravans of merchants, minstrels, and peasants met seasonally to display and sell products ranging from songs and salted meats to rare spices and silks. Most famous were the fairs of Champagne near Paris held in the twelfth and thirteenth centuries. They lasted anywhere from sixteen to fifty days.

At fairs, gingerbread was baked in the form of Saint Anthony's beloved pig, also commemorated in this stone church-stall carving.

The Bishop of Paris blesses a fair at the Abbey of St-Denis.

A poulterer clinches a sale in the market place.

Royal Rigors—and Rewards

Kings and knights may have had privileged positions at the medieval table, but they paid for them, and sometimes dearly. A seat above the salt more often depended on a man's military record in the field than on his virtue, social wit, or skill at a trencher—though the latter often proved helpful. If he drank too much, he risked being outmaneuvered by another guest for his liege's favor. If he ate too daintily, he might provoke rude comments among the servants, whose meals were often served just below the high table. Then, too, he could never be sure that the meat before him had not been poisoned by a jealous peer.

One of the duties that went with being noble was meting out alms to the poor, a chore engaging Saint Louis in the thirteenth-century manuscript drawing above. Opposite, Charlemagne observes the ceremony of assay—the tasting of food for poison. Below, an even more unappetizing ritual is undergone by a twelfth-century Irish king who, to win his crown, is taking a bath in horsemeat soup while he and his attendants eat blood sausages.

OVERLEAF: *The King of Portugal and his court entertain John of Gaunt.*

Fysshe Dayes

Grilling fish c. 1330, from the Holkham Bible

Fish was not only a popular and inexpensive dish in the medieval diet, but a fact of Christian life. Counting Fridays, Lent, and other fast days, meat was off limits for nearly half the year—to the profit of the fishmonger, left. Inland, many feudal estates like the German manor, right, stocked their moats with carp, trout, and other varieties of fresh-water fish to insure a weekly supply for the lord and his villeins. Some charged their tenants stiff rates for fishing rights, and though harsh punishment was meted out to trespassers caught with "angleroddes," poaching was widespread. Of coastal fish, herring was by far the most important. As an Englishman put it, "A red herring is . . . most precious merchandise, because it can be carried through all Europe. . . . The poorer sort make it three parts of their sustenance. It is every man's money, from the king to the peasant. . . . A red herring drawn on the ground will lead hounds a false scent. A broiled herring is good for the rheumatism. The fishery is a great nursery for seamen, and brings more ships to Yarmouth than assembled at Troy to fetch back Helen."

102

Camouflaged more for ceremony than for deception, huntsmen confront a buck, above. Clattering forth in a square-wheeled cart, below, they give their prey a better than sporting chance.

Good Form in the Forest

As in all noble pursuits, the sports of venery and hawking were attended by a complicated set of rules prescribing what to wear, how to handle weapons, and how to carve up the quarry afterward. The miniatures shown on these pages come from a fourteenth-century treatise by the French courtier Gaston Phoebus. Above, hunters dawdle over lunch spread in a clearing. A tablecloth was evidently *de rigueur*.

Of the poorly prepared artisan "He makes broth in a basket."

"Measure Is A Merry Mean"

While a select few could indulge in Rabelaisian repasts, the humbler folk of the later Middle Ages were of necessity more temperate in behavior. Just as the upper classes had their manuals of hunting etiquette, the *petite bourgeoisie* likewise had their guides for leading the correct life. Books of proverbs were both didactic and moral in purpose: through the combined force of word and picture, the reader was cautioned to follow the golden mean in his day-to-day activities. The *Proverbes en Rimes*, opposite, from a manuscript c. 1490, were written in the vernacular and were accompanied by illustrations literally interpreting the maxims, serving as models for those engaged in middle-class pursuits.

Of the imprudent husbandman "He eats his grain in the blade."

Of a slothful baker: "In the oven of a lazy cook the dough freezes."

Of small-town gossipmongers: "An oven and mill are nurseries of news."

Of the glutton: "He grabs with both hands, chews with both jaws."

Of a Jack-of-all-trades: "He who makes crosetz makes lasaigne."

Of a clever manager: "He can pick new spoons out of an old house."

On a sense of measure: "The knife is chosen according to the meat."

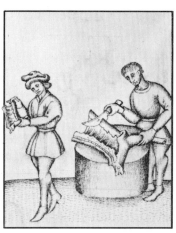

On shopping: "Of a little take a little, of a mickle take a mickle."

Of a complaisant scullion: "He who turns the spit never tastes a bit."

Of a wanton wench: "There's many a slip between mouth and spoon."

Of the foolish spendthrift: "He winnows his corn in the wind."

A Flemish merchant samples the wine, while a human treadmill loads casks in the town square.

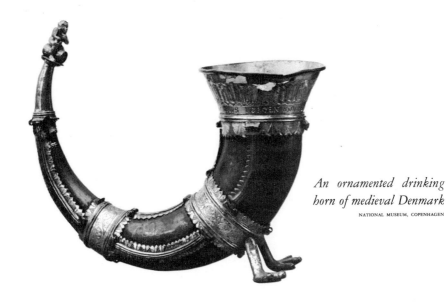

*An ornamented drinking
horn of medieval Denmark*

NATIONAL MUSEUM, COPENHAGEN

Good Cheer

One of the chief producers of wine was
the church, which maintained its own
vineyards. Part of the vintage went to
the brothers, part to the service of the
Mass; the remainder was sold to thirsty
travelers or was marketed in cities. The
cost of transporting it made wine more
often the rich man's tipple; beer, cider,
perry, and mead were the poor man's
cheer. Regulations were supposed to
keep tavern fare up to standard, and instances of doctored drink were dealt with
summarily. In 1364 one John Penrose of
England was given a penalty to suit his
crime: he had to drink his own brew.

OVERLEAF: *Honey collecting was hazardous
duty—a race between the keepers and bees.*

VATICAN LIBRARY, ROME

PIERPONT MORGAN LIBRARY, NEW YORK

Students carousing in a Strasbourg tavern

To the Manor Born

Women performed many tasks on the feudal manor. Here they pick spinach.

Digging truffles with a crude hoe

Taking a midday break in the shade

Baking white bread in a wall oven

Agriculture in the Middle Ages was centered in the feudal estate, where a tenant serf led the dawn-to-dusk routine portrayed in these illustrations from *Tacuinum Sanitatis*, a fifteenth-century Italian herbal. The serf was literally rooted to the soil; he passed with the lands when the manor changed ownership. In exchange for his labor, he was given a small plot, providing him with a simple fare of cereals and vegetables.

Depending on the vows of the order and the monastery's proximity to centers of commerce, a community might be secluded or very worldly indeed. Prosperity threatened to interrupt the contemplative life, particularly as agricultural surpluses were becoming sought on the open market; and overindulgence at table was a subject of numerous tracts by church reformers. Such sanctions did not discourage the brother at left, who is nipping at the cellar wine supply while filling the abbot's pitcher.

Peace or Prosperity

Kitchen work is interrupted by the arrival of the devil, above. Meals among the "Poor Clares" were not so diverting; opposite, they sup during a reading of the scriptures.

The festive "Marriage at Cana," transplanted to Renaissance Venice, by Veronese

RENAISSANCE
OF
THE TABLE

The year 1533 saw a trio of extraordinarily brilliant monarchs—the Tudor Henry VIII, the Hapsburg Charles V, and the Valois Francis I—seated on the leading thrones of Europe, each at the height of his prowess and display. It also saw a Florentine girl of fourteen arriving in France to marry a prince. Before long she would become the leader of a revolution in tastes of the table.

At Windsor Castle and Hampton Court, hearty Henry was stuffing in huge gobbets of food and disporting with Anne Boleyn, whom he was to wed that year in defiance of Pope Clement VII's refusal to grant him a divorce from Catherine of Aragon. On the Continent the austere Charles, heir to his family's domains in central Europe along with the crown of Spain, and since 1519 Holy Roman Emperor, was shuttling between his far-flung capitals at Madrid and Vienna, with little thought of comfort or pleasure. The year before, in 1532, he had thrown back the Turks along the Danube and had patched up a truce with

117

Luther's and Zwingli's rebellious Protestants at Nuremberg. Meanwhile, at Blois and his other châteaux in the French countryside, the prodigal, dashing Francis, devotee of arts and luxuries as well as of mistresses, was hard at work advancing his fortunes against the overweening Hapsburgs by means of alliances, marital and otherwise. His young son, aged fourteen, was that year to be the instrument of Francis' policy; and in casting about for a mate for the boy, the king shrewdly chose an heiress of the richest and proudest family in ducal and divided Italy. So it was that Catherine, daughter of Lorenzo de' Medici, landed in Marseilles in October to become there the child bride of the boy who was one day to succeed Francis as Henry II.

The match was arranged through the good offices of the girl's uncle, Pope Clement. Giulio de' Medici, as he was otherwise known, was a great lover of political machination and the arts. He had in fact been Catherine's guardian since the death of her father and her elder uncle Giovanni de' Medici, the munificent Pope Leo X, and thus held her as a pawn in international chess. Advantages would accrue to both sides in the match; for the Papacy, a political alliance with France; for Francis, a handsome Medici dowry and papal support. Young Catherine came bearing gifts of a more lasting sort, too. Trained at the papal court, she brought the elegant manners of Florence and a small army of Italian chefs. These *maîtres queux*, as the French called them, introduced to noble tables of France such refinements as artichoke hearts, sweetbreads, truffles, grated Parmesan, liver *crépinettes*, along with *quenelles* of poultry, and a taste for veal (thitherto unappreciated north of the Alps). Predictably, Italian cooks became fashionable in households of rank.

More was to come with Catherine and her entourage, or in their wake. Among new confections were delicate macaroons, zabaglione, custard cakes, "iced cream" (Florentine cooks prepared a different flavor for each day of her wedding festivities), and frangipane tarts, an invention of Count Cesare Frangipani, who made them for her before she left for France. Melons, which had been introduced from the East by way of Italy sometime before, now enjoyed new popularity, spurred perhaps by Jacques

Saddle with pockets for food and drink

Pons, professor of medicine, whose *Sommaire Traité des Melons* suggested fifty different ways of serving them. Imported for the French table were fine works of Venetian glassware, faience from Urbino, embroidered napery, and table silver wrought by artists such as Benvenuto Cellini. Also from Italy came that new tool of the cultivated, the *fuscina*, or fork, though its use north and west of the Alps remained rare until the seventeenth century. Catherine herself may never have used one; we do know, however, that the implement was to travel as far as England by 1582, when Queen Elizabeth received as a New Year's present a coral-handled fork. How esoteric it was to the English, even after the turn of the century, is apparent in the chronicle of the voyager Thomas Coryate, who wrote of his discovery following his venture into Italy: "I observed a custome in all those Italian cities and townes through which I passed, that is not used in any other country that I saw in my travels. . . . The Italians . . . do alwaies at their meates use a little forke when they cut their meat . . . their forkes being for most of yron or steels, and some silver. . . . The reason of their curiosity is, because the Italian cannot by any means indure to have his dish touched with fingers, seeing that all men's fingers are not alike cleane." Such fastidiousness was long regarded by Englishmen as an affectation of "fops and jackanapes."

Queen Catherine was both a precocious gourmet and a glutton. She loved her *tournedos* (another Florentine specialty), veal dishes, kidneys, and cocks' combs, sometimes to the point of excess particularly as she grew older: one observer at a round of royal feasts in 1576 remarked that she "ate so much that she almost burst and was terribly ill with diarrhea." She did, however, insist on great ceremony at board. Late in the fifteenth century, ladies of the French court had taken to absenting themselves from their lords' hearty, often boisterous tables, to dine in the privacy of their own chambers. A particular notion of delicacy had persuaded them that it would be unseemly for them to be seen eating in public, since mastication of food supposedly distorted the contours of their face and detracted from their beauty. Catherine changed all that. If eating had any effect on beauty, it was to enlarge the body, not deform the face. Imperious, unconcerned with her figure, and as vigorous in personality as her husband Henry was dull, she ordered the ladies of the court to attend stately banquets which, in form and protocol, were to be both the models of Elizabeth's dinner rites across the Channel a few decades later and the precursors of the splendors of Versailles.

Catherine de' Medici—the most influential, worldly, womanly presence and maker of taste since Eleanor of Aquitaine—was an embodiment and transmitter of that revival of classical manners and modes that had arisen in Italy several generations before her birth. Her native Tuscany was not only urban, in contrast to the isolated feudal estates and monastic communities of northern Europe, but urbane in its extensive life of commerce with East and West, its wealth of finance, and its resulting leisure time for self-improvement. The enterprising, rich, and cultured merchant of the Tuscan town of Prato, Francesco di Marco Datini, lived before 1400 in a prandial style very different from that of the Gothic north. His dinners began, not with a heaping of crude slabs of meat or bowls of stew, but with a *minestra*, or soup, that was often sprinkled with Parmesan, or a dish of *lasagne* or *ravioli*. Datini's chef also favored garlic and mushrooms—especially the small, delicate *prugnoli*—to lend savor to the cutlets that followed. His doctor expressly recommended veal: "Place it in your belly, in every way you can, for you can have no more wholesome victuals." The

La Dolce Vita

*E*ven among the pleasure-loving Tuscans, the people of Florence were renowned for their lusty appetites. It was commonly charged that they made better use of their glasses than their plates, and a contemporary estimated that the annual consumption of wine was more than five barrels for every man, woman, and child in the city. A month rarely passed without some excuse for an uninhibited *convivio*—like the pre-Lenten carnival procession pictured below, or the star-crossed feast of Calendimaggio (May Day) that introduced

the young Dante and Beatrice. For some, even a public disaster could be a sociable affair, as Giovanni Boccaccio records in the *Decameron*, a collection of tales told by a fictional group of men and women who have retreated to a villa outside Florence to escape the great plague of 1348. For ten days they outdo each other with stories of the cupidity and pretentiousness of their fellow men. Florentines, it seems, are so greedy that they are easy marks for con men and pranksters. On the eighth day of exile, one of the party tells the story of a foolish painter who sets out for a fabulous "Nomansland" where, he is told, they tie up the grape vines with sausages and a goose and gosling cost but a cent, and there is "a mountain of grated Parmesan cheese, inhabited by people who [do] nothing but make macaroni and ravioli . . . [and] a stream of white wine, the best ever drunk. . . ." Several tales later, one of the listeners tops them all with a story of a Florentine doctor who is duped into providing lavish board for two men on their promise to introduce him at an imaginary social club. Describing the hall where the club meets, one of the pretenders gives an exaggerated picture of the elegant entertainments which Renaissance aristocrats did, in truth, know. "It is a marvel to see the hangings . . . and the tables royally spread, and the quantity of handsome servants . . . and the basins and jugs and flasks and cups and other gold and silver vessels from which we eat and drink, and the many varied dishes of food according to each man's desire which are set before us. I could never describe . . . the sweet sounds of infinite musical instruments and the songs full of melody . . . nor all the wax candles which are burned . . . nor the quantity of sweetmeats consumed nor . . . the wines. . . ." Upon hearing that the con men dumped the doctor onto a manure pile en route to a club dinner, the listeners agreed he got his just deserts.

merchant also prized the tender beans growing in his garden.

In nearby Urbino in the next generation, Federigo da Montefeltro—the ruler of the duchy—was known for the high style of his table: among his five hundred household servitors there were five "readers aloud at meals." Later, the Duke of Milan commissioned Leonardo da Vinci to organize spectacular festivals. Under Lorenzo the Magnificent, there were Florentine carnivals with processions representing old Roman triumphs; and his son Giovanni de' Medici, the future Pope Leo X, even as a cardinal, rarely dined without the musical accompaniment of Italy's leading chamber musicians. In Venice there were water-borne dinner parties and regattas: one year at the Festival of the *Sempiterni*, a corporation of nobles, a splendid ball was literally launched in the Grand Canal.

About this time printed books of etiquette and cookery began appearing in numbers second only to Bibles. The first of these, Platina's *De Honesta Voluptate* of 1475, provided some sound advice on the value of avoiding disputes at table: "The stomach needs natural warmth, little motion and little mental agitation; otherwise it becomes weak and unable to produce its digestive juices." It also offered some novel recipes for advanced tastes—fish in aspic and a tart of chestnuts and cheese that may have prefigured the *quiche* of French cuisine. There was an Italian volume of 1480, *The Fifty Courtesies of the Table*, which cautioned its readers, "Do not stuff too large mouthfuls in both cheeks. Do not keep your hand too long in the platter and put it in only when the other has withdrawn his hand from the dish"—a presentiment, perhaps, of the fork. But far more important was the discovery of eight books by Apicius found in manuscript by the traveling Italian scholar Poggio Bracciolini at the library of the Fulda monastery in central Germany. Eventually these classical recipe texts, no doubt reworked by monastic scholars, were to be brought to the Vatican library and published in Milan just before 1500. The interest in them was such that the edition was pirated almost at once by Venetian printers.

Polished behavior and courtly dining also absorbed the Florentine-born prelate Giovanni della Casa, who published his own guide to good manners, *Il Galateo*. Della Casa inveighed against expressing one's self with gestures of the fork and emphasized the ceremonious presentation of an orderly sequence of dishes, some served from the *credenza*, or sideboard, decorated with the family silver, others carried in from the kitchen and pantries.

Perhaps the most influential of Italian Renaissance books concerning the table was Bartolomeo Scappi's *Cooking Secrets of Pope Pius V*, published in 1570, which presented menus that began with Neapolitan spicecakes and marzipan balls and proceeded through *prosciutto* cooked in wine and served with capers and strained grapes, "songbirds roasted on the spit, served cold, with tongues sliced over them," legs of goat, a soup of pigeons and almond paste, "stuffed fat geese, boiled in Lombard style. . . ." Scappi prescribed a change of napery, water for washing the hands, and toothpicks as a fitting close to a proper meal.

There were, to be sure, occasional dark rumors about the nefarious uses to which such elaborate foods could sometimes be put, particularly in the hands of a Cesare Borgia and his sister Lucrezia, supposed experts at hidden poisons early in the sixteenth century. One such was a white powder, *cantarella*, sugary and of a pleasing taste when added to a dish, but deadly. Alexandre Dumas in

Chicken dinner in a Renaissance household

his *Crimes Célèbres* described how the Borgias obtained a particularly virulent poison. The concoction was made, says Dumas, by forcing a bear to swallow a strong dose of arsenic. As the poison took effect, the beast was suspended by his hind legs, and a stream of foam poured from its mouth; this foam was collected on a silver plate and bottled by someone in the Vatican in expectation of some future mischief.

The taster of food and drink, who sampled dishes for evidence of foul play in the presence of his lord and lady before they dined, would remain a functionary immediately attached to the royal or high ducal table in many courts until the nineteenth century. Elizabeth of England, for instance, insisted on one (as for that matter did Adolf Hitler centuries

later). To dispense with "the proof of the test," as Henry IV of France did on one occasion when he was the guest of Madame de Montpensier, was a sign of special confidence. Then there were nasty little devices, mentioned in an Italian book on magic and potions, for making an unwelcome guest sick at table by mixing his wine with the filth of a dog's ear; or for driving him away by cutting up harp strings and strewing the small bits on hot meat, causing them to writhe like worms.

But such meannesses, accompanied by violence and occasional death, could not prevent Italian taste and style from becoming the exuberant toast of fashion-seeking western Europe. True, there were elements among the French *bourgeoisie* and the prospering English yeomanry in particular that scoffed at this southern incursion, and cooks were to be heard denouncing the foreign fork itself as a possible poisoner of food. The urbane essayist Montaigne, a leading interpreter of the Renaissance spirit in later sixteenth-century France, was to poke fun in one of his liveliest passages at the pretentiousness and self-importance of Italian *maîtres queux* as they flocked with their new dishes into France. In an essay entitled "Of the Vanity of Words," he wrote of a conversation he had with "an Italian who was in the service of the late Cardinal Caraffa until his death, in the capacity of major-domo. . . . He entertained me with a dissertation on the science of the gullet with the gravity and demeanour of a schoolmaster, as if he were discussing some important point in theology. He minutely explained that there was a difference in appetites: that which we have when fasting, that which comes after the second or third course; the means, now of simply gratifying it, now of arousing and stimulating it; the organization of sauces: firstly in general, then particularizing the qualities of the ingredients and their effects; the different salads according to the season, that which should be warmed, that which requires to be served cold, the manner of adorning and embellishing them to make them pleasing to the sight also."

Still, though a Montaigne might smile at its vanities, Europe was rapidly growing more stable under strong monarchs or at least uncontested dynasties; far wealthier and better schooled than before the spread of commerce and the growth of cities, men craved both pomp and polish. Perhaps the ultimate example of Italian opulence at table was reached at the regal banquet given in Mantua in 1581 to celebrate the marriage of that duchy's ruler. At the raised head table, under an immense *baldacchino*, or canopy, sat four cardinals, three dukes, and many other dignitaries. At the next table (to follow a contemporary description translated in Colin Clair's *Kitchen and Table*) there were "100 ladies beautiful beyond measure and most richly garbed." Four choirs in galleries at the four corners of the hall provided music. The finest Venetian glass crowded the sideboard; and the guests, "after having drunk, smashed the glasses they held in their hands as a sign of great joy." Richly embroidered tablecloths had been laid; "the napkins were marvellously folded in various manners with columns and arches, which presented a beautiful sight with innumera-

ble streamers of coloured cloth gilded with the arms of all the noble lords who were at table." The first "service" from the credenza consisted of "salads decked out with various fantasies such as animals made of citron, castles of turnips, high walls of lemons; and variegated with slices of ham, mullet roes, herrings, tunny, anchovies, capers, olives, caviar, together with candied flowers and other

Fish market during the busy Lenten season

preserves." The more serious eating began with "venison patties in the shape of gilded lions, pies in the form of upright black eagles, pasties of pheasant, which seemed alive, white peacocks adorned and re-clothed with their fanned-out tails, and decked with silken ribbons and divers colours, as well as long gilded confections which hung everywhere about the peacocks, which stood erect as in life, with a perfume emanating from the kindled wad in their beaks and an amorous epigram placed beneath their legs." And so on, to "three large statues in marzipan, each four hands high," representing famous mythological personages and events.

Imitation in France of such Italian delicacies and grandiosities, the novelist and gourmet Alexandre Dumas wrote in his *Dictionnaire de Cuisine*, was to reach a height under Catherine de' Medici's son Henry III, who reigned from 1574 to 1589 under the domination of the aging, obese queen mother. The Italian influence was to continue: *apéritifs*, sometimes iced, were introduced, and much later, indeed not until about 1660, ice creams and ices reached the Parisian public through the enterprise of a Sicilian named Francisco Procopio, who opened a shop on the Rue de l'Ancienne Comédie on the left bank.

The taste for new dishes and styles in France was by no means limited to the courtly and rich of Catherine's time. Everyday middle-class Paris was receptive to the dissemination of Italian ideas, though without the accompanying pomp. The type of glutton satirized by Rabelais (the first part of whose *Gargantua and Pantagruel* had appeared the year before Catherine's arrival) was disappearing, a remembrance of a rough, hungry age. The vice of drunkenness among the lower classes had indeed continued, to which Catherine's father-in-law Francis I had applied a corrective (after some disorders in Brittany caused by mobs under the influence of wine) in an edict that specified, "Any man convicted of being drunk will be condemned: on the first offense, to detention in prison on bread and water; on the second offense, to be whipped in the inner court of the prison; on the third offense, to be whipped publicly. . . . And on the fourth offense, he shall have both his ears cut off and be banished from the kingdom of France."

By mid-century, Paris, with its ample supplies of food, was becoming the seat of a well-ordered, varied life. Great sales

were held there on Wednesdays and Saturdays, when as many as two thousand laden drays rolled in through the city gates to what was to evolve into Les Halles, the central Paris food mart that survived until this decade; and nothing left unsold on one market day was allowed to be held over to the next. Vegetables came in from all sides, particularly after Olivier de Serres, a native gourmet of the late sixteenth century, had popularized them. Serres, who remarked to the Duc de Sully that "ploughing and grazing are the two breasts of France," owned an experimental farm whose yields were the richest in the country. New foods from distant lands, such as the potato, first praised by Serres, and the turkey, also arrived about this time. Great casks of Burgundy lumbered in from the Hospices de Beaune (a charitable but highly profitable lay foundation that had been set up a century and a half before to administer the holdings in the Côte d'Or), along with wains bearing *crus* of Pauillac and the Médoc.

Rabelais in his exuberant fashion lists his favorite wines as being "the Falernian, Malvesian [the Englishman's Malmsey], the Muscadine, those of Taige, Beaune, Moirevaux, Orléans, Picardent, Arbois, Coussi, Anjou, Graves,

Four cookboys with lever raising a heavy cauldron

Corsica, Vierron, Nerac, and others."

Fresh butter and milk (including that of asses) also came on the general market. There were wild strawberries, or *fraises de bois*, from the Fontainebleau woods. Oysters and salmon were available in season, and a middle-class specialty was a pâté of carp. Some oddities persisted: whale meat was still prized, particularly whale tongue which could be roasted and served with orange sauce or cooked in a court bouillon. A bishop of Sens appointed by Francis I was an advocate of donkey meat. Garlic was in vogue as a protector against disease. In fact, the food supply of Paris as well as its provincial capitals was so varied as to arouse the admiration of a Venetian ambassador who reported in 1577, "Since France abounds in woods, pastures and grain, the livestock is numerous and fat. Of the animals the sheep is the most esteemed, having the most succulent flesh. The beef is good, but not as good as in England. Calves are so plentiful that they cost no more than sheep. . . . Paris has in abundance all that one can wish for, for the merchandise of every country flows into it." He was also surprised by the irregularity of a Frenchman's dining hours. "They eat three, four, or five times a day without keeping to any fixed times or rules."

There had long been present in France a guild of *cuisiniers* or cooks and purveyors of food, who—remarkably—appear to have shown no organized opposition to the incursion of Italian chefs. There were many specialists in the trade: *charcutiers*, or pork butchers and sausage vendors; *rôtisseurs*, or roasters of poultry, game, and large saddles of meat, which they sold from their own cookshops; and *pâtissiers*, or pastry cooks and confectioners. There were also *tamisiers*, bread bakers, so named for the sieve

Crushing olives in an olive oil mill, c. 1570

which they used for their flour; and *vinaigriers* or *sauciers*, those who concocted sauces. Still another guild was the *maîtres queux cuisiniers et porte-chappes*, professional caterers, able to put together and deliver to a client's house a cooked meal—even a feast—almost on demand. An Italian marveled that "at less than an hour's notice . . . [they] can furnish a dinner for ten, twenty, or even a hundred persons."

At the same time a custom of dining out spread in Paris, Lyons, and other French cities with the growth of *cabarets* —establishments not to be confused with the night clubs of a much later Montmartre, but the precursors of that French invention, the restaurant. The medieval inn had been a gross and sometimes dangerous place, often offering no food (one brought his own), just drink, rough company, and stabling for horses. Chaucer's famous Tabard Inn at

Southwark, with its hospitality that started the Canterbury pilgrims on their way, had been advanced for its time. Late medieval Paris saw numerous *tavernes* and *auberges* arising outside its walls—rustic but welcome retreats amid trees or near vineyards and far from the dank, crowded alleys of the city. From these there developed in the city itself a type of hostelry that provided tables laid with cloth and cutlery and some food in addition to drink. The *rôtisseur*,

English silver tankard, 1602

already the owner of a cookshop, often became an eating-house keeper—a *cabaretier* or *traiteur*. Many jurisdictional squabbles arose, and under Henry III and Henry IV legislation had to be enacted to regulate the functions of those who sold wine, according to whether the wine was drunk on or off the premises.

At a good cabaret late in the sixteenth century one could get a substantial dish of chicken fricassee or stuffed gosling, roast partridge, or a carbonade of beef, and moreover possibly see celebrities at the next table. "Today," said a pamphlet of 1574 that described some of the leading French eating houses, "everyone goes to the More, or the Sanson, or the

Innocent, or the Havard, all of them nothing but ministers of luxury and extravagance." A stranger to Paris reported that "there are certain cabarets where one can dine at almost any price. . . . Princes of the blood and even the king himself patronize them on occasion." Henry IV was recorded as a visitor at the Trois Maures in the old Marais quarter. Moreover, many individual cabarets became the meeting places of poets and their intellectual friends. The Pomme de Pin, in the Rue de la Juiverie, was celebrated by Villon and Rabelais, and in a later day by Racine. La Fontaine, Boileau, and others patronized the Mouton Blanc in the Rue du Vieux-Colombier, later moving over to the Croix de Lorraine in the Place du Cimitière Saint-Jean. University students frequented La Corne, lawyers Le Petit Diable; and there were others of engaging names and sometimes of gamy reputations: L'Ecu d'Orléans, L'Epée Royale, Le Grand Cerf, La Fosse aux Lions, Le Sabot, the latter made famous by Ronsard. All were centers of lively talk and occasional entertainment; some appear to have been equipped with *chambres séparées* for intimate rendezvous.

Though not previously known for culinary genius, the inventive French showed an amazing aptitude for catching up with their Italian tutors of the table. On March 29, 1571, there took place in Paris a feast demanding extraordinary kitchen talents and a public levy of 300,000 livres; the city offered a banquet to receive Elizabeth of Austria, bride of Catherine's reigning son Charles IX, but the appointed day was a Friday. Since fast had to be observed, the din-

German coconut cup

ner was entirely without meat. The city's kitchens met the challenge handsomely. After Mass at Nôtre Dame, the royal party and its hundreds of courtiers were served with 2 barrels of oysters, 50 pounds of whale meat, 200 crayfish, 28 salmon, 10 turbot, 18 brill, 400 herring (half of them fresh, half salted), 50 carp, great platters of broiled lobster, steamed mussels, 18 trout, and 1,000 pairs of frogs' legs as well, the frog being regarded as fish food since it was aquatic. To stage such a banquet, with its innumerable variations in taste on one theme and without any recourse to meat, was a triumph of the art of the Parisian chef and his *sauciers*. By 1600 it was apparent that French *maîtres queux* were equal or superior to the *maestri di cucina* of Italy.

In England during these decades, the evolution of tastes and manners of the table generally proceeded at a much slower pace. Under the early Tudors the English people seemed to stand on an uncertain threshold between old and new—between their own roughhewn, baronial ways and the growing attraction of more polished and urbane living. No man embodied this time of transition more than the ravenous Henry VIII.

"The king ate enormously," one of his biographers writes, "stuffing the meat into his little mouth with his knife. As he munched, the meat and vegetables popping from cheek to cheek, his eyes shone with happiness. He jabbed his knife, greasy as it was, into the salt cellar, blew his nose on his napkin, spat into the washing bowl—he was the king. The meat was soaked with sauces of parsley, garlic, quince, pear, wine; there were great pastries, glittering with sugar, or hiding haunches of venison cooked to rags and powdered with ginger; there was veal boiled with sage and smeared with cinnamon, cloves, and saffron, stiffened with eggs, all buried under pastry dotted with dates. . . ." Yet this was the Henry who wrote occasional lyrics, composed airs for the lute, danced elegantly, patronized the painter Holbein, and fathered one of the most cultivated and regal women in the history of Europe.

Throughout the era the English held ambivalent attitudes toward the Continent. By the end of the sixteenth century, the Tudors had finally put an end to those marital alliances and military adventures that had brought their kingdom many victories across the Channel, but in the end little save grief. On one hand, England had turned away from the rest of Europe and back to its particular life at home ("This other Eden, demi-paradise; This fortress built by Nature for herself. . . ."), with royal ships cruising the Atlantic to ensure that this isolation would not be disturbed. But on the other hand, prospering, high-spirited, and ambitious—never more so than under the Virgin Queen—England was strongly attracted by Continental ways. The French were more suspect than ever in Tudor England, yet the Elizabethan chronicler Holinshed speaks of the presence of "musical-headed Frenchmen," favorite cooks of the English aristocracy. Italian intrigues, after Henry's schism with Rome over his divorce from Catherine of Aragon, were widely feared, and the activities of an Italian musician, David Rizzio, a favorite of Mary, Queen of Scots, confirmed many Englishmen in their prejudice; yet Venetian glass and napery were favorite imports, and Lombard Street in the City was named for the Lombard banking agents with whom Londoners traded there. Spain, after Henry's divorce, became an outright enemy. But Spain and its Canary Islands produced the Elizabethans' favorite wine, "sack" (a type of sherry). What could not conveniently be bought was seized. Francis Drake, out to "singe the beard" of King Philip at Cádiz in 1587, also captured 2,900 butts of the Spanish wine.

The English yeoman, whose status rose markedly in the Tudor age, was by nature resistant to the foreign influences that were working upon the aristocracy. Thomas Fuller, in his *Worthies*, writes with pride and the prejudice of his class that "at our yeoman's table you shall have . . . no meat disguised with strange sauces, no straggling joint of sheep in the midst of a pasture of grass beset with sallets [sic] on every side, but solid substantial food; no servitors (more nimble with their hands than the guests with their teeth) [who] take away meat before stomachs are taken away."

The yeoman's diet was certainly substantial. He began his day with "pot-tage" of boiled meat with vegetables and oatmeal, and a tankard of ale—the common breakfast beverages, tea and coffee, not yet having made their appearance. His main meal at midday might include either beef, mutton, lamb, veal, or "souse" (brawn of pork); he had also acquired a taste for cheese and took his "flapjacks, fritters [and] pancakes" with a goodly portion of butter, according to one man who praised his mother's cooking.

His ale was usually a home brew, made from malted barley without hops, the "pernicious weeds" used only in the "Dutchman's strong beere." But beer began to invade England during the sixteenth century, first made in London by "straungers, Flemyngis, Duchemen." Neither drink was served in upper-class households, for as Fynes Moryson wrote in his *Itinerary*, "Clownes and vulgar men only use large drinking of Beere or Ale . . . but Gentlemen garrawse onely in Wine, with which many mixe sugar." The English lower classes were equally partisan toward their brew: a song published in the mid-seventeenth century, but thought to be of popular origin in Elizabethan times, runs:

> *Submit, Bunch of Grapes,*
> *To the strong Barley ear;*
> *The weak wine no longer*
> *The laurel shall wear.*
> *Sack, and all drinks else,*
> *Desist from the strife:*
> *Ale's the only Aqua Vitae,*
> *And liquor of life.*

Amid these differences, a generally amicable life between classes in the Tudor age went on. There was never a

Francis Bacon

"To be free-minded and cheerfully disposed at hours of meat and of sleep and of exercise is one of the best precepts of long lasting . . . avoid envy; anxious fears; anger fretting inwards; subtile and knotty inquisitions; joys and exhilarations in excess; sadness not communicated. Entertain hopes; mirth rather than joy; variety of delights, rather than surfeit of them; wonder and admiration, and therefore novelties. . . ." Such a regimen of health, wrote Sir Francis Bacon, will carry a man comfortably to a benign old age. The essayist was not notably successful in following his own advice. Politically ambitious, forever embroiled in Elizabethan and Jacobean court intrigues, a man of remarkable literary and scientific inventiveness, he lived anything but a life of moderation. The chronicler John Aubrey gossiped that at Bacon's Twickenham Lodge, it "seemed as if the court had been there, so nobly did he live. Every meal, according to the  season of the yeare, he had his table strewed with sweet herbs and flowers, which he sayd did refresh his spirits and memorie." As for expense, King James himself remarked of his lord chancellor, "He and I shall both die beggars." Bacon protested in his essay on riches that money is only "the baggage of virtue," a sort of good man's burden. When Bacon was impeached for taking bribes and sent into retirement, his "baggage," including one of the finest wine cellars in all England, was quickly dispatched. Bacon returned to his thoughts and his essays: "Of Truth," "Of Envy," "Of Travel," "Of Gardens". . . . Never one to be daunted by lack of firsthand knowledge, Bacon even wrote an essay on intelligent husbandry in the New World. "[Notice] what kind of victual the country yields. . . . Then consider what victual or esculent things there are, which grow speedily, and within the year; as parsnips, carrots, turnips, onions, radish, artichokes of Hierusalem [*sic*], maize, and the like. For wheat, barley, and oats, they ask too much labour; but with peas and beans you may begin . . . because they serve for meat as well as for bread . . . and of rice likewise." He advised against uprooting the hired help, for people when "displanted" make it "rather an extirpation than a plantation." Bacon died, appropriately, searching for a way to preserve food: seized with the answer one wintry day, he bought a chicken, stuffed it with snow, and promptly contracted fatal pneumonia. His essay on death provided a fitting epitaph: "He that dies in an earnest pursuit . . . scarce feels the hurt."

lack of willing servitors of the great. Henry VIII once called upon four hundred to prepare a Christmas feast including a meat pie nine feet long, baked in a rectangle to symbolize the Christ Child's manger, and the traditional presentation of a boar's head, richly garnished. How amply servants and masters lived appears in the records of a middle-sized Tudor mansion, Ingatestone Hall, seat of Sir William Petre in Essex, where in the year 1552 the baronial family, their guests, and their twenty or so retainers managed to consume 20,000 loaves of bread, over a ton of cheese, 17 oxen, 14 steers, 4 cows, 29 calves, 129 sheep, 54 lambs, 2 boars, 9 "porks," 5 bacon hogs, 3 goats, 7 kids, 13 bucks, 5 does, and 1 stag.

Whether the Tudor English generally consumed more or less than their predecessors is a moot point. Certainly the preparation of what they ate and the way they ate it had changed conspicuously. The great Tudor country house itself provided an altered setting much akin to the new châteaux rising in the Ile-de-France and the Loire valley. The turrets, the battlements, the latticed, slit windows for defense, gave way to spacious, glazed windows overlooking great gardens and pleasances such as those of Hampton Court or Longleat. The ancestral moat became a decorative fishpond. The smoky, communal Great Hall of Yorkist and Lancastrian days with its imposing central hearth was gradually replaced by private dining chambers with side fireplaces; and nobility and retainers no longer necessarily took their meals together at ranked tables, though the custom of a dais for the first table

persisted. High tables became massive and ornamental pieces of furniture, as against the portable trestle tables common in the all-purpose hall. Chairs for lords and ladies superseded stools or benches, which were now restricted to children, lesser visitors, and servants.

As in France, silver and glassware gradually replaced pewter and earthenware in the houses of the rich, and they were proudly exhibited on sideboards in the dining halls. The yeomanry advanced from wooden spoons and cups of leather and earthenware to pewter spoons and tableware, and the time was not far ahead when a prosperous farmer named

Crest of the Fishmongers' Company

Giles Heard could list in his inventory eleven pewter dishes, nine porringers, six spoons, and two pewter "salts." Some yeomen even reached the stature of possessing silver.

Tudor royalty, for their part, had gone considerably beyond silver and had acquired a taste for gold wine goblets and enameled "standing cups." A good deal of gilded ware had come into the hands of Henry VIII through his dissolution and despoliation of monasteries, and foreign princes and ambassadors made lavish gifts of both silver and gold to Elizabeth, whose love of pomp and finery was well known throughout Europe.

Still, new-found elegance and traditional ways continued to mix, even at the royal level. At Nonsuch Palace, the presence chamber for Queen Elizabeth was hung with tapestries and laid with rugs where she was to tread, but the rest of the chamber was simply carpeted with straw, as were most great ducal houses. The gentry wore hats at table, doffing them only for the occasion of a toast—a custom that was to persist through much of the following century.

Meals still were a confusion of old and new. The commentator William Harrison speaks in 1577 of the heavy breakfast as falling into disfavor among many persons of taste, yet at Queen Elizabeth's court, poultry, rabbit, mutton, veal, and beef, along with wine and ale, were served to start the day. The gentry still took their dinner at about eleven, the merchants of the city advancing it toward noon. A proposed menu for a summer dinner for fifty, in a tract on table etiquette called *Two Bookes of Cookerie and Carving*, by John Murrel in about 1641, calls for a first course of twenty dishes including capons, pike, partridges, wild ducks, quails, "a Florentine of Puft-paste," a "forced boyld meate," a hash of venison, a swan, a "Fawne or Kid, with a pudding in his belly," a bustard, a chicken pie, a potato pie, and so on, even to a custard; a second course including kid, carp, heron, trout, a "Hartichoake Pie," a "sowst Pigge," a gull, more partridge and such, along with salmon, sturgeon, a "dried Neatestongue," and a cherry or gooseberry tart; this in turn to be followed by a seafood course of crabs, prawns, anchovies, lobsters, and oysters.

Such gastronomic chaos suggests how far English taste makers lagged behind their Italian and French mentors. To be sure, it was understood that a guest of breeding would by no means take a plate of everything presented, but would select from each course, or service, that which he preferred: it might be a fish here, a breast of fowl or cut of meat pie there, with sweets intermixed. As in medieval days, what was not chosen was sent on to retainers—in effect, the "second sitting." But the art of some order of presentation—from introductory dishes to main dishes to desserts, as it had been known in Rome—was not yet understood in England.

Restraints on self-indulgence, meanwhile, were being imposed both by edict and by an advancing taste. One act restricted the number of courses at table to three, though it was easily circumvented by the proliferation of dishes per course. The Dutch physician Levine Lemnie, who appears to have frequented many tables of the English rich at the time, comments that "although they be very sumptuous and love to have good fare, yet neither use they to overcharge themselves with excess of drink, neither thereto greatly provoke and urge others." Perhaps he had noted the custom in many good houses of removing the emptied glass or cup from the table, to be refilled only on request.

The Elizabethan table in any case was far more varied than before. Shakespeare in his plays speaks of apricots, mulberries, pomegranates, quinces, figs, gooseberries, and seems to have had a particular interest in strawberries, then considered by many to possess some special health-giving qualities. In *Henry V* a courtier likens the emergence of the young king's virtues after a misspent youth to the strawberry thriving under the nettle. Indeed, the fascination with medicinal plants and herbs long survived: to Shakespeare, rhubarb was known as a "physicke" (which, to be sure, it is), and cowslips, lungwort, liverwort, pennyroyal, were respected for their special qualities along with the mysterious mandrake—celebrated in the second line of John Donne's lyric, "Get with child a mandrake root. . . ."

Melons, currants, foreign cheeses, arrived, along with oranges (first known in some London markets as "portyngales," having come from Portugal). And the appearance in England of the first yam from the New World in 1564 (the common potato coming some four decades later) and of tobacco in 1565 was to have far-reaching effects, the one on menu, the other on manners.

In the evolving Elizabethan style at table, nothing was more conspicuous than the passion for sweet dishes of every sort, often served at the outset of a meal as well as between courses and at the end. There were custards, marmalades, jellies, meringues, "suckets" (candied fruits), and other "comfits" in profusion, reminiscent of the "sotelties" of an earlier day. Describing these elaborate showpieces, sometimes whole castles of pastry, the playwright Thomas Dekker called them "sinful suburbs of cookery." There was a fad for "marchpane," a combination of pounded almonds and pistachio nuts, sugar, flour, and various essences including vanilla, which made its first appearance in the confection prepared for Elizabeth. It was sometimes prized as an hors d'oeuvre (it survives today chiefly in central Europe, as *marzipan*, though as an accompaniment to the coffee hour or the close of dinner). In the numerous books of etiquette and cookery that began appearing in England, ladies were encouraged for instance to "gild" or glaze marchpane. They were given recipes telling how to "Candie Nutmegs or Ginger," to make "a sirup of Roses," or in Sir Hugh Plat's celebrated *Delightes for Ladies* of 1609, to create a "sugar plate" combining the colors and scents of flowers.

The "sack" that was widely drunk with meals was not "seke" or dry at all, but tasted perhaps somewhat like a modern sweet sherry. Some of the gentry preferred a still sweeter and richer drink called Hippocras, compounded of white wine, sherry, ginger, nutmeg, cloves, Jamaica pepper, and, again, sugar—a concoction that was to survive in later times as a Christmas or New Year's punch. Still others favored a very heavy wine known since medieval times as Bastard, after the Spanish Bastardo grape which was often used. Heavily sugared and perhaps fortified, it was no doubt the ancestor of the port wine that in the eighteenth century was thought to afflict so many English gentlemen with gout.

If the Elizabethans had an extraordinarily sweet tooth, no one surpassed the reigning queen herself, who constantly carried candies about with her in the folds of her gown, doted on fruit pies and on meringues, which became known as "kisses" because Elizabeth kissed the "faire cloth" of the table that held them. She consumed so many sweetmeats that her teeth eventually turned quite black. The intensity of the unmarried monarch's appetite for sweets is of interest to the psychologist. In other respects she was moderate at table. Unlike many other monarchs both before and after her time, she was not addicted to great and ostentatious feasting. On the contrary, she took many of her meals in the privacy of her chambers, surrounded only by the closest of her attendants, sometimes almost alone. The ceremony of utmost splendor that preceded this withdrawal served to emphasize the contrast. Her entrances, whether at Westminster, Windsor, Greenwich, or Hampton courts, or at one of the ducal mansions which she honored with a royal visit, or progress, were masterworks of stagecraft. Sometimes she did not deign to appear in person for a meal at all, and the elaborate ceremony went on without her. Thus, a German visitor who had the privilege of witnessing preparations for a royal dinner at Greenwich in 1598 wrote that while the queen was at prayer, noble gentlemen of the rod bore a saltcellar and other ornaments to the dining table and knelt before it; then came ladies of the court to "rub the plates with bread and salt, with as much awe as if the queen had been present"; they were followed in turn by yeomen of the guard "clothed in scarlet . . . bringing in at each turn a course of twenty-four dishes served in plate, most of it gilt." "Twelve trumpets and two kettledrums made the hall ring for half an hour" while each servant tasted the dish he carried for poison as the guests

looked on (presumably the food grew cold). Then a group of court ladies bore selected viands to Elizabeth, seated all the while in her inner rooms.

Other Elizabethan women could not so absent themselves. Indeed, with its increasing refinement and complexity, the late Tudor household and that of the succeeding Stuart period fell very considerably into the hands of the ladies. There were gentlemen ushers, gentlemen of the horse, auditors of the revenue, chaplains, stewards, butlers, secretaries, carvers, yeomen of the cellar, brewmasters, maltsters, pantrymen, chamberlains,

English trencher, from a set made in 1600

dairymen, candlemakers, gardeners, and so on down to scullions and turnspits (and Sir Peter Legh even kept a jester in the reign of James I); but the management of estates, often served by two hundred to four hundred domestics of ever-increasing specialization, called for the superintendence of intelligent wives. Did they, perhaps, have some influence on the movement for diet restraint and reform that began on the eve of the seventeenth century?

That there was such a movement, we know from scattered records. Doctor

Thomas Muffet published before his death in 1604 a popular tract entitled *Healths Improvement*, calling for "temperancy," avoidance of "surfeiting," and a return to good, plain cooking. The writer Nicholas Breton, in his *Fantasticks* of 1626, proposed "a wholesome dyet that breeds good sanguine juyce," based primarily on poultry, beef, and "morning milk fasting from the cow." Robert Burton, author of the esteemed *Anatomy of Melancholy* (1621), believed that "all black wines, over-hot, compound, strong thick drinks" were "hurtful" and inclined to lead to "head melancholy." A peasant known as Old Parr of Shropshire observed a far more healthy regimen, remembered in the following lines:

> *That green cheese was most wholesome*
> *(with an onion)*
> *Coarse maslin bread; and for his daily*
> *swig,*
> *Milk, butter-milk and water, whey*
> *and whig,*
> *Sometimes metheglin, and by fortune*
> *happy,*
> *He sometimes sipped a cup of ale most*
> *nappy.*

His contemporaries were all the more impressed because he had been convicted of fornication at the age of 105 and died at 152.

The seventeenth century brought numerous changes in the form and content of European eating and drinking. Many were handsome advances; others represented retreats. In France at the outset of the new era, Henry IV, a ruler of high polish, appointed the master *cuisinier*, La Varenne, to be a minister of state;

then came Louis XIII, whose tastes in food were gross, and Louis XIV, whose appetites were Gargantuan. England experienced in James I an alcoholic who made drunkenness fashionable at his court, and then in Charles I a king whose lofty fastidiousness contributed to his fatal unpopularity. In disordered Germany the age witnessed the hunger and bestiality of the Thirty Years' War. Vatel arose at Chantilly as creator of a cuisine far more subtle than that of the old Florentines, and new foods and tastes arrived from around the globe. In England the Puritans frowned on pleasures of the table, and a Roundhead like Colonel Hutchinson fined his soldiers for drinking on the Sabbath.

The seventeenth century brought, among other institutions of taste, the rise of the English coffeehouse and the French café. They were improvements, to be sure, on the old French cabaret and the English tavern or alehouse patronized by Ben Jonson and his company of talkers, players, feasters, pipe-smokers, wenchers, and other dubious characters who enjoyed "a pure cup of rich Canary wine." Nostalgically, the poet Robert Herrick, who outlived that good company, was to write:

> *Ah, Ben!*
> *Say how, or when,*
> *Shall we thy guests,*
> *Meet at those lyric feasts*
> *Made at the Sun,*
> *The Dog, the Triple Tun?*
> *Where we such clusters had,*
> *As made us nobly wild, not mad;*
> *And yet each Verse of thine*
> *Out-did the meat, out-did the wine.*

THE
PERPETUAL
PARTY

A pleasant exchange with the fruit and vegetable girl in a Paris market, c. 1630

Rich Bride, Poor Bride

Weddings were often boisterous and opulent occasions of banqueting and merrymaking that might last overnight or as long as ten days, depending on the capacities of the guests and the host's grip on his purse strings. One Elizabethan ascetic accused them of making a "brothel house of a bride house." In Italy the wedding of the Duke of Mantua was more refined if no less grand. Guests were entertained at a three-hour banquet by four choirs, and gifts of glass defied "competition from all the warehouses of Murano." Below, a panel painting from a cassone—a dowry chest—shows the typical Florentine wedding banquet of the times.

Gift cup for a new bride

For couples who could not afford the luxury of a banquet hall, there was always the street. Workers' weddings, left, were festive despite meagre dowries. What the rich spent on their entertainment and feasts would have lasted the poor through a lifetime.

The Way to a Woman's Heart

Botticelli's banquet, laid midst a surrealistic landscape of Renaissance arcades, was inspired by a tale from the Decameron, *in which the rejected suitor wins another hearing with his lady by inviting the whole family to dinner. After a fine meal and a scarifying lesson about the eternal damnation of cruel women, she willingly capitulates.*

To Set before a King

Much that glittered on the Renaissance table was indeed gold, or some other precious material. The decorative arts enjoyed almost as much attention as did painting and sculpture, and many an artist began his career as a metalsmith, shuttling between princely courts to keep their sideboards filled. Italy was the fount of all these industries: Venice exported glass of almost magical delicacy; the towns of central Italy produced brilliantly glazed earthenware including the fine majolica above; and Florence supplied superb goldsmiths, none more urgently sought than Benvenuto Cellini, who was enticed to the court of Francis I with the promise, "I will choke you with gold."

Cellini's enameled gold figures above, executed in 1543 for Francis I, represent Land and Sea, allegorical sources of the precious pepper and salt contained within. The potte below, which belonged to a chamberlain of Henry VIII, combines striped Venetian glass with a silver-gilt mounting of English workmanship, hallmarked 1546.

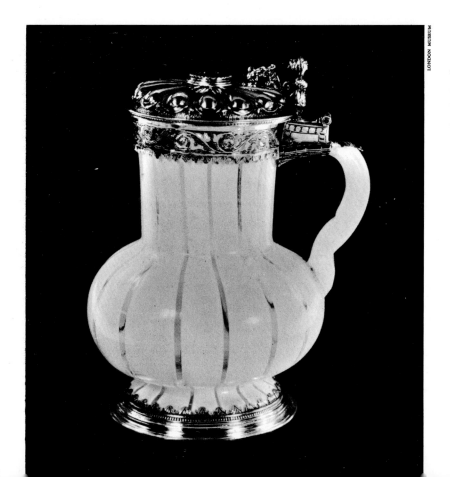

"Happy, Happy Burgundy"

142

So wrote Erasmus in 1532, when he praised the wine from the fruitful region where the grape harvest in the tapestry below takes place, stating that Burgundy "deserves to be called the mother of man, since she gives [him] such good milk from her breast."

Saint Jude tops one of a set of English apostle spoons.

A Sign of Breeding

If the dish be pleasant, either fleshe or fishe,
Ten hands at once swarm in the dishe;
And if it be fleshe ten knives shalt thou see,
Mangling the flesh, and in the platter flee.
To put there thy handes, in peril without fail
Without a gauntlet, or else a glove of mail.

As polite society took up the fork, the hand-to-mouth dining described in this Elizabethan ditty ceased. Many early examples of Renaissance cutlery were hinged for carrying in the pocket—a gentleman could not be too sure of his host's social graces—but as time passed even the most modest baron began to accumulate chests full of finely wrought pewter, silver, and sometimes gold. When the novelty of forks wore off, craftsmen turned to more specialized tools—from mulberry forks to apostle spoons: a set of twelve was a traditional gift at genteel baptisms.

Left: Bird bills serve as tines for an Italian fork.

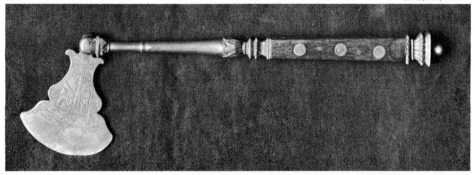

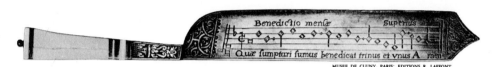

The cleaver at top is a miniature of an early battle-axe; the ivory-handled knife beneath it is scored with the words and music of the "Benedicite." Below are seven of a set of fourteen knives whose handles carry likenesses of English sovereigns from Edward V to James I.

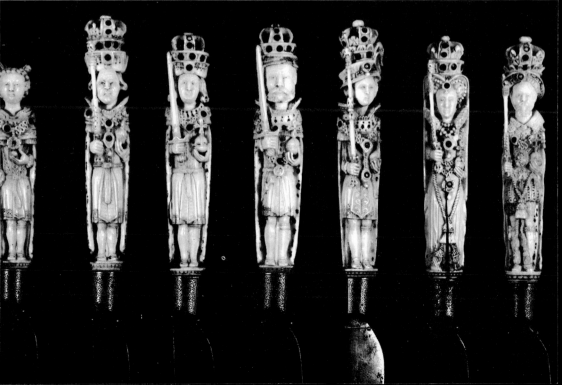

With a more liberal code of behavior, men and women began to appreciate each other openly and extravagantly. In Italy, where the orgy was as much art as entertainment, even the Papal Palace had its social season. For rest and recuperation, there were bathhouses which cleansed the body but did little to dampen the passions. Scented waters, companionable tub mates, and a proper meal constituted the "cure." A traveler wrote of the baths at Baden-Baden, "I think this must be the place where the first man was created, which the Hebrews call the garden of pleasure."

Good, Clean Fun

When courtesans came to dinner at the Hôtel Nesle, the fine French manor above, no one cared if dinner got cold. A gentleman could always get into hot water at the public bath (left) later.

OPERA DI
BARTOLOMEO
SCAPPI,

M. DELL'ARTE DEL CVCINARE,
con laquale si può ammaestrare qual si voglia Cuoco,
Scalco, Trinciante, o Mastro di Casa:

DIVISA IN SEI LIBRI.

NEL
Primo Libro si intende il ragionamento che fa l'Autore con Giouanni suo discepolo.
Secondo si tratta di diuerse viuande di carne, si di quadrupedi, come di volatili.
Terzo si parla della statura, e stagione de' pesci.
Quarto si mostrano le liste del presentar le viuande in tauola, cosi di grasso, come di magro.
Quinto si contiene l'ordine di far diuerse sorti di paste, & altri lauori.
Sesto, & vltimo si ragiona de' conualescenti, e molte altre sorti di viuande per gli infermi.

Con le Figure che fanno di bisogno nella Cucina.

Aggiontoui nuouamente il Trinciante, & il Mastro di Casa.

DEDICATE AL MAG. M. MATTEO BARBINI
Cuoco, e Scalco celeberrimo della Città di Venetia.

IN VENETIA, M. DC. X.
PRESSO ALESSANDRO VECCHI.

The Cook's Companion

One of the earliest printed cookbooks to appear in Italy was written by Bartolomeo Scappi, chef to Pope Pius V. Scappi's *Opera*, dated 1570, covered gastronomy from menus and recipes to diet and decorum. Like other Renaissance innovators, Scappi seems to have had a particular penchant for mechanical contrivances, including the clockwork turnspit on the title page opposite. In the woodcut below, he instructs the *maestro di cucina* in kitchen planning and layout of equipment (note the bristling knife rack to the right of the fire).

padella p fare oui frittolate

diuersi caldari

nauicella cõ piastrelle et quatro piedi

Conserua grande

Scappi's recommendations for the well-appointed kitchen include an assortment of pots and pans: from top to bottom, a pan for fritters; divers cauldrons; a four-legged steamer; a roasting pan; a frying pan; a "Dutch oven."

padella ouata

stufaroro

Nobilis.hinc.pater.et.illinc.est.c
Circumfula.sedet.digna.parti
Talis.erat.quondam.patriarchae
Menfa.fuit.Iobo: sic.cumulata.
Fac.Deus.ut.multos.haec.gignat
Germinet.ut.Iobi.ftirps.renova
Fercula.praeclaro.donafti.laeta
Haec.habeant.longos.gaudia.te
Ao. DN. 1567.

ÆTA 6

ÆTATIS SVÆ 5 GE

ÆTATI 1

2

Seen
But
Not
Heard

Although children were permitted to join their parents at the family table, the "seen but not heard" dictum was strictly observed. Il Galateo, a popular book on etiquette by Giovanni della Casa in the sixteenth century, admonished children: "not to eat too quickly, not to put one's elbows on the table, not to pick one's teeth, [and] not to spit as far as possible." The rules appear to be well enforced at the Elizabethan table, left, shown in a portrait of Lord Cobham and his brood.

Separate Tables

When Alexander VII gave a banquet in 1655 in honor of Sweden's Queen Christina, it was only the third time in history a pope had dined with a woman. To grace the occasion, leading artists fashioned trionfi, *the elaborate table decorations made from sugar, right. But honor or not, protocol required that Christina be seated at a table which was considerably lower—and quite apart—from that of her host.*

153

West meets East in seventeenth-century India and finds that parties are the same everywhere.

IN
QUEST
OF
SPICES

Shortly before his death in 1481, the Florentine physician and amateur geographer Paolo Toscanelli addressed a letter to a young seafarer who was then in Lisbon trying to win support for an extraordinary expedition to Asia. The letter began, "To Cristóbal Columbo . . . greeting: I observe thy great and noble ambition to pass over to where the spices grow. . . ." Toscanelli was one of the few who shared Columbus' belief that a westward voyage across unknown waters would lead more readily to the riches of Asia than the difficult passages then being explored around the huge land mass of Africa. But he was only one of many Europeans who were fired by the urge to reach Asia directly by sea. By the second half of the fifteenth century, extension of Turkish and Arab power had made travel overland and through the Middle Eastern gulfs forbidding to the West. The need for Eastern spices directly served to open the age of exploration, of colonial empires, and of the winning of the Americas.

The traditional course of a spice cargo to Europe involved in succession Chinese junks, Indian luggers, Arab dhows, pack camels, and Venetian freight galleys. Chinese traders from remote Canton would pick up a load in the East Indies—particularly the Moluccas, or Spice Islands, an archipelago bound on the north by the Philippines, on the west by Borneo and Java, and on the east by New Guinea—and transport it to the great Oriental mart of Malacca, on the Malay Peninsula. From there Malayan, Arab, or Indian shippers would carry the spice cargo on the monsoon winds across the Bay of Bengal to one of the ports on western India's Malabar

Eastern flora, by a Flemish artist, c. 1600

Coast—Calicut or Cochin or Goa—or possibly to Colombo in Ceylon. Next it would be borne across the western reaches of the Indian Ocean, to a harbor on the Persian Gulf—perhaps wealthy, strategic Hormuz—to be carried overland to Constantinople, or via the Red Sea to Mecca, then to Alexandria or a Syrian port. In these ports Venetian traders and shippers were on hand in numbers to buy for the European market.

But by 1453 the great Eastern Christian citadel of Constantinople had fallen to the Ottoman Turks, whose spreading empire soon commanded the littoral and overland routes of Asia Minor and Egypt. At Alexandria the price of pepper climbed 60 per cent when in 1428 a sultan created a state export monopoly and demanded higher tribute from traders. Imperialist Arabs were on the way to establishing a monopoly on sea trade between the vast Arabian peninsula and India and the islands beyond.

The West could still buy Eastern spices, but only at enormous cost. Some spices, by the time they reached Europe, were worth their weight in gold. Venice, so long the chief purveyor of Eastern goods to the Continent, was particularly threatened economically, trapped in a sea which Turks now virtually controlled, while Arab sway extended all along the North African coast to Gibraltar. There was, among kingdoms that fronted on the Atlantic, an opportunity as well as an impulse to escape the Mediterranean trap.

The Renaissance inspired the spirit of adventure. Learned Arabs, who had studied Ptolemy's celestial treatise the *Almagest* at Alexandria, along with the work of early Indian astronomers, added a wealth of mathematical and nautical studies which were brought to Europe and translated by Portuguese and Italian Jews. Arab sailors had long navigated by star sights; in the fifteenth century the astrolabe and the quadrant came into Western use to determine a ship's latitude (its position north and south) when out of sight of land. The more difficult problem of finding one's longitudinal (east-west) position remained elusive, sailors relying on dead reckoning—that is, observation of wind velocity, speed over the water, drift, and current—to determine their progress.

Moreover, fairly seaworthy vessels for deepwater work were being constructed in Europe, rigged with two or more masts and a combination of square and fore-and-aft sails that made them a great improvement over the traditional oared galleys of the Mediterranean or the lateen rigged ships of Arab skippers when it came to accomplishing long voyages or sailing close to the wind in heavy weather. Clumsy as these vessels may now seem, with their lofty poops or sterncastles, they could accommodate the compact but precious cargo from the East. In such ships Vasco da Gama, Columbus, and Magellan made their historic voyages, and Sir Francis Drake reconnoitered the East Indies for England.

The impulse to locate and tap the spice sources was also aided by scattered travel accounts that had come down over generations, some even from antiquity. The Egyptians, a millennium and a half before Christ, had used cinnamon as an aromatic, although the bark of the tree did not grow in their land, nor in Arabia either. Phoenician skippers—the most enterprising of ancient times—had sailed down the Red Sea and out into the Indian Ocean. Moreover, they had struck westward through the Mediterranean and past the Pillars of Hercules into the Atlantic, all the way down the West African bulge and around the Cape of Good Hope. Whether they actually reached the Eastern spice lands or merely bought their spices at some entrepôt such as Aden or Mecca on the great Arabian

peninsula has never been determined.

The Greek geographer Strabo in the first century B.C. wrote of southern Arabia as a center of spice production and trade, but ancient Arabs were secretive about the true source of those spices that were not native to their land. The Roman natural historian Pliny the Elder accused the Arab merchants of concealing the origin of their wares to keep their prices high. But soon Roman sailors and merchants came to know the west coast of India well, trading there for spices, perfumes, and luxurious textiles in exchange for Western gold coin, pottery, wine, and occasionally slave girls. Along with the pepper, ginger,

Radishes and peppers en route to market

cinnamon, and cardamom of the Malabar region, they imported a small amount of sugar from Indian cane fields and saffron, the flavoring made from the crocus of the Himalayan foothills.

Three centuries before, the Arabs had pushed farther on and established direct sea contact with China. They may have traded in the East Indies as well. Indians, after the decline of Rome, also turned to China and the islands for trade. They appear to have been skillful shipbuilders as well as navigators; one vessel of the fifth century A.D. carried two hundred crew and passengers. (Columbus' largest, the *Santa Maria*, carried only about forty.)

Though Western trade for Eastern delicacies was sporadic during the Middle Ages, the continuing contact between Christian and Moslem stimulated the European appetite for exotic flavors. Sugar, brought back from Syria by the Crusaders, is an instance. Its Arabic name *sukkar*, derived from the Sanskrit *sárkará*, or "pebble," passed almost unchanged into various European languages as *azucar*, *sucre*, or *Zucker*. With it came such sweet drinks of the Moslem world as aromatic rose water. The Arabs called it *julāb*—a term that evolved, according to the historian Philip K. Hitti, into the Western "julep." He also argues that the Western word "syrup" derives from the Arab term *sharāb*, a therapeutic solution of sugar in water, and that the

Brewing a physic, from a 1222 Arabic herbal

word "soda" as we know it (as in Scotch and soda, for example) in medieval Latin meant "headache," and meant "headache remedy" in the form *sodanum*, which derived from the Arabic *sudā*, meaning a "splitting pain in the head."

From the Arabs the Crusaders also learned the pleasures of sherbet, mel-

ons, and asparagus, while the Moors implanted in Spain a love of saffron flavored rice dishes (the *pilaf* of the Middle East, the *paella* of Iberia). Meanwhile, citrus fruits, which probably originated in Malaysia and spread from there to India, were gradually making their way to Europe. The very name "orange" comes from the Sanskrit *nāranga*—which with slight phonetic variations came into Western languages almost intact, save that the Germans were oddly to call the costly fruit *Apfelsine*. The lemon was the Arabic *laymūn*, which in turn derived from the Persian *līmūn*.

In the Middle East the strongholds of the Crusaders on the Levant coast soon fell to the Moslems. But Venetian traders, such as the clan that reared Marco Polo in the latter part of the thirteenth century, reached out undismayed beyond Constantinople to the Crimea on the Black Sea and as far as Bokhara. They found western Asian gardens flourishing with almonds, basil, pomegranates, peaches, apricots, plums, eggplants, and watermelons, the last exported all the way to Baghdad packed in ice. At the same time, Christian missionaries were reaching even farther, venturing into inner India and to the Himalayas, and sending back astonishing reports. One traveler, the Franciscan friar Oderic, wrote of his Eastern travels from 1318 to 1330 that "While I was in the province of Mancy [in India], I passed by the palace of a certain famous man, who hath fifty virgin damsels continually attending upon him, feeding him every meal as a bird feeds her young ones. Also he hath sundry kinds of meat served at his table, and three dishes of each kind; and when the said virgins feed him, they sing most sweetly." The bemused friar also told of a "mount" near the wall of the palace, "wrought with gold and silver, whereupon stand turrets and steeples and other delectable things for the solace and recreation of

Jeweled sweetmeat box, India

the great man." Oderic added that he had traveled as far as "a certain kingdom called Tebek [Tibet]," where the women "have two teeth in their mouths as long as the tusks of a boar" and "wherein I think there is more plenty of bread and wine than in any other part of the world." He was wildly exaggerating and distorting, since mountainous Tibet has been throughout history one of man's leanest and loneliest places.

Even the description he gave of India was highly colored. Most of India was existing on a vegetarian diet, induced partly by religion and partly by sheer poverty: vegetable curries, boiled or fried rice, or flat cakes of flour, the modern chapatis, fried in ghee (clarified butter) or vegetable oil. For sweets, the Indian chewed a slightly narcotic mixture of betel nuts and lime.

Europeans of discernment could discount the tales of Oderic, but there was detailed truth in the travel reports of Marco Polo, who at the age of seventeen set out in 1271 with his brothers for eastern Asia and the court of Kublai Khan. On his way he passed through the city of Mosul on the Tigris to find great spice shipments coming in. ("The merchants transport their goods to and from the Sea of India," he wrote, "the distance being computed at seventeen days' navigation. . . .") From there he pushed overland through the wild, robber infested Kurdish lands of northern Persia to reach the port of Hormuz at the mouth of the Gulf. Then his route led across Afghanistan, the Pamir highlands, and the Gobi Desert to the Yellow River, to take him in 1275 to the summer court of the Great Khan. He brought back reports of the glittering wealth of Peking; of ginger under cultivation in Shansi and Shensi provinces; of an island kingdom of Cipangu (Japan) off the Great Khan's coast; of islands in the China Sea lush with aromatic trees; and of distant Java to the south, an island that abounded in "pepper, nutmegs . . . cloves, and all other valuable spices and drugs . . . which occasion it to be visited by many ships laden with merchandise that yields to the owners considerable profit. . . ."

His observations, circulated in manuscript and by word of mouth, aroused European imagination as well as cupidity. Yet, like those of Friar Oderic, the stories of Marco Polo were also widely doubted. He was asked, when on his deathbed in 1324, to recant some of his more grandiose descriptions of the East, only to respond, "I have not told half of what I saw."

Amid much rumor and misinformation, tentative knowledge of the East gradually spread. Genoese merchants

159

A Scurvy Life

The epic voyages undertaken in quest of the spice treasures of Cathay were fraught with dangers, real and imagined. An explorer never knew when a sea serpent might rise from the inky depths to swallow his ship and crew, and navigators kept a wary eye on the horizon for fear they might sail off the edge of the world. But there was nothing mythical about the shortage of food supplies during long voyages. Slow starvation at sea was a common occurrence. Although historians have concluded from early manifests of ships' stores that a mariner's diet comprised thirty-five hundred calories daily, this was true only under ideal conditions. A short three months' sail from port could find the crew left with nothing more than stagnant water and soured hardtack which was shared with rats and weevils. During Magellan's trans-Pacific ordeal, his crew was reduced to gnawing oxhide thongs and jerkins, and many of the men literally rotted from scurvy—a disease resulting from a deficiency of Vitamin C. On the long runs from Portugal to India, scurvy claimed the lives of one out of every five seamen. The Portuguese were among the first to discover that citrus fruits prevented the disease, and they established plantations of oranges and limes on St. Helena, an island convenient to the caravels en route to India's Malabar Coast. English ships later became popularly known as "lime-juicers" because of an admiralty order requiring the distribution of lime juice rations to all hands. But the 190 sailors who shipped on the vessel carrying the provisions below did not enjoy such solicitous care—neither fresh fruits nor vegetables were in the hold:

11,400 POUNDS OF SALTED MEATS AND FISH
A FEW BEEF TONGUES
20,000 BISCUITS
30 BUSHELS OF OATMEAL
40 BUSHELS OF DRIED PEAS
1 1/2 BUSHELS OF MUSTARD SEED
1 BARREL OF SALT
100 POUNDS OF SUET
1 BARREL OF FLOUR
11 FIRKINS OF BUTTER
1 HOGSHEAD OF VINEGAR
10,500 GALLONS OF BEER
3,500 GALLONS OF WATER
2 HOGSHEADS OF CIDER

were in at least indirect contact with India and China via Arabia during the first half of the fourteenth century, and before the middle of the next the Venetian merchant adventurer Niccolò de' Conti returned overland from twenty-five years in India and southeast Asia with extraordinary and explicit news. He had seen the cinnamon trees of Ceylon. He had traveled up the Ganges and encountered both elephants and wealthy cities along its shores. He had gone as far as Burma, Malaya, Sumatra, and Java, observing religious rites there and partaking of their foods. What was most important, in a time before there was any accurate cartography of the East, he postulated that the waters about India and the islands were an open ocean. It followed that these areas could be reached by ship directly from Europe, thus avoiding the dangerous overland trek through Arabia.

The greatest collecting point of all such information was the remarkable observatory established in 1418 at Sagres on the southernmost promontory of Portugal by Prince Henry the Navigator. This remarkable intellect, the third son of King John I of Portugal, was bent upon studies of the globe as well as the pursuit of African and possibly Eastern wealth, in a new crusade against the powerful Moslems. He set up, as the maritime historian Samuel Eliot Morison describes it, "the ancestor of every marine observatory and hydrographic office today." Geographers and astronomers were assembled at his retreat on the desolate cliffs above Cape St. Vincent, and from 1418 on, captains who had been briefed there set out on in-creasingly distant voyages. The Canary Islands, the Madeira Islands, the Azores, were either located or rediscovered; the great western bulge of Africa was rounded, dispelling fears of a *mare tenebrosum*, or unmapped "green sea of gloom," to the south of it. Year after year Portuguese fleets brought home cargoes of western African pepper, elephant tusks, and slaves. Then in 1488 Lisbon—the most adventurous capital of the era—resounded with joy to the triumphal return of Bartholomeu Dias from his rounding of the Cape of Good Hope; the Genoese Christopher Columbus is said to have been at dockside to witness it.

While Dias was at sea, a Portuguese royal agent named Pedro de Covilhão was traveling to Calicut. Covilhão sent back secret intelligence to Lisbon on the location of thriving spice centers on the Malabar Coast and the prevailing winds of the Indian Ocean. Around 1493 the Genoese trader Girolamo da Santo Stefano, starting by an overland route, reached the eastern shore of India, Ceylon, Sumatra, and the Maldive Islands, bringing back more news of pepper and ginger. The Portuguese, attracted by reports of Eastern wealth and customs, promptly monopolized the trade. Upon learning that Columbus had failed to reach the Indies by a western route, the Portuguese determined to mount an expedition that would push on from the point Dias had reached and strike on to India by sea. The outcome was Vasco da Gama's arrival in the port city of Calicut in 1498, prompting the King of Portugal to proudly inform his royal neighbors at Madrid, "We learn that they did reach and discover India and other kingdomes and lordships bordering upon it; that they entered and navigated its sea, finding large cities, large edifaces and rivers, and great populations, among whom is carried on all the trade in spices and precious stones. . . . Of these they have brought a quantity, including cinnamon, cloves, ginger, nutmeg, together with the boughs and leaves of the same; also many fine stones of all sorts, such as rubies and others."

For the moment, the Portuguese had won a vast advantage—over Spain, over Venice, over the Arabs as well, and it now became their intention to establish not just trading posts but permanent strongholds from which to drive out the Moslems, subdue the Hindus, and rule as much of the East as they could reach. A view of the Indian world which they were entering is contained in a curious

Jade green ceramic mug, Persia

description by the Italian traveler Lodovico di Varthema, who visited the court of Calicut at just about the time the Portuguese were arriving:

"When the King of Calicut wishes to eat he uses the following customs . . . four of the principal Brahmans take the food which the king is to eat and carry it to the devil, and first they worship him in this manner: they raise their clasped hands over his head, and then draw their hands toward them, still clasped together, and the thumb raised upward, and then they present to him the food which is to be given to the king, and stand in this manner as long as a person would require to eat it; and then the said Brahmans carry that food to the king. . . . This food is in a wooden vessel, in which there is a very large leaf of a tree, and upon this leaf is placed the said food, which consists of rice and other things. The king eats on the ground without any other thing. And when he eats, the Brahmans stand around, three or four paces distant from him, with great reverence, and remain bowed down with their hands before their mouths. . . . When the king has finished his meal, the said Brahmans take that food which the king did not require and carry it into a courtyard and place it on the ground. And the said Brahmans clap their hands three times, and at this clapping a very great number of black crows come to this said food and eat it."

What was of far more interest to Vasco da Gama was his discovery that pepper could be bought directly at Calicut for as little as three ducats per hundredweight—and this at a time when it was selling through middlemen in Venice for as much as eighty. It is estimated that on his second expedition to India, which comprised an armada of twenty-five ships, twelve of them sent by the king in a display of military might and the rest belonging to Portuguese merchants, he brought home a cargo worth sixty times the cost of outfitting it. Within ten years of setting up bases at

Hormuz on the Persian Gulf and at Goa on the Malabar Coast, the Portuguese seized control of Malacca in Malaya and in 1513 sailed across the South China Sea to bring a ship into Canton— the first recorded European visit to the lands of the Great Khan since Marco Polo. At nearby Macao they established a permanent foothold, while from their vantage point on the Malacca Strait they also set sail for the Spice Islands. There they established an overlordship ruled from headquarters at Goa.

A small island just off the Indian shore, Goa was a colorful crossroads of Eastern trade. A Portuguese account describes the island as "very beautiful and luxuriant with numerous and tall groves of palm trees that give much wine, oil, vinegar, and jaggery [a coarse brown sugar made from palm sap], that almost tastes like sugar. It also has areca . . . with which betel is eaten. All this makes them much money, and now many Portuguese have large incomes from it. [The inhabitants] have also many gardens in which they grow numerous and very singular fruits of the earth. . . . They have a large amount of sesame from which they make excellent oil."

Peaceable as this sounds, a major struggle for spice and empire was in the making. Having all but swept the Arabs off the Eastern sea lanes and having found Indian and Malaysian peoples submissive, the Portuguese were to be confronted in turn by a jealous Spain, an ambitious England, and the enterprising Dutch. Within a hundred years their vast, new-found dominion was all but shattered.

The storm center was the Moluccas,

especially rich in cloves. Spain's rulers, smarting over Columbus' failure to find spices, had heard enough about the islands to regard them as a prime objective and claimed them as their own under an earlier demarcation treaty, in

Kublai Khan's brother sipping a bowl of milk

which the Pope had portioned out the world between Spain and Portugal. A century later the Protestant English and then the Dutch, not party to this presumptuous agreement, would have none of it. They would make sail for the Spice Islands too, with shotted guns.

Portugal's first major setback came with the defection of one of its most experienced sailors, Ferdinand Magellan, who, after being removed from command for alleged trading with the Arab enemy, entered the rival Spanish service and there accomplished another of history's great naval feats—the circumnavigation of the globe. Bravely sailing down to far southern latitudes to round unknown, storm-tossed Patagonia and driving on across the Pacific, he not only vindicated Columbus' belief in a western passage but opened the spice trade of the Indies to Spain—though he himself was to die in the Philippines as the result of a chieftain's treachery.

Magellan had aboard his ship an Italian chronicler, one Antonio Pigafetta of Vicenza, who survived to tell much of this great voyage and of what he saw, gathered, and incidentally ate. Thus when anchored in 1521 off a small island in the Philippines, Magellan and his

Pot and drinking tube for maté, Paraguay tea

captains were invited to a banquet with the local chief: "Each bite of meat," as the historian Donald F. Lach transcribes Pigafetta's account, "was accompanied by ceremonial [palm] wine drinking. Before the chief took the cup, he raised his fist toward the sky and brandished it at his companions. After he had taken the cup to drink, he flung out his left fist so sharply and abruptly that Pigafetta thought for a moment that the chief meant to strike him. When the European came to realize that the chief was merely offering a friendly toast, he replied in kind. . . . After a supper of pork and rice, the Europeans were taken to the chief's abode. . . ." There, squatting on bamboo mats, under torches "made from tree gum wrapped in palm and banana leaves," they were offered a concoction of fish and ginger.

Pigafetta and his companions saw much else in the Philippines—bananas, described as "long, delicious figs," breadfruit, and sago palms. But their goal was the Moluccas, where the survivors landed late in 1521. There they found precious clove trees and ginger roots (along with pygmies, cannibals, and a small colony of Moorish traders complete with its own harem). The Spanish and Portuguese now contended for control of these treasure islands; in 1529 the Portuguese king John III paid Spain a royal ransom of 350,000 gold ducats to abandon any further claims. Prophetically, the Portuguese traveler João de Barros wrote shortly after mid-century that "Evil and strife are endemic to the Moluccas, for the clove, though a creation of God, is actually an apple of discord and responsible for more afflictions than gold."

About this time the English also went to sea in force. In Magellan's wake Francis Drake circumnavigated the globe in 1577–80 and explored the Moluccas. Thomas Cavendish followed him in 1586. The defeat of the Spanish Armada in the English Channel in 1588 had further repercussions on the opposite side of the globe. Victorious Englishmen were soon to rival expansionist Spaniards in the Far East as Spaniards had rivaled Portuguese, and as the Portuguese had overtaken the Arabs before them. Shortly before her death, Queen Elizabeth, after a meeting of London merchants, chartered a monopoly of traders to be known as the East India Company, with percentages due the Crown. Their first spice fleet sailed in 1601. Meanwhile, the Dutch, who had also been scouting the Eastern promised land, aided chiefly by a skillful observer in the Portuguese service, one Jan van Linschoten, arrived on the scene with a fleet in 1595. They befriended local rulers anxious for deliverance from the Portuguese and soon formed their own East India Company as a national merchant combine chartered to exploit anything it could lay hands on between Magellan's Strait and the Cape of Good Hope. It could establish bases, make war, coin its own money—a potential imperium on a hemispheric scale. Investors' money streamed into these rival ventures. A Cologne representative of the Fugger family of Continental bankers, busy selling shares for the Dutch, wrote his clients in 1601 that "We are advised that the profits of the East Indian vessels recently arrived are to be distributed to shareholders. Each one is to receive 50

Indian scepter: a cocoa whisk

per cent." A merchant adventurer, it was said, could ship six spice cargoes from the East, lose five to pirates or shipwreck, and still make a handsome return. The third expedition of the London East India Company earned 230 per cent profit. The Spanish-Portuguese en-

tanglement in the East now diminished as a greater division of the spoils engaged England in India and the Dutch in the East Indies.

Most of the Eastern products for the table were familiar to Europe from times past—though now they could be had far more readily and cheaply. The coconut, the mango, and the banana made their first appearance on the tables of the rich, but the great source of new foods that were to enlarge the diet of the European common man lay elsewhere—just halfway around the globe.

On December 13, 1492, two months after his first landing, Columbus sent a party of men ashore on Española (Haiti), where they were well received by the Indians. The chronicle of the voyage records that "as soon as the natives had cast off their fear, they all went to the houses and each one brought what he had to eat, consisting of yams, which are roots like large radishes, which they sow and cultivate in all their lands, and is their staple food. They make bread of it, and roast it. . . ." This offering of yams was perhaps European man's first important encounter with the fare of the New World. But it was the white potato that was destined to be a staple of Europe's diet; cultivated in South America, the potato was discovered in the areas that were to become Peru and Bolivia by Spanish explorers searching for gold. Just how fast the potato's cultivation spread through Europe is a topic of continuing controversy. Some studies have held that it long remained a rich man's speciality; others, that it became familiar to everyday Spanish households as early as the 1570's. A traveler along the coast southeast of Lima wrote in 1586, "In the heights . . . are sown and gathered the seeds of the potato, which like cold ground. These are one of the best provisions which the Indians have in the said province, they are like truffles: and if we were to cultivate them in Spain in the manner they do there it would be a great help in years of famine. . . ." The likening of the sturdy potato to the delicate truffle is somewhat astonishing; one can only conclude that its finders considered it another delicacy. One of the first botanical studies of the potato called it *taratoufli*, Latin for "little truffle," a designation which survives in the German word for potato, *Kartoffel*. The potato was to serve Europe well—both in times of famine and good harvest.

On his second voyage, Columbus brought back the pineapple, known to the natives as *ananas*—the name it still bears in much of Continental Europe. It was a rare and costly import, the plant itself taking no hold even in the warm Mediterranean zone. (By contrast, on his outward passage, Columbus took with him the seeds of the first citrus trees to reach the New World.)

To the Spaniard Hernando Cortes and his men, a particularly pleasing discovery in Mexico was chocolate, which they may have first savored as guests of Montezuma. His table, as the expedition's chronicler Bernal Díaz del Castillo describes it, was both magnificent and barbarous. "For each meal," he writes, "over thirty different dishes were prepared by his cooks. . . . I have heard it said that they were wont to cook for him the flesh of young boys, but as he had such a variety of dishes, made of

so many things, we could not succeed in seeing if they were of human flesh or of other things, for they daily cooked fowls, turkeys, pheasants, native partridges, quail, tame and wild ducks, venison, wild boar, reed birds, pigeons, hares and rabbits, and many sorts of birds and other things which are bred in this country. . . ." But, Díaz adds, "I know for certain that after our Captain censured the sacrifice of human beings, and the eating of their flesh, [Montezuma] ordered that such food should not be prepared for him thenceforth." There was also an abundance of fruits and of tortilla cakes, made of corn meal and eggs. This was accompanied by a drink Díaz called *cacao*, served to him "all frothed up . . . in cup-shaped vessels of pure gold."

In his classic history of the conquest of Mexico, William Prescott elaborates, "The Emperor took no other beverage than chocolatl [*sic*], a potation of chocolate, flavored with vanilla and other spices, and so prepared as to be reduced to a froth of the consistency of honey, which gradually disolved in the mouth. . . . The Emperor was exceedingly fond of it, to judge from the quantity—no less than fifty jars or pitchers being prepared for his own daily consumption!" The Aztecs' drink was soon to become the rage in Europe, where it was served hot and topped with cream.

The conquistadors and others also encountered new varieties of beans in the Americas. The Lima bean, so called no doubt from the place where the Spanish may have first tasted it, proved hardy in transit and was a distinct addition to everyday European fare. Though Europe

Hafiz the Poet

Although the Persians were passionate defenders of Islam, they honored Mohammed's strictures on wine mainly in the breach; they not only lusted after the fruit of the vine, but as one visitor noted, drank "with freedom openly and with excess." Indeed, wine had been the sine qua non of Persians since ancient times—playing no small role in highlighting their sumptuous feasts, civilizing the barbarians that periodically conquered them, and stimulating their poetic instincts. By the fifteenth century they had a rich repertory of bibulous and erotic poetry, including the works of Omar Khayyám, Sadi, and above all Hafiz. Fate was especially kind to Hafiz, for he was born c. 1325 in Shiraz, at that time a haven for poets, philosophers, and artists, as well as the wine capital of Persia (the name Shiraz possibly coming from the Persian word for grape, *Sherab*). As a dervish Hafiz had earned his name by memorizing the Koran, but he soon decided that a loaf of bread was tasteless without a jug of wine to wash it down. He embarked on a new career, composing and singing amatory odes. In the lyrics below, Hafiz courts his monarch, Shah Shuja, ending with a note of self-praise common in Persian poetry.

The "Pain of Love," one story,
  Is told us o'er and o'er;
Yet, strange to say, by no one
  Tis worded as before. . . .

From fumes of wine grown heady,
  My friend gave hope—last eve—
But what today the promise,
  What will that head conceive?

How strange a branch of candy,
  HAFIZ, thy reed has grown,
That honey and pure sugar
  No fruit so luscious own!

Potations and paeans could not, however, bolster the shah's crumbling kingdom. Shortly before Hafiz' death in 1389, Tamerlane's Mongol armies invaded Persia. At a time of civil strife and anarchy, Hafiz' poetry exalting the fleeting pleasures of the senses provided an opiate for the world-weary citizens of Shiraz. The poems, interwoven with many themes like the patterns of a Persian carpet, permitted the reader to extract his own meanings, and profit thereby.

had broad beans from ancient times, *haricots*—the generic term that came into use in France to describe the species—appears to be a corruption of the Old Mexican word for bean, *ayacotl.* North America also provided several new types of beans, including the kidney, pinto, navy, and pea beans, all of which eventually found their way into European peasant cooking.

Indian corn, or maize, except that transplanted to northern Italy, had little effect on the European diet, but the root crop variously known to tropical American Indians as *manioc* or *cassava,* found acceptance. Manioc, when properly ground and prepared, is the source of tapioca, as well as other foods, all of which Europe welcomed. More important still was the American tomato and the pimento, introduced chiefly by the Portuguese and Spanish, and destined to have a great effect on the cuisine of southern Europe. The plants (both tomatoes and pimentos are classified generically as fruits) were successfully cultivated in the western Mediterranean. Northern Europe, however, did not take to them, and there was a long-lasting, obscure prejudice in Puritan England against tomatoes as injurious "love apples." (The Austrians, not averse to love fruits of any sort, named them *Paradeis.*)

New England provided other new food experiences for colonists. Thus Francis Higginson, in his promotional description *New England's Plantation,* published in 1630, wrote that "This country aboundeth naturally with store of roots of great variety and good to eat. Our turnips, parsnips and carrots are here both bigger and sweeter than is ordinarily to be found in England. Here are also store of pumpions [pumpkins], cowcumbers, and other things of that nature which I know not."

Above all, of course, there was the turkey. A seventeenth-century book on heraldry records that three centuries earlier a certain William Yoo of Devonshire emblazoned his coat of arms with "three Turkey-cocks in their pride proper." This would seem to indicate that the turkey was known in Europe long before the discovery of America and the Plymouth settlers' first Thanksgiving dinner. But, as the American historian of the turkey, A. W. Schorger, points out, the word "turkey" was used in England long before the bird we know ever arrived there. The name was taken

A British-run sugar mill in Barbados, 1667

from the land of the Turks, which since the Middle Ages had been the route if not the source of strange new flavors and foods. "Turkey" thus became the generic term for any large, edible, unfamiliar fowl. What William Yoo and others of his time were relishing were probably peacocks and peahens, domesticated or wild. According to Schorger, the actual turkey was probably seen by Spaniards during their early forays among the Indians of Mexico, perhaps during

Francisco de Córdoba's 1517 expedition to Yucatán. The historian of the expedition, Bartolomé de Las Casas, speaks of Córdoba's men being presented by the Indians with large, roasted *gallinas*; they were, he said, as large as peafowls, with a distinctive dewlap, and better in taste. The bird was brought back alive to Spain as early as 1511. It appears next to have been transported to Rome, where the naturalist Gyllius named it *gallo peregrino*, "wandering chicken," and confirmed that it had been brought from the New World. By 1538 it turned up in France as *poule d'Inde* (later shortened to *dinde*). The late eighteenth-century French gastronome and pioneer historian of taste, Brillat-Savarin, explains the French word derivation: "Superlatively knowing persons," he wrote with irony in his *Physiologie du Goût*, "maintain that the *Romans* were addicted to the turkey, that it was served at *Charlemagne's* wedding feast. . . . The French name of the bird, which, being *coq d'Inde*, clearly betrays its origin; for at first *America* was always known as the *Western Indies*."

Now the European table, enriched with great spice cargoes from the East and new foods from the Americas, was on its way to greater variety and flourish than had been known before. Another major innovation was to come in the seventeenth century—coffee.

The source of the coffee bean and the drink that was brewed from it appears to have been Ethiopia. From there it had spread through the Arab world, aided particularly by Mohammed's strictures against the consumption of wine: coffee was to be known as "the wine of Islam." Avicenna, famed eleventh century Arab physician and philosopher in remote Bokhara, was familiar with the drink (known to him as *k'hawah* and thought to have medicinal qualities).

The social life of the Middle East—then as later—revolved around the consumption of coffee at all hours of the

A Turk and his coffee in 1685

day, at home or in the bazaars. The Italian man of letters Pietro della Valle in his *Viaggi in Turchia, Persia ed India* tells of the Turks imbibing a "black beverage"; "During the summer they drink it to refresh and cool themselves, whereas in winter they find it warming; yet it is the same drink in both cases, similarly prepared. They take long draughts of it, extremely hot, but not during mealtimes, since this would remove their inclination to eat any more. It is consumed after the meal, as a dainty. It also promotes fellowship and conversation. . . . It is also said that when drunk after supper, it prevents those who consume it from feeling sleepy. For that reason, students who wish to read into the late hours are fond of it."

Throughout the Middle East there was a considerable similarity of diet, with regional variations. Lamb or mut-

169

ton—spitted as *kabāb*—was eaten everywhere except among the very poor. Sweet cakes and pastries, usually flavored with honey and often almonds, were also ubiquitous. Arabs had a particular fondness for date palm hearts and sugared fruits; Syrians, for baked eggplant and yoghurt; Persians, for melons and sherbets. But everywhere there was coffee, taken strong and sweet. Perhaps the first sample was brought back from the Levant in a ship that landed at Marseilles in 1634; but acquaintance with coffee in the West appears to have been limited until the Turks themselves brought it in—in one instance by diplomacy, in another by invasion.

In 1669 the Sublime Porte, then busy extending its power through the Balkans and toward the Danube, thought it might be wise to enter diplomatic relations with the court of Louis XIV of France as a possible ally against the Germanic peoples it was about to attack. That year an Ottoman emissary was received at Versailles in the person of Suleiman Aga, who brought with him large quantities of coffee in an equipage that also included an array of Turkish hangings, rugs, cushions, and other finery large enough to convert a mansion he had rented into an Oriental pleasure dome. Elegant, inquisitive Parisians flocked to his showplace, savored his strong brew, and—though some nobles resisted initially—soon became enraptured. The word of coffee spread downward from the aristocracy, and in 1672 an Armenian named Pascal opened the first Parisian coffeehouse.

Although Europeans had become used to the additions of new and exotic foods with each territory they conquered, coffee entered Vienna in 1683 in the baggage of Ottoman aggressors. The Turks by now had overrun all eastern Europe and were besieging the Hapsburg capital with a vast army. What happened next is related by Heinrich Jacob, author of the definitive history of coffee. An interpreter in the Austrian service, Georg Kolshitsky, who knew the Turkish language perfectly, managed to pass through the Ottoman lines in Eastern dress and get news of Vienna's plight to a relieving force headed by the Polish king John Sobieski. The relief was made, the siege was lifted, and the Turks retreating in disarray left behind vast spoils—perhaps the least of which were five hundred sacks of an unfamiliar bean of agreeable smell. While some wanted to throw the beans into the river or feed them to the animals, a few of the troops began to burn the sacks, but an extraordinary aroma rose to their nostrils. Kolshitsky, who knew good coffee when he smelled it, salvaged what was left. Before long, Vienna had learned to love coffee, especially when sugar and milk or cream were added. The city in its time was to become the great European entrepôt of coffee, developing no less than twenty ways of preparing it, from light to dark, from milky *eine Schaale Gold* to heavy *Mocha* and the murky Turkish brew topped with a mound of whipped cream. Thus, from the Danube, which the Turks had almost but not quite won, coffee traveled throughout Europe and then to the Americas. Needless to say, the proprietor of the first coffeehouse in Vienna was the enterprising Kolshitsky.

MORE
PRECIOUS
THAN
GOLD

Tropical fruits, the New World's gift to Europe, being sampled in an Ecuadorian market

Arab traders like the one above preferred buffeting sands to battering seas. Camel caravans brought spices overland from the Gulf of Suez to the markets at Cairo and Constantinople.

172

To Market, to Market

"The pepper business is profitable indeed; when the Lord God grants by His Mercy that none of the ships take damage either in coming or going, then the merchants wax rich." So ran the January, 1580, newsletter of the Fugger banking family, one of the principal investors in the spice trade. Pepper, being picked by natives in India, above, was the spice of life for most merchants, but ginger, nutmeg, and cinnamon also brought high prices on European markets. One shipment of cloves purchased in 1606 for £2,948 in the Spice Islands fetched no less than £36,287 in England. Opposite, a sixteenth-century map of Java and the Moluccas shows Europeans collecting and bartering for spices—while one wanders off to bag a deer. The boat at top has taken on cargo and is sailing for home.

EST

MOLVQVES

PETITE
IAVE

GRANDE IAVE

MER DE LINDE ORIENTALE

OVEST

Somewhere East of Suez

Artists like Théodore de Bry were not daunted by a lack of firsthand information in their depictions of faraway places. Though he rarely ventured beyond Frankfort, De Bry confidently interpreted the botanical, zoological, and social curiosities of the West and East Indies. The unrealistically well-ordered native market below is his conception of Bantam, Java, c. 1601.

A typical Arab coffeehouse in Constantinople

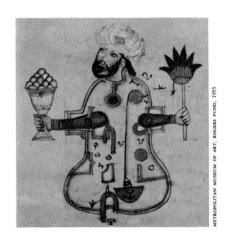

The Wines of Islam

Although the Koran frowned upon Mohammedans who indulged in wine, once out of sight of Mecca the rule was not strictly observed. Sometimes the fondness for drink was turned to imaginative ends, as in the mechanical man above, who the author explained, "drinks wine left by the king." As the right arm raises the cup, the other arm waves a blue lotus blossom, possibly to distract the pious. Like the vessel opposite, it originally appeared in a thirteenth-century book of wonders called the *Automata* and was created by the Arab inventor al-Jazarī for the amusement of his patron. But most true believers drank coffee, according to Persian legend first served to a sleepy Mohammed by the angel Gabriel. Prohibitionists seeking to rid Islam of the evils of alcohol called it "Islam's Wine."

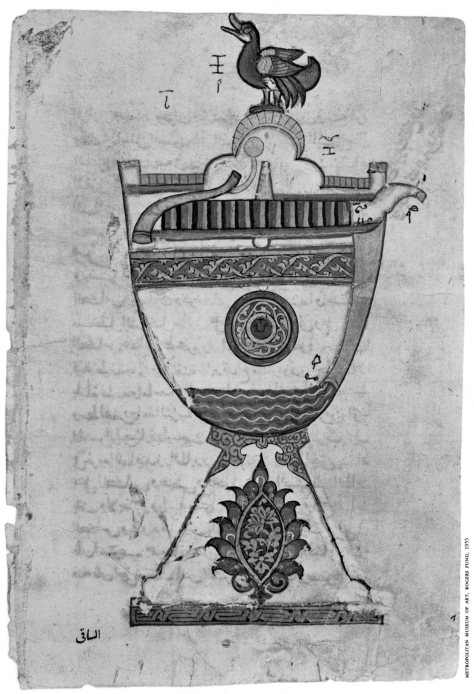

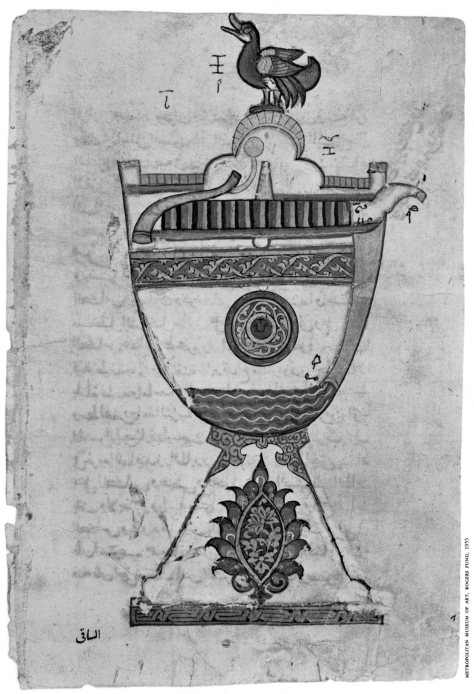

الساقي

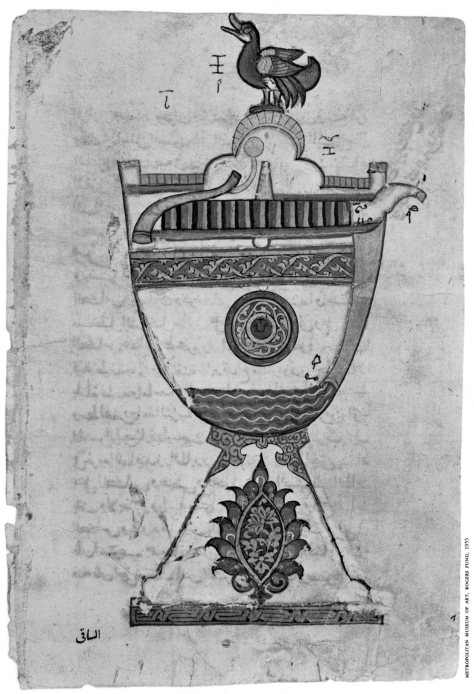

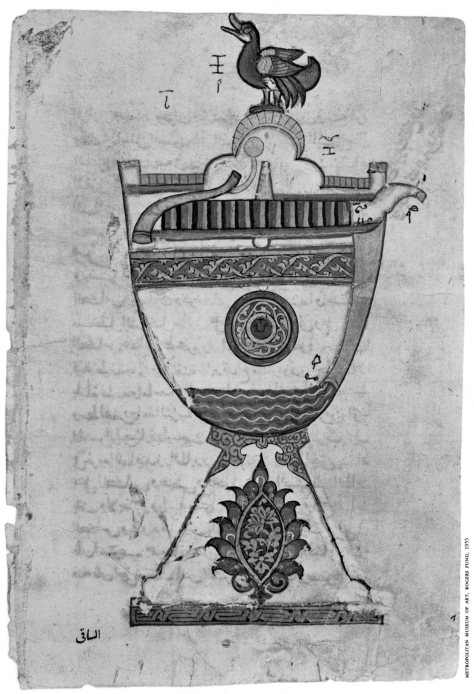

When this cup was filled with wine, so its inventor claimed, the bird would turn and whistle.

SMITHSONIAN INSTITUTION, FREER GALLERY OF ART, WASHINGTON, D.C.

Pleasant Dreams

When Jahangir of India dreamed of making peace with his enemy, Shah Abbas I of Persia, the imaginary encounter took place not over a ten-course banquet before an audience of hundreds, but intimately, over a light repast of fruit, nuts, and wine. The seventeenth-century miniature opposite, depicting the occasion, reveals both the high degree of refinement which European spice traders met in their Eastern travels and the crosscurrents of products and ideas that resulted. Decorative arts of Mogul India, like the cloisonné and gold water jug above, were often exchanged for such European *objets* as the Italian ewer and wine glass on Jahangir's table. The gilded stag on wheels, held by an attendant, right, is of German design, though it was inspired by the *Automata*

of al-Jazarī. Filled with wine, it will be set in motion, and when its mechanism has run down, the potentate nearest will empty it. Well-intentioned as Jahangir's dream of brotherhood was, the mercurial shah, kneeling, right, probably would have found such entertainment rather pallid. A visitor to his capital at Isfahan recorded that Abbas loved nothing more than to wander through the Maidan, "as spacious, as pleasant and aromatick a Market as any in the Universe," where he would shop among the stalls for wines and sweetmeats and rough companions. Though Occidentals as a rule did not find the curries and chapatis of Jahangir's India much to their liking, Abbas' Persian markets, redolent with fruits, raw vegetables, and roasting coffee, were the wonder and envy of all Europe.

OVERLEAF: *An eternal youth and a large-eyed maiden share much wine, many promises, and perhaps a Persian melon (bowl, left) in a scene that once decorated a wall of the shah's palace.*

The Gardens of Paradise

It was written in the Koran that on the day of judgment deserving Moslems would be served "wine, fruits, and flesh of fowl" in the gardens of Paradise. Meanwhile, Persians and Indians alike contemplated the pleasures of their earth-bound existence amongst shaded groves and gardens. Above, Persian cooks pre-pare an outdoor feast in a palace courtyard. In the Mogul miniature opposite, the treetop musings of a poet are interrupted by the arrival of lunch. While one servant prepares to climb the ladder with more wine, another fans the fire.

A New World

"Sail by the west into the east where spices grow," was the cry raised by explorers who groped for new and shorter passages to the Spice Islands and Cathay. Though the route ultimately proved too long and costly to be profitable, the early voyages of Columbus, Cabot, and Magellan had revealed a veritable horn of plenty—the Americas. The New World held many surprises, some pleasant, like the banquet shared with friendly natives, above. But other tribes were somewhat less cordial; mariners were aghast to learn that certain Indians preferred a sailor's well-tanned flesh to the salt beef of the ship's stores.

184

Europeans found that Indians were already exploiting the rich soil and lush climate of the New World; techniques were often crude, but crops were varied and plentiful. The scenes on this page, drawn by native artists, show (clockwise from top left) maize being planted, an early Mexican produce market, Indians picking corn, and two pages from an Inca calendar, with natives first spading the earth and then harvesting the potato crop.

Pineapple—Cuba

Maize jar—Peru

Cacao bean—Ecuador

Potato jug—Peru

Riches of El Dorado

"The abundant increase of corn proves this country to be a wonderment. Thirty, forty, fifty, sixty fold are ordinary here. Yea, Joseph's increase in Egypt is outstripped here with us." Maize, thus described in 1630 by Francis Higginson in his book *New England's Plantation*, was first known as "Turkey wheat" by the earliest settlers in the Americas. Though corn was never to become popular in Europe, many New World foods were soon to change Western menus and tastes. South American potatoes and yams became staple food for both rich and poor. Mexican chocolate and vanilla and a variety of beans and squashes were also imported. But few of the new foods caught the fancy of the homeland as did the turkey. The bird first reached European shores in 1511, after the Bishop of Valencia ordered Miguel de Passamonte to return from the Americas with ten "well-guarded" turkeys in the holds of his ships. Turkey raising quickly spread through Europe and by the early seventeenth century became so common that, according to Cardinal Jacques Davy Du Perron, farmers were "driving them from Languedoc to Spain in flocks like sheep." Through the good offices of the Portuguese, the bird also reached Goa, whence it was introduced to the Middle East.

Emperor Jahangir of India was so impressed by the turkey that in 1612 he commissioned the portrait opposite.

TOP TO BOTTOM: OVIEDO, *Coronica de las Indias*, 1547, N.Y. PUBLIC LIBRARY, RARE BOOK DIVISION; MUSEUM OF THE AMERICAN INDIAN HEYE FOUNDATION, NEW YORK; DUFOUR, *Tractatus Novi De Potu caphe*, 1685, N.Y. PUBLIC LIBRARY, RARE BOOK DIVISION; SMITHSONIAN INSTITUTION, MUSEUM OF NATURAL HISTORY, ARCHAEOLOGY COLLECTION, WASHINGTON, D.C.

Rapt in transcendental thoughts, a Chinese poet gazes on his companionable bowl of wine.

FROM
THE
GOOD
EARTH

China, which produced the first civili-
zation in the Far East, was from earliest times one of its greatest taste makers.
In due course it was to exert its influence upon the West as well. In the thirteenth century Genghis Khan's rough Mongolian tribesmen broke through
China's ancient walls and overran its heartland, only to take on in a generation
the aristocratic manners of the Peking they had captured. The Japanese, emerging from the obscurity of their island realm, borrowed many traditions from
Peking and cosmopolitan Hangchow. India, with which dynastic China had
entered into close trade relations especially during the fifth and sixth centuries
A.D., also absorbed Chinese influence. But ascetic Buddhism, followed by the
incursion of fervid Mohammedanism, set India far apart from the land guided
by the urbane precepts of Confucius and the mystical, romantic ideas of Lao-
tse. The principalities of Indonesia and southeast Asia, despite their penetra-
tion by early Chinese traders, were equally resistant, remaining worlds unto

189

themselves in social customs, religions, and culinary traditions.

A recent interpreter of China, Lin Yutang, wrote in *My Country and My People*, "If there is anything we are serious about, it is neither religion nor learning, but food." Coming from a man who was himself a scholar, the remark was no doubt intended as a whimsical exaggeration. He was, it would seem, out

Ancient ceremonial wine pitcher

to correct an impression held by some Westerners of a certain otherworldliness among highly educated Chinese of the past—as symbolized by the painting (see page 188) of the solitary scholar-poet gazing into his bowl of wine. China from its outset was a worldly civilization, craving not only food but very good food. In the time of its first flowering under the Chou dynasty, more than a millennium before Christ, it raised cookery to an art and dining to a ceremony beyond anything the Greeks had imagined.

Confucius himself (born in or about 551 B.C.) was not only an apostle of virtuous living but a gourmet and a stickler for excellence and ceremony at table. He set forth numerous rules for correct preparation and presentation of viands. As Lee Su Jan writes in *The Fine*

Art of Chinese Cooking, "His rice had to be polished white; his meat had to be finely minced, properly marinated, and served with the right sauce." If food was incorrectly combined, or if the table was not set to perfection as he saw it, he would not eat. It was from such influences as Confucius that there developed in China what has been called one of the world's two great cuisines—the other being the French.

But the preoccupation of the Chinese with their food, and their unique ways of preparing it, rest on many factors. Besides the classical Confucian ideal of gentleman-scholar-gourmet and of the meal as an expression of inner harmony through the ritual of friendship, there was the quite different Taoist school. It derived from the teachings of Lao-tse, a contemporary of Confucius, and emphasized simplicity, frugality, and a return to nature. This pursuit, apart from calisthenics, breathing, and certain sexual exercises, involved also a search for hygienic foods—particularly "life-giving" young and tender plants to be eaten raw or only half-cooked. From the former school there came much of the elegance and ceremony of Chinese cuisine; from the latter, its pleasure in very light, fresh, low-fat substances.

As in all other cultures, what was eaten was dictated by available resources —in China's case, an extraordinary mixture of scarcity and variety. It has been estimated that less than 15 per cent of China's land is today arable. What portion was arable in the time before Christ must remain conjecture, but we know that millet was the first recorded crop under cultivation there, followed by the soybean. The latter was a most valuable boon to the Chinese diet as a legume with a very high protein content (38 per cent), adaptable also to the making of curds, mashes, vegetable oils, and sauces, and moreover useful as fodder. In addition, the roots of the soybean had the rewarding quality of returning fertilizing nitrogen to the soil as the plant grew. The legendary father of Chinese agriculture, the emperor Shen Nung ("Divine Husbandman"), said to have lived c. 2700 B.C., had his clerks classify the plants of his realm, and listed the soybean as one of the five principal and sacred crops of China, the other four being rice, millet, wheat, and barley.

Still, despite intensive cultivation, recurrent famines and a tradition of undernourishment persisted in the land, and anything and everything that was edible had to be found and used, and nothing

Bronze cooking vessel, Han dynasty

wasted. This explains the inclusion in the Chinese diet of many foods that the Westerner finds forbidding if not repulsive. Locusts, silkworms, grubs, grasshoppers, snakes, and "thousand-year eggs" (actually only a few weeks old but preserved and ripened in a packing

of mud) were consumed. So were horses, mules, camels, rats, and alley cats. A chef in the imperial court of the khans around the time of Marco Polo's arrival wrote a three-volume cookbook which describes dishes using the meat of tigers, wolves, and monkeys. In the sixteenth century the Portuguese traveler Fernám Mendes Pinto wrote of food boats coming into Chinese harbors with otters, adders, and lizards for the market. He also saw compounds, or "parks" as he called them, where dogs were raised for the butcher's knife, and commented that dried orange peels were boiled up with dogs' flesh in victualing houses "to take away the rank savor and humidity" of the meat. And one Chinese tells of instances of cannibalism early in the twelfth century, when wars, invasion, and starvation had disrupted the empire. He reports that there were restaurants in Hangchow that served human meat under the name of "two-legged mutton." If this is true, it should be recalled that it occurred at the height of the Sung dynasty, renowned for its painters, mathematicians, inventors, and students of architecture and horticulture—a period when Chinese civilization was by all accounts the most advanced in the world.

Out of this background of need there developed an extraordinary, even playful, imagination in the seeking out of unusual foods. The roots of water lilies were enjoyed, along with pickled fir cones, seaweed, and kelp. A favorite dish was sharks' fins, soaked, marinated, and then simmered with ham or chicken, all of which took several days. Another was the famous "bird's-nest soup"—the nest being that of a particular species of offshore petrel that subsisted on certain types of seaweed to produce in its spittle an alkaline fluid with which it bound together its fragile roost. The resulting flavor, the Chinese found, was delectable, and immense care was taken in collecting, cleansing, and preparing broth from them. There was also a soup made of lotus seeds and a cake made of wisteria blossoms. There were even stranger dishes. A group of eighth-century A.D. poets, led by the renowned and alcoholic Li Po and calling themselves "the Eight Immortals of the Wine Cup," gave an annual banquet that included monkeys' lips, bears' paws, and something called dragon's liver—whatever that was.

Chinese cuisine was also affected by a persistent shortage of an essential element—firewood. Timber in the plains and valleys of the old provinces was extremely sparse, and stands in the remote highlands were all but inaccessible. Since fuel had to be used sparingly, it followed that cooking had better be quick rather than protracted, except where very low heat was used. Brief cooking time, as against the Western practice of slow-roasting large cuts of meat, required a great deal of preparation; foods had to be reduced to small pieces (sliced, diced, shredded, or minced) that would convert rapidly in thin, round-bottomed *woks*, or skillets. Moreover, the Chinese method was also economical in that brisk sautéing or "cook-stirring" kept down shrinkage and loss of precious juices and food values and preserved the tenderness and crispness of fresh vegetables as the Taoists had recommended.

But while scarcity or the threat of famine was ever-present, China by reason of its extensive land area—from the cold Manchurian north to the subtropical south—knew an extraordinary variety of foodstuffs. This, together with the foods that entered through conquest or foreign trade, gave China a range of diet far exceeding that of medieval Europe and in turn helped shape the diet of the West.

A court agricultural inventory made under the Han dynasty and covering the period from about the third century B.C. to A.D. 124, lists a total of 365 edible plants; not all of them can be identified

Informal lunch at a Chinese stall, c. 1300

from their ancient names. The modern writer Peh der Chen, more modest in his estimate, speaks of some 150 different types of vegetables as traditionally present and of Chinese pride in their variety. In the coastal region of Hangchow, it is reported that eighteen different kinds of beans were cultivated, along with nine varieties of rice, eleven of apricots, and eight of pears.

The Han period was one of particular luxury and expansion. Under the warrior emperor Wu Ti, who shortly before 100 B.C. extended his dominion westward toward Persia and southward beyond the Yangtze as far as Canton, oranges, grapes, pomegranates, walnuts, litchi nuts, and other novelties were introduced. (The period was also that in which glazed pottery appeared in China, along with the first experiments with porcelain—from which delicate and almost transparent bowls were to develop.) Han dynasty merchants grew rich traveling throughout the empire selling fine sauces, dried fish, dates, chestnuts, relishes, and such specialties as stuffed sheep's stomachs. Beginning in about the sixth century A.D., still more variety was introduced, reflecting Chinese contacts with Indochina, India, and the Middle East—pepper, sugar, almonds, figs, sesame, coriander, chives, onions, lettuce, garden peas, cucumbers, and probably olives. Later, carrots, kidney beans, and pistachio nuts appeared on the Chinese table, and there are records of Arab traders introducing the art of refining sugar to the Chinese.

Still later, in another instance of the transmigration that marks the history of the world's foods, maize, the sweet potato, and the peanut reached China: the corn, it is supposed, came via central Asia and the Moslem traders who got it from the Moors in Spain; the others came from Spanish traders in the Philippines. (On the other hand middle European sauerkraut can be traced to Chinese "sour cabbage"—that is, cabbage soaked in rice wine to preserve it over the winter. It is said to have been a favorite dish of Genghis Khan's invaders, who substituted salt brine for the rice wine and carried the recipe westward.) In the seventeenth and eighteenth centuries as foreign trade expanded, the pineapple and the white, or "Irish," potato appeared, as did squash and still more varieties of beans. Somewhat earlier, cultivation of the opium poppy, introduced from India, also took hold, with results at first pleasant when the seeds were used in cooking, but destined to be tragic for China when its consumers turned to the opium pipe.

The cumulative effect of all this (leaving aside the opium poppy) was a remarkable proliferation of dishes in China north and south. The common people, to be sure, subsisted primarily on a diet of rice, the soybean and its derivatives, fish, and various domestic animals and their intestines, supplemented by an occasional platter of pork. China's vast size and the range of its resources promoted numerous regional schools of cookery, each drawing on favorite and indigenous foods. The northern school of ancient Honan along the Yellow River leaned to sweet-sour dishes, using for instance the river's famous carp and the valley's delicate mushrooms. The more robust cuisine of inland southwestern Szechwan ran to highly spiced combinations, often including pimento; that of Canton on the southeastern coast, to rich sea food.

Peking, China's capital since the twelfth century, drew chefs from many provinces and developed a mixed style that at its most elegant and courtly was to be known under the Manchus as "imperial food." But perhaps the greatest variety existed at Hangchow, in effect a refugee center of Chinese gentry who emigrated down the Yangtze from northern Honan during the Mongol invasions. Hangchow boasted fresh-water fish from lakes and streams, game from nearby hills, catches from the sea, and local geese and ducks raised in huge hatcheries —some holding as many as ten thousand ducklings at once. Numerous restaurants dedicated to one or another speciality arose there. One thirteenth-century establishment offered only iced foods; another in the Mixed Wares Market concentrated on sweet soy soup; one specialized in pig cooked in ashes in front of the Longevity-and-Compassion Palace; Mother Sung's establishment outside the Cash-reserve Gate featured fish soup; still another in front of the Five-span Pavilion sold honey fritters.

Yet, however widely Chinese cooking varied from province to province and from class to class, it was governed by a general body of principles. Chinese precepts, reflecting a people of strong aesthetic and sensory bent, called for food that first must gratify all the senses —those of sight, touch, hearing, and smell no less than that of taste. Furthermore, dishes should strive for harmony coupled with contrast and accent, and always for a subtle blending of tastes. Innumerable elements entered into this scheme. Lin Yutang has explained, "We eat food for its *texture*, the elastic or crisp effect it has on our teeth, as well as for fragrance, flavor and color," and he adds that "a great part of the popularity of bamboo shoots is due to the fine resistance the young shoots give our teeth." (The use of water chestnuts, almost without taste themselves, but added to many dishes, whose flavor they absorb, is another instance of this fondness for texture; Lee Su Jan speaks of their "pleasing crunch.")

The pure whiteness of the polished rice on which Confucius insisted provided a background for the brilliant effects of color sought—the light emerald of very young vegetables, the golden brown of the swiftly sautéed morsels of duck, pork, or fish, the red of pimento. Clear, transparent broths were often graced with flower petals of a contrasting or subtly related hue: thus the light yellow chrysanthemum petals strewn in a bowl of amber chicken soup. The very bowls in which such dishes were served were works of remarkable artistry, sometimes richly colored, sometimes elegant in their sheer fragility, and were thought of as an essential ingredient to full enjoyment. An Arab merchant who visited China in the mid-ninth century, when the art of porcelain was developing, wrote that "there is in China a clay of superior quality from which are made cups (or bowls) as thin as bottles of glass; by reason of their transparency one may behold the liquid they contain."

The Chinese theme of harmony in foods was also subject to countless variations, harmony itself meaning both accord and diversity. The great eighteenth-century gastronome Yüan Mei—often referred to as the Brillat-Savarin of China—was to write, "Cookery is like matrimony. Two things served together should match. Clear should go with clear, thick with thick, hard with hard, and soft with soft." In a tone of revulsion he added, "I have known people to mix grated lobster with birds' nests, and mint with chicken or pork!" Yet he did not mean by this that all foods in the mating process should be alike. There should simply be an agreeable blend of foodstuffs on good terms with each

The Great Khan

Shortly after Kublai Khan consolidated his Tartar domain in China, he relinquished warfare in favor of less strenuous pastimes. When Marco Polo arrived at Khanbalik (Peking), he was greeted by a sinocized sovereign who wore the robes of a Chinese emperor, lived in a palace adorned with gilt dragons and lacquered ceilings, and like his new subjects, had a marked propensity for eating and drinking. Visitors from all parts of the empire came to the enormous hall where the khan held court. Before they could pay their respects and render tribute, they had to lower their voices, don white leather slippers, and equip themselves with lidded spittoons. Inside, Tibetan lamas reportedly performed such sorcery as sending goblets of koumiss (a Mongolian brew of fermented mare's milk) flying through the air to Kublai's mouth, and when empty, whisking them back with equal mystery. One banquet attended by as many as twenty thousand nobles is described by Marco Polo in splendid but probably accurate terms. Only about six thousand can be seated at tables; the others sit on carpets. "The tables are arranged . . . [so] that the Great Khan . . . on his elevated throne, can overlook the whole." Near the khan is a buffet, "hollow within, for . . . receiving a capacious vase, of pure gold, calculated to hold many gallons. On each of its four sides stands a smaller vessel . . . one filled with mare's milk, another with that of the camel." Gilt flagons, such as those in an illustration of Marco Polo's visit opposite, are each shared by two guests. "Stewards are continually . . . inquiring . . . whether any of them wish for wine, milk, meat, or other articles, in which case it is immediately brought. . . . At each door . . . stand two officers of a gigantic figure" armed with staves to prevent "persons from touching the

threshold with their feet [a bad omen]." If anyone is guilty, "these janitors take . . . his garment, which he must redeem for money; or . . . they inflict on him [a] number of blows. . . . As some . . . may be affected by the liquor, it is impossible to guard against the accident, and the order is not then strictly enforced." Kublai's waiters must "cover their noses and mouths . . . that his victuals or his wine may not be affected by their breath." Whenever he drinks, all servants and guests lie prostrate, and music plays until he has finished. Later, "tumblers and jugglers . . . exhibit their skill . . . to the . . . gratification of all."

other. He also recognized five primary flavors: sweet, bitter, sour, pungent, and salty, each with its complement.

Thus Yüan Mei: "Let salt fish come first, and afterwards food of more negative flavor. Let the heavy precede the light. Let dry dishes precede those with gravy. . . . Salt flavors must be relieved by bitter or hot tasting foods, in order to restore the palate. Too much wine will make the stomach dull. Sour or sweet food will be required to rouse it again into vigor. . . . Don't make your thick sauces greasy nor your clear ones tasteless. Those who want grease can eat fat pork, while a drink of water is better than something which tastes of nothing at all. . . . Don't over-salt your soups; for salt can be added to taste, but can never be taken away. *Don't eat with your ears*; by which I mean do not aim at having extraordinary out-of-the-way foods, just to astonish your guests. . . . *Don't eat with your eyes*; by which I mean do not cover the table with innumerable dishes and multiply courses indefinitely."

Yet it is erroneous to speak in terms of separate "courses" at all. More correctly, no two dishes offered must be alike. The Western scheme of a series of dishes ending on desserts or sweetmeats was unknown in China. Sweets appeared in the middle or even at the beginning of a meal. Guests were invited to sample from numerous platters or communal bowls what most appealed to them, and in the order they preferred, always having in front of them their personal bowl of rice. There was, furthermore, a division of foods in three main orders: those that called for just a touch of garlic or soy or other sauce to bring out their

natural flavors; those that involved what Lee Su Jan calls a whole "alchemy of condiments" enhancing one main ingredient; and still others comprised of two or more main ingredients and several condiments so that in the final dish the elements had undergone complete

Chinese porcelain water bucket

transfiguration. The result might be a "breakfast" such as the one served the emperor Ch'ien Lung in 1754, the eighteenth year of his festive reign.

The emperor rose at about four o'clock in the morning in the Imperial Palace at Peking, bathed, and was waited upon by a court eunuch with a dish of crystal sugar and swallows' nests. Afterward, he was carried to the audience hall in a palanquin to hear his courtiers, then returned to his chambers to rest a while. At about nine o'clock he was regaled by the following: a dish of fat chicken, pot-boiled duck, and bean curd, cooked by the master Chang Erh; a dish of swallows' nests and a julienne of smoked duck, cooked by the same; a dish of salted duck and pork, prepared by Jung Kuei; a dish of smoked chicken and Chinese cabbage; a bowl of clear soup; a dish of bamboo-stuffed steamed dumplings; another of rice cakes with honey; and the following, "served in a ceramic container patterned with hollyhock flowers": pickled cabbage, cucumbers in soy, pickled eggplant—and so on.

This was only the first of three meals of comparable magnitude during the day—though no doubt the emperor, following the custom, took only bits and pieces here and there with his porcelain soup spoon or his chopsticks. (The use of chopsticks—pidgin English for *faai jee* meaning "quick little boys"—was a sign of cultivation, in contrast to using one's fingers or the "barbaric" foreign fork. In polite society the table knife was also unheard-of, cutting in all its forms being the task of the chefs and servants, and never done at meals.)

A formal banquet would, of course, offer a far greater variety. There might be as many as fifty dishes, representing every category of food from land, sea, and air; a dinner of the empress dowager Tzu Hsi is reported to have included over a hundred. One Chinese book of dining goes further and mentions more than two hundred dishes that might be served at a very grand affair, including 41 of fish, shrimps, snails, pork, goose, duck, mutton, et cetera; 42 concocted from fruits and sweetmeats; along with 17 liquid refreshments, ranging from wine to pawpaw juice, litchi juice, and honey and ginger drinks. Since a basic principle of Chinese high cuisine was to offer only what was most fresh and to serve it immediately, the sheer logistical problems of assembling so many foods in prime condition for a given banquet must have been immense.

Another problem confronting the chef and his assistants was the selection of a site for such complex meals; in winter indoors, but in warmer seasons in some harmonious grove or pavilion or beside a lake or stream—the place was very much a part of the Chinese aesthetic. A banquet might be served on a terrace such as that of the ancient Han emperor Wu Ti where "amid the perfumed cassia trees, peacocks flocked together, monkeys screamed, kingfishers gathered, and phoenixes flew about," or in accompanying gardens lit by multi-colored lanterns. Or the court might decide to pick a remote spot for what the French call a *fête champêtre*. Banquets might also be served in pleasure barges. An eighth-century poet of the T'ang dynasty tells of such an evening in a brief fragment:

> *Forthwith we steered our boat in changèd course.*
> *A meeting with the Muse we fain would seek.*
> *We dressed our table with fresh food and wines.*
> *All lights gone out were lit up once again. . . .*

The custom had not changed by the eighteenth century. Of the later emperor Ch'ien Lung, a recent historian Lucille Su Chung Davis writes, "The greatest difficulty in serving the emperor came from the fact that there was no regular place for him to eat. The imperial cuisine was required to serve meals whenever and wherever the emperor demanded. For example, when the emperor was taking a walk, men of the refreshment division had to follow him with two round bamboo baskets containing plenty of refreshments, tea, and

197

a small stove so that food might be ready within minutes after it was ordered." Not only the portable stove, but iron cooking pots and pans, silver bowls, and fine porcelain cups had to be transported. This was "cook-stir" cuisine at perhaps its most demanding.

Dining and ceremony were inseparable. The greatest annual festival, that of *Sun Neen* (New Year's), involved special rituals concerning the god of the kitchen, who was supposed to ascend to Heaven to report on the virtues and vices of the family. A week before the New Year, the family gathered before his picture hung on the kitchen chimney to send him on his way: his lips were smeared with sticky sweets to prevent them from uttering evil, and then the image was taken down, set upon a straw or paper horse outside the house, and burned. On the last day of the year, his triumphal return to the kitchen was observed with fireworks and banqueting, and a new picture was placed upon the chimney.

Among the gentry not only banquets but even an everyday dinner with friends was governed by elaborate forms of reception, courtesy, and protocol of seating as well as of conversation. For more formal gatherings invitations were sent out—perhaps on red paper with gold inscription—to ten or a dozen guests, usually not more, mentioning the names of the others who had been invited, and thus giving each recipient a convenient way of excusing himself if he preferred not to join the particular company. (The West has not yet learned this subtle touch of "harmony.") The ultimate ceremonial, the state banquet, is described by Tien-Hsi Cheng, former member of the Chinese diplomatic corps, in his *Musings of a Chinese Gourmet*:

"1. The host stands on the west side of the hall a few yards from the dinner table. 2. The "Master of Ceremony" bows to the guest of honor and conducts him to a place on the east side of the hall not far from but opposite to where the host is standing. 3. The host bows to the guest, who bows in return. 4. The host ascends the hall up to the dinner table and bows to the empty chair on which the guest is to sit. The guest, now facing the host, bows in return. 5. The host walks to the chair and, with both sleeves, touches the cushion of the chair as a symbol of dusting it. After this, he bows to the chair and the guest bows in return. 6. The host, with a bow, raises the pair of chopsticks to be used by the guest, who bows in return. 7. The host, with a bow, raises the wine cup to be used by the guest, who bows in return. 8. The host returns to the place where he stood and bows to the guest, who bows in return. 9. The guest leaves and is conducted to his seat."

"Solemn but cheerful music" was frequently played at such festivities. The table was usually round, both to encourage general conversation and to provide all guests with equal access to the various dishes placed in the center, as against the European custom of a long table where one could converse comfortably only with his immediate neighbors and where food was served by footmen. The order of seating also ran counter to the European forms: the host, after mutual obeisances, sat opposite the guest of honor, who was placed nearest the family altar or farthest from the door. To be

198

seated at the left hand of the host was thought to be a higher honor than to be at his right. In polite houses there was a rule against religious, political, or other disputatious talk at table, which might disturb the friendship or conviviality of those present. One discussed art, philosophy, and no doubt one's neighbors—and above all, the food itself.

One also played table games at intervals during the meal. A chief purpose of these games was, clearly, to encourage drinking—the Chinese, with his elaborate sense of formality, evidently needed some "urging" to toss off another cup. Many responded to the urging quite

Mandarin banquet in an orchard, Ming dynasty

readily. There is ample evidence that from early times alcohol was consumed in quantity. Confucius himself admitted that he was sometimes "overcome by wine." A Chinese proverb claims, "No wine, no conversation; no conversation, no company." Poets told of the transcendental pleasures of becoming drunk. Li Po, one of China's greatest lyricists, wrote, "The rapture of drinking, and wine's dizzy joy, No man who is sober deserves." He is said to have drowned after falling overboard while in a state of drunken exultation, trying to seize the moon's reflection in a lotus pool.

By wine, however, the Chinese did not generally mean that made from grapes. The earliest sources of wine were fermented grains and a variety of fruits. An old tale has it that the drink originated in China when a palace cook placed some rice in a crock to soak and then forgot it. Several days later he returned to the crock wondering if the rice had spoiled. Not only was the rice delicious but the water had been transformed into something wonderful. He continued to sample the liquid, singing a happy song all the while.

The early yellow rice wine tasted, perhaps, somewhat like sherry. As Marco Polo observed on returning from thirteenth century Peking, the beverage the Chinese preferred was "a liquor which they brew of rice with a quantity of excellent spice in such fashion that it makes better drink than any other kind of wine; it is not only good, but clear and pleasant to the eye. And being very hot stuff, it makes one drunk sooner than any other wine." He was describing something similar to Japanese *sake*. There was also a stronger grain concoction resembling vodka; and rose petals, pears, oranges, and quinces were sometimes used. Wine made from grapes may have entered China in the second century before Christ, as a result of Han dynasty contacts with Persia. An envoy brought back seeds of *Vitis vinifera*, but for more than a millennium and a half grape wine remained an unfamiliar, imported luxury.

In early T'ang times, wine was apparently taken only after the meal, each guest awaiting his turn to raise his cup. In later centuries it was served through-

Games People Played

*I*n Chinese society playing games during the meal was not only good manners, it was almost *de rigueur*. Games kept the conversation flowing and discouraged discussion of sensitive subjects which had a way of souring the stomach. Since the Chinese also observed that the road to conviviality was paved with empty wine cups, most contests were designed to encourage drinking. One of the more popular mealtime entertainments was a Cantonese game called Guess the Unknown, which demanded stratagem, ruse, and digital dexterity. It involved two players, each of whom threw out on signal a hand showing one or more fingers extended, simultaneously calling out the total number of fingers between them. After each round, the loser—and often the winner—was consoled with wine. Another contest that probed the minds and capacities of guests was the "Wine Command." It relied not on guesswork but on erudition and was a favorite among the mandarins, the scholarly ruling class whose com-

petitive wits were well-honed at all times. Initially, the host chose a word, using it in a quotation from a literary classic. Depending on the position of the key word within the sentence, the player that many places to the left of the reciter then had to offer another sentence from the same work, using the chosen word. The "punishment" for failing to produce a quotation on cue was another cup of rice wine, a handicap that one with a faltering memory could ill afford. The diner's attainments as a muse might also be tested in a poetry contest—a theme was proposed by the host, and guests were expected to compose spontaneously a few lines. Whether born of the sheer joy of creation or the heat of competition, many of these poems have become classics. Tiring of such exercises and while waiting for a new siege of dishes, the assembly might debate the virtues of their favorite recipes for shark fin soup or the most refined blend of tea, each speaker trying to outdo his companions in evocative language. All these games presupposed an extraordinary degree of intelligence on the part of host and guests alike. Anyone planning a party among dullards could always resort to paid entertainers, highly specialized professionals such as riddle makers, tellers of obscene stories, imitators, slight-of-hand artists, and singers of songs. As European travelers visiting China for the first time discovered, capacities of mind as well as of stomach were required of the successful guest.

out the meal, still in cups and, as always, warmed. The warming served to overcome its "green" or harsh flavor, since it was consumed soon after fermentation. One thirteenth-century report, discussing Hangchow restaurants, taverns, and households, speaks of fifty-four different kinds of rice wines available. Evidently a quite remarkable selectivity of tastes had come into being by then. In the eighteenth century the fastidious Yüan Mei wrote with perception, "I am not much of a wine drinker, but this makes me all the more particular. Wine is like scholarship: it ripens with age; and it is best from a fresh-opened jar. The top of the wine jar, the bottom of the teapot, as the saying has it."

When the Chinese—and the Japanese who followed in their culinary wake— were not enjoying food or wine, their primary refreshment was of course tea, of which they made not only a ceremony but a cult. Tea, the national drink of China, was drunk at all hours and on all occasions—from breakfast at home to midnight and beyond at the many classes of teahouses. Business was (and is today) conducted over it. The first act of a host on receiving a visitor at his home or place of business was to offer a steaming drink, perhaps accompanied by almond cakes. Caravans, coaches, and then railroad trains stopped repeatedly at way stations to obtain boiling water from local purveyors for brewing the tea that individual passengers carried with them. The use of boiled water as a basis for refreshment, it might be remarked, in a land in which so many rivers and canals were polluted, had distinct advantages.

Although one legend attributes the discovery of tea to the emperor Shen Nung, another popular myth credits the founder of Zen Buddhism in India, Bodhidharma, with its origin. The saint, on a mission to China, decided to spend nine years in a sanctuary contemplating a wall, but exhaustion finally overcame him, and he fell asleep. As penance, he cut off his eyelids and threw them to the ground, where a strange bush sprang up. After tasting the leaves, Bodhidharma found that his drowsiness had passed, and he was able to continue his meditations without further interruption. Actually, it appears that the tea plant was indigenous to India where it thrived on steep slopes in poor acidic soil otherwise incapable of supporting crops. It may have entered China in about the third century A.D., after the Han empire had reached out to the subtropical regions south of the Yangtze valley. We know that tea was widely used in the eighth century, if only from a record of taxes imposed on it. Also about that time, a poet named Lu Yu is said to have traveled the countryside with cooking pots and a water tank to demonstrate methods of brewing the beverage.

Before long, an extraordinary proliferation of varieties of tea occurred in China, involving perhaps more subtleties of taste than exist among the wines of France. Since all tea comes from the same type of plant, its quality depends on the altitude; the month the leaves are harvested; whether or not the leaves are broken in handling; and whether the leaves are picked high (for better quality teas) or low on the bush. In the curing process certain teas are chemically altered by oxidation before they are dried, producing black teas; others are dried directly, hence green teas. Today, green teas are limited mainly to China. Most black teas come from Ceylon and India. Romantic and inviting labels are given to them: "Dragon's Whiskers," a delicate green growth of Shantung; "Water Nymph," "Eyebrows of Longevity," and "Clear Distance" of Kwantung; "White Clouds" and "Forest of Fragrance" of the region of Hangchow. Two extra-fine blends of dessert teas, known as *Tit-koon-yum* and *Tit-lo-hon*, of northern China were at last report still picked by monkeys trained to scale the heights and retrieve basketfuls of their tiny leaves. In early days, ginger, orange, or onion was used to add savor to the tea; in later times, jasmine blossoms or those of roses or crysanthemums or camellias added fragrance.

The ritual of tea prescribed that it be brewed not in the kitchen but in the presence of the guests themselves, usually in the individual cups they were to use; the Chinese as a rule used the pot for hot water only. Each cup was fitted with a lid, and when the cup was raised to the lips, its lid was lifted just enough to let the liquid flow but to hold back the leaves. A second or third cup brewed with the same leaves was generally thought to be an improvement on the

Embroidered covers on tea caddies, Japan, 1600's

first, and each pouring involved more ceremony and more compliments (the host, needless to say, denigrating the quality of his tea, though it might be the finest money could buy). A particularly graceful form of tea service took place as part of the marriage ceremony, when the bride presented tea in red (signifying joy) lacquer cups to her blood relatives and in-laws and the friends of both families, in order of precedence.

But if the offering of tea in China was a rite, in Japan it approached the status of a religion. It is said that the first Japanese ruler to taste the brew was the emperor Shomū, who accepted a cup from a party of visiting Buddhist priests in the year 729. He bestowed his approval, and soon the plant was being raised on the slopes of Mount Hiei; but it was not until much later that tea was taken for other than its medicinal properties or that the ritual of "teaism" developed. Out of the contemplative qualities of Zen Buddhism, the formalities of their own Shintoism, and their native aesthetic predilections, the Japanese developed during the sixteenth century the idea of the teahouse or tearoom attached to the house as a place to worship and to learn harmony, tranquillity, unselfishness, and dignity. Tea—not the clear, amber tea which was drunk with meals but a kind of soup whipped up from tea powder into a froth—became the substance and symbol of communion.

The classic "tea ceremony," *cha-no-yu*, of Japan was conceived far more in terms of symbols than substance. One came to a friend's teahouse not to enjoy a number of warming cups of *o cha* ("honorable tea") and conversation so much as to engage in a complex ritual. Following the teachings of the famed "tea master" Rikyu and successor *chajins*, even the tea-ceremony rooms were constructed according to precise specifications—a subtle play of assymetric proportions that were said to give full range to the imagination of the communicants. The ritual began with the invitation of the guests, usually four, after which each would call to express his *zenrei*, or polite thanks. Then, on the following day the guests would arrive, wearing properly muted kimonos and carrying their personal tea cloths and fans. After gathering in the waiting room, the group walked to the teahouse, preceded by the host or his gardener, who carried a bronze swordlike instrument which he brandished about as if to lop off branches that might obstruct the guests or snag their garments, this to symbolize the host's desire to give his guests every comfort. Before entering the chamber, everyone stopped for a ceremonious washing of face and hands and removal of sandals. Then, as Okakura-Kakuzo's classic *Book of Tea* records, "The guest will silently approach the sanctuary, and, if a samurai, will leave his sword on the rack beneath the eaves, the tearoom being pre-eminently the house of peace. Then he will bend low and creep into the room through a small door. . . . This proceeding [is] incumbent on all guests, high and low alike, and is intended to inculcate humility. The order of precedence having been mutually agreed upon . . . the guests one by one will enter noiselessly and take their seats, first making obeisance to the picture or flower arrangement on the *tokonoma* [a niche designed especially for their display]. The host will not enter the room until all the guests have seated themselves and quiet reigns with nothing to break the silence save the note of the boiling water in the iron kettle. . . ."

The rest of the ceremony went on in like ritual fashion, a sequence of precise movements being prescribed for the elevation of the cup to one's lips, as well as a practice, if a communal bowl was

Japanese invention for suspending kettle

used, of passing it around the table when emptied to be admired by the guests as a work of art. After each guest had made sucking sounds to signify his pleasure at his last sip, and the host his profound obeisances, the company departed through the same door by which they had entered.

When eating or drinking normally, the Japanese were not subject to such excruciating practices. Their basic diet (almost unchanged to this day) was akin to that of the coastal Chinese, both in foodstuffs and preparation, though there were many differences. Rice and soy were their staples, along with local seafood. The Japanese rice was served both steamed and in the form of rice cakes, or *moshi;* it was, in fact, so important to the diet that the word for rice, *gohan*, was also used to describe a whole meal. Soybeans appeared at table as bean paste and curd, vegetable oil, sauce, and as a fermented preservative for other foods. Fast or "instant" cookery of cut-up foods, also learned from China, was the rule. The Japanese also shared the Chinese' fondness for rice wine. A Chinese historian of the third century remarked that the Japanese "are given much to strong drink"; by the tenth century the amount of drinking had become formidable. The only time it was considered improper to drink was while eating rice.

Differences between Japanese and Chinese cuisine were due chiefly to the period of Japanese seclusion and Buddhist ascendancy beginning in the tenth century when Buddhist prohibitions against the killing of animals limited the orthodox to a vegetarian diet supplemented by fish. The meat of cattle, though Jesuit missionaries recommended it highly during the brief period of their access to Japan in the sixteenth century, continued to be despised as unfit for human consumption, and the real or imagined smell that accompanied meat eaters was deemed most disagreeable. But the nineteenth century was to see a turnabout, when Japanese came into close contact with carnivorous Americans and Europeans, and young intellectuals propounded the theory that red meat was advantageous to mind and body. In 1872 the emperor gave the signal by going over to beef himself; thereupon all Japan took to it, and beef eating, according to one Japanese historian, "was regarded as a sign of [an] advanced state of civilization." One result of this revolution is the dish most familiar to Westerners, the beef-and-vegetable *sukiyaki*, though Japanese gourmets look down upon it as untraditional and of peasant origin.

Like China, Japan from early times enjoyed its annual court festivals, all involving food and drink. Thus there was the ceremony of "The Medicinal Offerings and the Tooth Hardening," which an old court calendar describes as follows: "Various types of spiced wine are prepared by the Palace Medicinal Office and, after being tasted by specially appointed virgins, are offered to His Majesty as an elixir of long life. Radishes, mirror-shaped rice cakes, melons, and similar auspicious foods are presented to the Emperor in order to 'harden his teeth' [to ensure his good health] during the coming year." And for the "Festival of the Young Herbs," officials of the Imperial Storehouse went out to pluck the "seven lucky herbs" to mix with rice and make a gruel for the emperor; the same seven-herb gruel was also prepared in private households to ward off evil spirits and to protect the family from any dangers ahead. Another annual event was the exquisite chrysanthemum celebration in which the emperor and his court, after inspecting the blossoms in the royal garden, sat down to drink wine in which the petals had been steeped, to dine on white trout and compose poetry.

Such food ceremonies have long since disappeared. But China and Japan, despite their overwhelming changes in the last half century, remain profoundly attached to their traditions, and a meal is never really a meal without a bowl of good white rice and a cup of tea beside it.

LANDS
OF THE
LOTUS-EATERS

Kublai Khan and wife at a Mongolian cookout, from a contemporary Persian history

The Flowery Kingdom

不須更佩
宜男草
只合庭前
揉石榴
克光氏

According to Taoists, by observing the cyclic rhythms of nature, man could learn to live in harmony with the universe and even discover the secret of long life. Perhaps because Buddha (under a mango tree opposite) first attained perfect wisdom contemplating a Bo or wild fig tree, fruit trees such as the peach were particularly sacred. Chinese artists were inspired to capture the fragrance of pomegranate blossoms and the sweetness of the ripening fruit, above, or to convey the fragility of arbutus berries, below, with their brushes. A poet advised: "fruit trees should be painted in the chill of the evening. Then they lose their wildness. . . . Those who do not care for flowers need not look."

闊海夏深
初熟子
相儔第一
狀元紅
克光氏

207

Cultivating the paddy

Sowing in floodtime

The Hard-won Crop

Reaping the harvest

Bringing in the sheaves

Sifting

Winnowing

Preparing to transplant

Planting the seedlings

Rice was as basic to the Oriental diet as bread was to the European meal, but its cultivation was a far more demanding task. The good grace with which these Chinese peasants bend to their labors is purely imaginary, the romantic conception of the eighteenth-century Englishman who engraved the series. Except at harvest time, there was little joy in the rice paddy, and even the most bountiful yield, when polished to a properly Confucian white, provided little real nourishment.

OVERLEAF: *A British painter in Canton c. 1835 traces the progress of tea from its growth in the highlands, upper left, to its packing, sale, and shipment on the wharves, below.*

Threshing

Breaking the husks

Grinding

Offering thanks

Travel kit of eating and cooking tools, Korea, 1700's

Wine vessel, ancient China

The Perfect Setting

Porcelain dish, China, c. 1630

At the Oriental meal, form was as important as content. The distinctive diet of the East required tableware often very different from that of the West, and no dish or utensil was too insignificant to have its own standards of perfection. Above, a picnic set provided everything a nobleman needed for a cook-stir meal, including tongs for the fire, a marrow pick, and tiny cups for sipping a particularly refined brew of tea buds. Traditional drinking vessels in the shapes of animals are represented here in a bronze owl jar for sacramental wine, c. 1000 B.C., and in a seventeenth-century porcelain

Lacquered kettle, Japan, 1500's

CREDITS FOR PHOTOGRAPHS ABOVE, CLOCKWISE FROM TOP: CHARLES R. GRACIE AND SONS, INC.; THE MINNEAPOLIS INSTITUTE OF ARTS, ALFRED F. PILLSBURY BEQUEST; M. H. DE YOUNG MEMORIAL MUSEUM, ROY LEVENTRITT COLLECTION, SAN FRANCISCO; COURTESY OF DR. AND MRS. PAUL VIGNOS, JR.

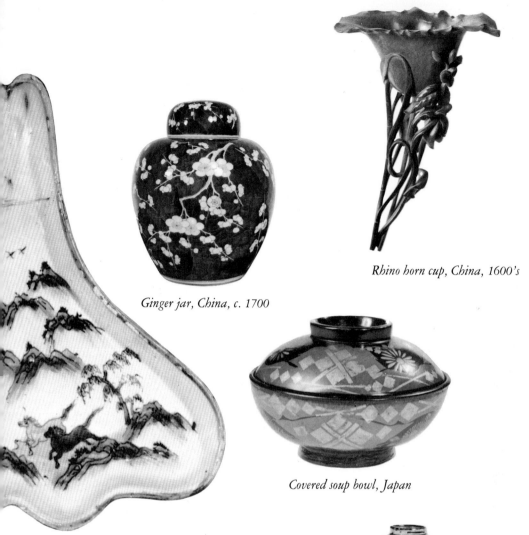

Ginger jar, China, c. 1700

Rhino horn cup, China, 1600's

Covered soup bowl, Japan

elephant bottle for table use. The cup carved from rhino horn in the shape of a lotus leaf combined the symbolism of a highly touted aphrodisiac and a dream-inducing plant. The ginger jar, in the cobalt blue and white perfected under the Ming dynasty, held sweetmeats sent to friends on the New Year. Chinese porcelain was also designed to suit foreign tastes —the dish in the shape of Mount Fuji was marketed for the Japan trade. Tableware created by the Japanese was often of a simpler, more robust design, like the kettle and the soup bowl, whose cover, when inverted, became a second dish.

Elephant bottle, China, c. 1600

The Floating World

"Living only for the moment, turning our full attention to the pleasures of the moon, the snow, the cherry blossoms and the maple leaves, singing songs, drinking wine, and diverting ourselves just in floating, floating . . ." was the not so elusive ideal of the newly risen feudal lords of sixteenth and seventeenth century Japan. The delicate Buddhist-inspired sensibilities of their predecessors were overthrown in favor of worldly diversions. Among these, the picnic held an especially favored place. The stylish couples opposite, depicted by the genre painter Shunsho, have taken to the countryside with a *samisen* (a three-stringed banjo) and a lacquer picnic box, wrapped in a cloth, but presumably like the four-tiered carrier above.

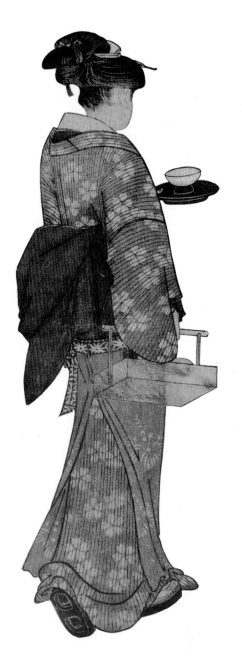

On the Road

Between the Imperial city of Kyoto and the shogunate in Tokyo, the traffic of Japanese pilgrims, bureaucrats, and feudal lords never slowed. For their protection, in 1601 the government established fifty-three way stations along the 305-mile Tokaido Road and ruled that no traveler could stay even a single night in a house other than a public inn. Though notable guests might appear for dinner and lodging at any time, innkeepers were in a special state of readiness every spring when a retinue of two hundred men set out from Tokyo for Uji, there to refill the Shogun's "precious tea canisters" and assorted lesser containers with the finest tea leaves of the country. On the return trip, messengers preceded the party to alert innkeepers, supervise the sweeping of the roadway, and halt all burning of fires or other activities which might flavor the tea. During these days, the usually attentive service to other clients might, understandably, suffer.

Opposite: The number of "waitresses" permitted by law was two; some proprietors gladly paid the fine.

Chop Chop in the Kitchen

For all the subtleties of Oriental cookery, the traditional kitchen was a rudimentary affair, uncluttered by batteries of utensils, ovens, and cutlery so dear to Western chefs. Below and opposite, the preparation of a samurai's meal, painted by an anonymous fourteenth-century artist, is divided among five men: two carving masters, cross-legged behind their low work tables, address a cormorant and a carp, the fish held upright between two chopsticks for filleting.

Their companions attend to the vegetables in round-bottomed pans over the fire pit, and ladle soup with a spoon fashioned from a scallop shell. The woman-run kitchen above has a more relaxed atmosphere, as drawn by the eighteenth-century artist Utamaro: left, one servant chats with the baby and gives a bowl a peremptory wipe, while another peels vegetables, washing them in the bucket at her side; right, they tend the fire, blowing on it through a pipe.

Both in China and in Japan, vendors of specialty foods called regularly at the kitchen door. The Chinese sweetmeat peddler at right carries a variety of preserved fruits— winter melon, kumquats, orange rinds—along with ginger and dried litchi. In season he also sells mosquito repellent. The Japanese boy below scurries through the streets with buckets of pure well water, a tray of cups, and a canister of tea leaves.

The Open Door
And
The Butter Stinkers

The young man at left, who has already equipped himself with a foreign pocket watch and an umbrella, is about to break one of old Japan's most sacred dietary taboos by eating meat. Not only did such acts of defiance raise conservative eyebrows, they also wrinkled noses. Westerners and their imitators were said to give off a strong odor of animal fats and were known as *bata-kusai*, or butter stinkers. Within three decades of Commodore Perry's arrival, trading ports boasted numerous Western-style restaurants: Rokumeikan, or the "Club of the Deer's Call," was Eastern in name only, recalling an ancient Chinese ode about hospitality. Inside, Oriental gentlemen in frock coats and trousers dined with ladies wearing the latest Paris fashions.

At the banquet above, tables are adapted for American comfort, but the raw fish is uncompromised. Opposite, a tar copes more manfully with a bottle of sake and a geisha robed in stars and stripes.

At a luncheon of French aristocrats, c. 1740, oysters take precedence over etiquette.

THE
TRIUMPH
OF
FRENCH TASTE

On a sultry August afternoon in 1661, young King Louis XIV climbed into his state coach at his château at the edge of the forest of Fontainebleau and, accompanied by the queen mother and a splendid cavalcade of princes of the blood, dukes, courtiers, *gardes du corps*, and pages, all in their richest array, bounced over thirty kilometers of rutted roads to attend one of the greatest festivities ever seen in France. The visit was to have unexpected and momentous results.

The occasion was a fete to celebrate the completion of the vast country seat erected by the young monarch's chief minister, Nicolas Fouquet, on a handsome slope beside a bend of the upper Seine. Fouquet's showplace, called Vaux-le-Vicomte, was a dazzling sight. As the king passed through the forecourt gateway, he saw a majestic white edifice encrusted with decoration and topped by a cupola. The structure was surrounded by a moat flanked by spacious outbuildings and was set in an immense preserve of gardens,

223

promenades, pools, grottoes, and some fifty fountains and cascades.

The most brilliant artists and designers of France had been enlisted to create it, along with an army of a thousand craftsmen. Le Vau was its architect, Le Nôtre its landscaper, and the painter Le Brun director in charge of its decor, from its ceiling frescoes to its tapestries and rugs. The entertainment for the king's evening was planned on the same

Faience platter depicting a rustic garden

splendid scale: the famed composer Lully would lead the orchestra; Molière would present a new play written for the occasion. Vatel, the rising *maitre d'hôtel* of genius, would supervise the chefs in preparing for some five hundred people a banquet that included ortolan, pheasant, quail, partridge, and assorted bisques and ragouts, along with the best wines of Champagne and Beaune. An outdoor ballet under countless lanterns, a display of fireworks, and a salute of cannon were to be the climax of the day.

On hand was the poet La Fontaine, who wrote in a strophe, "Le ciel en fut jaloux." But not only the heavens grew jealous. Louis was not amused. His minister had gone too far; he had displayed a magnificence far greater than that of the Crown. With his ever-present cour-

tesy, Louis remarked of the dinner service: "What admirable plate." Fouquet, falling into a trap, explained: "Pardon, Sire, it is not plate, it is gold." Whereupon the king, reportedly—and ominously—answered: "We have nothing like this at the Louvre."

Indeed both the old Louvre, hemmed in by dank city streets, and Louis' ancestral Fontainebleau were warrens of unpremeditated plan, thrown up over centuries—no match for Fouquet's smashing new palace and pleasure dome. The king's decision was soon made. He already knew of Fouquet's huge profiteering as the realm's minister of finance. The end was near. Within three weeks the minister was arrested, tried, and jailed for embezzlement, his property was declared forfeit, and Louis, just twenty-three years old, set out to build for himself a palace that would surpass Vaux—taking into his service the same Le Vau, Le Nôtre, and Le Brun. The result was Versailles, for well over a century to be the seat of Europe's greatest court, the scene of Europe's most lavish entertainment, and the embodiment of French hegemony of taste.

Louis XIII, a somewhat unprepossessing person as Bourbon rulers went, had owned a pleasant hunting lodge on the site his son chose for Versailles, but it had never occurred to him to enlarge it. Frugal yet tasteful, he liked on occasion to prepare with his own hands the game he had shot, and his skill as a cook was esteemed. He was also interested in gardening, to the extent of personally supervising the raising of spring vegetables at the small château, seeking to bring them in earlier than other producers in the area—and he was parsimonious enough to sell some of his own harvest to his neighbor Seigneur de Montauron, who kept a table more ample than his own.

This way of life bore little resemblance to that of his imperious son. When building the new Versailles, Louis ordered that the *grands appartements* of the royal family be flanked by wings, one to accommodate his mistresses and illegitimate children, the other to house several hundred courtiers in continuous attendance. There were quarters for some fifteen hundred officers and servants of the household, as well. To feed this many mouths every day, along with his numerous guests, was itself a vast undertaking. Versailles, though still called a château, became in effect a city; its kitchens, presided over by a hierarchy of stewards and *maîtres queux*, were the largest yet constructed, and its many service

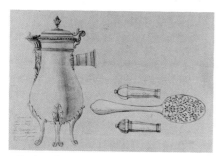

Designs for Louis XIV coffeepot and server

departments employed hundreds of men. Together, the bakery and wine cellars had fifty or more on duty. Mass feeding imposed its limits on cuisine.

In Louis XIII's time there had been, at fine houses such as Seigneur de Montauron's, a distinct effort at what might be called culinary reform—a search for a

better harmony and order of dishes to replace the riot of tastes inherited from the preceding century. That older disorder was satirized by Boileau, one of Louis XIV's leading court poets, when in the course of his *Festin Ridicule* he described a pyramid of meat:

> *On top of a hare flanked by six chicks*
> *Lay three rabbits, animals domestic,*
> *Who since their tender infancy in Paris*
> *were bred,*
> *Smelt still of the cabbage on which they'd*
> *been fed.*
> *Round this mass of meats piled high*
> *A long border of pressed larks did lie,*
> *And on the edge of the dish, six pigeons*
> *went,*
> *Exposing their burnt skeletons as reinforcement.*

Among the chefs before mid-century, none was greater than Francois Pierre de La Varenne, who may have learned the art of cookery as a young man at the court of Henry IV (for whom he also ran numerous amatory errands). An artist of sauces as well as a logician of menu planning, he tried to do away with the heavy spices and heaped-up dishes of the past. Meats were served in their own reduced juices. Fish were similarly prepared in a *fumet*, or stock of their trimmings. A sauce thickener known as *roux* (a carefully heated mixture of butter and flour) was introduced as a binder of flavors. Marinades, pâtés, mushrooms and truffles used as subtle accents, were also elements of La Varenne's art.

Recipes for sauces, along with rules governing the sequence of courses, were set forth in his *Le Cuisinier Français* of 1651, a treatise that became the bible of the "new cuisine." Among the first sauces perfected after La Varenne's teachings was a particularly fine white sauce called *sauce Béchamel* after Louis' lord steward. It was produced by adding chicken or veal stock to fresh cream and *roux*, and was a great advance over the tart *verjus* of sixteenth-century fare.

The king, however, was less interested in the art of the *cuisinier* than in the sheer gratification of his appetites, which were as formidable at board as they were in bed. As Louis remarked, "One eats

Forces of Lent attacking . . .

well who works well." In 1656, when he was not yet eighteen, he was served a banquet at the château of Pontchartrain that embraced 16 hot hors d'oeuvres and 8 potted meats and vegetables; 8 "broths" and 16 entrees of fine meats; 8 roast dishes and 16 vegetables cooked in meat stock; several pâtés of cold meats, fish dishes, and assorted salads; and as the fifth course, 24 different kinds of pastries and fresh and preserved fruits' for a grand total of 168 garnished dishes. Of course it was understood, as in times past, that the diner would be highly selective in picking from such an array.

The full achievements of French cuisine would have to await the eighteenth century. What Louis XIV did contribute to the table was a new grandeur and protocol. Le Roi Soleil made dining not only a ceremony but a spectacle, with himself as the principal actor. Once he was established at Versailles, his daily meals became rituals resembling tableaux, and they changed little from decade to decade. His day began with a *grand lever* at which a hundred or more courtiers with the right of entrance observed or assisted him in donning his first morning dress, after which he took a light breakfast of white bread, wine, and water. (Louis, it appears, though he lived on into a time when coffee, tea, and chocolate became fashionable, never consumed any of them; though in his later years, according to the court chronicler and gossip Saint-Simon, he enjoyed "an infusion of sage and veronica.") Then, after a morning of audiences with his ministers and Mass at 12:30, he took luncheon at one or two o'clock *au petit couvert*, dining alone or with his queen, the former Infanta Marie Thérèse of Spain, at a table beside the windows of his bedroom overlooking the central court of the palace.

Not that this was an informal or light meal. High officers of state, accompanied by an echelon of the king's guards, made ceremony of presenting it, marching through chamber after chamber of the palace crying, "the king's meat!" As the food passed, rapidly cooling in its long transit from distant kitchens, all the courtiers doffed their hats and bowed. Two archers followed by a gentleman usher and the lord chief steward, usually a prince of the blood, led the procession. Inside the apartments, the king's brother, Philippe, Duc d'Orléans ("Monsieur" in French court parlance), would sometimes be on hand to proffer a napkin and at the king's bidding might sit down but not eat; lesser nobles stood about in attendance. After the dishes were "tasted" by a gentleman in waiting, the king attacked his formidable lunch.

At ten o'clock the main meal was served *au grand couvert* in one of the state salons with the whole court in attendance, some of the nobles seated at the tables, the *petite noblesse* standing as spectators, along with such commoners as had been admitted. By this time Louis was again ravenous, and dinner began with a variety of soups, some very rich and thick, such as *soupe Colbert* topped with poached eggs and named after the finance minister who had succeeded Fouquet. Like many heavy eaters, Louis was but a light drinker, taking only a goblet or two of champagne. The champagne he drank, however, was not the bubbly drink we know today (the chemical invention of a Benedictine monk and cellarer named Pérignon in 1670); it was a still white wine of the province, mixed with water. Louis also favored the traditional syrupy "hippocras"—concocted of white or red wine, honey, and aromatics—and cordials, which, as Saint-Simon explained, were invented to provide "solace in his declining years."

Princess Palatine, Louis' sister-in-law, claimed to "have seen the King eat, and that very often, four plates of different soups, an entire pheasant, a partridge, a large plateful of salad, mutton cut up

in its juice with garlic, two good pieces of ham, a plateful of cakes, and fruits and jams." Madame de Maintenon, his final mistress *en titre*, who was also to become his second wife, is said to have remarked that if she ate half as much as he did she would be dead in a week. (It was discovered at his autopsy that his intestines were twice the length of an average man's.) His physician Fagon managed eventually to put him on something approaching a diet (this was the Fagon whom Molière satirized in

... *Mardi Gras* en garde

his comedy *Le Malade Imaginaire* as Doctor Paragon, the man who makes his king's life miserable by cutting off his favorite foods), and Saint-Simon was to go so far as to suggest in his memoirs that Fagon's regimen had contributed to the monarch's death. Saint-Simon particularly disapproved of the doctor's treatment for Louis' gout: the king was regularly sweated and fed iced, overripe fruit.

Louis' manners were impeccable, though from this distance it may seem odd that he firmly refused to use a fork, preferring to eat with his fingers, while

Ben Franklin

As representative of the rough, simple, and egalitarian Americans, and more especially as a victim of the gout, Benjamin Franklin was not really in a position to become an epicure during his eight-year visit to France. In fact, he learned that most of French society found his rustic table habits absolutely charming. He picked up his asparagus and bit off the tops, and he cracked his eggs into a cup and messed them about with salt, pepper, and mustard, making a veritable "philosophical ragout . . . like the kind of savage he was," as one of his few detractors churlishly put it. The attention he was unable to give to food he turned to wine. Franklin assembled an excellent cellar—for

health reasons, of course. He found no more efficacious tonic for aching joints and dull wits than three or four glasses of fine wine which on occasion moved him to write vinous thoughts to his friend Abbé Morellet. (It was almost as if Franklin were trying to create a French alter ego for his puritanical and pious American Poor Richard.) "'In vino veritas,' said the sage. . . . Before Noah, men, having only water to drink, could not find the truth. Accordingly . . . they became abominably wicked, and they were justly exterminated by the water they loved to drink. This good man, Noah, having seen that all his contemporaries had perished by this unpleasant drink, took a dislike to it; and God, to relieve his dryness, created the vine and revealed to him the art of making le vin. By the aid of this liquid he unveiled more and more truth; and . . . since this time all the best things, even the gods, have been called divine. . . . He made the wine to cheer us. When you see your neighbor at table pour wine into his glass do not hasten to pour water into it. Why would you drown truth? . . . know that the apostle Paul advised Timothy very seriously to put wine into his water for his health; but that not one of the apostles, nor any of the holy fathers, ever [watered] wine. P.S. In order to still more confirm you in your piety and recognition of divine providence, reflect on the position God has given the elbow . . . by its present location shown in fig. 5 [the figures above were obligingly drawn by Franklin's grandson to illustrate his letter], we see it designed so that we can drink at our ease, the glass comes just to the mouth. Let us then adore, glass in hand, that wise benevolence; let us adore and drink."

his grandchildren were being trained in the use of the new utensil. He wore his hat at table, and was punctilious in doffing it to ladies or raising it in various degrees to salute princes and nobles, with the result that his hat brim became covered with the grease of what he had just consumed.

Moreover, his tastes, though robust, were unpredictable. He had a great taste for delicate fruit, and in the course of relieving Fouquet of some of his treasures at Vaux, he transplanted to Versailles over a thousand orange trees—then exotic and costly rarities—setting them in long rows outdoors and in silver tubs in the salons, creating that particularly French form of conservatory, the *orangerie*. For his adored granddaughter-in-law, twelve-year-old Marie Adélaïde, he gave a ball in 1697 in the Hall of Mirrors, graced by numerous orange trees bearing hundreds of fruits which had been coated with sugar. He was also an ardent lover of fine peaches and pears, and so admired the manager of his exquisite orchards and gardens, Monsieur de La Quintinie, that he both befriended and ennobled him.

In the summers of his immensely long reign there were usually military campaigns to be fought (it was neither practical nor *comme il faut* to undertake them in winter), but even in the field a style not unlike that of Versailles was observed. The king and his general officers, often accompanied by their ladies, went into large and luxurious encampment: sieges rather than wars of movement were the order of the day, and often the whole court would turn out to watch Louis assault a fortified town. The pro-

tocol could be magnificent. Thus when Louis was investing Lille in 1667, its defender, the Comte de Brouais, discovering that the king was without ice for his provisions, sent him a supply every morning. When the king sent an emissary to ask for more, Brouais answered courteously that he would like to oblige but that he must conserve his resources, since the siege was likely to be a long one.

If there was not an actual battle in progress, Louis loved nothing better than to simulate one; he staged a mock assault at Compiègne one summer with some sixty thousand troops for the delectation of all who might like to watch. "There was never a spectacle so brilliant, so astonishing," wrote Saint-Simon, though he added that he was somewhat frightened by its magnitude. "There were innumerable tables, always freshly laid and ready at all times for the entertainment of any officers, courtiers, or spectators who might drop in— the merest sightseer was made welcome and served with courteous promptitude. . . . There was every sort of drink, hot and cold, that you can think of—French wines, foreign wines, and the rarest liqueurs flowed in abundance. There was every sort of game and venison, and the most unusual seafood was brought from Normandy, Holland, England, Brittany, and the Mediterranean fresh several times a day by means of a prodigious number of couriers." And when not taking to the field in the pleasant months of the year, Louis relished making regal descents with his entourage upon the estates of his greatest courtiers, as he had upon the unfortunate Nicolas Fouquet.

229

His Bourbon relative Le Grand Condé had acquired the services of Vatel, late of Fouquet's household, to make his own table at Chantilly one of the finest in France. Vatel was not a working cook, but something much higher—an *officier de bouche*, a gentleman-master of cooks, service, and cuisine. To be sure, he knew every detail of the culinary arts and could write in courtly fashion about them. In an essay on carving he declared, "A carver should be well bred, inasmuch as he should maintain a first rank among the servants of his master. Pleasing, civil, amiable, and well disposed, he should present himself at table with his sword at his side, his mantle on his shoulder .... He should make his obeisance when approaching the table, proceed to carve the viands, and divide them understandingly according to the number of guests .... A carver should be very scrupulous in his deportment, his carriage should be grave and dignified, his appearance cheerful, his eye serene. ...."

But Vatel's own serenity broke down when the king arrived at Chantilly in April, 1671, with a company evidently larger than had been expected. Various meats and fish that had been ordered did not arrive in time, and there was a shortage of food. Madame de Sévigné, one of France's great letter writers, hurried to write her daughter, Comtesse de Grignan, "I have just learned . . . of what passed at Chantilly with regard to poor Vatel. I wrote you last Friday, that he had stabbed himself; these are the particulars of the affair. The King arrived there on Thursday night; the walk, and the collation, which was served in a place set apart for the purpose, and

strewed with jonquils, were just as they should be. Supper was served, but there was no roast meat at one or two of the tables.... This affected [Vatel's] spirits, and he was heard to say several times, 'I have lost my fame! I cannot bear this

Expert directions on carving, 1647

disgrace!'" When, during the night, the fish ordered for the next day's lunch did not appear in adequate quantity either, it was too much: Vatel, like an old Roman, ran himself upon his sword.

The Olympian rounds continued. In 1715, when Louis at last reached his end, having outlived both his heir the dauphin, and the dauphin's own son and heir, the nobles and gentry breathed more freely. France felt young again. A new boy king, the patriarch's great-grandson Louis XV, was on the throne. A regent in the person of the boy's distant cousin, the second Philippe, Duc d'Orléans, set him an example of sybaritic gaiety, intimate pleasures, and gilded taste. Louis XV proved an apt and enthusiastic pupil.

In the years after 1715, elegance, not just grandeur, was the ideal. Exquisite porcelain, first imported at great cost from China, then from its adapters at Dresden, and finally in the reign of Louis XIV produced by France's own craftsmen at Sèvres, appeared in dining rooms and salons. The drinking of coffee, tea, and chocolate (the latter already promoted by the late Louis XIV's Spanish queen) became a late-afternoon social cult. The regent introduced the custom of the *petit souper*—an intimate supper at which a few noblemen and their ladies (usually their mistresses) could enjoy themselves without oppressive protocol. On such occasions the regent invited his male guests to join him and the cooks at preparing dinner.

Louis XV, when he came to his majority, enjoyed cooking, too. At the end of a hunting day, the new king particularly liked to gather around him a circle of lively spirits. Would-be guests put their names on a list from which the king might choose. One evening he invited the Prince de Beaufremont, the Ducs de Gontaut and de la Vallière, and the Marquis de Polignac to try their hand as *cuisiniers*, while he prepared the *poulets au basilic*. On another evening, according to the Prince de Cröy, "We were eighteen, squashed round the table, beginning at my right: Monsieur de Livry, Madame la Marquise de Pompadour, the King, the Comtesse d'Estrades, the Duc d'Ayen, the tall Madame de Brancas, the Comte de Noailles (governor of Versailles), Monsieur de la Suze, the Comte de Coigny, the Comtesse d'Egmont (the Duc de Richelieu's daughter), Monsieur de Croix, the Marquis de Renel, the Duc de FitzJames, the Duc de Broglie, the Prince de Turenne, Monsieur de Crillon. . . . The Maréchal de Saxe was there, but he never has supper so he walked about tasting bits of food, for he is very greedy. . . . We

were two hours at supper, all very free and easy but without any excess. Then the King went into the little salon, where he made the coffee and poured it out, there were no servants and we helped ourselves."

Sometimes Louis XV's *petits soupers* were a good deal more intimate. A scheme was devised for a disappearing table which dropped through an opening in the floor to be re-set below for the next course. Thus, one record has it, "Guests are not annoyed by the importunate glances of servants. They are freed of all embarrassment and need not blush on being caught unawares." On occasion, just two or three couples took part, the supper being planned as the

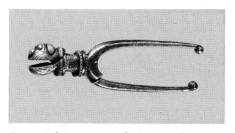

Brass and iron nutcracker, sixteenth century

prelude to other pleasures. The rakish Duc de Richelieu, a grandnephew of the illustrious cardinal, appears to have pursued this idea to the point of inviting a few couples to dine in the nude. His servants were models of discretion.

Almost everyone in France, it seems, was becoming concerned with fine cuisine, whether it led to *amour* or not. The Regency and the period of Louis XV were without doubt times of the most engaging invention in French dining. The era glorified the chef, for as the epicure Brillat-Savarin was to remark several decades later, "the discovery of a new dish confers more happiness on humanity than the discovery of a new star." Fresh discoveries were being made continually. Marin, the famed *maître d'hôtel* of the Prince de Soubise, wrote in his classic treatise *Les Dons de Comus* of 1739 that the "old cookery" had suffered from "an excess of spices. . . . [and] was very complicated and full of details; modern cookery is a sort of chemistry." Marin's own repertoire included a fluffy omelette made with cocks' combs and carps' roe which he invented for Louis XV.

Louis Sébastien Mercier, introducing his *Tableau de Paris* of 1781–82, echoed Marin's opinion: "The dishes of the present day are very light, and they have

Happy gourmand in an hour or two of ecstasy

a particular delicacy and perfume. The secret has been discovered of enabling us to eat more and to eat better, as also to digest more rapidly. . . . The new cookery is conducive to health, to good temper, and to long life. . . . Who could enumerate all the dishes of the new cuisine? It is an absolutely new idiom. I have tasted viands prepared in so many

ways and fashioned with such art that I could not imagine what they were."

One of the most spectacular demonstrations of the new cuisine was a *souper* given by the Duc de Richelieu (fully dressed) to a group of Hanoverian princes and princesses captured during a campaign of the Seven Years' War. Though his field supplies were reduced to a carcass of beef and some root vegetables, the enterprising duke, never at a loss, dictated the following elaborate directions: the table was to be decorated with his large *surtout*, a centerpiece adorned with the figures of great heroes of France. Then, a first course of beef consommé was to be served, followed by hors d'oeuvres of beef in various forms; then a rump of beef garnished with root vegetables; then such delicacies as oxtail with a purée of chestnuts, civet of beef tongue, *paupiettes* of beef à *l'estouffade* with pickled nasturtium buds, fillets of beef braised with celery, beef *rissoles* with hazelnut purée, beef marrow on toast, beef à *la mode* with pistachio nuts, fritters of beef brain steeped in Seville orange juice, and so on.

The Prince de Soubise took to the battlefield with a wagon train of complete kitchen equipment and table service. His campaigns were more distinguished for their dinners than for their victories: the Prussians overran his corps at Rossbach, but did not succeed in capturing his *batterie de cuisine*, his plate, or his chef, the renowned Marin.

Just how much the cuisine may actually have promoted health and longevity is an open question. It did promote refinements in cooking equipment: in wealthier households the days of cooking chiefly by spit or stewpot over the fire were past. A stove along with an array of copper or iron saucepans of various sizes and shapes accommodated the multitude of processes. New foods were constantly augmenting the diet

Wine taster made in Orléans, 1759

and challenging the chef. Lentils, long thought fit only as animal fodder, were made fashionable by Louis XV's queen, and the potato became the rage at court when an army pharmacist, Monsieur Parmentier, presented a bouquet of purple potato flowers to Louis XVI at a birthday reception. The king liked the blossoms so much that he placed one in his buttonhole and gave another to his queen Marie Antoinette; many courtiers followed suit, and the future of the *pomme de terre* was thenceforth assured.

The new and exciting dishes created were often named after members of the nobility, something a *maître queux* was only too happy to do in anticipation of reward. Thus there came into the French repertoire such creations as filet of sole *Pompadour* and chartreuse of partridge *à la Du Barry*, honoring Louis XV's chief mistresses. The most spirited ladies at court were not above devising dishes to seduce the king. Madame Du Barry arranged a *souper* that included such novelties as *coulis de faisan* (stewed pheasant), *salmis de bécassines* (ragout of young woodcock), *écrevisse* (crayfish) *au*

vin de Sauternes, and *fraises au marasquin* (strawberries in cherry liqueur); and the Marquise de Pompadour is credited with such diversions as *filets de volaille à la Bellevue* and *palais de boeuf* (palate of beef) *à la Pompadour.*

A few critics felt that preoccupation with good eating was going too far. In 1749 Voltaire warned his countrymen that their gluttony "would eventually numb the faculties of the mind." Though moderate at board, Voltaire was guilty of another form of self-indulgence: he was a slave to coffee, consuming as many as fifty cups a day. Madame du Châtelet, one of his closest friends before his exile, was noted for her intellectual dinners at which the conversation was brilliant but the food indifferent. (Like Voltaire, she took only one light meal a day.) Voltaire's secretary sniffed in disdain of her hospitality, "What wine! Burgundy made in Paris, and champagne of the same brand!"

But the *bonne table* rapidly became within reach of the middle classes, which were more interested in emulating the aristocracy than in following Voltaire. A typical bourgeois meal of about 1740 was recorded by Brillat-Savarin: first, beef bouillon; then an appetizer and an entree of veal cooked in its juices; then a turkey with vegetables and a salad; finally cheese, fruit, and preserves. In 1746 the gifted chef Menon produced for middle-class wives and their domestics his *Cuisinière Bourgeoise*, a book offering popular menus for those wishing only two or three dishes in a meal.

Brillat-Savarin, looking back, was able to sum up in his review of the latter part of the eighteenth century: "The ranks of every profession concerned with the preparation of food, including cooks, caterers, confectioners, pastry-cooks, provision-merchants, and the like, have multiplied in ever-increasing proportions. . . . Physics and chemistry have been called in to aid the alimentary art; the most eminent scientists have thought it not beneath them to apply their wisdom to the first of all our needs, and improvement has followed improvement, from the laborer's simple broth to transparent extracts that are never served but in vessels of crystal or of gold. . . . The wines of all countries have been cultivated or imported and make their appearance in regular order: Madeira to open up the way, French wines to accompany the main courses, and African and Spanish wines to crown the work. French cookery has annexed many dishes of foreign extraction, such as curry and the roast beef of England; relishes such as caviar and soy. . . . Coffee has come into general use, as a food in the morning, and after dinner as a tonic and exhilarating drink."

The working man, for his part, especially enjoyed starting the morning with a bowl of *café au lait*, sold at street corners by women vendors from huge tureens.

And there were visitors to France who did not have to wait for Brillat-Savarin to proclaim the genius of new French cookery. Benjamin Franklin, American emissary to Paris, wrote home: "I have never dined so handsomely as at Madame de Courtances' table." An English traveler in 1790 was one of the first to deplore the difference between what was being served to his countrymen under the name of food and what the French were enjoying. "The variety given by

their cooks to the same thing is astonishing," he reported. "They dress a hundred dishes in a hundred different ways, and most of them excellent; and all sorts of vegetables have a savouriness and flavour, from rich sauces, that are absolutely wanted to our greens boiled in water. . . . The English dinner of a joint of meat and a pudding, as it is called, or *pot luck,* with a neighbor, is bad luck in England; the same fortune in France gives, by means of cookery only, at least four dishes to one among us and spreads a small table incomparably better."

The period just preceding the French Revolution also saw the emergence of a new institution—the restaurant. It was to rise to great influence particularly after the estates of the *ancien régime* were seized or broken up, and from then on was to remain the center of French culinary genius. The renowned *maître queux,* so long a princely retainer, went into business for himself.

A superior hostelry known as the Tour d'Argent had been founded in 1582 on the Quai de la Tournelle outside the walls of Paris. Many historians have bestowed on it the honor of being the first restaurant. King Henry IV, who frequented the place as did many other monarchs, awarded it a coat of arms, thus distinguishing it from the other taverns or cabarets of the time. The Tour d'Argent (whose prestige, along with its regal prices, continues to this day) did not in its early years depart materially from the traditional tavern scheme of offering a "dish of the day" from the host's table *(table d'hôte).*

The well-to-do bourgeois of Paris, in search of a hearty fish stew, might so-

Best Behind Bars

To the hungry Parisians storming its walls on July 14, 1789, the Bastille symbolized the tyranny and corruption of the *ancien régime*. Ever since Louis XIV converted the medieval fortress into a state prison, rumors of dank dungeons, prisoners in rotting rags, and food "worse than would be given to a pig or a dog" were widely circulated. Though it was true that the inmates were held without trials, for indeterminate lengths of time, they were, nevertheless, "guests" of the king, and in this unique prison were treated as such. Jailers made sure that their wards had the amenities to which they had been accustomed, and politely catered to their whims, however eccentric. Nobles resided in spacious apartments equipped with fireplaces, into which they moved suites of furniture and a few retainers (before entering the Bastille a servant had to agree to remain until his master was freed). If a prisoner lacked the means, the king would foot the bill for his expenses, the amount varying according to his rank; three livres provided an adequate dinner for a common man; thirty-six for a *maréchal*. A morale-boosting meal might include green pea soup, a joint of fowl, sliced roast beef, meat pie garnished with sweet-breads, cocks' combs, asparagus, mushrooms and truffles, sheep's tongue *en ragoût*, biscuits, fruits, a bottle of Burgundy, and Mocha coffee. Occasionally complaints were voiced by such finicky eaters as the confidence man Danry, alias Vicomte Henri Masers de Latude. The prison commander noted that on fast days "He sends for us at eight . . . in the evening to tell us to send his turnkey to the market to buy fish . . . saying that he cannot eat eggs, artichokes or spinach. Danry is just as exacting on meat days. He swore like a trooper and said . . . 'when I'm given fowl, it should at least be well larded.'" Danry also collected silk shirts, and at one point possessed 162, from  which the ingrate wove a ladder and escaped; he was soon apprehended. A prisoner was free to pass his time attending parties, singing in ensembles, bowling, or breeding cats and dogs. Pens and paper were provided, but Danry insisted on writing in blood on linen or on slices of bread. Only seven prisoners remained in 1789. One, in the three months before his liberation, consumed 12 bottles of brandy, 121 bottles of beer, and 167 bottles of wine. Though meat pies *garni*, however fine, do not equal freedom, the mobs were rescuing victims of a despotism far more benevolent than that reigning outside.

journ to such traditional inns as the popular Relais du Gros Caillou on the banks of the Seine near the Invalides. Gentlemen and ladies, often disguised or masked, went slumming at such rough-and-ready resorts as the Taverne Hospitalière de la Coquille, or at Le Grand Salon on the Rue Lamartine. Cafés, which originally had provided only a

Commoners toasting the Third Estate, c. 1789

cup of coffee, had proliferated to some six hundred by 1750, often offering light meals (at the celebrated Café Procope, one might find Diderot and his fellow *philosophes*); but those were not restaurants as we understand the term. That connotation may have originated with a Parisian named Boulanger who was not a restaurateur at all, but the owner of a streetside stall whose fare was soups sold under the label of *restaurants*, meaning restoratives, and whose signboard is said to have proclaimed in near-liturgical Latin, *"Venite omnes qui stomacho laboratis, et ego restaurato vos"* ("Come all ye that labor with your stomach, and I will restore you").

Semantics aside, the true restaurant probably appeared in 1782 when the masterful chef Beauvilliers, former stew-

ard of "Monsieur," the Comte de Provence (the later Louis XVIII), made the bold experiment of setting up for the elite a formal dining-out place where he offered a long list of dishes, individually prepared *(à la carte),* and in surroundings just short of palatial. This was his Grande Taverne de Londres on the Rue de Richelieu, and it was a model for generations to come.

Beauvilliers, a master of protocol, presided in courtly dress, including sword and frilled shirt. Accomplished in five languages and aware of every political nuance of the day, he knew precisely where to seat ambassadors and ministers, royalists and republicans. As Brillat-Savarin was to write admiringly, "Beauvilliers was for more than fifteen years the finest restaurateur in Paris. He was the first to combine the four essentials of an elegant room, smart waiters, a choice cellar, and superior cooking." The Londres was not to be outdone for generations. It survived all upheavals and in 1835 was catering to European aristocracy with a menu that included fifty different *entremets* and at least thirty vintage wines. Although French chefs were not usually attracted to English cooking, Beauvilliers made a point of presenting in his treatise *L'Art du Cuisinier*, published in 1814 not long before Waterloo, some English recipes, including what he called *Wouelche rabette* (Welsh rarebit), *bifteck, plumbuting* (plum pudding), *machpotetesse* (mashed potatoes), and *ket-chop*, a sauce first popularized across the Channel.

Among the rival establishments that opened soon after Beauvilliers, were such fashionable meeting places as the

Café Conti and the sumptuous restaurant of Monsieur Véry—the latter featuring some 12 soups, 24 hors d'oeuvres, 24 entrees of fish, 15 of beef, 30 of game, and so on. The Café Conti eventually evolved into the famed Restaurant Grand Véfour; still later it incorporated with Monsieur Véry's restaurant, and continues to this day to occupy some of the old premises under the long arcade of the Palais Royal.

Louis XVI, the heavy, dull man who ascended the throne upon the death of his grandfather in 1774, played little part in this evolution of French taste. He dutifully followed court ritual—the public dinner *au grand couvert,* particularly on Sundays, though his queen Marie Antoinette hated to be stared at when eating, and usually absented herself. The Revolutionary Directoire, in power until Bonaparte seized sole control, far from reducing lavishness at table often gave dinners as splendid as those of the Louis'. Napoleon, for all his longing to acquire some polish, was the very opposite of a gourmet. He ate "at military speed," often wolfing a whole meal in just fifteen minutes, and moreover at wholly unpredictable hours. As his chronicler Las Cases recorded, "Never did one manage to make him eat his dinner while it was hot, for once he had settled himself to work no one knew when he would leave it. Therefore, when dinner time arrived, chickens were placed on the spit for him at half hourly intervals, and I have personally seen dozens of them so roasted before coming to the one finally presented to him." Distracted one day, gluttonous the next, fearful of putting on weight but likely to call for a huge meal at two or three o'clock in the morning, his habits resulted in chronic indigestion and early obesity.

The great tables of the empire were those of his foreign minister Talleyrand and his archchancellor Cambacérès. Not that Napoleon objected: on the contrary, he often advised foreign dignitaries to go to one or the other of their houses for a great repast. The two households naturally fell into competition. Cambacérès gave twice-weekly dinners for fifty or more distinguished persons, serving sixteen or eighteen dishes. State messengers were placed in his service to bring fresh game from his estate at Livet, and Alexandre Dumas père recalled a particularly magnificent dinner at which the archchancellor directed his footmen to pretend to stumble and drop the *pièce de résistance,* a rare Caspian sturgeon weighing some 170 pounds. Then, while the guests were still gasping at their loss,

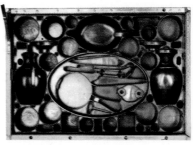

Fitted campaign kit for Napoleon's chef

the prodigal host called out, "serve the other sturgeon," and a second, still larger, fish was brought in.

Yet Talleyrand appears to have had the better of it, since he had recruited the great Antonin Carême (1784–1833), a man of genius. Born of humble parents and first trained as a *pâtissier,* he went on

237

in the next ten years to study the art of roasting and of making sauces and cold dishes under the leading chefs of France. Carême was as intrigued with the visual delights of pastry as with its taste. At one point he went so far as to say, "The fine arts are five in number, to wit: painting, sculpture, poetry, music, architecture—whose main branch is confectionery." Talleyrand liked to spend an hour each morning discussing with Carême what might be created for the evening's dinner. The minister's own principles were elegant and simple: two things were essential in life—"to give good dinners and keep well with women." In describing life under his culinary mentor, Carême wrote, "Only the most sanitary and the finest products were employed. Everything was ability, order, splendor. Talent was happy there, and highly placed. The chef governed the stomach. . . . Forty-eight course dinners were given in the halls on the Rue de Varenne. I have designed them and I have seen them served. What great tableaux [were] created! Who has not seen them has seen nothing."

Carême, whose genius at survival was equaled only by that of Talleyrand, was to serve Czar Alexander, Lord Castlereagh, Baron Rothschild, England's prince regent (the future George IV), and Louis XVIII. With a staff of forty cooks, he provided a great birthday feast for Czar Alexander following a review of Russian troops after Napoleon's defeat. He shared in presenting an even greater dinner for twelve hundred guests in the halls of the Louvre in 1815, upon Louis XVIII's Restoration. For this huge undertaking, a fifty-foot-long range

was installed in the principal hall of the palace; Carême took charge of the *entrées froid* and the *entremets du sucre*. He also wrote essays on every aspect of cuisine, emphasizing "lightness," "grace," "order," and "perspicuity" in the preparation of food. His was the crowning effort in the revival of gastronomy after the convulsions of the Revolution.

The Restoration also saw the emergence of such literary epicures as Grimod de La Reynière, who was fired by the impulse to systematize and refine French cuisine. He launched his *Almanach des Gourmands*, a guide to the restaurants and food purveyors of Paris, and organized a *Jury Dégustateur*. He tossed out such aphorisms as "A well-made sauce will make even an elephant or a grandfather palatable." In Brillat-Savarin, originally a country doctor, later a rotund provincial magistrate, the era found its philosopher of the table. His *Physiologie du Goût*, published in 1825 when he was seventy, became the classic work of the arts and sciences of gastronomy—though Carême himself sniffed at Brillat-Savarin because of his habit of consuming two dozen oysters at breakfast. Later still, in 1870, Alexandre Dumas père was to provide in his *Grand Dictionnaire de Cuisine* a compendium of lore concerning *grande cuisine*. The matter of fine eating was to be taken most seriously. After a banquet held in the celebrated restaurant Le Rocher de Cancale in 1834, one of the company recalled, "I remember the chairman, I can see him now, hear him saying to [his guests] in his most solemn voice, 'I advise discretion, gentlemen. No distractions. Remember. I know the menu. We shall be at table for three hours.'"

RECIPE
FOR
REVOLUTION

A baker, his helpers, and an old woman selling brandy, portrayed by Jean Michelin, 1656

LE DINE DV ROY A L'HOTEL DE VILLE DE PARIS

CALENDRIER POUR L'ANNEE BISSEXTILE MDCLXXXVIII.

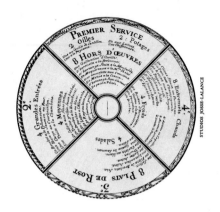

Chez Louis

What the French court gained in grandeur over the centuries, it lost in culinary amenities. Clever as the royal chefs were, they could not overcome the limitations of palace and protocol that made serving a hot meal impossible. The kitchens were often at great distances from the halls of state, and every dish was carried in solemn procession down long, drafty corridors, past ranks of admiring courtiers, tasters, and other functionaries, before it reached the royal consumer. Louis XIV did not balk at the system, but he added some light touches. He enjoyed pelting his guests with rolls; they were encouraged to return the fire. One lady in waiting, smarting from a well-aimed *pain*, volleyed with a salad. Under Louis XV state dinners became more elaborate than ever. Musical fanfares and complicated new rituals accompanied each dish. But, when his schedule allowed, the king enjoyed informal suppers, so *intime* that no servant entered the dining salon. Louis XVI, capitalizing on one of his few natural abilities, entertained his subjects by eating a spectacular meal in public every Sunday.

Opposite, Louis XIV and guests pause for a portrait during a dinner at the Hôtel de Ville. The menu at top was once served to Louis XV and Madame de Pompadour. Above, Louis XIII dines in splendor; below, Louis XVI eats crow in prison.

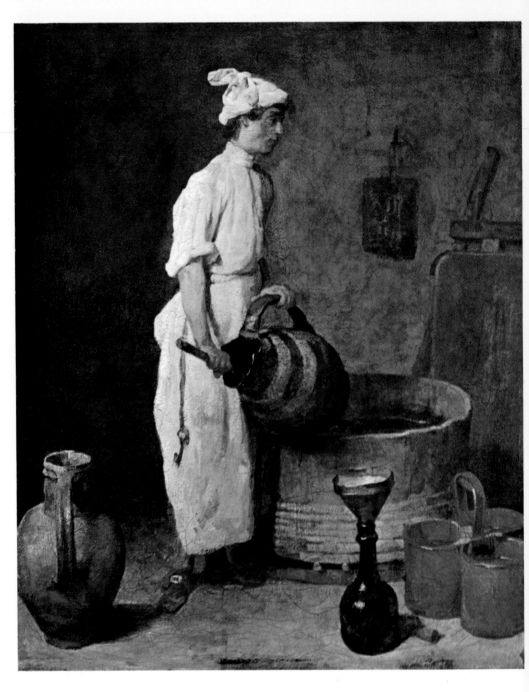

Life Belowstairs

The subjects of Chardin's paintings, above, perform their tasks in the depths of a *grande maison*. The poor scullery maid faces an endless succession of dirty pans, but the youth, while scrubbing out his wine pitchers, can at least dream of becoming head cook. Then he will exchange his rakish cap for a toque and

his modesty for the disposition of a martinet —only the king himself could outdo the *chef de cuisine* when it came to tyrannizing his subjects. The great eighteenth-century cook was, after all, an artiste of temperament so fragile and taste so delicate that he often had to be granted several days' rest and spe-cial diet to soothe his sensitive soul and ex-hausted palate. If the cellar boy is a more genial sort, he can aspire to become *maître d'hôtel*, director of the dining staff, whose brazen members, an American visitor com-plained, were "often observed in France inter-mingling in the conversation of the table."

Fun for All

The favorite haunt of many a member of the Third Estate was his neighborhood tavern, where he could buy a carafe of wine and watch the entertainment, sometimes planned, more often impromptu. Taverns on the outskirts of Paris had the added advantages of a verdant setting—and untaxed liquors. The uproar of the good times in the country cabarets wafted all the way back to the salons of the great, who began to appear in droves to "join in the amusements of the people" by dancing with fish-wives, drinking the good, cheap wine, and listening to slang "in all its native beauty."

Ramponneau, opposite, the proprietor of a tavern which could accommodate six hundred people, is portrayed with the symbols of his calling. Below is the sign of another cabaret. At right, top, customers purchase wine to take home, while others enjoy theirs on the premises. Below, patrons who tested their host's hospitality too far are shown the way out.

OVERLEAF: *Slumming was not the only outdoor recreation of the rich. Romanticized notions of the innocent pleasures of peasants had made gamboling about attired as swain or shepherdess a mandatory form of fun. Ollivier's painting of a picnic during the reign of Louis XVI illustrates another aspect of the noble back-to-nature movement. Before the guests gathered under the tent to eat, they undoubtedly had pushed one another on swings, played hide-and-seek, and trysted in the bushes. The fetes seemed less fun to the servants, who in planning and executing them had to make sure that none of the nature lovers lacked for any of the comforts of home.*

Habit de Cuisinier

Habit de Pescheur

Les Vendeurs

Habit de Poiſsonniere

Habit de Rôtisseur

Habit de Pâticier

Habit de Fruitiere

During the eighteenth century, Parisians bought most of their food from wandering vendors whose raucous cries made a sizable contribution to the cacophony that filled the streets. The engravings by Nicolas de Larmessin reproduced here show vendors clothed in imaginative costumes appropriate to their specialties.

Habit de Vinaigrié

Habit de Cabaretier

The Delicate Art of Porcelain

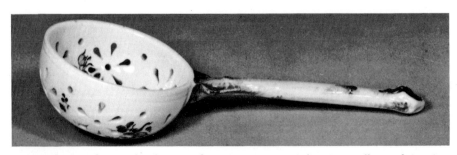

A pierced spoon for powdered sugar, from Mennecy, specialists in small porcelain pieces

A mustard jar from Rouen, c. 1645   *A small jam pot from Sceaux, c. 1770*

The soup tureen, top opposite, made for Madame Du Barry, and the *solitaire* coffee service, above, are both products of Sèvres, after 1753 the *manufacture royale*. Support of the porcelain industry had in fact begun with Louis XIV, who ordered his subjects to melt down their silver and gold plate to refill the impoverished treasury; but Louis XV was the first to give official sanction to a French factory. To attract the finest artisans, he restricted the use of decorative gold to the royal works and regulated firms under other patronage. Louis even worried about balancing Sèvres' books—to stimulate trade he personally auctioned off the annual inventory of porcelain to courtiers eager to show their good taste at any cost.

Café Society

The ten years of slaughter that Marie Antoinette was supposed to have sparked with her naïve suggestion, "Let them eat cake," left the poor who made the Revolution worse off than before. There were bread riots in the provinces, and in Paris it was difficult to find vendors who would sell food in exchange for the nearly worthless new currency with which working men were paid. The *nouveaux riches*—the speculators, the profiteers, the grafters, and the merchants who catered to them—had replaced the aristocrats as the group that was eating well. The milieu for dining had changed, too; the Revolution indirectly gave France its first fine restaurants. With most of the gourmet aristocrats destitute, departed, or dead, chefs of the *ancien régime* were forced to perform their magic in public establishments.

The ladies opposite, caricatured in 1827, were members of the new fashionable set that gathered every day in Parisian cafés to gossip over ices and Mocha. Two water colors at left by Carle Vernet show that citizens of the working class, eating at traveling snack bars, did not fare so well. The soldier at top, who drinks a cup of cocoa, probably has tasteless rations to look forward to; the sausage speared for the demobilized hussar may constitute his only nourishment for the day.

OVERLEAF: Frascati's near the Opéra was one of the most popular of dozens of cafés that sprang up in post-Revolutionary Paris. People gathered there to eat ice cream, sip liqueurs, gamble, and flirt. In the background is the ballroom, which could accommodate some two thousand dancers.

The Amphitryons

Carême, the pâtissier known as the "cook of kings and king of cooks."
CARÊME, L'Art de la Cuisine Française, 1854

Parmentier, who prophesied that potatoes would make starvation "impossible"
PHOTO BULLOZ

Dumas père, famed for his salads and his culinary dictionary of 1870
STUDIOS JOSSE-LALANCE

Brillat-Savarin, whose treatise separated gourmets from gluttons
PHOTO BULLOZ

Any gourmet wishing to keep his head and wits during the Revolution did well to follow the credo of Grimod de La Reynière: "Life is so brief that we should not glance either too far backwards or forwards. . . . therefore study how to fix our happiness in our glass and on our plate." In the aftermath, these amphitryons gave elegant dinners and formed such epicurean societies as the *Jury Dégustateur*. Its role as a supreme court of cookery was "to pass judgment on the quality of foodstuffs and their skill-

Grimod de La Reynière, author of etiquette guides for parvenu hosts
STUDIOS JOSSE-LALANCE

The Jury Dégustateur, *active from 1804 to 1812, assembled here to prove a pudding*
STUDIOS JOSSE-LALANCE

Cambacérès, president of the Jury, *although susceptible to meat balls*
BIBLIOTHEQUE NATIONALE, PARIS; SERVICE PHOTOGRAPHIQUE

Talleyrand, a diplomat who chose dinner tables over conference tables
BIBLIOTHEQUE NATIONALE, PARIS; SERVICE PHOTOGRAPHIQUE

ful preparation." Meeting weekly for five-hour séances at private homes or select restaurants, the jurors sampled food and drink donated by contributors who remained anonymous until every dish was voted on by secret ballot and an impartial verdict reached. The *Jury* awarded its certificate of *légitimation* charily. It could immortalize a talented *pâtissier*; conversely, it dealt out punishments fitting the crime, and a restaurateur living on his reputation might find the "truth" published all over Paris.

Plain and Fancy

Napoleon cared little for the niceties of *haute cuisine*. Not even a dinner for the czar and the King of Prussia, below, could change his habits noticeably. For the infrequent occasions when he entertained in the grand manner, the cupboards held a store of treasures worthy of an emperor: the Sèvres plate at right is one of a set depicting city views; the nef above, in which cutlery, napkins, goblets, and a poison tester were locked, was the gift of the city of Paris for Napoleon's coronation supper.

MALMAISON

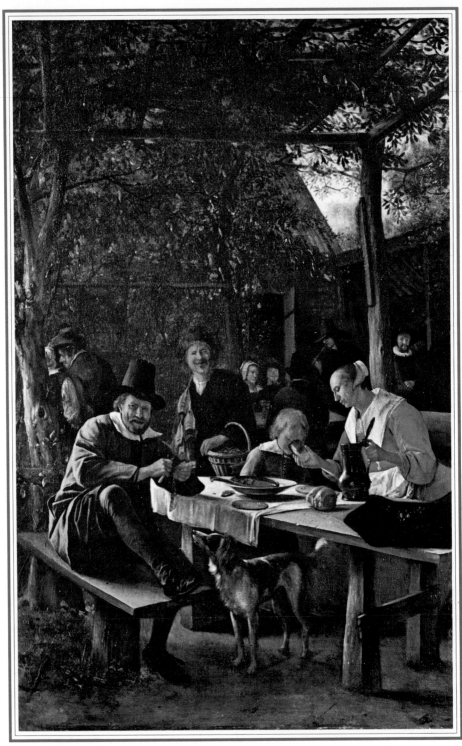

A family outing, by Jan Steen, seventeenth-century Dutch painter and tavern owner

THE
OTHER
EUROPE

From the reign of Louis XIV onward, French manners spread across Europe with astonishing speed. Following the king's revocation of the civil and religious rights of his Protestant subjects, Geneva became a center of French thought in exile, and of French cookery as well. Princelings in the gray flatlands of Schleswig and Pomerania vied for French tutors as well as *pâtissiers* to enhance their provincial courts. Young Czar Peter I of Russia, anxious to westernize and modernize his isolated domain, in 1697 set out from the Kremlin on an educational "grand tour" of the West that resulted in the building of a new, French-inspired capital and "window on Europe" at St. Petersburg. Frederick II of Prussia, a kingdom previously known chiefly for its production of turnips and stalwart grenadiers, responded to the French influence by entertaining in his new summer palace such men as Voltaire, conversing socially only in French, and making French cuisine *de rigueur* at the palace. The chefs of Empress Maria Theresa's table in

Vienna were either French or French trained. The university town of Leipzig became so taken up with French manners and cuisine, and with the Enlightenment radiating from the French capital, that a student who matriculated there in 1765, the poet Goethe, later bestowed on it the compliment *"ein klein Paris."*

Yet while the nobility fell under the French spell, there was another side of Europe that remained to a great extent untouched—the Europe become prosperous through heightened productivity, stability, and trade. The regional cuisines were not refined in the French sense: they were hearty and robust, varying from province to province in accordance with the produce most available, the commerce that was most profitable, and even the religious traditions of the people.

It was the world of the heavy Dutch stew called *hutsepot*, of the Belgian *hotchepot*, of German *Sauerbraten, Bierwurst,* and dumplings, of Scandinavian *smörgåsbord*

Danish bowl for Bishop's Cup

and herring pudding, of Austrian *Schnitzel*, of Hungarian *gulyás*, or goulash, of Polish and Russian *blini, pirozhki,* and cabbage soup. It was the world of coarse "black" bread, paprika, pickles, sour cream, and hot peppers; of such drinks as Dutch *genever*, or gin, German *Bier,*

Scandinavian *akvavit*, Bohemian *slivovitz*, and Russian *vodka* and *kvas*.

Solid bourgeois life perhaps flowered first in the urbanized Low Countries after the overthrow of Spanish rule. From the great Flemish and Dutch genre painters of the day, we get a general portrait of well-fed domesticity, of great attention to food and furnishings without ostentation, of a certain gravity coupled with a love of gatherings, processions, and joyous holiday feasts.

The center of the Dutch burgher's house of the seventeenth century was unquestionably the kitchen, often tiled with colored porcelain from Delft, and graced by a display of copper and pewter utensils gleaming fresh-scrubbed in their cupboards or above a marble sink. The middle-class Dutch obsession with cleanliness occasionally reached such lengths that only the boiling of water was permitted in the kitchen, with meals being prepared in the pantry and served in still another informal family room so as not to "dirty" the parlor and dining rooms. There was also usually a display of big, thick-stemmed wine goblets—for use on special occasions, since the everyday drink was beer, served in lidded mugs of pewter or porcelain.

Meals were formidable, as the resulting girth of many a stout *Stadtholder* or burgher painted by Rembrandt or Jan Steen indicates. Yet meals were perhaps more nourishing and varied than those of the time in other parts of Europe. Limited grazing area supported few beef cattle and little game, but the Low Countries were rich in vegetables, fruits, fish, and dairy cattle. Indeed, the use of butter in Dutch cooking gave dishes a lightness not common to cuisines dependent on vegetable oils, lard, and the like. At the main meal at midday, a prune and pea soup and a platter of herring or Rhine salmon might precede the *hutsepot* of stewed meat and vegetables, followed by an array of cheeses, puddings, fruits, and waffles. To tide the body over until supper, a midafternoon snack of bread and cheese, fruits and nuts, and beer or tea was also taken.

Prayers and readings from the Bible generally went before and after the domestic Dutch dinner. Yet the burgher and his wife, for all the composure and dignity they displayed to the portrait painter, enjoyed nothing better than a rousing good party. The Dutch of Rembrandt's time and after were addicted to banqueting—and the affairs were far from sedate. A French traveler recalled an engagement dinner in 1691, which he attended along with some highly respectable elderly couples and a number of local divines: eating and drinking continued for five hours, the guests "shouting out toasts, arm in arm, smashing glasses," and spilling Rhine wine on the table. To accommodate such celebrations, great inns and taverns arose. The Amsterdam police, observing in 1665 that as many as fifty different dishes were being served at such noisy festivities, clamped down on the number of courses and the size of the guest list in a token effort to quell disturbances.

There were also religious feasts, many carried over from Roman Catholic rite into the Protestant Church, and secularized. Martinmas, though Dutch Reformed ministers denounced it as a ceremony of Popery, continued to be observed on the eleventh of November. Saint Martin, the patron of wine growers, tavernkeepers, and reformed drunkards, was understandably a much-loved saint, and his day was celebrated with a traditional dinner of roast goose, perhaps in retribution for the cackling goose that once betrayed him. Twelfth Night and Shrove Tuesday were also retained. May Day, which derived from ancient pagan custom, was celebrated

Dutch butchers' escutcheon

with the erection of Maypoles, a procession of townspeople, and singing and dancing in the streets. But the climactic event of the year was the carnival known as the kermis, celebrating some special saintly patron or local tradition. After the Reformation, the kermis was secularized into an annual civic festival identified with liberty, political fraternity, and good cheer; it might continue for as long as three weeks, during which, as in the pre-Lenten Fasching or Mardi Gras in many Catholic areas, serious business was all but suspended.

Bakers, entertainers, wine and beer sellers, all had their stands at what was in effect a fair. Confectioners hawked special kermis cakes—griddle cakes with pink sugar icing and preserved fruit. As the historian Paul Zumthor writes in his account of the times, "The taverns were jammed. For many peasants the kermis in the neighbouring town was essentially an occasion to drink in unaccustomed surroundings. Long tables were placed out of doors, and people sat on benches, barrels or on the ground. The adults danced; the children yelled, chased each other and played the tambourine and penny whistle; fiddlers scraped away among the goods displayed in the stalls. Passers-by were sometimes seized by the scruff of the neck, and a glass of beer poured down their shirt, or their faces smeared with flour and wax. The kermis began to turn into an orgy. In some villages, a 'kermis ox' was solemnly paraded, wreathed with flowers, and then slaughtered in the market-place, roasted, and eaten by the population on payment of a contribution. . . . Everyone sang. Women's yells mingled with the creaking and groaning of the merry-go-rounds. The atmosphere[was]unbreathable. Ladies fainted."

So much for Dutch sobriety. Daily consumption of beer, among women as well as men, appears often to have begun quite early in the morning. In the following century, the young James Boswell, seeking out a quiet place to recuperate from his dissipated life in London, recorded in his journals the exuberance of the Dutch at table. He found them enjoying their potent geneva gin (a drink which is not to be ascribed to Geneva, but to *geneverbessenwater*, a distillation of grain flavored with juniper berries, whose discovery is attributed to a seventeenth-century professor of medicine in Leyden). Boswell indulged with

Distillery, c. 1580

Dutch students and on one occasion reproved himself, "Yesterday you recovered very well after your riot. . . . But remember how near you was to getting drunk and exposing yourself." A massive dinner at the house of his friend and tutor, Professor Trotz of Utrecht, was almost too much for him. He wrote:

Of learned Trotzius I have been the guest,
And with his heavy supper am oppressed.
Lazy and hot, most sensibly I feel
That I have eat roast rabbit and roast veal;
And though impatience goads my fretful brain,
Not one idea can I thence obtain.

The communities of neighboring Germany, meanwhile, were only in a few instances remotely describable as "a little Paris." The country, or rather the states, since German nationhood was not yet in sight, labored for generations under the memory of the ravages of the Thirty Years' War, in which in one principality alone some one thousand "witches and wizards" had been burned at the stake in the space of a year. Teutonic culture, after such horrors, was not

Oktoberfest

When Crown Prince Ludwig of Bavaria wed on October 12, 1810, forty thousand well-wishers gathered on the Theresienwiese, a Munich meadow, to stage a Bavarian bash worthy of the occasion. The party—if not the marriage—proved so successful that the day was promptly adopted as an annual affair. Part of the original celebrations had been wagon races among teamsters from the local breweries. Later, competition took a more commercial turn, with tents set up to sell beer and the fried and roasted delicacies of fish and chicken called *Schmankerlen*—and the day stretched into the Oktoberfest disrupting life for two weeks in the early autumn. More than 125 years later, the American Monk Webber, a character in Thomas Wolfe's *The Web and the Rock*, was alternately delighted and appalled by the fun. Munich, he observed, was a kind of German heaven (the scene from a Bavarian stein, right, of a burgher bound for paradise  astride a beer barrel bears this out). "It was an enchanted land of Cockaigne, where one ate and drank forever and where one was never filled. It was Scharaffenland—it made him think of Peter Breughel's picture of that name, which showed the little roast pigs trotting conveniently to serve your pleasure, with knives and forks stuck juicily in their tender, crackling hides, with pieces cut out of their hind quarters . . . and bottles dropping from the sky, and trees and bushes drooping down with growths of pastry and with fruits of food. . . ." In one *brauhaus* Webber saw "hundreds of tables with people sitting together devouring tons of flesh—ox flesh, great platters of sliced cold sausages, huge slabs of veal and pork—together with the great stone mugs that foamed with over a liter of the cold and strong October beer. There was a heavy and incessant rumble of voices full of food, an enormous and excessive clatter of heavy pottery and knives, that rose and fell in brittle waves." It seemed to Webber in his intoxicated condition that "In all the world there was nothing but Food—glorious Food. And Beer—October Beer. The world was one enormous Belly —there was no higher heaven than the Paradise of Cram and Gorge. . . . The doors of the great hall kept opening and shutting constantly as the incessant stream of beer drinkers pressed patiently in. From within Monk heard the shattering blare of a huge brass band and the roar of five thousand beer-drunk voices, rocking together in the rhythms of 'Trink, Trink, Brüderlein, Trink!'"

of a high level of refinement. Like the Dutch, the Germans leaned toward robust conviviality, and they developed a whole hierarchy of eating and drinking places. On the lowest level stood the ordinary *Wirtshaus*—the common man's rough tavern, virtually unchanged from the Middle Ages (and at whose tables, in some remote country districts, local people were to be seen even well into the twentieth century eating from a common stewpot, without plates of their own). Next was the *Gasthof*, a country inn which could be good, bad, or indifferent: in the eighteenth century, when German roads and travel amenities were far behind those west of the Rhine, a cross-country voyager of any class frequently had to put up with crude lodging and worse food. Boswell wrote during his "grand tour" in 1764:

> *Here am I, sitting in a German inn,*
> *Where I may penance do for many a*
>   *sin,*
> *For I am pester'd with a thousand*
>   *flies,*
> *Who flap and buzz about my nose and*
>   *eyes.*
> *A lumpish landlord has the easy chair;*
> *Hardly he speaks, but wildly does he*
>   *stare.*
> *In haste to get away, I did not dine,*
> *And now I've had cold beef and*
>   *cursed wine.*
> *And in five minutes, or a little more,*
> *I shall be stretch'd on musty straw to*
>   *snore.*

More rewarding and pleasant were the taverns—the *Keller*, the *Brauhaus*, and the outdoor terrace, which was often attached to or owned by a local brewery.

Along with the beer, hearty roasts and sausages were served, bands played, and huge salt-studded pretzels were provided at every table to promote thirst. The *Weinstube* was a similar establishment, specializing in wines. For the middle class the *Kaffee-Konditorei*, or combined café and confectionery, came into vogue, serving not only coffee but

German Easter egg

tea and hot chocolate as well, along with an array of heavy pastries. For the municipal dignitaries in the more prosperous German towns, there was the *Rathskeller*, which was located in the cellar of the town hall. There in the spacious vaults, the civic leaders assembled around the *Stammtisch*, or reserved main table, for their saddle of venison and red cabbage, their beakers of Rhenish wine, their puddings and cheeses, and probably a round or two of *Schnaps*—German spirits. Lastly, townsmen had their *Delikatessen*, a place selling delicacies, where they could buy prepared, sometimes imported, foods to take home.

The Germans were generally looked down upon by their English and French contemporaries for their supposedly boorish and unrestrained ways. A traditional *Schützenfeste*, or hunters' banquet, was prone to degenerate into a wild spree, ending with a memorable *Katzenjammer*, or hang-over, all around. One hostile report of the early seventeenth century had it that Germans, when traveling, often consumed only aquavit and gingerbread for breakfast. The ecclesiastical courts of Würzburg, Bamberg, and Fulda, cities in the German wine country, had a reputation for alcoholic overindulgence; and the lofty Lord Chesterfield, when making his own tour of Germany, called the diet "execrable." Boswell was somewhat more tolerant and fortunate, though he saw some things that astonished him. He went to a ball in Berlin at the house of Counsel of State Behmer, where he "saw the vivacity of German ladies and counts and captains and Herren. We had at ten o'clock a collation in the garden; three or four tables with cold meats and pastry and sweetmeats and fruits and wine of different sorts. Behmer was a big, gallant Allemand; his wife, hearty even to excess. . . . She had no cap, and her hair dangled about her head. While she ran from table to table, with bottles in her hand and health most florid in her face, she seemed quite a female Bacchanalian. I was just celebrating the *orgies*. Her daughter was little and lively and kind . . . . I eat [*sic*] much and drank much and found animal life of very great consequence. I danced a great deal, and was an easy man, without affectation."

The German diet was, to be sure, very limited in range. Unlike the Dutch, the Germans raised hardly any green vegetables commercially until well into the nineteenth century. Middle-class as well as lower-class families relied on their own garden patches and vineyards back of the kitchen or on the outskirts of town. Only staples such as rye, cabbage, wheat, and root crops were sold in the market place. The potato, destined to become indispensable to the Germans, was not generally cultivated until the 1770's, when Frederick the Great personally promoted it. The enlightened

Larder crown for hanging meats

ruler also assisted Prussian agriculture by draining some 300,000 acres of marshlands, distributing seed corn, and after the Seven Years' War, sending his army's horses to be used in his subjects' fields; but German agriculture remained backward until late in the century. On the Junker estates in Silesia, many of which were still worked by serfs bound to the land, the production of wheat acre for acre was only half that raised on comparable English soil. Herds of beef cattle were all but unknown, and most of the meat eaten was pork. Superior, thick-joweled hogs were raised in Westphalia, and local varieties of sausage abounded in every part of Germany. The principal fats used in cooking were lard and bacon fat. Except in Alsace, where French and German influences met to produce Strasbourg pâtés and delicate fish dishes, German cooking tended to be heavy and monotonous.

There was a considerable variety of soups, mandatory at almost every meal —lentil soup, cabbage soup, soup with liver dumplings, and the cucumber soup that Goethe favored. Thomas Mann, in his *Buddenbrooks*—the chronicle of a merchant family of Lübeck in the middle of the nineteenth century—describes a traditional local concoction known as bacon broth, "a bouillon made with sour cabbage, in which was served the entire meal—ham, potatoes, beet-root, cauliflower, peas, beans, pears, sour plums, and goodness knows what, juice and all—a dish which nobody except those born to it could possibly eat." But usually the soup, formidable as it might be (and always consumed from a large soup plate, never in small portions from a cup), was only the prelude to what was to come. In a celebrated episode in the same novel, Mann tells of a housewarming dinner at the mansion of Consul Buddenbrook in 1835 at which some of the family and guests were all but overcome. It began with cabbage soup and proceeded through fish and boiled ham served with an onion sauce, huge dishes of vegetables, and "Frau Consul's celebrated 'Russian jam,' a pungent fruit conserve flavored with spirits," to a rich dessert known as *Plettenpudding*, composed of "layers of macaroons, raspberries, ladyfingers, and custard." For the children there was also a blazing plum pudding. In addition, there were cheeses and fruits and, after the Rhenish and Bordeaux, several bottles of sweet golden-yellow Malmsey. There were toasts; the gentlemen considered unbut-

toning their waistcoats; all were a bit unsteady, and one had distinctly eaten too much. But it was the little son and heir of the Buddenbrooks who became ill and had to leave the party.

"It's nothing much, Frau Consul," assured one of the guests, the physician Doctor Grabow. "A touch of indigestion. . . . Better put him to bed and give him a Dover powder. . . . And a rigorous diet, you know, Frau Consul. A little

Scandinavian butter mold

pigeon, a little French bread. . . ." "I don't want any pigeon," the boy bellowed. "I don't want to eat anything, ever any more. . . ."

Then Doctor Grabow smiled to himself and mused that "He would soon eat again, this young man. He would do as the rest of the world did—his father, and all their relatives and friends: he would lead a sedentary life and eat four good, rich satisfying meals a day. Well, God bless us all!" The good Doctor "was not the man to upset the habits of these prosperous, comfortable tradesmen and their families. He would come when he was sent for, prescribe a few days' diet of a little pigeon, a slice of French bread, yes, yes, and assure the family that it was nothing serious this time. Young as he was, he had held the head of many an honest burgher who had eaten his last joint of smoked meat, his last stuffed turkey, and, whether overtaken unaware in his counting-house or after a brief illness in his solid old four-poster, had commended his soul to God. Then it was called paralysis, 'a stroke,' a sudden death. And he, Friedrich Grabow, could have predicted it, on all of these occasions when it was 'nothing serious this time'. . . . Well, God bless us all! He, Friedrich Grabow, was not the man to despise a roast turkey himself. That ham with onion sauce had been delicious, hang it!''

Though Thomas Mann was writing about nineteenth-century Germany, he could easily have been describing bourgeois life of the century before. The small provincial courts of the time of Frederick the Great were themselves quite *bürgerlich* in character, with only a thin French veneer of sophistication. A little principality like Gotha had an array of high-titled retainers, including an *Oberhofmarschall* (Lord High Marshal), an *Oberlandjägermeister* (Lord Master of the Hunt), and an *Oberschenk* (High Steward of Wine), but the prince had little to do but hunt, dine, play cards, and attend the local opera, while his ladies busied themselves with embroidery, sketchbooks, and water colors. Duke Ernst August of Weimar rose at midday after breakfast in bed, talked with his gardeners, and inspected and drilled his guard of thirty-three men;

Festive procession in eighteenth-century Germany

then, sometime in midafternoon, he settled down to a three to five hour main meal, after which he might play cards with his ladies in waiting. Apart from such pleasures, the role of the German woman of whatever class save the high nobility was that of housekeeper. A visitor from early Victorian England, William Howitt, wrote in 1842 in *The Rural and Domestic Life of Germany* that he was surprised to find that "Ladies of rank and fortune are still plentiful, who spend their mornings in the kitchen up to the elbows in flour."

Along steep slopes above the Rhine and Moselle rivers, and in favored hillsides of the Palatinate, German landowners made advances in one aspect of dining—the cultivation of their fragrant white wines. Great care was taken over the years to refine growths and to differentiate them by accurate place names of origin as well as by year of vintage. The first dated wine in Europe appears to have been bottled in the commune of Hochheim on the Rhine and labeled "1711." (Hochheimer became so prestigious that Englishmen derived from the name their generic term "hock" to denote Rhine wines in general.) It was at Johannisberg that the method of leaving the grapes of a fine growth on the vine well after normal harvest was developed. If the weather remained favorable, the grapes of the *Spätlese*, or late gathering, technique yielded an exquisitely aromatic wine, velvety in texture. With the *Beerenauslese* technique, a venturesome vintner might leave some berries on the vines a few weeks longer, then pick them one by one with small scissors, selecting moldy, overripe, half-shriveled grapes which yielded wine of an even rarer flavor. (The presence of *Edelfäule*, the "noble rot" sought by ancient Roman vintners and exploited later in the production of French Sauternes, evaporated the water from the juice of the grapes and concentrated the sweetness and flavor.) A bottle might bear such a magisterial label as "Deidesheimer Kieselberg Riesling Trockenbeerenauslese," meaning a late selection of dry Riesling grapes from the Kieselberg vineyard of the commune of Deidesheim. To consume such a treasure became for the discerning German a memorable gastronomic experience.

Though Austrians of every class had always been drinkers of wine (mostly white) rather than of beer (a taste for beer did not develop until later), their vineyards produced nothing so distinguished as the German wines. Nonetheless, Lady Mary Wortley Montagu—another of that lively company of English travelers who crisscrossed Europe, saw everybody, and wrote home about everything—appears to have shared the Viennese' fondness for their wines when she visited Vienna in 1716. She was en route with her husband on his diplomatic mission to Constantinople and paused in Vienna long enough to dine at all the best tables. She was particularly surprised, she wrote, by "the variety and richness of their wines." At one dinner a list of wines was placed before each guest, and Lady Mary "counted several times to the number of eighteen different sorts, all exquisite in their kinds." It is doubtful that she sampled all eighteen

Wooden cheese mold

wines; and, though the Austrians then and later were fond of displaying their own wines to foreign guests, one can assume that much of what she did sample was either German or French, with possibly a sweet Tokay from Hungary with the dessert.

But if the chemistry of the mid-Danubian soil and climate could not bring forth a Johannisberger any more than a Clos Vougeot, the land had other attributes that made both eastern Austria and Hungary more varied in produce than Germany. Though this plenty did not result in a high cuisine, it served to shape the pleasurable, easygoing, vivacious life of Vienna and Budapest in their prime. What also helped make this life so colorful was the circumstance that both capitals, especially Vienna, were meetingplaces of numerous influences—western European, Slavic, Balkan, and Mediterranean—and drew on foods and culinary traditions from every side.

As early as 1528, one year before the first Turkish invasion, a Venetian envoy had reported that in Vienna "Bread is cheap, the meat, beef as well as veal, excellent, and there is wine in abundance, though dear." A little less than two centuries later, Lady Mary wrote: "The plenty and excellence of all sorts of provisions are greater here than in any place I was ever in, and it is not very expensive to keep a splendid table. It is really a pleasure to pass through the markets, and see the abundance of what [in midwinter] we should think rarities, of fowls and venison, that are daily brought in from Hungary and Bohemia. They [lack] nothing but shellfish, and are so fond of oysters, they have them sent from Venice, and eat them very greedily, stink or not stink." By 1781 good fare in Vienna had become so ubiquitous that for a modest sum one could obtain a six-course à la carte meal including a choice of seven soups and five kinds of fish. A visiting Prussian bookseller and amateur musician named Nicolai observed with Prussian severity that such ease and cheapness of food led to gluttony and laziness. "The Viennese," he sniffed, "are not fond of hard work." Moreover, he noticed many florid faces and stout figures and acidly commented that many of the these self-indulgent people would no doubt die an early death of apoplexy.

Indeed the Viennese were more fond of good living than of hard work. Amid its growing prosperity the city had a large population of drifters and beggars who found themselves perennially aided by the dole and soup kitchens of a paternalistic government and by private handouts. In fact, with begging a recognized occupation and many of its professionals working well-defined stations in this or that district, some beggars even became affluent. At a late eighteenth century wedding feast given at an inn in the Viennese suburb of Penzing, the bride's parents were well-known almstakers who had become so prosperous that they were able to give their daughter a dowry of several thousand silver florins.

For common people, whether gainfully employed or not, the favorite resort was the Prater, a popular park and playground along the Danube, with band music and operatic concerts, booths selling *Wiener Würstchen* (the sausages that are the forerunners of the American "wieners"), and purveyors of Heurigen wine—the new "green" wine pressed perhaps only a few weeks before on the hillsides just outside Vienna. For those

Water ladle from a Slovakian kitchen

who could afford the price of a carriage, a trip up the slopes to Grinzing, the source of the Heurigen, was a regular diversion. There, at a rustic tavern, the new wine could be enjoyed at garden tables beside its vineyard to an accompaniment of zither players and fiddlers and a short distance from the Danube to the east.

Just as the cosmopolitan Viennese danced the czardas, the polonaise, and the quadrille, and later the waltz, the

271

Sancho Panza

*T*he exigencies of nature meant little to Don Quixote as he sallied through Spain. Sustained mainly by visions of "glorious Fame" and his fair Dulcinea, the knight occasionally ate roots and herbs or some pieces of salt cod known as "*Abadexo* in Castile, *Bacallao* in Andalusia . . . or Little Trout." Such food for thought, however, did little to alleviate the hunger pangs of his potbellied squire, Sancho Panza, who was more than eager to placate his adversaries for the sake of a meal. Abiding by the tenet that Spaniards might eat anything

except that which is "contrary to the holy mother church, to orthodoxy, and to good manners," Sancho always made do with the products at hand. In his native La Mancha he might stuff himself on leg of rabbit, roast pigeon, ewe's milk cheese, eggs and bacon, *gazpacho manchego* (a bread porridge with cooked game—quite different from the cold vegetable soup which the Moors popularized in Andalusia), and a skinful of Valdepeñas wine. Or, amongst shepherds on the dry plateau of central Spain, he would share a humble repast of kid stew, curds and whey, and acorns. Once when in jest a duke and duchess made Sancho lord of an "island" on their estate in Aragon, the squire was concerned more with the governance of his stomach than of his constituents. In preparing Sancho for his new office, Don Quixote advised him to avoid onions and garlic "Lest thy Breath betray thy Peasantry," but Sancho believed it was "Not with whom thou wert bred, but with whom thou hast fed" that made him qualified. During his brief incumbency, Sancho never developed a taste for such foods befitting his position as the aristocratic *guisados* (civets of fowl or hare), "*Moron* Partridges," or "*Lavajos* Green Geese." Sancho's likes were simple, and he relished above all an *olla podrida*, a "Hodgepodge of . . . many Sorts of Victuals . . . both wholesom and toothsom," including garbanzo beans, bacon, chicken, chorizo sausages, garlic, and pimentos cooked in an old earthen pot (and which in Cervantes' time as well as now was a Spanish national dish). Unfortunately, when this stew was set before him, his physician cried, "*Absit* . . . no Diet in the World yields worse Nutriment than those Mishmashes do. No, leave that [to] Masters of Colleges, and lusty Feeders at Country-Weddings: But let them not incumber the Tables of Governors." With that Sancho swore, "let me eat, or let 'em take their Government; for an Office that won't afford a Man his Victuals, is not worth two Horse-Beans."

polka, and the schottische with equal enthusiasm, their taste for sweets was catholic. The famed Viennese *Apfelstrudel* is said to have come from Hungary and before that from Turkey, where it took the form of *baklava*. The caramel encrusted, many-layered pastry known in Vienna cafés as the *Szegedinertorte* came from down-river Szeged in Hungary. The *Gugelhupf*, a fruitcake popular at domestic coffee parties, recalled Vienna's victory over the Turks (it was baked in the shape of the sultan's turban). The curious curled pastry called *Schillerlocken* (after the curly locks of Friedrich Schiller, a German poet deeply opposed to absolutism) had some political overtones as well. Vienna's most celebrated pastry was the *Sachertorte* —a chocolate-frosted cake with two layers of apricot jam; it bore the name of Franz Sacher, a noted confectioner and the proprietor of the city's liveliest hotel during the latter days of the empire. (From 1938 to 1962 a series of lawsuits regarding rights to the name "original *Sachertorte*" was waged in the Austrian courts to the vast entertainment of Austrians everywhere.)

Another instance of the eclecticism of central European cuisine was to be found in Hungary, ruled by Hapsburg Austria after the Turks were routed, but racially different from it. The Magyars who settled in Hungary in the ninth century had preserved many of the rough-and-ready eating customs of their nomadic Asian forebears. The traditional *bogrács*, a great copper kettle suspended from a tripod over a blazing fire, remained the proper vessel for cooking the hot Hungarian *gulyás*. The same vessel was used for making a pungent soup of fresh-water fish, including carp and perch, from the Tisza River. Hungary had stuffed sour-cabbage dishes, sour cream, seasonings of dill, aniseed, and pimento, mutton, and some of the finest poultry in Europe, including turkey and goose. Hungarians also liked macaroni and garlic. In this they were influenced perhaps by the Italian cooks whom Beatrice of Aragon brought with her when she arrived to become Matthias Corvinius' queen in the last half of the fifteenth century.

Paprika, today thought of as a vital ingredient of Hungarian cuisine, actually reached Hungary with the Turks, who occupied the country from 1526 to 1686; it was not widely used by Hungarians until the second half of the nineteenth century. Like the thick coffee which the Turks had brought to the Danube valley, paprika traveled upriver, and a Viennese addressing himself to a *Paprikaschnitzel mit Ungarischem Kraut* found himself consuming a truly international veal cutlet, the meat raised in Austria or Bohemia, the technique of sautéing the very thin slices of meat in batter Franco-Italian in origin, the principal condiment indigenous to India, and the sour cabbage a dish dating back to mongol incursions.

Spanish gentlefolk drinking chocolate, 1700's

273

It was after the Congress of Vienna, marking what appeared to be the end of the French threat and the setting up of a permanent order in Europe, that the middle class under the Hapsburgs fully came into its own. Domesticity mixed with pleasures outside the home. The Biedermeier house, with its circle of chairs for the family coffee gatherings, its potted geraniums in window boxes, its bird cages, its table under the arbor back of the house, was an upper middle-class setting portrayed by many sentimental painters of the period. At the same time, the Vienna cafés, with their mirrors,

Winter market in nineteenth-century Moscow

hangings, and deep plush seats, were always crowded with men escaping either their family or their office. Newspapers, writing materials, and chess sets were provided as a matter of course; one could sit as long as one wished over a single cup of coffee, the waiter bringing a fresh glass of water every half hour as a kind of time-clock courtesy. In the evening much of Vienna went out to dine and dance. Josef Lanner, a dashing composer of waltzes, led the orchestra at numerous balls held in Dommayer's Casino. His rival, the elder Johann Strauss, conducted at Sperl's. At the Coliseum, chefs were engaged in producing such dishes as a "Trout minuet," a "Fresco of boiled lobsters," and something called "Orpheus sailing on a giant salmon."

Beethoven late in his life echoed an old criticism when, during a meal after a walk in the woods, he was so oppressed by the amounts heaped on his table that he grumbled, "Why so many different dishes? Man sinks almost to the level of an animal when eating becomes his chief pleasure." Yet for most people there could not be enough of good things; such festivities as the annual round of Fasching balls brought six weeks of high living and dining, and there was every reason to assume that this happy condition would last indefinitely.

The fatal collision that was to come in 1914 would for many end such pleasures. The power struggle that arose among Vienna and Berlin and St. Petersburg made deadly enemies above, and proletarian friends below. As has often been remarked, the landed gentry, the closest thing Russia had to a middle class, was naïve politically, insecure in status, leaning westward in social aspiration but eastward in its slowness to convert from feudalism to a modern industrial state. Gogol, Pushkin, Tolstoy, Turgenev, Dostoevsky, Goncharov, and Chekhov have all written widely of these people, proud in their ways, often entrapped by their longings and their insufficiencies, yet all enjoying themselves volubly over samovars and at buffets and long dinners.

No literature, in fact, has set so many of its scenes around the table. One thinks of the student Raskolnikov indulging himself with champagne and rich dishes far beyond his means after committing murder in Dostoevsky's *Crime and Punishment;* of the lonely, provincial ladies offering the officers of the garrison lunch, a supper of roast turkey and apple tart, and almost continuous tea in Chekhov's *Three Sisters.* Tolstoy has a particularly thematic scene in *Anna Karenina* in which the sensual and polished Oblonsky and the spiritual Levin go out to dine together at a fashionable Moscow restaurant. Oblonsky wants to order elegant dishes in the French style: oysters, *soupe printanière,* turbot with a *sauce Beaumarchais,* capons *à l'estragon,* a *macédoine* of fruits;

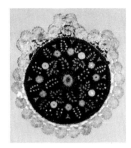

Embroidered matzo cover

Levin (who in Tolstoy's mind is evidently a symbol of virtuous Russian simplicity) is unhappy at this and would have preferred plain porridge, cabbage soup, bread, and cheese.

Gogol, in his satirical *Dead Souls,* sets a dinner-party scene that is equally revealing of upper-class tastes. Before entering the dining room, the gentlemen take a few appetizers and a tot of vodka. Then the meal begins: " 'The cabbage soup is particularly good today,' said Sobakevitch, taking spoonfuls of the soup and helping himself to an immense portion of a well-known delicacy which is served with cabbage soup and consists of sheep's stomach stuffed with buckwheat, brains, and sheep's trotters. 'You won't find a dish like this in town,' he went on, addressing his friend Tchitchikov, 'the devil only knows what they give you there!'

" 'The governor keeps a good table, however,' said Tchitchikov.

" 'But do you know what it is all made of? You won't eat it when you do know.'

" 'I don't know how the dishes were cooked . . . but the pork chops and the stewed fish are excellent.'

" 'You fancy so. You see I know what they buy at the market. That scoundrelly cook who has been trained in France buys a cat and skins it and sends it up to the table for a hare.' "

A dinner table dispute develops: " 'If you sprinkle frogs with sugar I wouldn't put them in my mouth, and I wouldn't taste oysters, either,' says the host Sobakevitch. 'Take some mutton. This is saddle of mutton with grain, not the fricassees that they make in gentlemen's kitchens out of mutton which has been lying about in the market-place for days. The French and German doctors have invented all that; I'll have them all hanged for it. . . . They talk of enlightenment . . . faugh!' " He goes on railing, while the mutton is followed by cheesecakes, each larger than a plate, then by "a turkey as big as a calf, stuffed with all sorts of good things: eggs, rice, kidneys, and goodness knows what." After that, saucers of radish preserve are offered, and the men, who had intended to talk business, settle sleepily into their easy chairs.

The most entertaining element of Russian cuisine remains that of the *zakuski,* an impressive display of hors d'oeuvres related to the Scandinavian *smörgåsbord*. An upper middle-class house would present platters of smoked sturgeon, herring fillets, suckling pig in horseradish, salmon, cucumbers in brine, little warm pâtés of meat baked in pastry (*pirozhki*), and small pancakes (*blini*) filled with sour cream and the finest caviar from the Caspian Sea. It was with the *zakuski* that exuberant drinking commenced. One never drank without eating; and the rich fish and tidbits that were small meals in themselves provided a firm foundation for tot after tot of vodka. Long regarded as indigenous to Russia, vodka now appears to have come from southwestern Europe. Or so the Russian historian Uspensky argued, stating that its distillation began on the island of Majorca and was transmitted by the Majorcan philosopher and alchemist Raymond Lully to the Genoese, who thereupon passed the technique to eastern Europe. The best Russian vodka was distilled from grain, the poorer varieties from potatoes. In either case, one could have it plain or iced, peppered (*pertsovka*) or flavored with a Siberian herb (*zubrovka*). And if one's purse matched his thirst, he could afterward indulge in what the Russians called *champanskoe*, served not just chilled, as in France, but half-frozen.

Yet, of all the European cuisines, none was more international than that of the Jews, the world's greatest migrants since the time of the Diaspora. Carrying their dietary laws, customs, and some of their ancestral dishes with them, they assimilated the foods of the many peoples among whom they settled. The traditional *knaidlach*, or dumplings made with *matzo* meal, are said to date back to the time of Moses; and for Austrian Jews, who observed a special rite at Passover, they symbolized the round stones which Moses threw against the wall that imprisoned the Jews in Egypt. *Matzos*, the only bread eaten during the Passover, were unleavened in memory of the hasty departure of the Jews and the unleavened dough which they baked in the desert sun. Jewish *blintzes*, inspired by Russian *blini*, were traditional at the spring festival of Shavouth and were usually filled with cheese, recalling that when the Jews returned from their long watch at Mount Sinai, the milk had soured in its jugs. Cheese or spinach turnovers called *borekas* were of Spanish-Jewish origin and closely resembled in name and taste the Middle Eastern *burek*, introduced on the peninsula perhaps by the Moors. *Gefüllte fish*, a dish prepared with ground, fresh-water fish such as pike or carp, and served on the Sabbath and during Passover, may have come into being in Holland, where Jews were welcomed after their expulsion from Spain in 1492. *Holishkes*, rolls of chopped meat cooked in grape leaves, are a traditional dish at the harvest festival of Sukkoth and commemorate the vineyards on the hillsides of the ancient Palestine homeland. They are, however, eaten by peoples throughout the Middle East and the Balkans. There was even a special curry of chicken, spices, peppers, and fruit which Jews, who had lived for centuries in Cochin, India, adopted from their Hindu neighbors and brought with them when they emigrated to the modern state of Israel. But had not every culture been borrowing from its neighbors since the beginning and making adaptations, even while priding itself on originality?

GOOD TIMES
AND
GEMÜTLICHKEIT

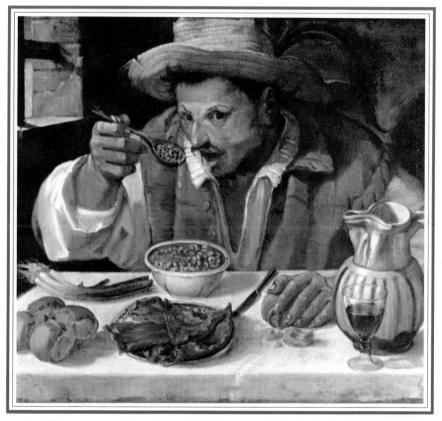

An Italian peasant wolfing dinner: "The Bean-Eater," by Annibale Carracci, c. 1585

In Celebration

Business, for the resolute, frugal Dutchman, always preceded pleasure, but when the day's work was done, some excuse for celebration could often be found, were it a religious holiday, a child's weaning, or another victory for the republic. The inverted "wager cup" at right was so designed that it could not be set down until empty. Practiced drinkers who could blow on the windmill and drain the cup before the sails stopped turning won a bet. Games, however, were not really needed to stimulate drinking at parties. Liquor flowed like water and was, considering the sanitation of the day, less dangerous.

The only stigma connected with drunkenness fell on the host who failed to get every man, woman, and sometimes child properly inebriated. The voracious Dutch made sure that plenty of food accompanied the wine, beer, and gin; special delicacies were prepared for feast days. In Jan Steen's painting of the Saint Nicholas Feast, opposite, traditional nuts and waffles fill the foreground. A lascivious old lady in the background beckons to her nubile granddaughter to look at what awaits her in the bedroom. If she does peek, the girl will find a *vrijer*, a gigantic cake shaped like a man, in her bed.

Pieter Bruegel's "Peasant Wedding," painted c. 1567, shows the Flemish in the flush of festivities. Unsteadied guests wisely keep their seats and leave the serving to sober cooks and waiters.

These cast-iron disks came in hinged pairs which, with handles attached, were used in the sixteenth century to cook German *Waffelen*. The iron above shows a hunting scene, that below, the holy day of Resurrection.

280

Pancake Day

From the frying pan to the waffle iron, flat breads have always enjoyed a special place in European tradition. As a symbol of the Eucharist, the wafer provoked a schism in the Protestant church. As the substance of self-indulgence, the rich, fat Shrovetide pancake was eaten in a ritual of pre-Lenten merrymaking that was celebrated from England to Russia. An Englishman, who may have perceived some sort of popish plot in such delicious fare, wrote, "there is a thing call'd wheaten floure, which the cookes do mingle with water, eggs, spice and other tragicall, magicall enchantments, and then they put it by little and little into a frying-pan of boiling suet, where it makes a confused dismall hissing, untill at last . . . it is transformed into the form of a . . . Pancake, which ominous incantation the ignorant people do devoure very greedillie." For the Dutch family in Pieter Aertsen's painting, c. 1560, above, the "magicall enchantments" of "Fat Tuesday" have already lost their charm. Perhaps their thoughts have turned to the forty lean days ahead. Undeterred, the old crone continues to cook while the waffles and pancakes cool.

In the Shops

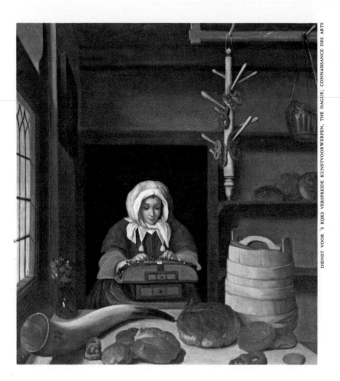

In the Netherlands self-regulation of trades permitted customers to shop with a confidence rare on the rest of the Continent. The bakery above sells bread whose contents, size, shape, and price are set by a local guild; the pocket scale, left, gives inspectors a quick reading on the specific weight—hence quality—of the grain that goes into various rye, barley, oat, buckwheat, and luxury wheaten flours. Hours are also regulated, and though this proprietress has only her tatting to occupy her while the next batch is in the ovens, she must remain open for business. When the breads are done she will summon clients with a blast on the ox horn at her elbow. The liquor store opposite, with its shelves of bottles and alembics for distilling spirits, is also regulated—what the guild does not supervise, the distiller's cashier-wife does. The dram of hospitality her husband dispenses must be accounted a short-term investment, a stimulant to new business, for as one foreigner remarked, "in dull air [liquor] may be necessary to thaw the frozen. . . brain."

On the Square

Butter, cheese, fish, meat, and produce were sold in outdoor markets, usually held in the town's main square, literally under the noses of the municipal authorities, who rented out stall space to farmers. Some markets were held once a week, but Pieter Aertsen's sixteenth-century vendor below most likely set up shop every day, for the Dutch doted on the vegetables—particularly beets, carrots, turnips, and parsnips—that their rich soil produced. In this they were advanced over other Europeans, one Englishman scoffing: "the poore Dutch men, like swine, digge up the rootes."

Dutch Treat

In the fourteenth century an enterprising Zeelander discovered a way to preserve herring by curing and pickling it in brine. The Netherlands promptly snatched the international herring monopoly from the northern Hansa towns. Their skill as sailors and as merchants, the latter based on a sturdy system of guilds, seems to have especially galled the English, one of whom complained in 1614, "We are daily skorned by these Hollands for being so negligent of our profite, and carelesse of our fishing, and they do daily floute us . . . at sea." The Spanish also attacked, hiring privateers in Dunkirk to destroy the Dutch fleet and, thereby, its prosperous economy. Though the French pirates sunk hundreds of boats during sixty years of harassment operations, it was herring as usual in Dutch households. They ate their profits fresh and raw when they were able; pickled, mashed, smoked, or boiled the rest of the year. They mixed herring with all manner of ingredients and consumed it zealously from dawn to dark.

Even the tableware celebrated Holland's good fortune; at left are Delft plates showing three phases of the herring industry: fishing, packing, and door-to-door selling. In Steen's "L'Offre Galante," opposite, salesmanship of another nature has won the heart of a buxom young maiden.

Bread and Bratwurst

Sandwich fixings have never reached more heroic proportions than in Germany, where in the eighteenth century the two demonstrations here took place. The *kuchen*, or sweet loaf above was prepared by the bakers of Dresden in 1730 in honor of a victory in Saxony. The recipe included 3,600 eggs and 126 pails of milk, and a twenty-foot-long knife was needed to cut it. The sausage below, which the engraver would have us believe is one single extrusion, is coiled around a long pole, the easier to parade it through the streets past an admiring throng of townspeople.

In a Spanish Kitchen

CHATEAU DE VILLANDRY; GIRAUDON

At a time when the Inquisition raged, even cookbooks warned that a señora with an unswept floor, a misplaced saucepan, or a neglected cooking oven would be duly punished by hell-fire. Thus, the Spanish housewife kept the kind of meticulously clean kitchen that inspired Velázquez' *bodegon*, or kitchen scene, above, with its brick oven, austere arrangement of copper and earthen soup pots, mortar and pestle, and shallow *paellera*, an iron skillet used for simmering Spain's classic rice dish. A different kind of fire flows through the veins of Goya's nineteenth-century peasant, below, who has consumed so much wine that he is well on his disheveled way to a not quite eternal siesta.

PRADO MUSEUM, MADRID

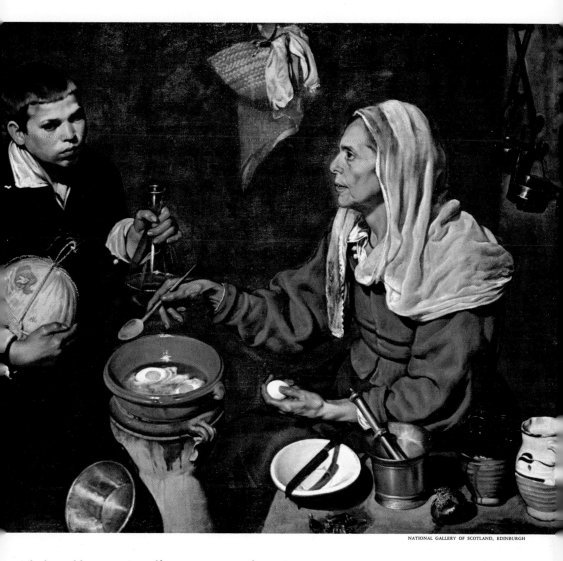

The lean old woman in Velázquez' painting of 1618 prepares her almuerzo, *or mid-morning meal, on a brazier. The eggs frying in olive oil, along with some onion, minced garlic, and pimento, may constitute her only meal of the day. Perhaps she can tempt the boy to share his wine and melon with her. Consoling but not filling is the native proverb "With a handful of olives and a crust of bread, one can live."*

Keeping the Feast

PICART, *Ceremonies Religieuses*, 1723

The German Jewish family above remains impervious to the elements as it celebrates the Festival of Tabernacles, or Laubhuttenfest. Instead of building the traditional *sukkāh*, or outdoor booth of latticework festooned with fruits, vegetables, vines, and branches, its members prefer the comforts of home; they have created a miniature *sukkāh* above the dinner table and have decorated the ceiling. The father, who has ushered in the holiday by lighting candles and saying a prayer, is now ready to dig into such delicacies as *gebrutenah euter* (roast beef udder), *kreplach* (stuffed dumplings), *holishkes* (stuffed vine leaves), *challah* (white bread twists), and *strudel* filled with fruits of the harvest. The eighteenth-century engraving at right portrays the bustle of a Jewish community baking *matzos* for Passover. Under a rabbi's careful scrutiny, a woman mixes the flour-and-water dough, while men roll out the round, flat wafers. Few foods are surrounded by more ritual than the matzo, or "bread of affliction," symbolizing the unleavened dough carried by the Jews in their hasty exodus from Egypt. On the top floor, a bespectacled man with a candle and a goose-feather brush searches for the *chometz*, or remaining crumbs of leavened bread, which he will sweep up and burn before Passover begins.

The nine-inch Gothic tower, left, made in Frankfort c. 1550 to contain spices, recalls the Middle Ages when spices were so precious that they
were locked in the strongholds of city halls.
The faience plate from Delft, above, inscribed
with "Rosh Hashanah" (New Year), is used
on the holiday to serve apples dipped in honey.

KIRCHNER, *Jüdisches Ceremoniel*, 1726

Pasta con Amore

The origins of pasta remain obscured in the vapors of ancient cookery. Except for parts of northern Italy, where *polenta* (corn meal mush) and *risotto* (a rice dish) traditionally prevail, pasta has been for centuries the daily bread of rich and poor alike. Marco Polo is often credited with introducing Chinese "spaghetti" to his countrymen, but an ancient tool identified as a macaroni-maker can be seen in the frescoes of an Etruscan tomb; and there is evidence that *ravioli* and *fettucini* made from semolina paste were prepared in the Middle Ages. By the seventeenth century, when the anonymous portrait of the merchant, opposite, was painted, business was so good that a crude sort of assembly line was often needed to satisfy the demand. At the back of shops like his, teams of muscular young men, stripped down to shorts and barefooted, waded into the dough to knead it. Then, after the dough was shoveled into a cylinder, more boys operated a huge wooden lever to press the dough through the *trafila*, a plate perforated to form the paste into one of the dozens of distinctive shapes that the local trade favored. There were marked preferences from one town to the next, and each variety, from the sublime *capelletti d'angelo* (angel's hair) to the ridiculous *ziti* (bridegrooms), was said to have its own flavor, though all were prepared from the same basic recipe. The final job was laying the pasta out to dry, a task in which the merchant, bearing a scepter of wet noodles, has taken a hand.

Whenever a Neapolitan was seized with a passion for pasta, there was a cooperative vendor nearby. At top, a pizza *salesman; above, a macaroni booth at rush hour; below, clowns eating handily.*

294

Tea and Hospitality

BELOW: HARRY W. BRENNER, NEW YORK

Enameled tea strainer

Khlebosolstvo—literally translated "bread and salt" but in practice the Russian word for "hospitality"— centered on the great samovar which every household owned. This uniquely Russian device for keeping tea water always at the boil ensured visitors a welcome all day long. It consisted of a charcoal-burning base, a central chimney surrounded by an urn of water, and a top rack for holding a pot in which the infusion steeped. The hoary gentlemen at the stall above evince a proper respect for their host's samovar by gathering around it for a portrait. The men are merchants, come to the east-west entrepôt of Novgorod for the summer trade fair; one of the major commodities they will buy is China tea, perhaps from this very stall. If the tea passes the test, it will be shipped in bales or bricks to their local markets. Meanwhile, the merchants sip, grit their teeth (to hold the piece of sugar that sweetens the tea on its way down), and listen to the latest news of business.

When Czar Alexander III gave a picnic, a staff of seven men with a battery of equipment reported for duty. One of the juggernauts above combines the function of samovar with cookstove. The other carries everything from caviar to camp stools, for when the party below "roughs it," everything must be just right.

Sanctum Sanctorum

HAMBURGER KUNSTH.

From London to Budapest, the café was the bourgeois gentleman's bastion of privilege, his political club, his amusement hall, his snack bar. A century after the Continent's first café had opened in Paris, the city of Vienna listed over a hundred establishments where coffee and conversation shared space with zithers, poetry improvisers, and billiard tables (a law required that the game be played on the ground level lest throngs of spectators come crashing down on coffee drinkers). In warmer climes, cafés spread out over the sidewalks, and when hotbloods were not planning a revolution, the passing scene was entertainment.

Except for the winsome cashier, women were not welcomed at Vienna's Silbernen Kaffeehaus, above, an establishment which boasted silver coat hangers and such distinguished patrons as waltz kings Lanner and Strauss. The Café Greco was, in 1850 when Passini painted the scene at left, a hangout and mail drop for foreigners in Rome—Mendelssohn, Schopenhauer, Buffalo Bill. It still stands near the Piazza di Spagna.

299

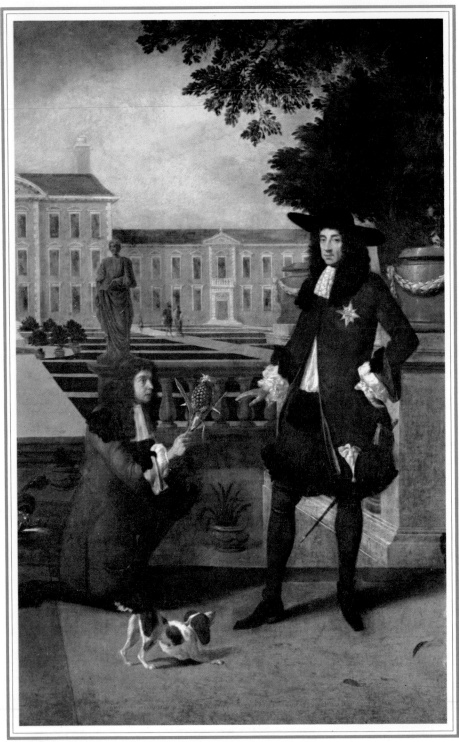

The first pineapple harvested in England, presented to Charles II by his gardener, c. 1670

PLEASURES
OF
ENGLISH
COMPANY

No people have held more tenaciously to their traditions than the British—or so the commonplace has it. Actually, few people have shown themselves so responsive to new whims of fashion, or so inventive in their customs of the table. After the stately exuberance of the Elizabethans and the hauteur of the first Stuarts, English manners passed within three centuries from the dour restraints of the Puritan Commonwealth, through the lustiness of the Restoration, the decorous period of Queen Anne, the robust self-indulgence of the Georgian era, and the dandyism of the Regency, to the ponderous and sometimes suffocating ways modeled by that commanding arbiter of English style, Queen Victoria.

These shifts found their embodiment in a succession of public and private institutions. In the seventeenth century the coffeehouse flourished as a major political and cultural center, one quite different in tone from the cafés and *Kaffeehäuser* of the Continent. From this evolved that particularly

301

English establishment, the exclusive gentleman's club. Great, comfortable country mansions and fashionable summer resorts also came to distinguish the English upper-class way of life. Finally, in the later years of Victoria's reign, the daring fashion of "dining out" in public was to lead to still another invention, that of the "grand hotel" with its fine restaurant, marked by the opening of the Savoy in the 1880's.

Startling contrasts also marked each period. Even as Restoration England cast off Puritan restraints, men of all classes who mingled at coffeehouses were enjoined by the management to avoid cards and dice; fines were imposed for swearing and quarreling; and anyone wanting alcoholic drinks usually took his trade elsewhere. Though exquisite silver, porcelain, and formalities of the tea table were fashionable in Queen Anne's day, a Swiss visitor of that time was aghast that even in the best society "belching at table, and in all Companies whatsoever, is a thing which the English no more scruple than they do Coughing and Sneezing. This is full strange to us that come from a Country where Custom has ordain'd that Belching should be a Privilege reserv'd totally to Hogs."

French cuisine was favored among the elegant, who imported French chefs, but the rest of England persisted in cooking in a generally unimaginative manner much as their Elizabethan forebears had, as if patriotism itself resided in boiled beef and cabbage. Thus, one Robert Campbell inveighed against highly seasoned French dishes in his tract *The London Tradesman* of 1747: "In the Days of good Queen *Elizabeth*, when mighty Roast Beef was the *Englishman's* Food, our Cookery was plain and simple as our Manners; it was not then a Science or Mistery. . . . But we have of late Years refined ourselves out of that simple Taste, and conformed our Palates to

Seventeenth-century spice box

Meats and Drinks dressed after the *French* Fashion: The natural Taste of Fish or Flesh is become nauseous to our fashionable Stomach; we abhor that anything should appear at our Tables in its native Properties; all the Earth . . . must be ransacked for Spices, Pickles, and Sauces, not to relish but to disguise our Food. Fish, when it has passed the Hands of a *French* Cook, is no more Fish . . . . It, and every Thing else, is dressed in Masquerade, seasoned with slow Poisons, and every Dish pregnant with nothing, but the Seeds of Diseases both chronick and acute."

Upper-class Englishmen and their ladies took most of their pleasures apart. Great hostesses were rare and nothing comparable to the French *salon* existed. Rather, great hosts were the rule, and lavish stag dinners the preferred entertainment; even when the sexes dined together, ladies generally retired soon after for cards and gossip, while the cloth was removed and men gathered closer over the mahogany for round after round of port. Yet, English women emerged as taste makers where French women had rarely ventured—as cookbook writers, beginning with the publication in 1670 of Hannah Woolley's *The Queen-like Closet: or, Rich Cabinet*, packed with household advice.

Were there no immutable English traditions? One thinks of the hearty breakfast. On New Year's Day, 1661, Samuel Pepys gave a breakfast party at which he regaled his friends with "oysters, neats' [oxen's] tongues, anchovies, wine, and Northdown ale." It was not as massive a morning meal as that taken at many a Tudor or early Stuart table (it appears to have included no mutton or beef), but it was in the handsome old style. Yet by the end of the seventeenth century, and throughout most of the eighteenth, a breakfast feast such as Pepys' was rare. The most that the gentry took then was a cup of coffee, chocolate, or tea, accompanied by bread or rusks or by that new invention, toast. ("The slices of bread and butter, which they give you with your tea, are as thin as poppy-leaves," reported the Swiss traveler Charles P. Moritz, who otherwise had little use for English cuisine; "But there is another kind of bread and butter usually eaten with tea, which is toasted by the fire, and is incomparably good. This is called toast.") Moreover, breakfast was often taken at about ten o'clock, after several hours of household activity—ladies instructing their servants, children receiving their lessons, fathers riding out or preparing their correspondence, and calls paid.

Less than two centuries later, breakfast customs had come full circle. We read, for instance, of a meal offered at one of the better provincial inns of England, the White Lion in distant Merionethshire, to fortify guests one rainy Sunday morning in 1854. The host offered a "pot of hare; ditto of trout; pot of prepared shrimps . . . tin of sardines; beautiful beefsteak; eggs, muffin; large loaf, and butter, not forgetting capital tea."

Equally substantial but less sociable were the breakfasts served in upper-class Victorian households. Sideboards were laden with silver-domed platters of eggs and bacon, grilled kidneys, sausages, kippers, plaice, from which the family took their choice. Punctuality at breakfast was counted among the Christian virtues. By eight o'clock everyone was expected to be in his place, and the head of the household was likely to be found already seated, surrounded by salvers of crumpets and pots of marmalades, reading from the immense pages of the morning *Times*.

Perhaps the sturdiest English tradition resulted from the "clubbable" character that Samuel Johnson noted in his friends, men who loathed being alone and who liked nothing better than to gather with friends and acquaintances for good talk and cheer. A "club," in the early part of the period, did not signify a formal institution housed in its own building; it was more accurately a circle of men of like interests who met frequently at their favorite tavern, chophouse, or, in later years, coffeehouse. Ben Jonson prefigured the custom by organizing the Apollo, a literary circle, at the Devil Tavern in Fleet Street. Rooms upstairs were reserved for the "private amusements" of the playwright and his fellow "clubbers." On the eve of the Restoration the Coffee Club of the Rota began to meet at Miles' Coffeehouse in New Palace Yard, Westminster; termed a "free and open society of ingenious gentlemen," it was, in effect, a debating circle. Pepys was one of its regular visitors, and the talk ranged far and wide over political as well as literary matters, the Rota often taking a vote on issues before Parliament.

The early years of the eighteenth century saw the nation bitterly divided between Whigs and Tories, particularly over the War of the Spanish Succession and the successor to Queen Anne herself: Should the next monarch be the Hanoverian George or Anne's exiled half brother, James, "the Pretender"? Men gravitated increasingly to political "clubs" of their own persuasion. Jonathan Swift was one of those who joined a Tory circle known as the October Club, which met at a tavern near the House of Commons. It was, he wrote, "a set of about a hundred Parliament men of the country who drink October beer at home, and meet every evening . . . to consult affairs and drive things on to extremes against the Whigs." In 1714 he formed his own Scriblerus Club of Tory partisans and men of letters, including the poet Alexander Pope, the statesman Lord Bolingbroke, and the playwright John Gay. The Whigs had their Kit-Kat Club, founded about 1700. It took its name from Katt, the proprietor whose reputation as a pieman had first attracted members there. Its luminaries included at various times such men as Addison, Steele, Congreve, Robert Walpole, and the architect Vanbrugh.

The Whig cause, because of prosperous middle-class support, ultimately prevailed, leaving Jacobites, when called upon to drink to His Majesty George I, to pass their wineglasses across their finger bowls in a covert toast to their exiled king "over the water." Finger bowls were consequently abolished, not to be restored until the twentieth century. Among themselves the Jacobites may have raised the following cheer:

God bless the king, our Faith's defender;
God bless—sure there's no harm in
   blessing—the Pretender;
But who Pretender is, and who is king,
God bless us all, that's quite another thing.

Yet peace and prosperity brought a degree of reconciliation, and no man in England was more clubbable than Johnson himself, who formed first the Ivy Lane Club, which met every Tuesday at the King's Head Tavern, a beefsteak house; then the Essex Head Club, meeting three evenings a week at the Essex Head Tavern off the Strand. He was also a regular at the Turk's Head Club, whose roles included Sir Joshua Reynolds, Oliver Goldsmith, Edmund Burke, and the actor David Garrick (though Johnson thought to blackball him for possible "buffoonery"). Here the select —first restricted to nine in number, though the quota was eventually raised to thirty-five—could match wits as well as drinks with the encyclopedic sage. Before long the Johnson circle had become, in effect, a congress of leading men of letters.

The coffeehouse was itself a club of sorts, but a democratic one, open to all who came. The first coffeehouse was

The Kitchen Conspiracy

"*T*he honour of every family," Jonathan Swift observes, "is deposited in the hands of the cook, the butler, and the groom." In his ironical *Directions to Servants*, written c. 1731, he offers some helpful advice on how to keep this sacred trust to the advantage of everyone but the "common enemy, which is your master and lady." No one, it seems, is better situated to wage internecine war than the female cook. Her first order of business is the affections of the butler: "Let there be always a strict friendship between you and the butler . . . the butler often wants a comfortable tit-bit, and you much oftener a cool cup of good liquor. However, be cautious of him, for he is sometimes an inconstant lover, because he hath great advantage to allure the maids with a glass of sack; or white wine and sugar." The cook's relations with the lower ranks are less agreeable. "To keep troublesome servants out of the kitchen, always leave the winder sticking on the jack to fall on their heads." Swift advises the footman to counterattack: "Whenever she turns her back, throw . . . a handful of salt in the pot, or smoking coals into the dripping-pan, or daub the roast meat with the back of the chimney . . . ." In the cook's dealings with tradesmen, too, strategy is recommended. "If you be employed in marketing, buy your meat as cheap as you can: but . . . set down the highest rate; which besides is but justice; for no body can afford to sell at the same rate that he buys. . . . Do not accept a treat of beef-stake and pot of ale from the butcher,

which I think in conscience is no better than wronging your master; but do you always take that perquisite in money. . . . If you find it necessary to go to market in a wet day, take out your mistress's riding-hood and cloak to save your cloaths." Management of the stewpots Swift leaves, for the most part, to the cook's imagination, though he does caution, "Never send up a leg of a fowl at supper, while there is a cat or dog in the house, that can be accused of running away with it: but, if there happen to be neither, you must lay it upon the rats, or a strange greyhound. . . . If a lump of soot falls into the soup, and you cannot conveniently get it out, scum it well, and it will give the soup a high French taste. . . . When you find that you cannot get dinner ready at the time appointed, put the clock back . . . and, if your dinner miscarries in almost every dish, how could you help it."

probably the Angel, which opened about 1650 in Oxford, at a time when no fewer than 350 alehouses were in operation there. By 1700, due to the rising vogue of coffee and the new political awareness of the middle classes, the popularity of these forums climbed to a point where more than two thousand were flourishing in London. Fifteen years later the number was close to three thousand. For the admission price of a penny, anyone could seat himself at a

Queen Charlotte frying sprats

table, pick up conversation, and gather news of the day. This was a boon in a time when newspapers were scarce and when political and commercial news was normally borne by word of mouth.

King Charles II was perturbed at the growth of coffeehouses, with their free talk and their potentialities as centers of dissent, and in 1675 he ordered them suppressed—a foolish move, never carried out and soon forgotten. Like the clubs, the coffeehouses gradually became specialized as men of varying businesses and professions congregated in their favorites. Lawyers were likely to be seen at the Rainbow in Fleet Street.

Shippers and buyers gathered at Edward Lloyd's in Lombard Street—a coffeehouse where so much maritime information was exchanged that it was to become not only the center of ship auctions but the headquarters of the famous body of underwriters known to the world as Lloyd's. Stock jobbers and financiers met at Jonathan's in Change Alley, where such schemes as the speculative "South Sea Bubble" were promoted. At Hogarth's Coffeehouse lessons in Latin were given daily at four o'clock to those who aspired to higher learning. As Macaulay remarked in his chronicle of the period, "the coffeehouse was the Londoner's home, and . . . those who wished to find a gentleman commonly asked, not whether he lived in Fleet Street or Chancery Lane, but whether he frequented the *Grecian* or the *Rainbow*." But above all, said Macaulay, "There was Will's [in Covent Garden] . . . sacred to polite letters, where earls in stars and garters, clergymen in cassocks, pert Templars, sheepish lads from Universities, translators and index-makers in ragged coats" could be found gathering about the chair of John Dryden, the poet laureate, who sat enthroned beside the fire in winter and on the balcony in summer, receiving literary aspirants and passing judgment on their work.

Alexander Pope was not yet twelve when he was presented to the presiding genius ensconced at Will's. He had already composed some verses ("I lisp'd in numbers, for the numbers came," as he later remarked proudly of his childhood efforts) and was long to write under the influence of the mighty, witty man in that high-backed chair. He had far less use for Joseph Addison, who decades later was the presiding spirit at the Whig coffeehouse known as Button's just across the street from Will's, and whom he castigated in savage verse:

Alike reserv'd to blame or to command
A tim'rous foe, and a suspicious
friend. . . .
Like Cato, give his little Senate laws,
And sit attentive to his own applause."

Jonathan Swift, in turn, had little use for Will's in its post-Dryden days, scoffing at the "wits" who assembled there: "The worst conversation I ever remember to have heard in my life."

These were the cutting edges of London life. Boswell, ever bent on adventure and welcoming almost any company, male or female, was not inclined to be so haughty. He "pub crawled" from one tavern and coffeehouse to the next. His *London Journal* of 1762–63 records a day-long tour in January with friends, beginning with "an excellent breakfast at the Somerset Coffeehouse," continuing with a visit to London Bridge to view the ice floes in the river, and a stop at a little "public house" in Whitechapel to drink "some warm white wine with aromatic spices, pepper, and cinnamon." After this the gay party adjourned to a private tavern room for "a jolly profusion of smoking, juicy beefsteaks." Next they proceeded to the Bedford Coffeehouse for coffee and tea. Thereupon they attended the theater and, undoubtedly sozzled, raised an uproar against David Malloch, the playwright. Finally, Boswell relates, "After the play we went to Lady Betty's" (who presided over a literary salon of dubious reputa-

tion) and, "as . . . we were very hungry after fatigues, we were set down in the parlour by ourselves to an excellent warm supper. We were in high glee. . . ."

By this time the serious and sober coffeehouse had passed its prime. Many had become sheer gaming resorts for well-dressed rakehells. Gentlemen of high rank and fashion, having savored the pleasures of the intimate circle, now desired permanent establishments of their own behind closed doors and away

George III toasting a muffin

from the rabble. So out of White's Chocolate House in St. James's Street grew the Tories' retreat, White's (founded in 1693), and out of William Almack's Assembly Rooms grew Boodle's (1762) in Pall Mall—the first clubs to have their own buildings, with liveried staff, fine furnishings, and well-stocked wine cellars. Together with Brooks' (1778) these clubs became enduring centers of English political and male social life at the top, and were the models for many others to come. (Such was the Reform Club, spacious headquarters of the new Liberal party from the 1830's onward and in whose kitchen the great chef

307

Alexis Soyer ministered, and the Athenaeum, opened in 1824, where leading patrons of the arts enjoyed superlative furnishings, classical busts, roomfuls of books, and a formidable table.)

Another reason for the decline of the coffeehouse was that the government, to foster trade with India and China, promoted tea drinking. Beginning with Charles II's queen, Catherine of Braganza, the court had taken to tea. Thus Alexander Pope, referring to teatime at Hampton Court during Queen Anne's reign, wrote a rhymed couplet using the then-current pronunciation of tea:

> *Here, thou, great ANNA! whom three*
> *realms obey,*
> *Dost sometimes counsel take—and some-*
> *times tea.*

Tea was also a favorite among English women of lesser rank, whose tastes were probably influenced by the fact that they were excluded from the coffeehouses. The "genteel" brew was served in pleasure gardens such as Vauxhall and Ranelegh. Tea drinking, particularly as tea tariffs were lowered, spread at such a rate that in the early decades of the eighteenth century annual imports rose from twenty thousand pounds to sixty thousand pounds, and by the end of the century, they had reached some twenty million pounds. Brewers, distillers, and importers of wine feared that tea would heavily cut in on their trade. Yet, the consumption of wines and spirits also rose enormously in the same period, from a half-million gallons of taxable gin in 1700 to five million in 1735, not to mention the illicit, and thus unaccounted, liquors drunk.

Mention of good claret and rich port also comes up constantly in the context of Georgian life. What wine a gentleman drank often reflected his politics or the dictates of English foreign policy. The immense popularity of port was an outgrowth of the power struggle between England and France for influence in Spain and of the Methuen Treaty of 1703: the Whigs, anxious to bring Portugal over to the English side and to boycott French trade, dropped the duties on Portuguese wines to only £7 a tun, raising those on French wines to a forbidding £55 a tun. Port, readily available, thus became the Whigs' patriotic drink; one proved his loyalty by the quantities he drank, while to resort to clarets or Burgundies was to drink the wine of the enemy. The Tories, on the

Brass nutcracker, 1700's

other hand, made a point of demonstrating their opposition to the war by acquiring the best French wines available, no matter what the price.

Another drink long identified with Whiggery and its political jollifications was punch. The drink derived its name from a Hindustani word meaning "five," a reference to its five basic ingredients

—rum, citrus-fruit juices, sugar, water, and spices—and was brought to England in the seventeenth century by merchants returning from India. Since it combined the principal imports from successful English enterprises in the West Indies, it enjoyed a double popularity. Punch was served hot or cold from great bowls, and in its potency and sweetness it resembled the spiced wines of the Middle Ages. At poorer clubs and taverns, the punch was often made with rum substitutes, either Eastern arrack— a distillation of coconut, rice, or sugar cane—or other nondescript brandies. By the 1780's it was one of the standard libations even at Tory Cambridge.

The rich never ate or drank so much as in Georgian England, and gout was the common price the overindulgent paid. If a man was long to survive a regimen of several bottles a day, he needed to pursue a highly active life to offset some of its effects, and this most gentlemen did. Amid all their clubbing and late evenings at wine, they were earnest horsemen, travelers, collectors, letter writers, amateur antiquarians, and above all mansion builders and developers of country estates. On a typical day in town, a Georgian gentleman might do business with his solicitor at breakfast; then ride out in St. James's park, pay social calls, take a light lunch at midday (the "dinner" hour in England, once observed before or close to noon, had been advanced to two o'clock at the beginning of the eighteenth century, and to three, four, and even five or six o'clock by the end of the century). After the meal he might visit London's smart art dealers to pass judgment on the latest fashion in painting and sculpture, or retire to his study to try a translation of Horace or Ovid (a fashionable exercise of the time) before showing his prowess at the dinner table. Then, on to his club for an hour or two; and afterward to Parliament where, if steady enough, he might deliver a speech; after adjournment he would visit his mistress.

Silver gilt punch bowl, c. 1715

In the country the gentleman's life took another turn. Generally, his wealth came from his lands, which had to be tended carefully if they were to thrive. Unlike the French courtier who under the spell of Versailles often saw little from year to year of his own holdings, the English landlord, from duke to squire, spent months on end at his estate, conferring with overseers, visiting tenants, serving as local justice of the peace, and supervising crop management. Many a landed lord, absenting himself from clubs and boudoirs, particularly during the spring and summer, became an expert on selective cattle breeding, crop rotation, and experiments with new vegetables and fruits. The effort he expended was salubrious for both his health and his table.

Many wealthy and titled heirs—Bathursts, Pembrokes, Burlingtons, Oxfords, Leicesters, Bedfords—took to erecting ostentatious country showplaces designed after the style of Palladio, Inigo Jones, Sir Christopher Wren, and Sir John Vanbrugh. From these handsome seats they administered self-sufficient sources of varied food supply, tending their own orchards, raising poultry, cattle, hogs, and often producing their own cheese, ale, and cider. Tobias Smollett, author of the Georgian novel *The Expedition of Humphry Clinker*, wrote authentically, if in high-flown style, when he had one of his characters, Matthew Bramble, describe life at his own Brambleton Hall in the Midlands: "I drink the virgin lymph, pure and crystalline as it gushes from the rock, or the sparkling beverage home-brewed from malt of my own making . . . my bread is sweet and nourishing, made from my own wheat, ground in my own mill . . . my table is, in a great measure, furnished from my own ground; my five-year-old mutton, fed on the fragrant herbage of the mountains . . . my delicious veal, fattened with nothing but the mother's milk . . . my poultry from the barn door, that never knew confinement but when they were at roost; my rabbits panting from the warren; my game fresh from the moors; my trout and salmon struggling from the stream. . . . My salads, roots, and pot-herbs, my own garden yields in plenty and perfection. . . ."

Some estate owners, in their efforts to outdo one another, leaned to the exotic. The extravagant Duke of Chandos—who maintained at Canons an aviary of rare birds, along with 93 household servants, 19 gardeners, and an orchestra of 27 players—called upon overseas suppliers to furnish him with unusual produce: "From Captain Massey in Carolina came rice, kidney beans (said to grow prodigiously, like hops or vines), ananas (or pineapples), and pickles, not to mention certain fauna—a Mexican squash [*sic*], 'which we take to be a little beaver,' rough coated, very tame and entertaining, and flamingos. Mr. Ashley of the Barbados [sent] pineapples, cinnamon, coffee trees and berries, and 'Avigator [*sic*] Pears'. . . . Messrs. Harriman of Leghorn supplied broccoli seed and fennel . . . orange-flower water, capers, *muscatello di Castello* vinegar, preserved citron, anchovies. . . . While from Oporto the Duke procured Lamiego hams, more appetizing, let us hope, than those from Pennsylvania, and, from Lisbon, sugar, raisins of the sun . . . currants, lemons, oranges, musk and water-melon seeds." The Duke of Bedford, at Woburn, rejected the offer of a tiger from a supplier abroad, but accepted a huge turtle. "His Grace had about twelve ladies and gentlemen at the eating of it," his steward reported. "We dressed it after the West India manner and the Duke said he never eat [*sic*] a better in his life."

However the fare might vary from one great country house to the next (de-

Before: top-hatted Britisher landing in France

pending largely on whether the owner had imported a French chef), it was customary that the company be large. The day might find the house guests broken into small groups, pursuing various diversions and sports in the surrounding "park" and the preserves beyond; but the dinner hour brought the company together in the drawing room for a formal entrance into the dining room, each lady on the arm of a gentleman. Liveried house servants lined the way, sometimes with the personal attendants of the visitors forming a second rank. Lord Hervey recalled an extended visit to Robert Walpole's stately Houghton Hall in Norfolk—a rural palace surmounted by domes and statuary: "we used to sit down to dinner a little snug party of about thirty odd, up to the chin in beef, venison, geese, turkeys, etc.; and generally over the chin in claret, strong beer and punch." In a later generation we hear of a house party of forty at the Duke of Devonshire's Chatsworth, and of eighty at Thomas Coke's Holkham Hall. At Woburn, in 1800, at a four-day-long Sheepshearing Party, nearly two hundred people, ranging from noblemen to yeomen from the countryside—a company reminiscent in size of Tudor days —sat down together for dinner at three.

Despite the profusion of servitors in attendance on such occasions, dining procedure in many mansions appears to have been self-service. The table was set with platters before the guests entered, and each gentleman helped himself and his table partner to the dishes nearest him; if he liked some other dish several places away or across the table, he asked for a helping to be passed to him or sent a servant to fetch it. In the eyes of the German prince Pückler-Muskau, visiting estates during the Regency, this was "a very troublesome custom," and he was pleased to discover that "some of the most elegant travelled gentlemen have adopted the German [and French] fashion of sending servants round with the dishes."

As for wine, the prince observed that "It is not usual to take [it] without drinking to another person. When you raise your glass, you look fixedly at the one with whom you are drinking, bow your head, and then drink with the greatest gravity." Such toasting was another custom hallowed by generations of the gentry, a French visitor having written as early as 1698 that "To drink at table without drinking to the health of some one in especial, would be considered drinking on the sly, and as an act of incivility." The larger the company, the more numerous the pledges. After this, and the port and the cards and the other indoor games that followed, the house guests retired to gather strength for the next day's exertions.

Though the urban upper middle classes possessed no Woburns or Holkham

After: rolling home with a well-developed paunch

311

Alexis Soyer

*T*he finest chef in mid-nineteenth-century England was a Frenchman. Dining at the Reform Club, where Alexis Soyer was head chef, was the goal of every gourmet in London. The talented, flamboyant, egocentric character could have capitalized on his reputation socially, but he chose to use it to launch some of the projects that crowded his brain. The astonishingly vulgar ambience and delectable food of The Gastronomic Symposium of All Nations, a restaurant that he designed, decorated, and operated, attracted a thousand customers a day, but he happily sold recipes to the firm of Cross & Blackwell so that the poorer, stay-at-home public could sample his culinary artistry, too. In spare moments he invented things—stoves, jelly molds, mime scenery— and even there succeeded with surprising frequency. But Soyer was above all

a humanitarian. Organizing soup kitchens for starving Britons and providing nourishing food on the Crimean battlefield were his proudest achievements. His enormously popular cookbook for the rich was followed by one for poor cottagers. His style can best be described as purple, his English fractured; but Soyer's advice was always thorough and appropriate for the audience he meant to reach. The following is from his *Shilling Cookery*, which is set up as an exchange between two ladies gathering recipes. "*Mr. B.* [husband of one of the ladies] 'In my wife . . . you see almost an accomplished woman (hearing such praise, Mrs. B. retired, saying, 'How foolish you talk, Richard'); she . . . as an amateur, is rather proficient in music, but her parents, very wisely considering household knowledge to be of the greater importance, made her first acquainted with the keys of the storeroom before those of the piano.' " Mrs. B.'s recipe for toast: "Procure a nice square loaf . . . that has been baked one or two days previously (for new bread cannot be cut, and would eat very heavy) . . . contrive to have rather a clear fire; place a slice of the bread upon a toasting fork . . . then begin to move it gradually to and fro until the whole surface has assumed a yellowish-brown color . . . have some fresh or salt butter (which must not be too hard, as pressing it upon the toast would make it heavy); should you require six such slices for a numerous family . . . cut each slice into pieces as soon as buttered . . . as often in cutting through four or five slices with a bad knife, you will squeeze all the butter out of the upper one and discover the under one, at the peril of its life, swimming in an ocean of butter at the bottom."

Halls, they were not far behind their betters in the pursuit of good living. And in the country, even a man of lesser means might be found serving an original and varied dinner. A particularly gregarious host, a rural parson named James Woodforde, recorded an entertainment he had given (on a clerical salary of some £400 a year) to a small party in 1770: "I gave them for dinner a dish of fine Tench . . . Ham and 3 Fowls boiled, a Plum Pudding; a couple of Ducks rosted, a rosted neck of Pork, a Plum Tart and an Apple Tart, Pears, Apples and Nutts after dinner; White Wine and red, Beer and Cyder." The meal began at four o'clock. At six he served coffee and tea. Later, at ten, he offered a supper of "Hashed Fowl and Duck and Eggs and Potatoes, etc." Four years later he told of a more "elegant" dinner he had presented on his stipend: "The first course was, part of a large Cod, a Chine of Mutton, some Soup, a Chicken Pye, Puddings and Roots, etc. Second course, Pidgeons and Asparagus. A Fillet of Veal with Mushrooms and high Sauce with it, rosted Sweetbreads, hot Lobster, Apricot Tart and in the Middle a Pyramid of Syllabubs and Jellies." There were fruits as well as Madeira and port to wind up the evening, and "We were all very cheerful and merry."

Regarding desserts, Mrs. Raffald in *The Experienced English Housekeeper*, a compendium of some eight hundred recipes published in 1769, advised her many readers to "lay up" in summer all manner of preserves and dried fruits for the January table; such unexpected fare in winter would be "entertaining to the company," making "a pretty appearance after the cloth is drawn"—that is, after the table was cleared for dessert. She counseled that all sweetmeats and fruits be readied in China dishes or baskets; that it would be easy to make "five different ices" for the centerpiece, "with four plates of dried fruit round them, apricots, green-gages, grapes, and pears —the four outward corners, pistacho [*sic*] nuts, prunellas, oranges, and olives —the four squares, nonpareils, pears, walnuts, and filberts—the two in the centre, betwist [*sic*] the top and the bottom, chestnut and Portugal plums—for six long dishes, pine-apples, French plums, and the four brandy-fruits, which are peaches, nectarines, apricots, and cherries." For reasons that were never made clear, each course in a given meal was to have the same number of dishes —twenty-five in the meal whose dessert is described above.

Such good eating required food industries on a scale never before known. Large specialty markets dotted London in the eighteenth century—fish at Billingsgate, poultry at Leadenhall, fruits and vegetables at Covent Garden and Spitalfields, meat at Smithfield. Over 75,000 head of cattle were driven to London yearly in the first half of the century; some 100,000 toward the end. Salmon came from Scotland, oysters from Colchester, butter from Yorkshire and East Anglia (the trip by sea left some of it tasting like "train-oil thickened with salt," said Smolett), and the cheesemongers of London maintained a fleet of more than a dozen ships to bring huge wheels of Cheshire cheese around Land's End from the port of Liverpool.

Still, amid this prosperity, the laboring class fell prey to the gin craze of which William Hogarth has left vivid testimony. The *laissez-faire* attitude of the government was, without doubt, partially at fault. It had long regulated the sale of ale and beer, requiring that they be dispensed only at licensed houses. But it had imposed no like restrictions on spirits, and only the lightest of taxes. It appears to have been unprepared for

Milk for sale in St. James's Park, 1790

the sudden proliferation of back-alley gin mills—where signs such as "Drunk for a penny, dead drunk for twopence, straw provided free" lured many of the cities' poor to their ruin. The "gin," moreover, was often not a true product of grain and juniper at all, but a potion of lethal substitutes. One recipe called for oil of vitriol [sulphuric acid], oil of almonds, oil of turpentine, spirits of wine, lump sugar, lime water, rose water, alum, and salt of tartar. The novelist Henry Fielding, in outrage, wrote in 1751 of "that poison called *gin* . . . the principal sustenance (if it may be so called) of more than a hundred thousand people in this metropolis." Though belated steps were taken to bring spirits

under control, by taxation and curtailment of illicit stills, enormous social damage had been done.

Other social ills overtook the poorer classes from about mid-century on. The "enclosure" movement, under the pretext of putting more land under cultivation, benefited rich landowners while uprooting many a cottager from his farm land and pasturage. The deprived and the landless were forced into the cities, there to become the work force of the new Industrial Revolution. Food prices soared, particularly during the Napoleonic Wars, and the Corn Laws of 1815 made matters worse by restricting grain imports and keeping home prices high. Adulteration of foods by unscrupulous producers, along with a high rate of spoilage due to the increasing distances and inadequate roads over which food was brought into teeming cities—all this added to turmoil and unrest. The quality of English bread so deteriorated that an uproar was raised against both its price and content. Critics charged that chalk or alum was added to make it white, and one pamphleteer, in *Poison Detected, or Frightful Truths*, charged that bakers were snatching bodies from the morgue and grinding up the bones for flour. Some vegetables were made to look greener with poisonous copper oxide additives. Milk was almost unknown to the urban poor, except in a watered or half-spoiled state (though in the fashionable West End of London, cows were still driven through the streets and milked at curbside for wealthy clients).

In novels such as *Oliver Twist* and *Nicholas Nickleby*, Charles Dickens described the ravages of near starvation among the poorest of all, the children of the poor: "Pale and haggard faces, lank and bony figures, children with the countenances of old men . . . boys of stunted growth, and others whose long meagre legs would hardly bear their stooping bodies." In the 1840's—the "Hungry Forties," as they are often called—wages were to sink to their lowest level in a century, and the diet of the poor, then composed chiefly of potatoes and gin, reached its nadir. The disease which destroyed the Irish and English potato crops, and the resultant famine of 1845–46, sent a specter through the land, and vacant-eyed, corpse-like figures could be seen in numbers in gutters from Thamesside to Merseyside. There were innumerable reformers on hand, to be sure, to proclaim that the best medicine for poverty was temperance.

Perhaps few men cared less about the condition of the poor than the raffish George IV, whose first notable act as regent for his insane father was to invite two thousand guests to Carlton House for a stupendous banquet and benefit for artists in 1811. As if to emulate Louis XIV at Versailles, he had an artificial rivulet constructed for the festivities. It sprang from a silver fountain housed in a "temple" in front of his own chair, ran

Street cars carrying hot and cold drinks, 1842

through a channel in the main table, and was spanned by numerous little bridges; "gold and silver fish were by a mechanical invention made to swim and sport through the bubbling current." At Brighton the regent erected the gossamer pavilion that was his Oriental pleasure dome, and he imported the great Carême to be his chef at a salary of £1,000 a year. To be stylish under the Regency, one needed to be carefree, a trifle exotic, and Francophile; yet, as the Frenchman Louis Simond wryly observed after a tour of great houses in 1810–11, it was remarkable that English gentlemen who prided themselves on their "scrupulous delicacy" of taste adhered to an odd custom—that of using a chamber pot placed in a corner of the dining room to relieve themselves as the hours over wine wore on.

Nor were the privileged classes of the early Victorian age greatly concerned with the state of England's society as a whole. They were much more involved in the change of manners affecting upper and middle classes. Everything was in flux, from mealtime hours to food and method of table service. The gradual advance of dinner to the evening hours (Queen Victoria, at the time of her coronation in 1837, took dinner as late as eight o'clock) resulted in a general upheaval of the established eating order and the introduction of two new forms, the substantial luncheon and the ritual of afternoon tea. The confusion over what to call each meal seems to have been so troublesome that Thomas De Quincey offered his readers an all-purpose definition: "dinner" was "that meal, no matter when taken, which is

315

the principal meal, i.e. the meal on which the day's support is thrown . . . in which [meat] predominates."

In 1853 *The Family Friend* counseled wives that luncheon be taken about five hours after breakfast, "to allay the cravings of nature, but not entirely to destroy the appetite." With this the magisterial arbiter Isabella Beeton agreed, instructing ladies in her *Book of Household Management*, published in 1861, that the "solidity" of luncheon "must of course in some degree be proportionate to the time it is intended to enable you to wait for your dinner and the amount of exercise you take in the meantime." And as the fashionable dinner hour grew later and later, the more important became the palliative of afternoon tea, which evolved from its origins as a polite refreshment into a virtual sub-meal involving tea cakes, sandwiches, and scones, and thus into an institution.

Traditional English fare and Continental cuisine, and their various manners of presentation, were also a subject of dispute. No man was a warmer advocate of the joys of the hearty English meal uncontaminated by foreign influences than Dickens, with his glowing descriptions of great beefsteaks and smoking potatoes, of flaming Christmastide plum puddings, of a board "groaning beneath the weight of fowls, fish, boiled beef . . . [and] heavy vegetables," accompanied by tankards of "the most stupendous Wiltshire beer." Generally, the meal was set before diners all at once.

But for the upper class it became the fashion in Regency times to present a dinner *à la française*—a bastard scheme in which standard English dishes high-

lighted by some Frenchified dishes were served in the French manner, that is, in ordered sequence. A menu at a party for eighteen given by the Duke of Richmond in London in the 1830's offered twenty-eight dishes, ranging from lightly garnished calf's head and ramekins of cheese to such elaborate dishes as mutton cutlets with soubise sauce, cassolettes of salpicon of beef palates, lark patties with truffles, and so on, apportioned or carved at table. Much later, the modern idea of serving *à la russe* came in—joints were fully carved by stewards, arranged on platters, then formally presented in well-defined courses to each diner.

Meanwhile, perhaps chiefly as a result of Prime Minister Gladstone's relaxation of import duties on table wines in 1861, the drinking of French wines came into favor once again. Port was no longer the preferred drink of the aristocracy. No doubt their health improved. They continued to eat heartily. Prime Minister Lord Palmerston was reported by a companion at a dinner in 1865 to have consumed "two plates of turtle soup; he was then served very amply to a plate of cod and oyster sauce; he then took a pâté; afterwards he was helped to two very greasy looking entrees; he then dispatched a plate of roast mutton; there then appeared before him the largest, and to my mind the hardest, slice of ham that ever figured on the table of a nobleman, yet it disappeared, just in time to answer the inquiry of his butler, 'Snipe, my Lord, or pheasant?' He instantly replied 'Pheasant,' thus completing his ninth dish of meat at that meal." The prime minister was then eighty-one and in thriving health.

COFFEE,
TEA,
OR GIN

Three ways to hold a Chinese tea cup, demonstrated by an eighteenth-century family

Robert Wass, the Red Lion's most pop-
ular waiter, is seen in the sketch above
carrying a bowl of punch, perhaps to
some coffee-sated patrons. Most coffee-
houses made extravagant health claims
like those in the broadside below and
sold tokens (below right) redeemable in
coffee. The seventeenth-century paint-
ing at the right conveys the conviviality
that turned customers into habitués.

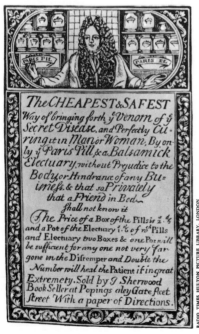

The CHEAPEST & SAFEST
Way of bringing forth ye Venom of ye
Secret Disease, and Perfectly Curing it in Man or Woman; By only ye Paris Pill, & a Balsamick
Electuary, without Prejudice to the
Body, or Hindrance of any Bu=
iness, & that so Privately
that a Friend in Bed
shall not know it
The Price of a Box of the Pills is 2:6
and a Pot of the Electuary 1:6 of ns Pills
and Electuary two Boxes & one Pot will
be sufficient for any one not very far
gone in the Distemper and Double the
Number will heal the Patient if in great
Extremity. Sold by I Sherwood
Bookseller at Popings aley Gate fleet
street With a paper of Directions.

Seminaries of Sedition

Puritans condemned England's love of coffee as excessive and coffeehouses as dens of dalliance; Charles II saw them as centers of political dissent; tavernkeepers and vintners resented the inroads coffee made on their business; and one alarmist termed it "the black enemy of sleep and copulation." Despite these churlish demurrers, coffeehouses prospered from Dublin to Edinburgh. Drawn by the delicious aroma and an atmosphere of sobriety difficult to find elsewhere during that hard-drinking age, assorted groups of wags and intellectuals, bards and blackguards, gathered in their favorite haunts, day after day, to match wits with their peers.

The Beaten Path

Before the days of the Salvation Army, there was little organized attempt to instill temperance in the masses. At the height of the gin era in the 1740's, every fourth slum dwelling sold cheap gin; and people on the verge of starvation went to any length to secure their "Royal Poverty," defined by a contemporary lexicographer as a "nickname for the liquor called geneva. . . . When beggars are drunk they are as great as kings."

William Hogarth, whose "Gin Lane" appears above, was one of the few to realize the dangers of the gin craze and to pressure Parliament into passing the "Tippling Act" of 1751 which taxed and checked the illicit sale of liquor. Here, drink has drained the energy of the underfed populace, and the pawnbroker alone does a thriving trade. While one woman pours a shot of the potent pacifier down her baby's throat, another neglected child plunges to his death. To entice the people back to the fold, Hogarth advocated beer as a more healthful drink. In "Beer Street," opposite, prosperous cockney laborers pause for a tankard of "that invigorating liquor" and some good-natured banter. As two fishwomen read a ballad about herring, a blacksmith displays his strength. Even the sign painter is likely to be rewarded with the Barley Mow's brew.

The Beefeaters

"I eat like a very Turk, or rather indeed like a very John Bull, whose supreme joy is good beef," Boswell confided to his diary. Beef was not only a joy; it was the essence of inviolable English tradition, prompting Henry Fielding to quote a patriotic song in its praise. One verse ran: "Then, Britons, from all nice dainties refrain, Which effeminate Italy, France, and Spain; And mighty roast beef shall command on the main." At right, Hogarth's "Calais Gate" takes another swipe at food across the Channel. A cook returns from the docks with a juicy side of beef, imported by a Calais hotel catering to English travelers, but not before the soup-eating soldiers have cast a lean and hungry look his way and the friar has given the meat a covetous poke. The cartoon above draws a comparison between food prices and wages, indicating that to a laborer in 1795 symbols of plenty had a hollow ring.

323

Cucumbers by the cartload

Oysters on the half shell

Sweet milk, sweeter words

Hot cross buns in season

Casseroles from the baker

Cherries for cheer

Alive, Alive, Oh!

By 1850 thirteen thousand hawkers were doing a brisk trade in London's streets. Some sold pies, sausages, breads, and other foods that were literally "homemade" in neighborhood cookshops and houses. Other vendors resold at small profit produce bought at outlying farms or at one of a dozen entrepôts like Billingsgate Fish Market above. Though anyone was free to buy from these cheaper markets, stalls were so filthy and smells so bad that customers risked "carrying home the shop-bill upon their clothes," as one veteran complained. Haggling on one's own doorstep, to judge from Thomas Rowlandson's scenes opposite, was a far more pleasant exchange.

"Prince of Whales"

This 1792 sketch by the caricaturist James Gill-ray, entitled, "A Voluptuary Under the Hor-rors of Digestion," is actually a picture of the future George IV at table. It is not difficult to understand why contemporary satirists referred to him as a fat Adonis and the Prince of Whales.

The prince regent who became George IV was a prodigious drinker, eater, and whoremonger; he was also able to find time to spend the state's money building and rebuilding various residences. His greatest extravaganza was Brighton Pavilion, an Oriental pleasure palace that was the scene of activities as unorthodox as the decor. The prince conducted drinking bouts from which no man could easily excuse himself; female guests fulfilled their roles, in part, by supporting the swaying sovereign on the dance floor, pretending the while that it was they who had overindulged. As befitted a man of his interests, George gave Brighton's kitchen (below opposite) special attention. Not only did it carry on the decorative themes of the grand dining room (above); it was adequately equipped to serve hundreds. Its facilities comprised a veritable showcase of the latest cooking gear: "contrivances for roasting, boiling, baking, stewing, frying, steaming, and heating; hot plates, hot closets, hot air, and hot hearths." In 1816 the regent persuaded Carême to preside over the belowstairs wonderland, but the famous French chef left within eight months. He confided to an English lady that "the tastes of his royal majesty were too bourgeois." George, however, knew what he liked—and usually got it. In later years, when he was so corpulent he had to be lowered onto his horse by a machine, and a specially tailored coat failed to hide the well-corseted royal paunch, George IV, publicly exposed, abandoned Brighton.

The Norfolk coach speeding toward London with a cargo of fresh-killed geese and turkeys

A merry throng of shoppers converging on the baker's for traditional Twelfth Night cakes

Four generations of a family finishing their second gigantic Christmas meal of the day

Twelve Days of Christmas

Victorian sentimentality swelled to a climax during the Christmas season; apparently, the only way Englishmen could stop choking on the lumps in their throats was to keep eating and drinking. The season traditionally began with a plump bird and a plum pudding, the latter steamed to a soggy deliciousness in a huge cauldron like that pictured above. Artist Robert Seymour's cook presumably worked for a household where the merriment lasted a full twelve wassailing days, but even the likes of Bob Cratchit could look forward to at least one memorable meal. As Dickens described the occasion, "There never was such a goose. . . . Its tenderness and flavor, size and cheapness, were the themes of universal admiration. Eked out by apple-sauce and mashed potatoes, it was a sufficient dinner for the whole family." At the climactic moment, Mrs. Cratchit brought forth the pudding, "like a speckled cannon-ball, so hard and firm, blazing [with] ignited brandy. . . . O, a wonderful pudding!" As the century wore on, many families added tree decorating (a custom imported with the German Prince Albert) to the agenda. The decorations of gingerbread and bonbons were almost a meal in themselves.

The Breakfast Habit

Melton Mowbray in Leicestershire is renowned for its Stilton cheese, pork pies, and most especially its fox hunting, all in a day's pleasure for the gentlemen above. The engraving, after a painting by Sir Francis Grant, records a hunt breakfast held in 1839 at one of the district's many estates, and the morning meal which they have just finished is a traditionally sumptuous if leisurely preparation for a brisk ride to hounds. While a late-comer is served, the others are free to read the paper, scribble a few lines, or just wait impatiently.

Servants and Serviettes

To many Victorians nothing was more important than gentility, even if achieving it meant being vulgar. One way to be considered genteel was to entertain on a scale more lavish than one could afford. Only the very rich could muster the large corps of waiters necessary for a dinner party from their own household staffs. The others did what William Thackeray confessed to in an essay on dinner-giving snobs: "[I] hire sham butlers and attendants; have a fellow going round the table with still and dry Champagne, as if I knew his name, and it was my custom to drink those wines every day of my life." The properly ostentatious Victorian (whose elegant dinner is about to be enjoyed, above) also served more dishes than any normal guest could sample. It was considered fair to spirit away an untouched platter after only a slight pause, thereby preserving it for the admiration of the next night's crowd. But a good player like Thackeray's dining-out snob could easily out-maneuver his host: "Whenever, for my part, I see the head man particularly anxious to escamoter [take away] a *fricandeau* or a *blancmange* I always call out, and insist on massacring it with a spoon." A third important element of a dinner party was table decoration. A much-sought-after accomplishment in a housemaid was the ability to fold napkins into fanciful shapes, but as such a talent was not to be found just anywhere, there were many manuals of instruction in the art. A page of directions for the "Rose and Star," surrounded by several completed creations such as a double horn of plenty, slippers, and an archbishop's miter, is shown opposite.

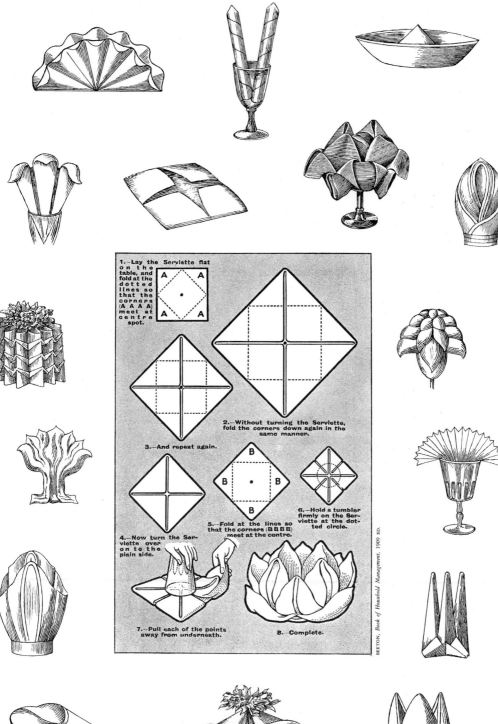

1.—Lay the Serviette flat on the table, and fold at the dotted lines so that the corners (A A A A) meet at centre spot.

2.—Without turning the Serviette, fold the corners down again in the same manner.

3.—And repeat again.

4.—Now turn the Serviette over on to the plain side.

5.—Fold at the lines so that the corners (B B B B) meet at the centre.

6.—Hold a tumbler firmly on the Serviette at the dotted circle.

7.—Pull each of the points away from underneath.

8.—Complete.

BEETON, *Book of Household Management*, 1909 ED.

As the Queen Went, So Went the Nation

Though a few English gourmets of the Victorian era were advocating one dish per course, state banquets continued to offer a wide selection of dishes, each as dull as the next. Among the unexotic choices on the wedding menu above are fried sole, lamb chops, and chicken livers.

The thoroughly bourgeois morals and tastes of grandmotherly Queen Victoria quite naturally were adopted by the hordes of new-rich Englishmen who had no taste at all. Her majesty sponsored the 1851 show at the Crystal Palace, where table implements like the cream ladle and fish fork, below, and furnishings of the same ilk were displayed. A catalog of the Exhibition burbled that such items ideally suited "the taste . . . and domestic refinement of those classes [for whose] use the articles were manufactured." It is not surprising, therefore, that the tables of parvenus all over England were soon writhing with silver and glass. Victorian interest in the appearance of things lapped over into the kitchen, too, producing such follies as the cake opposite, which graced the bridal table of Victoria's grandson George. Wine, however, did not flow freely at the queen's table, and after-dinner port sessions were cut short, for she objected to the bibulous and bawdy. As if to make up for it, she insisted that no one leave the table hungry. Her subjects, noting the royal behavior and waistline, dutifully overate for Crown and country.

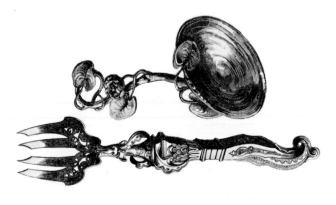

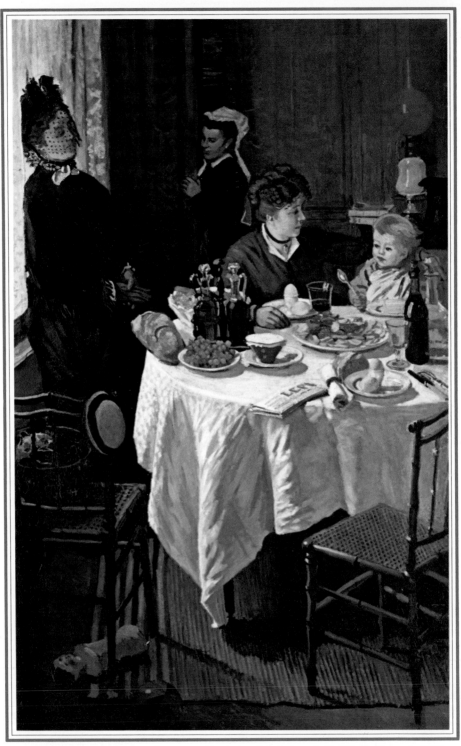

The midday meal, affectionately portrayed by the head of the household, Claude Monet, in 1868

TOWARD
AN
INTERNATIONAL
STYLE

Two men of plebeian origin, born within four years of each other in obscure Alpine villages, rose in the last decades of the nineteenth century to become all but sovereign arbiters of the privileged tables of Europe. The society into which they climbed stood at its zenith of regal splendor. Yet no one sought to bar their ascent. Georges Auguste Escoffier, born in 1846, the son of a blacksmith in Villeneuve-Loubet in Provence, and César Ritz, born in 1850, the thirteenth child of a Swiss peasant couple in Niederwald near the Simplon pass, ruled together like the royalty and millionaires to whom they ministered.

Their arrival on the scene in the 1880's was well timed. The fashionable world was beginning to lose its old ingrown exclusivity and was bursting with new money, with new personalities who found Queen Victoria staid and Emperor Franz Josef stuffy, and with a craving for new pleasures and sensations. To all this the ambitious duet of Escoffier and Ritz was remarkably attuned. Quitting smithy and farm, they had both commenced their careers at a very young age (the thirteen-year-old Escoffier as a scullion in his uncle's restaurant in nearby Nice, the fifteen-year-old Ritz as an apprentice wine steward in a hostelry in neighboring Brig). Both soon gravitated to Paris, Escoffier to become the *saucier* at the smart Restaurant du Petit Moulin, and Ritz to rise from

Auguste Escoffier

assistant waiter to *maître d'hôtel* at a series of restaurants. When at length Ritz invited Escoffier to become chef of the Grand Hotel at Monte Carlo, of which he was then manager, both were men of proven brilliance.

Escoffier, a culinary innovator of the first order, was out to do nothing less than revolutionize the whole scheme of French cookery. Ritz, for his part, was the first great entrepreneur of the fashionable hotel and resort. Over the years he extended his operations from Monte Carlo, Baden-Baden, and San Remo to London's Savoy, Carlton, and Ritz hotels. He operated additional establishments in Frankfort, Biarritz, Rome, Palermo, Madrid, Johannesburg, and

Cairo. Unlike Vatel or Carême, neither Ritz nor Escoffier ever took service in the household of a great lord. They served a select public who came to them. Taste makers of genius, both were inveterate showmen and impresarios, with all the verve of *arrivistes* and a high degree of acquired snobbery.

The era upon which Frenchmen, glowing with memories, were eventually to bestow the name *la belle époque*, was one of constant movement both in the social and geographic senses. Luxurious railroad transportation played an increasing role, enabling leisure classes to pursue more readily the cycle of the seasons, traveling across Europe from resort to resort with their servants and mountains of luggage. The list of fashionable watering places extended from Ostend and Aix-les-Bains to Hamburg and Karlsbad. Russian grand dukes arrived from distant estates in *wagons-lits* to meet with maharajas and South American cattle magnates at the tables of Monte Carlo. The Prince of Wales, the future King Edward VII and for decades Europe's biggest glass of fashion, regularly visited Biarritz, Marienbad, and Baden-Baden, and in doing so made them especially prestigious in international society. (His professed objective, like that of other frequenters of spas, was to take what was called the "cure", to remedy the effects of too much good eating—which, however, did not interfere with his having a five-course luncheon, afternoon tea, and a seven-course dinner, with intermediate "snacks."

In Paris, as the turn of the century approached, the *Grande Saison*, or social high season, commenced ten days after

Easter and ended with the running of the Grand Prix in mid-June, after which the gentry dispersed to the seaside or the mountains. In the fall there were hunting parties at châteaux, followed in December by a *Petite Saison* of formal dinners, opera, theater, and balls in town, ending in late winter, when it was time to sojourn to the French Riviera. In England the high season began early in May, with Ascot Sunday in June, after which came the Henley boat races on the Thames. The season ended in August with the Cowes Regatta of the Royal Yacht Squadron—so brilliant under Edward's reign that the waters of the Solent might be crowded with such tall-masted yachts as the king's *Victoria and Albert* (accompanied by a battleship), Czar Nicholas' *Standart*, Kaiser Wilhelm's *Hohenzollern*, Alfonso of Spain's *Hispania*, and J. P. Morgan's *Corsair*. After banquets afloat and fireworks, lines of festooned gigs brought guests back to shore. The next thing to do was to shoot grouse in Scotland or possibly visit the Swiss lakes and mountains.

In Austria, as soon as the aging Emperor Franz Josef had closed the season's formalities at Schönbrunn palace in Vienna and retreated to his hunting lodge at Bad Ischl, the aristocracy withdrew to livelier playgrounds. (A dinner at Schönbrunn was a quite excruciating affair: several hundred places might be set, with a footman assigned to each guest, but the first person served was of course the emperor, who ate sparingly and with extraordinary rapidity. Etiquette required that the moment he had finished a course, all others suspended any further eating, with the result that many never got so much as a morsel. It was common practice in Vienna, when invited to the imperial table, to fortify one's self with a substantial dinner at Sacher's in advance.)

In England the mobility of the era showed itself in the quite sudden love affair with the grand hotel and restaurant. Until the 1880's there had been no restaurants of respectable standing in London, and none of good table other than the

César Ritz

noisy Café Royal in Regent Street; and this, owned by a Frenchman, was long patronized almost entirely by *émigrés* and visitors from the Continent. A few places such as Romano's in the Strand catered to journalists, women of "the lighter stage," and bohemian types. Kettners' nearby had numerous private dining rooms whose uses—like those in the old taverns—were notorious. But restaurants and hotels were not for the English gentry when on home ground, so it was thought. Gentlemen would not emerge from their clubs, nor ladies from their town houses, to be seen dining in public.

Yet in the 1880's Richard D'Oyly Carte, the London theatrical promoter who had enriched himself by producing Gilbert

339

A Gourmet's Guide

*T*he first automobile drivers were genuine adventurers, wandering where their cars would take them, daring breakdown and washout, innless nights and restaurantless days. Gradually, automobiling became a tamer sport, and in 1900 André Michelin, a French tire manufacturer, seized the opportunity to pump up good will for his product by publishing a directory of lodgings, gas stations, and repair shops throughout France. Today's annual *Guide Michelin*, some thousand pages bristling with a formidable array of symbols, blocks of text, and maps, has exactly the same goal as the first one—to provide any practical information that might contribute to the success of a trip. To restaurateurs and many of the guide's readers, the book has come to represent something else. It is the supreme judge of the quality of food served in French restaurants, and many people who purchase it are interested only in its culinary pronouncements. At present Michelin has eleven inspectors who are bona fide gourmets and connoisseurs of fine wines. The man from Michelin arrives unannounced and eats thoughtfully, comparing what he finds with last year's rating (although to avoid identification no one man appears in the same place more than once every eight years). He makes mental notes about the setting and decor, the men's room and the table linen, and is especially critical about the service. He then presents himself to the horror-stricken owner (who is often the chef too) and asks to be shown around the kitchen. The guide has

some hundred thousand correspondents a year, classified by Michelin's editors as *sympathique*, *hépathique* (jaundiced), or *fléchi* (thoughtful); if there are many complaints about the restaurant on trial, the inspector discusses them and perhaps makes suggestions for improvements, but never until the guide comes out will the anxious *propriétaire* learn what his new rating is. One qualification for an inspector is an iron stomach, for whatever his personal inclinations, professionally he must seek out and try dining rooms with meals for under $2 as often as he inspects the very expensive ones. Small owners therefore get the benefit of expert advice, too, and consequently so do drivers of *deux cheveaux*. Restaurants are rated as to the level of luxury; more important to gourmets are the stars (like those worn above by the bulbous tiremen used to illustrate the book) rating culinary excellence. No place can win more than three stars, and only twelve kitchens in France can now claim that distinction.

and Sullivan operettas at the Savoy Theatre, conceived the daring idea of building a luxury hotel next door as a haven for his patrons. While in the process of planning his new project and taking a "cure" in Baden-Baden, he was struck by the magnetism of César Ritz, presiding there at his own restaurant and hotel together with Escoffier. If these men could command the praise of the English aristocracy abroad, D'Oyly Carte would engage them in London. His Savoy became the first hotel in Europe to offer modern comforts; it boasted seventy bathrooms (the Savoy's closest rival had four bathrooms for five hundred guests) and a restaurant on a really *grand luxe* style. A new day of London fashion had begun.

Ritz, a perfectionist even in his personal attire, would answer the private bell that warned of the arrival of royalty by placing a fresh white carnation in the buttonhole of his frock coat or evening tails on the way to the lobby. He was the master of protocol, of seating, of housekeeping, of every detail. Did Grand Duke Sergei prefer his turbot prepared in a certain way? It would be done. Did Lady so-and-so fancy a particular size of bed? It would be provided. Lighting was staged in tints to set off ladies' complexions and jewels to best advantage. Dinner music, another Ritz innovation, had to be of the best— on occasion, Johann Strauss the younger was engaged to lead his own Viennese orchestra—and evening dress, if one expected to be seated in the great dining salon rather than in the accompanying grillroom, was *de rigueur*.

The bold scheme worked. Soon such fashionable hostesses as the Duchess of Manchester, Lady Randolph Churchill (mother of Sir Winston), Lady Dudley, and the American heiress and Duchess of Marlborough, Consuelo Vanderbilt, were giving style-setting dinner parties at Ritz' Savoy. Backstage, Escoffier displayed wit and genius sometimes compounded with mischief. On one occasion he served the middle-aged, sybaritic Prince of Wales a creation mysteriously and invitingly called *Cuisses de Nymphes à l'Aurore*, "Nymphs' Thighs at Dawn." The future Edward VII savored it and then learned that what he was eating for the first time was frogs' legs. On another occasion, Escoffier was coaxed from his kitchens at the Savoy to the galleys of the recently launched Hamburg-America luxury liner the *Imperator*, where he produced for Kaiser Wilhelm II a phenomenal creation of salmon steamed in champagne. "How can I repay you?" asked the emperor, summoning the chef into his presence. "By giving us back Alsace-Lorraine" was Escoffier's reply.

Escoffier's basic scheme, with which he liked to regale those not simply bent on stuffing themselves, was to construct a dinner somewhat like a symphony of contrasting movements yet with a related theme. Soups, he said, should perform like "an overture in a light opera [divulging] what is to be the dominant phrase of the melody throughout." Each diner, like the listener at a concert, was to experience the same progression. Escoffier was the first to take seriously the precept pronounced by Brillat-Savarin, namely that "The order of food in a dinner is from the more substantial to the lighter." He popularized the new style of service, *à la russe*, rebelling against the tradition in which all the entrees were put on the table at once. In place of vast centerpieces of game, of forty or more simultaneous entrees and entremets, he introduced rhythm, if not restraint.

A dinner prepared by Edward's own chef at Buckingham Palace in 1902 showed the Escoffier influence, though it lacked the refinements of the master. A rather heavy sequence of hot and cold consommés was followed by fillets of trout or whitebait, quail and chicken, then mutton and ham garnished with vegetables, followed by ortolans and salad, succeeded by asparagus vinaigrette, and a dessert course including *"gâteau Punch,"* a sweet soufflé, pastries, and, inexplicably, canapés of anchovies. A progression of Escoffier's own making tended to be more subtle. Thus, the menu he offered at Ritz' Carlton Hotel to celebrate the coronation of George V in 1911 deserves to be given in full:

Caviar
Cantaloupe

Clear Turtle Soup
Cold Velouté of Chicken Soup

Roast Chicken George V

Saddle of Welsh Lamb
Peas à l'Anglaise

Duckling Breasts in Port Wine Aspic

Quail with Grapes

Salade Orientale
Hearts of Artichokes Grand Duc

Peaches Queen Mary
Petits Fours
Fruits

Such a dinner, with its graceful overtures and its *pièce de résistance*, the quail, rep-

resented the climax of the most polished Escoffier cuisine. Glancing over the menu today, a diner might wonder whether after the soups, the chicken, and the lamb, he might really wish to go on to a round of jellied duck and quail with grapes. But there was always respite in a change of wines—Escoffier and Ritz did their best to promote dry clarets, Burgundies, and champagnes, while discouraging that old mid-prandial palliative, sherbet.

The upper-class English, encouraged by men like Ritz and Escoffier, were rapidly becoming leading consumers of fine French wines. Another dinner served at Buckingham Palace early in Edward's reign was accompanied by an old Madeira of 1816 with the soup, a Johannisberger of 1886 as the "hock" to go with the fish, magnums of 1884 Möet et Chandon champagne with the fowl, a Chambertin of the great year 1875 with the venison, a Château Latour of the same year with asparagus with mousseline sauce, and, for good measure, a Château Margaux of 1871 in addition to the usual after-dinner port, sherry, and heirloom brandy.

None was a finer judge of wines than George Saintsbury, the renowned scholar of English literature at Edinburgh, who amid his major literary treatises wrote *Notes on a Cellar-Book*, describing his delight in "laying-down" on a scholar's pay racks of the great clarets of 1858, "not very plentiful, and getting a trifle old," of 1864, "in perfection, but very dear," and of 1874 and 1875, "drinkable at forty years old [but] always what wineslang calls 'dumb.'" (The ruinous Phylloxera disease blighted French growths for several decades following.) Saintsbury was against the emerging vogue of the pre-dinner cocktail, and of whisky and soda, although he liked a tot straight on occasion. He was to grow ripe in years, dying at eighty-eight, leaving the jot-

Short-order staff, Paris, c. 1870

tings of his *Notes* as a classic of English response to French attraction.

While Continental cookery, hotelkeeping, and fine wines invaded England, English styles and manners captivated the *gratin*, or upper crust, of France. Paris *boulevardiers'* clothes were patterned on those of Savile Row, garden parties and five o'clock tea were introduced in the Faubourg St-Germain, and the English country house party was copied in ancient châteaux. Parisian sporting fellows aspired to membership among *les clubmen*—banded together at such English-style clubs as the Jockey or Royale.

Yet Parisian life retained its own particular flavor, though this too was fast changing. The *belle époque* saw the *grande cocotte* graduate from a playgirl or a *chanteuse* performing at the Folies-Bergère or the Bal Tabarin to a dashing

beauty kept by princes, magnates, or foreign potentates. Flashing with diamonds and trailing ermine or chinchilla, she often swept into Maxim's on the Rue Royale for late supper. The most gorgeous and desirable of these creatures —*les grandes horizontales*—took on spurious, aristocratic names as they rose to fame, such as Liane de Pougy, Emilienne d'Alençon, Cléo de Mérode, and Clémence de Pibrac, though this fooled nobody. Wealthy Russian nobles were particular habitués at the supper tables of Maxim's. There they could find a favorite to make the all-night "Tour of the Grand Dukes," or round of cabarets. Spectacular parties were frequent; at one the Grand Duke Sergei of Russia presented the *horizontale* Augustine de Lierre with a twenty-million-franc pearl necklace served on a bed of oysters. One bold entertainer of men who declined to adapt her name to fit Europe's social register was the devastating Catalonian gypsy known as *"la belle Otéro,"* adept at jumping on the tables of Maxim's to perform a wild fandango. Otéro, who made millions only to lose them all at the gambling tables, reached such notoriety that when she was found seated at the Comédie Francaise on an evening also honored by the Russian czar's presence, she was smartly ejected, shouting to the royal box as she left the theater, "I'll never eat caviar again!"

Maxim's was the liveliest dining place in France and perhaps the world, and one never took his wife there. Hugo, the *maître d'hôtel*, kept a discreet notebook for leading guests. It contained the names of the chief *horizontales* known to the establishment, and some notations

343

in code as to their current availability. One was "R.A.F.," meaning *rien à faire,* in other words, "occupied." Another rating was "Y.M.C.A.," which, far from implying any connection with a young men's Christian association, signified *Y a moyen de coucher avec*—or "highly cooperative."

Paris society was divided into numerous circles, the old, the newly rich, the decadent, the international, the anti-Dreyfus, and pro-Dreyfus. (In many houses that sought to keep dinner-table peace at the height of the furor, a sign was posted like a centerpiece, *"Ici on ne parle pas de l'Affaire."*) No hostess was more imperious than Madame Aubernon, who at her twice-weekly intellectual evenings jingled a large silver bell to gain the company's full attention. No host was more eccentric than the perfumed Comte Robert de Montesquiou (a model for the Baron Charlus of Marcel Proust's novel). On one occasion he gave a soirée in a darkened room suffused with exotic essences. All eyes were focused on a live turtle, its shell encrusted with diamonds, sapphires, and amethysts, that crawled among the diners. For another evening he sent out engraved cards inviting his elite friends to the christening of his cat.

But even Montesquiou was no match for the flamboyant Comte Boni de Castellane. By marrying Anna Gould, the very plain daughter of the American millionaire Jay Gould, Comte Boni gained a dowry of fifteen million dollars. He ran through her money fast, building his fantastic Palais Rose in Paris on royal, seventeenth century proportions, and at his château keeping six hundred servants in

livery to match the changing decor. For Anna's twenty-first birthday he staged a fete that among other embellishments called for 80,000 Venetian lanterns, an orchestra of 200 musicians, the complete *corps de ballet* of the Opéra, 15 kilometers

Detail from a menu sketched by Renoir

of red velvet carpeting, and 600 torches carried by lackeys in scarlet livery.

It was a great epoch for all those with bank accounts. The *demi-monde* had long been following the *haut monde* from resort to resort, often with the result of raised lorgnettes on the part of dowager duchesses. But by now all circles, from the aristocrats to the *horizontales,* were beginning to mix. In the daily morning drive in the Bois de Boulogne, the Barons Rothschild, the Aga Khan, Prince Galitzine, and Leopold II of Belgium might be found taking the air almost in tandem with the writers Edmond Rostand and Colette, and with Liane de Pougy, Cléo de Mérode, and *"la belle Otéro."* At Ritz' loftiest international establishment, the hotel that bears his name at 15 Place Vendôme, the guests regularly included, along with an array of lords and ladies, the highest-priced courtesans of the town.

Ritz and Escoffier had taken leave of the Savoy, after a falling-out with its directors, when in 1905 the Wall Street financier George Kessler staged there his startling "gondola dinner." At a cost of £4,000, the equivalent of $20,000, he had the Savoy's courtyard flooded, and the walls decorated with depictions of St. Mark's, the Doges' Palace, and other well-known Venetian landmarks; he hired Enrico Caruso to serenade his two dozen guests who were afloat in a gondola under huge representations of the Lions of St. Mark's in ice. Nor did Ritz and Escoffier have anything to do with another affair given at the Savoy before the curtain of 1914 fell, a "blowout" at which a man who had broken the bank at Monte Carlo in a series of plays on red at the roulette table ordered a massive feast, all in red. The very lights and hangings of the restaurant were changed to red, the waiters were all costumed in red, down to their gloves; and the thirty-six guests were served only red dishes, including lobster, rare beef, wild duck in Bordeaux, red cabbage, beet salad, a mousse of strawberries, red wines, and so forth, on a red and black tablecloth that was designed as a huge roulette board. Ritz and Escoffier would have thought this was going rather far.

Such was one side of life on the eve of World War I. At the other extreme was the life of the everyday workingman, who in Britain, the most industrialized and prosperous of the European nations, was reported in 1913 as earning an average wage of only about twenty shillings (somewhat below five dollars) a week. "How does a working man's wife bring up a family on 20s. a week?" asked the author of an angry tract; "Assuming that there are four children, and that it costs 4s. a week to feed a child, there would be but 4s. left on which to feed both parents. . . ." Many families subsisted almost entirely on bread and tea,

and one study of the situation in York found that infant mortality in the poorest class was running to 247 per thousand. As James Laver writes in his *Manners and Morals in The Age of Optimism, 1848–1914*, "Perhaps the most shocking thing . . . was the complacency with which this state of affairs was accepted. When some poor old woman died of starvation in an East End attic the verdict of the coroner was 'self-neglect.'"

Still, the position of the working class was not entirely bleak. A 1904 official study found that on an average weekly family income of thirty-six shillings there was an outlay of twenty-two shillings for food, the biggest item by far being meat, followed by vegetables and fruit, cheese, bread and flour, butter, and fresh milk— a great change for the better in terms of

Advertisement for a bourgeois cookbook, c. 1850

proteins over the predominantly carbohydrate diet of Corn Law times. This improvement, gradual as it was, reflected a subtly changing economic balance.

The overriding factor was the "population explosion"—herald of the explosions to come in Asia—which between 1800 and 1900 doubled the number of Europe's inhabitants. Emigration, chiefly to the Americas, under stress of hunger, politics, and economic aspiration, drew off a part of this, but the Old World was confronted with a huge increase in mouths to feed. Fortunately, this burst of population was matched by a vast increase in industry and in food production. As cities became factories, so agricultural producers found new and larger markets for their foodstuffs. Farm machinery raised crop yields on both continents (the Americans McCormick and Hussey had first shown their grain reapers abroad at the London Great Exhibition of 1851). New chemical fertilizers succeeded the

Soup-to-nuts service by the ideal waiter

less productive organic fertilizers. Plant and animal breeding had become a science. European migrants were opening up vast new areas of land in the Americas, South Africa, Australia, and New Zealand to farming and livestock.

Long-distance rail and sea transport helped to revolutionize Western man's daily diet, especially when coupled with a new technology of food preservation. The ancients knew that cooling a food served to postpone decay, and the ever-curious Francis Bacon, ruminating on this point, had experimented with freez-

ing early in the seventeenth century. And, around 1795, the Frenchman François Appert had limited success "canning" foods, subjecting them to very high temperatures and storing them in sterilized glass jars for as long as three months. Yet, as we have seen, common preservation methods were long confined to sun-drying, smoking, salting, pickling, preserving in sugar, and fermenting, with all the loss or distortion of flavor and food values these processes entailed. Beginning in the mid-nineteenth century, however, a great breakthrough occurred. Men as various as the experimental dairyman Gail Borden of Litchfield, Connecticut, the meatpackers Gustavus Swift and Philip Armour of Chicago, the German food processer Baron Justus von Leibig, and the great French bacteriologist Louis Pasteur figured in it. The problem of getting fresh milk to growing urban markets before it spoiled had long defeated dairymen. By 1865, though, some refrigerated milk was reaching London by train, and experiments were under way in France to build ammonia-cooling plants. Nine years before, Borden had obtained a United States patent for a "fresh country milk from which the water is nearly all evaporated and nothing added"—a condensation of milk that was pure, economical, and readily transported. (Pasteur was then conducting studies on the sterilization of milk.)

Meanwhile in the 1860's, the meatpacking industry was established in Chicago, where fattened Western cattle met several Eastern railheads. With the development of freezer freight cars in the next decade, the industry was able to supply Europe with beef from the Western plains and pork products from the Iowa corn country. In 1877 the first frozen mutton was successfully shipped from Buenos Aires to Le Havre. Due to a collision, the voyage took six months, but the meat arrived in good condition. Meat from Australia and New Zealand began reaching England soon thereafter. As one of the major shippers there remarked, "Where the food is the people are not, and where the people are the food is not. It is however . . . within the power of man to adjust these things." A *Daily Telegraph* reporter marveled in 1880 that the

Automated dining for the weary

imports could not "by any peculiarity . . . be distinguished from freshly killed English meat."

In 1863 Baron Haussmann, as part of his grand plan for transforming Paris into a metropolis able to serve the increasing population, had designed the central, hygienic slaughterhouse of La Villette. Pasteur, by developing a method of inoculating sheep and hogs against the dread disease anthrax, vastly improved the practice of animal husbandry as well as public health. Inoculation of cattle, scientific dressing and process-

ing, factory canning of a growing list of products, pasteurizing of milk—all these processes changed the whole configuration of supply from the old days of small, filthy market stalls and dependence on the latest wagon or boatload of what the nearest fields or fisheries had to offer. Underdeveloped nations of Latin America, the Middle East, Africa, and the Orient did not—and in large measure still do not—participate in these advances, a fact which made their own population explosions the more critical.

Along with new methods of food production, handling, and distribution in the West, there also came into being the gradual mechanization of the household. This, too, had its profound effects on food customs, and ultimately on the structure of social life. Until about 1830, cooking throughout Europe had depended on the age-old open hearth and the wood-fired oven—cumbersome installations demanding an immense amount of arduous labor. All was well so long as labor was accessible and cheap. Then came the "red-hot monster," as Dickens called it, the iron range, with its more compact and efficient utilization of wood or coal fuel. An even greater labor-saver, a crude version of the gas range, had been patented at the beginning of the nineteenth century, and an improved model was shown at the Great Exhibition of 1851, but except in hotels, it did not come into use until the 1880's when coal gas became widely available. In place of laying fires and cleaning out clinkers, all one had to do then was turn a handle. The next step was the electric range, first shown in London in 1891. Domestic refrigera-

Miss Toklas and Company

*T*he late Alice B. Toklas may not have been the finest chef ever to wield a spatula, but she certainly fed the most interesting collection of diners of her day. As cohostess of Gertrude Stein's Paris salon in the first decades of the 1900's, Miss Toklas met almost every great and potentially great artist and writer of the modern movement. Dancers, critics, royalty, and Iowans also appeared at the door on Rue de Fleurus, hoping to be invited to one of the celebrated dinners. Between callers, she gathered notes for *The Alice B. Toklas Cook Book*, which became as much a collection of anecdotes and musings about her famous friends as of recipes; it was written in a witty and crisp style that makes it far more widely read today than the brilliant, arcane works of Miss Stein. Miss Toklas' recipes were often as eccentric as her appearance—the sketch below by Roger Baker captures the peculiar integrity of his friend. A recipe for hashish fudge suggests just how wicked the maiden lady could be. Except for telling the reader where to buy the forbidden ingredient, her directions for making fudge are as precise as anyone could wish, but there are other recipes as impressionistic as *Bass for Picasso*. "Before coming to Paris I was interested in food but not in doing any cooking. When in 1908 I went to

live with Gertrude Stein . . . she said we would have American food for Sunday evening supper . . . the servant would be out and I should have the kitchen to myself. So I commenced to cook the simple dishes [of] California. . . . My repertoire . . . expanded as I grew experimental and adventurous. One day when Picasso was to lunch with us I decorated a fish in a way that I thought would amuse him. I chose a fine striped bass and cooked it according to a theory of my grandmother who had no experience in cooking. . . . She contended that a fish

. . . once caught, should have no further contact with the element in which it had been born and raised. She recommended that it be roasted or poached in wine or cream or butter. . . . I covered the fish with an ordinary mayonnaise and, using a pastry tube, decorated it with a red mayonnaise, not colored with catsup—horror of horrors—but with tomato paste. Then I made a design with sieved hard-boiled eggs, the whites and the yolks apart, with truffles and finely chopped *fines herbes*. . . . when it was served Picasso exclaimed at its beauty. But, said he, should it not rather have been in honour of Matisse than of me."

tion, another boon, had appeared in the 1860's, as had first attempts at a mechanical dishwasher—an indication that there was already a "servant problem."

At the country house of Longleat, seat of the Marquesses of Bath, the normal complement of indoor staff at the turn of the century ran to forty-three, from house steward and housekeeper down to lamp boy. At Chatsworth, the 273-room palace of the Dukes of Devonshire, the entire house staff ran to a hundred or more shortly after World War I. The wage of a good butler or cook in London in those years appears to have averaged £50 annually—in addition to which there was, of course, room, board, and such "fringe benefits" as guests' tips, kickbacks from suppliers, accepted access to the ale and wine in the master's cellar. All this soon changed. New York's lofty Mrs. Hamilton McK. Twombly, daughter of William H. Vanderbilt and granddaughter of Cornelius, the former ferryboat owner who had become a railroad magnate, was one of those to upset the pattern when in 1917 she hired the Escoffier-trained Joseph Donon to be chef of her mansions at a salary rumored at $25,000. By the 1920's a highly trained cook or butler in a well-to-do private house on either side of the Atlantic could command a salary many times that paid before 1914—too much, it soon appeared, for all but the most prosperous. The between-wars generation needed and wanted to rid itself of the tyranny of the servant. The triumphant end result in America was the technocratic, all but servantless house, its kitchen processes simplified by blenders, mixers, pressure cookers, and auto-matic cooking controls, its staple foods duly packaged, branded, and often premixed or precooked by great corporations with their own dietitians and recipe writers, and the family's food reserve from the supermarket laid down safe and sound for months to come in the arctic recesses of the freezer.

The proprietor and chef of one of the most prestigious restaurants of recent decades, Alexandre Dumaine of the Hôtel de la Côte-d'Or in Saulieu, France, remarked to a visiting American gastronome one day that "Frozen food is dead food," and took his guest along to watch him carefully test and buy only the freshest and finest of produce in the local market to prepare for that day's luncheon. Another great French *cuisinier*, the late Fernand Point, worked in the same fashion, searching for perfection from stall to stall and from one *vignoble* to the next for his restaurant, La Pyramide, in Vienne, where an air of intimacy quite removed from the flamboyance of Ritz and Escoffier prevailed. These men were the ultimate refiners. Nothing, according to the skilled taster Joseph Wechsberg, was ever quite so perfect as Point's gratin of crayfish tails. One leaves La Pyramide's great chef with a poignant picture of him gathering of a morning some thirty bunches of tiny watercress from the riverbank for a purée to delight his few guests.

It is easy—perhaps all too easy—to wish the revival of traditional individualized cuisine such as that found today only in the finest European restaurants. It is easy to mock the modern condition, with its bland efficiency, its producers' promises of "uniform quality guaranteed," and its ultimate offense, the pre-cooked "dinner" consumed by millions from tin containers, without so much as the small pride of one's own bowl or platter, while gazing raptly at the latest Western. Yet such abasement of cookery has been accompanied also in our time by its internationalization, and in a larger sense, by its democratization.

The American housewife, long supplied with good advice, but only recently with a more sophisticated audience for her ministerings, has risen to the occasion by adding all manner of highly specialized, semiprofessional equipment: French omelette pans, Dutch cutlery, Italian pasta presses, Chinese *woks*, Spanish paella pans. Abroad, such American "specialties" as tunafish salad, hot dogs, hamburgers, milk shakes, steak, and corn on the cob had migrated with the G.I.'s and the tourists. Canning and refrigeration had also aided the commingling of Western and Eastern influences. Caspian Sea sturgeon, Malossol caviar, Bering Sea crabmeat, and Aus-

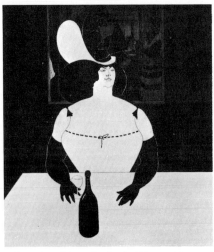

Aubrey Beardsley's sketch of "The Fat Woman"

tralian kangaroo tails could readily reach Kansas City, just as North and South American beef could be moved, for instance, to Istanbul. Scotch grouse, once air freight was established, were to be found among purveyors and restaurateurs in New York only a day or two after the Highland hunting season had opened, just as Hudson River shad roe became available at Paris and London branches of Prunier's soon after the first March nets were cast off Tarrytown. A few hours' flight could bring the fresh-caught makings of a bouillabaisse from Marseilles to Le Pavillon.

Once fully launched, the process of global interaction of tastes was not to be stopped. Results were sometimes astonishing. In Moscow it became a fad in some official circles to abandon the traditional drinking of vodka straight and to adopt the capitalistic habit of the cocktail—mixed, often, in an electric blender, an innovation which was itself a Western import. One such Muscovite cocktail, named *vostorg* ("delight"), consists of a frappé of cognac, cherry liqueur, lemon juice, cherries, and ice. At the same time, the West was taking to vodka with such enthusiasm as to drive traditional producers of gin and whiskeys to near panic.

Westward in the Philippines, whose indigenous culture had been dominated by Spaniards for 350 years, then "liberated" by the Americans at the turn of the century, then overrun again by Japanese and truly liberated by the Americans after World War II, West and Orient met in extraordinary disarray. Though the archipelago had originally attracted Europeans for its spices and native fruits, a dinner given in the early 1960's at the presidential palace in Manila in honor of the returning General MacArthur began with canned American fruit salad. A correspondent writing for the *Saturday Review* spoke of Manila as looking "like a sprawling, unwieldy city in the United States. Its traffic-clogged avenues are blighted by billboards proclaiming American merchandise in high-pitched Madison Avenue jargon; sleazy drive-ins offer 'colossal' hot dogs, hamburgers, and other gastronomic imitations."

Postwar Japan served a breakfast of bacon and eggs, along with the traditional morning fare of seaweed wafers, rice, and bean soup. A branch of Maxim's opened in a basement under Tokyo's Ginza complete with Toulouse-Lautrec posters and copies of French china and silverware; young Japanese preferred to drink Scotch rather than *sake* and eat *hottu doggu* rather than the traditional sliver of raw fish called *sashimi*. Hamburgers, steak, *crème caramel*, and ice cream were served on Japanese dining cars, themselves somewhat of an innovation since Japanese travelers had traditionally taken their own food aboard. France's national institution, the café, fell into catastrophic decline, with some thirty thousand of these establishments closing their doors in the last decade, from the famed Select and La Rotonde in Paris to innumerable zinc counters in the back streets of Lyons and Marseilles. Such voguish establishments as "Le Drugstore," with its American sodas and high-speed sandwiches, overtook some. The increasing home comforts provided by television, refrigeration, and central heating overtook others. The

prolonged two-hour lunch favored by the business and professional classes, often followed by a brief snooze before returning to work, gave way to a quick platter at the "snack bar." (Indeed, under President de Gaulle inducements were offered officials who would cut

Pristine waiters before the dinner hour

down on their luncheon time.) In the Marne valley, which for so long held sacred the slow and painstaking production of some of the West's finest cheeses, a factory opened that according to *The New York Times* "turns out cheese in a fast, continuous strip, like a steel mill." Machines were devised in Brittany to produce crepes on an assembly line; another in Besançon to fabricate the long, slim French loaf in an endless ribbon, chopped off in short lengths for the consumer. America created the supermarket, but Paris went a step further and computerized it. The *Super-Marché de Poche*, set up in 1967, was the first successful completely mechanized food establishment, in which one could see but not touch packaged samples of the food sold (Frenchmen have

351

always had a weakness for probing every-thing on the market stalls); the cus-tomer, gathering a punch card for each selection, turned them in to a clerk who transmitted the order to a computer for toting up the bill; thereupon, the order was transmitted to the stockroom where duplicates of the merchandise on dis-play were bagged for taking home.

The elite string of hotels, like those Ritz had commanded, have been over-taken by Hilton, whose International division as of 1968 operated 47 hotels in 32 countries. Built by Conrad Hilton, who got his start as the operator of small-town hotels in Texas, the chain provides cornflakes and U.S. Prime steer beef to guests around the globe. To order a breakfast of waffles and deerfoot sausages at the Istanbul Hilton as pre-pared by a Turkish cook who has never laid eyes on such strange fare before, can lead to surprises. And in London the high-rise Hilton monolith that now dominates Hyde Park, far from insisting on American foods, features—of all things—a Polynesian dining room.

Who influences whom when it comes to dining? A distinguished French chef of our day, René Verdon, White House chef under President and Mrs. Kennedy, abruptly resigned his position when under the Johnsons a "kitchen econo-mizer" was hired and Verdon was or-dered to use frozen vegetables. Yet an-other leading French chef in America, Pierre Franey, trained at Drouant's in Paris and celebrated as chef of New York's distinguished Le Pavillon res-taurant for two decades, resigned his position in 1960 to become *chef de cuisine* of the Howard Johnson chain of some 785 roadside eateries, along with 18 Red Coach Grills, and their retail packaged foods division. He has since developed "quick-frozen gourmet foods" such as beef Bourguignon, whose recipe for 13,000 servings calls for $2\frac{1}{2}$ tons of cubed beef, 600 pounds of mushrooms, 700 pounds of onions, 60 gallons of Burgundy, and 465 gallons of sauce. Franey foresees a time when Howard Johnson's will even serve caviar.

Great Britain has also invaded Ger-many—in a fashion hard to believe. In 1967, as if striking at the heart of the greatest beer-producing country in Eu-rope, the Watney-Mann brewery of Lon-don opened the Victoria, an "authentic" British pub in Düsseldorf, and the Sir Winston Churchill in Paris. There are even plans afoot to establish pubs in Florence and Madrid.

Yet all this lively interchange might also be transitory. Who can tell? Despite all the advantages of nature, science, and imagination available to man, there has been present at the tables of the world a haunting knowledge of hunger and in-sufficiency. Fully half of mankind, it was established by United Nations experts in 1966, was inadequately fed. In another fifteen years, they predicted, there will be an additional fifteen billion mouths to feed. "Half the world's children of preschool age," as Drew Middleton summed up in *The New York Times*, "are so undernourished that their physical and mental growth is retarded and mor-tality among these children in the under-developed countries is 60 times as great as in more advanced societies."

Those who enjoy a good table cannot quite escape the thought of this.

THE
BANQUET
YEARS

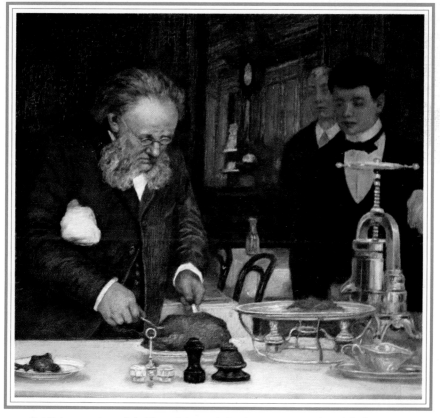

Frédéric, proprietor of the Tour d'Argent in Paris, preparing its famed duck, c. 1890

Absinthe-minded

Harper's Magazine, APRIL, 1889

Toward the *fin de siècle*, music halls like the Folies-Bergère were the most egalitarian of Parisian institutions, catering to those with "overworked digestions and underworked intelligences . . . foreigners, shop assistants on the spree, and little ladies on the make." Undiscriminating audiences relished the nightly fare of sentimental ballads, dirty jokes, and risqué dances. The barmaid, however, in Edouard Manet's painting of the nightspot opposite, has long been inured to the performances on stage as well as off, and waits impassively as a customer chooses a bottle. People in search of more solitary dissipations could drink absinthe at a local café such as the one above. Introduced to France about 1850 by soldiers returning from Algeria, the wormwood flavored liqueur quickly became a favorite of the decadents. Absinthe reputedly doubled the potency of anything taken afterward; overindulgence could cause blindness, delirium, madness. It was outlawed in 1915.

355

To get their jobs les forts *carried 440 pounds on their heads. Their uniform was the broad-brimmed hat which kept the blood of fresh-killed carcasses from dribbling down the neck. Their trade was moving the markets' produce from farmers' carts to stalls like that in the 1898 photo at left, then back onto wagons for delivery to retailers like the butcher opposite, who poses with his family, his employees, and a canopy of well-dressed meats.*

356

"The Belly of Paris"

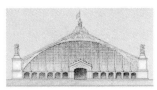 Les Halles, condemned now to make way for sky-scrapers, stands on a site which since the twelfth century has been the central market place for all France. The present markets, ten giant iron and glass sheds, were begun under Napoleon III, following the sort of aesthetic-cum-political brouhaha of which only Parisians are capable and after such far more revolutionary designs as that in the inset above were rejected. Les Halles was, in fact, only one of dozens of wholesale food markets designed during the nineteenth century to accommodate the needs of Europe's burgeoning cities, but it has always had a special charm. Add to its architectural interest the bustle of merchants and roustabouts, the ambrosial smells of flowers, fruits, and fish, the brilliant colors of bloody meats and fresh vegetables, and most particularly the onion soup served at neighboring cafés, and one has a last glimpse of Paris' famed late-night-to-dawn tourist spectacular.

357

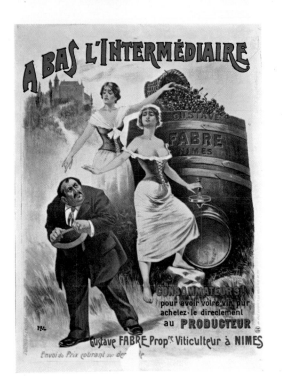

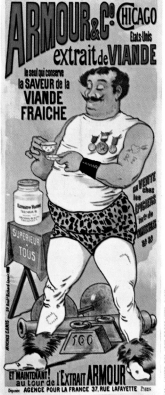

By the late 1800's the tea package had given birth to mass marketing complete with brand names and chain stores. It was time for advertising, and as these posters demonstrate there was no lack of talent to produce it. On the facing page, at upper left, two maidens promote sales for a local vintner. Haughty despite their dishabille, they shout, "Down with the middleman." To the right is an ad for the "only working baby bottle with its own guarantee." At bottom, Fouquet and Company, today a thriving restaurant and delicatessen, promises firstrate merchandise, which it still delivers. On this page, clockwise from left, a swaying housemaid, a nattily dressed chorus, and a strong man push two flavors of tapioca, chicory coffee, and the only broth "conserving the flavor of fresh meat."

359

Finishing touches are added in the dessert room.

Bushels of oysters are shucked in the ice room.

In the cold pantry butter and aspics are molded.

All That Glitters

Napoleon III's new imperium had to sparkle—the nation that called it into being expected no less. The head of state willingly obliged by spending lavishly on travel, clothes, and entertainments. To be sure, all that glittered was not gold; that had been stolen during the uprising of 1848. But the new electroplated table-ware would hardly be noticed by the guests above, gathered in the Galerie de Diane of the Tuileries for a ball in 1869. Led by Napoleon and Eugenie, they take their customary tour of the tables before dining. Meanwhile, the food, brought up by dumb-waiter from the elaborate kitchens, left, turns lukewarm *à la française*.

A la Carte

Dufy's water color celebrating the liberation of Paris, 1944

Renoir's juggling chef, 1878

Gauguin's colonial satire, c. 1900

Toulouse-Lautrec's modiste, *1893*

Before the nineteenth century, diners had to find their way through dinner without a written menu. It took the Parisian restaurateur to introduce the *carte* to polite society. Since it was to be decoration as well as guide, noted artists were often called on to execute the illustrations, sometimes for money, sometimes in exchange for supper. Renoir prepared menus for his favorite patrons. Toulouse-Lautrec, himself a gourmet, sketched menus for meals to which he was invited. Even Gauguin in his Tahitian retreat gave banquets complete with anticolonial menus. Production of such ephemera in our own century has been rare, but a day of national joy could still inspire the remarkable display of artistic-gastronomic enthusiasm opposite.

Disgorging the sediment　　　*Inserting the cork*　　　*Fastening the cork with string*

Bottling the Bubbles

The crew poses with the top-hatted owner and two "nurses," workmen entrusted with turning the bottles.

The inhabitants of Champagne had known for a long time that the wine of their region underwent a second fermentation in the spring which transformed it into a sparkling delicacy, but they had to wait until the late 1600's when Dom Pérignon made a cork that withstood the pressure built up by gases in the bottle. Further experiments taught local vintners to blend the products of different vineyards and to add a little sugar before the spring fermentation to encourage the bubbles. Ever since Champagne presented its gift to a grateful world, the pop of the cork has signaled a celebration. These engravings of workers in Pierry accompanied the musings of one ardent admirer in an 1855 issue of the *Illustrated London News*. "A *souchet* of flounders—a *compote* of pigeon—and a salad of strawberries. Well, one may struggle with such a repast. . . . This is Ida's birthday, and she must be toasted as becomes the lady of my heart . . . the only draught worthy of such an honor—a bottle of champagne iced to a degree. This bumper I drink in silence. How grateful—how delicious! Remove those grosser matters, and leave me alone with this sublimated liquor—created for love's libations. What other draught born of the grape goes direct to the heart like this and in a moment makes the pulse beat quicker? What pleasant memories are associated with this reaming glass, remembering as we do the silent tongues it has made eloquent, and the anxious hours it has converted into mirthfulness. Who has not led some bashful maiden down to supper and thought the task a bore until a glass—perhaps two—of this elixir has converted her into the sweetest prattler that was ever listened to? Or who has not seen some scornful lady that has slighted the heart devoted to her through a whole program of quadrilles and polkas, smile at last when humanized by a *tazza* of champagne?"

Securing the wire cap

Putting on the tinfoil

Wrapping the bottle in paper

Fête Champêtre

"The world was a ripe peach and we were eating it," wrote Sir Osbert Sitwell about the "smart set" reigning during the 1920's. The "ripe peach" would rot in their hands in the next decade, but in the years between the war and the depression, the beautiful people moved in a surrealistic whirl of gaiety and brilliant conversation, exotic costume and exquisite food. To them the *fête champêtre* came as naturally as it had to their hedonistic predecessors in the courts of the Louis'. In the painting at right Kees Van Dongen, psychological portraitist of the age, has caught all the kaleidoscopic color of a picnic at a French estate. The party is just getting under way—the sun is high in the summer sky, flirtations are still at the hand-kissing stage, and the champagne supply seems limitless. What better way to launch *le weekend*?

Hôtel de Paris

Monaco has long been a meeting place of the monied and titled. The caricaturist of the twenties, Sem (who appears at bottom on the lady's left), sketched notable patrons at play in the famous hotel's dining salon. Each year's drawings were compiled as a "souvenir" of the Monte Carlo high season, but they were not without malice. At left, for instance, a well-known count has a drink with the mysterious "Lady M," whose back is discreetly turned.

The Enduring Art

COLLECTION WALTER; GIRAUDON

Claude Derain's homely still life above focuses on cooking implements not unlike those found in the Egyptian pyramids or the tombs of ancient Etruria. Edouard Vuillard's lithograph opposite catches the mood of relaxed satisfaction of a woman cleaning up after the family dinner. Both works, executed in this century, suggest the timelessness of the culinary adventure. Only the details have been changed: the faster pace of life has brought about a demand for lighter, less elaborate meals; technological changes like the improved stove and running water have taken most of the drudgery out of cooking; rapid transportation, canning, and freezing mean that almost all ingredients from albacore to zucchini are widely available. Any aspiring gourmet now has the means with which to experiment, with the result that our era boasts more fine cooks than ever before—and an enormous brotherhood of knowledgeable eaters to appreciate their productions.

ACKNOWLEDGMENTS

The following is a list of picture credits for front matter and text. Page numbers appear in boldface type.

Front cover Biblioteca Ambrosiana, Milan; Scala **4** N.Y. Public Library, Prints Division **6** Studios Josse-Lalance **12** Romain Robert **13** Louvre, Paris; Tel-Vigneau **14** Valeriano, *Hieroglyphica*, 1586, N.Y. Public Library, Rare Book Division **15** American Museum of Natural History, New York; Lee Boltin **16** By Permission of the Trustees of the British Museum **17** Louvre, Paris; Giraudon **18** Metropolitan Museum of Art, Harris Brisbane Dick Fund, 1957, New York **20** Archepiscopal Museum, Ravenna; Anderson **21** Museo Nazionale, Rome; Boudot-Lamotte **22** top, Roger-Viollet; bottom, Courtesy of *Life* Magazine; Frank Scherschel **24** Younger, *Gods, Men, and Wine* **25** By Permission of the Trustees of the British Museum **43** By Permission of the Trustees of the British Museum **44** Metropolitan Museum of Art, Fletcher Fund, 1938, New York **47** Museo Nazionale, Naples, Anderson **48** Musée des Antiquités Nationales, St-Germain; S. Guiley-Lagache **51** Brooklyn Museum **52** Museum of Fine Arts, Boston; Gift of H. P. Kidder **54** Gabinetto Fotografico Nazionale, Rome **76** Archives Photographiques, Paris **78** Folger Shakespeare Library, Washington, D.C. **79** Rheinesches Landesmuseum, Bonn **81** George Whicher, *The Goliard Poets* **82** Bibliothèque Nationale, Paris **85** Bibliothèque Nationale, Paris, Service Photographique **86** Montagné, *Larousse Gastronomique* **87** *Kuchenmeisterei*, 1490 (facs. ed.), N.Y. Public Library, Rare Book Division **88** By Permission of the Trustees of the British Museum **89** By Permission of the Trustees of the British Museum **90** Lehner, *Folklore and Odysseys of Food and Medicinal Plants* **118, 124** *Opera Di M. Bartolomeo Scappi*, 1643, N.Y. Public Library, Rare Book Division **120, 122, 123, 125** N.Y. Public Library, Prints Division **126** Sotheby & Co.,

London **127** Graf Eltz **129** Nat'l. Portrait Gallery, London **130** Stow, *Survey of London*, 1633 **133** Victoria and Albert Museum, London. Crown Copyright **156** De Bry, *East Indies*, Pt. 4, N.Y. Public Library, Rare Book Division **157** De Bry, *East Indies*, Pt. 4, N.Y. Public Library, Rare Book Division **158** Metropolitan Museum of Art, Rogers Fund, 1913 **159** Museum of Fine Arts, Boston; Heeramaneck Collection **160** Library of Congress, Washington, D.C. **162** Smithsonian Institution, Freer Gallery of Art, Washington, D.C. **163** By Permission of the Trustees of the British Museum **164** By Permission of the Trustees of the British Museum **165** Dufour, *Tractatus Novi de Potu Caphe; de Chinensium The; et de Chocolata*, 1685, N.Y. Public Library, Rare Book Division **167** By Permission of the Trustees of the British Museum **168** Dutertre, *Histoire Generale des Antilles*, 1667–71, N.Y. Public Library, Rare Book Division **169** Dufour, *Tractatus Novi de Potu Caphe; de Chinensium The; et de Chocolata*, 1685, N.Y. Public Library, Rare Book Division **190** Smithsonian Institution, Freer Gallery of Art, Washington, D.C. **191** Royal Ontario Museum, University of Toronto **192** Art Institute of Chicago, Kate S. Buckingham Fund **195** Bibliothèque Nationale, Paris; Service Photographique **196** M. H. de Young Memorial Museum, San Francisco; Roy Leventritt Collection **199** Fine Arts Gallery of San Diego **200** N.Y. Public Library, Prints Division **202** Courtesy of Inosuke Setsu, Tokyo **203** Seattle Art Museum **224** Louvre, Paris; Giraudon **225** National Museum, Stockholm; Giraudon **226** Bibliothèque Nationale, Paris; Service Photographique **227** Bibliothèque Nationale, Paris; Service Photographique **228** American Philosophical Society, Philadelphia **230** Bibliothèque Nationale, Paris **231** University of St. Thomas Art Department, Houston **232** Bibliothèque Nationale, Paris; Service Photographique **233** Archives Photographique, Paris 235 Bulloz 236 Giraudon 237 Carnavalet; Bulloz 262 National Museum, Copenhagen 263 Musée Municipal de Lakenhal, Leyden 264 Mattioli, *Commentaires,* 1578 265 Wendy Buehr Collection 266 Museum Fur Volkerkunde, Basel 267 University of St. Thomas Art Department, Houston 268 Pinto Collection of Wooden Bygones 269 N.Y. Public Library, Prints Division 270 Liptov Museum, Ruzomberok 271 Liptov Museum, Ruzomberok 272 Metropolitan Museum of Art, Rogers Fund, 1927 273 Museo de Artes Decoratives, Barcelona 274 Anne S. K. Brown, Military Collection 275 Picture Archive, Jewish Seminary, New York; Frank J. Darmstaedter 302 Courtesy of Ronald A. Lee 305 By Permission of the Trustees of the British Museum 306 By Permission of the Trustees of the British Museum 307 By Permission of the Trustees of the British Museum 308 Marshall B. Davidson Collection 309 Cleveland Museum of Art, Gift of Mr. and Mrs. Warren H. Corning 310 N.Y. Public Library, Prints Division 311 N.Y. Public Library, Prints Division 312 Morris, *Portrait of a Chef* 314 Metropolitan Museum of Art, Harris Brisbane Dick Fund, 1953 315 By Permission of the Trustees of the British Museum 339 Bettmann Archive, New York 340 *Guide Michelin* 343, 345 Studios Josse-Lalance 344 Collection Robida, Paris 346 Bettmann Archive, New York 347 Bettmann Archive, New York 348 Virgil Thomson Collection 350 The Tate Gallery, London 351 *Yellow Book,* July, 1894 384 Antique Co. of New York, Inc., Incorporating the Antique Porcelain Co.

Grateful acknowledgment is made for permission to quote from the following works:

Andrieu, Pierre, *Fine Bouche,* copyright © 1956 by Pierre Andrieu and Editions Causse. Published by Cassell and Company Ltd., London.

Apicius, *The Roman Cookery Book,* translated by Barbara Flower and Elisabeth Rosenbaum, copyright © 1958 by George G. Harrap and Company Ltd., London.

Bickerdyke, John, *The Curiosities of Ale and Beer,* published 1965 by Spring Books, London.

Cheng, F. T., *Musings of a Chinese Gourmet,* copyright 1954 by F. T. Cheng. Published by Hutchinson and Co. Ltd., London.

Clair, Colin, *Kitchen and Table,* copyright © 1964 by Colin Clair. Published by Abelard-Schuman Ltd., New York

Diaz del Castillo, *The Discovery and Conquest of Mexico,* copyright © 1956 by Farrar, Straus, and Cudahy, New York.

Drummond, J. C., and Wilbraham, Anne, *The Englishman's Food,* copyright © 1957 by Jonathan Cape Ltd., London.

Herodotus, *The Histories,* translated by Aubrey de Selincourt, copyright 1954 by Penguin Books Ltd., London.

Higham translation, *Oxford Book of Greek Verse,* copyright 1930 by The Clarendon Press, Oxford.

Jacob, Heinrich Edward, *Coffee,* copyright 1935 by The Viking Press, New York.

Lach, Donald F., *Asia in the Making of Europe,* copyright © 1965 by University of Chicago.

Lopez, Claude-Anne, *Mon Cher Papa, Franklin and the Ladies of Paris,* copyright © 1966 by Yale University, New Haven.

Mitford, Nancy, "Madame de Pompadour's Staircase," *History Today,* Volume IV, No. 1, 1954. Published by Bracken House, London.

Montagné, Prosper, *Larousse Gastronomique,* copyright © 1961 by Crown Publishers, Inc., N.Y.

Montaigne, *Essays,* translated by E. J. Trechman, copyright 1935 by Oxford University Press, New York.

Petronius, *The Satyricon,* translated by William Arrowsmith, copyright © 1959 by William Arrowsmith. Published by University of Michigan Press, Ann Arbor.

Plumb, J. H., *Sir Robert Walpole,* copyright © 1956 by John Harold Plumb. Published by Houghton Mifflin Company, New York.

Pottle, Frederick A., ed., *Boswell in Holland 1763–1764,* copyright © 1956 by Yale University. Published by McGraw-Hill Book Company, New York.

Rugoff, Milton, ed., *The Great Travelers,* Volume 1, copyright © 1960 by Simon and Schuster, Inc., New York.

Seranne, Ann, and Tebbel, John, eds., *The Epi-*

cure's Companion, copyright © 1962 by Ann Seranne and John Tebbel. Published by David McKay Company, Inc., New York.

Simon, André, *Food*, copyright 1949 by Burke Publishing Company Ltd., London.

Thompson, James Westfall, *Economic and Social History of the Middle Ages*, copyright©1959 by Frederick Ungar Publishing Company, Inc., New York.

Toklas, Alice B., *The Alice B. Toklas Cook Book*, abridgment of pp. 29–30 (hardbound ed.), copyright 1954 by Alice B. Toklas. Reprinted by permission of Harper and Row, New York.

Wason, Betty, *Cooks, Gluttons, and Gourmets*, copyright © 1962 by Elizabeth Wason Hall. Published by Doubleday & Company, Inc., New York.

Whicher, George F., *The Goliard Poets*, copyright 1949 by George F. Whicher. Reprinted by permission of New Directions Publishing Corporation, New York.

Younger, William, *Gods, Men, and Wine*, copyright © 1966 by Elizabeth Younger. Published by The World Publishing Co., Cleveland.

Zumthor, Paul, *Daily Life in Rembrandt's Holland*, English translation, copyright © 1962 by George Weidenfeld and Nicolson Ltd., London.

The editors wish to express their deep gratitude to the institutions and individuals mentioned below for their help in providing pictorial material and for supplying information and advice.

Wine consultant: Pierre Bennerup, New York

Historical research: Mrs. Helen Prince, New York

Photography: London—R. B. Fleming and Co. Ltd.; New York—Century Photo Service, Inc., Max Steinbook; Oliver Baker Associates, Geoffrey Clements; Paulus Lesser Photography, Inc.

Napkin illustrations on page 333 drawn by Cal Sacks

Ing. Paolo Agnesi, Imperia

Bayerische Staatsbibliothek, Munich

Bibliothèque des Arts Décoratifs, Paris
  René Salanon, Chief Curator

Bibliothèque Nationale, Service Photographique, Paris, *Madame Le Monnier*, Chief Curator

Bibliothèque Royale de Belgique, Brussels
  Martin Wittek

Mrs. Jane Horton de Cabanyes, Madrid

Carnavalet Museum, Paris

Germanisches Nationalmuseum, Nuremberg
  Dr. Bernward Denekee

Hamburger Kunsthalle
  Dr. Otfried Schroeder

Jewish Theological Seminary, New York
  Frank J. Darmstaedter

Kunsthistorisches Museum, Vienna
  Dr. Erwin M. Auer, Director

Arpag Mekhitarian, Paris

Metropolitan Museum of Art, New York
  Miss Ellen Franklin
  Miss Nora Scott

Michelin & Cie., Paris

Musée d'Art et d'Histoire, Geneva
  Madame Anne de Herdt

Musée d'Art et d'Industrie, St-Etienne
  Madame Yvonne Allemand

Musée de la Manufacture Nationale de Sèvres

Musée Municipal de Lakenhal, Leyden

Museo Nazionale, Naples
  Dr. Giuseppe Maggi

National Museum, Copenhagen
  Miss Fritze Lindahl

National Museum, Stockholm
  Dr. Pontus Grate

National Palace Museum, Taipei
  Dr. Chiang Fu-Tsung, Director

New York Public Library
  Astor, Lenox, and Tilden Foundations
  Mrs. Maud D. Cole
  Mrs. Philomena C. Houlihan
  Miss Romana Javitz
  Miss Elizabeth Roth
  Lewis M. Stark

Osterreichische Nationalbibliothek, Vienna
  Hofrat Dr. Hans Pauer, Curator

Rijksmuseum, Amsterdam

Rosgarten Museum, Constance

Dr. Roudinesco, Paris

Georges Sirot, Paris

Miss Bianca Spantigati, Rome

Mrs. Maria Fossi Todorow, Florence

Max Willibald, Erbgraf zu Waldburg-Wolfegg, Schloss Wolfegg, Algau

INDEX

Page numbers in italic type indicate that the subject is illustrated.

192, 195, 197, 198, 199, *199*, 204; Dutch, 263–64, 278–81 *passim;* early Christian, 12, *72–73*, 73; Egyptian, 18, 26, 38, *38–39;* Etruscan, 49; French, 126–27, 223–24, 225, 226, 229, 245, *246–47;* Gallic, 77; German, 265, 274, *288–89*, 289; Greek, 11, 14, 18, 19–20, 21, 42–43, 49, 50, 56, 65; Indian 154; Italian, 121; Japanese, 204, *214–15*, 215, 221, *221;* Jewish, 12, 20, 21, 276, 292, *292–93;* Macedonian, 48; Persian, 11, 167, 182, *182;* Peruvian, 14; Philippine, 164; Roman, 12, 14, 41, 45, 47, 49, 54, 55, 64, *64–65*, *66–67*, 73, *73;* Syrian, 54–55; betrothals and weddings, 90, 118, 123, 136, *136–37*, 137, 271, 278–79, *278;* birthdays, 11, 238; carnivals and Lent, 120, *120*, 121, *226*, 227, *227*, 263, 274, 281; Christmas, 14, 89, 130, 278, 279, 328, 329; coronations and enthronements, 26, 77, 90; death, 11, 90; Easter, 89; Feast of the Pheasant, 90–91; fire, 14; harvest and thanksgiving, 11, 12, 14, 20, 90, 168; Halloween, 14; Kermis, 263–64; Martinmas, 78, *78*, 264; May Day, 14, 120, 263; Michaelmas, 89; Midsummer's Night, 14, 89; New Year's, 12, 14, 22, 89, 303; Oktoberfest, 265; Sheep-shearing, 90, 311; Whitsuntide, 89
FERMENTATION, 13, 21, 22–23
FESTIN RIDICULE, 225
FIELDING, HENRY, 314, 322
FIESOLE, 51
FIFTY COURTESIES OF THE TABLE, THE, 121
FINE ART OF CHINESE COOKING, THE, 190
FIRE, mythology of, 12, 14
FISH, 8, 17, 21, 24, 33, 41, 46, 50, 102, *102*, 164, 193, 194, 197, 221, 271, 276, 285; albacore, 371; anchovies, 46, 51; bass, 348; carp, 83, 102, 193, 218, *218, 273;* cod, 82; dogfish, 45; eel, 58, 83; haddock, 82; harpfish, 45; herring, 82, 84, 102, 263, 276, 286, *286;* jellyfish, 46; kippers, 303; mackerel, 44; octopi, 51, 58; perch, 19, 273; plaice, 303; rays, 45; salmon, 83, 125, 263, 276, 313, 341; sardines, 51; shad, 350; skate, 58; sole, 233; squid, 51; sturgeon, 44, 83, 237, 276, 350; trout, 83, 102, 204; tuna, 45, 50, 350
FISHERIES, 17; Aegean, 50; Atlantic, 82; Mediterranean, 50; North Sea, 82, 286; Seine, 83
FISHMONGERS, 102, *102*, 130, *130, 248*
FLANDERS, 82
FLOUR. *See* Grains and Cereals
FLOWERS, in food, 192, 194; in tea, 202; in wine, 199, 204
FONTAINEBLEAU, 223, 224
FOOD ADULTERATION, 314
FOOD ADVERTISING, *358–59*, 359

FOOD MIGRATION, 15–16, 51, 164–69, 186, 193
FOOD PRESERVATION, 22, 46, 84–86, 346; canning, 346, 370; curing, 83, 287; drying, 78, 346; freezing, 346, 370; pickling, 13, 46, 80, 287, 346; salting, 78, 82, 346; smoking, 346
FOOD PROCESSING, 346–47
FORKS, 118, 119, 122, 144, *144*, 227–29. *See also* Eating Implements
FORME OF CURY, THE, 87
FORNAX, 61
FOUQUET, NICOLAS, 223, 224, 227, 229, 230
FOUQUET AND COMPANY, 358
FOWL. *See* Birds and Fowl
FRANCE, 12, 26, 41, 52, 74–97 *passim*, 117–19, 123–27, 134–35, 142–43, *222*, 223–59 *passim*, 336–71 *passim*
FRANCIS, SAINT, 75
FRANCIS I, King of France, 117, 118, 124, 125, 140, 141
FRANEY, PIERRE, 352
FRANGIPANI, COUNT CESARE, 118
FRANKINCENSE, in food, 18
FRANKLIN, BENJAMIN, 228, 234
FRANKS, 77
FRANZ JOSEF, Holy Roman Emperor, 337
FREDERICK II, King of Prussia, 261
FRENCH COOKERY, 84, 126–27, 190, 225–26, 229–38 *passim*, 261–62, 302, 338; American influence on, 351; Italian influence on, 118, 123–24. *See also* France
FROGS, THE, 43
FROGS' LEGS, 16, 341
FRUITS, 15, 24, 33, 50, 53, 80, 160, 166, 168, 170, 171, *171*, 179, 182, 191, 197, *206–7*, 207, 219, 229, 263, 313, 345, 350; apples, 16, 24, 50, 51, 82, 293; apricots, 24, 131, 158, 192, 313; arbutus berries, 207, *207;* avocados, 15; bananas, 164, 165; breadfruit, 164; cherries, 16, 24, 324; citrus fruits, 82, 158, 160, 168, 229, lemons, 51, 82, 158, limes, 159, 160, oranges, 132, 158, 160, 191, 192, 199, 202, 219, 229, 313; coconuts, 165; dates, 17, 24, 26, 34, 85, 193; figs, 17, 18, 23, 24, 33, *33*, 50, 131, 164, 193; gooseberries, 131; grapes, 20, 23, 34, 132, 167, 193, 199, 313, *see also* Vineyards; guava, 15; kumquats, 219; mangoes, 165, *206*, 207; melons, 24, 118, 132, 158, 170, 179, *180–81*, 204, 219, 291; mulberries, 131; nectarines, 313; peaches, 16, 158, 229, 313; pears, 50, 51, 192, 199, 229, 313; pineapples, 15, 166, 186, *186*, 193, 300, *300*, 313; plums, 16, 51, 82, 158, 313; pomegranates, 33, 50, 51, 131, 158, 193; quinces, 50, 82, 131, 199; strawberries, 82, 125, 132, 233
FUGGER FAMILY, 165, 172
FULLER, THOMAS, 128

G

GALATEO, IL, 121, 151
GALILEE, 25
GAMA, VASCO DA, 157, 161–62
GARGANTUA AND PANTAGRUEL, 75, 91, 124
GAUGUIN, PAUL, 363; water color by, *363*
GAUL, 48, 51, 52, 63, 69, 77, 78
GEORGE IV, King of England, 315, 326, 326
GERMAN COOKERY, 16, 262, 265–69
GIBBON, EDWARD, 56
GILFILLAN, SEABURY COLUM, 56
GILLRAY, JAMES, 326; sketch by, *326*
GIRALDUS CAMBRENSIS, 83
GOATS. *See* Meat and Meat Products, goat
GOETHE, JOHANN VON 262, 268
GOGOL, NIKOLAI, 275
GOTHS, 77; Ostrogoths, 56; Visigoths, 56
GOYA, FRANCISCO, 290; painting by, *290*
GRAINS AND CEREALS, 12–15, 17, 18 20, 21, 22, 24, 33, 50, 51, 52, 63, 71, *71* 79, 84, 85, 113, 166, 225, 283, 294. *See als* Barley, Corn, Millet, Oats, Rice, Wheat
GRAND DICTIONNAIRE DE CUISINE LE, 124, 238, 256
GRANT, SIR FRANCIS, 331; painting by *331*
GREECE, 8, 14, 16, 18, 25, 41–56 *passim*, 64 65, *64–65*, *66–67*
GRIMOD DE LA REYNIERE, 8–9, 238 256, 257, *257*
GUYENNE, Duchy of, 92
GYLLIUS, 169

H

HADES, 18
HAFIZ, 167
HAMPTON COURT, 117, 130, 133, 308
HANSEATIC LEAGUE, 17, 82
HARRISON, WILLIAM, 131
HEALTHS IMPROVEMENT, 134
HEARD, GILES, 130
HEBREWS, 25
HENRY II, King of England, 92
HENRY IV, King of England, 90
HENRY V, King of England, 132
HENRY VIII, King of England, 117, 12' 28, 130, 141
HENRY II, King of France, 26, 118
HENRY III, King of France, 124, 126
HENRY IV, King of France, 122, 126, 13 225, 234
HENRY THE NAVIGATOR, 161
HERACLIDES, 45
HERB GARDENS, 74, *74*, 80, 86
HERBS, *See* Spices and Seasonings
HERODOTUS, 11, 18, 21, 24, 48, 49

PART TWO

Menus and Recipes

The

HORIZON
COOKBOOK
and Illustrated History of
Eating and Drinking
through the Ages

by

THE EDITORS OF HORIZON MAGAZINE

EDITOR IN CHARGE

WENDY BUEHR

RECIPES EDITOR TATIANA McKENNA

HISTORICAL FOODS CONSULTANT MIMI SHERATON

PUBLISHED BY

AMERICAN HERITAGE PUBLISHING CO., INC.

BOOK TRADE DISTRIBUTION BY

DOUBLEDAY & COMPANY, INC.

TABLE OF CONTENTS

❦ A WORD OF EXPLANATION ❧

HOW THE RECIPES WERE SELECTED: We have tried to include in this book recipes for the most delectable and interesting dishes prepared throughout history around the world. Manuscripts, old cookbooks, historic menus, and other original documents have been our sources. The recipes have been adapted for use in today's kitchens to take full advantage of modern equipment and of current packaged and frozen foods. Such foreign ingredients as are called for are now widely available, if not in supermarkets, then in gourmet and specialty food shops throughout the United States. Each recipe has been tested and all the recipes, we hope, retain the flavor and appeal of the original.

ORGANIZATION OF RECIPES: To make selection easy, recipes are grouped by course—under Soups, Desserts and Sweets, and similar headings. Each of these sections contains recipes that span many centuries and several continents; when the background and traditions associated with a particular dish are of unusual interest, as is frequently the case, an accompanying note appears in green type. Ingredients are listed in order of use; if a given ingredient is to be added in parts rather than all at once, we alert readers by writing that step of the recipe in italic. Wherever a choice of names for a dish has existed, we have tended to favor the native name, adding sometimes in one or more variations the names and slight differences by which it is known in other lands (as with the corn meal mush that Rumanians call Mamaliga, Italians serve as Polenta, and West Indians prepare as Stamp-and-Go).

HISTORIC MENUS: On pages 392 to 412 are nineteen menus adapted from old documents and the literature of other days and places. Some of these menus, that served to Ludwig II of Bavaria in 1885, for example, are taken directly from the pages of history. Others, such as the sixteenth-century supper with Pope Pius V, are compilations of dishes known to have been favored in a particular time and place. Still others, like the Christmas Eve dinner traditional in Poland, are based on the religious and social customs of a nation. Ambitious both in size and richness, these menus are intended as guides from which the modern hostess may wish to plan her own meals. Asterisks appear beside those dishes for which recipes may be found in the index.

MENUS

A HOUSE PARTY FOR HER MAJESTY

Although the cost was shocking, there was keen competition among Queen Elizabeth's subjects to entertain Her Majesty when she passed through their counties on one of her numerous summer progresses. In 1578 Sir Roger North was honored at his estate by the "Queen's Majesty's coming thither on Monday the first of September to supper and tarrying until Wednesday after dinner." The honor cost Lord North about £ 770, most of which was paid to serve the queen and her enormous entourage meals like that below. The lord's account books show that among other things he purchased "a cartload and two horseloads of oysters, 430 pounds of butter, and 2,522 eggs." In anticipation of the glorious event he had put up a banqueting house and some new kitchens, and he hired special cooks from London to augment the dozens of people already on his serving and kitchen staff. For most of Elizabeth's hosts such generosity paid off, not only in preferments but, equally important, in the friendship of the monarch. Years later when Elizabeth heard that Lord North was "violently attacked with dullness of hearing," she paid him a supreme compliment. She wrote out for him her own prescription; like her subjects she believed that diet and the external application of foodstuffs affected one's psyche and physiology alike. "Bake a little loaf of bean flour, and being hot rive it in halves, and into each half pour three or four spoonfuls of bitter almonds; then clap both halves to your ears at going to bed . . . and keep your head warm."

Smoked Sturgeon   Mussels with Sweet Herbs*

Pease Potage*

Roasted Cygnets, Quails, and Snipes   Oysters, Bacon, and Pullets*

Mutton with Cucumbers*   Neat's Tongue Roasted with Rhenish Wine*

Venison Pastie   Boiled Beef with Sauce Robert*

French Puffs with Greene Hearbes*   Salat*

Maids of Honour*   Mince Pie*   Apple Cream*

Peris in Syrippe*   Clouted Cream*   Syllabub*

Mulled Cider*   Mead*

MARTINMAS

Scandinavian Liver Pastei *

Blood Soup *

Roast Goose with Peaches *

Cinnamon Apples   *Sauerkraut* *

Crêpes *

New Wine

The November 11 Feast of Saint Martin began in the Middle Ages as a harvest festival. It honors the fourth-century Bishop of Tours whose act of charity in sharing his cloak with a shivering beggar is preserved in the many customs of hospitality which surround this day. Two ingredients are basic to the thanksgiving celebration: new fall wine, recalling Martin's reported habit of planting vines wherever he preached, and a plump goose, in retribution for the bird whose cackle is said to have betrayed Martin when hiding from his pursuers. To this each nation adds its own specialties: Germans serve sauerkraut; Swedes precede the main event with blood soup; the Dutch favor pancakes and tart medlars; and the French, who consider Saint Martin one of their own, make a rich *pâté de foie gras* which, eaten with too much enthusiasm, may account for the seasonal stomachache called *mal de Saint Martin*. In England, where superstition holds that failure to share the goose with a needy person will bring hard times on the house, most citizens have willingly given the day its due and caroused accordingly. As the Elizabethan poet Barnabe Googe put it, "To belly cheare yet once againe doth Martin more incline, Whom all the people worshippeth with roasted geese and wine . . . They him unto the skies extoll with prayse devine, Drinking deepe in tankardes large and bowles of compasse wide."

THE JEWISH SABBATH SUPPER

Ever since God allegedly told Moses, "I have a precious gift in my treasure house, and its name is Sabbath. . . . make it known to [Israel]," Jews have observed a seventh day of rest. As Sholem Aleichem has depicted in his folk tales of nineteenth-century Russian Jewry, it is a time not only of prayers but also of good food. Since cooking is forbidden from sundown Friday to sundown Saturday, the womenfolk have prepared in advance the traditional dishes for the three meals to come. One character waxes poetic over the fish: "I can guarantee . . . you haven't eaten [any] like my wife's . . . not even in a dream"; the roast, "a delicacy from heaven"; and the cholent (served in orthodox households at the midday meal Saturday), "you know what that smells like when you take it out of the oven and take the cover off the pot." Whatever the table provides, the Sabbath is a joyous occasion, one that helps Sholem Aleichem's people face another week in an alien land.

*Challah**

Chopped Liver   *Chopped Herring*

Gefüllte Fish with Horseradish*

Dill Pickles   *Radishes*

Chicken Soup with Matzo Balls

Pot Roast   *Cholent**

*Carrot Tzimmes**

Strudel   *Fruit Compote*

Wine   *Cognac*   *Cherry Cider*

394

A SIXTEENTH-CENTURY SUPPER WITH THE POPE

Sausages Cooked in Wine*

Ravioli Fiorentina*

Aspic of Capon*   *Duck with Turnips**

Brain Fritters with Orange Sauce*   *Lamb with Rosemary**

Stuffed Artichoke Bottoms*   *Tender Peas with Bacon*

Golden Rissoles* of Pork on Skewers   *Veal Pie**

Lettuce Salad   *Orange Salad*   *Torta di Sparagi**

Nuns' Cake*   *Puff Pastry* Filled with Custard*

Pears in Wine*   *Apple Florentine**   *Savory of Wild Cherries**

Assorted Cheeses   *Marzipan*

Stalks of Sweet Fennel   *Toothpicks in Rose Water*   *Bunches of Flowers*

Many of the predecessors of Pope Pius V (1566–72) had used the Vatican as headquarters for riotous eating, drinking, and merrymaking. The good Pius hoped to work a renaissance in the Church like the one that was taking place in the arts. He forbade every impropriety from swearing to whoring, and, theoretically at least, he even clung to his vows of poverty after his election. Perhaps the most convincing evidence of his saintliness is that although he himself ate frugally, he encouraged Bartolomeo Scappi, a veritable Da Vinci of the kitchen, to exercise his imagination and talents for the papal entourage. The listing above is a compilation of dishes from the menus and recipes in Scappi's 900-page *Opera.* A typical supper menu provided for some thirty-five dishes with delicacies like goat's feet salad, boiled calf's head with borage flowers, and dormouse pie to be served in the three courses. The work makes it clear that Italy was in the advance guard of sophisticated table habits too. While other European aristocrats were lofting their beef bones to slavering hounds, Renaissance Italians were setting down their knives and forks and daintily wiping their lips on clean white napkins after each course. Fortunately, in the next decades envoys like Marie de' Medici, armed with Scappi's book, carried such niceties throughout Europe.

DINING IN OLD RUSSIA

Caviar with Lemon Juice

Herring with Mustard Dill Sauce*

Radishes   Minced Mushrooms

Vodka   Kvass*

Shchi* with Pirozhki*   Borsch*

Ring Mold of Sterlet   Coulibiac of Salmon*

Roast Partridge   Roast Turkey   Roast Duckling with Potatoes

Karavai*   Guriev Kasha*   Fruits   Nuts   Pastilles of Fruit*

Unlike the sirens of Greek mythology whose singing so enticed sailors that they forgot to eat, the tempter in Chekhov's *The Siren* of 1887 makes his victims forget everything *but* food. Four Russian judges listening to their secretary's tantalizing description of a dinner are transformed into ravenous wolves, each "ready to make a meal of [his] own father." The easiest prey is the fattest judge, who hardly needs any vodka to salivate at the suggestion of herring, "salted pink mushrooms, minced fine as caviar," and *coulibiac*, a pie from which "butter drips . . . like tears, and the filling is fat, juicy, rich." When another judge cynically asks, "Is there nothing to live for but mushrooms and meat pie?" the secretary invokes images of huge tureens containing cabbage, beet, and vegetable soups, followed by platters of Caspian sterlet. A third judge suffering from a stomach ulcer is told his malady is merely the result of "pride and free-thinking," and he is seduced with thoughts of roast turkey and duckling. Unaware that two of his quarry, caught up with rumblings of the stomach, have run out to eat, the secretary warbles on with sugarcoated words about the "sweet eclipse" following the meal when the "body is basking, the soul is transported," and the "crowning touch [is] two or three glasses of spiced brandy." Finally the remaining judges hastily retreat to a restaurant, to leave the uninvited secretary alone—feasting on his thoughts.

396

A MOUNTAIN MEAL WITH LUDWIG OF BAVARIA

Theodor Hierneis, a cook at the court of Ludwig II of Bavaria, described his employer as a man of "unapproachable grandeur" evidently more like a romantic Wagnerian hero than a nineteenth-century ruler with a psychotic "lifelong passion [for] designing [and building] fairy-story castles." On impulse the king would leave his Munich *Residenz* and go to one of his numerous palaces or hunting lodges in the Bavarian Alps. Since he expected formal meals wherever he went, the kitchen staff was forced to precede him with the necessary "cooking utensils, table cloths, damask napkins and . . . an entire service of China" and often had to work in primitive and makeshift surroundings. Even mealtimes were erratic, for Ludwig sometimes rose for breakfast about 6 P.M., took dinner at 2 A.M., and supped at 6 or 7 A.M., so that the royal cooks "had to turn night into day." They also had to prepare food enough for four, because Ludwig, dining alone, imagined himself to be in the company of French kings. Though Bavaria, the archetypal land of beer and *wurst*, reputedly had the best cuisine in Germany, Ludwig still insisted that dishes (except for exclusively German ones) be given French names and be served in the style of Louis XIV. The menu for a typical "mountain expedition" dinner given in the Tirol appears below. Due to Ludwig's tooth trouble, his chefs created such finely minced dishes as brown consommé with dumplings and hechtenkraut, a traditional favorite of German royalty, consisting of layers of pike and sauerkraut. A wine ice flavored with woodruff preceded the Bavarian specialty of roast venison. Ludwig's fairytale world eventually collapsed; declared insane and deposed, he drowned himself on June 13, 1886.

*Consommé with Liver Dumplings**

*Hechtenkraut**   *Trout with Hollandaise Sauce**

Chicken Fricassee

*Sorbet von Waldmeister**

*Saddle of Venison with Red Cabbage**

Roast Beef with Petits Pois   *Roast Mountain Goat*

*Fruit in Wine Jelly**   *Tutti-frutti Ice Cream with Orange Sauce*

BRILLAT-SAVARIN'S GASTRONOMIC TESTS

Certain guests of M. de Talleyrand winced whenever Brillat-Savarin joined the company. They regarded the magistrate, appropriately from Belley, as a boorish bumpkin who ate more than the dictates of politeness allowed, added little to the repartee, and committed the grand gaffe of dozing at the table. However, the modest Brillat-Savarin, unbeknownst to his dinner companions, was writing *La Physiologie du Goût*, which in 1825 would elevate him to the gastronomic hall of fame and silence his smug critics. In his treatise the author covered all topics related to the art of good eating. One entry, a test called *les éprouvettes gastronomiques*, calculated to separate the true gastronome from his indifferent confreres, consisted of various delicacies served in heaping portions so as not to inhibit anyone's intake. The dishes were to be "of known savour and such indisputable excellence, that the sight of them alone must rouse all the gustative powers of a man of right constitution." Conversely, "those in whose countenance no kindling of desire is seen, nor any glow of ecstasy, can justly be marked down as unworthy . . . of the occasion and the pleasures thereto pertaining." Since circumstance does not necessarily breed a gourmet, Brillat devised three menus of ascending refinement, "suited to the faculties and habits of the different classes of society." Hence, a man of humble means passed his particular test if he commented, "Ha, this looks good; come on, we must do it justice"; a *bourgeois gentilhomme* at the next stratum distinguished himself with "Dear friend, what a lovely apparition! This is indeed a feast of feasts"; and, in the upper echelons it would suffice for a minister of state to effuse, "Ah, *Monsieur* . . . what an admirable man your cook must be! One never meets such things anywhere but here!"

La Première Eprouvette

Fillet of Veal

Roast Turkey* with Chestnut Stuffing   *Roast Pigeons*

Sauerkraut*

Oeufs à la Neige*

La Deuxième Eprouvette

Boiled Turbot

Truffled Turkey

Venison with Gherkin Sauce   *Fillet of Beef*   *Leg of Mutton**

Early Green Peas*

La Troisième Eprouvette

Pâté de Foie Gras

Rhine Carp à la Chambord   *Stuffed Pike with Sauce Nantua**

Capon Demi-deuil*   *Truffled Quails à la Moelle*

Ortolans à la Provençale   *Roast Pheasant en Toupet*

Asparagus in Bouillon

THE POLISH WIGILIA

The Christmas feast of vigil, or Wigilia, observed in Catholic Poland began with the announcement of the first star of evening. The table had been laid with a bed of straw beneath the white cloth to symbolize the manger in Bethlehem, a place set for the Christ Child, and a candle lighted for Him in the window. Sheaves of grain stood in the corners of the room in a silent prayer for the next year's harvest. Superstition dictated that the number of diners be even and the number of dishes be odd. The meal began with each member of the family breaking a piece from the *oplatek*, a large unleavened wafer stamped with scenes of the Nativity, and then the traditional dishes—all of them meatless in observance of the fast day—were brought in. Mushrooms and carp, two Polish favorites the year round, and *kutya*, a wheat pudding that is often served but seldom eaten, were ritual dishes. A compote of twelve stewed fruits, symbolizing the Apostles, was also mandatory. When the last delicious bite had been savored, the host rose to bless the company, and at a signal—for to move too soon would be to chance death in the next year—the others would rise together; then on to the opening of gifts. The Wigilia ended at midnight when the church bells called the household to *Pasterka*, or Shepherds' Mass.

Blini *

Mushrooms in Sour Cream *

Borschok *

Pike with Hot Horseradish Sauce *   *Bohemian Christmas Carp* *

Noodles * with Poppy Seeds*   *Beans with Plums* *   *Sauerkraut* *

Vareniki *   *Medivnyk* *

Compote of Stewed Fruits

Vodka

Coffee

SAINT NICHOLAS EVE PARTY

Speculaas*   *Peppernoten**   *Gingerbread*

Letterbankets   *Marzipan* Candies*   *Doughnuts**

Bishop*   *Hot Chocolate**   *Hoppel Poppel**

Because Saint Nicholas reputedly ransomed three maidens from slavery by dropping bags of gold down their chimney, the December 6 feast honoring the patron of the poor has been associated with gift giving. The holiday, popular in the Netherlands since the thirteenth century, was especially dear to children, for they were given license to sing, dance, eat, and drink—though at one point town authorities reprimanded parents for letting their darlings run riot in the streets. Today on Saint Nicholas Eve, families cordially receive *Sinterklaas*, who austerely clad as a bishop (instead of in the red garb familiar to Americans), drops nuts and candy on a sheet near the door. While the adults fortify themselves with bishop and schnapps and the young stuff their stomachs with sweets, the Saint takes a toll of everyone's deeds for the year. Proclaiming the outcome in gently satirical verses, he distributes presents to the deserving. Then the guests, their places at the table marked by *letterbankets*, or pastry initials, sit down to gorge on such treats as marzipan, Speculaas, and gingerbread. Before going to bed, the children leave fodder in wooden shoes for Saint Nicholas' horse, which the kindly gift-bringer will usually replace with more sweetmeats—however, a naughty child is apt to find only birch rods as recompense.

A MEXICAN COMIDA

Pretty, Scottish-born Fanny Calderón de la Barca arrived in Mexico in 1839, the wife of the first Spanish ambassador to the republic. She soon developed a liking for bullfights and pulque (an ancient Indian drink made from the fermented sap of the agave plant) and even acquired a taste for Mexican dishes, accomplishments described in her ebullient *Life in Mexico*. Recalling a trip to the provinces to attend a native *herradero*, or bull-branding festival, she marveled, "Such roaring, such shouting, such an odour of singed hair and *biftek au naturel*, such playing of music, and such wanton risks as were ran by the men!" Appetite still intact, however, she plumped herself down on a heap of white moss thoughtfully gathered at the edge of the *plaza de toros* for an alfresco meal. Some dishes like the chili, the author confessed, "I have not yet made up my mind to endure," but pulque, added Fanny with undisguised enthusiasm, could be sipped à discretion."

*Guacamole**

Chili con Carne   *Mole de Guajolote**   *Puchero**

*Frijoles Refritos**   *Fried Bananas*   *Tortillas*

Cream Cheese with Guava Shells   *Camote y Piña**

*Chocolatl de Molinillo**   *Pulque*   *Coffee*

MUSTAFA EFFENDI'S HAREM DINNER

Anchovy Cakes   Imam Bayaldi*

Dolmates* of Chopped Meat and Spiced Rice

Cinnamon Wine Soup*

Chickens Stuffed with Herb and Olive Pilaf*

Cucumber and Yoghurt Salad*

Bourma*   Sharbatee Gulab*   Lemonade   Turkish Coffee*

"There are probably few nations in the world," wrote Miss Pardoe on a visit to Constantinople in 1835, "that observe with such severity as the Turks that domestic precedence and etiquette, which, while it may certainly prevent any disrespectful familiarity, has a tendency to annihilate all ease." Certainly dinner at the harem of the Egyptian Chargé d'Affaires Mustafa Effendi was a more elaborate and structured affair than the convivial dinner party of Miss Pardoe's native England. Not only were the women strictly segregated, but etiquette within the harem was rigidly determined by one's household position. Thus the first wife and guest occupied the upper portion of the low divan, while the other women arranged themselves in descending order to their marital status. The ladies were served by nine slaves, who formed a relay from the door to the table. As for the repast itself, Miss Pardoe was somewhat discomfited by the absence of knives and forks. The poultry was torn asunder and eaten with the fingers. The only utensils were spoons, with which, when required, the ladies partook directly from a common dish—a custom "rendered less revolting than it would otherwise be, by the fact that each individual is careful . . . always to confine herself to one spot." Having washed their hands with tepid rose water poured by a procession of slave girls, the company retired to the principal apartment to sip thick, sweet Turkish coffee, without which no Turkish meal is complete. The fare at the venerable Mustafa Effendi's was modest in comparison with some Turkish tables. At another meal the English visitor was presented with "nineteen dishes, of fish, flesh, fowl, pastry, and creams, succeeding each other in the most heterogeneous manner . . . terminated by a pyramid of pillauf." While Turkish courtesy did not demand it, the persevering Miss Pardoe sat through the whole performance, fascinated to the last.

403

SMÖRGASBORD IN THE LAND OF THE MIDNIGHT SUN

Gravad Lox Swedish Anchovies Caviar*

Kogt Torsk Smoked Salmon with Poached Eggs*

Herring Salat Herring Fillets*

Cucumbers Fried Sausages Smoked Goose Breast

Smoked Reindeer Meat

Cumin Cheese Hard-boiled Eggs

Swedish Crisp Bread White Bread Rye Bread

Aquavit Ale Schnapps Vodka

Norwegian Fish Pudding with Lobster Sauce

Red Glazed Ham Swedish Baked Beans*

Spanish Cake Wienerbrod*

The Swedish smörgåsbord, and its Norwegian, Finnish, and Danish variations, began as an informal herring buffet that accompanied the drinking of aquavit. The custom of eating it as the appetizer to a festive meal, and the multiplication of dishes that now comprise the course, is no more than three centuries old. Paul Du Chaillu, an American who visited Gothenburg in the 1880's, was so impressed with a party meal he was served there that he described the smörgåsbord which, with adaptations, appears above. "We dined at 3 P.M.," he reported, adding with chagrin that he committed the gaucherie of appearing without dress coat and white cravat, about which "the Swedes are very particular. . . . Dinner in Sweden is invariably preceded by a *smörgås*, a series of strange dishes eaten as relish. I was led to a little table called *smörgåsbord*, around which we all clustered. . . . Everything was tastefully arranged upon a snowy cloth—the plates, knives, forks, and napkins, [but] I was at a loss how to begin; the meal was eaten standing. Observing my predicament, the hostess came kindly to my rescue, and helped herself first. . . . I observed the proceedings warily all the time, in order to know what to do next. . . . The *smörgås*, however, was only a preliminary. . . ." Dinner followed.

A WEE BIT O' BREAKFAST

"If an epicure could remove by a wish in quest of sensual gratification, wherever he had supped, he would breakfast in Scotland," wrote Samuel Johnson after a visit in 1776. The menu below, from an early-nineteenth-century cookbook by Mistress Margaret Dods, contrary to the notion of proverbial Scottish frugality, illustrates the kind of Highland meal that made the learned doctor and his friends feel "treated like princes in their progress." Though Johnson's hosts would serve such whets as ale, rum, or a spirit called *scalch* with breakfast, for women of his time tea was the standard eye-opener and bracer for an early morning stroll.

Oatmeal with Cream

Smoked Herring   Sardines with Mustard   Broiled Trout

Cold Meat Pies*   Broiled Kidneys   Scotch Woodcock*

Sausages with Mashed Potatoes

Tongue with Hot Horseradish Sauce*

Singing Hinnies*   Bannocks*   Barmbrack*

Honey   Conserves   Marmalade

Tea   Coffee

CONFUCIUS' EIGHT DELICACIES

Westerners confronted with their first Chinese banquet are always astonished at the elaborate ritual that attends even the most incidental parts of the meal. Though they are seldom able to deduce exactly what they have been served—poetic names such as "Ten Thousand Arrows Piercing through the Clouds" being of little help in identifying a soup of sharks' fins and eggs, for example—they often make a brave attempt at reporting something of the protocol. A British diplomat writing in the December, 1900, issue of *Blackwood's* Magazine described one three-hour dining "adventure" to which he had been invited at a restaurant, it being considered presumptuous to entertain other than relatives at home. "The hour named was 4 P.M.; and, in accordance with Chinese etiquette, here we are, at six, about to set out. . . . The table is ready laid with an imposing show: a regulation number of regulation dishes, marshalled in regulation order. [Following Confucius' prescription that "eight delicacies" be served at banquets in accordance with the eight fundamental elements in the universe, most menus offer multiples of the number, though the total may run as high as forty dishes or more.] When all are seated ready for the fray the host raises his cup—'Let us drink!' We reply, 'Thanks! thanks!' then set to—with chopsticks [silver or ivory implements, supposed to turn black in the presence of poison, are traditional at banquets]; picking now from one dish, now from another, in piquant contrast of sweet, sour, and salt. . . . Finally comes a bowl or two of white boiled rice. . . . The guests shortly afterwards disperse, the host apologizing for the wretched dinner he has dared to set before them, the guests politely protesting." A more modest feast, no less Confucian in its offering of sixteen delicacies, follows.

Won Ton Soup*   *Spring Rolls**   *Marbelized Tea Eggs**

Szechwan Pepper Prawns*   *Sweet and Sour Fish**

Asparagus with Walnuts*   *Fried Rice**   *Smashed Radish Salad**

Sesame Chicken*   *Braised Duck with Pear and Chestnuts**

Suckling Pig*   *Lion's Head Cabbage**   *Spareribs**

Honeyed Apples*   *Eight Precious Pudding**   *Peking Dust**

406

A FOUR BOY CURRY TIFFIN

Shrimp Curry Soup*

Nargis Kofta*   *Pakoras Fritters**

Chicken Tandoori*   *Murghi Biryani**

Vindaloo Curry*   *Koorma Curry**

Kitcherie*   *Dal**   *Dum Aloo**

Mint Chutney*   *Pickled Onion Relish*   *Fruit Chutney**

Puri*   *Chapatis**

Fresh Fruits   *Barfi**

Tea

In nineteenth-century England anyone mixing in worldly society could not avoid for long an encounter with the hot, spicy cooking of colonial India. The first meeting could be painful, as Thackeray's Becky Sharp discovered when she tried to impress the eligible young Joseph Sedley with her culinary adventurousness. "Oh, I must try some, if it is an Indian dish. . . . I am sure everything must be good that comes from there." Gasping over her first mouthful, but still game, she was urged on to still more painful taste sensations by Sedley, whose years in Calcutta had made him forget the initial shock of an authentic curry. Like most British colonials he was accustomed to "tiffing" or lunching in the native style, often and well. Indeed, rivalries developed among different companies of officers and businessmen as to who served the most prestigious Indian meals. A four boy curry, requiring a mere four boys to serve the main part of the meal, was considered minimal, and the chief steward of Honest John Company, as nostalgically remembered by one observer, "rejoiced . . . to give 'tiffin' parties at which he prided himself on sending round eight or nine varieties of curry with diverse platters of freshly-made chutneys." An Indian tiffin, too much for a Miss Sharp but pleasing to a Mr. Sedley, might include the above.

A SHOOTING LUNCHEON

Mulligatawny Soup   Scotch Broth*   Mock Turtle à la Diable

Devonshire Squab Pie*   Partridge Pie   Beefsteak Pie

Sauté of Game   Duck with Turnips*   Haricot of Mutton

Braised Beefsteak   Braised Mutton   Civet of Hare

Irish Stew   Venison Stew*

Plum Pudding*   Mince Pie*   Apple Charlotte*

In Victorian England the design of a hunt lunch could be a matter of almost moral considerations. The grander it became the more suspect was the character of the hunters who willingly partook. A critic writing anonymously in an 1885 issue of the London *World* faced the issue squarely. "Lowest of all we place the bestial profusion of the hot lunch, in which a precious hour of December daylight is all too often wasted . . . . An overgrown lunch is justly abhorred by all men who are really keen on sport." The author then offered what he judged suitable for a lunch when "the shooting is moderate, the weather cold . . . and it is possible to have it in a cottage or shooting lodge."

VICTOR EMMANUEL'S BANQUET CHAMPETRE

Although Victor Emmanuel's aristocratic lineage could be traced back to a certain Humbert of the White Hands, the squat, unkempt Italian monarch was at heart a peasant, variously described by other European blue bloods as a "royal buffoon," a man appearing "to have lived more in camps than in courts," and the only Knight of the Garter who "looked as if he would have the best of it with the dragon." He loved sports, like shooting snipe in the Piedmont rice fields, and had a voracious appetite for food as well as for females. Official banquets bored the king, and a guest at one noted that he "neither tasted a morsel of food nor took a drop of water . . . but sat like a statue of marble, with both hands resting on the hilt of his sword." Instead, Victor Emmanuel preferred to dine informally on such characteristic dishes of northern Italy as roast game, savory *bollito* (a stew redolent with onions and garlic), and hearty *risotto*, made with the rice, butter, cheese, wine, and pungent white truffles of Piedmont. Even if the menu below for an 1857 picnic was of Gallic inspiration, the chef, Genin, did acknowledge the king's tastes with the bear cub, the mountain trout, and the chamois (a species of antelope). The occasion marked the beginning of the first of the great transalpine tunnels, intended to replace the hazardous Mont Cenis pass which had served as the crossing for travelers to Italy since the days of Hannibal.

Hors d'Oeuvres Variés

Risotto Piemontese*

Lake Trout with Green Sauce*

Filet de Boeuf à la Victor Emmanuel

Bear Cub Cutlets Sauce Mauresque

Galantine* of Truffled Turkey

Roman Punch*

Roasted Haunch of Chamois   Juniper-seasoned Thrushes on Canapés

Spinach à la Piemontese   Petits Pois à la Crème*

Biscuit de Savoie*   Vanilla and Raspberry Ices

Café Express

THE GREEK EASTER

For Greeks the most solemn event in the Christian calendar is the Feast of the Resurrection, or Pasch (from the Hebrew word for Passover). Many of its traditions stem from such pagan festivals as the springtime rites of the Eleusinian mysteries observed as early as the seventh century B.C. Initiates in the cult devoted to Demeter, the goddess of vegetation, tried to ensure the year's forthcoming growth of grain by undergoing a preliminary fast, sitting through an all-night vigil and taking a communion of barley water from a sacred goblet. Similarly, devout Greeks today abstain from eating meat during Lent, and on Holy Week eliminate even eggs, milk, and fish from their diet. Communion is taken the day before Easter, and a church service beginning early that evening terminates at midnight when the priest chants, "Christ has risen from the dead, bestowing death unto death, and awarding to those in the graves eternal life." At this, members of the congregation kiss one another, explode fireworks, and commence merrymaking, or as one nineteenth-century visitor aptly put it: "The Versatile Greeks [are now] as ardent and eager in the pursuit of pleasure as they [were] but an hour previously in that of salvation." Returning to their homes people breakfast on hitherto forbidden treats like the lamb soup mayiritsa, Easter bread with feta (goat's cheese) and honey. Boiled eggs dyed red to symbolize the blood of Christ are served "merely in compliance with the national custom, as an Easter emblem; for on this the day of emancipation from the thrall of fast, [few have] a thought to bestow on such fare." Instead, the eggs are part of a ritual, one person cracking another's and exclaiming "*Christos Anesti*" (Christ has been resurrected), to which the affirmative reply is, "*Alithos Anesti*" (He has indeed risen). It is much later on Sunday, however, that feasts of Homeric magnitude begin. Complying with the Macedonian proverb that "Easter without lamb is a thing which cannot be," families begin the roasting on huge outdoor spits. To stave off hunger they munch such *mezedes*, or appetizers, as taramosalata, Greek caviar, and kokoretzi (grilled lamb's liver and intestines). Surfeited with dinner, retsina (wine flavored with resin), and too much dancing, people attempt to ward off indigestion with a dish of yoghurt. The holiday for the pleasure-loving Greeks by no means ends here; shortly after, in celebration of the Feast of Saint George, people named George visit from house to house . . . and the rounds of food continue.

Break Fast

Mayiritsa*

Hard-boiled Eggs   *Easter Bread**

Feta Cheese   *Honey*

Coffee

Mezedakia

Greek Olives   *Mashed Chick-peas**

Taramosalata*

Pickled Jellied Fish* in a Cross-shaped Mold

Greek Apéritifs

Easter Dinner

Roast Lamb with Rosemary*

Pilaf*   *Baked Eggplant*

Green Salad

Baklava*   *Kourabiedes**   *Fruits*

Yoghurt

Retsina

A BALL SUPPER

Oysters

Consommé à la Royale   *Crème de Volaille**

*Sole Normande**   *Mayonnaise of Lobster*

*Galantine**   *Pheasant*   *Larks in Aspic*

Turkey à l'Impératrice

Cold Sliced Ham   *Melton Mowbray Pie**

Queen's Cakes   *Maids of Honour**   *Bavarian Cream**

To be accepted in Victorian London society, observed an American diplomat, "one must be great or famous, or one must dance. . . . The average London man of society thinks dancing a very slow amusement. He is
either athletic, and prefers hunting or yachting, or he is dissolute, and
simple pleasures pall upon his jaded appetite. As a rule, too, important
young men do not dance. The greater a man is, the more he is careful to
abstain from anything that will make him entertaining." Small wonder
that the hostess of a private dance felt compelled to offer a lavish spread
to supplement the music—and appreciated all the professional advice
she could get. The menu above is from a popular book called *Breakfasts,
Luncheons, and Ball Suppers*, published in 1887. The author, a mysterious
Major L . . . , offered some peripheral advice: "I shall give only four Bills
of Fare. Anyone who gives *more* than *four* balls in one year will probably
be in a lunatic asylum before the next, so will not require more."

RECIPES

APPETIZERS

"Be wisely frugal in thy preparation, and freely cheerful in thy entertainment: if thy guests be right, it is enough; if not, it is too much; too much is a vanity; enough is a feast." Thus the seventeenth-century English poet Francis Quarles cited the rules for launching a successful party dinner. It was in Scandinavia, however, that the custom of serving preprandial drinks with a formal assortment of piquant dishes started. The aquavit table, as it was called, migrated from there to Russia, where *zakuski* (little bits) absorbed the native vodka. In the nineteenth century, France adopted the Russian tidbits and renamed them *hors d'oeuvres à la russe*, "hors d'oeuvres" meaning outside the chef's main work. Variations on the appetizer theme include the German *Vorspiesen*, the Italian *antipasti*, the Middle Eastern *mesé*, the Spanish *tapas*, the South American *entremeses*, and the Japanese *zatsuki*. To abate the effects of the alcohol served with them, these foods are typically rich in oil and cream, often made with expensive, luxury ingredients, and served in small quantities.

SOUPS

"The word *soupe*," said the eighteenth-century *Dictionnaire de Trévoux*, "is French, but extremely bourgeois; it is well to serve *potage* and not *soupe*." These social subtleties aside, there are two distinct subdivisions in the recipes that comprise this course, and in many European countries the French names prevail. By *soupe* Frenchmen mean clear broths into which minced herbs, diced meats or vegetables, toast, and other garnishes are added. In peasant households the hearty *soupe* often provides the main dish of the *souper*, or supper. *Potage* is a more subtle mélange in which the broth is thickened with egg yolks and cream, a starch, or a purée of vegetables, and to which garnishes may or may not be added. The Italians call anything containing a starch such as pasta, rice, or potatoes a *minestra*; all other broths, clear or thickened, are called *zuppa*.

BROTH

To the French, stocks are known as the *fonds de cuisine* because these preparations provide the bases for a variety of soups, sauces, stews, aspics, and glazes. Well-flavored broths—whether called stocks, bouillons, or consommés—have been essential to the cooking of every country.

1 3-pound beef shin and 2 pounds chuck or 1 5-pound soup chicken with giblets or 1 3-pound veal shank and 2 pounds veal shoulder
2 pounds veal or beef marrow bones
3 quarts water
1 onion, peeled and studded with 3 cloves
1 large leek, with green tops, split and well washed
2 large carrots, scraped and cut in half lengthwise

2 stalks celery, with leaves
1 white turnip, peeled and quartered (optional)
Root vegetables, such as $\frac{1}{2}$ scraped parsnip, 1 scraped Italian parsley root, and 1 small knob celery root, peeled and cut in half (optional)
3 to 4 sprigs parsley, preferably Italian
1 small bay leaf
Pinch of thyme
5 peppercorns
Salt

Place cut-up meat or quartered chicken and marrow bones in a tall soup kettle or marmite. Add water, which should cover meat and bones completely; if it does not, the pot is too wide and shallow. Do not add more than 3 quarts water. Bring to a boil, reduce heat, and simmer gently, covered. Skim off foam and scum as they rise to the surface. When surface is clear, add all other ingredients, including salt to taste. Cover and continue simmering slowly for 3 to 4 hours. Soup should never boil. Do not add more salt during cooking. When done, strain soup through a double thickness of cheesecloth that has been wrung out in cold water or through a very fine, double-mesh sieve. Discard vegetables and bones and, if desired, reserve meat or chicken for salads, hash, pot pies, or similar dishes. They may also be cut up and served in the broth. Season strained stock, cool, and refrigerate. If stock is to be reduced, do not add more salt or other seasonings at this point. To reduce stock further, simply simmer it uncovered until it is as strong as desired and adjust seasonings. Makes 12 cups.

VARIATIONS: *Double Consommé*: Reduce stock by one half. *Clarified Stock*: For every 4 cups of broth, have on hand 2 egg whites and 2 crushed egg shells. Bring stock to a boil. Add shells and beaten egg whites, bring to a boil again and stir for 1 to 2 minutes. Remove from heat and pour through a sieve that has been lined with a double thickness of cheesecloth wrung out in cold water. Heat thoroughly if this is to be served as a soup, and adjust seasoning. Clarifying reduces flavor, so season as needed. If this is to be used as an ingredient in a recipe, reheat or not, as called for. *Brown Stock*: To add color to stock for gravies and for stews, brown the bones in hot oven before adding them to the soup. Also use 1 unpeeled onion browned in the oven. If preferred, a peeled, diced onion may be browned in a little fat, but the flavor will be less delicate. *National Variations*: In northern and central Europe the optional root vegetables are always added, while the bay leaf, thyme, and cloves are eliminated. A few sprays of dill are usually included. In Italy a tomato or a little canned tomato juice is added to broth when it is to be served as a soup. In the Middle East lamb meat and bones are used in place of other meats. When preparing national dishes that call for stock, prepare the stock accordingly to maintain the authentic flavor of the dish.

SOUP GARNISHES

Garnishes have always been a favorite way to embellish simple soups. Mille Fanti (Soup of a Thousand Infants) and Minestra del Paradiso were gathered by the Florentine gastronome, Pellegrino Artusi, at the end of the nineteenth century. Each of the following garnishes is planned for 6 servings unless otherwise indicated.

MILLE FANTI

2 eggs, well beaten
$\frac{1}{4}$ cup semolina, farina, or cream of wheat
1 tablespoon grated Parmesan cheese
Pinch of nutmeg (optional)
$6\frac{1}{2}$ cups hot broth

Mix eggs, semolina, cheese, and nutmeg until well blended and smooth. Stir in *one-half cup broth* and pour mixture slowly into *remaining 6 cups boiling broth*. Simmer for 3 to 5 minutes, or until egg is cooked, and serve.

BRUNOISE

1 small onion
2 small carrots
1 turnip
2 small leeks
3 stalks celery
$\frac{1}{2}$ teaspoon salt,

1 teaspoon sugar
4 tablespoons butter
1 cup broth
$\frac{1}{2}$ cup cooked peas
Fresh minced chervil for garnish

Wash and scrape all vegetables as necessary, except peas, and finely dice. Sprinkle with salt and sugar and sauté for 1 minute in hot melted butter. Cover and cook gently for 10 minutes, stirring frequently, until vegetables are tender and faintly golden brown. Add broth and simmer for another 15 minutes. Just before serving, stir brunoise into 6 cups of broth, add peas, and sprinkle with chervil.

COLBERT

Vegetable brunoise, prepared
   according to above recipe

6 poached eggs
Fresh minced chervil

Garnish each serving of chicken broth with some of the vegetable brunoise, 1 poached egg, and a sprinkling of chervil.

MARROW TOAST

12 thin slices French bread
3 to 4 tablespoons butter

3 to 4 4-inch lengths of marrow bone

Fry bread in hot melted butter, turning once so that both sides become golden brown. Remove marrow from bones carefully so it does not break and cut into $\frac{1}{2}$-inch slices. Place slices in cold water in a saucepan; then heat to just below boiling point. Remove from heat and add cold water to reduce heat rapidly. Let stand in water until ready to serve. Spread toast with marrow; serve with broth or Petite Marmite (see Portugal Broth, page 424).

MINESTRA DEL PARADISO

4 eggs, separated
4 teaspoons fine, dry bread crumbs
4 teaspoons grated Parmesan cheese

Pinch of nutmeg
6 cups beef broth

Beat egg whites until they are stiff but not dry. Beat yolks lightly and fold into egg whites along with bread crumbs, cheese, and nutmeg. Bring 6 cups beef broth to a boil and drop batter from a teaspoon to form tiny puffs. Remove from heat and cover pot. Let stand for 7 to 8 minutes or until dumplings are puffed up and thoroughly cooked.

MATZO BALLS

2 eggs, lightly beaten
2 tablespoons rendered chicken fat
½ cup water

1 teaspoon salt
¼ teaspoon white pepper
¾ cup matzo meal

Beat together eggs, chicken fat, water, salt, and pepper. Gradually beat in enough matzo meal to make a soft, porridge-like paste. Chill for 3 to 5 hours. With wet hands, shape into balls, each about the size of a lime. Drop gently into 2 quarts boiling, lightly salted water. Reduce to a simmer, cover, and cook for 30 to 35 minutes. To remain light, matzo balls should cook at a steady, though gentle, simmer. Remove from water with a slotted spoon and serve in hot chicken broth. Leftover cooked matzo balls may be sliced when cold and fried in butter. Makes 18 to 20 matzo balls.

GERMAN LIVER DUMPLINGS

5 slices white bread or 4 small rolls
1 cup lukewarm milk
¾ pound beef liver, all tubes and
   membranes removed
2 ounces kidney fat
1 small onion

2 eggs
1 teaspoon salt
Pinch of marjoram
Grated rind of 1 lemon
½ to 1 cup bread crumbs
8 cups beef broth

Dice bread or rolls, with crusts. Soak in warm milk until milk becomes cool; squeeze out excess milk. Grind together bread, liver, kidney fat, and onion through the fine blade of a food chopper. Stir in eggs, salt, marjoram, and lemon rind. Gradually add bread crumbs, 1 tablespoon at a time, until mixture can be shaped into dumplings, each about 1½ inches in diameter. Dumplings can be shaped most easily with wet hands. Drop dumplings gently into boiling beef broth. Reduce to a steady but slow simmer and cook uncovered for 15 to 20 minutes or until dumplings float. Serve in soup. 10 to 12 dumplings will serve 6 to 8.

419

SHIRUMONO

Like the French, the Japanese classify their soups, *shirumono*, into two groups: Suimono, which are clear broths to which various garnishes are added, and Miso soups, broths thickened with mashed, fermented soy bean paste, which may also be garnished. At a formal or festive dinner, both types may appear, the clear Suimono at the start, and the Miso somewhere in the middle of the meal. Simple Miso soups are also standard breakfast fare. A fish-flavored stock, Dashi, is also frequently used in Japanese cooking; combined with chicken broth, it is served as a soup.

SUIMONO

Bones and giblets from large chicken or
  1 small stewing chicken
8 cups water
2 slices fresh ginger root or 1 teaspoon
  powdered ginger

3 scallions with green tops or 1 leek
  with green top
Soy sauce
Salt
Monosodium glutamate

Simmer chicken or bones in water with ginger and scallions for $1\frac{1}{2}$ hours. Skim scum and fat as they rise to surface. Strain and reduce broth to about 6 cups. Serve with soy sauce, salt, and monosodium glutamate. Serves 4 to 6.

EGG AND GREENS SUIMONO

6 sheets uncoated typing paper
  ($8\frac{1}{2}$ by 11 inches)
6 eggs

18 trefoils or sprigs of Italian parsley
6 small strips lemon rind
6 cups Suimono broth (page 420)

Fold each sheet of paper in half from top to bottom, then in half again from side to side. This will produce a small rectangle. Bring some water to a boil in a small, straight-sided saucepan. Break 1 egg into a cup and gently pour this into the front pocket of 1 sheet of folded paper. Fold top of paper over to form a triangle and close the pocket. Set paper triangle upright in water, point down, and simmer gently for 7 to 8 minutes or until egg is completely set. Do not attempt to cook more than 1 egg at a time. As each egg is finished, place it in the refrigerator, still in the paper. When all eggs are cooked and thoroughly chilled, slip them out of the paper. Wash parsley and knot stems together in bunches of three. Blanch parsley in hot water for a few seconds, then plunge it briefly into cold water. Place 1 egg and 1 bunch of parsley in each serving of suimono broth and garnish with a strip of lemon peel. If Japanese soup bowls are used, cover and serve. Serves 6.

MISO

6 ounces miso paste
5 cups water
½ pound lean pork shoulder,
  cut into 1-inch cubes

1 pound fresh spinach, chopped, or 1
  package frozen chopped spinach
1 slice ginger root or a pinch of
  powdered ginger
2 scallions, greens and bulbs, minced

Blend miso paste into water until smooth. Bring to boil and add pork. Simmer for 30 minutes or until pork is cooked. Add spinach and simmer for 5 minutes more. If using powdered ginger, add it with spinach. If fresh ginger is used, grate it into the finished soup. Serve garnished with minced scallion. Serves 6.

VARIATION: Miso soup may be made as above with any minced solid meats, fish, shellfish, and vegetables added to it. Diced eggplant, minced dried and soaked mushrooms, chicken, clams, shrimps, carrots, Japanese radishes, or bean curds may be included singly or in any preferred combination.

DASHI

2 tablespoons dashi no moto (mixture of
  bonito shavings and seaweed) or
  1 tablespoon katsuobushi (dried bonito

  shavings) and 1 tablespoon kombu
  (seaweed), rinsed
4 cups boiling water

If you can get packaged dashi no moto, follow instructions on the box. Otherwise, add bonito shavings and seaweed to boiling water in lidded pot. Boil for 3 minutes, raising the lid several times to stir broth. Strain. Serves 4.

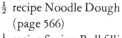

WON TON

½ recipe Noodle Dough
  (page 566)
½ recipe Spring Roll filling (page 569)

1 egg, beaten
1 quart water, lightly salted

Roll dough out to paper thinness; cut into 2-inch squares. To fill each square, turn it with one point toward you, so that square is in a diamond shape. Place 1 generous teaspoonful of filling on the point nearest you. Make two tight turns, jelly-roll fashion, so that square is half rolled. Dab a little beaten egg on the two wide opposite points and pinch them together around rolled filling. There should be a loose flap of dough opposite the filled portion. Bring 1 quart of lightly salted water to a boil. Add won ton and boil for 5 to 7 minutes. Rinse quickly under cold water and serve in hot chicken broth. Makes 12 won ton.

421

ESAU'S POTTAGE

According to the Old Testament, Esau sold his birthright for a "mess of pottage," a hearty lentil soup which has ever since been a staple in peasant households throughout the Middle East and Europe.

1 ham bone or smoked ham butt	Salt and pepper
7 cups water	Bouquet garni (pinch of thyme, 3 cloves,
1½ cups lentils	4 peppercorns, 3 sprigs of parsley,
1 large onion	1 bay leaf, 1 clove garlic, tied in
2 stalks celery with leaves, chopped	cheesecloth)
1 large carrot, sliced	

Simmer ham bone in water for 1 hour. Wash and pick over lentils. Add them to the ham bone and stock along with the onion, celery, carrot, ½ teaspoon salt, and the bouquet garni. Bring to a boil, reduce heat and simmer, partially covered, for about 1½ hours or until lentils are thoroughly cooked. Remove ham bone or butt and bouquet garni. Purée soup through a strainer or in a blender. Return to pot, heat thoroughly, and season with salt and pepper to taste. Serve in soup plates, sprinkled with a little parsley. If using ham butt, dice meat and serve it in the soup, or slice and serve as a separate course. Serves 6.

VARIATIONS: *Crème Esau*: Follow above recipe but use only 5 cups water in cooking lentils. After puréeing, stir in 2 cups scalded half-and-half (milk and cream). *Lentil Soup à la Paysanne*: Put all vegetables and herbs in cheesecloth bag for easy removal. Do not purée soup. Serve with bite-size pieces of ham and sliced cooked frankfurters in each portion. *German Lentil Soup*: Follow basic recipe but dice all vegetables and garlic and sauté in 3 tablespoons butter or bacon fat until light golden brown, then add to soup. Do not purée. Serve with diced ham meat, sliced frankfurters, and bits of crumbled, crisply fried bacon. *Armenian and Middle Eastern Lentil Soup*: Make with lamb stock rather than ham. Add 2 to 3 peeled, seeded, and chopped tomatoes or stir in ½ cup tomato purée during cooking. Chopped mint may be substituted for thyme and bay leaf in bouquet garni.

AERTER MED FLÄSK

The Swedish custom of eating this yellow split pea soup on Thursday dates back, it is said, to King Eric XIV, who died on a certain Thursday in 1577 after having eaten pea soup into which his brother was suspected to have slipped some poison.

1½ cups yellow split peas	1 teaspoon marjoram
10 cups water	Pinch of powdered ginger
1 pound piece of lean salt pork or bacon	Salt and pepper
2 onions, peeled and sliced	

Wash and pick over peas. Follow directions on package, soaking if needed. If so, cook the following day in the same water. Cook for 1½ to 2 hours, skimming off shells as they rise to the surface. Peas may be puréed at this point or left whole. Add pork, onions, marjoram, and ginger; simmer gently but steadily for 1 hour or until pork and peas are tender. Season with salt and pepper to taste. Remove pork from soup, slice, and serve on a platter with mustard and accompanied by chilled aquavit. Serves 4 to 6.

VARIATIONS: *Gule Aerter (Danish Pea Soup)*: Add 1 peeled and cubed knob celery or 3 stalks chopped celery, 2 sliced leeks, 3 diced carrots, and 3 peeled and diced potatoes to the soup, along with the onions and pork. Shortly before serving add 1 pound sliced Canadian bacon and a few sliced Vienna sausages or frankfurters to the soup and simmer until they are hot. Serve meat on the side. *Snuten and Puten (Dutch Pea Soup)*: Follow basic variations with vegetables indicated for Danish version. The meats to be added are 4 fresh pig's knuckles and, if you can get it, a pig's snout. *Erbsensuppe auf Berliner Aert (Berlin Pea Soup)*: Follow directions for the Danish version but also add ½ diced scraped parsnip and 1 peeled and diced parsley root with the other vegetables. Use any or all the meats and garnish with Spaetzle (page 567). This soup is often thickened as follows: sauté 1 small minced onion in 3 tablespoons butter until golden brown. Stir in 3 tablespoons flour and sauté, stirring frequently, until flour turns light brown. Beat into finished soup and simmer just below boiling point for 10 minutes, stirring occasionally until soup is smooth and thickened.

MY LORD LUMLEY'S PEASE-POTAGE

Most of the peas in this soup are strained. The reason for leaving some of them whole, says Digby, "is only to shew that it is Pease-potage."

5 tablespoons butter	2½ cups fresh or frozen green peas
1 leek, minced	4 cups chicken broth
½ small onion, minced	1 teaspoon sugar
½ head Boston lettuce, shredded	1 cup light cream
1 tablespoon flour	Salt
¼ teaspoon powdered coriander	1 teaspoon chopped fresh chervil or
¼ teaspoon white pepper	½ teaspoon dried chervil

Melt 3 *tablespoons of butter* in a large saucepan and stew the leek, onion, and lettuce until lettuce is wilted. Add the flour and cook for 2 minutes over low flame. Add coriander, pepper, peas, broth, and sugar; simmer until peas are just tender. Pick out and reserve ½ cup whole peas; purée remaining peas and vegetables. Return to the fire, add cream and season with salt to taste; heat to the boiling point. Swirl in *remaining butter* and serve with a sprinkling of whole peas and chervil. Serves 6 to 8.

VARIATION: *Potage Fontanges*: Follow above recipe, eliminating lettuce and coriander. After soup is done and cream has been added, stir in 4 tablespoons puréed sorrel or spinach, or ½ package thawed frozen spinach, and about 3 tablespoons butter.

PORTUGAL BROTH AS IT WAS MADE FOR THE QUEEN

This recipe for Portugal Broth, taken daily by Queen Henrietta Maria of England for her health, comes from *The Closet of the Eminently Learned Sir Kenelm Digby Kt. Opened*, 1669. Similar soups are Poule-au-pot, which Henry IV hoped would feed all France, and Pot-au-feu.

1 veal knuckle, cracked
3 pounds beef, flank, rump, or chuck, neatly tied
2 pounds neck or shoulder of lamb or mutton (optional)
1 4- to 5-pound stewing chicken, quartered
4 quarts cold water
2 large onions, quartered
4 leeks, with green tops

Bouquet garni (1 clove garlic, 1 bay leaf, 6 sprigs parsley, $\frac{1}{2}$ teaspoon thyme, 2 cloves, 5 peppercorns, and optional herbs such as $\frac{1}{2}$ teaspoon dried mint, 2 crushed coriander seeds, and $\frac{1}{4}$ teaspoon saffron, tied in cheesecloth)
Salt and pepper
1 small cabbage, shredded (optional)
Slices of toast
3 tablespoons minced parsley

Place bones and meat in a large soup kettle or marmite. Cover with cold water—about 4 quarts in all. Bring to a boil, reduce heat, cover, and simmer gently. Skim scum off as it rises to the surface. When no more appears, wipe sides of kettle and add the onions, the leeks, and the bouquet garni. Cover and simmer slowly but steadily for $3\frac{1}{2}$ hours or until all meats are tender. Season with salt and pepper to taste. Simmer cabbage in 1 cup of the broth for about 10 minutes or until tender. Remove meat from broth and strain. Remove fat from the surface. Meat may be diced and added to soup or reserved for other dishes. Pour soup into a tureen, add cabbage, and serve over slices of toast in soup plates. Garnish with fresh minced parsley. Shredded sorrel, endive, or lettuce may be added as garnishes along with herbs such as dill, fennel, or borage. Serves 10 to 12.

VARIATIONS: *Pot-au-feu* and *Petite Marmite*: Prepare exactly as above, eliminating mutton or lamb and the optional herbs. Add 2 scraped carrots, 2 stalks of celery with leaves, 1 peeled white turnip with the onions and leeks called for above. This should be made in an earthenware marmite, but an enameled cast-iron or heavy aluminum soup pot may be used. Serve with cabbage, as described above, and garnish with rounds of Marrow Toast (page 418) or Hot Horseradish Sauce (page 637). Chicken may be served on the side. To give broth a deep golden color, if desired, place onions and leeks in a moderate oven for about 30 minutes or until they are golden brown before adding them to the broth. *Poule-au-pot*: Prepare exactly as above, eliminating the beef and lamb and adding 1 more chicken. If desired, the chickens may be cooked whole, stuffed with a mixture of $\frac{1}{2}$ pound minced ham, $\frac{1}{2}$ pound minced pork, 3 to 4 chopped chicken livers, 2 small minced onions, minced parsley, and salt and pepper. Serve soup with vegetables, then serve sliced chicken with a little soup.

GARBURE

Béarn, in southwestern France, claims this traditional vegetable soup. Its name could come from the Spanish *garbias* (stew), or the Béarnais term *garburatye* (any collection or mixture of green vegetables). A delightful variation of Garbure is Goudale. When the diner has eaten all the bread and vegetables from the soup, he adds a cup of red or white wine to the remaining broth and drinks up.

1 medium cabbage, shredded	1 sprig thyme or pinch of dried thyme
4 potatoes, finely chopped	Salt and pepper
4 leeks, finely chopped	2 quarts water
1 turnip, finely chopped	1 red sweet pepper, diced
2 carrots, finely chopped	$\frac{1}{2}$ pound string beans, diced
1 medium onion, finely chopped	1 1-pound piece salt pork
1 cup kidney beans, previously soaked, if necessary	Small can preserved goose (optional)
	$\frac{1}{4}$ cup chopped parsley
2 cloves garlic, minced (optional)	12 to 16 slices toasted French bread

Put cabbage, potatoes, leeks, turnip, carrots, onion, kidney beans, and garlic in a soup kettle. Season with thyme, salt, and pepper. Add 2 quarts water or enough to cover the vegetables. Simmer for $1\frac{1}{2}$ hours; add the sweet pepper, string beans, salt pork, and goose. Simmer for 1 hour longer. Correct seasoning. Add parsley. Serve in individual soup plates in which 1 to 2 slices of bread have been placed. Sliced pork and goose are to be passed on separate platter and added to soup. Serves 6 to 8.

CALDO VERDE

As a visitor to Portugal in 1787, William Beckford observed: I never beheld eaters or eateresses . . . lay about [their food] with greater intrepidity." The Portuguese were among the first Europeans to cook with potatoes, one of their favorite dishes being the fortifying soup Caldo Verde, made from kale and potatoes.

4 potatoes	Salt and pepper
3 tablespoons olive oil	2 pounds kale or green cabbage
8 cups water	$\frac{1}{2}$ pound smoked garlic sausage

Peel and slice potatoes. Combine with olive oil and water and cook for 20 to 30 minutes or until potatoes are very soft. Purée potatoes through a sieve and return to liquid. Season with salt and pepper to taste and simmer gently for 30 minutes. Wash kale or cabbage, discarding all tough leaves and ribs, and cut into shreds. Add to potatoes and cook for 30 minutes. Add cooked, sliced sausage. Correct seasoning and serve. Serves 6 to 8.

SCOTCH BROTH

Samuel Johnson ate as prodigiously as he wrote. On tasting Scotch Broth for the first time, while touring the Hebrides, he downed several plates of it at one sitting and said enigmatically, "I don't care how soon I eat it again." This recipe is adapted from one in Hannah Glasse's *The Art of Cookery made Plain and Easy.*

1 pound boneless stewing lamb, cut
  into small cubes
1 pound lamb bones in cheesecloth
$2\frac{1}{2}$ quarts water
1 cup chopped onion

1 cup diced celery
1 cup diced carrots
Salt and pepper
$\frac{1}{2}$ cup pearl barley
$\frac{1}{2}$ cup chopped parsley

Place all ingredients except salt and pepper, barley, and parsley in a soup kettle. Bring to a boil and skim carefully. Reduce heat and season with 1 teaspoon salt and $\frac{1}{2}$ teaspoon pepper. Simmer covered for $1\frac{1}{4}$ hours; add barley and cook for 45 minutes or until meat and barley are both very tender. Remove bones and correct seasoning. Serve generously sprinkled with chopped parsley. Serves 8 to 10.

COCK-A-LEEKIE

According to Scottish tradition, this dish evolved from cockfighting. The loser was tossed into the pot, with leeks for flavor, and spectators all shared the soup. Some say Cock-A-Leekie is just an adaptation of a fourteenth-century English dish called Ma-Leachi, "ma" meaning fowl.

1 stewing chicken, cut up
1 calf's foot or veal knuckle,
  cleaned and split
2 quarts water
1 carrot, sliced
Bouquet garni ($\frac{1}{2}$ teaspoon marjoram,
  $\frac{1}{4}$ teaspoon thyme, 1 bay leaf,
  $\frac{1}{2}$ teaspoon chervil, 2 cloves,
  4 sprigs parsley, 4 peppercorns,
  tied in cheesecloth)

1 onion, finely chopped
$\frac{1}{4}$ cup pearl barley
5 leeks, finely chopped
2 tablespoons butter
12 prunes (optional)
Salt and pepper
8 slices toasted bread
2 tablespoons chopped parsley

Simmer chicken and calf's foot in 2 quarts water, skimming surface. Add carrot, bouquet garni, and onion and simmer for 2 hours. Add barley and simmer for 40 to 45 minutes. Sauté leeks in the butter until soft but not brown. Add leeks and prunes to soup. and season with salt and pepper to taste. Simmer for 15 minutes. Discard bouquet garni. Take chicken and calf's foot from soup and bone them. Cut meat in bite-size pieces and return to soup. Serve in a tureen, over toasted bread. Sprinkle with parsley. Serves 8.

CREME DE VOLAILLE FEDORA

Adolphe Dugléré, the famed chef at Café Anglais in Paris, created this soup in 1882 to honor Victorien Sardou and Sarah Bernhardt, the author and star of the new theatrical *succès fou, Fédora.*

8 cups well-flavored broth made with
   1 4-pound chicken and a veal bone
Breast of the soup chicken, skinned,
   boned, and julienned
6 ripe tomatoes, peeled and seeded, or
   $\frac{3}{4}$ cup canned tomato purée
1 cup cooked rice

$\frac{1}{4}$ cup milk
$\frac{1}{4}$ cup water
$\frac{1}{4}$ pound vermicelli
Salt and pepper
2 egg yolks
$\frac{1}{2}$ cup heavy cream

Keep broth hot but not boiling. Spoon a little soup over the julienne strips of chicken and keep warm. Rub peeled and seeded tomatoes through a sieve into the broth or add tomato purée to broth. Combine cooked rice with milk and water and simmer gently until all liquid is absorbed and mixture is creamy, about 5 to 8 minutes. Turn rice mixture into soup. Simmer until smoothly blended, stirring frequently. Cook vermicelli in salted water until tender and drain well. Beat egg yolks with cream. Gradually add about 1 cup of hot broth to egg yolk mixture, beating constantly. Pour back slowly into remaining soup, beating constantly. Season with salt and pepper to taste; heat thoroughly but do not boil. Place a little vermicelli in each bowl, add soup, and garnish with julienne strips of chicken. If there is any meat on the veal bone, it may be finely shredded and added to the soup along with the chicken. Serves 6 to 8.

TO MAKE AN ONION SOOP

Cream distinguishes this eighteenth-century English variation on the old French soup. Hannah Glasse offered it along with such helpful prescriptions as "a certain Cure for the Bite of a Mad Dog."

10 tablespoons butter
6 large yellow onions, sliced
8 cups strong beef broth
$\frac{1}{4}$ cup cognac (optional)
Salt and pepper

2 egg yolks
$\frac{1}{2}$ cup light cream
12 slices toasted French bread
Parmesan cheese, freshly grated

Melt the butter in a soup kettle and stew onion rings slowly for 30 minutes, without browning. Add beef broth and simmer for 20 minutes. Add cognac (optional) and season with salt and pepper. Beat the yolks into the cream. Slowly add a little hot soup, beating constantly, and slowly pour the yolk-cream mixture back into the kettle, beating constantly. Put 2 slices of toasted French bread in each soup plate and add soup. Pass Parmesan cheese. Serves 6.

BORSCH

Endless, excellent varieties of Borsch are made throughout the Slavic countries. These recipes include a hefty meat-and-cabbage Borsch (almost a meal in itself) from the Ukraine and a clear, all-beet Borschok common to many Slavic lands.

2 pounds lean beef, rump or round
2 pounds beef bones
3 onions, quartered
4 stalks celery, diced
4 carrots, quartered
3 small leeks, chopped
Handful parsley, with stems
2 large white turnips, diced
2 parsnips, diced

8 peppercorns
6 large beets, julienne
1 cabbage, cut into small wedges
1 large can tomatoes or 6 fresh tomatoes, peeled, seeded, coarsely chopped
Salt and pepper
2 tablespoons wine vinegar
1 teaspoon sugar
2 cups sour cream

Wipe meat and bones and put into a soup kettle. Cover with 4 quarts water; bring to a boil and skim carefully until only white foam appears. Wipe the sides of the kettle. Add vegetables to the soup, with the exception of the beets, cabbage, and tomatoes. Add 1 tablespoon salt, cover and simmer for 3 hours. Strain, reserve the meat, and return broth to clean kettle. Discard bones and vegetables. Add beets, cabbage, and tomatoes. Season with salt and pepper to taste and simmer for 1 hour. Add vinegar and sugar. Serve with meat cut up in the soup. Pass a bowl of sour cream to be used for garnish. The longer this soup cooks the better it tastes. Serve with meat Pirozhki or Pirog (page 508). Serves 10.

BORSCHOK

5 to 6 beets, chopped
6 cups strong beef broth
1 onion
2 teaspoons sugar, or to taste
Salt and pepper

1 to 2 tablespoons lemon juice or vinegar, or to taste
3 tablespoons minced dill (optional)
1 cup sour cream

Simmer beets in water to cover until tender—about 15 to 20 minutes. Simmer beef broth with onion for about 15 minutes. Remove onion and combine broths. Season to taste with sugar, salt and pepper, and lemon juice or vinegar. Mix dill into sour cream. If soup is served hot, top each portion with a spoonful of the sour cream-dill mixture. Soup may also be served chilled, with the sour cream-dill mixture stirred into it. A tablespoon of minced, seeded cucumber may be added to the chilled version. Serves 6 to 8.

OUKHA

This fish soup has been a traditional dish in Russia for centuries. Four kinds of Oukha, made of pike, perch, zander, and carp, appear on a list of eatables prepared for a fast day at the house of a wealthy Russian boyar on February 14, 1656.

1 pound fish (such as halibut, sole, or striped bass), cut into 2-inch pieces
2½ pounds fish trimmings
1½ cups dry white wine
3 medium onions, chopped
1 parsley root, scraped (optional)
2 stalks celery, chopped
3 mushrooms, chopped

3 tablespoons minced fresh dill or 1½ tablespoons dried dill
1 bay leaf
4 peppercorns
2 quarts water
Salt and pepper
¼ cup butter
3 to 4 scallions, chopped

Wipe the fish and set it aside. Put fish trimmings, wine, onions, parsley root, celery, mushrooms, *half the dill*, bay leaf, and peppercorns into a soup kettle with 2 quarts water and 2 teaspoons salt, ¼ teaspoon pepper. Simmer gently for 1 hour. Strain carefully. Clarify stock if desired (page 417). Melt the butter and gently sauté the fish. Turn fish, add scallions, sauté for 5 to 6 minutes and season with salt and pepper. Add to the broth. Serve sprinkled with *remaining dill*. Serves 6 to 8.

SHCHI

It mattered greatly to Nicholas I of Russia, who was essentially of German persuasion and tastes, to be accepted as a good Russian monarch. Thinking that the safest way to his people's heart was through his own stomach, he displayed a preference for Shchi and for Kasha (cooked buckwheat). He continued to feed furtively on his German favorites.

1 pound sauerkraut
2 large onions, chopped
1 stalk celery, diced
3 tablespoons butter
2½ quarts hot beef broth
2 pounds lean beef, cut into cubes, or 8 sliced frankfurters

Bouquet garni (½ bay leaf, 6 peppercorns, pinch of thyme, tied in cheesecloth)
Salt and pepper
8 small potatoes, boiled in their skins
2 tablespoons chopped fresh dill or 1 tablespoon dried dill
1 cup sour cream

Rinse the sauerkraut in cold water and drain well. Stew onion and celery slowly in butter until soft. Add sauerkraut and sauté until slightly golden. Add broth, meat, and bouquet garni; simmer for 2 hours. Discard bouquet garni, season with salt and pepper to taste, and serve with whole, peeled potatoes, dill, and sour cream. Serves 6 to 8.

INDIAN SHRIMP CURRY SOUP

1½ pounds shrimps, cooked, shelled, and deveined
1 large onion, grated
2 cloves garlic, minced
2 thin slices ginger root, minced, or ½ teaspoon powdered ginger
½ teaspoon powdered turmeric
¼ teaspoon powdered cumin

Salt and pepper
¼ cup butter
1 hot green chili pepper or dash of Tabasco
3 cups chicken broth
1½ cups Coconut Milk (page 632)
1 cup thick Coconut Cream (page 632)
1 cup cooked rice

Reserve a *few whole shrimps* for garnish. Mince the *remainder* and pound to a paste or purée in blender. Make a paste of the onion, garlic, ginger, turmeric, cumin, ½ teaspoon salt, and add a spoonful or two of water if needed. Heat the butter and cook the spice paste for 3 to 4 minutes. Add shrimp paste, chili pepper or Tabasco, and chicken broth. Stir and simmer for 20 minutes. Add the coconut milk and *half the coconut cream*. Bring to a boil. Correct the seasoning and serve with 2 tablespoons rice to each serving and a *spoonful of coconut cream* as topping. Garnish with *remaining whole shrimps*. Serves 4 to 6.

POTAGE PARMENTIER

France continued to spurn the potato long after it had been accepted in other European countries, dismissing it as food for pigs and a possible cause of leprosy. Antoine-Auguste Parmentier knew better. As a war prisoner of the Germans, he survived on potatoes for a year. In 1779 he entered the *Solanum tuberosum* in a French contest for "Plants that can best replace cereals in time of famine," and won first prize.

4 tablespoons butter
6 leeks or 2 large onions, chopped
3 stalks celery, diced
8 medium potatoes, peeled and quartered
Bouquet garni (8 peppercorns, few sprigs parsley, 1 bay leaf, pinch of thyme, tied in cheesecloth)

½ pound spinach or sorrel (optional)
2 quarts water
Salt and pepper
3 egg yolks
1 cup heavy cream, scalded and cooled
Chopped chervil or parsley
1 cup croutons

Melt the butter in a soup kettle and gently stew leeks or onion and celery until transparent. Add water, potatoes, the bouquet garni, and the spinach or sorrel, if desired. Season with 1 teaspoon salt and ¼ teaspoon pepper. Bring to a boil, cover and simmer for 20 minutes or until potatoes are very soft. Remove bouquet garni and purée through a sieve and return to the fire. Beat the yolks into the cream. Slowly add a little hot soup, beating constantly, and slowly pour mixture back into the kettle, beating constantly. Add salt and pepper to taste. Serve sprinkled with chervil or parsley and croutons. Serves 8 to 10.

SOPA DE AJO

Ever since garlic was introduced by the Romans, the herb has been a basic ingredient of Spanish cooking. Dishes like Sopa de Ajo not only satisfied hunger, but were believed to cure maladies ranging from snake bites to acid indigestion. Aristocrats, however, have occasionally turned up their noses at the pungent cloves; and in 1330 King Alfonso XI of Castile banished all knights reeking of garlic from his court for a month.

16 large cloves garlic, thinly sliced
4 tablespoons olive oil
8 cups water
Salt and black pepper

4 to 8 eggs
8 slices French bread, lightly fried in olive oil
4 tablespoons grated Parmesan cheese

Fry garlic slices very slowly in olive oil until they become golden brown on both sides—about 10 minutes. Bring water to a boil and add to garlic and oil, seasoning to taste with a little salt and pepper. Cover and simmer gently for 15 minutes. Check seasoning and correct. Garlic may be left in soup as is or removed with a slotted spoon, puréed, and blended back into soup. Poach 1 egg per serving in the soup or in water. Place 1 to 2 slices of toast in each bowl, top with cheese and finally with a poached egg. Add soup and serve at once. Serves 4 to 8. For soup with a little more body, cook garlic in 7 cups of water and 1 cup of beef stock. Do not use more stock than that or it will overpower the flavor of the garlic.

AVGOLEMONO

The Greeks have always had a penchant for piquant seasonings; relying on lemon juice to flavor practically every course of their meals from the popular Avgolemono soup onward. As the philosopher Theophrastus in the third century B.C. wrote: "if any one boils the inner part of the fruit in broth . . . and then swallows it, it makes his breath smell sweet."

8 cups chicken broth
½ cup rice
4 eggs, well beaten

Juice of 2 lemons
3 tablespoons minced dill or parsley
Salt and white pepper

Bring broth to a boil and cook rice in it until tender. Remove from heat. Slowly pour about 1 cup of hot soup into eggs, beating constantly. Slowly pour egg mixture back into remaining hot soup, beating constantly. Heat but do not boil. Stir in lemon juice, add dill or parsley, and season with salt and pepper to taste. Serves 4 to 6.

VARIATIONS: *Mayiritsa (Greek Easter Soup)*: Prepare 8 cups of lamb stock using 2 pounds lamb bones with some meat on them, 1 small onion, 2 stalks of celery, and a little salt and pepper. (Traditionally, lamb innards are cooked with this, but may be eliminated.) Strain lamb broth after it has simmered for 2 hours. Prepare as described above.

431

GAZPACHO

Since meat and poultry were traditionally scarce in southern Spain, Andalusian peasants devised nourishing substitutes with such staples as olive oil, garlic, and vegetables. Iced Gazpacho provided the poor with a cooling midday meal and the rich with a liquid salad to accompany other courses. Today there are some thirty classic versions of the soup. As the French traveler Théophile Gautier wrote in 1840, "strange as it may seem the first time one tastes it, one ends by getting used to it and even liking it."

4 large ripe tomatoes
2 green peppers
1 large cucumber
2 cloves garlic
3 slices white bread, crusts removed
7 to 8 tablespoons olive oil
3 tablespoons red wine vinegar
6 cups ice water

Salt
Garnishes: $\frac{1}{2}$ cup small croutons; $\frac{1}{2}$ cup minced onion, chives, or scallions; $\frac{1}{2}$ cup peeled and diced cucumber; $\frac{1}{2}$ cup seeded and chopped green pepper; $\frac{1}{2}$ cup peeled, seeded, and chopped tomato

Blanch tomatoes in boiling water for 1 minute or until skins wrinkle; peel. Remove seeds and cut tomatoes into small pieces. Seed and coarsely chop green peppers. Peel and coarsely chop cucumber. Slice garlic. Soak white bread in a little water, then squeeze out excess water. Purée tomatoes, green peppers, cucumber, garlic, and bread in a blender at low speed. Gradually and alternately add oil and vinegar until soup is smooth-textured with a piquant flavor. Adjust amounts of oil and vinegar to taste. Beat in *1 cup ice water*. Run soup through a fine sieve, add *remaining ice water*, and season with salt as needed. If soup is not to be served at once, chill after rubbing through a sieve, and stir in the 5 cups of ice water just before serving. Ladle into individual bowls and pass garnishes in separate dishes on the side. Serves 6 to 8.

VARIATIONS: *Gazpacho Sevillano* is made without soaked bread and is garnished with minced hard-boiled egg in addition to the vegetables and croutons. *Green Gazpacho* is a specialty of the Extremadura region of Spain and of Portugal as well. Follow above recipe but eliminate all tomatoes and use both soaked bread and 2 raw eggs in the blender mixture. Adjust oil and vinegar to taste and stir in ice water. Chill and serve with all garnishes except tomato.

CREAM OF CUCUMBER SOUP

2 large cucumbers, peeled, seeded,
   and minced
3 tablespoons minced onion
3 tablespoons butter
2 tablespoons minced parsley
4 tablespoons flour

2 cups chicken broth
2 cups milk or half-and-half (milk
   and cream)
1 teaspoon salt
Pinch of each: black pepper, cayenne
   pepper, and nutmeg

Simmer minced cucumber and onion in butter until cucumber begins to soften—about 3 minutes. Add parsley, cover, and braise over low heat for 5 minutes, stirring to prevent scorching. Sprinkle with flour and stir until flour is absorbed—about 2 to 3 minutes. Add chicken broth and milk and simmer covered for 10 minutes. Add salt and spices to taste and simmer for 2 to 3 minutes longer. Serves 6.

PISTOU

This soup originated in Genoa and emigrated to Nice when the House of Savoy occupied that part of France. The name comes from the thick paste of herbs and olive oil which is served with the soup.

$\frac{1}{4}$ cup olive oil
1 large onion, diced
3 tomatoes, peeled, seeded, and chopped
6 cups water
Salt and pepper
$\frac{1}{2}$ pound string beans or 1 package
   frozen string beans
$\frac{3}{4}$ cup half-cooked white kidney beans
2 zucchini, diced
3 large potatoes, peeled and diced
2 leeks, bulbs and greens, chopped

2 stalks celery, with leaves, chopped
2 tablespoons minced parsley
$\frac{1}{4}$ pound vermicelli, broken into
   short pieces
4 cloves garlic
Pinch of salt, preferably coarse
12 sprays of fresh basil or $\frac{1}{4}$ cup dried
   basil steeped in hot water and drained
2 tablespoons chopped parsley
4 to 5 tablespoons olive oil
Grated Parmesan or Gruyère cheese

Heat olive oil in a soup kettle and in it sauté onion until it just begins to take on color. Add chopped tomatoes. Simmer, uncovered, until tomatoes are soft—about 10 minutes. Stir frequently. Add the water and a little salt and pepper. Bring to a boil and add string beans (cut into 1-inch lengths), white beans, zucchini, potatoes, leeks, celery, and parsley. Simmer for 20 minutes. Parboil vermicelli in salted water. Drain and add to soup and continue cooking for another 10 minutes or until all vegetables and vermicelli are cooked. While soup cooks, prepare paste: peel and slice garlic and place in a mortar with a little salt to act as an abrasive. Pound until garlic is crushed and add basil and parsley. Pound to a thick, smooth paste. Slowly and gradually trickle in olive oil, working it into the paste with the pestle. Stir into the soup just before serving, along with grated cheese. Serves 6.

BLACK AND SOUR SOUP

Upon eating a meal of black broth among the Spartans, a visiting Sybarite commented that he no longer wondered at his hosts' valor. "The greatest coward on earth would rather die a thousand times than live and endure such [fare]." Contrary to this minority opinion, black broths are still widely eaten and enjoyed throughout Europe where less sanguine peoples substitute a brown roux and a little red wine for the traditional lamb or poultry blood. The following variation is especially favored in Germany.

3 pounds duck or goose giblets, necks, wings, livers, gizzards, and hearts
8 to 10 cups water
2 carrots, scraped and sliced
2 onions, diced
Salt
6 cloves
Pinch of marjoram

12 peppercorns, lightly crushed
1 pound mixed dried prunes and apples, soaked and drained
1 cup goose or duck blood (optional)
2 tablespoons flour
White vinegar to taste
Sugar to taste

Clean and scald meat as necessary, Bring water to a boil. Add meat, vegetables, 1 teaspoon of salt, cloves, marjoram, and peppercorns. Cover and simmer slowly for about 40 minutes or until giblets are tender. Add prunes and apples and simmer for 20 minutes. Mix blood with flour and stir into boiling sauce. Simmer for 5 minutes. Add vinegar and sugar to taste, producing a mild sweet-sour flavor. Serve giblets, fruits, and vegetables with sauce poured over them. Serves 4 to 8.

VARIATION: If you cannot get duck or goose blood, melt 6 tablespoons butter and stir in 6 tablespoons flour. Sauté slowly until flour turns a deep brown color. Add to stock and bring to a boil, stirring until well blended. Add a little red wine to taste.

CINNAMON WINE SOUP

3 cups dry red wine
1 stick cinnamon
1 strip lemon peel

3 tablespoons cornstarch
3 to 4 tablespoons sugar
2 egg yolks, beaten

Simmer wine with cinnamon and lemon peel for 10 minutes. Blend cornstarch to a paste 3 tablespoons cold water. Stir into 3 cups water and simmer for 5 minutes. Strain into hot wine mixture and simmer for 5 more minutes. Remove cinnamon and lemon peel and add sugar to taste. Gradually ladle about 1 cup of hot, not boiling, wine soup into egg yolks, beating constantly. Pour this mixture back into soup slowly, beating constantly. Heat but do not boil. Adjust seasonings and serve. This soup may also be served chilled. Serves 6.

HALASZLIE
(Hungarian Fisherman's Soup)

$\frac{1}{4}$ cup butter
3 onions, finely chopped
4 stalks celery, chopped
2 carrots, finely chopped
1 tablespoon paprika
Bouquet garni (1 clove garlic, 1 bay
   leaf, 8 peppercorns, 1 sprig thyme,
   10 sprigs parsley, tied in cheesecloth)
3 pounds fish trimmings
$\frac{1}{2}$ cup dry white wine or 2 tablespoons
   lemon juice or 2 tablespoons vinegar

Salt and pepper
$\frac{1}{2}$ cup green peas
$\frac{1}{2}$ cup diced green beans
$\frac{1}{2}$ cup diced carrots
$\frac{1}{2}$ cup diced onion
$2\frac{1}{2}$ pounds fresh-water fish (2 or more
   varieties, such as whitefish, carp, and
   pike), cut into 2-inch pieces
2 tablespoons chopped parsley

Melt the butter in a soup kettle and slowly stew the onion, celery, and carrots for 5 to 6 minutes until soft but not brown. Stir in paprika and cook for 2 to 3 minutes more. Add bouquet garni, fish trimmings, wine, and salt and pepper to taste. Cover with water and bring to a boil. Turn down heat and skim with care. Cover and simmer for 1 hour. Strain carefully through a dampened cloth or fine sieve. Return broth to a clean kettle. Add vegetables and simmer for 15 minutes. Add fish and poach gently for 7 to 8 minutes. Correct seasoning and serve sprinkled with parsley. Serves 8 to 10.

MEHLSUPPE

Mehlsuppe, based on ground wheat and butter, is served in rural regions of Switzerland, Germany, and Austria. This version from the Bernese Alps is flavored with caraway and cheese and resembles a fondue.

4 tablespoons butter
$\frac{1}{2}$ cup flour
4 cups water or beef broth
1 tablespoon caraway seeds
1 clove garlic

Salt and pepper
Nutmeg
$\frac{1}{2}$ cup milk
$\frac{1}{4}$ pound Swiss cheese, grated
8 slices toasted French bread

Melt butter and when it is hot, stir in flour. Cook over low heat, stirring almost constantly until flour is a rich golden brown. Do not let flour burn or turn black. Stir in water or beef broth and add caraway seeds, garlic, and salt, pepper, and nutmeg to taste. Bring to a boil, reduce heat, cover and simmer slowly for 30 to 40 minutes, stirring frequently and adding a little water if soup gets too sticky or lumpy. Stir in milk, heat for 2 to 3 minutes, but do not boil. Place grated cheese in preheated soup bowls or cups and add soup. Serve with toast on side, to be used for dunking or to be eaten in soup. A nice accompaniment is a glass of iced kirsch or pear brandy.

OKROSHKA
(Russian Minced Vegetable and Meat Soup)

$\frac{3}{4}$ cup cooked beef, diced

$\frac{3}{4}$ cup cooked ham, diced

$\frac{3}{4}$ cup cooked tongue, veal, or chicken, diced

1 large cucumber, peeled and diced

1 pickled dill cucumber, diced (optional)

1 bunch scallions, bulbs and greens, chopped

2 to 3 sprigs each dill and parsley, minced

3 hard-boiled eggs

1 teaspoon prepared mustard

1 teaspoon sugar

$\frac{3}{4}$ cup sour cream

Salt and pepper

1 quart Kvass (page 753)

Ice cubes

Combine all diced meats and vegetables. Separate egg whites and yolks. Chop whites and reserve. Mash yolks in a soup tureen or a large serving bowl and stir in mustard, sugar, sour cream, and salt and pepper to taste. Slowly pour in kvass; add meats and vegetables. Chill. Place 1 to 2 ice cubes into each bowl and ladle soup over ice. Sprinkle with reserved chopped egg white. Serves 6. To make okroshka without kvass follow above recipe stirring $2\frac{1}{2}$ cups of broth and 1 cup of white wine into the yolk, mustard, and sour cream mixture. Add vegetables and meat. Just before serving add 1 cup of club soda.

CSERESZNYELEVES
(Hungarian Cream of Cherry Soup)

2 pounds fresh or frozen cherries (a mixture of sweet and sour)

4 cups water

1 stick cinnamon (optional)

$\frac{1}{2}$ cup sugar, or to taste

4 tablespoons flour

$\frac{1}{2}$ cup cold water

1 cup sweet or sour cream

1 cup dry red wine (optional)

Wash fresh cherries; remove stems and stones. Frozen cherries need not be thawed. Cook cherries in 4 cups water with the stick of cinnamon for about 10 minutes or until they are soft. Remove cinnamon and add sugar to taste. (Practically no sugar will be needed if frozen cherries are used as they will already be sweetened.) Combine flour and $\frac{1}{2}$ cup water in a screw-top jar. Close tightly and shake vigorously until flour and water are smoothly blended. Pour into hot cherry soup, stir, and bring to a boil; simmer for 3 to 4 minutes. Chill thoroughly, preferably overnight. Stir in sweet cream or beat in sour cream and flavor with red wine, if desired, just before serving. Serves 6 to 8.

VARIATIONS: *Northern European Cherry Soup* is made in a slightly different way. The cooked cherries are puréed through a sieve and the soup is thickened with 2 tablespoons cornstarch dissolved in a little water instead of the flour, and it is flavored with a dry white wine. Cream is not added to the soup itself, but each serving is garnished with a dab of unsweetened whipped cream or sour cream and a few uncooked, stoned cherries. *Fruit Substitutes*: Pared and diced apples, stoned and halved ripe plums, peaches, or nectarines may replace the cherries in the above recipe. Adjust sugar as necessary and flavor with red or white wine.

SOPA DE ZAPALLO
(South American Pumpkin Soup)

1 onion, diced
6 scallions, bulbs and greens sliced
  separately
5 cups chicken broth
2½ cups pumpkin purée, canned or fresh

Salt and cayenne pepper
2 cups light cream
2 tomatoes, thinly sliced
1 cup heavy cream, whipped

Cook onion and *bulb portions of scallions* in chicken broth until vegetables are very soft—about 15 minutes. Purée through a sieve and return to broth. Stir in pumpkin purée and simmer for 10 to 15 minutes or until soup is smooth and thickened. Season with salt and pepper to taste and chill thoroughly. Stir in 2 cups light cream just before serving and adjust seasoning. Ladle soup into cups or cream soup bowls and top each serving with 2 slices of tomato, a dab of whipped cream, and a sprinkling of sliced *green tops of scallions*. Serves 6 to 8.

YAYLA CHORBASHI

Yoghurt is a basic ingredient in the cuisine of the Middle East. This yoghurt soup is traditionally served during the picnic outings of "Hidrellez," the Turkish spring festival held each year on the first of May.

2 tablespoons butter
2 large onions, chopped
½ cup pearl barley
4 cups chicken broth

¼ cup chopped mint leaves or
  1 teaspoon dried mint
2 cups yoghurt, well beaten
½ cup chopped parsley
Salt and white pepper

Heat the butter in a soup kettle and stew the onion until transparent but not brown. Add barley and chicken broth and simmer for 45 minutes or until barley is tender. Add mint, yoghurt, and *half the parsley*. Season to taste with salt and pepper and simmer for 5 minutes. Serve sprinkled with *remaining parsley*. Serves 6.

FISH

Dr. Nicolas Venette, in his seventeenth-century *Tableau de l'Amour*, informed readers that "we have observed in France that those who live almost entirely on shellfish and fish . . . are more ardent in love than others. In fact, we ourselves feel most amorously inclined during Lent." The aphrodisiac powers of fish were not a new idea. Many ancient cults forbade the eating of fish among their priests while encouraging the rest of their people to consume formidable amounts. (The eccentric Queen Gatis of Syria decreed that none of her subjects was to eat fish without first inviting her.) And Brillat-Savarin retold an old tale brought back by the Crusaders of the ascetic dervishes who were confined to Saladin's palace so that the sultan might observe how firm their continence. Fattening them on a diet of meat, he then presented them with "two odalisques of surpassing loveliness [but the] saints emerged from their soft ordeal as pure as the diamond of Vizapoor." Saladin then had the ascetics fed on fish, brought the ladies back, "and this time the too happy cenobites succumbed most marvelously."

COURT BOUILLON

Even in the first century A.D., the Romans relied on an all-purpose sauce, *garum*, made from a stock of fish entrails boiled in brine to which herbs and sometimes "must" were added; its desired effect, as Apicius commented, was that "no one at table will know what he is eating." Court Bouillon, perhaps a descendant of *garum*, is used as a liquid for poaching fish, the recipe below being adapted from Robert May's *The Accomplisht Cook, or the Art and Mystery of Cookery* (1660).

2 stalks celery, with leaves, chopped
1 medium onion, chopped
Bouquet garni (4 sprigs parsley, small
   bay leaf, 10 crushed peppercorns,
   pinch thyme, tied in cheesecloth)

2 white-meat fish trimmings
1 teaspoon salt
1 bottle dry white wine
2 quarts cold water

Place all the ingredients in a large saucepan. Bring to a boil, lower heat, and simmer for 25 minutes, uncovered. Strain carefully through a double cheesecloth first wrung out in cold water. Cool before using for poaching fish. Freezes well. Makes 2 quarts.

438

KAMANO LOMI
(Hawaiian Salmon)

1 pound smoked salmon, thinly sliced	1 teaspoon coarse salt (kosher salt)
3 tomatoes, peeled, seeded, and diced	$\frac{1}{3}$ cup ice water
10 scallions, with greens, finely minced	Lettuce leaves

Soak the salmon for 3 to 4 hours in cold water. Drain well and pat dry. Cut into julienne strips. Combine salmon and tomatoes and mash to a paste with a fork. Crush the scallions with the salt and add to fish. Stir in ice water; chill thoroughly. Serve in large individual lettuce leaves or in small individual bowls. Serves 8 as an appetizer.

TARAMOSALATA

> By the sixteenth century when Rabelais spoke of "caviat" in *Pantagruel*, the lightly pressed, salted roe had long been considered a delicacy. Caviar is prepared from the eggs of such fish as Caspian sturgeon, Gironde carp, and Columbia River salmon. Although connoisseurs prefer to eat it plain, many Englishmen spread it on their baked potatoes, and Russians enjoy it with sour cream in *blini*. The Greek Taramosalata is made from the puréed red roe of cod and is served, typically, as an appetizer.

3 slices white bread, crusts removed	1 tablespoon minced onion
$\frac{1}{4}$ cup water	1 egg yolk
5 ounces tarama (fish roe, available in jars)	1 cup olive oil
	2 tablespoons lemon juice
	2 teaspoons chopped parsley

Crumble the bread and soak in water. Put tarama and onion in a blender and blend until puréed, but not liquid. Scrape sides with a rubber spatula. Squeeze out excess water from bread and blend bread with tarama. Add yolk and blend at medium speed. Pour in oil in a slow stream as for mayonnaise (the last of the oil may have to be stirred in). Add lemon juice to taste. Pile in a serving dish and chill. At serving time sprinkle with parsley. Serve with toast, sesame crackers, or Arabic bread. Makes about $2\frac{1}{4}$ cups.

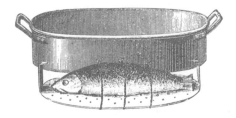

HERRING SALAT

"Herring is one of those productions which decide the destiny of Empires," the nineteenth-century naturalist Lacépède declared, and, indeed, such medieval Hansa towns as Bergen, Amsterdam, and Hamburg were all but built upon the herring shoals that cruised the North Sea. In Norway this recipe is a traditional Christmas accompaniment.

3 salt herrings, soaked overnight
1½ cups diced cooked veal, lamb,
   or beef
1½ cups diced cooked beets, with juice
1½ cups diced apples
2 cups diced boiled potatoes

2 pickled cucumbers, cubed
½ cup dry red wine or wine vinegar
5 tablespoons sugar
2 to 3 tablespoons olive oil
Pepper
4 hard-boiled eggs

This recipe must be started 1 to 2 days ahead. If soaked herrings are still too salty, soak again. Dry and cut into fillets after removing skins and bones. Cut fillets into bite-size pieces. Mix with meat, beets, apples, potatoes, and pickles. Mix wine, sugar, and oil with the juice from the beets. Season to taste with pepper and pour into salad. Marinate for 10 to 12 hours in refrigerator. Serve decorated with sieved hard-boiled eggs. Serves 8 to 10.

ESCABECHE DE PESCADOS

Escabeche is a dish common to all Hispanic countries. It takes its name from the Arabic word *sikbaj* (diced meat cooked in vinegar) suggesting that it may date back to the period of Moorish domination in Spain.

2 pounds small fish fillets
   (pompano, flounder, bass, halibut)
Flour for dredging
1¼ cups olive or corn oil
2 cloves garlic, minced
1 medium onion, sliced
¼ teaspoon black pepper
1 tablespoon chopped parsley
½ teaspoon crushed cumin seed

¼ teaspoon powdered ginger
¼ teaspoon powdered saffron (optional)
¼ cup vinegar
2 tablespoons lemon juice
¾ cup water
Salt
½ cup minced scallion
4 lemon slices
2 small bay leaves

Lightly dredge the fish with flour. Heat *one-quarter cup oil* and fry the garlic and onion until soft but not brown. Remove with a slotted spoon and reserve. Fry the fish in the same oil until golden. Drain and arrange in a shallow, wide serving dish. Mix *remaining cup of oil*, spices and herbs, vinegar, lemon juice, water, and salt to taste. Pour over fish. Sprinkle with reserved onion and garlic and chopped scallion. Add lemon slices and bay leaves. Marinate for 24 hours in refrigerator. Serves 6 to 8 as an appetizer.

SINGAPORE LOBSTER CURRY

$\frac{1}{2}$ cup butter
2 cups chopped onion
2 cloves garlic, minced
$\frac{1}{2}$ teaspoon powdered cumin
1 teaspoon cinnamon
$\frac{1}{2}$ teaspoon allspice
$\frac{1}{2}$ teaspoon powdered cloves
$\frac{1}{4}$ teaspoon nutmeg
1 good pinch cayenne pepper
2 tablespoons curry powder
3 cups Coconut Cream (page 632)

2 small cucumbers, peeled, seeded,
  and cubed
2 2-pound boiled lobsters
  or rock lobster tails
6 thin slices ginger root, minced, or
  1 teaspoon powdered ginger
1$\frac{1}{2}$ cups broth from lobsters
  or chicken broth
2 tablespoons lime juice
Salt
4 to 6 bowls hot cooked rice

Melt the butter and stew the onion and garlic until soft but not brown. Add the next 7 spices and the coconut cream. Stir and simmer for 8 to 10 minutes. Blanch the cucumber in boiling water for 2 minutes. Drain and add to sauce. Remove lobster meat from shells, cut in bite-size pieces, and add to sauce along with ginger root. Add the lobster or chicken broth and simmer for 15 minutes on very low heat. Add lime juice and salt to taste and simmer for 5 minutes. Serve with rice. Serves 4 to 6.

CHUPE
(*Peruvian Fish Stew*)

1 pound shrimps, shelled and deveined
1 pound scallops, or firm white-meat
  fish (sliced thick), or abalone meat
1 cup water
$\frac{1}{2}$ cup dry white wine
2 cups minced cooked clams
1$\frac{1}{2}$ cups soft white bread crumbs
1 cup milk
$\frac{1}{2}$ cup olive oil
4 medium onions, chopped
1 clove garlic, minced and crushed

4 tomatoes, peeled, seeded,
  and chopped (optional)
2 stalks celery, chopped
1 bay leaf
2 cups heavy cream
Salt
$\frac{1}{4}$ to $\frac{1}{2}$ teaspoon hot pepper, cayenne,
  or hot chili peppers, crushed
4 hard-boiled eggs, quartered
$\frac{1}{3}$ cup Parmesan cheese

Combine shrimps and scallops with water and wine and simmer for 4 to 5 minutes. Reserve broth and a few shrimps. Mince remainder of fish and combine with clams. Soak bread crumbs in the milk. Heat the oil and fry the onions. Add garlic, tomatoes, celery, and bay leaf and simmer for 5 to 6 minutes. Add reserved fish broth, fish, and milk mixture and cream. Season with salt and hot pepper to taste. Add quartered eggs and reserved whole shrimps. Heat through and serve. Pass grated cheese as garnish. Serves 6. Bread crumbs may be replaced by 3 large diced potatoes cooked in the broth and milk before returning fish to broth.

TEMPURA

Tempura, deep-fried seafood and vegetables, is thought to have been introduced by Jesuit missionaries to Japan in the late 1500's. The name derives from the Portuguese word for Lenten "Ember Days" when meat and poultry were proscribed to Christians.

$1\frac{1}{2}$ to 2 pounds assorted raw fish and shellfish in season (such as flounder, sole, whiting, bass, smelts, whitebait, eel, squid, scallops, shrimps, lobster, mussels, clams, and oysters)

Assorted vegetables (such as eggplant, zucchini, green peppers, scallions, onions, mushroom caps, bamboo shoots, chrysanthemum leaves, cauliflower, sweet potatoes, and water lily or lotus roots)

Batter:

1 egg, separated

$\frac{3}{4}$ cup water and $\frac{3}{4}$ cup dry white wine or sake, or $1\frac{1}{2}$ cups water

$\frac{1}{4}$ cup cornstarch and $\frac{1}{4}$ cup rice flour, or $\frac{1}{2}$ cup cornstarch

$1\frac{1}{2}$ cups flour

Pinch of salt

Oil for deep frying:

2 parts sesame oil to 1 part corn oil

Sauce:

$\frac{1}{3}$ cup sweet rice wine or dry sherry

$\frac{1}{3}$ cup soy sauce

1 cup Dashi broth (page 421) or clam juice

$\frac{1}{4}$ teaspoon monosodium glutamate (optional)

Garnishes: grated white radish, chopped fresh or pickled ginger

Select at least 2 kinds of fish and 3 kinds of shellfish plus 3 vegetables for an interesting tempura assortment. *Prepare fish as follows*: White-meat fish should be filleted and cut into chunks no larger than 2 bites each. Small fish may be left whole. Eel should be filleted and cut into $1\frac{1}{2}$-inch pieces. Squid should have cuttlebones and ink sacks removed; tentacles should be cut in half and the body of the squid cut into strips and rings. Small scallops should be left whole but large ones should be cut in half crosswise. Shrimps should be shelled with tails left on; they should be deveined and pressed into butterfly shapes. Cut lobster meat into chunks. Mussels should be shelled, bearded, and left whole. Clams and oysters may be left whole unless they are very large, in which case cut them in half. *Prepare vegetables as follows:* Peel eggplant and cut into cubes. Cut zucchini into 1-inch thick round slices or chunks. Cut seeded green peppers into rings or strips. Leave scallions whole with bits of green tops left on. Cut onions into chunks or rings. Leave mushroom caps whole. Cut bamboo shoots into slivers. Leave chrysanthemum leaves whole. Break cauliflower into flowerlets. Cut peeled sweet potatoes in round slices and do the same with water lily or lotus roots. *To prepare the batter*: Mix egg yolk with the water and wine, add the cornstarch and rice flour, the regular flour, and salt. A wire whisk is best for this. When batter is fairly smooth, beat egg white until stiff and fold in with a rubber spatula. Use at once. Heat combined oils to 360°. Dry fish and vegetables thoroughly and dip into batter just before frying. Fry until golden brown. It is best to fry mild-flavored fish and vegetables first and then proceed to the stronger flavors. Drain on pieces of paper towel for a moment and serve at once. Each guest should have a small sauce bowl for dipping, containing a mixture of the sauce ingredients. Grated radish and ginger should be served on separate dishes, to be added to the sauce to taste. Serves 4 to 6.

TO STEW PRAWNS, SHRIMPS, OR CRAWFISH

Directions for stewing these sea creatures appeared in Robert May's *The Accomplisht Cook* of 1660.

36 shrimps (average size)
6 tablespoons sweet butter
$\frac{1}{4}$ teaspoon nutmeg
1 cup heavy cream

$\frac{1}{2}$ teaspoon salt
Freshly ground pepper
1 tablespoon orange juice
Paprika

Add shrimps to lightly salted water and simmer for 3 minutes. Cool, shell, and devein. Melt the butter; add the seasoning, the shrimps, and the cream. Stir until smooth and simmer together until cream thickens a little—about 5 minutes. Season to taste with salt and pepper and add the orange juice. Serve in large scallop shells or in a buttered rice ring, and sprinkle with a little paprika. Serves 6

SZECHWAN PEPPER PRAWNS

Traders on the Yangtze probably first introduced shellfish to Szechwan, a fertile inland province of China noted for its spicy cuisine.

2 pounds large shrimps, shelled
and deveined
$\frac{1}{2}$ cup cornstarch
Corn oil for frying
1 clove garlic, crushed
2 scallions, with greens, minced
(optional)

4 hot chili peppers or Tabasco or
Chinese pepper sauce to taste
2 slices ginger root, shredded, or
$\frac{1}{2}$ teaspoon powdered ginger
$1\frac{1}{2}$ tablespoons soy sauce
2 tablespoons dry white wine
1 to 2 teaspoons salt
$\frac{1}{4}$ teaspoon monosodium glutamate

Dredge shrimps lightly with cornstarch. Heat oil to 365° and fry shrimps until they are a light golden color. Remove, drain, and keep warm. Place $\frac{1}{3}$ cup corn oil in a skillet and in it fry garlic, scallions, chili peppers, and ginger root for 3 to 4 minutes. If using Tabasco or Chinese pepper sauce, add to the following soy sauce-wine mixture. Add soy sauce, wine, salt, and monosodium glutamate and bring to a boil. Add shrimps and heat. Serves 6.

YAM KOONG MA MUANG
(Thai Shrimp and Mango Salad)

2 pounds medium-size shrimps
2 large green or red sweet peppers
2 mangoes
Lemon juice
2 tablespoons peanut or sesame oil
2 cloves garlic, minced
2 tablespoons minced shallot

$\frac{1}{2}$ teaspoon anchovy paste
1 tablespoon soy sauce
2 tablespoons crushed roasted unsalted
  peanuts
1 to 2 cups Coconut Cream (page 632)
2 red or green chili peppers or 2
  teaspoons dried, crushed red pepper

Broil shrimps until done—about 8 minutes—turning once. Shell, devein, and cut each into 4 slices. Hold peppers on a fork over a flame, turning slowly until all the skin is charred. Peel off skin and slice peppers into thin strips or dice, discarding seeds and inner filaments. Peel mangoes and cut into thin strips. Sprinkle with lemon juice. Combine shrimps, peppers, and mangoes. Heat oil and in it sauté garlic and shallots until golden brown. Add, with pan fat, to shrimp mixture. Blend anchovy paste and soy sauce, add to shrimp mixture, and toss lightly. Sprinkle with peanuts, then add the coconut cream gradually until there is enough to coat all the ingredients. Season to taste with more soy sauce or anchovy paste. Garnish with chili peppers and serve at room temperature. Serves 6 to 8.

VARIATION: If desired, 2 medium-size apples, peeled, cored, sliced, and sprinkled with lemon juice, may be substituted for the mangoes.

CUSCUZ SAO PAULO

Brazilian Cuscuz is an adaptation of North African Couscous, brought to South America by Negro slaves in the sixteenth century. In place of African semolina, it uses two local staples, corn meal and manioc flour.

1 hot pepper (or more), minced
4 large tomatoes, peeled, seeded,
  and coarsely chopped
2 sweet green peppers, seeded and diced
$1\frac{1}{2}$ cups vegetable shortening or olive oil
1 large onion, finely chopped
3 cloves garlic, minced
Salt and pepper
2 pounds shrimps, shelled and deveined
1 can hearts of palm, sliced in rounds
$1\frac{1}{4}$ cups chicken broth

1 package frozen peas
1 cup black Spanish olives, pitted
  and chopped
2 cups yellow corn meal
$\frac{1}{2}$ cup manioc flour or farina
3 scallions, with some greens, minced
3 tablespoons chopped parsley
2 hard-boiled eggs, chopped
Garnish: 4 hard-boiled eggs, 1 head
  Boston lettuce, $\frac{1}{2}$ cup black olives,
  2 large tomatoes cut in wedges

Liquefy hot pepper, tomatoes, and sweet peppers in a blender with $\frac{1}{2}$ cup water. (This may have to be done in 2 batches.) Heat *three-quarters cup oil* in a large skillet and sauté the onion and garlic for 2 to 3 minutes. Add the tomato-pepper liquid and simmer briskly. Season with salt and pepper as needed. Reserve 6 *shrimps*. Coarsely chop *remaining shrimps* and add to the hot mixture. Simmer for 3 minutes. Reserve 8 *palm rounds*. Add *remaining palm rounds* to hot mixture. Add the chicken broth. When boiling, add peas and chopped olives. In another large pan heat *remaining three-quarters cup oil* to boiling hot. Mix the corn meal, manioc flour, scallions, parsley, and 1 teaspoon salt and add to the fat. Stir briskly for 1 to 2 minutes. Add shrimp mixture and the chopped hard-boiled eggs. Oil a 5-quart pudding pan and garnish the bottom with the reserved shrimp (halved lengthwise), the 8 rounds of hearts of palm, and *1 hard-boiled egg* (sliced). Pour in the cuscuz. Put the pan on a rack in a larger pot filled with boiling water to a 1-inch depth. Cover with a cloth and a lid and place on low direct heat to steam for $1\frac{1}{2}$ to 2 hours, replenishing water as needed. Remove from steamer and invert on a platter, first placing platter over pan and turning both over quickly. Let set for 10 minutes before removing pan. Garnish with lettuce leaves, *remaining 3 hard-boiled eggs* (quartered), olives, and tomato wedges. Serves 10 to 12.

ECREVISSES AU SAUTERNES
(Crawfish in Sauternes)

40 fresh (or thawed frozen) crawfish or 40 medium-size shrimps	Salt and pepper
2 onions, thinly sliced	Cayenne pepper
2 carrots, chopped	$\frac{1}{4}$ cup cognac
2 shallots, minced	$2\frac{1}{2}$ cups Sauternes
5 to 6 tablespoons butter	$1\frac{1}{2}$ cups tomato purée
Bouquet garni (1 bay leaf, parsley, thyme, celery leaves, 5 peppercorns, tied in cheesecloth)	Beurre Manie (page 630), as needed
	1 cup rice or 4 to 6 slices toasted French bread (optional)
	2 tablespoons minced parsley

Wash crawfish and remove black intestines from center. Do not remove shells. If shrimps are used, shell and devein. Sauté onion, carrot, and shallot in butter until they are soft but not brown. Add bouquet garni, a dash each of salt, pepper, and cayenne pepper, and the cognac. Boil rapidly for 1 minute and add Sauternes. Simmer for 5 minutes and add crawfish or shrimps. Simmer uncovered for 5 to 7 minutes or until crawfish are bright red. Remove bouquet garni. Stir in tomato purée and adjust seasoning. Sauce may be thickened with beurre manie, if necessary. Serve in deep bowls with rice or toasted rounds of French bread. Garnish with minced parsley. Serves 4 to 6.

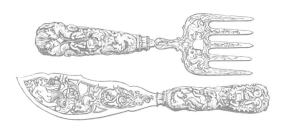

HOMARD AU COURT BOUILLON

March is a time, wrote the ebullient Baron Brisse in his nineteenth-century cookbook, "to fall back on the sea for our resources, not by throwing ourselves into it from a rock, like the unhappy Sappho, but by welcoming myriads of turbot, brill, soles, lobsters . . . which are better now than at any other time of the year." Following is his prescription for preparing lobster.

1 cup Madeira wine	1 tablespoon Dijon-style mustard
3 tablespoons butter	1 teaspoon soy sauce
6 sprigs parsley	8 shallots, minced
1 teaspoon dried, crushed red chili pepper	1 tablespoon minced parsley
1 tablespoon salt	1 tablespoon minced fresh tarragon or 2 teaspoons dried tarragon
4 live lobsters	2 tablespoons anisette
Liver and roe of lobsters	Juice of 2 lemons
1 cup olive oil	Coarsely ground black pepper

Add Madeira, butter, parsley, crushed peppers, and salt to 3 quarts of water. Bring to a boil, add lobsters, and cook for 20 to 25 minutes or until lobsters are done. Cool lobsters in broth, then drain and chill. Broth may be reserved to use as the base for a soup or sauce. Split lobsters and remove liver and roe, if any. Mash together and cream into olive oil. Blend in mustard and add soy sauce, shallots, parsley, tarragon, and anisette and beat with a spoon until all ingredients are well blended. Add lemon juice, and pepper to taste, and beat again. Serve sauce separately with the cold lobsters. Serves 4 to 8.

LOBSTER ARMORICAINE

Brittany, known in ancient times as Armorica, is thought to be the ancestral home of this recipe for lobster in tomato sauce. Bonnefoy's, a fashionable restaurant of mid-nineteenth-century Paris, was probably the first to serve the refined version of the provincial dish.

2 1½-pound live lobsters	1 cup dry white wine
¼ cup olive oil	½ cup concentrated fish stock (made with fish trimmings, 1 bay leaf, 1 onion, 1 small carrot, celery leaves, parsley sprigs, peppercorns, and a pinch of thyme)
4 tablespoons butter	
4 shallots or 1 small onion, minced	
1 clove garlic, crushed	
4 large tomatoes, peeled, seeded, and diced	¼ cup cognac
3 tablespoons tomato paste	Salt and cayenne pepper
2 tablespoons minced parsley	

Split lobsters and remove legs; cut the tails into slices following the markings. Remove coral and liver and reserve for sauce. Crack claws. Lobsters should be cut up as close to cooking time as possible. In a large heavy frying pan heat the oil and cook the lobster pieces, turning them until shells are bright red. Remove the lobster and reserve. Add 3 *tablespoons butter* to the pan and sauté the shallots and garlic for 2 to 3 minutes. Add the tomato, tomato paste, parsley, wine, and fish stock and simmer for 25 to 30 minutes. Return lobster to the pan, pour in the cognac, and flame. Simmer for 15 minutes, covered. Add coral and liver, season with salt and cayenne pepper, and simmer for 5 minutes. Stir in *remaining butter*. Serves 2 to 4.

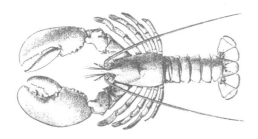

LOBSTER THERMIDOR

How this recipe for lobster came to be named for the eleventh month in the Republican calendar is uncertain. Some date its origin from the Napoleonic era, but more likely it was created in honor of Victorien Sardou's play *Thermidor*, which opened to favorable notices in 1891.

2 2-pound live lobsters	4 teaspoons minced fresh tarragon or
Salt	2 teaspoons dried tarragon
1 cup olive oil	2 cups thick Béchamel Sauce
1½ cups dry white wine	(page 618)
1½ cups fish stock or clam juice	2 teaspoons powdered mustard
4 shallots, minced	Cayenne pepper
4 teaspoons minced fresh chervil or	½ cup grated Parmesan cheese
2 teaspoons dried chervil	½ cup butter, melted

Split live lobsters lengthwise down the middle and remove center vein. Sprinkle with salt, cover with oil, and roast in preheated 425° oven for about 20 minutes, brushing with additional oil once or twice. Remove claws, crack, and take out meat. Reserve shells. Remove all meat from the tails. Dice meat and mix with any of the green liver or roe that might have been in the lobsters. Cook wine, stock, shallots, and herbs rapidly until they are reduced to a thickish, slightly liquid, paste. Stir this into the béchamel sauce with the mustard and a little cayenne pepper to taste, adding salt if necessary. Heat sauce and stir until smooth and well blended. Mix lobster meat into sauce, reserving a little of the sauce on the side as a topping. Fill shells with lobster and coat each half with reserved sauce. Sprinkle with cheese and spoon on melted butter. Brown in preheated 400° oven and serve at once. Serves 4.

447

SOFT-SHELLED CRABS WITH FIG FRITTERS

This recipe for *molecche*, or soft-shelled crabs, was prepared in the seventeenth century for a Bolognese banquet honoring Pope Urban VIII's nephew and chief legate, Cardinal Antonio Barberini.

24 dried figs	4 to 5 cloves
24 almonds, shelled and blanched, or	Double recipe Fritter Batter (page 583)
$\frac{3}{4}$ to 1 cup pine nuts	Corn oil for deep frying
1 cup red wine, heated	12 to 18 very small soft-shelled crabs
1 small stick cinnamon	

Place figs in a steamer or in a strainer over a pot of boiling water. Cover and steam for about 30 minutes or until figs are completely soft. Stuff the center of each fig with 1 almond or a few pine nuts. Place figs in a small bowl and cover with red wine, adding the cinnamon and cloves. Steep for 15 minutes. Dry each fig, dip into batter, and fry in oil (heated to 360°) until golden. Drain and keep warm until crabs are ready. Clean and dry each crab, dip into batter, and fry a few at a time in deep fat heated to 375°. Keep temperature constant until all crabs have been fried. When crabs are golden brown on both sides, drain on paper towel. Serve with fig fritters. Serves 6 to 8.

EELS IN GREEN SAUCE

No fish enjoys a wider habitat nor a more colorful reputation than the eel. It is found in almost all countries and climates, in fresh water and salt, and is variously credited as an aphrodisiac, a cure for alcoholism, and an aid to discovering fairies. The recipe below is Belgian.

2 pounds eel meat, cut into	1 teaspoon chopped fresh tarragon
2-inch chunks and halved	1 tablespoon chopped fresh chervil
$\frac{1}{2}$ cup butter	$\frac{1}{2}$ teaspoon dried thyme
6 shallots, minced	$1\frac{1}{2}$ teaspoons salt
$\frac{1}{2}$ cup finely chopped parsley	$\frac{1}{2}$ teaspoon pepper
1 cup finely chopped sorrel or spinach	3 cups dry white wine or light beer
leaves	3 egg yolks, beaten
1 tablespoon chopped fresh sage	Juice of 1 lemon

Wipe the eel and quickly sauté in *4 tablespoons butter*. Add *remaining butter* and shallots, sauté for 5 minutes. Add all the herbs, greens, and salt and pepper. Stir for 3 minutes or until sorrel or spinach is limp. Add the wine, cover, and simmer gently for 15 minutes. Slowly beat some hot broth from the eels into the beaten egg yolks. Pour slowly into eel pan, beating constantly; stir gently over low heat for 5 minutes. Do not boil. Season to taste, adding lemon juice as needed. Pour into a serving bowl, cool, and chill. Serves 6.

VOL-AU-VENT D'HUÎTRES A LA MAINTENON

At a time when women cooks were a rarity, Louis XIV's second wife, Madame de Maintenon, upset tradition by founding St-Cyr, the first school to teach girls the culinary arts. The best *cuisinières* won blue ribbons and the academy eventually became the famed Cordon Bleu. Another Maintenon triumph was Vol-au-vent d'Huîtres (literally translated "flying in the wind"), a puff pastry filled with oysters, mushrooms, and truffles; it was reputedly invented to appeal to the aged, dyspeptic, toothless king. Over-a century later Carême rhapsodized: this dish "is almost always eaten with pleasure for its extreme delicacy and lightness."

1 quart shucked oysters
½ cup butter
Salt and pepper
Juice of 1 lemon
¼ teaspoon nutmeg
2 large truffles, minced (optional)

½ pound mushrooms, sliced and
   sautéed in butter
3 cups fish Velouté (page 616)
6 Vol-au-vents (see Puff Pastry, page
   684) or purchased patty shells

Drain the oysters, reserving any liquid. Melt the butter and gently stew the oysters until edges start to curl. Add salt, pepper, lemon juice, nutmeg, truffles, and mushrooms. Add oyster juice and stir in the velouté sauce. Fill vol-au-vents with oyster mixture and top with centers. Serve on individual plates. Spoon remaining oyster mixture around the pastries. Serve immediately. Serves 6.

JAPANESE OYSTER PANCAKES

1 pint small, shucked oysters and
   their liquor
¼ cup minced scallions or shallots
1 tablespoon chopped parsley
4 eggs, beaten
½ teaspoon salt
Pinch of pepper

½ cup flour
½ teaspoon baking powder
2 to 3 tablespoons corn, peanut,
   or sesame oil
1 teaspoon soy sauce
½ cup cider vinegar
1 teaspoon Japanese hot pepper sauce

Strain the oysters and reserve the liquor. Chop coarsely. Mix oysters, scallions, parsley, beaten eggs, salt, and pepper. Sift flour and baking powder together and stir into oyster mixture, adding about ½ cup oyster liquor or milk to thin out. Heat a pancake griddle, oil lightly, and make 3- to 5-inch pancakes, dropping the batter from a tablespoon. Turn pancakes when golden on one side—about 1 minute; cook 1 more minute to brown second side. Keep warm in a low oven until ready to serve. Combine soy sauce, vinegar, and pepper sauce to be served as dip. Serves 4 to 6. Oysters may be replaced by chopped clams.

MUSSELS WITH SWEET HERBS

The source of this recipe is *The Accomplisht Cook* by Robert May. Written upon the author's return from France in 1660, the recipe closely resembles the Gallic *moules marinières*.

48 mussels	Salt and freshly ground pepper
$\frac{3}{4}$ cup butter	4 egg yolks
1 clove garlic	1 cup heavy cream
$\frac{1}{3}$ cup chopped shallots or onions	2 tablespoons chopped chives
1 bay leaf	$\frac{1}{4}$ cup chopped parsley
$1\frac{1}{2}$ cups dry white wine	Juice of 1 lemon

Scrub the mussels with a stiff brush and remove the beards. Discard any mussels that have opened or that are unusually heavy. Wash in several waters. In a very large kettle melt the butter and stew the garlic and shallots without browning. Add the bay leaf and wine. Add the mussels, cover tightly, and steam until they open, discarding any that remain closed. Remove 1 shell of each mussel and place mussels on half shells in a deep serving dish or soup tureen. Keep warm. Strain broth very carefully. Return to a clean kettle. Season with salt and freshly ground pepper. Beat yolks into the cream, add some hot broth to egg mixture, beating constantly. Pour back into remaining broth, beating constantly. Heat over low heat, stirring until thickened. Do not allow to boil. Add chives, parsley, and lemon juice to taste. Add broth to mussels. Serves 2 as main course or 4 as first course.

ESCARGOTS A LA BOURGUIGNONNE

Edible snails have been gourmet fare since the Homeric age. The Lacedaemonians called them "interrupters of banquets" and ate them between bouts with more substantial dishes. Romans demanded snails in such quantities that one Fulvius Lupinus set himself up in business with a snail farm, fattening his black beauties on a diet of boiled wine and flour. Nowadays, the best snails are found in Burgundy where, at their own discretion, they thrive on grape leaves.

6 dozen snail shells
1 recipe Snail Butter (page 628)
6 dozen snails (canned)

Scrub shells and dry. Place *one-quarter teaspoon snail butter* inside each shell. Push in a snail and seal completely with *remaining snail butter*. Set in snail pans and place in a preheated 450° oven for 10 minutes. Serves 6.

BEIGNETS DE GRENOUILLES

Robert May, a seventeenth-century author-cook, devised a recipe for a pie that concealed live frogs. May wrote that when the pie was opened the frogs would leap up "and Cause the ladies to squeak and hop about." A more sedate dish, traditional in northern France, follows.

18 large frogs' legs, fresh or frozen	Vegetable shortening for deep frying
$\frac{1}{3}$ cup flour	Fried parsley for garnish
Salt and pepper	Lemon wedges for garnish
1 recipe Fritter Batter (page 583)	

Wash and dry the frogs' legs. Season the flour with salt and pepper and dredge the frogs' legs in the flour, shaking off excess. Dip in batter and deep fry in shortening (heated to 360°) until puffed and golden. Drain on paper towels and keep hot in a low oven until all legs are done. It is better to fry a few at a time so that fat remains at same temperature. Serve on a bed of fried parsley with lemon wedges placed around edge of platter. Serve with tartare sauce, tomato sauce, or Aioli (page 638). Serves 4 to 6.

WATERZOÏ

"This is rather a Dutch dish, and for [a] change no bad one," remarked an eighteenth-century English visitor, adding that "to make this in perfection you should have several sorts of small fish, flounders, gudgeons, eels, perch, and a pike or two." A sort of northern bouillabaisse, Waterzoï is traditional in Belgium.

$\frac{1}{3}$ cup butter	3 pounds assorted fish (such as eel,
1 cup diced celery	pike, carp, sea bass, and cod) cut
3 leeks, chopped	into large, even chunks
2 onions, chopped	1 cup dry white wine
3 parsley roots (optional)	2 quarts fish stock or water
Bouquet garni (6 sprigs parsley,	Salt and pepper
$\frac{1}{2}$ teaspoon sage, $\frac{1}{2}$ teaspoon thyme,	6 to 8 slices buttered toast
$\frac{1}{2}$ bay leaf, tied in cheesecloth)	

Melt the butter in a soup or fish kettle and stew the vegetables for 5 to 6 minutes without browning. Add bouquet garni, fish, wine, and stock or water and bring to a fast boil. Turn heat down and simmer until fish is cooked—about 10 to 12 minutes. Discard bouquet garni and parsley roots. Season with salt and pepper to taste. Serve immediately, poured over toast in soup plates. Serves 6 to 8. If desired, stew may be thickened by adding 2 egg yolks beaten into $\frac{1}{2}$ cup heavy cream just before serving.

VARIATION: Fish may be replaced by stewing chicken, and stock by chicken broth.

BOUILLABAISSE

The ancestry of Bouillabaisse begins with the Phoenicians who made a stew with *rascasse*, a fish found only in the Mediterranean. The Romans added herbs and spices, the Arabs, saffron, and finally, with the discovery of America, the tomato found its way to the stewing pot. The same ingredients are used today in the Bouillabaisse of Marseilles. Although purists maintain there is no Bouillabaisse without the *rascasse*, there are infinite variations of the recipe, a number of which do not even contain fish. William Thackeray in *The Ballad of Bouillabaisse* has immortalized the stew and the confusion of definition which surrounds it:

This Bouillabaisse a noble dish is —
A sort of soup, or broth, or brew,
Or hotchpotch of all sorts of fishes . . .

3 to 4 pounds assorted fish (such as eel, striped or sea bass, haddock, whiting, red snapper, sole, flounder, and halibut)
2 large or 3 small lobsters
24 mussels
24 clams
½ cup olive oil
2 large leeks, bulbs only, sliced
2 large onions, chopped
4 cloves garlic, minced

3 fresh tomatoes, peeled, seeded, and chopped, or 2 canned tomatoes, drained and chopped
Bouquet garni (fennel, bay leaf, thyme, 3 sprigs parsley, tied in cheesecloth)
Pinch of powdered saffron
1 strip dried orange peel
Salt, pepper, and cayenne pepper
10 to 12 slices toasted French bread, rubbed with garlic
Rouille (page 638) (optional)

Choose at least 3 different kinds of fish but try to include eel. Have all fish cut into convenient serving pieces. Slices (about 1½ inches thick) are better than fillets, which tend to fall apart. Heads may be used for making stock if desired. Lobsters should be cut up live. Remove and crack claws, split bodies in half and then in half again, removing center vein and sandy sack between the eyes. Scrub and beard mussels. Scrub clams. Heat olive oil in a Dutch oven and in it sauté leeks, onions, garlic, and tomato over high heat for 2 to 3 minutes. Add bouquet garni, saffron, orange peel, and heavier fish such as eel, haddock, halibut, or bass. Cook rapidly, uncovered, for about 8 minutes. Add lobster and lighter fish and enough boiling water, clam juice, or stock to barely cover. Cover kettle and boil rapidly for about 12 minutes. Season with salt, pepper, and cayenne to taste. Add mussels and clams. Cover and cook until they open, discarding any that do not. Remove fish to a deep, hot serving dish. Remove bouquet garni and orange peel from sauce and boil sauce rapidly for 8 to 10 minutes.

Pour over fish. Toast should be placed in individual soup bowls and the fish and sauce ladled over it. Serve plain or with rouille on the side. Serves 6 to 8.

VARIATIONS: *Zuppa di Pesce*: The Italian version of bouillabaisse differs mainly in that it never includes saffron, leek, or orange peel and usually has $\frac{1}{2}$ cup dry white wine added to the onion and garlic after they have been sautéed. Basil is substituted for thyme. The fish and shellfish assortment is the same but squid is almost always added. Have 1 pound squid cleaned and cut into rings. Tentacles should remain intact. Add to oil with onion and garlic, cover, and braise for 20 minutes before going on with the recipe. *Mussel Soup* and *Clam Soup*: Both very popular in Italy, these soups are made in exactly the same way as zuppa di pesce except that they include only scrubbed and bearded mussels or scrubbed clams, and only 1 cupful of water or stock is added to the pot during cooking. Steam for about 7 minutes or until shells open. Serve in soup plates with a little sauce poured over.

BOURRIDE

A 1744 edition of La Chapelle's *Le Cuisinier Moderne* recommends this spicy "sea-soup" from Provence. "Bourride," the writer comments, "is a soup excellent good for a Seaman, and almost all the officers ask for some, in the Morning."

1 pound fish trimmings	$2\frac{1}{2}$ cups Aioli (page 638)
1 onion, diced	6 to 8 slices French bread
1 leek, sliced (optional)	3 tablespoons olive oil
1 bay leaf	1 clove garlic, cut in half
Pinch of each: thyme and fennel	2 to $2\frac{1}{2}$ pounds assorted fish fillets or
3 sprigs parsley	slices (such as bass, cod, haddock,
1 strip dried lemon or orange peel	halibut, flounder, whiting, snapper,
1 cup dry white wine	and sole)

Place fish trimmings in a saucepan with onion, leek, bay leaf, thyme, fennel, parsley, lemon or orange peel, and white wine. Add water to cover (about 4 cups). Bring to a boil, reduce heat, cover, and simmer gently for about 20 minutes. Strain stock and let it cool. Meanwhile, prepare aioli sauce. Fry bread slices in olive oil until both sides are golden brown. Rub 1 side of each slice with a cut clove of garlic. Reserve. Just before serving, place fish fillets or slices in cooled stock and poach gently, covered, for about 10 minutes or until fish flakes when tested with a fork. Carefully remove fish to heated serving dish. Place *1 cup aioli sauce* in a heavy saucepan or in the upper half of a double boiler. Gradually ladle into it 1 cup of the hot fish stock, beating constantly with a wire whisk. Slowly pour this into remaining hot stock, beating constantly. Cook stock over simmering water or low direct heat, stirring constantly, until it is thick enough to coat wooden mixing spoon. Place 1 or 2 slices of toast in each soup bowl and add stock. Ladle a little stock over the fish to keep it hot. Serve fish as a separate second course or in the stock. The *remaining aioli sauce* should be passed separately in a sauceboat and may be stirred into the stock or served as a sauce with the fish. Serves 4.

BASS FOR PICASSO

1 recipe Court Bouillon (page 438)
  made with wine and no water
1 5-pound striped bass
2 cups mayonnaise
1½ tablespoons tomato paste

3 hard-boiled eggs, whites
  and yolks separated
3 tablespoons finely chopped
  fines herbes
2 truffles or 4 black olives,
  chopped or sliced

Simmer the court bouillon for 30 minutes and cool. Tie the bass in cheesecloth, leaving long ends for easy removal of fish from kettle. Place fish and court bouillon in a long, narrow kettle. Bring to a boil and simmer for 20 minutes. Remove from heat and let fish cool in the court bouillon. When cool, place bass on a serving platter. Remove cheesecloth and lift off skin with care. Dry the bass thoroughly, patting it with paper towel. Coat smoothly with *half the mayonnaise*. Add tomato paste to *4 tablespoons mayonnaise*, put into a pastry bag with a small, serrated tube, and make decorative squiggles of red mayonnaise on the bass. Garnish with sieved egg whites and yolks, the fines herbes, and the truffles. Pass *remaining mayonnaise* separately. Strain court bouillon and reserve for other uses. Serves 6.

COULIBIAC OF SALMON

There are many varieties of Coulibiac, a hot fish pie. It is a favorite Russian accompaniment for soup. A nineteenth-century cookbook says that St. Petersburg cooks preferred to make these pastries with salmon, but on state occasions they used sterlet.

1¼ cups butter
4 onions, sliced
½ pound mushrooms, sliced
3 pounds center-cut salmon steaks
6 shallots, finely chopped
⅓ cup dry white wine
Salt and pepper

1 recipe: Puff Pastry (page 684) or
  Brioche dough (page 653) or Cream
  Cheese Pastry (page 680)
4 cups cooked rice
3 hard-boiled eggs, chopped
3 tablespoons minced dill or
  1½ tablespoons dried dill
½ cup bread crumbs

Melt *one-half cup butter* in a large skillet and slowly stew the onions until very soft and transparent—about 20 minutes. Remove and reserve. Add *one-quarter cup more butter* and sauté the mushrooms over high heat for about 7 minutes or until dry. Meanwhile, butter an oven-proof dish with *one-quarter cup butter*, arrange salmon and shallots in the dish, add the wine, season with salt and pepper to taste, and cover with foil. Bake in a preheated 400° oven for 20 to 25 minutes. Remove bones and skin and cool completely. Reserve fish stock. Roll out pastry on a floured cloth into a large rectangle (18 by 14 inches) about ⅛-inch thick. Mix onions, mushrooms, rice, hard-boiled eggs, and dill. Season with salt and pepper to taste.

454

Spread ½ the rice mixture on the length of the dough, leaving a 4-inch border of dough at the sides and a 1-inch border at both ends. Place fish and shallots on rice, cover with remaining rice. Melt *remaining butter* and pour over rice with fish stock. Fold pastry over and seal. Slip a buttered cookie sheet close to the coulibiac, hold edge of cloth with both hands, and roll coulibiac over onto cookie sheet. Make 2 small vents in pastry. If using yeast pastry, let rise for 20 minutes. Brush with melted butter and sprinkle with bread crumbs. Bake in a preheated 400° oven for 35 to 40 minutes or until golden brown. Serve hot with a bowl of melted butter. Serves 8 to 10. Fish may be poached in court bouillon instead of baked, and broth clarified and served in cups with the coulibiac.

ZARZUELA

The Catalonians have never forgotten that they once comprised an independent kingdom in Spain, and they take particular pride in their distinct culinary tradition. Although matters of home rule mean little to the provincial fisherman, his catch of *tallinas* (clams), *bagavante* (lobster), mussels, and crawfish is the basis of the Catalonian specialty Zarzuela. Meaning a "musical comedy," the name dates back to the seventeenth-century performances given at Phillip IV's palace, La Zarzuela. The version below substitutes Pernod for the traditional Catalonian absinthe while the Basques add cognac to theirs.

½ cup olive oil

2 pounds halibut, fillets of sole, sea bass, or haddock, cut in chunks

2 squid, cut in rings (optional)

Salt and freshly ground white pepper

3 tablespoons flour

2 dozen large shrimps, shelled and deveined (reserve shells)

32 mussels or clams

2 medium onions, finely chopped

2 large tomatoes, peeled, seeded, and chopped, or 1 cup canned tomatoes, drained and chopped

¼ cup blanched almonds or hazelnuts

2 cloves garlic

2 tablespoons minced parsley

½ cup dry white wine

2 to 3 tablespoons Pernod, heated

Heat the oil in a large flameproof casserole. Sprinkle fish and squid with salt and pepper. Dredge with flour and fry until golden on both sides. Remove fish and reserve. Add shrimps and cook until light pink. Remove and reserve. Meanwhile, simmer shrimp shells and well-scrubbed mussels in 1 cup water with a little salt for 5 to 6 minutes or until mussels open. Discard those that do not open. Strain broth carefully and reserve. Fry onions in the oil. Add tomatoes and simmer gently for 5 minutes. Add ½ the broth from the mussels. Put the nuts and garlic through the blender with the remaining shellfish broth. Add to onions and tomatoes. Add the parsley and wine and simmer for 3 to 4 minutes. Return fish, squid, and shrimps to stew. Pour in Pernod and flame. Return mussels to stew in the shell or shelled as preferred. Correct seasoning and heat through. If too thick, a little water may be added. Serve immediately, preferably in the casserole. Serves 8. Cognac may be substituted for Pernod.

SUQUETTE
(Catalonian Fish in Almond Sauce)

$\frac{1}{3}$ cup olive oil	$\frac{1}{2}$ teaspoon dried basil
3 medium onions, finely chopped	1 large bay leaf
2 cloves garlic, minced	Salt and pepper
1 small can Italian plum tomatoes, drained	1 cup slivered blanched almonds
1 cup dry white wine	1 pound fish fillets (such as sole, flounder, lemon sole, or halibut)

Heat the oil and sauté the onion until soft but not brown. Add garlic, tomatoes, wine, basil, and bay leaf. Season to taste with salt and pepper and simmer for 45 minutes to 1 hour. Meanwhile, put almonds through a blender or pound them to a paste in a mortar. Strain the cooked tomato sauce through a fine strainer. Combine with the almonds and return to a large, shallow saucepan. Poach the fish in the sauce until it flakes easily—about 10 to 12 minutes. Serve with rice. Serves 3 to 4. If desired, 1 tablespoon grated bitter chocolate may be added to the sauce when fish is nearly cooked.

KOGT TORSK

Cod, perhaps because it is so abundant and so cheap, has always been identified with peasant fare in Europe. Fleets from as far away as Catholic France, Spain, and the Basque countries have vied for centuries with ships of Scandinavia, England, and the Low Countries for this North Atlantic fish. Southern peoples, of necessity, have commonly eaten cod salted and dried, but northerners, near the fishing banks, prefer it fresh. Kogt Torsk, or boiled cod, is a Danish delicacy.

3 pounds fresh codfish, in 1 piece	3 hard-boiled eggs, chopped or sliced
3 tablespoons salt	$\frac{1}{2}$ cup chopped parsley
2 small bay leaves	$\frac{1}{4}$ cup capers (optional)
1 cup butter, melted	2 cups chopped pickled beets (optional)
Lemon wedges	3 tart juicy apples, grated (optional)
Parsley sprigs	1 cup grated horseradish (optional)
6 to 8 hot boiled potatoes	Hollandaise Sauce (page 625) (optional)
6 chives, minced	Mustard Dill Sauce (page 641)

Wash and wipe the fish. Sprinkle with *1 tablespoon salt* and let stand in a cool place for 1 hour. Rinse and dry. Cover with cold water, add *remaining salt* and bay leaves, bring to a boil, turn down heat, and simmer for about 20 minutes or until fish flakes when tested and is white. Drain well and place on a heated platter. Cover with hot melted butter and surround with lemon wedges and sprigs of parsley. Serve with boiled potatoes and remaining condiments and sauces in little bowls for guests to serve themselves. Serves 6.

BRANDADE DE MORUE

The restaurant Trois Frères Provençaux, patronized by such luminaries as Napoleon and Josephine, was famous for its preparation of this salt cod stew. In his *Grand Dictionnaire de Cuisine*, Alexandre Dumas suggests that the word *brandade* derives from the French verb *brandir*, to stir forcibly, the very method by which the cod is transformed into a creamy consistency, "as easy to digest as vanilla-flavored bread and milk."

2 pounds dried salt codfish	Salt and white pepper
2 cloves garlic, crushed	Toast points
1 cup olive oil	Black truffles (optional)
1 cup milk or half-and-half (half cream, half milk)	

Soak salt cod overnight in cold water to cover. After 24 hours remove from water, place in enameled pan, cover with fresh water, and simmer for 5 to 8 minutes. Remove from water. Take out all bones and flake the fish. Add crushed garlic. Heat olive oil and milk until barely warm in separate saucepans. Add gradually and alternately to hot fish, beating constantly, until fish is smooth and about the consistency of mashed potatoes. Season with salt and white pepper. Serve warm with triangular slices of bread fried in olive oil. Brandade should be shaped into a dome in a deep bowl. Garnish with slices of truffles. Serves 8 as an appetizer.

BACALAO VERACRUZANO
(*Mexican Codfish Stew*)

2 pounds dried salt codfish	1 chili pepper, minced, or $\frac{1}{2}$ teaspoon crushed hot red pepper
Bouquet garni (2 cloves, 6 peppercorns, 1 bay leaf, tied in cheesecloth)	1 bell pepper, diced
3 cloves garlic	2 pimentos, diced
$\frac{3}{4}$ cup olive oil	1 cup coarsely chopped pitted black olives
3 large onions, chopped	$\frac{1}{4}$ cup minced capers
2 pounds tomatoes, peeled, seeded, and coarsely chopped	Salt and pepper

Soak the salt fish in cold water for 24 hours, changing the water once or twice. Boil the cod with the bouquet and *2 whole cloves garlic*, covered with fresh cold water. Simmer for 1 hour. Drain and reserve $\frac{1}{2}$ cup stock. Heat *one-half cup olive oil* and fry *remaining clove garlic*, sliced; when brown, remove garlic from oil. Add fish to oil and cook to heat through. Heat *remaining oil* in another saucepan and cook onions until transparent. Add tomatoes and simmer for 15 minutes. Add $\frac{1}{2}$ cup strained reserved stock and remaining ingredients except capers. Simmer for 5 to 6 minutes. Dome fish on a heated serving dish. Add capers to sauce. Season to taste with salt and pepper and pour over fish. Serves 6.

HECHTENKRAUT
(German Pike with Sauerkraut)

2 pounds of pike or other firm
   white-meat fish, cut in fillets
Water or fish stock, to cover
3 onions
1 stalk celery, with leaves
6 peppercorns
Salt
8 slices bacon, diced

1 cup fine, dry bread crumbs
1 recipe Sauerkraut (page 595)
$\frac{1}{2}$ cup butter
3 tablespoons flour
$\frac{1}{4}$ cup sour cream
Paprika
6 to 8 cooked crawfish tails or
   shrimps (optional)

Poach fish in water or stock along with *1 sliced onion*, celery, peppercorns, and a little salt. When flaky, remove fish; strain and reserve stock. Fry bacon and as fat becomes rendered add *2 diced onions*. Fry slowly until bacon and onion are golden brown. Butter a 6-cup soufflé dish and sprinkle bottom and sides with bread crumbs, tapping out excess. Place a layer of sauerkraut in the dish, add a layer of the onion and bacon mixture and another of fish. Repeat layers in that order until dish is full, ending with sauerkraut. Melt *3 tablespoons butter*, stir in flour, and sauté over low heat for about 5 minutes or until flour begins to take on color. Measure stock and, if necessary, add enough water to make 2 cups. Add to butter and flour mixture along with the sour cream. Stir until smooth. Season with salt and paprika to taste. Place crawfish or shrimps around top of sauerkraut. Add sauce and a generous layer of bread crumbs dotted with *remaining butter*. Bake in preheated 375° oven for about 30 minutes or until sauce is golden brown and bubbling. Serves 6.

BOHEMIAN CHRISTMAS CARP

Carp is synonymous with holidays in many Catholic countries where fish is a time-honored symbol of Christianity. In Polish folklore carp is also a symbol of strength. It is often eaten during Lent but is most elaborately prepared for the feasts of Christmas and New Year's.

3 to 4 pounds carp
Salt
3 cups water, or 1 cup dark beer
   and 2 cups water
1 carrot, sliced
1 stalk celery, sliced, or $\frac{1}{2}$ knob celery,
   peeled and sliced
1 leek, sliced
1 small onion, sliced
Small piece of parsley root (optional)
2 or 3 sprigs parsley

$\frac{1}{4}$ cup vinegar
1 bay leaf
3 tablespoons dark molasses
6 gingersnaps, crushed
$\frac{1}{3}$ cup blanched, coarsely chopped
   almonds
6 to 8 prunes, soaked,
   pitted, and sliced
$\frac{1}{4}$ cup walnuts, chopped
$\frac{1}{4}$ cup golden raisins, soaked
Sugar to taste

Have fishman clean carp thoroughly. Reserve the head. Cut carp into 1- to 1½-inch slices. Sprinkle lightly with salt and let stand for 30 minutes. Cook carp head in water with vegetables, vinegar, and bay leaf for 15 minutes. Strain stock. Rinse and dry salted carp, add it to stock, and simmer slowly for 25 minutes or until done. Remove fish to a heated platter. Add molasses, crushed gingersnaps, almonds, prunes, walnuts, and raisins to stock. Simmer for 10 minutes or until hot and thick, stirring frequently. Season to taste adding vinegar, sugar, or salt as needed. Pour over cooked fish and serve. Serves 4 to 6.

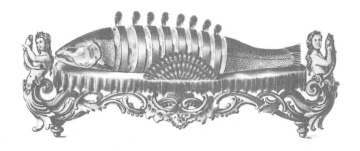

PICKLED JELLIED FISH

The art of pickling foods in salt and vinegar takes its place with sun drying and smoking as the oldest known methods of food preservation. There is evidence that both Chinese and Babylonian cooks stored fish in brine, and Athenaeus records in *The Deipnosophists* that "The Athenians were so fond of pickled fish that they enrolled as citizens the sons of Chaerephilus the seller of salt fish." Some twenty centuries later, Europeans continue to pickle fish, in the manner below.

4 pounds whitefish, pike, carp, trout, or eel
Salt, preferably coarse
2 large onions, sliced
4 cups water
½ cup white vinegar

1 tablespoon mixed pickling spices, tied in cheesecloth
1 bay leaf
1 carrot, scraped and sliced
1 tablespoon sugar

Fish should be cut into 1½- to 2-inch slices without being skinned or boned. Wash, rub with salt, and let stand in refrigerator for 1 to 2 hours. Rinse before cooking. Cook sliced onions in 4 cups water for 15 to 20 minutes. Add vinegar, pickling spices, bay leaf, sliced carrot, and sugar. Bring to a boil, add fish, and reduce heat; cover pan and poach gently for about 30 minutes until fish is done but not falling apart. Remove fish to crock, jar, or ceramic bowl. Taste stock and adjust seasoning with vinegar, sugar, and salt. Remove sack of pickling spices. Pour stock, with onions, carrots, and bay leaf, over fish. Cover and chill for 24 to 48 hours before serving. Serve with jellied stock, sliced onion, and carrot. Serves 4 to 6.

459

FILETS DE MAQUEREAU AUX FENOUIL ET GROSEILLES

Despite its French name, this recipe for mackerel comes from an eighteenth century English cookbook. In addition to fennel, it is flavored with gooseberries, a fruit unknown in most of Europe until the fifteenth century when it was apparently carried north by Castilian sailors.

1 3-pound mackerel, filleted
Salt and pepper
7 tablespoons butter
2 fish roes, if available
¾ cup dry white wine
1½ cups beef broth
3 stalks celery, sliced, and a pinch of dried fennel seed, or 3 stalks fresh

fennel, with greens, and one scallion, bulb and greens, sliced
3 tablespoons flour
4 slices lemon
¼ teaspoon nutmeg
1 pint fresh gooseberries, cooked, or 1 No. 2 can gooseberries, drained
2 tablespoons orange juice

Sprinkle mackerel fillets with salt and pepper. Spread *2 tablespoons butter* in a baking pan. Add fish and roe; dot with *2 tablespoons butter* and add white wine to pan. Bake for 20 to 25 minutes in preheated 350° oven. Remove cooked fish to heated serving dish. Pour beef broth into pan, bring to boil, and scrape bits of fish into broth. Sauté sliced celery with dried fennel seed or fresh fennel with scallion in *3 tablespoons butter* until vegetables soften but are not brown. Add flour and sauté slowly, stirring constantly until flour begins to turn golden brown. Add beef broth and lemon slices. Cover and simmer for about 7 minutes or until sauce is smooth and thick. Add nutmeg and gooseberries. Simmer for 3 to 4 minutes and season with orange juice and salt and pepper. Spoon over fish. Serves 4.

KILIC BALIGI SISDE
(Turkish Swordfish)

2 pounds swordfish steak
Juice of 1 lemon
½ cup olive or sesame oil
2 tablespoons grated onion

Salt and pepper
4 medium-size tomatoes
3 medium-size onions
18 to 20 bay leaves

Cut swordfish steak into 1-inch cubes. Marinate for 2 hours in a mixture of lemon juice, oil, grated onion, salt, and pepper. Cut tomatoes into chunks and onions into wedges. Thread fish cubes onto skewers, alternating with pieces of tomato, onions, and bay leaves. There should be a bay leaf between every 2 pieces of fish. Brush with marinade and broil over hot charcoal or in a preheated broiler. Turn frequently, brush with marinade, and broil until fish is golden brown on all sides—about 15 minutes. Serve with lemon wedges. Serves 4 to 6.

SWEET AND SOUR FISH

Many Chinese dishes exploit the play of opposite flavors and textures. Sweet and sour preparations are a specialty of Honan, ancient provincial capital in the agricultural heartland of China.

1 2-pound fish (such as striped or sea bass, carp, perch, or mullet)
3 tablespoons dry sherry
2 teaspoons salt
2 tablespoons cornstarch

2 tablespoons flour
Sesame, peanut, or vegetable oil for deep frying
Sweet and Sour Sauce (page 620)

Score fish on both sides with 3 slashes. Mix sherry, salt, cornstarch, and flour. Spread over fish. Heat oil to 360° in a shallow pan and fry fish until golden brown, about 7 to 10 minutes on each side. Drain and put on a heated platter. Pour sweet and sour sauce over fish. Serves 4.

POISSON AU RHUM GUADELOUPE

"The chief fuddling they make in the island is rum-bullion alias kill-divil and this is made from sugar-canes distilled, a hot, hellish, and terrible liquor." Thus a seventeenth-century manuscript described the industry that dominated the history of the West Indies for centuries. French colonists in Guadeloupe also found rum an excellent flavoring for fish in the recipe below.

3 tablespoons butter
2 tablespoons olive oil
1 medium onion, chopped
1 clove garlic, chopped
1½ pounds fish (such as sole, halibut, or sea bass) or shelled and deveined shrimps, lobster, or crabmeat

2 tablespoons light rum
2 tomatoes, peeled, seeded, and diced
¼ pound mushrooms, thinly sliced
Juice of 1 lemon
½ cup dry white wine
Salt and pepper
1 teaspoon curry powder

Heat the butter and oil in a large skillet and simmer onions and garlic. Add the fish (cut into chunks) and brown lightly on all sides. Spoon rum over fish and flame. When flames die out, add tomatoes, mushrooms, *half the lemon juice*, and the wine and season with salt and pepper. Cover and simmer gently for 15 to 20 minutes. Dilute curry powder in *remaining lemon juice* and add to fish. Let it simmer 1 to 2 minutes while stirring. Serve with steamed rice. Serves 4.

FILLETS OF SOLE

The European sole is considered the most delectable and versatile member of the flatfish family. The fillets, accompanied by elegant sauces, are an important item in the French repertoire. In 1837 chef Langlais invented Sole Normande, a tribute to the Normandy coast where the fish abounds. Another sole recipe bears the name of Adolphe Dugléré, chef of the chic Café Anglais; another, the name Marguery, "the place in Paris for banquets, political luncheons, reunions of old comrades, of future deputies . . . celebrating some festive occasion with more noise than manners."

SOLE MARGUERY

12 mussels
2 cups dry white wine
4 shallots or 1 small onion, chopped
4 large fillets of sole
Salt and pepper
4 tablespoons butter

3 tablespoons flour
12 cooked shrimps, shelled and
    deveined
2 egg yolks
$\frac{1}{2}$ cup heavy cream

Scrub and wash mussels, removing beard. Steam with $\frac{1}{2}$ cup water in a covered pot until mussels open—about 5 minutes. Discard any mussels that remain closed. Shell mussels and remove black portions. Strain and reserve stock. Put the wine and shallots in a wide skillet with a cover and simmer for 5 minutes. Place sole fillets in the wine, season with salt and pepper, cover, and simmer gently for 5 to 7 minutes or until fish flakes when tested with a fork. Remove fish with a slotted spatula to a heated serving platter. Add stock from mussels to sole stock and simmer briskly for 5 minutes. Melt 3 *tablespoons butter* in a saucepan, add the flour, stir, and cook for 3 minutes. Add strained fish stock (about 1 cup) and stir until thickened. Simmer for 5 minutes. Add mussels and shrimps. Beat yolks into the cream; gradually add some sauce to cream and pour all back into saucepan on very low heat. Stir until smooth and thickened but do not boil. Remove from heat and swirl in *remaining tablespoon butter*. Pour sauce over sole fillets. Serves 4.

SOLE NORMANDE

8 mussels	8 shucked oysters
4 large mushrooms	1 cup fish Velouté (page 616)
2 shallots, minced	1 tablespoon butter
1 cup dry white wine	1 teaspoon lemon juice
Salt and pepper	2 egg yolks, beaten
4 fillets of sole	8 cooked shrimps, shelled and deveined

Scrub the mussels and remove beards. Cut mushroom stems level with caps; peel, reserving peels. Put chopped stems, washed mushroom peelings, and shallots in a saucepan with *half the wine*. Add mussels and bring to a boil. When mussels open, simmer for 2 to 3 minutes. Remove mussels from shells, discarding any unopened mussels, and reserve broth. Salt and pepper the fish. Fold fillets lengthwise and place in a lightly buttered pan with a cover. Add strained mussel broth and *remaining wine*. Simmer for 10 minutes, add oysters, and simmer for 3 minutes or until oysters curl at the edges. Remove fish to a heated platter; cover and keep warm. Reserve oysters in a little warm broth. Reduce fish stock to 1 cup. Add to hot fish velouté and simmer, stirring. Meanwhile, poach the mushroom caps for 6 to 8 minutes in a little water, 1 tablespoon butter, ½ teaspoon salt, and the lemon juice. Add this liquid to the sauce and reserve mushroom caps. Pour a little hot sauce into beaten egg yolks, beating constantly, and pour back into saucepan, beating constantly. Add mussels and shrimps, correct seasoning; heat and stir but do not boil. Arrange fish on a platter, and cover with sauce. Place oysters down the center and top each fish fillet with a mushroom cap. Serves 4.

VARIATION: *Sole Riche*: Add 2 to 3 tablespoons Lobster Butter (page 629) to the hot sauce and garnish with finely chopped truffles.

SOLE DUGLERE

6 tablespoons butter	½ small bay leaf
4 fillets of sole	⅓ cup dry white wine or dry vermouth
2 shallots or 1 small onion, minced	Salt and pepper
2 tomatoes, peeled, seeded, and diced	1 tablespoon flour
1 tablespoon chopped parsley	½ cup light cream
¼ teaspoon dried thyme	

Using *1 tablespoon butter*, butter a large skillet that has a cover. Arrange the fillets of sole in it and cover them with shallots, tomatoes, parsley, thyme, bay leaf, wine, salt, and pepper. Dot with *2 tablespoons butter*. Cover, bring to a simmer, and cook for 10 to 15 minutes or until fish flakes when tested with a fork. Remove fillets carefully to a heated platter, using a slotted spatula; keep warm. Reduce broth by a third. Meanwhile, cream *2 tablespoons butter* with the flour. Stir it slowly into the simmering broth. When thickened, simmer for 5 minutes longer. Add the cream and simmer for 2 to 3 minutes; remove from heat and stir in the *remaining tablespoon butter*. Pour sauce over fish. Serve with lemon wedges. Serves 4.

GEFÜLLTE FISH

3 pounds assorted fish (such as yellow
   pike, whitefish, and carp)
Fish trimmings
Fish roe, if any
6 medium-size onions
2 eggs
¼ cup ice water

2 to 3 tablespoons matzo meal
2 teaspoons salt
½ teaspoon white pepper
1 teaspoon sugar
3 carrots, scraped and sliced
2 stalks of celery, sliced

Use pike, whitefish, and, if it is absolutely fresh, carp. Have fish cut into fillets but keep trimmings and roe. Salt fish lightly and place in refrigerator for 3 to 4 hours. Pat dry. Grind fish and *2 onions* twice through the fine blade of food chopper. Turn into a chopping bowl and, with a hand chopper, gradually chop and work in the eggs, the water, and enough matzo meal to give the mixture the consistency of thick oatmeal; add the salt, pepper, and sugar. Let stand for 30 minutes. Place fish trimmings, *remaining 4 onions*, diced, and sliced carrots and celery in the bottom of a kettle. Add water to cover (about 6 to 8 cups) and bring to a boil. With wet hands shape fish into balls about 2 inches in diameter. Drop gently into boiling fish broth, cover, and simmer gently but steadily for about 1 hour. Add water if needed during cooking. Let cooked fish cool in broth for 30 minutes. Remove fish and carrot slices to a deep bowl, and strain broth over fish. Chill thoroughly, preferably overnight. Serve fish with a little jellied broth, finely diced, some roe, a few of the carrot slices, and bottled red or white horseradish. Serves 4 to 6. Reserved strips of fish skin may be wrapped around fish balls before poaching; or have fishman fillet fish, leaving skin intact. Wrap force-meat in whole skin and poach in a fish kettle, producing a fish that is truly *gefüllte*—stuffed.

FISKEFÄRCE
(Norwegian Fish Pudding)

2 pounds fresh haddock or halibut
⅓ cup butter
4 egg whites
2 teaspoons potato or all-purpose flour
2 teaspoons salt

½ teaspoon white pepper
½ teaspoon nutmeg
4 cups milk
Lobster Sauce (see Hummer Sao,
   page 619)

Skin and bone the fish and mince twice through the finest blade of a meat grinder with the butter. Put in a bowl and pound with a wooden pestle or spoon, adding the egg whites gradually until fish is a thick paste. Rub through the finest strainer twice. Dissolve potato flour in a little milk and add with the salt, pepper, and nutmeg. Pound again until smooth. Add milk very slowly, a spoonful or two to begin with, and beat for 25 minutes by hand or for 8 to 10 minutes with an electric beater at medium speed. Pour in a buttered 10-cup ring mold and bake for about 1 hour in a preheated 350° oven or until pudding is firm. Unmold and serve with lobster sauce. Serves 8.

MIDYE DOLMASI
(Stuffed Mussels)

24 mussels
$\frac{1}{4}$ cup olive oil
1 large onion, minced
$\frac{1}{2}$ cup rice
1 cup hot chicken broth

2 tablespoons chopped pine nuts
2 tablespoons currants
2 tablespoons chopped parsley
Salt and pepper to taste
$\frac{1}{4}$ teaspoon cinnamon

Scrub mussels well, removing beards. Steam mussels in $\frac{3}{4}$ cup water, covered, with *1 tablespoon olive oil* until they open. Remove from the heat and cool. Discard any mussels that did not open. Remove black part from open mussels without removing mussels from shells. Strain and reserve broth. Heat *remaining olive oil* in a saucepan and sauté the onion. Add the rice and sauté for 3 to 5 minutes. Add the hot chicken broth, the reserved broth from the mussels, and remaining ingredients. Stir once, cover, and simmer for 15 minutes or until rice is tender but still firm. Pack shells with rice and chill. Garnish with lemon wedges. Serves 4 to 6.

QUENELLES DE POISSON

It is believed by some that these forcemeat dumplings got their name from the Anglo-Saxon word *knyll* (to pound or grind), because to make Quenelles, the fish used must first be finely ground.

1 pound boned, skinned pike or
  other firm fish
3 cups crumbled stale white
  crustless bread
1 cup milk
1 cup butter
1 teaspoon salt

$\frac{1}{4}$ teaspoon nutmeg
$\frac{1}{4}$ teaspoon white pepper
4 egg whites
1 cup heavy cream (optional)
1 tablespoon minced truffles (optional)
Sauce Nantua (page 619)

Grind pike 2 or 3 times using finest blade of food chopper. Rub through the finest strainer and chill. Combine bread crumbs, milk, *2 tablespoons butter*, salt, nutmeg, and pepper in a saucepan over low heat and work with a wooden spoon into a very smooth, thick paste. Spread on a plate and cool, then chill. Fill a large bowl with ice and set a second smaller bowl in the ice. Put in the fish and work in the egg whites, one by one, pounding the fish smooth. Add the panade (bread and milk) and continue blending the mixture. Work in softened *remaining butter* bit by bit. Gradually stir in the cream, a teaspoon at a time. Mix in the truffles. Shape into dumplings with 2 wet tablespoons or into $1\frac{1}{2}$- by 4-inch sausages. Place side by side in boiling water and immediately reduce heat so water just simmers; poach uncovered for 10 minutes. Remove with a slotted spoon and drain well. Put some sauce nantua at the bottom of an ovenproof serving dish, place quenelles over this sauce, cover with more sauce, and heat in low oven for 10 minutes to swell quenelles. Serves 4 to 5.

OTAK-OTAK

The ancient Greeks cooked their shrimps in fig leaves, and the practice of baking food in protective foliage persists today in many areas of the world. In Malaya native fish is often wrapped in banana leaves.

4 banana leaves or 4 pieces aluminum foil (8 by 12 inches)
⅔ cup freshly grated coconut or 1 can grated unsweetened coconut
4 dried red peppers or 1 teaspoon crushed hot peppers
2 cloves garlic, minced

½ teaspoon turmeric or curry powder
Salt
⅔ cup thick Coconut Cream (page 632)
1 pound swordfish, halibut, or fillets of sole
24 small cooked shrimps, shelled, deveined, and halved

If banana leaves are available, blanch first in boiling water. Spread leaves ready to stuff. Spread the coconut on a cookie sheet and toast in a preheated 425° oven until golden brown. Pound the peppers, garlic, turmeric, ½ teaspoon salt, and the toasted coconut to make a paste, or purée in a blender. Add coconut cream and put in a double boiler; cook until thick. Let cool completely. Cut the fish into thin slices. Partially frozen fish will slice easily. Mix the shrimps and coconut cream. Spread half the shrimp mixture into 4 portions on the leaves or foil. Arrange fish slices on this and top with remaining shrimp mixture. Wrap leaves or foil around fish and secure with toothpicks. Bake for 20 minutes in preheated 400° oven or roast over a charcoal fire. Serves 4.

SEVICHE

Many versions of the seafood cocktail Seviche appear throughout Latin America. In Acapulco it is made with *huachinango* (red snapper), pompano, and scallops, but any raw fish will do. The acid action of the lime juice actually "cooks" and tenderizes the fish.

2 pounds halibut fillets (or any firm white-meat fish fillets) or scallops
½ cup lime juice
1 bay leaf
1 large onion, minced
1 clove garlic, minced (optional)
4 large tomatoes, peeled, seeded, and diced

1 teaspoon dried thyme
⅛ teaspoon powdered cloves or cumin
¼ cup olive oil
12 black olives
Salt and freshly ground pepper
1 can chilies serranos or 1 hot red pepper, minced, or dash Tabasco
1 tablespoon Worcestershire sauce

Cut the fish into slices ½ inch thick and 2 inches long. Place slices in a shallow, wide dish. Pour in lime juice and add bay leaf. Marinate fish for 2 hours at room temperature, turning frequently. Remove fish from lime juice and pat dry. Mix with remaining ingredients and marinate for another 2 hours in the refrigerator. Place in serving dish. Serves 6 as an appetizer.

SASHIMI

In feudal Japan the preparation of Sashimi, or sliced raw fish, was an elaborate ritual. After sharpening his knife, the deft Sashimi Master would keep the blade in water overnight so that the smell of the whetstone would not affect the delicate flavor of the tuna or bream. When cut, the paper-thin strips were symmetrically aligned on a platter, garnished with seaweed and *daikon* (white radishes), and served with soy sauce.

8 fillets firm white-meat fish (such as trout, halibut, bass, or snapper)
$1\frac{1}{4}$ cups shredded carrots
$1\frac{1}{4}$ cups shredded radishes
1 tablespoon powdered Japanese
horseradish or 1 teaspoon bottled horseradish
$\frac{1}{3}$ cup soy sauce
4 teaspoons sake or dry sherry
2 teaspoons sugar

Slice the fillets on the slant to obtain the thinnest possible slices. Mix the carrot and radish and divide on 4 serving plates as a bed for the fish slices. Arrange slices in overlapping pattern. Mix the horseradish with about 1 tablespoon water to a smooth paste. Add soy sauce, wine, and sugar. Mix well and pour into 4 small bowls as dip for fish. Serves 4.

SWEDISH GRAVAD LOX

$2\frac{1}{2}$ pounds center-cut fresh salmon, in 1 piece
$\frac{2}{3}$ cup sugar
$\frac{1}{3}$ cup salt
$\frac{1}{4}$ teaspoon white pepper
2 tablespoons dried dill seed
1 large bunch fresh dill
Mustard Dill Sauce (page 641)

Salmon should be split in half but not skinned. Have the large center bone removed. Run fingers over the flesh of the fish and, using a pair of tweezers, extract all the tiny bones that can be found. Rinse fish and pat dry. Combine sugar, salt, and white pepper. Rub this mixture into the flesh of the fish halves. Place one piece of fish, skin side down, in a glass or ceramic dish. Sprinkle with *1 tablespoon dill seed* and top with *8 to 10 sprigs of fresh dill*. Sprinkle with *remaining dill seed* and cover with second piece of fish, flesh side down on the dill mixture. Arrange *remaining sprigs of dill* around fish in the dish and add any of the sugar-salt mixture that you may not have been able to work into the fish flesh. Cover with a sheet of waxed paper. Top with a plate slightly smaller than the baking dish and weight down. Place in refrigerator for 48 hours, turning fish every 12 hours and replacing plate and weight. Do not drain off liquid that accumulates around fish; it will eventually cover it completely. Before serving, remove fish, drain, and scrape off all dill and spices from the surface of the flesh. Cut salmon in paper-thin slices, holding knife with blade in a horizontal position and cutting diagonally down from the surface to skin in undercuts. Do not cut skin off with salmon slices. Serve on thin Danish or Westphalian pumpernickel squares with mustard dill sauce and a small spray of fresh dill. Makes about 20 canapés or 8 first-course servings.

POULTRY

Since air is less dense than earth, reasoned Aristotle, birds ought to stand higher in esteem than quadrupeds. To judge from the number of sumptuary laws directed specifically against overindulgence in poultry dishes, mankind has needed no urging. Fowl are the oldest of domesticated creatures and their delicate flavors have doubtless inspired more imaginative cooking than any other food.

CHICKEN VARIUS

The only cookbook that has come down to us from classical civilization was written by Apicius in the first century A.D. The section entitled "Birds" includes "Sauces for Ostrich," "Fig-Peckers," and "Peacocks." Two of his recipes for chicken follow.

2 to 3 tablespoons olive oil
1 large onion, chopped
1 carrot, chopped
2 stalks celery, chopped
2 2-pound chickens, disjointed
Bouquet garni (2 leeks, 4 sprigs
 parsley, 4 crushed coriander seeds,
 4 peppercorns, $\frac{1}{2}$ teaspoon summer
 savory, tied in cheesecloth)
Salt and pepper

1 cup dry white wine
Sauce:
2 tablespoons pine nuts,
 pounded to a paste
2 tablespoons butter
2 tablespoons flour
2 egg yolks
$\frac{1}{2}$ cup heavy cream
2 tablespoons lemon juice
1 tablespoon dry sherry

Heat the oil in a wide casserole with a cover. Simmer the onion, carrot, and celery until soft but not brown. Add chicken, bouquet garni, 2 teaspoons salt, $\frac{1}{2}$ teaspoon pepper, wine, and enough water to cover. Simmer chicken covered until tender—about 40 minutes. Strain off broth, reserving $1\frac{1}{2}$ cups. Keep chicken warm and make the sauce.

To make the sauce: Pound the pine nuts and add to $1\frac{1}{2}$ cups reserved broth. Heat the butter and add the flour, stirring for about 2 minutes. Add the broth mixture and stir over low heat until smooth and thickened. Simmer for 15 minutes over very low heat. Beat egg yolks into cream; gradually add some hot sauce, stirring constantly. Return to pan and stir until very hot. Add lemon juice. Season to taste. Add sherry just before serving. Serves 4 to 6.

CONCHICLA
(Casserole of Chicken with Calf's Brain)

1 calf's brain	$\frac{1}{4}$ teaspoon each: crushed coriander,
1 tablespoon butter	cumin, lovage, and celery seed
2 tablespoons olive oil	Salt and freshly ground pepper
1 3$\frac{1}{2}$-pound chicken, disjointed	1 cup large dried prunes, pitted
1 medium onion, minced	3 cups cooked peas
1 cup dry white wine	1 teaspoon cornstarch
2 cups chicken broth	2 tablespoons minced parsley

Soak the calf's brain in ice water for $\frac{1}{2}$ hour. Plunge into boiling salted water and poach for 5 minutes. Cool, wipe, and remove membranes. Cut into cubes and reserve. Heat the butter and oil and lightly brown the chicken. Add the onion; when brown, add the brain, wine, broth to cover, and the dried herbs and spices. Cover and simmer for about 20 minutes. Add prunes and simmer for 10 minutes longer, uncovered. Purée *two and one-half cups peas* with a spoonful of the chicken broth. Pour purée in the bottom of a casserole. Strain chicken, reserving broth. Place chicken, brain, and prunes over pea purée. Top with *remaining peas* and bake in preheated 350° oven for 10 minutes, covered, just to heat through. Mix cornstarch with a little water and gradually pour into strained broth. Place over moderate heat and simmer until thickened. Stir in parsley. Pass gravy separately. Serves 4 to 6.

CHICKEN SLICES WITH PISTACHIOS

Vincent La Chapelle, borrowing from the Italians, adds a flavorful nut known since Roman times to this eighteenth-century recipe.

1 cup butter	$\frac{2}{3}$ cup chicken broth
2 large chicken breasts, split	2 egg yolks
Salt and pepper	$\frac{1}{2}$ cup heavy cream
4 shallots or 1 onion, finely chopped	$\frac{1}{3}$ cup chopped pistachio nuts
4 large mushrooms, sliced	$\frac{1}{4}$ teaspoon dried tarragon
1 tablespoon flour	1 tablespoon lemon juice
$\frac{1}{3}$ cup dry white wine (optional)	

Melt *one-quarter cup butter* in a large skillet, and when it is hot and bubbly, sauté the chicken breasts on both sides. When chicken is golden, season with salt and pepper, remove, and set aside. Sauté shallots in pan for 5 minutes. Add mushrooms and continue cooking for 5 minutes, adding more butter if needed. Add the flour and cook for 3 minutes, stirring. Add wine and broth and stir until slightly thickened. Return breasts to pan. Cover and cook for 15 minutes on a low heat. Beat the egg yolks and cream. Add some hot sauce to them and return to the pan with the pistachios and tarragon. Stir on a very low heat until slightly thickened and heated. Add lemon juice and correct seasoning. Serves 4.

SQUAB A LA DUXELLES

The mushroom sauce which accompanies this squab dish is supposed to have been created in the seventeenth century by La Varenne, the remarkable chef and social secretary to the Marquis d'Uxelles.

2 slices bacon, minced
4 squabs or Cornish game hens
6 tablespoons butter
3 young scallions, minced
3 shallots, minced
$\frac{1}{4}$ pound mushrooms, minced
Salt and pepper
$\frac{1}{4}$ teaspoon dried thyme

$\frac{1}{4}$ teaspoon dried basil
2 teaspoons minced parsley
$\frac{1}{2}$ cup dry white wine
$\frac{3}{4}$ cup beef broth
4 slices ham
4 slices bread, crusts removed
Juice of $\frac{1}{2}$ lemon (optional)

Fry bacon until crisp in a casserole. Remove bacon and reserve. Brown birds in bacon fat, breasts down. Turn the birds; add *2 tablespoons butter*, the scallions, shallots, and mushrooms. Sprinkle with salt and pepper and cook for 5 minutes. Add the herbs, white wine, and broth. Simmer for 5 minutes. Cover and bake in a preheated 350° oven for 40 minutes. Meanwhile, fry the ham and the bread in the *remaining butter*. Place ham on fried bread on a heated platter. Place a bird on each piece of ham, add bacon pieces and lemon juice to sauce, and pour over birds. Serves 4.

POULET MARENGO

There is no question that this entree was named for the battle at which Napoleon defeated Austria in 1800, but there is much speculation about its creation. The general's cook, Dunand, is most often given credit and the improbable combination of ingredients, so the story goes, were scavenged by Bonaparte's aides in the Piedmontese countryside.

2 frying chickens, disjointed
Salt and pepper
$\frac{2}{3}$ to $\frac{3}{4}$ cup olive oil
1 pound mushrooms, washed and sliced
18 small white onions, peeled
$2\frac{1}{2}$ tablespoons flour
$\frac{1}{4}$ cup brandy
1 cup dry white wine, heated
1 cup hot water
9 tomatoes
Bouquet garni (2 teaspoons thyme, 5 to 6 sprigs parsley, 2 bay leaves, tied in cheesecloth)

4 shallots, peeled and crushed
2 cloves garlic
15 small olives, pitted (optional)
6 to 8 eggs, deep fried in olive oil (optional)
Cayenne pepper
12 to 18 slices French bread, fried in olive oil
12 to 18 anchovy fillets (optional)
16 to 20 cooked crawfish or large shrimps (optional)

Sprinkle chicken pieces lightly with salt and pepper. Heat *one-half cup oil* and when it is smoking add chicken and brown slowly on all sides, adding more oil if necessary. Remove chicken pieces. Add mushrooms and fry until they begin to brown. Remove and reserve. Add onions and brown lightly on all sides. Remove and reserve. Return chicken to pan and sprinkle with flour. Turn pieces over low heat until all flour is absorbed. Add brandy and boil rapidly until it almost evaporates completely. Add hot wine and water. Peel, seed, and dice 6 *tomatoes* and add them to the chicken along with bouquet garni, the shallots, and the garlic. Return mushrooms and onions to pan. Cover tightly and simmer gently but steadily for 30 or 40 minutes or until chicken is done. Add olives for last 10 minutes of cooking time. Peel *remaining 3 tomatoes*, cut them in half, remove seeds, and sauté for 3 minutes in a little olive oil. Prepare eggs. When chicken is done, season sauce with salt and cayenne pepper to taste. Place chicken on platter, pour sauce over it with mushrooms, onions, and olives. Garnish with toast slices, tomato halves, fried eggs topped with anchovies, and crawfish or shrimps. Serves 6 to 8.

A CHICKEN-PYE WITH ITALIAN MASCARONIS

No sooner had the proper Englishman mastered the Italian fork than he felt competent to try pasta. In 1685 Robert May directed readers to make with "a piece of paste . . . some great and some very little, rouls or stars" and combine them with capons and cheese. Vincent La Chapelle, the influential eighteenth-century chef, offered a more refined version (much like the American Chicken Tetrazzini) in *The Modern Cook*.

4 cups cooked elbow macaroni
4 cups thin Béchamel Sauce (page 618)
½ teaspoon dried tarragon
1½ cups cooked ground veal
Pinch each: mace, thyme, sage, and
   rosemary
2 tablespoons finely chopped parsley
1 tablespoon chopped chives

Salt and freshly ground pepper
½ cup grated Parmesan cheese
1½ cups finely diced cooked ham
2 large chicken breasts, cooked
   and sliced
1 recipe Short Pastry (page 682)
1 egg yolk

Butter a 12-cup casserole. Mix the macaroni, *3 cups béchamel sauce*, and the tarragon. Put half the macaroni mixture in the casserole. Mix veal, mace, thyme, sage, rosemary, *2 teaspoons parsley, 1 teaspoon chives*, and salt and freshly ground pepper to taste. Spread over macaroni. Sprinkle *1 tablespoon grated Parmesan* over veal, cover with ham, sprinkle with *2 teaspoons parsley* and *1 teaspoon chives, 1 tablespoon cheese*, and a sprinkling of pepper. Place chicken slices over ham, season with salt and pepper, *remaining parsley and chives*, and *1 tablespoon cheese*. Cover with remaining macaroni. Mix *remaining cup of béchamel sauce* with *remaining cheese*. Season to taste and pour over filling. Roll out pastry to ¼-inch thickness. Cover casserole with pastry. Seal and flute. Brush with egg yolk beaten with 2 teaspoons water. Prick with a fork or make little slits in a ring for vents. Bake in a preheated 425° oven for 15 minutes, lower heat to 350°, and bake until golden, about 25 minutes. Serves 8 to 10.

POULET BASILIQUE

2 2-pound chickens, disjointed
Salt and pepper
1½ cups butter
2 cups dry white wine

2 tablespoons chopped fresh basil or
1 tablespoon dried basil
Lemon juice

Sprinkle chicken pieces with salt and pepper. Heat *three-quarters cup butter* and in it brown chicken slowly on all sides. Cover and cook slowly for 10 to 12 minutes, shaking the pan frequently to prevent scorching. Remove pieces of white meat and continue cooking dark meat for another 10 minutes. Be sure that heat is low enough to prevent butter from burning. Remove all chicken from pan and pour off excess butter. Add wine and basil to pan, bring to a boil, and scrape coagulated pan juices into wine. Boil rapidly until wine is reduced by ½. Swirl in *remaining three-quarters cup butter* and season with salt, pepper, and a dash of lemon juice. Place chicken on heated platter and spoon sauce over it. Serves 4 to 6.

CHICKEN ON CINDERS

La Chapelle, chef to the Prince of Orange and Nassau and author of *Le Cuisinier Moderne*, notes contradictorily at the end of this recipe that the chickens are not actually cooked over cinders. "I hope that it will not be taken amiss, that I direct the Dressing of them in a stew-pan, because they retain their Gravy, taste better this Way, and are not liable to be burnt, as they are on Cinders."

4 squabs or Cornish hens, with livers
Salt and pepper
¾ cup butter
½ cup chopped shallots
4 large mushrooms, minced
4 slices white bread, crumbled
¼ cup chopped parsley
¼ teaspoon each: marjoram, tarragon, and basil
1 large truffle, minced (optional)

1¼ cups beef broth made with
1 bouillon cube
1 large onion, thinly sliced
4 thin slices veal, pounded and cut into julienne strips
4 slices Virginia ham, cut into julienne strips
4 slices bacon
¼ cup dry sherry

Singe the squabs and wipe them. Season the cavities with salt and pepper. Mince livers. Melt *4 tablespoons butter* in a frying pan and sauté the shallots, mushrooms, and livers. Season to taste with salt and pepper. Add the crumbled bread, parsley, herbs, and truffle. Add just *enough beef broth* to moisten slightly. Divide the mixture equally to stuff the four birds. Skewer and truss birds. Rub each with *1 tablespoon butter* and salt and pepper. Melt *remaining 4 table-spoons butter* in a roasting pan and cover bottom of pan with onion, veal, and ham. Add game hens and top each with a slice of bacon. Roast in a preheated 400° oven for 40 minutes, basting twice. Discard bacon. Keep birds hot on serving platter. Spoon ham, veal, and onions around them. Remove fat from the pan and add *remaining beef broth*, and bring to a boil, stirring co- agulated pan juices with a spoon. Simmer for 5 minutes; add sherry, simmer 1 minute longer, and season to taste. Pour gravy over birds. Serves 4.

TO BAKE A CHICKEN WITH GRAPES

In his *New Book of Cookerie*, 1631, John Murrel promises to reveal "the most commendable fashion of Dressing, or Sowcing, either Flesh, Fish or Fowle," including this recipe for roast chicken.

$\frac{1}{2}$ teaspoon dried mace
1$\frac{1}{2}$ teaspoons salt
$\frac{1}{2}$ teaspoon black pepper
1 4-pound roasting chicken
$\frac{3}{4}$ cup butter
2 small onions, sliced
$\frac{1}{2}$ cup dry white wine
1 cup chicken broth
2 cups seedless grapes, fresh or canned
Juice of $\frac{1}{2}$ orange

Stuffing:
$\frac{3}{4}$ cup butter, melted
1 onion, minced
1 chicken liver, diced
2 cups croutons
$\frac{1}{2}$ cup chicken broth
1 teaspoon dried sage
$\frac{1}{4}$ teaspoon dried thyme
Freshly ground pepper and
　　salt to taste
1 cup seedless grapes, fresh or canned

To make the stuffing: Melt 6 *tablespoons butter* and in it sauté onions for 2 to 3 minutes. Add *remaining 6 tablespoons butter* and the diced liver and sauté until liver is cooked but not brown. Add remaining stuffing ingredients and toss well. Salt to taste.

To prepare chicken: Combine mace, salt, and pepper. Rub outside of bird with *3 tablespoons butter* and sprinkle with spice mixture. Rub inside of bird with salt and pepper. Stuff and truss securely. Add *one-third cup butter* to roasting pan. Place chicken on rack in pan, breast down. Add onions. Roast in preheated 425° oven for 30 minutes. Turn chicken on its back, lower heat to 350°. Baste and bake for 30 minutes more, adding *remaining butter* as needed for bast- ing. When legs move freely in sockets, or juices run clear when chicken is pierced in the joint, remove to heated platter and keep warm. Place pan over medium heat and stir in wine. Sim- mer and scrape in coagulated pan juices. Add broth and simmer for 5 minutes. Strain into saucepan, add grapes and orange juice, and simmer for 5 minutes. Season to taste. Carve chicken and cover with a little of the sauce. Pass remaining sauce separately. Serves 6.

OYSTERS, BACON, AND PULLETS

Robert May prefaced his eight-volume cookbook with the modest admission that "God and my own Conscience would not permit me to bury these my Experiences in the Grave." When *The Accomplisht Cook* was first published in 1660, he had served some fifty-five years as professional cook in a dozen noble households. May's "experiences" were fast becoming *démodé* in a nation infatuated with French cuisine, and in such dishes as the following he took his readers back to "those Golden Days wherein were practiced the Triumphs and Tragedies of Cookery [when men strove] to be good rather than to seem so."

2 2-pound broiling chickens	2 cups fresh bread crumbs
Salt	$\frac{1}{2}$ teaspoon each: pepper, thyme,
1 pint oysters and their liquor	and marjoram
4 shallots or 1 small onion, minced	$\frac{1}{4}$ teaspoon nutmeg
4 tablespoons butter	$\frac{1}{2}$ cup chicken broth
$\frac{1}{4}$ pound bacon, in one piece	

Wipe the broilers and salt the cavities. Simmer the oysters in their liquor until the edges barely curl. Strain and reserve liquor for basting. Cook the shallots in *1 tablespoon butter*. Dice the bacon, fry it for 5 minutes, and drain. Mix the oysters, shallots, bacon, bread crumbs, and seasonings. Stuff the birds and truss. Spread each bird with *1 tablespoon butter*. Use *remaining tablespoon butter* to butter a roasting pan. Place birds in the pan and roast in a preheated 400° oven for 45 minutes, basting twice with the oyster liquor after the first 20 minutes. Keep chickens warm. Deglaze the pan on a low fire by pouring in chicken broth and scraping all the drippings. Simmer for 3 minutes. Serve separately in a sauceboat. Serves 4 to 6.

WIENER BACKHUHN
(*Viennese Fried Chicken*)

2 frying chickens, disjointed	3 eggs, beaten with
Juice of 1 lemon	3 tablespoons water
Salt and pepper	Bread crumbs
Flour	Lard or vegetable shortening
	$\frac{3}{4}$ cup melted butter

Remove skin from all chicken pieces except the wings. Flatten breast pieces, removing bones as necessary so they will fry evenly. Sprinkle chicken with lemon juice and let stand at room temperature for 1 hour. Pat dry, sprinkle with salt and pepper, and dredge lightly with flour. Dip each piece into beaten egg, letting excess drip off. Dredge with bread crumbs. Let stand at room temperature for 20 minutes. Heat lard or vegetable shortening in a deep skillet; there should be a 2-inch depth of melted fat. Add chicken and fry slowly, turning once so that both sides become golden brown. When brown, lower heat, and fry for another 8 to 10 minutes on each side. Total frying time should be about 25 minutes. Arrange fried chicken pieces in a single layer in an open baking pan. Pour a little melted butter over each piece and bake in preheated 325° oven for 10 minutes or until breading is dry and crisp. Serves 4 to 6.

CAPON IN A BAG

"This collection . . . needs no Rhetoricating Floscules to set it off. The Author as is well known, having been a Person of Eminency for his Learning and of Exquisite Curiosity in his Researches. . . . His name does sufficiently Auspicate the Work." The author thus described on the title page of a seventeenth-century English cookbook was Sir Kenelm Digby, the remarkably durable friend of Court and Commonwealth, sometime naval officer, great traveler, and promoter of a highly-touted panacea. His recipe for curing a wound was to remove the bandages and, at a safe distance, soak them in his "Powder of Sympathy." Digby's recipe for capon, probably more efficacious, may have been borrowed from the French; the layer of truffles veiling the chicken closely resembles the classic *demi-deuil* (literally half-mourning).

1 5- to 6- pound capon	6 stalks celery, cut into 6-inch pieces
3 large truffles, sliced	Bouquet garni (4 sprigs parsley, pinch
Salt and freshly ground pepper	thyme, 3 sprigs celery leaves, 1 small
1 onion, stuck with 2 cloves	bay leaf, 5 to 6 peppercorns, crushed,
$\frac{1}{3}$ cup butter	tied in cheesecloth)
1 teaspoon dried tarragon	3 to 4 cups chicken broth
1 teaspoon chopped chives	4 egg yolks
4 to 5 shallots, chopped	$1\frac{1}{2}$ cups heavy cream

Wipe the capon inside and out. Slice *2 truffles* into 6 slices each. Using a sharp paring knife, loosen the skin of the capon carefully, starting from the cavity. Slide 2 slices of truffle between the meat and skin on the breasts, 2 on the legs, and 2 on the 2 joints. Care must be taken not to puncture the skin. Season inside and out with salt and pepper. Put the onion, *half the butter*, and *half the tarragon and chives* inside the capon. Place in a large sheet of heavy-duty foil with the shallots, *remaining butter, tarragon, and chives*, celery, and bouquet garni. Seal foil and place in a second sheet to encase the bird from 2 directions. Put on a rack in a pot holding 3 inches chicken broth. Keep simmering, covered, for 2 hours, adding broth. Carefully open the foil and strain all the liquid into a saucepan. Beat yolks and cream and add a little liquid from saucepan, beating constantly. Return mixture to saucepan. Simmer over low heat, stirring until thickened, about 10 minutes. Carve the capon on a heated platter, arrange the celery around the bird. Correct the seasoning of the sauce and pour a little sauce on the bird. Mince *remaining truffle*, add to the remaining sauce, along with liquid from truffles can. Pass sauce separately in sauceboat. Serves 6.

CHICKEN PAPRIKAS

Turks, invading Hungary in the sixteenth century, introduced the sweet pepper (indigenous to India) that would later be identified with Hungarian cuisine. Initially the plant was regarded as a decorative shrub. When in 1793 a count was advised by his provincial hosts to season his meat with paprika, the red powder made from the crushed pepper pods, he found it "pungent, but only for short times," making "the stomach feel very warm!" Such favorable reactions to the spice quickly spread, and by 1850 "rose," or sweet, paprika was nationally accepted.

2 3-pound chickens, disjointed	Salt, pepper, and cayenne pepper
$\frac{1}{2}$ cup butter or chicken fat	1 to 2 cups chicken broth
2 yellow onions, chopped	2 tablespoons flour
2 tablespoons sweet paprika	1 cup sour cream

Wipe chicken pieces. Heat butter in a heavy covered casserole and brown chicken on all sides. Remove and reserve. Sauté onions in butter until soft but not brown. Add paprika, salt, pepper, and a dash or two of cayenne. Stir and sauté for 2 minutes. Return chicken to pan and add enough broth to barely cover chicken. Cover, bring to a boil, reduce heat, and simmer gently for 30 to 40 minutes or until chicken is tender but not falling apart. Blend flour into sour cream. Stir into sauce and simmer for 3 to 4 minutes. Serve with buttered Noodles (page 566), Spaetzle (page 567), or Tarhonya (page 566). Serves 6.

RUSSIAN CUTLETS KIEV

2 large chicken breasts, split	Salt and pepper
$\frac{1}{2}$ cup butter	1 cup dry bread crumbs
Flour for dredging	Vegetable shortening for deep frying
2 eggs	

Ask butcher to split and bone the chicken breasts, leaving a small piece of the wing bones intact. Have him pound them flat and very thin. Divide the butter into 4 portions and roll into compact sausage shapes. Roll them in flour and put in freezer for $\frac{1}{2}$ hour. Place one butter roll on each piece of chicken. Beat eggs with 2 tablespoons cold water and brush some of the mixture on edges of chicken. Sprinkle with salt and pepper. Roll and fold the chicken so butter is completely sealed in. Dredge chicken with flour, roll in beaten egg, and then in bread crumbs. Chill in the freezer for 10 minutes. Fry in deep fat heated to 360° until golden brown—about 10 minutes. Serve immediately with a little paper frill on the bone. Serves 4.

VARIATIONS: In place of $\frac{1}{2}$ cup butter, 4 tablespoons butter may be used and mixed with 4 tablespoons pâté de foie gras. Or the $\frac{1}{2}$ cup butter may be mixed with chopped fresh tarragon or chives, or 4 tablespoons minced and sautéed mushrooms, chilled.

PASHTET
(Russian Chicken Pie)

3 onions, sliced
¾ cup butter, melted
3 cups cooked rice
4 tablespoons minced dill
4 hard-boiled eggs, sliced

1 4-pound roasted chicken,
    boned and sliced
Salt and pepper
Cream Puff Paste (page 725)

Cook the onion slowly in *4 tablespoons butter* until soft and golden. Mix the rice with *4 tablespoons butter* and the dill. Butter a 9- by 11-inch baking pan and arrange a layer of rice, a layer of onions, a layer of sliced hard-boiled eggs, then the chicken. Repeat layers of onions and eggs, finishing with rice, seasoning each layer with salt and pepper. Cover with the cream puff paste. Insert a plain, large pastry tube in the center and bake in a preheated 425° oven for 20 minutes, lower the heat to 350°, and bake for another 20 minutes. Pour 4 tablespoons *remaining butter* through the pastry tube and serve hot. Serves 6.

CIRCASSIAN CHICKEN

The warlike people who once inhabited Circassia, a region on the eastern coast of the Black Sea, were famed for their beautiful women. Today their descendants are noted for this dish of chicken with walnuts.

2 chicken breasts, split
1 onion, sliced
1 carrot, sliced
2 stalks celery, with leaves
Bouquet garni (1 small bay leaf, 6 sprigs
    parsley, 4 peppercorns, tied in
    cheesecloth)

Salt and pepper
2 cups walnut meats
3 slices white bread, crusts removed
½ cup heavy cream
1 tablespoon sweet paprika
½ cup walnut or sesame oil (optional)

Poach the chicken breasts in water to cover with onion, carrot, celery, and bouquet garni. When done, add salt to taste. Strain and reserve stock. Remove skin and bones from chicken and slice meat into serving portions. Set aside. Blanch walnuts in boiling water for 5 minutes. Dry and rub off as much skin as possible. Put walnuts through the finest blade of the food chopper 4 to 5 times or until oil begins to flow from them freely. Press oil out of ground walnuts and reserve. Soak bread in cream until softened and squeeze out excess cream. Add paprika and bread to ground nuts and grind again 4 to 5 times or until there is ½ cup oil. (If this seems too tedious purée nuts and soaked bread in a blender. Mix paprika and ½ cup walnut or sesame oil and reserve.) Thin bread-nut paste by slowly beating in enough chicken stock to make sauce the consistency of sour cream. Flavor with salt and pepper as needed. Spoon sauce over chicken portions, dribble a little red walnut oil over the top of each, and serve at room temperature or slightly chilled. Serves 4 as first course, 8 as an appetizer.

CHICKEN TANDOORI

In northern India food is commonly cooked in the primitive *tandoori* oven, built with a combination of straw, cow dung, and wet mud. While the chicken roasts directly on the hot coals, the dough for *nan*, a flat bread, is slapped on the sides of the oven to bake.

1 3-pound chicken, quartered	1 teaspoon powdered cinnamon
2 cups yoghurt	$\frac{1}{2}$ teaspoon powdered cardamom
4 cloves garlic, minced and crushed	1 teaspoon crushed hot red pepper,
1 teaspoon turmeric or curry powder	or cayenne pepper to taste
1 $\frac{1}{2}$-inch piece ginger root, minced, or	3 large bay leaves, crumbled
1 teaspoon powdered ginger	Salt to taste
$\frac{1}{2}$ teaspoon powdered cloves	3 tablespoons butter or sesame oil

Prick the chicken all over with a fork. Combine yoghurt and garlic and marinate chicken for at least 4 hours, turning frequently. Blend remaining ingredients with the butter to make a paste. Rub well into chicken and let stand for 2 to 3 hours. Bake in a preheated 450° oven for 45 to 60 minutes, or broil or barbecue, turning frequently. Serves 4.

MURGHI BIRYANI

From Pakistan comes this traditional chicken and rice dish flavored with several of the aromatics for which the Indian subcontinent is known. According to John Gerard, an Elizabethan herbalist, the rose water has been especially esteemed because "Mahumetans say that [the flower] sprang of the sweat of Mahumet."

1 4-pound chicken	2 slices ginger root, minced, or
Salt	1 teaspoon powdered ginger
2 cups yoghurt	$\frac{1}{2}$ teaspoon powdered cinnamon
$\frac{1}{3}$ cup butter	$\frac{1}{2}$ teaspoon powdered cumin
1 large onion, finely chopped	4 to 5 sprigs fresh mint, leaves only
4 cloves garlic, minced	2 cups long-grained rice
5 green chili peppers, diced, or cayenne	$\frac{1}{2}$ teaspoon saffron
pepper to taste	1 tablespoon rose water
4 to 5 whole cloves	

Have the chicken disjointed and each piece cut in half. Put chicken in a shallow dish, sprinkle with 1 teaspoon salt, and cover with yoghurt; leave for $\frac{1}{2}$ hour. In a large saucepan melt the butter and sauté the onion for 3 to 4 minutes. Add the garlic, chili peppers, cloves, ginger root, cinnamon, cumin, and mint. Place chicken in pan and simmer for 30 minutes. Add the rice and 2 cups water. Season with salt, swirl in the saffron so the rice is streaked with orange rather than uniformly colored. Cover tightly and steam for 20 to 25 minutes. Add rose water. Serve on a heated dish. It is usual to have the spices whole and crushed, but powdered spices may be used. Serves 4 to 6.

SAMBAL HATI-HATI

The *rijstafel* (rice table) is Indonesia's contribution to culinary history. The name reflects the influence of the Dutch whose domination of the archipelago dates from the seventeenth century, but in practice the spread is a mixture of Chinese, Indian, and Malaysian dishes. At the typical rijstafel (an Eastern smörgåsbord of sorts), a variety of curries, spiced vegetables, pickled fruits, and skewered meats are accompaniments to rice. Sambal Hati-Hati (chicken giblets) is typically Malaysian.

10 each: chicken livers, gizzards, and hearts
3 tablespoons corn, peanut, or sesame oil
1 large onion, chopped
3 hot red chili peppers, minced
3 cloves garlic, minced
1 teaspoon anchovy paste
1 teaspoon turmeric or curry powder

2 slices ginger root, minced, or ½ teaspoon powdered ginger
½ teaspoon powdered coriander
2 bay leaves
1½ cups Coconut Cream (page 632)
6 hard-boiled eggs, quartered
2 tablespoons tamarind or lime juice
Salt

Cut livers in half, slice gizzards and hearts. Heat the oil and fry onion, chili pepper, and garlic for 2 to 3 minutes; add anchovy paste and stir; add turmeric, ginger root, coriander, and bay leaves. Stir and simmer for 2 minutes. Add chicken livers, gizzards, and hearts. Stir and fry for 3 minutes. Add coconut cream and simmer for 25 minutes, covered. Add eggs and tamarind juice. Simmer 5 minutes, remove bay leaves, and season. Serves 6 as an appetizer.

479

POULTRY IN CHINA

Poultry had been prized in China for nearly three thousand years when the eighteenth-century gourmet-poet Yüan Mei listed chicken and duck among "the four heroes of the table." Legends had grown up about the birds: the rooster, believed to be the incarnation of the masculine cosmic force (*yang*), possessed such virtues as "literary spirit" symbolized by his crown and "faithfulness" manifested by his crowing at dawn; the duck, because of his affection for his mate, represented marital fidelity. Today the Chinese have numerous poultry recipes. Some call for feet, gizzards, even tongues of fowl, which Chinese markets, unlike those in the West, will sell separately.

LEMON CHICKEN

Lemons, used here to flavor a popular Hong Kong dish, were introduced to China from India between the sixth and ninth centuries A.D. The first written reference to them occurs in a court chronicle which states: "In the fourth year of K'ai Pao [971] two bottles of lemon juice were allowed to be presented to the Emperor."

1 4-pound chicken
1 teaspoon dried tangerine or orange peel, soaked and minced
2 slices ginger root, minced, or $\frac{1}{2}$ teaspoon powdered ginger
1 clove garlic, minced
1 teaspoon salt
$\frac{1}{4}$ teaspoon pepper
$\frac{1}{2}$ teaspoon cinnamon
1 teaspoon sugar

$\frac{1}{4}$ cup minced parsley
1 lemon, thinly sliced
1 cup chicken broth
3 tablespoons soy sauce
Cornstarch
Corn oil for deep frying
2 teaspoons lemon juice
1 teaspoon grated lemon rind
Lemon wedges
Parsley sprigs

Wipe the chicken with a damp cloth and truss neatly. Mix the next 8 ingredients. Put the chicken on a trivet or rack in a heavy pot with a lid. Spread the mixed herbs and spices over the chicken and arrange the lemon slices on top. Pour 1 cup chicken broth into pot, cover, and steam for 20 minutes. Turn the chicken and steam for 20 minutes longer. Remove chicken, brush with soy sauce, and dust with cornstarch. Return chicken to pot and steam for 10 to 15 minutes until done but not falling apart. Have hot oil ready in a deep pot. Bone and cut chicken into small pieces, reserving broth. Deep fry chicken, turning to brown evenly. When golden and crisp, remove from fat. Strain chicken broth, season with lemon juice and rind. Pour sauce over chicken and serve garnished with lemon wedges and sprigs of Chinese or ordinary parsley. Serves 4 to 6. Dried orange or tangerine peel may be made by placing fresh peel in a preheated 250° oven until dried out.

SUGAR-SMOKED CHICKEN

In the eighteenth century, under the patronage of the gourmet emperor Ch'ien Lung, envoys traveled throughout China collecting recipes for the royal kitchens at Peking. The king so admired this Soochow dish of chicken, smoked over burning sugar and served with cabbage, that the chef's employer bequeathed his cook to the imperial court.

1 2½-pound chicken, split in half
1 onion
Salt
2 tablespoons dry sherry
¼ cup soy sauce

½ cup corn, sesame, or peanut oil
1 teaspoon powdered aniseed (optional)
1 teaspoon cracked black pepper
1 clove garlic, crushed
½ cup dark brown sugar

If possible a special smoking pan should be used to prepare this dish. Otherwise, use an old, heavy pan with a tight-fitting cover. Line pan with heavy-duty foil to prevent sugar from burning bottom of pan. Line the inside of the lid as well. If the lid does not fit tightly, seal with foil. Cook chicken until tender in boiling water (to cover) with 1 onion and 2 table-spoons salt. Remove chicken from broth and pat dry. Combine sherry, soy sauce, *one-quarter cup corn oil*, aniseed, pepper, and garlic. Marinate chicken in this mixture for 30 minutes. Pat dry, brush with *a little corn oil*, and place on rack in pan over *one-quarter cup brown sugar*. Cover tightly and place over moderately high heat and smoke for 8 minutes. Remove chicken, rack, and foil. Reline pan with foil and add *remaining brown sugar*. Return rack with chicken, cover, and smoke for 8 to 10 minutes more or until sides of the chicken are a rich mahogany brown. It is not necessary to turn the chicken. Brush with *corn oil* and serve. Serves 2 to 4. Boiled duck or raw fish may be smoked in the same way.

KOREAN SQUAB IN LETTUCE CUPS

¼ cup peanut oil
2 squabs or 1 chicken, minced
¼ pound lean pork, minced
1 6½-ounce can water chestnuts, finely diced
6 dried mushrooms, soaked and minced
2 stalks celery, minced

½ cup finely diced bamboo shoots
1¼ cups chicken broth
2 teaspoons soy sauce
½ teaspoon salt
¼ teaspoon pepper
1 tablespoon cornstarch
1 head soft-leaf lettuce

Heat the oil in a large frying pan. Add the squab and pork and cook, stirring, at high heat for 2 to 3 minutes. Add the vegetables, stir, and cook for 2 minutes. Add *1 cup broth* and the soy sauce. Cover, lower the heat, and simmer for 10 minutes. Season with salt and pepper. Mix cornstarch with remaining cold broth and add to squab. Stir until thickened and very hot. Serve in a chafing dish over hot water with a bowl of the separated lettuce leaves to be used as cups. Put a spoonful of squab mixture in a leaf, roll leaf, and eat with the fingers. Serves 6.

481

SESAME CHICKEN

Sesame oil is to Chinese cuisine as butter is to French. The pressed seeds of the sesame plant, introduced to China in about the fifth century A.D., provide a basic cooking fat. When toasted, they impart a delicate nutlike flavor to dishes such as chicken.

1 5-pound roasting chicken or 4 large chicken breasts	*Sauce*: 2 tablespoons sesame seeds
1 egg	$\frac{1}{2}$ cup sliced mushrooms
2 teaspoons rice wine	1 teaspoon lemon juice
Salt and pepper	Salt and pepper
$\frac{3}{4}$ cup cornstarch	2 tablespoons cornstarch
Corn or peanut oil for frying	$\frac{1}{4}$ teaspoon monosodium glutamate
	$\frac{1}{2}$ cup light cream

Have butcher split and bone the chicken and cut it into $\frac{1}{4}$-inch slices. Beat the egg with the wine, $\frac{1}{2}$ teaspoon salt, and $\frac{1}{8}$ teaspoon pepper. Dip chicken slices in egg mixture, then dredge with cornstarch. Heat 1 inch of oil to 375° and deep fry the chicken slices a few at a time until they are golden—about 5 minutes—turning them so that they brown evenly on both sides. Remove from pan and keep warm.

To prepare sauce: Toast the sesame seeds in a skillet until golden and jumping; reserve. Put the sliced mushrooms, lemon juice, 1 teaspoon salt, and $\frac{1}{8}$ teaspoon pepper in $1\frac{1}{2}$ cups water and simmer for 5 minutes. Dissolve the cornstarch in $\frac{1}{2}$ cup cold water and add to mushrooms. Add monosodium glutamate and cream; stir until thickened and hot. Pour over chicken slices. Sprinkle with sesame seeds. Serves 4 to 6.

CHICKEN VELVET

To conserve fuel, the Chinese have devised many techniques for chopping meat into small pieces, which cook faster than large chunks. The blunt edge of a cleaver is traditionally used to mince the ingredients of Chicken Velvet so that they have a smooth consistency without tasting of the chopping board.

1 cup ground chicken meat	*Sauce:*
$\frac{1}{2}$ teaspoon salt	1 cup chicken broth
1 teaspoon cornstarch	1 chicken bouillon cube
5 egg whites	1 to 2 teaspoons dry sherry
2 tablespoons minced smoked ham or tongue (optional)	$\frac{1}{4}$ teaspoon salt
	2 teaspoons cornstarch
3 tablespoons corn or peanut oil	

To prepare sauce: Mix *three-quarters cup chicken broth* with the bouillon cube to make a rich stock. Add sherry and salt. Mix *remaining one-quarter cup broth* with 2 teaspoons cornstarch and add to first mixture. Heat in a saucepan until thickened and hot. Keep warm in a double boiler over low heat.

To prepare chicken: Grind chicken several times through the finest blade of meat grinder. Add salt, 1 tablespoon water, 1 teaspoon cornstarch, and *1 unbeaten egg white*. Work and pound in a mortar into a smooth paste. Then add $\frac{1}{4}$ cup water drop by drop, working it in. If the water is added too fast, mixture will not hold together. Beat the *remaining 4 egg whites* until stiff but not dry and fold in along with the minced ham. Heat the oil to just warm in a medium frying pan. Pour the chicken mixture into the oil. Take pan off the fire and stir rapidly to blend in the oil. Replace on the fire and cook on medium heat until mixture is set but not brown. Slide quickly onto a heated platter, pour on sauce, and serve immediately. Serves 4. Chicken may also be dropped by tablespoonfuls into hot fat and cooked until just set.

PAPER-WRAPPED CHICKEN

Cooking food in paper to preserve its natural flavor and tenderness is a practice known to chefs throughout the world. A Szechwanese banquet dish of chicken and smoked ham is "gift-wrapped" in rice paper, fried in oil, and presented for the guests to open at the table.

2 chicken breasts, split, boned, and sliced into 40 very thin slices	2 to 3 tablespoons sesame oil
20 paper-thin onion slices or $\frac{1}{2}$ cup minced scallions	20 pieces of wax paper, cellophane, or foil (4 by 4 inches)
1 tablespoon sherry	20 snow pea pods
2 tablespoons soy sauce	20 paper-thin slices smoked ham, cut same size as chicken slices
20 very thin slices ginger root	Corn or peanut oil
$\frac{1}{2}$ teaspoon each: salt, pepper, and sugar	Parsley sprigs

Chicken will be easier to slice if it is slightly frozen. Marinate chicken slices with onion, sherry, soy sauce, ginger root, salt, pepper, and sugar. Meanwhile, lightly oil the wax paper on 1 side. Place paper with 1 point toward you. Arrange 2 slices chicken, 1 pea pod, 1 slice onion, 1 slice ginger root, and 1 slice ham a little off center toward you. Dribble any remaining marinade over filling. Fold flap nearest you over chicken, then fold on left, then on right side. Finally fold over the furthermost flap and tuck it in securely. Heat fat to boiling. Drop packets in gently, a few at a time, frying them for 4 minutes on each side, turning with tongs. Keep oil at boiling point. Place packets on hot platter. Garnish with parsley. Serves 6 to 8.

YAKITORI

When Japan began to admit foreigners in the 1850's, the American consul, Townsend Harris, noted that "the only animal food used by the Japanese are Fish and Poultry." As early as the fourteenth century Buddhist injunctions against meat eating were not strictly observed, and a popular food of the time was skewered roasted game fowl. Today, Yakitori (grilled bird) is commonly made with chicken or duck cooked on tiny bamboo skewers over a cypress fire.

1 2- to 2½-pound broiling chicken
4 chicken livers (optional)
4 gizzards (optional)
4 chicken hearts (optional)
½ small duck (optional)
8 to 10 scallions (optional)
1 can quail eggs (optional)
½ cup soy sauce

½ cup dry sherry
½ cup peanut, sesame, or corn oil
1 clove garlic, crushed
2 thin slices ginger root, minced, or
    1 teaspoon powdered ginger
Soy sauce for dipping
½ cup grated white radish

To serve an authentic yakitori of assorted foods on skewers, use optional ingredients. Or, if you prefer, prepare with just chicken or chicken livers. Skin chicken and cut meat off the bones into 1-inch cubes. Reserve bones for stock. Cut livers, gizzards, hearts, and duck meat into 1-inch cubes. Cut scallions into 1½-inch pieces. Leave quail eggs whole. Combine soy sauce, sherry, oil, garlic, and ginger root and marinate ingredients at room temperature for 30 minutes. Thread onto small metal or bamboo skewers, using only one kind of meat to each skewer, adding a piece of scallion to some of the skewers. Broil over hot charcoal or under broiler for about 5 minutes, brushing with marinade several times and turning so food browns evenly. Serve with soy sauce mixed with grated radish to taste. Serves 12 as an appetizer.

OYAKO DONBURI

Oyako Donburi, translated "mother and child," is so named because it contains both chicken and eggs. The casserole is a favorite at Japanese picnics, the portions being packed in lacquer boxes for each guest.

2 cups rice
2 large chicken breasts, cooked, split, boned, and chilled
1 cup chicken broth
$\frac{1}{4}$ cup soy sauce

$\frac{1}{4}$ cup sake or dry sherry
1 cup thinly sliced mushrooms
2 scallions, diagonally sliced
4 eggs, lightly beaten

Put rice in 1 quart water, bring to boil, cover, reduce heat to low. Simmer for 14 to 15 minutes. Do not uncover, turn off heat, and let rice absorb steam for another 15 minutes. Slice chicken meat as thinly as possible. In a saucepan mix chicken broth, soy sauce, and wine. Simmer, adding chicken slices, mushrooms, and scallions, and continue simmering for 3 to 4 minutes or until chicken and vegetables are tender. Divide the rice into 4 serving bowls. Add eggs to chicken mixture and cook, stirring occasionally, until nearly set. Divide into 4 portions and turn the mixture into individual rice bowls. Serves 4.

SATAY

These Malayan grilled chicken pieces are a favorite "street" dish in Singapore. The Satay vendors begin grilling early in the evening, keeping their stalls open into the early hours of morning.

2 cloves garlic
1 tablespoon peanut butter
6 to 8 coriander seeds
1 teaspoon sugar
$\frac{1}{4}$ teaspoon aniseed
Peanut oil
3 cups cubed chicken
$\frac{1}{2}$ cup Coconut Cream (page 632)

Sauce:
1 medium onion, minced
1 clove garlic, crushed
1 tablespoon peanut oil
4 dried chili peppers
$\frac{1}{2}$ cup peanut butter
$\frac{1}{2}$ cup broth

Make a paste of the 2 cloves garlic, 1 tablespoon peanut butter, coriander, sugar, and aniseed with a little peanut oil. Spread this mixture on the chicken. Thread on 4 small metal or bamboo skewers and brush with peanut oil or coconut cream. Let marinate for 2 hours. Broil or grill over coals or in broiler turning frequently until golden brown. Serve on skewers with following sauce as a dip. Serves 4 to 6 as an appetizer.

To prepare sauce: Fry the onion and garlic in 1 tablespoon oil until golden. Add peppers, peanut butter, and broth; stir and simmer until sauce is thick and smooth. Makes $1\frac{1}{2}$ cups.

BRAISED DUCK WITH PEAR AND CHESTNUTS

An Augustinian monk, impressed with the thriving duck trade in six-teenth century Canton, wrote in an exaggerated account that "they sustaine a great part of the country therewith." Actually, the pleasures of duck eating were limited to the wealthy. Cooking students in Peking were required to take a one-year course in the art of force feeding (similar to the French method of fattening geese), slaughtering, and dressing the bird for their patrons' tables.

1 5-pound duck	2 tablespoons soy sauce
1 pound can chestnuts in water or	2 slices ginger root, minced, or
$\frac{1}{2}$ pound fresh chestnuts	$\frac{1}{2}$ teaspoon powdered ginger
3 to 4 tablespoons peanut oil	1 large ripe pear
1 cup beef broth	1 teaspoon sugar
3 tablespoons dry sherry	

Have butcher chop the duck, with bones, into 2-inch chunks. Wipe the duck pieces well with a damp cloth. Drain and rinse the chestnuts and reserve. (If using fresh chestnuts, cut a cross on the rounded side of $\frac{1}{2}$ pound chestnuts and boil for 10 to 15 minutes. Peel carefully while warm and wet, removing both skins.) Heat the oil in a large frying pan, brown duck pieces quickly, a few at a time. Drain off most of the fat and return all duck to the pan. Add broth, sherry, soy sauce, and ginger root. Bring to a boil, cover, then lower heat. Simmer for $\frac{1}{2}$ hour. Add chestnuts and simmer for 10 minutes more, shaking pan to turn chestnuts. Peel and core the pear, slicing it into 8 pieces. Dredge with sugar. Add to duck and simmer covered for 3 to 4 minutes, shaking the pan to cover pear and duck with juices. Serves 2 to 4.

CANARD A LA BIGARADE

Brillat-Savarin was very particular about saucing his ducks, denouncing some combinations as "monstrous, degrading, and dishonorable," but he shared the Gallic enthusiasm for the traditional dish below. Our version is from Menon's influential *Nouvelle Cuisine*, 1753. The bitter oranges which flavor the sauce likely owe their existence to Arab traders, who introduced the citrus fruit to Spain and the south of France in the fourteenth century.

2 oranges, rind and juice	1 cup beef broth
$\frac{1}{2}$ lemon, rind and juice	$\frac{1}{4}$ teaspoon anchovy paste (optional)
1 tablespoon sugar	2 teaspoons cornstarch
1 6-pound duck	1 tablespoon currant jelly (optional)
4 tablespoons butter	$\frac{1}{4}$ cup Madeira wine
Salt and pepper	4 oranges for garnish

486

Remove the rind from the oranges and lemon without any pith (white) and slice very thin. Poach in a very little water with the sugar for 10 minutes and reserve. Wipe the duck and pierce skin in several places with a fork. Spread with *2 tablespoons butter*. Spread *remaining 2 tablespoons butter* in a roasting pan. Roast duck in preheated 400° oven for 20 minutes, then lower heat to 350°. Prick duck with a fork several times during roasting. Season with salt and pepper and roast for an additional $1\frac{1}{4}$ hours or until legs can be moved easily in their sockets. Remove duck and keep warm. Pour fat from pan and add broth. Bring to a boil, scraping all the coagulated pan juices into stock. Simmer for 5 to 6 minutes. Strain into a saucepan, add anchovy paste and orange and lemon juice. Dissolve cornstarch in 2 to 3 tablespoons cold water and add to sauce. Stir and simmer until thickened—about 1 minute. Add currant jelly and melt on low heat. Add wine and drained orange and lemon peel. Carve duck and serve decorated with sections of peeled oranges. Pass sauce on the side. Serves 4.

VARIATIONS: *Duck with Cherries,* or *Montmorency*: Roast duck as for bigarade. Deglaze pan with broth and add Madeira. Poach $\frac{1}{2}$ pound pitted black cherries in the sauce for 5 minutes. Place cherries around carved duck. Add 2 tablespoons cherry brandy to sauce. Serve in a sauceboat. For cold duck Montmorency, coat with brown Chaud-froid Sauce (page 634) to which has been added 2 tablespoons cherry brandy. Surround with cooked pitted cherries in pastry or orange shells. *Brazilian Duck with Orange Sauce*: Baste duck with orange juice while roasting. Add the grated orange rind to the pan along with 2 bananas, sliced lengthwise and halved, 1 bay leaf, and $\frac{1}{4}$ cup dark rum. The sauce is made by discarding all the fat, adding $1\frac{1}{2}$ cups beef broth to pan, and bringing broth to a simmer, thickening with 2 teaspoons cornstarch diluted with 2 tablespoons cold water. Add $\frac{1}{4}$ cup finely ground or chopped Brazil nuts and a few dashes of orange liqueur. Serve the duck with fresh orange sections and cooked bananas. Pass the sauce separately.

MANDARIN CRISP ROASTED DUCK

1 5-pound duck	4 to 5 slices ginger root, minced, or
1 cup dry sherry	1 teaspoon powdered ginger
1 teaspoon salt	3 tablespoons cornstarch
1 teaspoon sugar	1 egg, beaten
2 teaspoons five-spice powder, or	Corn, peanut, or sesame
1 teaspoon cayenne pepper and	oil for frying
$\frac{1}{2}$ teaspoon powdered aniseed	Cracked peppercorns
1 leek, sliced	

Marinate duck in sherry for 20 minutes; drain off excess sherry. Mix salt, sugar, and spice powder and rub the duck with mixture. Put the duck in a bowl with the leek and ginger root. Put bowl in a steamer, cover, and steam for $1\frac{1}{2}$ hours. Remove duck and cool. Mix cornstarch with a little water to make a paste and add to egg. Coat the duck with this mixture. Fry in smoking oil until crisp and deep brown, about 15 minutes. Sprinkle with cracked peppercorns and serve immediately. Serves 2 to 4.

DUCK WITH TURNIPS

Turnips were to ancient Roman cookery what potatoes are to modern cuisine, and citizens cited with approval Manius Curius, the general who was so well satisfied with eating turnips that he could not be corrupted with offers of gold. More self-indulgent Romans liked to combine them with duck, as in the recipe from Apicius below.

1 6-pound duck
Salt and pepper
2 tablespoons butter
$\frac{1}{2}$ cup dry white wine
1 onion, chopped
2 stalks celery, with leaves
1 small carrot, quartered
1 cup beef broth
$\frac{1}{4}$ teaspoon powdered coriander
$\frac{1}{4}$ teaspoon powdered cumin
12 white turnips
2 teaspoons cornstarch

Wipe the duck carefully. Rub the cavity with salt and pepper. Butter the duck with *1 tablespoon butter* and salt and pepper it. Spread *remaining butter* in roasting pan. Put duck in the pan and roast it in a preheated 400° oven for 30 minutes. Drain off and reserve all but 2 to 3 tablespoons fat. Add the wine and simmer for 5 minutes. Add the next 3 vegetables, the broth, and the spices. Lower the heat to 325°. Cover the pan and braise for 1 hour, basting twice. Discard celery and carrots. Meanwhile, peel and quarter the turnips, shaping the quarters in the shape of olives. Sauté them quickly in a little reserved duck fat and add them to the duck pan. Continue braising the duck for 30 minutes more. Carve the duck, surround with turnips, and keep warm. Reduce the juices by about one-third. Skim fat. Mix the cornstarch with a little cold water and add to pan juices. Bring to a boil, lower heat, and simmer for 5 minutes, stirring often. Pass gravy separately in a sauceboat. Serves 4.

CANARD AUX PERLES

From the Trois Frères Provençaux, one of the first restaurants to open in Paris after the Revolution, comes this recipe for duck, first served in 1833 at a dinner party given by the waiters for their favorite customers. The duck came with "a string of pearls wound round it from neck to tail" as one of the diners reported.

3 cups thick Béchamel Sauce (page 618)
Cayenne pepper
1 tablespoon tomato purée
1 cup sliced cooked button mushrooms, fresh or canned
2 cups cooked lobster meat
2 to 3 black truffles, diced (optional)
1 5- to 6-pound duck
Salt and pepper
2 to 3 tablespoons butter, melted
Garnish: 1 long rope imitation pearls

Prepare béchamel sauce and season with cayenne pepper; add tomato purée. Stir in well-drained mushrooms, lobster meat cut into small chunks, and truffles. Chill thoroughly. Clean and singe duck and sprinkle cavity lightly with salt and pepper. Close neck opening by pinning crop to back of duck with skewers. Spoon lobster sauce into body cavity, tipping duck back so that sauce will not run out. Sew opening closed with small, tight stitches. Sprinkle duck with salt and pepper, pierce skin in several places with the tines of a fork, and tie legs and wings in place. Place duck on a rack in an open roasting pan. Roast in preheated 325° oven for about 2 to 2½ hours, pricking skin several times during roasting, and basting with pan drippings. Brush with melted butter for last 20 minutes of cooking time. Duckling is done when skin is crisp and golden brown and legs can be moved easily in their sockets. Place on serving platter and wind rope of pearls around duck from end to end. Remove pearls before carving. Spoon sauce from cavity of duck onto carved portions. Serves 4.

ROAST GOOSE WITH PEACHES

Since the days of ancient Egypt, the goose has suffered domestication with distinction. A vigilant goose alerted the Roman capital to the invading Gauls, and Pliny the Elder reported that "wonderful to relate, the bird comes all the way from Morino [near Naples] to Rome on its own feet—the weary geese go before, and those following by natural pressure urge them on." With some help from Roman colonists, geese also found their way to northern Europe, where they have been ever since a favorite holiday bird. A variety of stuffings provide the distinctive national flavor.

1 10-pound goose	1 onion, quartered
½ cup butter	1½ cups beef broth
Salt and pepper	12 Elberta peach halves (canned)
1 recipe Persian Cracked Wheat and Apricot Stuffing (page 499)	2 tablespoons cognac
	2 tablespoons orange liqueur

Singe and wipe the goose. Rub inside of goose with *2 tablespoons butter*, softened. Season with salt and pepper. Fill neck and body cavity with stuffing. Fold neck skin over and secure with small skewer. Sew up body cavity, truss bird, prick skin all over with a fork. Spread with *1 tablespoon butter*, softened, and butter a roasting pan with *1 tablespoon butter*. Place bird in pan with onion. Roast in a preheated 400° oven for 30 minutes. Pour off fat, season with salt and pepper, and pour on port wine from soaked fruit in stuffing. Lower heat to 350° and roast, basting 3 or 4 times, for 1½ hours or until legs move freely in their sockets. Keep bird warm. Remove fat from roasting pan, pour in beef broth, and simmer for 5 minutes on top of stove, scraping the pan of all brown particles. Meanwhile, melt *remaining 4 tablespoons butter* and sauté well-drained peach halves until golden. Carve goose, arrange peach halves around it. Add cognac and liqueur to sauce and simmer for 5 minutes. Serve in a sauceboat. Serves 8.

VARIATION: *Roast Goose with Noodle or Potato Stuffing* (pages 498 and 499): Proceed as above, basting with butter instead of port wine, and eliminating peach garnish.

489

GALANTINE

When the master cook of Richard II of England compiled his *Forme of Cury* c. 1390, he included a recipe for "Galyntyne," a spicy sauce, but over the centuries the name has come to describe boned meat—commonly poultry—symmetrically molded in aspic. In France, where it is most often served, etymologists maintain that the name evolved from the Old French word for chicken (*galine*), but Englishmen look to the ginger-like galingale that flavored the original sauce.

1 8-pound turkey or	2 teaspoons salt
1 7- to 8-pound capon	$\frac{1}{2}$ teaspoon white pepper
$\frac{1}{2}$ pound veal, ground twice	1 teaspoon allspice
$\frac{1}{2}$ pound lean pork, ground twice	1 teaspoon nutmeg
$\frac{1}{2}$ pound tongue, cut into $\frac{1}{2}$-inch strips	1 large onion, minced
$\frac{1}{2}$ pound ham, cut into $\frac{1}{2}$-inch strips	3 tablespoons butter
$\frac{1}{2}$ pound fat back, cut into $\frac{1}{2}$-inch strips	2 eggs, lightly beaten
$\frac{1}{2}$ pound pâté de foie gras or diced	$\frac{1}{2}$ cup chopped pistachio nuts, blanched
truffled liver paste	4 quarts chicken stock
$\frac{1}{2}$ cup Madeira wine	Chaud-froid Sauce (page 634)
$\frac{1}{4}$ cup cognac	Aspic (page 635)

Have butcher bone the bird without piercing the skin. Remove all flesh, leaving the skin intact. Use bones to make stock. Cut the leg and breast meat into $\frac{1}{2}$-inch cubes and reserve. Grind remaining bird meat as fine as veal and pork; reserve. Marinate tongue, ham, fat back, and pâté in the combined wine and cognac for 1 hour. Season the ground turkey, veal, and pork with salt, pepper, and spices. Cook the onion slowly in the butter until soft but not brown. Cool slightly and add to the ground meats. Drain marinade from sliced meats and add it to ground meat mixture. Reserve slices. Add eggs to mixture and beat with wooden spoon until light. Lay the turkey skin (outside down) on a large pastry board, tuck in the leg and wing parts so they will not dangle. Spread half ground meat mixture on skin. Sprinkle *half the pistachios* on the meat, then arrange the sliced meats and turkey cubes in alternating strips on the ground filling. Sprinkle *remaining pistachios* on these and top with remaining ground meat. Bring up the sides of the skin of the bird (on its length) to meet in a sausage shape and sew with doubled coarse white thread. Tie the ends with cotton strings, then tie at 2-inch intervals with more string. Shape into even roll with hands. Roll tightly into a clean cloth, first dampened and wrung out. Tie the end securely and tie again at intervals.

Place in long saucepan such as a fish kettle. Pour in enough well-seasoned chicken stock to cover. Put on lid, bring to a boil, turn down heat, and simmer gently for $1\frac{1}{2}$ hours. Let the galantine cool in the stock. Remove from the broth, top with a platter, and weight it down. When cold, remove cloth, strings, and sewing threads with care. Chill well. Cover with chaud-froid sauce. Decorate with some of the following, cut into geometric designs: tarragon leaves, sliced olives or truffles, carrot flowers, egg slices, pimento. Coat with a clear aspic. Use remainder of aspic as garnish, either scrambled with a fork or cut into shapes. Serves 10 to 12.

BRAZILIAN TURKEY

What to call the *Meleagris gallopava* was a problem that once occupied many naturalists and gourmets. Some Frenchmen called it *Jesuit* in the belief that the brothers first discovered the bird; others, thinking it came from the mysterious East, called it *D'Inde* or "Turkey." Colonials in Brazil settled on "Peru" as its name and origin. Brillat-Savarin had the final word, pronouncing the turkey "one of the prettiest presents which the Old World had received from the New."

1 12- to 15-pound turkey	1 cup olive oil
5 cloves garlic, minced	1 cup white wine vinegar
4 scallions, minced	4 cups dry white wine
2 tablespoons chopped parsley	$\frac{1}{2}$ cup lemon juice
3 sprigs fresh mint or	2 cups orange juice
1 teaspoon dried mint	1 recipe Brazilian Chestnut
1 hot pepper, minced, or	Stuffing (page 497)
$\frac{1}{2}$ teaspoon hot pepper sauce	1 recipe Farofa Stuffing (page 497)
$\frac{1}{8}$ teaspoon powdered cloves	Salt and pepper
1 bay leaf, crumbled	$\frac{1}{2}$ cup butter
Freshly ground pepper	1 cup beef broth (optional)

Wipe the turkey. Mix the next 8 ingredients with the olive oil and purée in a blender. Rub this paste all over and inside the turkey and let stand for 2 hours. Put turkey in a deep glass or ceramic bowl and add vinegar, wine, and lemon and orange juice. Let marinate for 12 hours, turning once or twice. Reserve marinade. Before roasting, stuff the turkey with chestnut stuffing and the neck cavity with farofa stuffing. Truss the bird, season with salt and pepper, and put in a well-buttered roasting pan. Spread bird with 4 *tablespoons butter*, softened. Melt *remaining butter*, dip a large piece of cheesecloth in the butter, and spread over bird. Cover legs with foil. Roast bird in a preheated 425° oven for 30 minutes. Pour $\frac{1}{2}$ cup marinade on turkey, reduce heat to 350°, and roast, basting frequently with marinade, for $2\frac{1}{2}$ to 3 hours, depending on size of turkey. Remove cheesecloth and foil and roast for 20 minutes longer or until skin becomes deep golden brown and legs move easily in their sockets. To make gravy, deglaze roasting pan with beef broth. Simmer for 5 minutes, strain, and pass in a sauceboat. Serves 12.

DINDE DES ARTISTES

Not content with defining the etymology of the turkey in his *Grand Dictionnaire de Cuisine*, 1873, Alexandre Dumas included the following cautionary tale about an encounter between the bird and one of France's illustrious poets. "Boileau, when a child, was playing in a courtyard where . . . there happened to be a turkey. Suddenly the child fell, his dress went up, and the turkey . . . flew at him and with his beak so wounded poor Nicolas that, forever barred from becoming an erotic poet, he became a satiric one and maligned women, instead." Other artists, Dumas thought, could still enjoy a good roast bird. His recipe below, forsaking the luxury of truffles in the stuffing, is dedicated to them.

1 15-pound turkey	$\frac{1}{2}$ pound sausage meat
Salt and pepper	$\frac{1}{2}$ pound blood sausage, casing removed
2 cups fresh bread crumbs,	1 teaspoon dried sage
soaked in milk	$\frac{1}{2}$ teaspoon dried thyme
2 large onions, finely chopped	$\frac{1}{2}$ teaspoon dried marjoram
2 stalks celery, finely chopped	2 tablespoons chopped parsley
1 cup butter	2 eggs, slightly beaten
1 pound veal, ground	1 large can chestnuts in water, drained
2 cups ground chicken meat	1 cup chicken broth (optional)

Sprinkle turkey inside and out with salt and pepper. Squeeze out excess milk from bread. Simmer onions and celery in *3 tablespoons butter* until transparent. Mix meat and herbs and work to a fine light mixture with the eggs. Crumble the chestnuts and add to stuffing. Stuff the turkey and truss. Spread with the *one-half cup butter* and sprinkle with salt and pepper. Cover with cheesecloth dipped in *remaining butter*, melted, and roast in a preheated 425° oven for 30 minutes. Lower heat to 350° and roast for 3 to $3\frac{1}{2}$ hours (about 20 minutes per pound), basting frequently. Test for doneness by moving turkey leg. If loose, bird is done. Remove cheesecloth, let turkey set for 15 to 20 minutes before carving. If desired, deglaze pan with chicken broth for pan gravy. Serves 14 to 16.

POULET D'INDE A LA FRAMBOISE
(Turkey with Raspberry Sauce)

1 8-pound turkey	$1\frac{1}{4}$ cups beef broth
$\frac{1}{2}$ cup butter	Rind of $\frac{1}{2}$ lemon
Salt and pepper	Orange rind, 2- by 1-inch piece
2 onions, quartered	1 pint fresh raspberries or
$\frac{1}{4}$ cup raspberry jelly	2 packages frozen raspberries,
2 tablespoons lemon juice	defrosted and drained (optional)
$\frac{1}{2}$ cup Madeira or tawny port wine	

Wipe and fill the turkey with any preferred stuffing. Truss the bird, spread with *4 tablespoons butter*, softened, and season with salt and pepper. Set in a buttered roasting pan. Dip a large double piece of cheesecloth in *remaining 4 tablespoons butter*, melted, and spread over turkey. Add onions to pan. Roast in a preheated 425° oven for 30 minutes; lower heat to 350°, and roast for 1½ hours, basting frequently. Simmer raspberry jelly, lemon juice, wine, *one-quarter cup beef broth*, and lemon and orange rinds until jelly is melted. Remove cheesecloth from bird, pour on sauce, and continue roasting for 1 hour, or until turkey is cooked, basting frequently. Place turkey on serving platter. Let set for 10 to 15 minutes before carving. Skim off fat, deglaze pan with *remaining broth*, and strain gravy into a sauceboat. If desired, add fresh raspberries to sauce. Serves 8 to 10.

MOLE DE GUAJOLOTE

Ever since the Aztecs, in an ill-fated gesture of friendship, offered the Spaniards a meal of *guajolote* (turkey), the bird has symbolized Mexican hospitality. The *mole* (from the Aztec word for sauce or stew) recipe below is attributed to seventeenth-century nuns from Puebla, who honored a visiting viceroy by composing a turkey sauce of chocolate and chili peppers. Today the national dish is served at virtually every fiesta: carrying the custom to an extreme, the Zapotec Indians of southern Mexico validate their marriages only when the groom provides three turkeys and mole ingredients, including twenty-five pounds of chocolate. Around Veracruz, departing souls are given stylish send-offs at wakes where guests drown their sorrows in delectables like turkey and mole.

1 10- to 12-pound turkey, disjointed	4 tortillas (canned), toasted in oven
1 cup lard or rendered turkey fat	6 large tomatoes, peeled, seeded,
2 onions, chopped	and chopped
4 cloves garlic, minced	¼ cup chili powder
2 green peppers, seeded and chopped	1 teaspoon salt
2 teaspoons powdered cumin	¼ teaspoon cinnamon
½ teaspoon powdered aniseed	Pinch of black pepper
4 tablespoons sesame seeds, toasted	3 ounces bitter chocolate, grated
¾ cup unsalted peanuts, roasted	3 cups turkey stock

Cook turkey in salted water to cover until done (about 1½ hours). Reserve stock and cut meat into serving pieces. Pat dry, and brown pieces on all sides in *one-half cup lard*. Place in casserole and keep warm. Add chopped onions and garlic to fat in pan and sauté until soft but not brown. Place onions in a blender with all remaining ingredients except stock. Blend at medium speed to a fine paste. Add *remaining lard* to skillet and in it heat paste, stirring constantly. Slowly stir 3 cups turkey stock into paste and pour over turkey. Simmer for about 30 minutes or until turkey is thoroughly heated and sauce is thick. Add more stock as necessary. Shake pan and stir frequently to prevent scorching. Serve with rice. Serves 8.

NORWEGIAN GAME BIRDS WITH COGNAC AND CREAM

2 Cornish game hens
Salt and pepper
1 onion, halved
$\frac{1}{2}$ cup butter
4 shallots or 1 onion, chopped
$\frac{1}{2}$ cup dry white wine
1 cup beef broth
$\frac{1}{2}$ teaspoon dried sage

3 large apples
$\frac{1}{2}$ cup sugar
1 1-inch piece vanilla bean
1 cup water
1 cup heavy cream
2 tablespoons cognac
$\frac{1}{2}$ cup preserved lingonberries
Watercress for garnish

Wipe the birds, season the cavities with salt and pepper, and insert $\frac{1}{2}$ onion in each. Melt *4 tablespoons butter* in a large oven casserole and brown the birds, breast down first, then on the sides. Add *remaining 4 tablespoons butter* and shallots, and turn birds on their backs to finish browning. Remove birds, pour in wine and broth, and scrape casserole of brown particles with a wooden spoon. Season birds with salt and pepper and sage, return to casserole, and cover. Put in a preheated 400° oven and roast for 30 minutes, basting frequently. Uncover and roast for 10 to 15 minutes. Meanwhile, peel and core the apples and cut each into 3 thick rings. Make a syrup of sugar, vanilla, and water, boiling it for 5 minutes. Lay the apple rings side by side in a wide skillet, pour on syrup, and poach until just tender, from 5 to 10 minutes. When birds are done, put on serving platter. Add cream to casserole and stir over low heat on top of burner. Simmer for 2 to 3 minutes and correct seasoning. Off the heat, add the cognac and strain into sauceboat. Carve birds and place a ring of drained apple slices around them. Fill apple centers with lingonberries. Garnish with watercress. Serves 4.

CHARTREUSE OF PARTRIDGE A LA DU BARRY

1 large green or white cabbage
2 cups beef broth
$\frac{1}{2}$ cup butter or rendered duck
  or goose fat
1 large onion, finely chopped
4 large carrots, sliced and blanched

4 to 5 white turnips, sliced
  and blanched
6 roasted partridges or squabs
  or small Cornish game hens
Freshly ground pepper
$2\frac{1}{2}$ cups Demi-glace Sauce (page 623)

Shred the cabbage and simmer slowly in the beef broth for 20 to 30 minutes. Drain cabbage and reserve broth. Melt *3 tablespoons butter* in a large saucepan and brown the onion. Add the cabbage, mix well. Melt *3 tablespoons butter* in 12-cup covered casserole. Line with half the cabbage and top with *half the carrots and turnips*. Arrange the partridges in a circle on the vegetables, season with freshly ground pepper, and add *remaining carrots and turnips* and top with remaining cabbage. Brown *remaining 2 tablespoons butter* and dribble over the cabbage along with *1 cup demi-glace sauce*. Cover and bake in a preheated 350° oven for 50 to 60 minutes. Uncover and bake for 10 minutes. Serve in the casserole with *remaining hot demi-glace sauce* passed in a sauceboat. Serves 6.

BAVARIAN ROAST PHEASANT AND SAUERKRAUT

2 pheasants
Salt and freshly ground pepper
1 large onion, halved
½ cup butter
2 apples, peeled, cored, and diced
2 large onions, finely chopped

3 pounds sauerkraut, rinsed and drained
Bouquet garni (12 juniper berries,
   ½ bay leaf, 6 peppercorns,
   tied in cheesecloth)
1 bottle dry white wine or champagne
1 cup beef broth

Season pheasants with salt and pepper, insert *one-half onion* in each bird, and truss. Melt *one-quarter cup butter* in a large enameled kettle and slowly stew the apple and chopped onion until soft but not brown—about 10 minutes. Add the well-rinsed and drained sauerkraut, the bouquet garni, salt, freshly ground pepper, the wine, and enough water to cover. Bring to a boil, turn heat down, and simmer slowly, partially covered, stirring occasionally for 2½ to 3 hours or until liquid has evaporated. When sauerkraut has cooked for 1½ hours, spread the trussed pheasants with *remaining one-quarter cup butter*. Place in a buttered roasting pan, season with salt and freshly ground pepper, and roast in a preheated 400° oven for 30 minutes. Lower the heat to 375° and roast for 1 hour, basting 2 or 3 times. Remove pheasant from oven and let set for 10 minutes. Discard bouquet garni from sauerkraut. Put sauerkraut in a serving casserole. Cut pheasant into serving portions and bury in the sauerkraut. Deglaze roasting pan with beef broth and pour over sauerkraut. Put in a preheated 350° oven for 15 minutes and serve. Serves 6 to 8.

GUINEA HEN STUFFED WITH PATE

The Romans first found the guinea hen in Carthaginian Africa. This recipe is adapted from one prepared at the Renaissance court of Henri II by his queen's Italian cooks.

2 guinea hens or large Cornish
  game hens
2½ ounces canned pâté de foie gras or
  goose liver spread with truffles
1 tablespoon butter, softened
½ small can chestnuts in water, chopped
4 slices white bread (crusts removed),
  crumbled
½ to ¾ cup milk
1 egg, lightly beaten
¼ teaspoon dried thyme
¼ teaspoon dried sage
1 tablespoon cognac

Salt and pepper
1½ ounces canned truffles, minced
  (optional)
1 cup dry white wine
4 cups chicken broth
1 onion, stuck with 1 clove
1 carrot, quartered
2 celery stalks, with leaves
Bouquet garni (4 sprigs parsley,
  ½ bay leaf, ¼ teaspoon thyme,
  3 peppercorns, 6 juniper berries,
  slightly crushed, tied in cheesecloth)
1 pound spinach leaves (optional)

Wipe the birds. Cream the pâté and whip until light with the soft butter. Mix the chestnuts. Moisten the bread with milk, beat in the egg, and add to the goose liver. Season with thyme, sage, cognac, and salt and pepper to taste. Add the minced truffles. Fill the birds with the stuffing. Truss neatly and place in a soup kettle with wine, chicken broth, the onion, carrot, celery, and bouquet garni. Bring to a boil and lower heat so mixture simmers. Cook covered for 30 minutes. Season with salt and pepper to taste and continue simmering for another 15 to 20 minutes or until the birds are tender. Birds need not be covered with liquid, but rather steam cooked, and may even be put on a trivet in the broth. Remove birds to a marmite or soup tureen and keep warm. Strain broth, return to clean kettle, bring to a boil, and add spinach; cook until spinach is limp but still green and add to marmite. Carve the birds at the table and serve in soup plates along with broth. Serves 4.

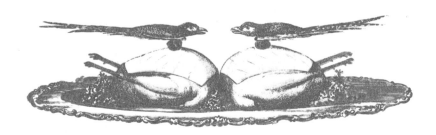

FAROFA STUFFING

The Christmas turkey is so highly regarded in Brazil that it often rates two stuffings, one for the gullet and one for the cavity. The common ingredient in both recipes below is manioc flour, ground from Brazil's chief staple, the manioc root. Toasted, it is the Farofa of the first recipe. The chestnuts which flavor the second are descendants of trees planted centuries ago by colonists from Spain. Both there and in Brazil the nut still serves as a nourishing and abundant staple of the peasant diet.

Turkey giblets, heart, and liver
4 tablespoons butter
1 small onion, finely chopped
1 clove garlic, minced
2 large tomatoes, peeled,
   seeded, and diced
$\frac{1}{4}$ cup pitted chopped green olives
$\frac{1}{4}$ cup seedless golden raisins

$\frac{1}{2}$ cup manioc flour or farina, spread on
   cookie sheet and toasted in medium
   oven until slightly golden
2 teaspoons chopped parsley
1 hard-boiled egg, chopped
1 $\frac{1}{4}$-inch-thick slice ham, chopped
Salt and pepper to taste

Sauté the giblets, heart, and liver in *2 tablespoons butter* for 3 minutes. Add *remaining 2 table-spoons butter* and sauté onion and garlic until golden brown. Chop the giblets, heart, and liver into small pieces and return to pan. Add the diced tomatoes and simmer for 5 minutes; add remaining ingredients and stir well. Makes about $2\frac{1}{2}$ cups, enough to stuff neck cavity of turkey (see Brazilian Turkey, page 491). To stuff both the neck and body cavities of a medium-size turkey (10 to 14 pounds), triple the recipe.

BRAZILIAN CHESTNUT STUFFING

$2\frac{1}{2}$ pounds chestnuts or 2-pound can
   peeled chestnuts in water, drained
$\frac{1}{4}$ cup corn oil
3 cups beef broth
4 tablespoons butter
1 medium onion, finely chopped
2 cups manioc flour or farina

$\frac{1}{2}$ pound dried prunes,
   pitted and chopped
$\frac{1}{2}$ pound seedless golden raisins
$\frac{1}{4}$ teaspoon dried thyme
$\frac{1}{4}$ teaspoon dried marjoram
Salt and pepper

If using fresh chestnuts, cut slits in the flat side of the chestnuts and cook briskly for 5 minutes in a frying pan with the oil, shaking the pan constantly. Cool and peel chestnuts, removing shells and inner skin. Put in a saucepan and simmer with beef broth to cover for 20 minutes. Meanwhile, heat the butter and sauté the onion until soft. Add manioc flour or farina and brown lightly. Add the prunes and raisins. Season with thyme, marjoram, salt, and pepper. Break up the chestnuts and mix into stuffing. Makes about 8 to 9 cups, enough to stuff body cavity of a 12- to 15-pound turkey.

AFRICAN YAM STUFFING

When Senegalese slaves first discovered the strange sweet tuber growing in the West Indies, they named it *nyami*, their word for "to eat."
Yams were soon brought to West Africa where they thrived in the subtropical soil, became staples of the native diet, and inspired much tribal
ritual. During the Feast of the Yams in Nigeria, the king was given a
special dispensation to come out and dance before his subjects, although
he could not leave his palace at any other time.

12 cooked yams	shredded pineapple
2 tablespoons butter	$\frac{1}{2}$ teaspoon poultry seasoning
1 large onion, minced	Salt and pepper
$\frac{1}{2}$ green pepper, minced	1 egg, well beaten
2 large tomatoes, peeled, seeded, and diced, or $\frac{1}{2}$ cup	3 tablespoons heavy cream

Cut yams into small pieces. Melt the butter and cook the onion and pepper without browning; add tomatoes and stew for 5 to 6 minutes or until juices have evaporated. Add the yams
and season with poultry seasoning and salt and pepper to taste. Cool slightly, add egg and
cream. Makes about 6 cups, enough to stuff a 5- to 6-pound chicken.

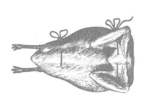

HUNGARIAN NOODLE STUFFING

1 pound egg noodles	1 tablespoon minced parsley
$\frac{1}{2}$ cup butter	Salt and pepper
1 medium onion, chopped	1 tablespoon paprika
Liver (from bird), diced	$\frac{1}{2}$ teaspoon poultry seasoning or
$\frac{1}{2}$ pound pâté de foie gras or liverwurst, diced	powdered sage

Cook noodles in boiling salted water until tender. Drain thoroughly and keep hot. Melt
butter and in it sauté onion until it is soft but not brown. Add liver and pâté or liverwurst
and sauté for about 5 minutes or until liver begins to take on color but is not brown. Add to
noodles, along with any fat left in the pan. Add parsley, salt, pepper, paprika, and poultry
seasoning or sage. Toss well with a fork until all ingredients are evenly distributed. Makes 8
cups, enough to stuff body cavity and neck of a 12-pound bird.

CZECHOSLOVAKIAN POTATO STUFFING

3 pounds boiling potatoes, peeled
4 tablespoons rendered goose or
   turkey fat, or butter

Liver (from bird), diced
1 onion, diced
Salt and pepper

Boil potatoes until soft. Drain, return to pot, and shake over low heat until potatoes are completely dry. Mash and keep hot. Heat rendered poultry fat or butter and sauté diced liver and onion until golden. Mix liver and onion, with fat, into potatoes. Season with salt and pepper. Makes 5 to 6 cups, enough to stuff body cavity and neck of a 10-pound bird.

POLISH VEAL AND ANCHOVY STUFFING

5 slices bacon, diced
1 medium onion, chopped
½ pound lean veal, minced
4 cups cubed bread, crusts removed
½ cup milk
2 teaspoons anchovy paste

½ cup butter, softened
5 egg yolks
Salt and pepper
Rind of 1 lemon, grated
3 egg whites, stiffly beaten

Fry bacon until fat becomes rendered. Add onion and sauté with bacon until onion is light golden brown. Add veal, stir, and fry until it begins to take on color. Cool thoroughly. Sprinkle bread with enough milk to moisten it slightly. Squeeze out excess milk and add bread to veal mixture. Work anchovy paste into softened butter and beat with egg yolks. Stir this into veal and bread until thoroughly blended. Season with salt, pepper, and lemon rind; fold in egg whites. Makes 6 cups, enough to stuff body cavity and neck of a 10-pound bird.

PERSIAN CRACKED WHEAT AND APRICOT STUFFING

½ pound dried apricots, pitted
1 cup tawny port wine
2 cups cracked wheat (burghul)
¼ cup butter
2 medium onions, chopped
2 celery stalks, finely diced

1 teaspoon dried sage
Salt and pepper
½ pound dried prunes,
   pitted and halved
⅓ cup pine nuts
1 cup beef broth

Soak the apricots in the port overnight. Reserve port to baste bird. Soak the cracked wheat in 4 cups water for 2 hours. Drain well. Melt the butter and fry the onion and celery, add the well-drained cracked wheat, and sauté for 5 minutes. Season with sage, and salt and pepper to taste. Mix in prunes, pine nuts, drained apricots, and broth and simmer for 20 minutes. Makes about 6 cups, enough to stuff body cavity and neck of a 10-pound bird.

MEATS

A well-balanced diet is a fairly new concept, as this excerpt from an Elizabethan grace, devoted almost entirely to meat, suggests:

Gloria deo, sirs, proface
Attend me now whilst I say grace . . .
For flesh and fish, and every dish;
Mutton and beefe, of all meates cheefe:
For Cow-heels, chitterlings, tripes and sowse,
And other meate thats in the house:
For backs, for breasts, for legges, for loines,
For pies with raisons, and with proines. . . .

CHOLENT

The Cholent is a traditional beef stew whose ancestry is traced back to medieval Italy, where a great renascence in Jewish writing and cooking occurred. By that time rabbinical law had forbidden any physical labor from sundown on Friday to sundown on Saturday, a stringent interpretation of the Biblical words, "And on the seventh day God finished His work which He had made; and He rested on the Seventh day." So the woman of the house toiled for two days to prepare all the food for the Sabbath and lit a great fire which would keep the oven warm until it was over. Into the oven went the Cholent in a tightly sealed kettle, to be served at the first meal of the day on Saturday.

2 large onions, sliced
4 tablespoons rendered chicken fat
3 pounds beef chuck, brisket, or flanken
Salt and pepper
1 calf's foot, split and cleaned, or
   1 veal marrow bone (optional)

6 medium-size boiling potatoes,
   peeled and halved
1½ cups dried lima beans, presoaked
2 cloves garlic
1 bay leaf (optional)

Sauté onion in fat until it is soft but not brown. Add meat and brown slowly on all sides. Sprinkle with salt and pepper. Place in large Dutch oven or casserole and add calf's foot or marrow bone, potatoes, and lima beans. Slowly add enough boiling water to cover meat. Add garlic, bay leaf, 1 teaspoon salt, and a little extra black pepper. Cover tightly and bake in preheated 250° oven overnight. Or simmer gently for about 3½ hours. Serves 6 to 8.

RAGOUT IN THE MANNER OF OSTIA

Athenaeus lauded Homer for portraying his heroes as simple roast-meat eaters, suggesting that such a habit would "turn us away from the intemperate indulgence of our appetites." It is highly doubtful that the third-century gourmet followed his own advice, for like all his contemporaries he loved fiery meat dishes like this one from Apicius.

2 pounds bottom round beef, cut into 3- by ½-inch slices	2 cups dry red wine
2 tablespoons cracked peppercorns	1 tablespoon honey
½ teaspoon each dill and powdered cumin	4 tablespoons olive oil
1 bay leaf, crumbled	3 tablespoons butter
Salt and pepper	2 leeks, bulbs only, chopped
	1 onion, chopped
	2 teaspoons cornstarch

Wipe the meat carefully. Mix the cracked pepper, dill, cumin, and bay leaf with 1 teaspoon salt. Pound this mixture into the meat. Place in a glass or enameled pan just large enough to hold the meat pieces side by side. Pour in the wine, mixed with the honey and *2 tablespoons olive oil*. Marinate overnight. Pat the meat dry, reserving the marinade. Melt the butter and *remaining 2 tablespoons oil* in a heavy casserole with a lid. Brown the meat on one side, turn, and add the leeks and onion. When well browned, add the marinade and just enough water to cover. Bring to a boil, cover, lower the heat, and simmer for 2 hours or until meat is tender. Dilute the cornstarch with a little cold water and add to the stew. Stir and simmer until thickened. Correct seasoning. Serve with buttered rice. Serves 4 to 6.

STIFATHO

According to Athenaeus, Homer advised his heroes to eat "Viands of simple kinds" and "wholesome sort." He never put "rissoles, or forcemeat . . . before his princes, but meat such as was calculated to make them vigorous in body and mind." Such is this traditional Attic stew.

⅓ cup olive oil or butter	2½ pounds small white onions
2½ pounds beef or veal, cut into 1-inch cubes	Salt and pepper
1 large yellow onion, finely chopped	½ cup dry red or white wine
2 cloves garlic, minced (optional)	1 cup canned tomato purée
	1 bay leaf

Heat the oil. Brown the meat, chopped onion, garlic, and whole onions, stirring to brown evenly. Season with salt and pepper, add wine, tomato purée, and bay leaf. Cover and cook over low heat, stirring occasionally, until meat is tender—about 2 hours. Uncover and cook until sauce is very thick. Correct seasoning and serve very hot. Serves 6.

BOEUF A LA MODE EN GELEE AUX PISTACHES

Alexis Soyer, noted nineteenth-century restaurateur-historian, wrote in his *Pantropheon* that even the "whimsical" J. J. Rousseau, despite his denunciation of animal slaughter, could always be silenced with a serving of Boeuf à la Mode. Soyer went on to describe a very old celebration dedicated to its antecedent, the *boeuf gras*, or fatted ox, which appreciative Parisians observed each Shrovetide. "The horns of the animal are gilded; he is afterwards decorated in a sumptuous manner, and led through the principal thoroughfares. . . . Troops of butchers . . . both on horseback and on foot, are preceded by bands of music, and the heathen divinities, drawn by eight horses in a richly gilt triumphal car, form one of the most splendid and grotesque pageants of modern times."

1 5-pound beef rump tied with string	3 or 4 sprigs parsley
6 to 8 strips larding pork or bacon	1 bay leaf
1 bottle dry red wine	1 teaspoon dried thyme
Salt and pepper	1 strip dried orange peel
$\frac{1}{4}$ pound fresh pork fat, diced	1 large clove garlic, crushed
2 calf's feet or 1 large veal knuckle, split	2 cups beef broth
5 carrots, sliced or shaped into nuggets	$\frac{1}{2}$ cup Madeira wine
12 to 15 small white onions	2 tablespoons tomato purée or
2 large onions, sliced	1 tablespoon tomato paste
$\frac{1}{3}$ cup brandy	$\frac{1}{2}$ cup chopped unsalted pistachio nuts

Lard beef with pork strips. Place it in a deep, narrow ceramic bowl and cover with red wine. Marinate in the refrigerator for 24 hours, turning 2 or 3 times. (Always turn by the string; do not pierce the surface of the meat at any time during marinating or cooking.) Remove meat from marinade and dry thoroughly before cooking or it will not brown. Reserve marinade. Sprinkle with salt and pepper. Heat diced pork fat and in it slowly brown meat on all surfaces. Remove meat from pot and add calf's feet or bones, carrots, and white onions. Sauté until golden brown. Remove from pan and reserve. Pour off excess fat leaving 2 tablespoons in pot. Add sliced onions to pan and sauté slowly until they are golden brown. Add the brandy, heat for a minute, then ignite it and let it burn off. Return the meat to the pot, along with the calf's feet, parsley, bay leaf, thyme, orange peel, and garlic. Add the broth and enough marinade to almost cover the beef. Bring to a boil, cover, reduce heat, and simmer gently for 3 to 4 hours or until meat is very tender. Add the browned carrots and small white onions for the last 20 minutes of cooking time. Remove meat from sauce. Remove carrot slices and white onions and reserve separately. Add Madeira and tomato purée. Strain gravy, pressing as much as possible from the cooking vegetables. Chill meat, reserved vegetables, and gravy (preferably overnight). When cold, skim all fat that has hardened on top of gravy. Slice meat and arrange on flat serving dish or baking dish with white onions and carrot slices set around it attractively. Sprinkle with pistachio nuts. Heat jellied gravy until it is melted but not yet hot. Pour over meat and vegetables. Chill for 5 to 7 hours or until set. Serves 8 to 10.

BIFTEK AU POIVRE

4 tablespoons butter
2 shallots, finely chopped
1 cup Sauce Espagnole (page 622)
⅓ cup dry red wine
¼ cup cracked pepper
4 filets mignons, 1½ to 2 inches thick

Salt and pepper
¼ cup beef broth
3 truffles (optional)
2 tablespoons cognac (optional)
4 rounds of fried toast

Melt *1 tablespoon butter* in a saucepan and brown the shallots. Add the sauce espagnole and the wine and simmer for 15 minutes, skimming as needed. Press the pepper into both sides of the meat. Heat the *remaining 3 tablespoons butter* to sizzling in a large frying pan and sear the filets for 4 minutes on each side for rare. Season with salt. Reserve and keep hot. Deglaze the frying pan with the beef broth and pour into sauce. Add *2 truffles*, minced, and cognac to sauce. Simmer for 5 minutes. Slice *remaining truffle* into 4 pieces. Place beef on fried toast on a heated serving platter, pour 1 tablespoon sauce over each filet, and top with slice of truffle. Garnish with watercress. Pass sauce separately in a sauceboat. Serves 4.

BEEF STROGANOV

Though the cultivated gentleman of pre-Revolutionary Russia was devoted to his homeland, he was at the same time enamored of things French. This duality was deliciously resolved in Beef Stroganov: the sour cream sauce was Russian, the method of preparation French. It is named for one of St. Petersburg's chief families of merchant-noblemen.

1½ pounds sirloin or tenderloin
Salt and pepper
3 tablespoons flour
½ cup butter
2 medium onions, chopped
1 tablespoon tomato paste

1½ cups beef broth
½ pound mushrooms, sliced
½ cup heavy sweet cream
1 cup sour cream
1 tablespoon Worcestershire sauce
1 teaspoon prepared mustard

Cut the meat into thin strips, 1½ inches long, ½ inch wide. Season with salt and pepper and dredge in flour. Melt *3 tablespoons butter* and sear the meat and onions quickly at high heat until meat is no longer red. Add tomato paste and broth. Stir until smooth and simmering. Melt *remaining butter* in a separate pan and sauté mushrooms for 5 to 7 minutes. Season with salt and pepper to taste and add to meat; add sweet cream and warm sour cream. Stir until thick and smooth, season with Worcestershire and mustard. Serve with rice. Serves 4.

CARBONNADE FLAMANDE

Flanders, now partly Belgian, partly French, was during the Middle Ages a distinctive culture with its own language and cuisine. Carbonnade, which uses the native drink beer in the stewing, is one of the best-known dishes of this wine-poor region.

3 pounds chuck, rump, or bottom round beef cut into 1-inch cubes
Flour for dredging
Salt and pepper
3 to 4 tablespoons olive or salad oil
5 large onions, sliced
3 garlic cloves, crushed or minced

Bouquet garni (parsley sprigs, celery tops, 1 large bay leaf, 1 teaspoon thyme, 3 or 4 peppercorns, crushed, tied in cheesecloth)
1 to 2 cups strong beef broth
1 to 2 cups dark beer
1 tablespoon brown sugar
1 tablespoon wine vinegar

Wipe the meat. Dredge cubed meat in about $\frac{3}{4}$ cup flour with 1 teaspoon salt and $\frac{1}{2}$ teaspoon pepper. Shake off excess. Heat the oil in an iron or heavy stew pot with a lid. Brown the meat in batches with the sliced onions, adding oil as needed. When all pieces are brown remove excess oil and return meat to the cooking pot. Add crushed garlic, bouquet garni, and enough broth and beer to just cover the meat. Simmer covered for 2 to $2\frac{1}{2}$ hours on top of the stove, or place in preheated 300° to 350° oven or at a temperature that will keep broth at a gentle simmer. Add more broth and beer if stew seems dry. When meat is tender, remove bouquet, correct seasoning, add sugar and vinegar, and simmer about 10 minutes more. Serve with parsley potatoes. Serves 6 to 8.

BEEF BIRDS

Robert May, in his introduction to *The Accomplisht Cook* (1660), said, "I have so managed for the general good that [for] those whose Purses cannot reach to the Cost of Rich Dishes, I have descended to their meaner expenses." Beef Birds date back to a time when real birds were prohibitively expensive, and this savory means of stretching meat became known as the poor man's "bird," due to its shape.

8 slices top round beef, pounded thin
1 onion, minced
6 tablespoons butter
4 slices crisp bacon, crumbled
$\frac{1}{4}$ teaspoon each: dried thyme, chervil, and mace
1 teaspoon chopped parsley

8 olives, minced
Salt and pepper
3 tablespoons flour
$\frac{1}{2}$ cup dry red wine
$\frac{3}{4}$ cup beef broth
1 package frozen artichoke hearts, defrosted

Pound the beef to 6-inch rounds between sheets of waxed paper. Brown the onion in *2 tablespoons butter*. Add the bacon, herbs and spices, and olives. Season with a little pepper. Spread some mixture on each of the beef slices, fold in the sides, and roll them up. Tie or skewer them. Mix the flour with salt and pepper and dredge the beef lightly. Heat *remaining 4 tablespoons butter* in the same skillet used for the onion and brown the meat on all sides. Add the wine and broth and simmer covered for 10 minutes. Add the defrosted artichoke hearts and simmer until heated through. Arrange the beef birds and artichoke hearts on a heated platter. Spoon pan juices over meat. Serves 4.

SURSTEG
(*Danish Sour Roast*)

1 3-pound slice beef, such as bottom round or chuck	$\frac{1}{8}$ pound salt pork or bacon, cut into small pieces
1 large onion, chopped	Salt
3 bay leaves	4 tablespoons butter
6 cloves	1 cup dry red wine
$\frac{1}{4}$ teaspoon powdered ginger	2 cups beef broth
6 peppercorns, crushed	2 tablespoons flour
Red wine vinegar to cover	2 teaspoons brown sugar, or to taste

Pound the meat or have the butcher do it. Put in an enamel, glass, or ceramic dish with the onion, *1 bay leaf*, cloves, ginger, and peppercorns. Cover with vinegar and marinate in refrigerator for 24 hours, turning once or twice. Dry meat thoroughly, strain marinade, reserve the onion. Make little slits in the meat and lard with the pieces of salt pork. Rub the meat with salt. Melt *2 tablespoons butter* in a large saucepan or skillet and brown the meat well. Dry the onion and brown with the meat. Add *remaining bay leaves*, wine, and broth. Cover and simmer slowly for 2 hours or until meat is tender, turning once. Remove meat and pour off broth. Add *remaining 2 tablespoons butter* to skillet and brown the flour. Return broth to the flour and stir until thickened and smooth. Add the brown sugar. Correct seasoning. Slice the meat, pour a little gravy over it, and pass the remainder in a sauceboat. Serves 6.

SWEDISH MEATBALLS

2 slices white bread, crusts removed	1 pound lean beef, ground
$\frac{1}{4}$ cup milk	$\frac{1}{2}$ pound veal, ground
1 egg	$\frac{1}{2}$ pound pork, ground
1$\frac{1}{2}$ teaspoons salt	$\frac{1}{2}$ cup fresh minced dill
$\frac{1}{2}$ teaspoon pepper	or $\frac{1}{4}$ cup dried dill
$\frac{1}{4}$ teaspoon nutmeg	1$\frac{1}{2}$ cups beef broth, or as needed
1 large onion, finely chopped	$\frac{1}{2}$ cup sour cream or sweet heavy cream
8 tablespoons butter	

In a large bowl soak the bread, milk, and slightly beaten egg. Add salt, pepper, and nutmeg. Mix well, making a "panade" or soft paste of the bread and liquid. Brown the onion in *2 to 3 tablespoons butter*. Add the beef, veal, pork, onion, and *one-third of the dill*. Mix very well. Wet hands and make 1$\frac{1}{2}$-inch meatballs. Heat the *remaining butter* in the same pan in which the onions were fried, and sauté the meatballs, turning to brown evenly. Add the broth and simmer for 5 minutes. Heat sour cream or scald sweet cream. Combine cream and *half the remaining dill* with meatballs. Stir well and heat to the boiling point. Sprinkle with the *last of the dill*. Serves 6. May be made smaller and served as an appetizer.

RHEINISCHER SAUERBRATEN
(Rhineland Sauerbraten)

1 5-pound beef rump roast or	1 large carrot, sliced
top or bottom round	4 slices bacon and 2 tablespoons butter,
Bacon or salt pork for larding	or 5 tablespoons drippings of kidney
Salt and pepper	fat, bacon, or beef fat
3 cups white vinegar	2 tablespoons butter
3 large onions, sliced	3 tablespoons flour
3 bay leaves	2 tablespoons sugar
18 cloves	Lemon juice to taste
8 peppercorns	$\frac{1}{2}$ cup soaked golden seedless raisins
1 tablespoon pickling spices	Tomato purée or sour cream (optional)

Lard meat with strips of bacon or salt pork and tie securely with string so meat will hold its shape and may be turned easily. Sprinkle with salt and pepper and place in deep earthenware or glass bowl. Combine vinegar with 3 cups water and simmer for 5 minutes with *1 sliced onion, 2 bay leaves, 9 cloves*, peppercorns, pickling spices, and carrot. Cool and pour over meat to cover completely. If necessary, add water and vinegar in equal amounts until meat is covered. Cover and marinate in refrigerator for 3 to 5 days, turning 2 or 3 times each day. Remove meat from marinade and dry thoroughly. Strain and reserve marinade. Fry bacon in butter, or heat other fat, in a 5-quart Dutch oven. Brown meat slowly on all sides in the hot fat. Remove. Add *remaining 2 sliced onions* to fat and brown. Place meat on top of onions. Add enough strained marinade to half cover meat. Add *remaining bay leaves and cloves,* bring to a boil, cover pot, reduce heat and simmer very slowly but steadily for 3½ to 4 hours. Turn meat 2 or 3 times during cooking. Add more marinade to pot if needed. Meat is done when it can easily be pierced with a long-pronged fork, but do not make this test before 3½ hours. Remove meat to a platter and strain gravy. Wipe pot. Pour gravy back into pot. Melt butter in a saucepan and stir in flour and sugar. Fry slowly, stirring constantly until sugar turns a deep golden brown. Add to hot gravy and beat smooth with a wire whisk over low heat. Season to taste with lemon juice. Add raisins, return meat to pot, and simmer for 10 minutes. Stir in 2 tablespoons tomato purée or 4 tablespoons sour cream and simmer. Slice meat and serve with gravy on the side. Serves 8. If desired, 6 to 8 crushed gingersnaps may be added to the sauce for the last 10 minutes of cooking time.

BOEUF BOURGUIGNON

½ cup flour
1½ teaspoons salt
½ teaspoon pepper
3 pounds lean stewing beef, cut into
   1½-inch pieces
¼ pound salt pork, diced
2 tablespoons olive oil
1 pound button mushrooms
3 medium yellow onions, chopped
¼ cup cognac

2 tablespoons tomato paste
3 cups red Burgundy wine
1 cup beef broth
Bouquet garni (1 clove garlic, 1 bay leaf,
   ½ teaspoon thyme, 3 sprigs parsley,
   4 peppercorns, tied in cheesecloth)
24 small white onions, parboiled
2 tablespoons butter
1 teaspoon sugar
¼ cup finely chopped parsley

Mix the flour, salt, and pepper, and dredge the meat. Parboil the salt pork for about 3 minutes. Drain well on paper towels. Heat the olive oil in a casserole with a lid. Brown the diced pork, stirring occasionally. Remove meat with a slotted spoon and reserve. Sauté the cleaned mushrooms. Season with salt and pepper and reserve separately from the pork. Brown the beef in two batches in the hot oil, adding oil if needed. When turning over the second lot of meat, add the onions. When meat is done, remove all pieces from pot, skim fat, and deglaze the pot with the cognac. Return meat to pot, add the tomato paste, wine, and enough broth to barely cover the meat. Stir well and bury the bouquet garni in the center of the stew. Bring stew to a boil, turn down the heat, and simmer covered for 2 hours, adding broth or water as needed. The stew may also be put in a preheated 325° to 350° oven. Liquid should just quiver and the stew should be stirred occasionally. Sauté white onions in the butter with sugar. Add onions and mushrooms to the meat when it is nearly tender. Simmer another ½ hour or until meat is quite tender and remove any remaining fat. Serve in a heated dish and sprinkle with chopped parsley. Serves 6 to 8.

PIROG

Pirog are as Russian as the Volga boatman and as old, at least, as the seventeenth-century boyars who served them at banquets. They also appeared at Name Day celebrations (the Saint's Day on which a Russian child was baptized) when two relatives would break a large Pirog over the celebrant's head. If any of the stuffing fell on him a wish was made that he be similarly showered with gold and silver. Then, as a more practical gesture, the Pirog was divided and eaten accompanied by vodka. Pirozhki, often served as appetizers (*zakuski*), are a smaller version of the Pirog.

¾ cup butter	Salt and pepper
2 large onions, finely chopped	¾ cup chopped fresh dill
3 pounds lean ground beef	1 recipe Cream Cheese Pastry
2 eggs	(page 680)
2 tablespoons beef broth	¼ cup bread crumbs

Melt *one-half cup butter* in a large skillet and cook the onions. Add the beef and keep stirring with a fork until meat loses red color; do not brown. Remove from heat and add the eggs and beef broth. Season to taste with the salt and pepper. Add the dill. Add *all but 1 tablespoon of the remaining butter*, melted. On a floured dish towel, roll the pastry into an oval about 16 by 14 inches. Place filling in the center, leaving strip of dough about 4 inches on each side. Fold long sides over filling, seal neatly with a little cold water, and shape pirog into an oval. Using towel, invert onto a buttered cookie sheet. Prick well with a fork. Brush with the *remaining butter* and sprinkle with the bread crumbs. Bake in a preheated 425° oven for 13 to 15 minutes, lower heat to 350°, and bake 20 to 25 minutes longer or until golden brown. Serve hot with Broth (page 416) or Borsch (page 428).

VARIATIONS: *Pirozhki*: Cut dough into 4-inch squares, fill, and fold into triangles or 3-inch rounds folded in half. Omit bread crumbs and brush with cream. Bake 10 minutes at 425° and 10 minutes more at 350°. *Cabbage Filling*: Shred 2 large heads of cabbage. Salt generously to draw out water, squeeze out excess water. Melt ½ cup butter in a large frying pan and sauté 2 chopped onions on low heat. When transparent, add chopped cabbage. Raise heat slightly. Cook, stirring until cabbage is tender and has taken on color (about 20 minutes), and add 4 tablespoons butter. Season generously with salt and pepper. Add ½ cup minced fresh dill; cool. Mix with 6 chopped hard-boiled eggs. Spread on dough and proceed as above.

EMPANADAS

According to a Spanish explorer who reached South America in 1516, the first meal he witnessed there consisted of some of his crew who were stewed up and eaten by the Indians. The natives gradually turned from Spaniards to Spanish dishes for nourishment; this turnover became the most popular. In South America it takes the place of the sandwich and is prepared with a great variety of fillings, to be sold at street corner stands everywhere.

4 tablespoons butter
1 large onion, chopped
½ clove garlic, minced (optional)
½ pound lean beef, ground
1 large tomato, peeled, seeded, and chopped
1 teaspoon sugar
8 pimento-stuffed green olives, finely chopped

3 tablespoons raisins
Salt and pepper
1 hard-boiled egg, chopped
1 recipe Short Pastry (page 682) made with ¼ cup shortening (half butter, half lard) or 1 recipe Cream Cheese Pastry (page 680)
Vegetable shortening for frying

Heat butter, fry the onion and garlic, add the meat, and fry until it is no longer red. Add next 4 ingredients and cook about 8 minutes, stirring well. Season to taste, with generous amount of pepper. Add egg. Cool mixture before using. Make pastry and let rest about 20 minutes. Roll out to about ¼-inch thickness on a floured board. Cut into 3-inch rounds. Place a tablespoon of filling on one side of round. Fold dough to form semicircle and seal by wetting the edges with cold water and pressing with the tines of a fork. Heat fat to 360° and fry a few turnovers at a time, spooning fat over them. Temperature of fat should remain constant. Brown both sides. Drain and keep hot in a preheated 300° oven. Makes about 24.

PICADHINO
(South American Savory Beef)

3 tablespoons butter
1 large onion, thinly sliced
1 pound round steak, ground
2 large tomatoes, peeled, seeded, and diced
½ teaspoon dried thyme or oregano

Salt and pepper
1 cup beef broth
3 cups cooked rice
½ cup chopped green olives
2 hard-boiled eggs, chopped

Melt the butter, add the onion, and cook for 2 minutes. Add the meat and stir until meat is browned. Add tomatoes, thyme, salt and pepper to taste, and the broth. Cook over very low heat, covered, for 20 minutes. Uncover and cook until liquid has evaporated. Pour over hot cooked rice and sprinkle with chopped olives and chopped hard-boiled eggs. Serves 4.

MATAMBRE

Stuffed flank steak, whose name translates literally as "hunger-killer," is served throughout South America; but it is at its best in Argentina, where some of the world's finest beef cattle are raised.

4 pounds flank steak	1 cup chopped, cooked spinach
¼ teaspoon dried thyme	1½ cups bread crumbs
1 clove garlic, mashed	3 to 4 tablespoons milk
3 tablespoons chopped parsley	3 chorizos or Italian hot sausages
1 large onion, chopped	1 egg
½ cup red wine vinegar	4 hard-boiled eggs, chopped
1 bay leaf	½ pound salt pork, cut in thin strips
6 peppercorns	for larding
Salt and pepper	2 cups beef broth
1 bunch scallions, minced	

Pound the steak to a thin square shape. Marinate in a glass or earthenware dish for 4 hours with the thyme, garlic, *1 tablespoon parsley*, the onion, vinegar, bay leaf, and peppercorns. Reserve marinade. Lay steak flat and sprinkle with pepper. Mix scallions, spinach, bread crumbs soaked in milk, *remaining parsley*, and sausage removed from casing and diced. Add beaten egg and season with salt and pepper. Spread on the meat to within 1 inch of edge. Spread with chopped eggs. Arrange the salt pork strips all over the meat. Roll flank steak up like a jelly roll and sew carefully so stuffing will not come out. Put in a long roaster with a cover. Brown in a little fat. Pour in broth and remains of marinade. Cover. Braise in preheated 350° oven for 3 hours, turning meat occasionally and basting often. Test with fork for doneness. Cool under weight such as heavy platter. Serve cold in thin slices. Makes 16 slices.

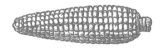

PASTEL DE CHOCLO
(South American Corn Stew)

⅓ cup butter	¼ teaspoon pepper
3 medium onions, finely chopped	½ cup raisins, soaked in water
2 green peppers, peeled and chopped	8 stuffed green olives, chopped
3 tomatoes, peeled, seeded, and chopped,	3 hard-boiled eggs, sliced (optional)
or 1 No. 2 can plum tomatoes, drained	12 ears of corn, grated, or 3 cups
2 pounds beef or veal, ground	drained canned or frozen corn
½ teaspoon powdered cumin	kernels, ground in meat grinder
½ teaspoon dried marjoram	¼ cup flour
3 tablespoons sugar	1 cup milk
1½ teaspoons salt	6 eggs

Melt *half the butter* and brown the onions and peppers in a 10-cup casserole. Add the tomatoes and simmer for 10 minutes. Add the meat and cook, stirring until it is no longer red. Add the cumin, marjoram, *1 tablespoon sugar, 1 teaspoon salt*, and the pepper. Mix well. Add the raisins and olives. If using hard-boiled eggs, place a layer of sliced eggs over mixture. In another saucepan melt *remaining butter* and put in the corn, *one-half teaspoon salt*, and *1 tablespoon sugar*. Mix the flour with the milk, add to the corn, and cook, stirring until well thickened. Cool slightly. Beat the eggs into the corn mixture, one by one. Pour corn mixture over the meat. Sprinkle with *remaining sugar*. Bake in preheated 350° oven for 45 to 60 minutes or until puffed and golden. Serve from the casserole. Serves 6 to 8.

STUFFED CABBAGE

Stuffed cabbage leaves, and their close relation stuffed vine leaves, are eaten throughout eastern Europe. Among the Jews they are called *holishkes* and are eaten on Sukkoth, a holiday celebrating the harvest.

1 3-pound head of green cabbage	3 whole cloves
1 pound beef, ground	1 small bay leaf
$\frac{1}{2}$ cup rice	Juice of 1 lemon
2 onions	2 tablespoons brown sugar
1 egg	3 to 4 tablespoons tomato purée
Salt and pepper	$\frac{1}{2}$ cup raisins
2 cups beef broth or water, or as needed	8 or 9 gingersnaps, crushed

Using a thin, long-bladed paring knife, cut the core out of the head of cabbage and discard. Loosen the leaves carefully and remove individually. Use only the large, outside leaves; there should be about 12. Steam or blanch large leaves until they are flexible. Place rib side up and trim off heavy center rib. Turn leaves over. Mix meat with rice, *1 onion*, grated, egg, salt, and pepper. Place 1 tablespoonful of meat mixture at rib end of leaf. Roll toward the tip, jelly roll fashion, tucking sides in. When all leaves are filled place them in a deep pot and add beef broth or water to cover completely. Stud *remaining onion* with cloves and add to pot along with bay leaf, lemon juice, brown sugar, and tomato purée. Cover and simmer slowly for 1 hour. Add raisins and gingersnaps and simmer for 15 minutes more. Stir sauce gently from time to time so that it will be smoothly blended. Arrange cooked cabbage rolls in a single layer in a flat baking pan 3 to 4 inches deep. Season sauce to taste and pour over cabbage rolls. Bake in a preheated 375° oven for about 30 minutes or until the sauce is thick and the cabbage rolls are brown. Serves 4 to 6.

BEEF TERIYAKI

The best Japanese cattle know no home on the range. To keep their flesh tender enough for such dishes as Teriyaki they are raised in stalls; to keep them suitably lean they are massaged daily by teams of young women. Draughts of beer, mosquito-repelling incense, and hot water bottles also go to make their short lives content.

2 pounds steak (shell, sirloin, or fillet), cut into ½-inch slices, or 1 whole sirloin steak

Marinade:
1½ cups soy sauce

½ cup sugar
1 clove garlic, crushed
1 tablespoon sake or dry sherry
2 tablespoons minced ginger root, or 2 teaspoons powdered ginger

Combine marinade ingredients and heat, stirring, long enough for sugar to melt. Cool completely. Pour over meat and marinate for 2 hours. Drain the meat and grill over coals or under broiler, basting with the marinade to preferred doneness. Serves 6. Marinade will keep a few days under refrigeration. The same marinade may be used for pork, lamb, chicken, or fish.

SUKIYAKI

Not until the Meiji restoration of the 1860's did meat become a respectable food in Japan. Earlier, anyone inclined to trespass against Buddhist doctrine found it the better part of discretion to cook *(yaki)* his beef out in the fields on his shovel *(suki)* where the smell would quickly waft away. With the arrival of a decidedly vigorous race of beef-eating Westerners, the enlightened new emperor gave his blessings to meat and to one of Japan's now traditional dishes.

1½ pounds shell or sirloin steak, sliced paper thin
2 medium onions, thinly sliced
1 cup carrots, cut into julienne strips
¾ pound spinach leaves
1½ cups bamboo shoots, split and sliced
¾ pound chrysanthemum leaves (shungiku), blanched (optional)
1½ cups diced celery
10 scallions, sliced on the slant to 1½ inches
1½ cups sliced mushrooms
1 cup lotus or water lily root or water chestnuts, sliced

1½ cups bean sprouts
2 cakes baked bean curd, cut into 12 pieces each
2 cups Dashi (page 421) or 3 cups beef broth
⅔ cup soy sauce
⅓ cup sake or dry sherry
3 tablespoons sugar
¼ teaspoon monosodium glutamate
½ cup peanut oil
6 bowls cooked white rice
1 raw egg yolk per person (optional)
Grated white horseradish

Arrange meat on large platter. Arrange raw vegetables and bean curd on the same platter, keeping each separate. Heat an electric skillet or hibachi to medium heat. Combine dashi, soy sauce, sake, sugar, and monosodium glutamate and put in a pitcher. Pour *one and one-half tablespoons oil* in the skillet. Fry a few meat slices, tossing them around with a fork or chopsticks to prevent sticking or scorching. Push aside when lightly browned and cook some of each of the vegetables, starting with the onion, for 3 minutes. Add remainder in the order given and brown quickly. Do not cook too much at once. Add some soup stock and simmer for 3 to 4 minutes. Keep each vegetable separate. Add the bean curd, cook 1 minute, and serve on hot plates with the bowls of rice. Repeat until all the food is cooked. Serve with egg yolk, soy sauce, and grated white horseradish as dips. Serves 4 to 6.

KOREAN FRIED GREEN PEPPERS

3 green peppers
1 pound lean beef, ground
1 tablespoon sesame oil
1 clove garlic, crushed
$\frac{1}{8}$ teaspoon pepper

Soy sauce
Flour for dredging
1 egg, beaten
$\frac{1}{4}$ cup peanut or vegetable oil

Wash and dry peppers; cut them in half lengthwise, remove seeds, membranes, and stems. Mix the lean ground beef with the sesame oil, garlic, pepper, and 2 tablespoons soy sauce. Stuff the pepper halves. Dredge the meat side with flour and coat entire halves with beaten egg. If peppers are large, 1 more egg may be needed. Heat the oil in a frying pan and fry the peppers slowly until both the meat and the peppers are tender, about 35 minutes. Makes 6 halves. Serve with soy sauce.

A VEAL PIE

The *Archimagirus Anglo Gallicus or Excellent and Approved Receipts from a Choice Manuscript of Sir Theodore Mayerne Knight*, London (1658), was among the first English cookbooks to sanction veal as suitable food. Since Saxon times, killing a healthy calf had been considered wanton and typical of the odious behavior of conquering Normans.

3 pounds boneless veal, cut into 1-inch pieces
1 onion, stuck with 2 cloves
1 carrot, quartered
4 slices lemon
1 bay leaf
$\frac{1}{4}$ teaspoon dried thyme
Salt and pepper

5 tablespoons butter
5 tablespoons flour
$\frac{1}{4}$ teaspoon powdered mace or nutmeg
2 egg yolks
$\frac{1}{2}$ cup heavy cream
2 tablespoons capers
$\frac{1}{2}$ recipe Puff Pastry (page 684) or Short Pastry (page 682)

Cover the veal with cold water in a large saucepan, bring to a boil, simmer for 4 to 5 minutes, drain the meat and rinse pot. Replace meat in saucepan. Cover it with 5 cups cold water or enough to cover the meat. Add the onion, carrot, lemon slices, bay leaf, thyme, 1 teaspoon salt, and $\frac{1}{4}$ teaspoon pepper. Bring to a boil again; cover and simmer gently for 1 hour or until the meat is tender. Discard the onion, carrot, lemon, and bay leaf. In a separate saucepan, melt the butter, add the flour, and cook, stirring until the flour starts to barely color. Add $3\frac{1}{2}$ cups of the strained broth from the meat and stir until it is thick and smooth. Season to taste with salt and pepper. Add the mace or nutmeg. Beat the egg yolks with the cream. Pour a little of the sauce into the eggs and pour this back into the sauce. Remove from heat and stir well. Add meat and capers. Butter a deep pie dish and pour in the meat and sauce. Cover with a $\frac{1}{2}$-inch layer of pastry, leaving a vent for steam to escape. Bake in a preheated 425° oven until pastry is puffed and golden, about 20 to 25 minutes. Lower the heat if it browns too fast. Serve immediately. Serves 6.

RULLEPÖLSE
(Danish Pickled Veal Roll)

1 $3\frac{1}{2}$-pound veal breast
2 teaspoons salt
1 teaspoon white pepper
1 teaspoon powdered allspice
$\frac{1}{2}$ teaspoon powdered cloves
1 cup finely minced or grated onion
1 teaspoon saltpeter
3 tablespoons chopped parsley and dill, mixed

$\frac{1}{2}$ teaspoon sugar
$\frac{1}{2}$ pound fat back (or ham, bacon, or pork), very thinly sliced
Pickling mixture:
8 cups water
$\frac{1}{4}$ cup salt
$\frac{1}{2}$ teaspoon saltpeter
2 tablespoons sugar

Have the butcher bone the veal and remove any sinews. Trim meat to a neat square or rectangle, sewing it up where needed. Mix salt, pepper, spices, onion, saltpeter, herbs, and sugar and spread on the meat to within $\frac{1}{2}$ inch from edge. Lay the thinly sliced fat back and any veal trimmings on the spices. Roll up tightly as for a jelly roll and sew up ends and flap to seal completely. Tie with white cotton string at 1-inch intervals. Wrap in a clean muslin cloth and sew this up. Put ingredients for the pickle in a saucepan and cook long enough to dissolve salt, saltpeter, and sugar. Cool completely. Put pickle and veal sausage in a glass or earthenware bowl; weight the sausage down so it is covered with pickle. Let the sausage remain in the pickle in refrigerator for 4 to 5 days. Remove from pickle and put to boil in cold water for $1\frac{1}{2}$ hours. Remove and cool under a weight, such as a platter with a heavy object set on it. Remove from cloth, cut away strings and threads. Serve cold, sliced very thin, on buttered pumpernickel bread. Serves 6 to 8.

CUTLETS POJARSKY

Some contend that these cutlets were named for the seventeenth-century general who liberated Moscow from the Poles. Others trace the name and recipe to Pojarsky's tavern, a stopover on the road between St. Petersburg and Moscow in the years before the railroads were built.

$1\frac{1}{2}$ pounds boneless veal or white meat of chicken, or combination of both	$\frac{1}{3}$ cup butter, softened
1 cup crumbled white bread	1 teaspoon salt
$\frac{1}{2}$ cup milk	$\frac{1}{2}$ teaspoon pepper
1 egg white	$\frac{1}{4}$ teaspoon nutmeg
$\frac{1}{2}$ cup heavy cream	$\frac{1}{2}$ cup dry bread crumbs
	$\frac{1}{2}$ cup Clarified Butter (page 630)

Have the butcher grind the meat very fine. Soak crumbled bread in the milk for 10 minutes; squeeze out excess milk. Mix veal, bread, egg white, cream, $\frac{1}{3}$ cup butter, salt, pepper, and nutmeg. Work with a wooden spoon until very well mixed. Divide into 6 oblong cakes, flatten slightly, roll in bread crumbs, and sauté in $\frac{1}{2}$ cup clarified butter until deep golden brown on both sides. Makes 6.

VARIATIONS: *Cutlets Maréchal*: Form meat mixture into oblong cakes and push some chopped truffles into the center of cutlets. Close opening with meat mixture. *Russian Bitkis*: Prepare above recipe using 3 tablespoons butter and 1 egg in the meat mixture, along with 1 teaspoon meat glaze and cooked, finely chopped onion. Roll into 3-inch meat patties and sauté in clarified butter. A sauce may be made by deglazing the frying pan with $\frac{1}{2}$ cup of beef broth and adding sour cream to taste. Strain and pour over meat cakes.

BRESOLLES

The creation of this ragout is credited to the *valet de chambre* of the Marquis de Bresolles. One version has it that the valet needed some way to pass the time while his master was off fighting the Seven Years' War.

$\frac{1}{4}$ pound sliced ham, minced
$\frac{1}{2}$ cup olive oil
1 tablespoon minced parsley
1 teaspoon chopped fresh tarragon or
$\quad$ $\frac{1}{2}$ teaspoon dried tarragon
1 cup minced mushrooms

1 clove garlic, minced
9 thin slices veal, pounded
Salt and pepper
$\frac{1}{4}$ cup dry white wine (optional)
$\frac{1}{4}$ cup unsweetened chestnut purée
$\frac{1}{2}$ cup beef broth

Mix the ham, *half the oil*, parsley, tarragon, mushrooms, and garlic. Put $\frac{1}{3}$ of this mixture in a casserole. Place a layer of 3 slices of veal on this, season with salt and pepper to taste. Trickle on *some oil* and wine. Repeat layers until ham mixture and veal are used up. Cover and simmer for 35 minutes. Remove meat to a hot platter. To the liquid in the casserole add the chestnut purée diluted with the broth. Simmer gently for 5 minutes, stirring. Remove fat and pour over bresolles. Serves 4.

WIENER SCHNITZEL

Wiener Schnitzel and its Italian counterpart, Cotoletta Milanese, involved two Hapsburg domains in a culinary quarrel. Both branches of the family, Austrian and Italian, claimed credit for the invention of the dish, the latter branch tracing their claim all the way back to a banquet given in 1134 for the canon of Milan's St. Ambrogio Cathedral.

6 large veal cutlets
$\quad$ (scallopini), pounded thin
Lemon juice (optional)
Salt and pepper
Flour for dredging

3 eggs, beaten with 3 tablespoons
$\quad$ cold water
Bread crumbs for dredging
Butter, lard, or vegetable shortening
$\quad$ for frying

Veal cutlets may be lightly sprinkled with lemon juice 30 minutes before they are breaded or they may be cooked unmarinated. Pat cutlets dry and sprinkle one side of each with a little salt and pepper. Dredge lightly with flour, dip into beaten eggs, letting excess drip off, and dredge with bread crumbs. Let stand at room temperature 20 minutes before frying. Heat fat in a large skillet. There should be about a 1-inch depth of melted or liquid fat. Fry a few cutlets at a time, slowly, turning once so both sides become golden brown. Allow 4 to 6 minutes for each side. Drain on paper towel. Keep finished cutlets warm in 250° oven while others are frying. Serves 6. For *Schnitzel à la Holstein*, top each cutlet with 1 fried egg, 2 or 3 anchovy fillets, and a few capers.

VITELLO TONNATO

Tunnied veal, a standard dish in many parts of Italy, may be no older than the recipe that appeared in the Livornese cookbook *Il Cuciniere Italiano Moderno* (1844) where it was explained that in the absence of the luxury tuna, veal could be disguised with anchovies or other salted fish to taste almost like the real thing.

1 3- to 4-pound boned leg of veal, skinned and tied in a roll	1 large carrot
1 small can anchovy fillets	3 or 4 sprigs parsley
2 cloves garlic, slivered (optional)	1 7-ounce can tuna fish
Salt and pepper	$\frac{3}{4}$ to 1 cup olive oil
1 large onion, studded with 3 cloves	Juice of 1 or 2 lemons, or to taste
1 bay leaf	3 to 5 tablespoons capers, drained
	Lemon slices

Make 4 or 5 incisions in veal and put *1 anchovy fillet* and *1 sliver of garlic* in each. Rub lightly with salt and pepper. Place in deep pot, add onion, bay leaf, carrot, parsley, and boiling water to cover. Simmer for $1\frac{1}{2}$ to 2 hours or until veal is tender. Remove meat from broth and chill. Strain broth and reserve, discarding vegetables. Purée tuna fish in a mortar or blender. Add *5 or 6 anchovy fillets* and continue blending or mashing, adding olive oil gradually as for mayonnaise. Add lemon juice to taste and capers. Add reserved veal broth if needed to thin sauce to consistency of beaten yoghurt or very heavy sweet cream. Season to taste. Cut veal into thin slices and arrange in glass or ceramic serving dish. Cover with sauce and marinate in refrigerator for 24 to 48 hours. Garnish with lemon and capers. Serves 8 as appetizer, 6 as entree.

SALTIMBOCCA

Pellegrino Artusi, a visiting Florentine gourmet, found a Roman *trattoria's* version of Saltimbocca good enough to justify its fanciful name—literally "jump in the mouth." He set it down in his late-nineteenth-century cookbook, *La Scienza in Cucina*.

6 large veal cutlets (scallopini), pounded paper thin	Leaf sage, fresh or dried
Salt and pepper	12 slices prosciutto ham
	Butter for frying

Cut each large scallopini in half diagonally making twice as many smaller cutlets of close to same shape as the larger ones. Sprinkle each piece lightly with salt and pepper and sprinkle a few leaves of sage on one side. Top sage with 1 slice of prosciutto and tie together with string or fasten with 1 or 2 toothpicks. Heat butter and sauté veal side first for about 5 minutes. Turn and sauté ham side for about 2 minutes. Do not fry ham longer than that or it will harden. Place on platter and remove string or toothpicks, serve with pan juices. Serves 6.

OSSO BUCO

Veal knuckles with marrow or, as the Milanese call them, "hollow bones," are a specialty of Lombardy, Italy's major cattle-raising region.

3 veal shanks, each cut into 3 pieces	4 tomatoes, coarsely chopped
Salt, pepper, flour, for dredging	Bouquet garni (parsley sprigs, 1 small
⅓ cup olive oil	bay leaf, 6 peppercorns, tied in
2 cloves garlic	cheesecloth)
1 large onion, finely chopped	1 teaspoon sugar
1 large carrot, finely diced	1 cup beef broth
1 large stalk celery, finely diced	Rind of 1 lemon, grated
½ cup dry white wine	¼ cup minced parsley

Sprinkle meat with salt and pepper. Dredge with flour and shake off excess. Heat *half the olive oil* in a large ovenproof, lidded casserole. Brown *1 clove garlic* until golden; remove and set aside. Brown the veal shanks carefully, turning them to brown on all sides without losing the marrow. Add the onions, carrots, and celery, adding more oil if needed, and cook for about 4 minutes, stirring so vegetables do not burn. Add the white wine and reduce for a minute or so. Add the tomatoes, bouquet garni, and cooked garlic, minced. Reduce briskly. Add the teaspoon of sugar if tomatoes are acid. Pour in the broth, stir well, and bring to a boil. Cover and place in a preheated 350° oven for 1 hour. Uncover and correct seasoning. Continue cooking for 10 to 15 minutes. Meanwhile, prepare classic garnish, gremolata, by mincing the *remaining clove of garlic* and mixing it with the lemon rind and parsley. Transfer the osso buco to a heated platter and sprinkle the gremolata over the meat. Serve with Risotto alla Milanese (page 558). Serves 6.

DILLKÖTT PA LAMM

Dill is an herb of ancient reputation. It is recorded in the medicinal rolls of ancient Egypt, and in the Middle Ages was accounted an excellent deterrent to witches, a reliable aid to flagging lovers. Today, in Sweden, its use is commonly confined to the kitchen where one of its characteristic uses is as seasoning for boiled lamb.

4 to 5 pounds boneless shoulder of lamb, cut up for stew	Salt and pepper
2 tablespoons fresh minced dill or 1 tablespoon dried dill	3 tablespoons butter
1 onion, stuck with 3 cloves	3 tablespoons flour
Bouquet garni (1 small bay leaf, 6 peppercorns, 4 sprigs parsley, tied in cheesecloth)	2 tablespoons wine vinegar or lemon juice
	1 teaspoon brown sugar, or to taste
	2 tablespoons capers (optional)
	1 lemon, sliced (optional)

Wipe the lamb thoroughly and put in a kettle with *half the dill*, the onion, the bouquet garni, 1 tablespoon salt, and $\frac{1}{2}$ teaspoon pepper. Cover with warm water—about $1\frac{1}{2}$ to 2 quarts. Bring to a boil, skim carefully. Cover, leaving a vent for steam to escape, and simmer for about 2 hours or until meat is tender. Strain stock, keep meat warm. Simmer stock until reduced to 4 cups. In another saucepan melt the butter and brown the flour. Add the reduced stock and stir until thickened and smooth. Simmer for 10 minutes. Add vinegar, sugar to taste, and *all but 1 tablespoon remaining dill*, minced. Return the lamb to the sauce, heat, and serve with *remaining dill* sprinkled on top. Garnish with capers and lemon. Serves 6.

KIBBEH BI SANIEH

To Lebanese expatriates the national dish, Kibbeh, invokes a well-spring of memories such as the ritual of pounding lamb (the Near East's principal meat) with a mortar and pestle, and the convivial *ghada* (noon meal) at which it is served. The version below is eaten hot; the second, a Lebanese equivalent of steak tartare, is consumed cold.

Basic mixture:
$1\frac{1}{4}$ pounds lean lamb, ground
1 large onion, finely chopped
$1\frac{1}{2}$ cups cracked wheat (burghul)
2 teaspoons salt, or to taste
$\frac{1}{2}$ teaspoon pepper
1 to 2 tablespoons ice water, as needed

Stuffing:
$1\frac{1}{2}$ cups butter
1 cup chopped onions
$\frac{3}{4}$ pound lean lamb, ground
$\frac{1}{2}$ cup chopped pine nuts
Salt and pepper to taste
$\frac{1}{2}$ teaspoon cinnamon

To prepare the basic mixture: Grind lamb and onion 3 times through the finest blade of a food chopper or pound to a paste. Wash the cracked wheat (burghul) in cold water and drain. Mix with lamb and grind twice more, adding salt, pepper, and enough ice water to blend mixture to a paste. *To prepare the stuffing*: Melt *one-half cup butter* and sauté onions until soft but not brown. Add lamb, nuts, and seasonings. Cook until lamb begins to brown. Butter an 11- by 9-inch baking pan and spread in it just less than half basic lamb mixture. Spread stuffing over it and top with remaining basic mixture. Score a diamond pattern over meat. Melt *remaining butter* and pour over meat. Bake in a preheated 400° oven for 20 minutes or until well browned. Serve hot or at room temperature. Serves 8.

VARIATION: *Raw Kibbeh*: Prepare only basic lamb mixture. Spread on a serving dish, score in diamond pattern, and serve as an appetizer, similar to steak tartare. Mixture may be shaped into tiny balls and served with toothpicks or on sesame crackers.

KUFTEH TABRIZ
(Persian Giant Meatball)

1 2½-pound shoulder of lamb	⅛ teaspoon powdered cloves
3 large onions	¼ cup black currants
½ teaspoon powdered turmeric	6 prunes, pitted and chopped
Salt and pepper	2 tablespoons shredded, dried
1 cup split peas	tangerine or orange peel
1¼ cups rice	4 large hard-boiled eggs, chopped
1 tablespoon fresh chopped dill or	¼ cup shelled, blanched, coarsely
1½ teaspoons dried dill	chopped pistachio nuts
1 tablespoon chopped scallions	¼ cup coarsely chopped walnuts
1 tablespoon chopped chives	½ cup lemon juice
1 tablespoon chopped parsley	2 teaspoons brown sugar
½ cup butter	½ teaspoon curry powder
½ teaspoon dried saffron, steeped in	2 teaspoons fresh minced mint or
2 tablespoons boiling water	1 teaspoon dried mint

Have butcher bone lamb and grind meat. Put lamb bones in a soup kettle with *1 onion*, coarsely chopped, turmeric, salt and pepper, and 6 cups water. Bring to a boil. Skim carefully, lower heat, and simmer gently for 1 hour. Meanwhile, separately cook split peas and *1 cup of rice* in salted water until very soft. Regrind the lamb and *1 onion* twice. Stew herbs in *4 tablespoons butter* until bright green. Mix the meat, cooked rice and peas, herbs, steeped saffron, and powdered cloves and season to taste with salt and pepper. Knead thoroughly to a smooth paste. Rinse a 12-cup bowl with cold water and fill with ½ the meat mixture, packing it in to take the shape of the bowl. Cover with currants, prunes, *1 tablespoon tangerine peel, 2 chopped eggs*, pistachios, and walnuts. Fry the *1 remaining onion*, cut into fine rings, in *2 tablespoons butter* and place on top of the dried fruit and meat mixture. Cover with remaining meat, rolling the meatball in the bowl to give it a completely round shape. Tie in cheesecloth and immerse in strained lamb broth, adding water to cover. Add *remaining one-quarter cup rice*, pounded to a powder or broken in a blender. Cover and simmer for 1 hour or until meat is well done. Add lemon juice, brown sugar to taste, curry powder, and *remaining tangerine peel* to broth. Simmer 5 to 10 minutes more. Sauté the mint in *remaining 2 tablespoons butter*. Remove meatball from cheesecloth and put on a serving platter; pour on a ladle or two of broth. Sprinkle with mint and *remaining 2 chopped eggs*. Slice meat like a melon. Serve broth separately as a sauce. Serves 8.

SHAMI KABOB
(Hindu Meat Patties)

4 medium onions
⅓ cup butter
2 cloves garlic, minced
1 tablespoon minced ginger root or
   ½ teaspoon powdered ginger
2 hot green peppers, minced (optional)
½ teaspoon crushed, dried,
   hot red chili pepper

1 teaspoon powdered cumin
½ teaspoon fresh coriander leaves
   or Italian parsley
1½ pounds lamb or beef, ground
⅓ cup split pea flour or
   very fine bread crumbs
Salt
2 limes

Chop *2 onions* and sauté in *half the butter*. Add garlic, ginger root, green and red pepper, cumin, and coriander leaves. Stir for about 1 minute and cool. Mix with the ground meat and split pea flour and season with salt. Form into 6 patties. Heat *remaining butter* in the same frying pan and sauté meat patties for 4 to 5 minutes on each side for medium rare lamb, and to taste for beef. Serve with *remaining onions*, sliced and in rings, and lime wedges as garnish. Serves 4 to 6.

VARIATION: *Seekh Kabob*: This same mixture, prepared without the split pea flour, may be rolled into 2- to 3-inch sausage rolls, slipped onto skewers, and broiled. Baste with oil and turn so kabobs brown evenly.

KHORESCHE ESFANAJ

Varieties of *khoresche* (stew) have been served in Persia for centuries. Esfanaj, one of the oldest, is a traditional night-time dish during the months of Muharram and Ramadan, when the faithful fast all day and gather for public dinners and religious celebrations at sundown.

1 4- to 5-pound shoulder of lamb,
   with bones, cut for stew
2 medium onions, finely chopped
½ cup olive oil
Salt
½ teaspoon pepper
1 teaspoon powdered turmeric
1 cup beef broth

¾ cup lemon juice
6 scallions, tops only, minced
2 bunches celery, leaves only, minced
1½ pounds spinach leaves, chopped
2 tablespoons fresh minced dill or
   1 tablespoon dried dill
½ cup dried pea beans, soaked for
   several hours

Brown the meat and onions in *2 tablespoons oil* in a casserole. Season with salt and pepper, turmeric, add broth and lemon juice. Cover and simmer for 10 to 15 minutes. Wilt the vegetables in a frying pan without adding water, stirring constantly. Add *remaining oil* and fry for 5 minutes. Add vegetables and dill to meat. Add pea beans and simmer for 45 minutes or until pea beans and meat are tender. Serves 6.

SHASHLIK

Kabobs, small pieces of meat broiled over an open fire, were for centuries skewered on nomads' swords. They are eaten throughout eastern Europe and the Middle East—the version below is from the Caucasus.

1 leg of lamb, boned and cut into 2-inch cubes	3 large onions, finely chopped
$\frac{3}{4}$ cup olive oil	1 clove garlic, minced (optional)
1 teaspoon dried thyme	$\frac{1}{2}$ cup lemon juice
4 crumbled bay leaves (optional)	3 or 4 dashes cayenne pepper
	Salt and pepper

Toss the meat thoroughly in the oil. Add the remaining ingredients, except salt and pepper, and mix well. Marinate for 5 hours. Skewer lamb. Brush with the marinade, season with salt and pepper, and broil under a high flame, or on coals, for 4 to 5 minutes on each side. Serve with a saffron rice or white rice pilaf. Serves 6 to 8.

VARIATIONS: Add $\frac{1}{2}$ cup dry red wine to marinade. Meat may be placed on skewers alternating with pieces of bacon, tomato, mushroom caps, green pepper, onion, and unpeeled eggplant, all brushed with oil before broiling. *Shashlik Karsky* is a thick rack of lamb marinated whole overnight and roasted whole on a spit or in the oven. *Lebanese and Turkish Kabobs* are marinated with a little oil, finely chopped onion, lemon juice, and yoghurt, and are highly seasoned. *Greek Souvlakia* are kabobs of lamb or mutton kidney cut in half and skewered with pieces of tomato, green pepper, and onion, brushed with oil, seasoned with salt and pepper, and broiled. For Indian skewered meat cumin powder or curry powder may be added.

DOLMATES
(Middle Eastern Stuffed Grape Leaves)

50 vine leaves (approximately), fresh or in jars	1 teaspoon fresh mint, chopped, or $\frac{1}{2}$ teaspoon dried mint (optional)
1 pound lamb, ground	$\frac{1}{4}$ teaspoon pepper
$\frac{1}{2}$ cup rice	1 teaspoon salt
2 medium onions, finely chopped	3 tablespoons butter
$\frac{1}{2}$ cup chopped parsley	2 cups beef broth
$\frac{1}{2}$ teaspoon powdered aniseed	Avgolemono Sauce (page 624)

Blanch the vine leaves for 2 to 3 minutes in boiling water, drain, and cool. Mix all the ingredients with the exception of the butter, broth, and sauce. Place vine leaves, dull side up, on a board. Place a generous tablespoon of the mixture on each leaf (use 2 leaves if they are small) and fold like an envelope; fold loosely, as stuffing will swell. Place in a buttered wide skillet, folded side down. Cover with broth and butter. Place a plate on the dolmates so they will not unwrap. Simmer slowly for 35 to 40 minutes; drain. Serve hot with avgolemono sauce. Makes about 25 to 30 dolmates.

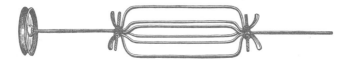

SOMALI LAMB WITH ROSE WATER

4 breasts of lamb, sliced
   into separate ribs
Juice of 3 lemons
Grated rind and juice of 2 oranges
2 tablespoons rose water
½ teaspoon powdered cloves
1 teaspoon powdered ginger

2 teaspoons salt
½ teaspoon cayenne pepper
½ cup chopped parsley
½ teaspoon pepper
1 cup beef broth
1 teaspoon cornstarch
½ cup golden seedless raisins (optional)

Place ribs in an oblong dish deep enough for ribs and marinade. Pour over ribs the next 5 ingredients, well mixed. Marinate ribs for 1 hour, turning a few times. Drain and dry ribs. Mix salt, pepper, and chopped parsley. Place dried ribs in floured pan, sprinkle with parsley mixture, and place in a cold oven which has been set at 350°. Bake for 1 hour. Remove to heated platter. Pour beef broth into roasting pan and scrape with a spoon over low heat. Add 1 teaspoon cornstarch mixed with a little cold water and simmer for a few minutes. Sprinkle ribs with raisins. Pass pan drippings in a sauceboat. Serve with buttered okra and baked plantain. Serves 4.

LEBANESE STUFFED LEG OF LAMB

1 7-pound leg of lamb, boned
2 cloves garlic
⅔ cup butter
1 onion
½ cup rice
1 cup beef broth

¼ cup pine nuts or
   slivered blanched almonds
3 tablespoons seedless raisins
⅛ teaspoon each: powdered allspice,
   nutmeg, and cinnamon
Salt and pepper

Have the butcher bone the lamb and have him scoop out about ½ pound of meat from the inside of the leg without damaging the outer shell. Grind this meat and reserve. Push little slivers of *1 clove of garlic* deep into the leg of lamb. Melt 4 tablespoons *butter* in a large saucepan and brown *1 onion*, chopped. Add rice and *remaining clove of garlic*, minced. Add ground lamb and stir until meat is no longer red. Add *one-half cup broth*, nuts, and raisins and season with spices and salt and pepper. Simmer for 10 to 12 minutes. Correct seasoning. Stuff the lamb with this mixture and sew it up well. Place in a large roasting pan well buttered with the *remaining butter*. Roast for ½ hour in a preheated 425° oven. Lower heat to 375° and roast slowly, basting often with *remaining one-half cup broth*, for about 1¼ hours. Serves 6 to 8.

ABBACCIO AL FORNO

Lamb as traditional Easter fare traces its origin to the Jewish Passover when, the Bible relates, the Lord commanded the Children of Israel to "take every man a lamb . . . without blemish" and slaughter it. He further commanded that they should smear the blood outside their doors that when He came to punish the Egyptians, He might know the Jews and pass over their houses. Thenceforth they were to prepare a feast of whole-roasted lamb each year in remembrance. In the intervening centuries Christians have adopted the Pascal lamb as a symbol of sacrifice and purity. The following recipe for *abbaccio* (milk-fed baby lamb) is an Easter specialty in Rome, where the roasting is often entrusted to the neighborhood *fornaro*, or baker.

1 5-pound leg of baby lamb	2 tablespoons dried rosemary
6 cloves garlic	1 teaspoon black pepper
1 tablespoon salt	$\frac{1}{2}$ to $\frac{3}{4}$ cup olive oil

Remove skin from lamb. Cut *2 cloves garlic* into thin slivers. Make several gashes in lamb with sharp pointed knife and insert a garlic sliver in each. Crush *remaining garlic* and combine with salt, rosemary, and pepper. Pound to a paste, adding olive oil gradually to make a fairly thick, spreadable paste. Spread over lamb, rubbing in well, and let stand at room temperature for 3 hours. Roast in a preheated 375° oven for 1 to $1\frac{1}{2}$ hours. Baste frequently with olive oil. Slice and serve with skimmed pan juices. Serves 6 to 8.

TO MAKE A DEVONSHIRE SQUAB PIE

During the Middle Ages any dish of meat, fowl, or fish with a top crust was called a pie. Usually they served as accompaniment to the great roasts at the baronial table. On occasion an enormous nonedible pie was carried to the banquet table containing a surprise for the guests. The best remembered banquet bonus is four and twenty blackbirds but the favorite of the time was a dwarf springing through the pie crust headlong into a bowl of custard. Even Devonshire pie has its own surprise. Beneath its crisp crust there is no squab. The pie is traditionally made with lamb but the old name has remained.

$\frac{1}{4}$ cup butter	$\frac{1}{2}$ teaspoon powdered nutmeg
$2\frac{1}{2}$ pounds boneless lamb, cut into 1-inch pieces	$\frac{1}{2}$ teaspoon powdered cinnamon
Salt and pepper	4 large onions, thinly sliced
8 large apples, peeled, cored, and sliced	1 cup Brown Sauce (page 620)
2 tablespoons brown sugar	1 cup beef broth
	$\frac{1}{2}$ recipe Short Pastry (page 682)

Heat the butter and brown the meat. Season with salt and pepper. Put a layer of meat in an 8-cup casserole and cover with a layer of apples. Sprinkle these with a little of the sugar and spices. Put over this a layer of onions. Repeat layers ending with apples, sugar, and spices. Half fill casserole with mixed sauce and broth. Roll out the pastry and cover the pie. Press pastry to sides of dish and flute it. Prick all over with a fork. Cover pie with foil to prevent burning. Put in a preheated 425° oven for 10 minutes, lower heat to 350° and bake for 1 hour and 20 minutes. Remove foil for last 10 to 15 minutes. Serves 6 to 8.

CHINE DE MOUTON AUX CONCOMBRES

William Verral, master of the White-Hart Inn in Sussex, England, guaranteed in his *Complete System of Cookery* (1759), that even "the meanest Capacity shall never err" in achieving good results. Verral, who had once been apprenticed to a Continental chef, could not resist flaunting his learning by giving French titles to his recipes.

1 6-pound shoulder of lamb
Salt and pepper
1 teaspoon powdered mace
$\frac{1}{4}$ pound lean bacon, minced
$\frac{1}{2}$ pound mushrooms, minced or ground
4 shallots, finely chopped
2 onions, finely chopped
1 cup bread crumbs

$\frac{1}{2}$ teaspoon each: thyme, marjoram, summer savory, and tarragon
2 tablespoons chopped parsley
1 egg
$\frac{1}{2}$ cup butter
$1\frac{1}{2}$ cups beef broth
8 cucumbers
2 to 3 tablespoons flour
Juice of $\frac{1}{2}$ lemon

Have butcher bone but not tie the meat. Season it with salt and pepper and mace. In a large casserole, render the bacon and fry the mushrooms, shallots, and *half the onions*. Mix with the bread crumbs, herbs, *half the parsley*, and the egg, slightly beaten. Spread the meat with the stuffing and tie neatly. Add *3 tablespoons butter* to the casserole and brown the meat and *remaining onions*. Add *1 cup broth* and cover. Put into preheated 375° oven for about $1\frac{1}{2}$ hours for medium rare meat. Peel and cut the cucumbers into 2-inch sticks. Put in a bowl and salt generously. Let stand $\frac{1}{2}$ hour and press out the water. Roll them in flour seasoned with pepper and fry in *remaining butter* to a golden color. Carve meat and add *remaining one-half cup broth* and lemon juice to taste to meat drippings. Pile cucumbers to one side of the meat, pour on sauce and sprinkle with *remaining parsley*. Serves 8. Zucchini may replace cucumber as garnish.

EPIGRAMME D'AGNEAU

Among lettered men of the mid-eighteenth century, epigrams were a favorite form of dinner table repartee. When a less learned marquise, however, heard that one of her guests had feasted on "excellent epigrams," she ordered her chef to prepare the same. Finding no reference to the recipe in any cookbook, he did what any good French chef would do; he improvised and created the lamb dish which, in spite of its malapropos title, has been a delicacy ever since.

2 pounds boned breast of lamb
1 large onion, chopped
4 tablespoons butter, melted
Bouquet garni (1 clove garlic, 1 bay
  leaf, 4 sprigs parsley, 3 sprigs
  celery leaves, 6 crushed peppercorns,
  $\frac{1}{4}$ teaspoon thyme, tied in cheesecloth)

$1\frac{1}{2}$ cups beef broth
6 rib lamb chops
2 eggs, beaten
Salt and pepper
$\frac{3}{4}$ cup dry bread crumbs
$\frac{1}{2}$ cup Clarified Butter (page 630)
Watercress or asparagus tips for garnish

Brown the breast of lamb and onions in the hot melted butter; add the bouquet and broth and simmer for 1 hour or until meat is tender. Reserve broth. Cool meat under a weight. Cut into pieces the size and shape of chops. Dip the shaped pieces and the chops in the eggs seasoned with salt and pepper. Roll in bread crumbs and fry in clarified butter until golden brown. Arrange alternating pieces of lamb breast and chops in a circle. Serve lamb braising liquid as sauce and watercress or asparagus tips as garnish. Serves 6.

RATONNET OF LAMB

The French always speak of milk-fed baby lamb in the most sentimental terms. Dumas wrote that *agneau* (lamb) is derived from the Latin *agnoscere*, to recognize, because the lamb "recognizes its mother as soon as it is born." Similarly, the figurative meaning of Ratonnet, a recipe which appeared in his *Dictionnaire*, is "little pet" or "darling."

1 leg of lamb, cut into thin slices
  as for scallopini
1 tablespoon mixed green herbs (such as
  chervil, chives, tarragon, marjoram)
2 tablespoons chopped parsley
5 scallions, bulbs and green tops,
  minced
2 cloves garlic, minced
$\frac{1}{2}$ cup olive oil

Juice of 1 lemon
$\frac{1}{2}$ cup dry white wine
Salt and pepper
1 cup ground cooked chicken or veal
$\frac{1}{2}$ cup ground mushrooms, cooked
  in butter
$\frac{1}{4}$ teaspoon powdered nutmeg
1 cup Sauce Italienne (see Sauce
  Duxelles, page 623)

Pound lamb slices to flatten and widen them. Place in a wide enameled pan and sprinkle with herbs, parsley, scallions, garlic, olive oil, lemon juice, wine, and ½ teaspoon pepper. Marinate for 2 hours. Meanwhile, mix chicken with mushrooms, salt and pepper to taste, and nutmeg. Drain lamb and pat dry. Reserve marinade. Spread slices with chicken stuffing and roll as for Beef Birds (page 504). Skewer and broil, basting with marinade and turning meat to brown evenly. Add drippings and remaining strained marinade to sauce Italienne and simmer for 5 minutes. Pass separately. Serves 6 to 8.

COTELETTES A LA MAINTENON

In his last will and testament, the poet Scarron not only gave his wife carte blanche to remarry, but he also wrote: "I have forced her to fast, and that should have given her a good appetite; let her enjoy it then a little." Thus, to honor his dying wish, Madame de Maintenon married Louis XIV and developed a taste for luxurious foods. At her request the court chefs prepared such culinary masterpieces as these lamb chops. Indeed, such *savoir-faire* so impressed Louis that years later, on his deathbed, he not only insured Madame de Maintenon a pension but, as she related, asked her to "forgive him for not having been kind enough."

12 rib lamb chops
2 large onions, finely chopped
½ cup butter
¼ pound mushrooms, minced

Salt and pepper
1 cup Béchamel Sauce (page 618)
½ cup fresh bread crumbs

Broil the lamb chops on 1 side only, 3 inches from a hot flame. Meanwhile, cook the onions in *3 tablespoons butter* until soft and transparent. In *3 more tablespoons butter* cook the mushrooms for 5 to 6 minutes. Season with salt and pepper. Mix the béchamel sauce, onions, and mushrooms. Coat the uncooked side of the chops with a thick layer of this mixture. Top with bread crumbs and dot with *remaining butter*. Place in a preheated 400° oven for 8 minutes, then put under the broiler until brown and bubbly. Serve in a ring on a heated platter. A double amount of béchamel, onions, and mushrooms may be made and half of it thinned out slightly with milk or broth and passed as a sauce. Serves 6.

SUCKLING PIG

By Charles Lamb's definition the life of the suckling pig ends when it is "under a moon old." Under the Roman Empire consumption of the unweaned animal reached such proportions that the pig-world was nearly depopulated, and laws had to be passed prohibiting the slaughter of virgin swine. Thereafter, the suckling pig became holiday food. It is traditionally roasted on a spit and basted with beer in Cuba, garnished with apples in England and four-leaf clovers in Hungary, and stuffed with green maize in South Africa. As the poet Pouvoisin apologized: "Regret not, little pig, thine early fate: Honours are thine beyond the fattening sty,—We eat thee, brother, and incorporate Thy substance, thus, in our humanity." Below are Spanferkel in the Bavarian manner, Cochinillo Asado as prepared since the early eighteenth century at Madrid's Restaurante El Sobrino de Botín, and a recipe originating in China.

1 12- to 14-pound suckling pig	2 to 3 cups water
Salt	1 pint bottle dark beer
Marjoram	1 lemon or small apple for garnish
Caraway seeds	1 tablespoon flour
1 cup melted butter, or	$\frac{1}{2}$ cup sour cream
$\frac{1}{2}$ pound bacon, sliced	

Wipe pig with damp cloth and sprinkle inside with a little salt, marjoram, and caraway seeds. Stuff pig with crumpled aluminum foil so it will hold its shape. Tie front legs forward and tie back legs under body. Prop mouth open with a block of wood. Pierce skin in several places with the tines of a fork. Rub with salt, marjoram, caraway seeds, and butter. If using bacon, place 4 strips across back of pig. If using butter, brush on back. Place pig on rack in an open roasting pan and cover ears and tail with double thicknesses of aluminum foil so they will not burn. Add water to cover bottom of pan. Roast in preheated 350° oven allowing 30 minutes per pound. Add water to pan as needed. Brush pig with additional butter several times during roasting or replace bacon strips as they become crisp. Pierce skin several times during roasting and baste frequently. Remove foil from ears and tail for last 30 minutes of cooking and baste with beer 4 or 5 times during this last roasting. To serve, remove wood from mouth and place a lemon or apple in it. Place on heated platter. Skim pan juices, add a little water to pan and bring to a boil, scraping coagulated pan juices into sauce. Dissolve flour in 1 to 2 tablespoons cold water, stir into gravy, and simmer until thickened. Stir in sour cream until smooth, heat thoroughly, and serve in heated gravy boat. Serves 8 to 10.

VARIATIONS: *Cochinillo Asado (Suckling Pig, Spanish Style)*: Stuff pig with a mixture of 4 cloves of garlic, minced, 3 onions, minced, 2 cups of minced parsley, and a pinch each of thyme and marjoram. Sprinkle outside with salt and pepper, pierce skin with fork and place on rack in open roasting pan. Pour in equal amounts of dry white wine and water to cover bottom of pan. Roast as above, basting frequently with pan juices. Stop basting for last 30 minutes and rub the pig with bacon or melted butter, or brush with olive oil to brown. Do not baste again.

Chinese Roast Suckling Pig: Roast pig split and flattened, with head and tail intact. Pour boiling water over skin and pat dry. Rub both sides with five-spice powder and brush with soy sauce and honey. Marinate for 1 hour. Broil, turning every 10 minutes for 1 to 1½ hours, brushing with honey several times. Roast until juice runs clear and meat is red. Serve cut in pieces with Sweet and Sour Sauce (page 620).

MORVAN HAM A LA CREME

1 10- to 12-pound precooked ham	8 peppercorns, ½ teaspoon thyme,
2 stalks celery, chopped	1 bay leaf, tied in cheesecloth)
2 medium onions, chopped	1 cup dry Madeira or red port
6 mushrooms, chopped	1 cup beef broth
1 carrot, sliced	1 cup heavy cream
Bouquet garni (4 sprigs parsley,	Salt and pepper

Simmer ham in water for 30 minutes. Cool slightly and remove skin. Place in a roasting pan with the celery, onions, mushrooms, carrot, bouquet garni, and wine. Cover and bake in a preheated 325° oven for 1 hour, basting frequently. Keep ham warm. Remove all fat from the drippings, strain, and simmer drippings on top of the stove with the broth; reduce by a third. Add cream and season to taste with salt and pepper. Simmer for 5 to 6 minutes or until sauce thickens. Slice ham, pour strained sauce over it, and pass remainder in a sauceboat. Serves 12 to 14.

HONEY-GLAZED HAM WITH FIGS

The ancients attributed magical, medicinal powers to the sweet and juicy fig. Athenaeus went so far as to state that "the fig is the most useful of all the fruits which grow on trees." Apicius prescribes it as an ingredient in this classical Roman recipe.

1 10-pound precooked ham	10 crushed peppercorns
2 pounds dried figs	$\frac{1}{2}$ cup honey
3 bay leaves, crushed	Cloves
2 cups dry white wine	

Place the ham and all remaining ingredients, with exception of the honey and cloves, in a roasting pan. Add enough water to barely cover the figs. Bake in a preheated 350° oven for 1 hour. Remove the skin from the ham. Score fat in diamond pattern, spread with honey, stud with cloves, and bake in a preheated 400° oven for $\frac{1}{2}$ hour, adding a little water or wine so figs do not burn. Serves 12 to 14.

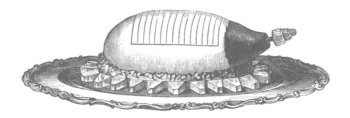

RED GLAZED HAM

Tart, red barberries were traditionally used to color this ham, adapted from an eighteenth-century Swedish cookbook by Johan Winberg.

1 10- to 12-pound precooked ham	3 tablespoons sugar
3 egg whites	Red food coloring
2 tablespoons red fruit syrup (lingonberry, raspberry, or strawberry)	

Parboil ham in boiling water for 20 minutes or long enough to remove rind easily. Cool completely, remove rind, and score fat. Mix egg whites with a fork until broken up but not frothy. Mix in syrup and sugar. Add red coloring—about 6 drops for a rich red. Cover ham with a thick coating of mixture and bake in a preheated 325° oven for 50 minutes, brushing with additional glaze every 10 minutes. Serves 10 to 12. The ham may be decorated with candied cherries, attached with toothpicks, after the first glazing.

JAMBON PERSILLE
(French Easter Ham in Parsley Jelly)

1 8-pound precooked ham	$\frac{1}{2}$ teaspoon each dried tarragon
1 cracked veal knuckle	and chervil
1 calf's foot, cleaned and split	2 bottles dry white wine
Soup greens, cut up (2 onions, 1 carrot,	1 tablespoon wine vinegar
celery tops)	White pepper to taste
Bouquet garni (1 bay leaf, 1 clove garlic,	2 cups chopped parsley
2 cloves, 8 peppercorns, 6 shallots,	
6 sprigs parsley, tied in cheesecloth)	

Put everything except the parsley into a large stew pot. Add enough water to just cover. Cover and simmer slowly for 3 hours or until ham is loose on the bones. Remove the ham and bone it. Strain, clarify, and cool the broth. Break the ham into small pieces with a fork and pack into a bowl. When the broth is slightly thickened, mix with parsley, pour over the ham, and mix well. There should be $\frac{1}{2}$ inch of jelly over the ham. Chill well. Sprinkle with remaining parsley, serve and slice in the bowl. Serves 20 to 24 as an appetizer. If calf's foot is not available, add 1 envelope softened gelatin to each 2 cups warm clarified broth and let thicken slightly before adding parsley.

CARNE DE PORCO CON AMEIJOAS
(Portuguese Pork and Clams)

3 pounds boneless pork for stewing,	3 large onions, diced
cut into 1-inch cubes	3 tomatoes, peeled, seeded, and chopped
Salt and black pepper	1 small jar pimentos
2 tablespoons paprika	18 clams, in shells, scrubbed
5 cloves garlic, crushed	Tabasco to taste
3 bay leaves	Minced parsley
2 cups dry white wine	12 slices French bread, fried in olive
4 tablespoons melted lard or bacon fat	oil and rubbed with garlic

Sprinkle pork with salt, pepper, and a *pinch of paprika*. Combine *remaining paprika*, garlic, bay leaves, and white wine and simmer for 10 minutes. Cool and pour over seasoned pork. Marinate overnight in refrigerator, turning once or twice. Heat *2 tablespoons lard* and in it sauté onions until soft but not brown. Add tomatoes and pimentos and simmer until mixture is dry. Season with a little salt and pepper and add clams. Cover and simmer until clams open—about 3 minutes. Remove pork from marinade. Reserve marinade. Dry pork thoroughly and brown in *remaining fat*. Add enough marinade to barely cover pork and simmer rapidly for 30 minutes or until pork is tender. Uncover and simmer until mixture is fairly dry —about 15 minutes. Combine pork and clam mixture and stir together. Season with Tabasco. Simmer for 10 minutes and serve garnished with minced parsley and garlic toast. Serves 6.

PYG IN A COFFIN
(Old English Ham in Pastry)

1 12- to 14-pound precooked ham
2 large onions, sliced
Bouquet garni (8 sprigs parsley,
   2 bay leaves, $\frac{1}{2}$ teaspoon thyme,
   6 shallots, 10 peppercorns,
   3 cloves, tied in cheesecloth)
1 bottle dry white wine
2 recipes Short Pastry (page 682) made
   with 2 eggs and milk instead of water
   or 1 recipe Brioche dough (page 653)
   made with 3 eggs instead of 6
4 slices bacon
1 onion, finely chopped
$\frac{1}{2}$ pound mushrooms, minced
1 pound pork, ground

$\frac{1}{4}$ teaspoon dried sage
1 teaspoon dried rosemary
Freshly ground pepper
$\frac{1}{3}$ cup shelled, unsalted pistachio nuts
$\frac{1}{2}$ cup currants, plumped in boiling water
2 egg yolks
1 cup Madeira wine
2 envelopes unflavored gelatin
2 beef bouillon cubes
$\frac{1}{4}$ cup currant jelly
1 tablespoon brown sugar
1 tablespoon Dijon-style mustard
2 teaspoons cornstarch
2 tablespoons butter

Place ham on sliced onions in a deep, narrow kettle. Add the bouquet garni and wine. Add enough water to barely cover ham. Cover tightly and let ham simmer gently for 1 hour. Cool in the broth. Strain and reserve broth. When cool enough to handle, remove rind from ham. Meanwhile, prepare pastry and chill for 2 hours. Prepare the stuffing: Fry the bacon in a large skillet until crisp, remove, crumble and reserve. Fry the chopped onion and mushrooms for 5 minutes and add the ground pork. Cook for 10 minutes. Season with sage, rosemary, and freshly ground pepper. Mix in crumbled bacon, pistachios, and currants. Cool. Roll out the pastry in an oval large enough to wrap the ham in completely. Spread the cooled stuffing on the pastry about the same size as the ham. Pat ham dry and place it top-side down on the stuffing and wrap in pastry, sealing it neatly. Invert into a shallow, buttered pan. Cut any leftover pastry into decorative shapes with cookie cutter and apply to ham by brushing pastry with egg yolks mixed with a little cold water. Brush the casing with egg yolks. Cut an opening in the middle of the pastry for steam to escape and put $\frac{1}{2}$-inch collar of pastry around it. Bake in a preheated 425° oven for 20 minutes, lower heat to 350°, and continue baking for about 1 to $1\frac{1}{2}$ hours or until crust is golden. If it browns too quickly, cover loosely with foil. Remove from the oven and pour in *one-half cup Madeira* through the small vent. Soak the gelatin in $\frac{1}{3}$ cup cold water. Remove all fat from ham broth. Reduce briskly by boiling to 3 cups liquid. Add bouillon cubes and *remaining Madeira*. Pour half the broth into shallow pan, add the gelatin, and chill until set. Make a sauce with the remaining broth as follows: Melt the currant jelly in the broth with the brown sugar and mustard. Dissolve the cornstarch in 1 to 2 tablespoons cold water, add to the sauce, and simmer for 1 minute. Swirl in the cold butter. Serve ham warm, or cold with diced aspic around it. Pass sauce separately, hot or cold, depending on how ham is served. Serves 14 to 16.

MADEIRA HAM WITH CINNAMON

1 to 2 pounds ham steak
½ cup Madeira wine
6 cloves
10 crushed peppercorns
½ teaspoon dried marjoram
1 teaspoon powdered cinnamon
2 tablespoons olive oil

1 large onion, thinly sliced
2 medium tomatoes, peeled,
  seeded, and sliced
2 white turnips or large carrots, sliced
1 apple, peeled, cored, and sliced
½ cup pitted green and black olives
Pepper

Marinate the meat in the wine with the cloves, peppercorns, marjoram, and cinnamon for about 2 hours, turning once. Spread olive oil in bottom of roasting pan. Arrange the sliced vegetables, apples, and olives in the pan. Drain marinade from ham and pour on vegetables. Sprinkle with pepper. Bake in a preheated 350° oven for 1 hour, uncovered. Add the ham, sprinkle with pepper, cover and continue baking for 50 minutes. Serves 4 to 6.

PIEDS DE PORC A LA STE-MENEHOULD

Alexandre Dumas' recipe for breaded grilled pigs' feet began: "Singe as many feet as a pig has, generally 4." Such explicitness was hardly necessary, for the French had been familiar with the dish ever since the fifteenth century when it was invented by peasants at Ste-Menehould in northeastern France. While fighting the English, Charles VII stopped at the town which had been so badly ravaged that the only food remaining for the king to eat were a few chickens and pigs' feet improved as below. In America, pigs' knuckles are often substituted for the trotters.

4 pigs' knuckles
1 large onion, stuck with a clove
1 small carrot, quartered
Bouquet garni (1 bay leaf, 4 sprigs
  parsley, 1 clove garlic, celery leaves,
  pinch thyme, tied in cheesecloth)
1 cup dry white wine (optional)

1 tablespoon salt
½ teaspoon pepper
4 egg yolks
4 teaspoons milk
⅔ cup bread crumbs
½ cup butter, melted

Put the well-cleaned and washed knuckles in a large kettle with the onion, carrot, bouquet garni, wine, salt, and pepper. Cover with cold water, bring to a boil, and skim carefully. Lower heat and simmer gently until very tender—about 1½ hours. Remove knuckles from broth. Strain broth and reserve for other use (clarified and flavored with Madeira, it makes a very delicate aspic). Remove bones from knuckles and pat dry. Mix yolks with milk and beat slightly. Dip knuckles in egg, then roll in bread crumbs. Roll again in egg and bread crumbs. Grill under the broiler, turning and basting frequently with melted butter until deep golden brown. Serve with Sauce for a Poor Man (page 636) or tomato sauce. Serves 4.

MELTON MOWBRAY PIE

Such is the fame of pork pies from the English town, Melton Mowbray, that a poem was written by Richard Le Gallienne in tribute:

Strange pie that is almost a passion!
O passion immoral for pie!
Unknown are the ways that they fashion
Unknown and unseen of the eye.
The pie that is marbled and mottled,
The pie that digests with a sigh:
For all is not Bass that is bottled,
And all is not pork that is pie.

$2\frac{1}{2}$ pounds lean pork loin or chops, with bones	$\frac{1}{4}$ teaspoon rosemary, pounded to a powder
1 small bay leaf	1 teaspoon salt
$\frac{1}{4}$ teaspoon powdered mace	$\frac{1}{2}$ teaspoon pepper
1 medium onion	1 recipe Hot Water Dough
2 teaspoons chopped chives	(page 680)
2 teaspoons chopped parsley	1 egg yolk

Put meat, bay leaf, mace, onion, herbs, salt, and pepper in a saucepan with enough water to barely cover and simmer for about 2 hours. Reserve stock. Cool, remove bones, and dice or grind the meat and onion. Correct seasoning. Line an oiled 4-cup deep mold, preferably an oval one, with two-thirds of the dough rolled out to $\frac{1}{4}$-inch thickness, leaving $\frac{1}{2}$ inch overlapping edge of dish. Put in filling and $\frac{1}{2}$ cup of the stock. Reserve rest of stock. Cover with remaining dough rolled out for the lid. Trim. Seal edges well with cold water, and crimp. Roll out any leftover bits of dough to make decorative shaped pieces, wet slightly on underside and attach to pie. Make a hole in center of pie and surround with small collar of dough. Beat egg yolk with a little cold water and brush on crust. Bake in a preheated 425° oven for 10 minutes. Lower heat to 325° and bake for 2 hours. Cover with foil if crust browns too fast. Remove from the oven and pour in remaining heated stock. Cool the pie completely before serving. Cut into wedges. Serves 6.

PORK LOIN WITH PRUNES AND APPLES

The Danish sometimes refer to the dish below as "mock duck," prunes and apples being a favorite stuffing for their roast duck as well.

2 5-pound pork loins, boned	$\frac{1}{2}$ cup butter
Salt and pepper	1 to 2 cups beef broth or water
Powdered ginger as needed	1 tablespoon flour
$\frac{1}{2}$ pound prunes, parboiled and pitted	2 tablespoons red currant jelly
3 large apples, peeled, cored, and sliced	$\frac{1}{2}$ cup sour cream (optional)

Sprinkle cut sides of pork loins with a little salt, pepper, and ginger. Combine prunes and apples and place on top of one loin. Cover with second loin. Tie securely with string. Rub outside of meat with salt, pepper, and ginger. Heat butter and brown pork loin slowly on all sides. Add enough broth or water to cover bottom of pan. Cover tightly and braise slowly for about $1\frac{1}{2}$ hours or until meat is tender. Add broth or water as needed. Remove meat to heated platter. Skim excess fat from gravy. Dissolve flour in 1 to 2 tablespoons cold water and stir into gravy. Add jelly and stir over low heat until melted. Add sour cream and heat thoroughly. Season to taste. Slice pork loin and serve gravy separately. Serves 8 to 10.

FRICASSEE WITH APRICOTS

The Romans discovered the apricot during their campaigns in Armenia. They dubbed it *praecocia* because of its precocious June ripening, and by the first century A.D. they had succeeded in transplanting it to their capital. Apicius recommended combining the fruit with pork as follows.

3 tablespoons butter	$\frac{1}{2}$ teaspoon each: dried mint, dill,
2 tablespoons olive oil or salad oil	cumin powder, and pepper
2 pounds boneless pork,	Salt
cut into small cubes	2 teaspoons honey
6 shallots or 1 large onion,	1 tablespoon wine vinegar
finely chopped	1 cup dried pitted apricots,
1 cup dry white wine	previously soaked for 2 hours
1 cup beef broth	1 teaspoon cornstarch

In a heavy pot with a lid, mix *2 tablespoons butter* with the oil. Brown the meat, adding shallots half way through. Add the wine and cook briskly for 5 minutes. Add the broth. Pound the herbs and spices together with 1 teaspoon salt and add to the meat. Dilute honey in the vinegar and add to meat along with the apricots. Cover and simmer gently for $1\frac{1}{2}$ to 2 hours or until meat is very tender. Dilute cornstarch in a little cold water and add to the sauce. Stir until thickened. Turn off heat, swirl in *remaining tablespoon butter*, and serve immediately in a heated dish. Serves 6. This recipe may also be made with leftover cooked pork or lamb.

GOLDEN RISSOLES

For centuries pork formed the basis of the English yeoman's diet. Slaughtered in the late fall, the family pig provided a variety of fresh, smoked, and salted meats throughout the winter. This recipe for meatballs with a golden crust was popular in the Middle Ages. Less tender cuts of beef or veal were also prepared in this manner.

1 recipe Fritter Batter (page 583) made with sugar, white wine, and a few drops almond extract
1 pound pork, beef, or veal shoulder, ground
1 teaspoon salt
$\frac{1}{8}$ teaspoon black pepper

$\frac{1}{4}$ teaspoon powdered allspice
$\frac{1}{8}$ teaspoon powdered nutmeg
$\frac{1}{4}$ teaspoon powdered ginger
$\frac{1}{2}$ teaspoon dried sage
$\frac{1}{2}$ teaspoon dried thyme
4 eggs, separated
Corn or peanut oil for deep frying

Prepare fritter batter. Mix pork thoroughly with salt, pepper, allspice, nutmeg, ginger, sage, and thyme. Beat egg whites until stiff and mix gently into meat. Beat yolks lightly and reserve. Heat oil to 360°. Shape meatballs about the size of limes and drop a few at a time into oil. Deep fry for 8 to 10 minutes or until balls float on surface and are firm. Drain on paper toweling until they are as dry as possible. Coat with batter and refry at 375° for 3 to 5 minutes or until they are light golden but not brown. Drain well and thread onto skewers. If skewers are large, several balls can go on each but leave $1\frac{1}{2}$ inches between them. Dab well on all sides with thick coating of egg yolk. Broil in a preheated broiler, turning frequently so that all sides become golden. Dab on more egg yolk if necessary. Remove from skewers and serve plain or with Cumberland Sauce (page 635). Makes 10 to 12 balls. Serves 4 to 6 as an appetizer. Balls may be made much smaller (about the size of walnuts) for cocktail parties.

ROAST PORK WITH LEMONS AND ORANGES

It was a culinary rule of thumb in medieval England to accompany pork with some of the same things that fed and flavored the omnivorous pig, such as wild sage or garlic, and windfall apples. Later, when citrus fruits were imported, they were used as well. This recipe is adapted from *The Compleat Cook*, published anonymously in London in 1655.

2 loins of pork, about 7 chops each
4 anchovy fillets, each cut into 4 pieces
6 tablespoons butter
$\frac{1}{2}$ teaspoon dried thyme
1 teaspoon powdered mace
1 teaspoon salt

$\frac{1}{2}$ teaspoon pepper
3 onions, chopped
1 lemon, thinly sliced
1 orange, thinly sliced
1 cup dry white wine
2 cups beef broth

Have the butcher separate the bones for easy slicing of the meat. With a sharp-pointed paring knife make slits in the meat and insert the pieces of anchovy fillets. Mix *4 tablespoons butter*, thyme, mace, salt, and pepper to make a paste. Spread over the roast. Spread the remaining *2 tablespoons butter* in a large roasting pan and place the meat in it. Surround with onions and the sliced lemon and orange. Place in a preheated 400° oven. Roast for 30 minutes. Add the white wine and *one-half cup broth*. Reduce oven temperature to 350° and roast for 2 hours, basting once every ½ hour and *adding broth as needed*. When roast is done, keep hot on a heated platter. Remove fat from roasting pan, add *remaining beef broth*, and deglaze the pan. Simmer for 5 minutes and strain. Serve in a sauceboat. Serves 6 to 8.

SZEKELY GULYAS

The modern gulyás, a word meaning "herdsmen's meat," evolved from an improvised stew of the ancient Magyars of Hungary. Originally it consisted of whatever fresh meat, vegetables, and seasonings the no-mads could gather during their daily travels, each man dropping his con-tribution into the communal cauldron, or *bogrács*, on his return to camp at night. Székely Gulyás, which adds sauerkraut to the basic recipe, comes from the Transylvanian region, now part of Rumania.

3½ pounds sauerkraut	2½ cups dry white wine
2 large onions, chopped	3 pounds boned loin of pork,
¼ cup bacon fat, melted	cut into ½-inch slices
1 teaspoon caraway seeds	1 tablespoon paprika
½ teaspoon dried tarragon	2 cups sour cream, heated
Salt and pepper	

Rinse the sauerkraut and drain. Fry *half the onion* in *half the bacon fat* in a heavy saucepan until golden. Add the sauerkraut and fry, stirring until it begins to turn golden brown. Stir in caraway seeds, tarragon, ½ teaspoon pepper, *2 cups wine*, and enough water to cover. Bring to a boil and simmer for 3 hours, adding water or wine if too dry. Meanwhile, heat *remaining bacon fat* and fry the pork slices, add *remaining onion* and finish browning. Pour off excess fat, season with salt and pepper and paprika, and cook slowly for 2 to 3 minutes. Add *remaining wine* and ⅓ cup water, cover, and cook very slowly for 1½ hours, adding water if too dry. Combine pork, sauerkraut, and sour cream and serve immediately. Serves 8 to 10.

537

LION'S HEAD CABBAGE

Meatballs, whose shape reminds Chinese of the revered lion, and mustard cabbage, a vegetable indigenous to the Orient, are the principal ingredients of this recipe.

$1\frac{1}{2}$ pounds boneless pork, not too lean
8 dried Chinese mushrooms, soaked $\frac{1}{2}$ hour
3 thin slices ginger root, minced, or 1 teaspoon powdered ginger
15 water chestnuts (2 small cans), minced
3 scallions, bulbs and green tops, minced
2 eggs, beaten

5 teaspoons cornstarch
1 teaspoon sugar
1 teaspoon salt
Sprinkling of pepper
Vegetable oil for deep frying
1 head mustard cabbage
3 tablespoons vegetable oil
$1\frac{1}{2}$ cups chicken broth
2 tablespoons dry sherry

Have butcher grind the pork coarsely. Dry the soaked mushrooms and mince. Mix pork, mushrooms, ginger root, water chestnuts, and scallions. Mix with beaten eggs and *2 teaspoons cornstarch*, sugar, salt, and pepper. Toss lightly together until just mixed. Wet hands and divide and mold pork into 6 large meatballs. Heat frying oil to 375° and put meat in a frying basket, lower into oil, and fry for 5 to 6 minutes. Remove and drain on paper towels. Remove core from mustard cabbage, separate the leaves, and cut into large pieces. Heat the 3 tablespoons oil and fry the cabbage for about 2 to 3 minutes or until slightly limp. Add meatballs to cabbage. Pour on *one and one-quarter cups broth* mixed with sherry, cover and simmer for about $1\frac{1}{2}$ hours. Remove cabbage to hot platter, leaving broth in the pan. Arrange meatballs over cabbage. Add *remaining cornstarch* to *remaining cold broth*. Add to hot broth in the pan and stir until thickened and hot and pour over meat and cabbage. Serves 6.

ADOBO

Even after four centuries of Spanish rule, the only influence to rub off on the classic Philippine stew, Adobo, is alien garlic. Preparation of the poultry and pork differs from Western procedures: the meats are boiled until tender and then fried. The Spanish name describes dressed leather and dressed meat alike.

2 pounds boneless pork, cut into $1\frac{1}{2}$-inch cubes
3 pounds chicken, cut into $1\frac{1}{2}$-inch pieces
$\frac{3}{4}$ cup cider vinegar
5 cloves garlic, crushed

2 teaspoons salt
$\frac{1}{2}$ teaspoon freshly ground pepper
1 bay leaf
1 tablespoon soy sauce
2 cups beef broth
Corn oil for frying

Mix all the ingredients with the exception of the broth and oil in a glass or earthenware bowl. Marinate for 1 hour, turning meat and chicken twice. Put meat and marinade in a saucepan with broth to cover and bring to a boil. Lower heat and simmer for 30 minutes. Remove chicken and simmer pork 15 to 20 minutes longer. Uncover the pan to reduce juices during last 10 minutes. Heat 2 to 3 tablespoons oil in a frying pan and fry the boiled pork, chicken, and garlic until brown, adding oil as needed. Discard bay leaf and simmer meat juices. Pour over meats. Serve with rice. Serves 8 to 10.

SPARERIBS

> According to ancient Chinese legend, it was a clumsy peasant boy, Bo-Bo, who in burning down his father's pigsty first tasted the joys of cooked pork. As Charles Lamb relates in his "Dissertation upon Roast Pig," imitators were soon building and burning down pigsties at such a rate that only the fortuitous arrival of a genius with a cooking grill saved the science of architecture from being lost altogether. Since then the Chinese have learned to prepare pork in dozens of more subtle ways. This sweet and sour dish emanates from the Honan region.

2 pounds pork spareribs, bones cracked	2 tablespoons Haisein sauce (optional)
3 tablespoons sugar	$\frac{1}{2}$ teaspoon five-spice powder
2 teaspoons salt	2 tablespoons dry sherry
$\frac{1}{2}$ cup soy sauce	2 tablespoons honey
3 to 4 cloves garlic, crushed	

Rub the ribs with 2 teaspoons sugar and 2 teaspoons salt and let stand for 1 hour. Mix all the remaining ingredients except honey and pour over ribs in a shallow pan. Marinate for $1\frac{1}{2}$ to 2 hours, turning frequently. Place on a rack over a pan of hot water and bake in a preheated 350° oven for 1 hour, basting with the marinade and turning the ribs to cook evenly. Brush with the honey and bake for an additional 20 minutes or until ribs are a rich brown. Serve with Chinese mustard and plum sauce. Serves 4.

OLLA PODRIDA

Olla is the name of a deep earthenware pot and *podrida* means, literally, "rotten," referring either to this stew's pungent bacon or to the pot which in olden days was infrequently washed. Since the sixteenth century the Spanish stew has been a favorite of peasants and royalty alike; when Marie Thérèse married Louis XIV in 1660, she had the dish served at the French court. The recipe below is adapted from the *Arte de Cocina* of Francisco Martinez Montiño, head chef to Phillip III.

1 1-pound smoked ham butt or thick slice ham steak
1 1½-pound piece beef brisket, chuck, or flanken
1 ½-pound piece salt pork or bacon (optional)
1 stewing chicken, disjointed
1 pound chick-peas, soaked overnight
Salt
2 leeks, cut in half lengthwise
5 carrots, cut in half lengthwise
5 or 6 sprigs parsley
2 turnips, cubed
6 cloves
1 head cabbage, coarsely chopped
4 Spanish chorizos or Italian pepperoni sausages

1 1-pound garlic pork sausage, such as Italian coteghino (optional)
1 tablespoon caraway seeds
2 onions, chopped
2 cloves garlic, chopped
3 tablespoons butter or bacon fat
8 medium potatoes, peeled and halved
Pepper to taste
Pinch each powdered cinnamon and saffron
Sauce:
1 boiled potato
1 clove garlic
2 tablespoons chopped parsley
1 tablespoon wine vinegar
3 tablespoons olive oil
1 tablespoon tomato purée

Place ham, beef, salt pork or bacon, chicken, and soaked and drained chick-peas in a large earthenware or enameled cast-iron soup pot. Add water to cover—about 3 quarts or more if needed—and 1 tablespoon salt. Bring to a boil, reduce heat, and simmer, skimming off scum as it rises to the surface. When broth is clear, add leeks, carrots, parsley, turnips, and cloves. Cover and simmer slowly for 2 hours. Meanwhile, in a separate pot, cook cabbage, barely covered with lightly salted water, whole chorizos or pepperoni, and the garlic sausage which has been pierced with a fork in several places to keep it from bursting. Simmer for 1 hour. Add cabbage, sausage, and their broth to meat pot. Add caraway seeds. Brown chopped onions and garlic in butter and add to other ingredients with potatoes and a generous dash of black pepper. Cover and simmer together for 30 minutes or until cabbage and potatoes are done. Add cinnamon and saffron and simmer for 10 minutes. Season to taste. Skim fat from surface. *To make the sauce*: Mash potato, purée garlic and parsley in a mortar or blender and work into potato. Add vinegar and pour oil in slowly, beating constantly as for mayonnaise. Stir in tomato purée and enough broth from olla podrida to make a thick sauce. Season with salt and pepper. Serve broth, plain or with cooked rice or noodles, as a first course. Arrange sliced meats and vegetables on a serving platter and serve with sauce. Serves 8 to 10.

FEIJOADA

"From the increase of eight pigs have come the pigs found everywhere . . . in the Indies, all which ever were there and ever will be, which have been and still are endless," marveled Bartolomé de Las Casas of the cargo carried by Columbus on his second voyage to the New World. The admiral was also foresighted enough to bring seeds for the first citrus trees. Both pork and oranges found a place as ingredients of the stew which became Brazil's truly national dish, Feijoada. Beans were an Indian contribution and the hot spices were probably attributable to African slaves, commonly the cooks in colonial households.

4 cups dried black beans, soaked overnight
1 pound dried beef, soaked overnight
1 smoked tongue, soaked 5 to 6 hours
$\frac{1}{2}$ pound chorizos or hot Italian sausage
$\frac{1}{2}$ pound salt pork
4 tablespoons butter or corn oil
2 large onions, chopped
2 cloves garlic, minced
$\frac{1}{4}$ cup sausage meat
3 hot chili peppers or pinch cayenne pepper
6 cups hot cooked rice
1 green cabbage, simmered with onions, green squash, or collards
4 oranges, peeled and sliced

4 large sweet onions, thinly sliced
Toasted manioc flour or farina
Sauce:
2 large tomatoes, peeled, seeded, and chopped
3 to 4 hot peppers, minced, or hot pepper sauce to taste
2 cloves garlic, minced
Juice of 2 lemons
$\frac{1}{2}$ cup wine vinegar
2 medium onions, finely chopped
4 scallions, minced
6 sprigs parsley, minced
$\frac{1}{4}$ teaspoon white pepper, or to taste
1 cup broth from feijoada
Salt and cayenne pepper

Drain the beans. Place in a saucepan and add water to cover. Bring to a boil, lower heat, and simmer gently, covered, for 30 minutes. Meanwhile, drain soaked meats. Place tongue and dry beef in fresh water. Bring to a boil, simmer for 5 minutes, drain, and rinse. Replace in the pot with warm water and simmer gently for 1 hour. Add chorizos, pricked all over with a fork, and salt pork. Simmer for 10 minutes. Drain and cool slightly. Remove skin from the tongue and slice or cube the meat. Heat *2 tablespoons butter* and brown the tongue. Add to the beans. Add thinly sliced chorizos, salt pork, and dried beef to the beans. Cover and simmer for 2 hours. Heat *remaining 2 tablespoons butter* and sauté onions and garlic. Add 1 cup very soft beans, the sausage meat, and chili peppers or cayenne pepper. Mash and stir for 10 minutes. Return half the mixture to bean pot, simmer 30 minutes longer. *To make the sauce.* Put the first 3 sauce ingredients through the blender. Add remaining sauce ingredients and season with salt and cayenne to taste. Sauce should be peppery. Makes about 3 cups. Arrange the sliced meats attractively on a large platter. Pour remaining black bean and sausage sauce mix over meat. Serve the beans, the rice, and the vegetables separately. Have sliced oranges, sliced onions, feijoada sauce, and toasted manioc flour or farina as condiments. Serves 12.

BIGOS

The ancient manors of the Polish nobility were often the scene of great hunting parties. The dish traditionally served to the ravenous hunters was Bigos washed down with great quantities of vodka.

1 large cabbage
Salt and pepper
4 tablespoons butter
$\frac{1}{4}$ pound bacon, diced
$\frac{1}{2}$ pound each: boneless veal, pork, lamb, and beef, cubed

2 large onions, chopped
2 large tart apples, peeled and chopped
2 cups beef broth
$\frac{1}{2}$ Polish sausage

Shred the cabbage and sprinkle lightly with salt. Let stand for 1 hour. Meanwhile, melt *2 tablespoons butter* in a heavy pot with a lid and fry the bacon cubes. Remove with a slotted spoon and reserve. Brown cubed meat well and add onions and apples to brown. Season with salt and pepper. Press out the water from the cabbage. Add to the meat along with *remaining butter* and fry lightly, turning mixture over with a fork. Add broth to stew. Put the lid on the pot, leaving a small vent, and simmer slowly for $2\frac{1}{2}$ hours. Slice sausage and add to stew. Add reserved bacon and simmer for $\frac{1}{2}$ hour longer. Serves 6 to 8.

LEYDEN HUTSEPOT

Dutchmen's darkest hours in their revolt against Spain occurred in the summer of 1574 when Leyden was besieged. During the struggle fresh provisions were cut off from the burghers, who had to rely on ingenuity, plus stale beef and such long-lasting vegetables as onions and carrots, to make their traditional hutsepot. Today the Leyden version is served, along with herring and bread, at the annual liberation feast on October 3.

3 pounds beef brisket or flanken
5 onions, diced
6 carrots, scraped and diced
6 potatoes, peeled and cubed

2 or 3 knockwurst (optional)
3 to 4 tablespoons rendered beef suet, chicken, duck, or goose fat
Salt, pepper, and cayenne to taste

Simmer beef in lightly salted water to cover for 1 hour. Add vegetables and knockwurst and continue simmering for about 30 minutes or until meat is tender and vegetables are soft enough to mash. Remove meat and knockwurst. Drain vegetables and reserve broth. Mash vegetables and stir in rendered fat. Season to taste. Beat until mixture is smooth and fluffy. Remove casing from knockwurst and slice. Fold into vegetables. Slice meat and place over vegetable purée. Broth may be served as a sauce or reserved for future use. Serves 6 to 8.

LANCASHIRE HOT-POT

$2\frac{1}{2}$ pounds lamb necks, cut
    into 1-inch slices
2 large onions, chopped
1 bay leaf
Pinch of dried thyme
3 cups beef broth or water
$\frac{2}{3}$ cup butter
$\frac{1}{4}$ teaspoon sugar

Salt and pepper
6 lamb kidneys, cleaned and sliced
4 large carrots, sliced (optional)
18 oysters, shelled
$\frac{1}{2}$ pound mushrooms, sliced
6 to 8 potatoes, peeled and
    sliced to $\frac{1}{4}$-inch thickness
2 tablespoons flour

Bone the lamb necks, or have the butcher do it. Put lamb bones, *half the onion*, the bay leaf, thyme, and beef broth in a saucepan. Bring to a boil, skim, and simmer gently for 40 minutes; reserve. Meanwhile cut the lamb into pieces and brown in *2 tablespoons butter* for about 5 minutes. Turn the pieces, add *remaining onion*, the sugar, and a sprinkling of salt and pepper and continue browning for 5 to 6 minutes more. Put the lamb and onions in a deep 12-cup oven casserole with a lid. Add *1 tablespoon butter* to the pan and just barely sear the kidneys. Place on lamb pieces. Sprinkle with a little pepper. Brown the carrots in *2 tablespoons butter* in the saucepan used for the meats for about 5 to 6 minutes. Put over kidneys. Cover with the oysters. In *2 tablespoons butter* simmer the mushrooms for 2 to 3 minutes and put over the oysters. Season lightly. Top with the sliced potatoes. Add *remaining butter* to the browning pan and stir in flour. Cook, stirring until brown but not burned. Strain broth from bones and add 2 cups to the flour. Stir until smooth and slightly thickened. Season to taste, pour over hot-pot. Cover with buttered foil and the lid and bake in a preheated 375° oven for 1 hour. Remove lid and foil. Brush potatoes with a little melted butter. Return to the oven and bake for about 15 to 20 minutes or until potatoes are golden and crusty. Serves 8 to 10.

HASENPFEFFER

Greeks thought eating hare caused insomnia. Romans ate it for seven days to cure ugliness. Germans are content to enjoy it as below.

$\frac{1}{2}$ recipe Red Wine Marinade (page 640)
1 5-pound hare or rabbit, with giblets,
    cut into serving pieces
Salt and pepper

5 tablespoons butter, rendered lard,
    or bacon fat
5 tablespoons flour
$\frac{1}{2}$ to 1 cup sour cream (optional)

Prepare and cool marinade. Pour over cut-up hare and giblets in a ceramic or glass bowl. Marinate in refrigerator for 2 days, turning meat several times a day. Remove from marinade and dry thoroughly. Strain and reserve marinade. Dry meat and sprinkle with salt and pepper and brown slowly on all sides in butter. Sprinkle with flour; stir and sauté until flour is absorbed and turns cocoa color. Add strained marinade and simmer covered for 45 minutes to 1 hour or until meat is tender. Stir in sour cream, season to taste, and simmer for 5 minutes. Serves 6.

MONGOLIAN HOT-POT

This elaborate fondue is Mongolian in origin. At its simplest it was eaten by nomads squatting around the campfire, each man cooking his own chunks of meat in the communal kettle. The more refined Chinese devised a small table stove for the purpose, exchanged fine silver forks or bamboo skewers for impromptu sticks, added many subtle relishes, and made it into a dish for festive occasions.

½ pound sirloin or fillet of beef, sliced paper thin

½ pound leg of lamb meat, sliced paper thin

½ pound breast of chicken meat, sliced paper thin

½ pound Chinese cellophane noodles, blanched

¼ pound soft bean curd cake, cut into small cubes

½ pound spinach leaves, well washed

½ head Chinese cabbage, coarsely shredded

½ pound bamboo shoots, thinly sliced

1 cup Chinese hot pepper sauce

1 cup sesame oil

1 cup soy sauce

1 cup vinegar

½ cup bean curd paste

1 cup peanut butter

1 cup minced Chinese parsley (cilantro or fresh coriander leaves) or Italian parsley

1 cup minced scallions, bulbs and greens

½ cup minced ginger root, fresh or pickled

10 to 12 cloves garlic, minced

8 to 10 cups chicken or beef broth, or as needed

All sliced meats, noodles, bean curd cake, spinach, cabbage, and bamboo shoots may be arranged on separate large platters and passed around the table. Or divide each ingredient into 6 portions and give each guest a single, assorted plate. Place hot pepper sauce, oil, soy sauce, vinegar, bean curd paste, peanut butter thinned with peanut oil to dipping consistency, minced parsley, scallions, ginger root, and garlic in separate serving bowls. Provide each guest with a small bowl for combining these ingredients to taste. Set a Chinese hot-pot, a deep saucepan, or a chafing dish over a moderately high flame. Pour hot broth into pot and set in center of table. When broth begins to boil, each guest, using chopsticks or long-handled fondue forks, cooks his dinner himself, holding each piece of meat in pot until cooked. Each piece is dipped into the sauce as it is eaten. Noodles and cabbage may be dropped into broth to be removed as they are cooked. When all meats and vegetables and noodles have been eaten, ladle remaining broth into sauce bowls and drink. Have extra broth on hand to be added to pot if needed. Serves 6.

VARIATIONS: *Korean Sin-Sul-Lo*: This is the same hot-pot as the above except that all ingredients are brought to the table simmering in the broth. The Korean version usually includes hard-boiled egg quarters, chunks of fried fish, ginkgo nuts, fresh dates, shrimps, and pieces of roasted pork. *Japanese Mizutaki*: This is similar to the Chinese version and is always cooked by the diners at the table. It is usually made with only one meat—chicken, lamb, or beef— and includes such vegetables as seaweed, thinly sliced lotus root, and mushrooms.

COUSCOUS

The granaries of North Africa, once the breadbasket of ancient Rome, have since Biblical times supplied the peoples of Algeria and Morocco with *couscous*, the hard wheat semolina basic to this dish. It is traditionally prepared in a two-tiered *couscousière*, the copper bottom for boiling meats, vegetables, and stock, the top of perforated earthenware or loose-woven grass for steaming the grain. Diners, seated cross-legged and in a circle around a low table, eat from a communal bowl. Etiquette prescribes that they hold their wooden spoons in the right hand, and that they eat from the outer edges of the bowl, leaving the center for "the blessing of heaven to descend upon it." The Arab meal concludes with the passing of a communal bowl of milk or water followed by coffee.

2 pounds coarse semolina
6 cups boiling salted water
$\frac{1}{2}$ cup olive oil
$1\frac{1}{2}$ pounds boneless lamb,
   cut into 1-inch pieces
$1\frac{1}{2}$ pounds bottom round or chuck beef,
   cut into 1-inch pieces
1 4-pound chicken, cut into
   2-inch pieces
6 large onions, chopped
1 teaspoon each salt and black pepper
5 to 6 dashes cayenne pepper, or to taste

$\frac{1}{2}$ teaspoon powdered turmeric
1 teaspoon saffron
$1\frac{1}{2}$ quarts beef broth or water
2 cups cooked chick-peas (garbanzos
   or ceci), rinsed and drained
4 tomatoes, peeled, seeded, and chopped
2 zucchini, or yellow squash,
   cut into cubes
3 carrots, thinly sliced
$\frac{3}{4}$ cup seedless raisins
$\frac{1}{2}$ cup butter

Place the semolina in a large bowl and pour on *2 cups boiling salted water*. Let stand for 20 minutes. The grains will swell as they absorb the water. Repeat twice. Place in the cheese-cloth-lined top part of steamer as indicated below. Heat the oil in a heavy frying pan and brown the meat and chicken in small batches, adding oil as needed. Transfer meat to the bottom part of a steam cooker, such as a small clam steamer or a large double boiler with a perforated top, or if available, a regular couscous cooker. Add oil to the frying pan and brown the onions; add to the meat. Deglaze the frying pan with a little broth and pour over meat and onions. Season with salt, pepper, cayenne pepper, turmeric, and saffron. Cover with the broth and bring to a simmer. Place soaked semolina in cheesecloth-lined top part of steamer or in a large strainer placed over an ordinary large heavy saucepan. Place over but not touching the stew. Make sure steam is not escaping between stewpot and colander. If necessary seal with foil. Cook for 1 hour. Toss semolina with fork to separate grains. Add chick-peas, tomatoes, zucchini, and carrots to stew. Simmer for 45 minutes. Add raisins and simmer 15 minutes longer. Toss semolina with butter. Mound on a large platter. Remove meat and vegetables from stewpot and place on top of semolina. Keep warm. Reduce the sauce and remove the fat, although traditionally fat remains. Correct seasoning—the sauce should be very peppery. Pour over meat and serve at once. Serves 10 to 12.

GODIVEAU

The origins of this French recipe for forcemeat balls are so far back in history that even the etymology is uncertain. Most likely Godiveau was first made with veal, but other meats and fish have also served nicely.

1 pound boned veal, chicken, or pike, ground twice
$\frac{1}{4}$ to $\frac{1}{2}$ teaspoon nutmeg
1 teaspoon salt
$\frac{1}{4}$ teaspoon white pepper
$\frac{3}{4}$ pound kidney fat, with all sinews removed, ground twice or minced

1 cup chicken or veal Velouté (page 616), well chilled
4 eggs
$1\frac{3}{4}$ cups finely shaved ice or well-chilled heavy cream

Season the ground veal with nutmeg, salt, and pepper and pound it to a paste in a mortar. Pound the kidney fat to a paste. Mix veal and fat and pound until completely blended. Add the well-chilled velouté. Continue pounding and add eggs, one by one, without stopping, constantly working the mixture. Purée through the finest strainer. Spread on a platter, cover with waxed paper, and chill overnight. Place in a bowl set in a bowl of ice and pound again, adding the shaved ice gradually and in very small amounts, until all is absorbed. Test by dropping a teaspoon of the mixture into simmering water. If too solid, add a little more ice; if too loose, pound in 1 unbeaten egg white. Shape into small balls about the size of a large olive with wet hands or with a pastry bag with a plain tube. Poach in salted simmering water for 10 minutes. Drain. These may be served mixed with diced poached sweetbreads in Sauce Suprême (page 617) in vol-au-vents or as a soup garnish. Makes about 50.

TRIPE A LA MODE DE CAEN

Tripe was banquet fare among the ancients, but it was not until the fourteenth century when Benoît, a chef in the city of Caen, secured for it a place among the classics of French gastronomy. His touch of genius was adding *cidre* and Calvados, the "wines" of his native Normandy.

6 pounds tripe (fat belly, white and brown honeycomb, in equal quantities)
Salt and freshly ground pepper
1 ox hoof, split and halved, or 2 calf's feet
10 large onions, chopped
8 large carrots, sliced
8 leeks, tied in a bunch

Bouquet garni (4 cloves, 6 sprigs parsley, celery leaves, $\frac{1}{2}$ teaspoon thyme, 1 large bay leaf, 4 cloves garlic, $\frac{1}{2}$ teaspoon dried tarragon, tied in cheesecloth)
$\frac{1}{2}$ teaspoon nutmeg
$\frac{1}{2}$ cup Calvados or applejack
2 quarts apple cider
Flour for sealing lid

Wash tripe thoroughly and soak overnight in cold water. Parboil in salted water for 15 minutes, drain, rinse well, and cool. Cut into 1½-inch squares. Put tripe in a deep casserole or bean pot with a cover, in layers, seasoning with salt and pepper, about 1 teaspoon salt per pound, or to taste. Bury the ox hoof in the center with the onions, carrots, leeks, and bouquet garni. Sprinkle with nutmeg. Pour in Calvados and add cider to cover completely. Make a thick paste dough with flour and some hot water. Seal pot cover with the dough. Place in a preheated 275° oven and bake for 10 hours. Unseal, remove crust, discard bouquet garni, vegetables, and ox hoof bones. Skim off as much fat as possible. Tripe may be served in individual heated bean pots or in very hot soup plates with the cooking liquor strained and poured over. Another jigger of Calvados may be added at serving time. Serves 10 to 12.

CASSOULET

Three cities of old Languedoc claim to produce the original version of France's celebrated peasant dish, Cassoulet. Common to all are white beans, a variety of American lentil unknown in Europe before the seventeenth century. Local variations depend on the meats used: Castelnaudary's casserole, the simplest and probably the oldest, relies on pork; to this base, Carcassonne adds mutton; Toulouse embellishes it still further with its local specialty, *confit d'oie*, or preserved goose. The name of the dish derives from the *cassole*, or casserole, in which it cooks.

2 pounds dry white beans (navy beans, pea beans, or white kidney beans)
2 large onions, sliced
8 thick slices bacon, diced
2 large tomatoes, peeled, seeded, and chopped
Black pepper
4 cloves garlic, crushed
½ teaspoon dried thyme
4 or 5 sprigs parsley
1 large bay leaf

4 cups meat stock (preferably lamb)
1 pound leg or shoulder lamb, cut into cubes and browned in olive oil
1 pound pork shoulder, cut into cubes and browned in olive oil
1 pound sausages (French saucisson à l'ail, Italian coteghino, or Polish kielbasa) cut into slices 1 inch thick
1 duck or ½ goose, half-roasted, cut into serving pieces
Bread crumbs for topping

Soak beans as directed on package and cook in water to cover for about 2 hours or until beans are almost soft. Fry onions and bacon until onions are soft but not brown and bacon begins to brown. Add tomato, a generous pinch of pepper, garlic, thyme, parsley, and bay leaf. Add stock and simmer for 15 minutes. Place *half the well-drained beans* in the bottom of a deep earthenware casserole. Top with meats and then with *remaining beans*. Add onion-bacon-tomato mixture and broth in which it cooked. Stir beans gently to mix with bacon and onions. Top with a generous layer of bread crumbs. Bring to boil over low flame, cover and bake in a preheated 325° oven for 1 to 1½ hours or until beans are cooked. Liquid should be absorbed and a good crust formed on top. Serves 6 to 8.

BLACK FOREST VENISON STEW

"Hunters go into Paradise when they die, and live in this world more joyfully than any other men," wrote Henry IV's master of game. As to their share of earthly joys, there can be little argument, for no one but princes of noble birth were permitted to hunt in medieval Europe, and anyone caught poaching on the royal prerogative or even harassing the rabbits at lunch on his crops was subject to imprisonment. Hunting remained for centuries the chief amusement of kings and courtiers, with Germany's Black Forest providing some of the finest hunting grounds. German cooks obliged with many exceedingly fine recipes for game, among them the venison stew following.

4 pounds venison stew meat	3 onions, chopped
4 cups Red Wine Marinade (page 640)	4 tablespoons flour
10 juniper berries, tied in cheesecloth	2 cups beef broth
1 teaspoon dried marjoram	Salt and pepper
$\frac{1}{2}$ teaspoon dried rosemary	1 cup sour cream
$\frac{1}{4}$ cup butter	

Wipe the venison meat and put in a wide, shallow dish. Pour in marinade. Add juniper berries, marjoram, and rosemary. Stir well. Marinate 24 hours in refrigerator, stirring frequently. Drain venison, reserving marinade. Pat the meat dry. Melt the butter and quickly brown venison on all sides—about 10 minutes. Remove meat, add onions, and brown. Add the flour and brown for 3 to 4 minutes, stirring. Return meat to pan. Add broth and 2 cups marinade and stir until simmering and slightly thickened. Season with salt and pepper to taste. Cover and simmer for about 1 hour or until meat is tender. Skim off fat. Add sour cream. Stir and heat without boiling. Serve with Spaetzle (page 567) and with stewed pears decorated with a dab of red currant jelly. Serves 8 to 10.

KÖNIGSBERGER KLOPSE
(German Meat Dumplings)

$1\frac{1}{2}$ pounds ground pork, veal, and beef, in equal parts	$\frac{1}{4}$ teaspoon white pepper
3 slices stale white bread	Pinch of nutmeg (optional)
$\frac{1}{2}$ cup lukewarm milk	4 cups beef broth
1 medium onion	Sauerkraut (page 595)
6 anchovy fillets	*Sauce:*
2 eggs	1 tablespoon butter
$1\frac{1}{2}$ tablespoons minced parsley	$\frac{1}{2}$ small onion, minced
Rind of 1 lemon, grated	$1\frac{1}{2}$ tablespoons flour
$\frac{1}{2}$ teaspoon salt	2 tablespoons capers
	2 to 3 tablespoons sour cream (optional)

Regrind all meats together through the fine blade of a food chopper. Soak bread in milk for 10 minutes; squeeze out as much milk as possible. Regrind combined meats with soaked bread, onion, and anchovies. Mix in eggs, parsley, lemon rind, salt, pepper, and nutmeg and mix thoroughly. Wet hands in cold water and shape meat into large balls, about the size of lemons. Bring broth to a boil, add meat dumplings and reduce heat. Simmer uncovered for 15 minutes or until meatballs float in broth and one tests done. Meanwhile, melt butter and sauté minced onion until golden brown. Add flour and sauté slowly until it is medium brown. Beat this into broth and simmer until smooth and thick. Add capers and sour cream to sauce and season to taste. Place meatballs on sauerkraut and cover with caper sauce. Serves 4 to 6.

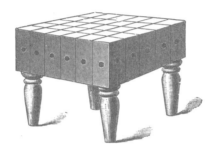

BOHNEN, BIRNEN, UND SPECK

Salted, smoked bacon has been for centuries the meat most often served in German peasant households. The very word probably derives from *bachen*, the wild pigs which once roamed the forests of Germany. When the legendary Meistersinger, Hans Sachs, sang of a Glutton's Paradise, he naturally built his houses of bacon, "fat and crisply fried." It is one of the principal ingredients in the *Eintopfgerichte*, or "one dish" meal, which the people of Hamburg still favor. The stew is very like the hearty bacon broth served by Thomas Mann's *Buddenbrooks* family.

1 pound dried white kidney or fava beans	4 large half-ripe pears, peeled, cored, and cubed
1 pound unsliced smoked bacon, cut into 1-inch cubes	1 large onion, sliced (optional)
3 tablespoons butter	1 teaspoon salt
	$\frac{1}{2}$ teaspoon black pepper
	Minced parsley

Soak beans overnight if necessary or parboil according to instructions on package. Fry bacon in butter in a Dutch oven until brown on all sides. Drain soaked or parboiled beans and add them to bacon along with pears, onion, seasonings, and enough water to barely cover. Simmer covered for 1 hour or until beans are done. The pears should become soft enough to fall apart. Season to taste and serve sprinkled with parsley. Serves 6.

TORTA DI PASQUA
(Italian Easter Pie)

1 recipe Puff Pastry (page 684) or ½
  recipe White Bread dough (page 643)
3 eggs, beaten
1½ pounds ricotta cheese, drained in
  a strainer overnight
½ pound hot or mild Italian sausage,
  sliced and fried lightly in olive oil

8 to 10 slices prosciutto ham,
  coarsely chopped
½ pound mozzarella cheese, diced
⅓ cup grated Parmesan cheese
2 tablespoons minced parsley
Freshly ground pepper
Salt to taste

Prepare puff pastry or bread dough. Beat eggs into ricotta cheese, add all remaining ingredients, and season to taste. Roll out ½ the dough and line an 11-inch, buttered pie plate. Pour in filling and cover with remaining ½ of dough. Seal, flute and trim edges, brush with egg yolk mixed with 1 teaspoon cold water. Prick with a fork or make 2 or 3 slits in the top crust. Bake in a preheated 350° oven for 40 to 45 minutes or until golden brown. Serve warm or at room temperature. Serves 8.

SAUCISSON EN CROUTE

Smoking or salting meat to preserve it probably goes back to the time of the ancient Egyptians. Although sausage is usually made of pork, there is virtually no meat that cannot be used. Sausage-eating customs differ as much from one country to another as the spices used in making them. In Germany every type of sausage has its hour—or meal—when it is traditionally eaten. The French prefer sausage as an appetizer.

1 ¾- to 1-pound garlic sausage (Italian
  cotteghino or French saucisson à l'ail)

½ recipe Cream Cheese Pastry (page 680)
  or Puff Pastry (page 684)

Poach sausage gently in water to cover in a deep wide saucepan or skillet for 1 hour. Turn sausage several times during cooking, being careful not to puncture the casing. Remove from water and cool. Gently remove casing. Roll out dough according to instructions to ¼-inch-thick rectangle. Place cold sausage in center of dough. Fold dough around sausage and pinch edges closed, using a little water or beaten egg yolk to seal them. Chill for 1 hour. Set on unbuttered baking sheet. Bake in preheated 350° oven for 10 to 15 minutes or until pastry is golden and crisp. Using a sharp knife, cut into slices ½ to ¾ inch thick. Serve warm with Dijon mustard and French potato salad. Serves 6 as first course.

VARIATION: *Saucisson en Beaujolais*: Parboil sausage in water to cover for 15 minutes. Drain off water. Cover sausage with Beaujolais wine and poach gently for 45 minutes. Turn sausage several times but do not puncture the casing. When done, cut sausage without removing the casing. Serve hot with hot Beaujolais spooned over it. Serve with cornichons (sour gherkins) and French potato salad.

TOAD IN THE HOLE

An uncomplimentary 1797 reference to Toad in the Hole compares the dish to a London theater in which the great tragedienne Sarah Siddons was appearing. "Mrs. Siddons and Sadler's Wells . . . seem . . . as ill-fitted as the dish they call toad in the hole . . . putting a noble sirloin of beef into a poor paltry batter pudding." The modern version uses sausage which the writer would have found a more suitable combination.

2 eggs, separated	Pinch each ginger and nutmeg (optional)
1 cup milk	10 to 12 link pork sausages
1 cup flour	2 tablespoons melted butter or
Salt, pepper, and cayenne to taste	rendered fat from sausages

Beat egg yolks with milk. Add flour gradually, beating constantly until batter is smooth and creamy. Add seasonings. Fry sausages according to instructions on package. Pour melted butter or rendered sausage fat into 10-inch pie plate or square baking dish, brushing some fat around sides of pan. Beat egg whites until stiff and fold into egg yolk batter. Arrange fried sausages in pan and pour batter over them. Bake in a preheated 400° oven for about 30 minutes or until batter is puffed and golden brown on top. Cut into wedges or squares into single portions and serve hot. Serves 4 to 6. Sausages and batter may be baked and served in individual pie plates or baking dishes.

CREPINETTES

Napoleon, demanding to know why he was never served pork crepinettes, was told that they were "not a choice dish." The emperor notified his *maître d'hôtel* that he would have some anyway. The battle of wills ended in a tie: the official served his master pheasant crepinettes—and Napoleon liked them so much he had three helpings. Other Frenchmen are well satisfied with the hearty peasant version below.

2½ pounds pork, lean and fat	Pinch of thyme, marjoram, or sage
1½ teaspoons salt	3 to 4 tablespoons brandy
¾ teaspoon black pepper	½ cup butter, melted
¼ pound mushrooms, minced	1 cup bread crumbs
3 or 4 minced black truffles (optional)	Butter for frying

Grind lean and fat pork together 3 times through fine blade of food chopper. Mix in salt, pepper, mushrooms, truffles, and any other spices or herbs being used. Gradually knead in ½ cup water and brandy. Shape into small patties using 1 heaping tablespoonful of meat mixture for each. Brush with melted butter, dredge with bread crumbs, and fry in butter for about 8 to 10 minutes on each side. Serves 8 to 10.

PATE DE CAMPAGNE

2 medium onions, finely chopped
$\frac{1}{4}$ cup butter
2 cloves garlic, minced
$\frac{1}{2}$ teaspoon each: rosemary, thyme,
  and marjoram
$\frac{1}{4}$ teaspoon each: allspice and nutmeg
$\frac{1}{8}$ teaspoon powdered cloves
$1\frac{1}{2}$ teaspoons salt
Cayenne and freshly ground black
  pepper to taste
$\frac{1}{2}$ pound chicken livers

$\frac{1}{2}$ pound unsalted pork fat, ground
$\frac{1}{2}$ pound fresh boneless pork, ground
$\frac{1}{2}$ pound veal, ground
3 eggs, slightly beaten
$\frac{1}{4}$ cup cognac
1 cup heavy cream
$\frac{1}{2}$ pound smoked ham steak or tongue,
  cut into long strips $\frac{1}{2}$ inch wide
2 small bay leaves
$\frac{1}{4}$ cup chopped parsley

Brown the onions in the butter, add the garlic, and cook 1 more minute. Add the herbs and spices, and cool. Mince chicken livers. Regrind the pork fat, pork, and veal together, or have the butcher do it. In a bowl mix onions, livers, and meats. Work in eggs, cognac, and cream and mix well. Put $\frac{1}{3}$ pâté mixture in an oblong or oval 8-cup terrine with a cover. Smooth down and arrange *half the ham strips* on this. Cover with $\frac{1}{3}$ more pâté, *remaining ham strips*, and cover with rest of pâté. Insert $\frac{1}{2}$ bay leaf at each end and on the sides of terrine. Cover, set in a pan $\frac{1}{2}$ full of hot water, and bake in a preheated 350° oven for 2 hours. Uncover and bake for 20 to 30 minutes longer. Weight down pâté and chill overnight before using. Sprinkle with chopped parsley and serve sliced from the terrine. Pass crisp, sliced French bread and a small crock of sweet butter. Serves 8 to 10.

WHOLE ROASTED CALF'S LIVER

Calf's liver is prepared in many delicious ways in Italy, where it is usually cooked in thin slices. This recipe for a whole liver is from *Il Cuoco Galante* (1786), by the Neapolitan Vincenzo Corrado.

6 slices bacon or fat prosciutto,
  cut into small pieces
Freshly ground pepper
1 tablespoon minced fresh tarragon or
  $1\frac{1}{2}$ teaspoons dried tarragon
1 teaspoon dried basil
2 tablespoons cognac
1 whole calf's liver (about 2 pounds)
$\frac{1}{2}$ teaspoon powdered mace

$\frac{1}{2}$ teaspoon powdered allspice
2 tablespoons chopped parsley
2 bay leaves
$\frac{1}{2}$ cup olive oil
$\frac{1}{2}$ cup dry white wine
2 tablespoons white wine vinegar
1 large onion, sliced
Salt

Marinate the bacon with pepper, *half the herbs*, and the cognac for $\frac{1}{2}$ hour. Make little slits in the liver and lard it with the bacon pieces. Put *remaining herbs* and any remaining bacon marinade in a large bowl. Add spices, parsley, bay leaves, oil, white wine, vinegar, onions, and the liver. Marinate for 2 to 3 hours, turning frequently. Place in a roasting pan and season with salt and pepper. Drain onions from the marinade and add to the liver. Roast in a pre-heated 400° oven for 10 minutes, lower heat to 350°, pour on heated marinade, and continue roasting for 50 minutes, basting 3 or 4 times. Glaze with meat glaze and serve with A Thick Sauce with Pepper (page 621). Serves 6 to 8.

LEIBERSPIESSCHEN

In 1336 disgruntled members of thirteen Zurich guilds united and declared their independence from the city's corrupt rulers. The coup not only established a constitutional government, but it also promoted excellent Swiss cooking, for the guilds promptly built themselves fine halls and finer kitchens. On holidays like the spring Sechseläuten, celebrating the setting ahead of the town clocks, guilds would vie with one another in making specialty dishes. Leiberspiesschen, calf's livers grilled on skewers, was traditional to the tailors.

1 pound calf's liver	$\frac{1}{3}$ cup butter
6 slices bacon cut in 2-inch pieces	1 medium onion, chopped
Fresh sage leaves	Salt and pepper

Slice the liver into 2-inch-long pieces, $\frac{1}{4}$ inch thick. Thread on small metal or wooden skewers, alternating with pieces of bacon and a sage leaf. Melt the butter in a large heavy skillet. Add onion and brown for 3 minutes, then add the skewered liver. Sauté until brown on each side, for about 3 to 4 minutes. Season with salt and pepper and serve immediately. If fresh sage is not available, $\frac{1}{2}$ teaspoon dried sage may be added to the butter. Serves 4.

SCANDINAVIAN LIVER PASTEI

The Greeks and Romans were great fanciers of pâtés, cramming both geese and pigs with such odd fodder as dried figs, wine, and honey to enlarge their livers. Geese are still bred and fed for this high office, but other animals have since been left to produce livers according to their natural wonts. Northern Europeans eat great quantities of the soft, steamed liver paste below.

1 pound calf's or pork liver
1 pound pork fat or bacon
2 medium onions, chopped
1 teaspoon pepper
1 tablespoon salt
½ teaspoon allspice

¼ teaspoon powdered cloves
¼ teaspoon dry mustard
1 recipe medium Béchamel Sauce (page 618)
3 eggs, separated
1 egg white

Remove membranes and tubing from liver and grind with pork fat or bacon and onions 3 or 4 times using finest blade of meat grinder. Add pepper, salt, and spices to béchamel sauce. Cool. When cold add to liver. Mix in the well-beaten egg yolks and fold in the 4 egg whites, beaten stiff. Pour into a buttered 8-cup loaf pan. Set in a pan of water and bake in a preheated 350° oven for 1½ hours, adding water as needed. Cool in pan. Serve sliced. Serves 10 to 12.

MEXICAN ENCHILADAS

2 cups minced onions
¼ cup butter or corn oil
2 pounds lean beef, pork, or chicken, ground
1 tablespoon chili powder
1 teaspoon salt
2 cups peeled, seeded, and diced tomatoes

Sauce:
⅓ cup butter
2 medium onions, minced
3 tablespoons flour
2 tablespoons chili powder
2 cups tomato juice
Salt
12 tortillas, canned or homemade
½ pound sliced jack cheese or unprocessed cheddar

Brown the onion in ¼ cup butter for 2 minutes. Add the meat and stir until meat begins to brown. Season with chili and salt. Add tomato pulp and simmer gently for 10 to 15 minutes.

To make the sauce: Melt the butter and brown the onion. Add the flour and brown it, stirring to prevent burning. Add chili powder and cook, stirring, for 1 minute. Add tomato juice and stir until thickened and smooth. Season with salt to taste. Makes about 3 cups. Dip the tortillas in the hot sauce and fill with the meat; roll up like jelly rolls and lay side by side in a buttered baking dish. Cover each with a slice of cheese and pour on remaining sauce. Bake in a preheated 375° oven for 20 to 25 minutes. Serves 6.

TOURTIERE
(French-Canadian Meat Pie)

1 recipe Short Pastry (page 682) made
 with an egg and milk instead of water
$\frac{3}{4}$ pound veal, ground
$\frac{3}{4}$ pound pork, ground
1 large onion
1 clove garlic
$\frac{1}{2}$ teaspoon salt

$\frac{1}{4}$ teaspoon pepper
$\frac{1}{4}$ teaspoon mace
$\frac{1}{4}$ teaspoon dried summer savory or sage
3 tablespoons bacon fat
$\frac{1}{2}$ cup beef broth
1 tablespoon chopped parsley
Heavy cream as needed

Make the pastry and chill well for 1 hour. Regrind meats together with onion and garlic. Season with salt, pepper, mace, and summer savory. Heat bacon fat in a large frying pan, add meat mixture, and brown for 5 to 6 minutes, stirring. Add *half the broth* and simmer covered for 20 to 25 minutes, stirring occasionally, adding broth if needed, so mixture does not become dry. Cool completely. Roll out pastry into 2 circles, one larger than the other. Line a buttered 8-inch pie dish with the smaller circle of pastry. Mix pork and veal mixture with parsley and pile high in pie dish. Cover with second round of pastry, seal, trim, and flute. Prick with a fork and brush with cream. Bake in a preheated 425° oven for 15 minutes. Lower heat to 350° and continue baking for 40 minutes longer or until the pie is golden brown. Cool and serve at room temperature. Serves 6.

BOLLITO MISTO
(Italian Boiled Dinner)

1 3- to 4-pound smoked beef tongue
1 3- to 4-pound piece boiling beef
 (flanken, brisket, chuck)
1 3- to 4-pound piece veal shoulder or
 boneless rump, tied in a roll
2 onions
3 carrots
3 stalks celery, with leaves

6 sprigs parsley
1 stewing chicken or 1 capon
1 or 2 1-pound Italian coteghino or
 zampone sausages
Salt and pepper to taste
8 to 10 large potatoes, boiled
Salsa Verde (page 627) or mustard

Wash tongue, cover with cold water in a large pot, bring to a boil, and simmer for 10 minutes. Pour off water. Add fresh boiling water to cover. Cover pot and simmer slowly for 45 minutes. Add beef and veal and simmer for 1 hour more, skimming scum as it rises to the surface. Add onions, carrots, celery, parsley, chicken, and sausage and simmer for 1 hour more, skimming scum as it rises to the surface. Cook until all meats and poultry are tender. Season broth to taste with salt and pepper. Remove meats to heated platter. Peel tongue. Slice all meats. Spoon a little broth over them to keep them hot. Reserve remaining broth for future use. Pot vegetables are not usually served with this. Serve with boiled potatoes and salsa verde or mustard. Serves 8 to 10.

BRAIN FRITTERS WITH ORANGE SAUCE

Readers of Bartolomeo Stefani's *L'Arte di ben cucinare*, published in Mantua in 1662, were directed to prepare brains in the following manner.

2 calf's brains	4 or 5 black peppercorns, crushed
1 tablespoon lemon juice	Fritter Batter (page 583) made with
1 small onion, sliced	white wine and a pinch of cinnamon
1 stalk celery (optional)	Vegetable oil for deep frying
3 or 4 sprigs parsley	Sauce Maltaise (see Hollandaise Sauce,
Salt	page 625) or orange juice

Soak brains in ice water with lemon juice for 2 to 3 hours. Drain and parboil gently for 10 minutes in water to cover along with onion, celery, parsley, salt, and peppercorns. Drain and cool, and remove tubing and membranes. Pull apart into bite-size pieces. Dry thoroughly. Dip into batter and fry in oil heated to 375° for about 3 minutes or until golden. Drain on paper towel and serve with sauce maltaise or a sprinkling of orange juice. Serves 4 to 6. Sweetbreads may be prepared in the same way.

SALPICON

Salpicon—in Spanish parlance a ragout of chopped meats or fish and vegetables in sauce—may date from the fourteenth century. French chefs adopted the name and the method, as in the old recipe following.

1 pound veal sweetbreads	$\frac{1}{2}$ recipe veal or chicken Godiveau
Juice of 1 lemon	(page 546), made into 1-inch balls
$\frac{1}{2}$ pound button mushrooms or	and poached for 10 minutes
quartered large mushrooms	2 ounces truffled goose liver, diced
1 tablespoon butter	$\frac{1}{2}$ pound cooked Virginia ham, diced
Salt and pepper	$1\frac{1}{4}$ cups Sauce Espagnole (page 622)

Soak sweetbreads in cold water for 3 to 4 hours. Remove membranes and filaments. Poach in salted water and *half the lemon juice* for 8 to 10 minutes. Cool before using. Scrub mushrooms; remove woody part of stems. Simmer for 5 minutes in very little water with *remaining lemon juice*, butter, salt, and pepper. Cool and drain. Combine mushrooms, diced sweetbreads, godiveau, liver, and ham with the sauce espagnole. Simmer very gently to heat through and blend flavors. Serve plain or on fried toast or in vol-au-vents. Serves 4.

VEAL KIDNEYS APICIUS

Prehistoric warriors believed that kidneys imparted courage. In Roman times, whence this recipe dates, they were eaten mainly for their own sake, although in the famous banquet scene in Petronius' *Satyricon* kidneys were served as edible symbols of the Gemini.

$\frac{1}{3}$ cup butter

2 shallots or $\frac{1}{2}$ small onion, minced

4 veal kidneys, with a little fat left on, thinly sliced

$\frac{1}{2}$ cup Madeira or sherry

Salt and freshly ground pepper

1 cup Sauce Robert (page 623)

2 cups cooked rice

$\frac{1}{4}$ cup pine nuts

2 coriander seeds, crushed to a powder

Melt 3 *tablespoons butter* in a frying pan and sauté shallots for 1 minute. Add kidneys and sauté quickly until red disappears. Add Madeira, simmer briskly for 2 to 3 minutes, add salt, freshly ground pepper, and sauce robert. Heat thoroughly without boiling. Mix *remaining butter* with hot cooked rice and toss with pine nuts, coriander powder, salt, and pepper. Mound rice in the center of a heated dish, surround with kidneys. Serves 4.

NEAT'S TONGUE ROASTED WITH RHENISH WINE

1 $4\frac{1}{2}$-pound fresh tongue

Bouquet garni (2 bay leaves, 2 cloves garlic, $\frac{1}{2}$ teaspoon thyme, 6 sprigs parsley, 6 peppercorns, 4 to 5 crushed coriander seeds, tied in cheesecloth)

3 cups Rhine or semidry white wine

2 small onions, each stuck with 2 cloves

Salt and pepper

2 tablespoons butter

2 shallots, chopped

$1\frac{1}{4}$ cups Brown Sauce (page 620)

$\frac{1}{4}$ teaspoon dried basil

$\frac{1}{4}$ teaspoon dried tarragon

$\frac{1}{8}$ teaspoon powdered mace

Orange or lemon juice to taste

Put tongue, bouquet garni, wine, onions, 1 tablespoon salt, $\frac{1}{2}$ teaspoon pepper, and 3 quarts water (or enough to cover tongue) in a tall straight-sided pot. Cover; bring to a boil and skim. Lower heat and simmer for 2 to 3 hours or until bones fall away and meat is tender. Remove the skin and root. Melt the butter in a braising kettle with a lid, and brown the shallots. Add the tongue, brown sauce, $1\frac{1}{4}$ cups liquid from tongue, the herbs, and mace. Cover and put into preheated 350° oven for 45 minutes. Turn the tongue and cook for another 45 minutes. Remove tongue to a platter. Skim fat from gravy; add orange or lemon juice to taste. Slice the tongue and pour a little sauce over it. Pass remainder in a sauceboat. Serves 4.

RICE
AND OTHER
GRAINS

"Mother, feed me, I am hungry," prays the Philippine peasant as he commences the day's labors in the rice fields, repeating a ritual that has barely changed since Neolithic times. Like the maize cultivated by the peasants of Latin America, the growing of rice in Asia is steeped in traditions based on a belief in a soul that lies within each grain of rice. Though India was the probable site of the first cultivated crop, many Eastern countries have a rich mythology to prove their own claim to that honor. In Java it is related that Shiva, a Hindu god, took a fancy to the goddess Retna Dumila, who agreed to submit to him only after he had created the perfect food. Failing, Shiva enlisted the help of his lieutenant, Kala Gumerong, who in turn was thwarted by another reluctant goddess, Dewie Srie. Virginal to their deaths, the two enchantresses were buried by their grieving suitors, and from their tombs sprang the perfect food, Rice.

RISOTTO ALLA MILANESE

Rice, the chief grain of northern Italy, was considered by ancient Romans to be a calorific cure for consumption. Apicius employed it as a thickener, and the Tuscans adapted the *risotto* by simmering it with meat in a broth. It was not until the Renaissance when traveling Italians tasted French fish stews, Spanish paella, or Turkish pilaf that rice was combined with saffron (made from stigmas of the crocus flower). The Milanese specialty below was purportedly invented in 1574 by a certain Zafferano, named for his trade of "gilding" foods with the precious yellow spice, who sampling a poorly prepared *risotto*, doctored the dish with saffron and other savory ingredients to save Milan's culinary reputation.

2 cups long-grained rice
5 tablespoons butter
1 medium onion, finely chopped
7 or 8 threads of saffron or a pinch
   of powdered saffron

4 to 5 cups chicken broth
$\frac{1}{2}$ cup grated Parmesan cheese
Salt

Do not wash rice; place it between two kitchen towels and rub until grains are shiny. Heat *3 tablespoons butter* in a heavy-bottomed saucepan and sauté onion slowly until soft and bright yellow but not brown. Add rice, stir well, and sauté for about 5 minutes or until grains become glassy and translucent. Dissolve saffron in hot chicken broth for 10 minutes. Add *1 cup boiling chicken broth* to rice. Cover and simmer gently until broth is absorbed. Add *remaining broth*, a cup at a time, as needed. Cook until rice is tender but not too soft—about 15 to 20 minutes depending on the type of rice used. Add *remaining butter*, Parmesan cheese, and salt to taste and toss lightly with a fork. Serves 6.

VARIATIONS: Add $\frac{1}{2}$ cup white wine to sautéed rice and simmer until wine evaporates before adding broth. Sautéed minced chicken livers or mushrooms may be tossed in with risotto after it is cooked. *Risotto Piemontese*: Follow basic recipe, eliminating onion and saffron. Sauté rice in butter until glassy and translucent and add chicken broth as directed. When rice is tender, add 3 tablespoons butter and 3 tablespoons grated Parmesan cheese. Toss lightly through rice with fork, turn into serving dish, and top with a border of 4 or 5 thinly sliced canned Italian white truffles. Serve additional cheese on the side. *Seafood Risotto*: Follow basic recipe, eliminating saffron. Add white wine to rice after it has been sautéed. Simmer until wine evaporates, then add fish broth instead of chicken broth. Heat about 3 cups of cooked, cut-up shellfish (shrimp, lobster, squid, whole mussels, or clams) in a little butter and stir into rice. If desired, 2 large peeled and seeded tomatoes, fresh or canned, or 3 tablespoons tomato purée may be added with the broth. Herbs such as thyme or minced parsley may also be added.

RISI E BISI VENEZIANA

By commandeering the overland spice routes between Europe and Asia in the sixteenth century, Venice also acquired a cosmopolitan cuisine. Turkish pilaf, combined with peas as in the recipe below, went into the traditional Venetian soup served to the Doges on the April 25 Feast of Saint Mark. Ingredients would arrive in the lagoon-locked city, as Samuel Johnson's crony Mrs. Piozzi noted in the 1780's, "from *terra firma* loaded with every produce of nature, neatly arranged in . . . flat-bottomed conveyances [gondolas]."

1 large onion, minced	1 teaspoon salt
$\frac{1}{3}$ cup butter	Pinch of pepper
1 cup rice	1 cup shelled young peas or 1 package
$2\frac{1}{2}$ cups beef broth	thawed frozen peas
1 bay leaf	$\frac{1}{2}$ cup grated Parmesan cheese

Stew the onion in *half the butter* until transparent. Add the rice and sauté for 3 minutes more or until rice is glassy. Add the broth, bay leaf, salt, and pepper. Stir once, cover, and simmer for 12 minutes. Add peas and cook until peas and rice are tender, adding a few spoonfuls of broth or water if needed. When done, toss with *remaining butter* and cheese and serve immediately. Serves 4.

MOROS Y CRISTIANOS

With the name of this dish, Cubans recall centuries of coexistence between Moors and Christian Spaniards. Similar combinations of black beans and rice are found throughout Latin America, and, though eaten almost daily, they carry a special omen of good luck on New Year's Day.

1 pound dried black beans
1 ham bone or 1 1½-pound smoked ham butt or ½ pound cubed salt pork, fried
1 teaspoon salt
3 cloves garlic, minced
1 bay leaf
¼ teaspoon dried thyme
3 or 4 sprigs parsley
2 tablespoons olive oil or rendered bacon fat

1 large onion, chopped
1 green pepper, seeded and chopped
1 large tomato, peeled, seeded, and chopped (optional)
1½ tablespoons vinegar
Black pepper to taste
4 cups hot cooked rice
Garnishes: chopped hard-boiled eggs, minced onion, olive oil, lemon wedges

Soak beans overnight in water to cover. Drain and place in pot with ham bone, cover with water (about 6 cups), and add salt, garlic, bay leaf, thyme, and parsley. Simmer slowly for about 1 hour or until beans are almost tender. Heat olive oil or bacon fat and sauté onion and green pepper until soft. Add tomato and vinegar, simmer for a minute or two, and add to beans. Season to taste and simmer for another 20 to 30 minutes or until beans are tender. Serve beans on bed of rice with garnishes on side. Sliced ham may be served separately or with the beans. Serves 6 to 8.

VARIATION: Red kidney beans or lentils may be substituted for black beans. In the Orient, soy sauce and rice wine or dry sherry to taste are added to boiled red kidney beans and tossed with cooked rice.

FRIED RICE

4 cups cold cooked rice
3 eggs, well beaten
Salt and pepper
½ cup sesame or peanut oil
4 scallions, bulbs and greens, minced
1 cup cubed roast pork, chicken, or duck
¼ pound ham, diced
10 cooked shrimps, shelled and deveined, or ½ cup diced lobster or crabmeat

1 cup bean sprouts, bamboo shoots, or chopped celery, blanched
6 dried mushrooms, soaked and chopped
2 tablespoons soy sauce, or to taste
½ teaspoon sugar

Separate the grains of rice with a fork so they do not stick. Beat the eggs with a little salt and pepper. Heat 3 *tablespoons oil* in a large frying pan. Pour in the eggs, forming a thin pancake.

Cook on low heat until just set. Remove from pan, set aside until cool, and shred. Add another *3 tablespoons oil* and cook the scallions for 2 to 3 minutes. Add *remaining oil*, meats, shellfish, and vegetables. Turn heat high and add rice. Stir and fry quickly until hot. Add soy sauce, sugar, pepper to taste, and shredded egg pancake; toss. Serve very hot. Serves 6 to 8.

CONGEE

In China, where rice is almost a religion, even the imperial court were expected to do their share to ensure a bountiful crop. Each year at the beginning of the planting season, and with great ceremony, they plowed their appointed rows—three for the emperor, six for his sons, and so on down to the mandarin's fifteen. The peasant, whose days in the rice paddies were more arduous than those of their rulers, might go home to a bowl of Congee, a rice porridge flavored with leftovers.

1 cup long-grained rice, or $\frac{3}{4}$ cup long-grained rice and $\frac{1}{4}$ cup glutinous rice
$\frac{1}{2}$ pound cubed raw meat or fish (chicken, beef, pork, ham, shelled shrimps, lobster, or crabmeat)
6 scallions, minced
2 slices ginger root, minced, or $\frac{1}{2}$ teaspoon powdered ginger

1 teaspoon salt
$\frac{1}{4}$ cup dry sherry
1 tablespoon sesame oil
1 tablespoon soy sauce
8 to 10 cups water or broth
2 eggs, beaten (optional)

Place all ingredients except eggs in a deep pot. Bring to a boil, cover, and simmer gently for 30 to 45 minutes, adding water if needed. Cook until rice has reached a porridgelike consistency. If glutinous rice is used, cooking time should be increased to $1\frac{1}{2}$ to 2 hours. Stir eggs into cooked congee just long enough to set. Correct seasoning. Serves 6.

PELLAO WITH PLANTAINS

Pellao, the rice of India, is traditionally cooked with other ingredients. Gold and silver leaf—thought by some to be digestive aids—decorate the upper-caste Pellao on festive occasions. Slices of plantain, a species of banana, suffice for the less affluent. The banana is native to the tropical regions of Asia. It was the forbidden fruit of Hindu legend, and certain varieties of the "Tree of Paradise" were cultivated only in monasteries where they provided shade and sustenance for sages and holy men.

$\frac{1}{2}$ cup butter	$\frac{1}{2}$ teaspoon powdered cumin
2 pounds boneless lamb, cubed	$\frac{1}{4}$ teaspoon powdered cardamom
2 large onions, sliced	$\frac{1}{2}$ teaspoon powdered cinnamon
1 tablespoon minced fresh ginger root	$\frac{1}{2}$ cup sugar
or $\frac{1}{2}$ teaspoon powdered ginger	Juice of 3 limes
1 teaspoon pounded coriander seeds	2 cups rice
or $\frac{1}{2}$ teaspoon powdered coriander	Freshly ground pepper
$\frac{1}{4}$ teaspoon powdered cloves	6 plantains or large bananas
1 teaspoon salt	

Melt *4 tablespoons butter* in a casserole or heavy kettle and brown the meat for 5 to 6 minutes. Turn it and add the next 8 ingredients. Cook for 6 to 8 minutes or until meat and onions are browned. Add $2\frac{1}{2}$ cups water and simmer. Cook sugar with $\frac{1}{4}$ cup water on low heat for 5 minutes, covered. Cool. Add 1 tablespoon sugar syrup and the *juice of 1 lime* to meat. Boil the rice for 6 to 8 minutes in salted water. Drain well and add to meat and gravy. Stir rice, bring to a boil, simmer on low heat for 10 minutes, adding a little water or beef broth if needed. Add *remaining butter*, cover, and simmer gently for 5 minutes longer. Season to taste with freshly ground pepper. While meat and rice are cooking, poach the plantains or bananas (halved lengthwise) in remaining syrup and *lime juice*—20 minutes for plantains, 5 minutes for bananas. Serve the pellao with the plantains on top. Serves 6.

KITCHERIE

Rice and lentils, flavored with various curry spices, are the basis of this Indian breakfast food. British colonials, substituting leftovers of fish for beans, renamed it Kedgeree.

1 clove garlic (optional)	1 teaspoon salt
1 large onion, sliced	1 cup lentils or yellow split peas,
6 tablespoons Ghee (page 630)	soaked and drained
2 teaspoons curry powder or pinch each	1 cup rice
powdered cloves, mace, cardamom,	2 to 3 cups water as needed
ginger, and black pepper	2 hard-boiled eggs, quartered

Sauté garlic and onion in *4 tablespoons ghee* until soft and golden—about 10 minutes. Stir in curry powder or spices and salt and sauté for 2 to 3 minutes. Add lentils or peas and rice; stir until blended with butter and spices. Add 2 cups boiling water, cover, and simmer slowly for about 20 to 30 minutes or until rice and beans are tender. Add a little more boiling water if necessary. When tender, uncover and place over low heat until water evaporates and mixture is dry. Garnish with hard-boiled egg quarters and *remaining ghee*. Serves 6.

PAELLA VALENCIANA

By bringing rice and saffron to Spain, the Moors provided the basis for the world-renowned Paella Valenciana, a dish of chicken, shellfish, and vegetables simmered together in a broad, flat pan. Its ancestor was, perhaps, the Persian *pilaf* of rice, nuts, chicken, lamb, and seasonings, invented about the time of Darius I in the fifth century B.C. Practically every country has a related rice dish: the Indians have *pellao*; the Africans, *perleau*; and in early-nineteenth-century New Orleans eclectic chefs created *jambalaya*, a combination of ham (*jambon*) and *paella*.

1 teaspoon dried saffron	2 cups rice
4 to 5 cups broth, half chicken, half clam	2 large tomatoes, peeled, seeded, and diced
1 cup olive oil	2 small lobsters, cut into chunks
2 cloves garlic	12 mussels or clams or both, scrubbed
1 3-pound chicken, cut into 2-inch pieces	12 shrimps, shelled and deveined
Salt and pepper	2 chorizos or Italian sausages
1 large onion, finely chopped	1 small jar pimentos
	$\frac{1}{2}$ cup cooked green peas

Bring saffron and broth to a boil and keep hot. In a 12- to 14-cup casserole or paella pan heat *half the oil* and fry the garlic until brown; remove and discard it. Fry the chicken pieces until golden. Season with salt and pepper, turn, and add oil as needed. Add the onion and cook until brown, add *more oil* and rice, and cook, stirring about 3 minutes or until slightly browned. Add tomatoes and simmer over low heat for 2 to 3 minutes. Add 4 cups broth to rice mixture and stir once. Bury lobster pieces, mussels, clams, and shrimps in the rice and cover and simmer for 12 to 15 minutes or until rice is done and fish is cooked. Discard any unopened shells. If rice needs more cooking, add broth as needed. Put paella in a preheated 450° oven for 10 minutes, uncovered. Meanwhile, slice and fry the chorizos in *2 tablespoons olive oil*, reserve. Cut the pimento in even sections and heat slightly in oil. Mix peas and chorizos into paella. Arrange pimento in a decorative circle over rice. Serve very hot. Serves 8 to 10. Any cooked vegetables may be added (artichoke hearts, zucchini, yellow squash). The paella may also be made with chunks of fish. Heat oil and garlic, discard garlic, cook onion until golden, brown 2 pounds solid fish and continue recipe as above, minus shellfish.

563

TURKISH PILAF

$\frac{1}{2}$ cup butter

1 onion, finely chopped

2 cups rice

$\frac{1}{2}$ teaspoon powdered cinnamon

$\frac{1}{2}$ teaspoon powdered allspice

$\frac{1}{4}$ teaspoon powdered mace

$\frac{1}{8}$ teaspoon powdered cloves

5 cups strong beef broth

Salt and pepper

$\frac{1}{4}$ cup pine nuts

$\frac{1}{4}$ cup slivered almonds

$\frac{1}{4}$ cup black currants

Melt *half the butter* in a large saucepan. Brown the onion, add the rice, and stir for 3 to 5 minutes while rice browns. Add the spices and the broth. Stir well once, lower the heat, cover, and simmer for 15 minutes. Test for doneness. Rice should be firm. Drain any excess broth. Season to taste with salt and pepper. Meanwhile, sauté the pine nuts, almonds, and currants in the *remaining butter*. Mix with the rice. Serve in a heated serving dish as an accompaniment to lamb or chicken. Serves 6.

VARIATION: *Herb and Olive Pilaf*: Substitute $\frac{1}{2}$ teaspoon each dried thyme and marjoram for spices, and $\frac{3}{4}$ cup chopped black olives and $\frac{1}{4}$ cup chopped parsley for nuts and currants.

MAMALIGA

The maize that goes into this corn meal mush first came to Europe in the holds of Columbus' returning ships, but, like the potato, it was slow to be recognized as food for human consumption. The Portuguese tried to grow corn in Java in 1496 and in China in 1516, but rarely planted it at home. The Venetians, when they found the Turks a ready market, gladly sold all their seeds to the infidels. (By a curious twist Mohammed had told of a plant in Paradise that "grows in the twinkling of an eye . . . in sheaves like mountains," and his followers fell to cultivating the Venetians' cast-off maize with something like the joy of men in the Promised Land.) So successful were the Turks in their new agricultural venture that the rest of Europe took to calling the plant "Turkie Corne"; and when, in the seventeenth century, the Italians reconsidered matters and began to cultivate it on their own northern plains, they turned to the Turks for assistance. Because corn was rougher than other grains and less adaptable to baking (one naturalist said, "it is hard and dry as Bisket is, and hath in it no clamminesse at all, for which cause it . . . is of hard and evil digestion"), Europeans have generally eaten their corn in porridge form. Rumanians call it Mamaliga; Italians, Polenta. In Jamaica, where the mush is made into portable little cakes, it is known as Stamp-and-Go, local slang for traveling, like the American Journeycake.

1 quart boiling water

$1\frac{1}{2}$ teaspoons salt

1 cup yellow corn meal

Bring water and salt to a rolling boil in a large heavy-bottomed saucepan. Lower heat and trickle corn meal into water so that water continues to boil. Stir briskly, keeping water at a boil. When slightly thickened, cover, and simmer gently for 12 to 15 minutes. Serve immediately with a lump of butter or pour into a small, oiled loaf pan, cool completely, slice, and fry in butter until golden on both sides. Serves 6.

VARIATIONS: Cook 1 recipe mamaliga for 5 minutes. Pour *half the hot mamaliga* into a 10-inch pie plate liberally greased with bacon fat. Sprinkle with 4 slices fried bacon, crumbled, and $\frac{1}{2}$ cup grated dry cheddar or Parmesan cheese. Cover with *remaining mamaliga*, another 4 slices bacon, crumbled, and $\frac{1}{2}$ cup more cheese. Bake in a preheated 400° oven for 15 minutes. Cut into wedges and serve hot with salad. *Mamaliga Dumplings*: Form cold mamaliga into balls and push a hole in the dumplings. Stuff with chopped ham, crumbled bacon, chopped hard-boiled egg, or diced cheese. Seal dumplings with more mush, roll in flour, and deep fry in hot (360°) vegetable shortening for 4 to 5 minutes or until golden brown. Drain on paper towels and serve with sour cream or spear with toothpicks as a hot appetizer. Makes about $2\frac{1}{2}$ dozen.

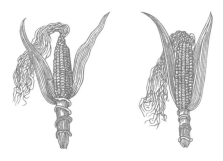

KASHA AND MUSHROOMS

Kasha, a dish of cooked groats, has been a staple of the Russian diet for many centuries. It was a particular favorite of the *chumak* merchants, purveyors of salted and dried fish, who never set out on one of their long journeys inland without a hefty supply of buckwheat or other grain with which to prepare their campfire dinners.

$\frac{1}{2}$ cup butter	$\frac{1}{4}$ pound chopped mushrooms, sautéed
$1\frac{1}{2}$ cups kasha	in butter, or 1 recipe Mushrooms in
1 teaspoon salt	Sour Cream (page 591)

Heat the butter in a large frying pan. When bubbling hot add the kasha and stir it on a medium heat for 6 to 8 minutes until well coated with butter and slightly browned. Put into a 2-quart oven dish and add boiling water to 1 inch above the kasha. Add the salt, stir once, cover, and place in a preheated 350° oven for 1 hour. Add a little boiling water if necessary, but do not stir the kasha. Uncover for final 15 minutes to let steam escape; it should be dry and stand out grain by grain. Combine with mushrooms in an ovenproof dish and reheat in a 350° oven. Serves 4 to 6.

PASTA, PANCAKES,
AND
DUMPLINGS

NOODLE DOUGH

Noodles are said to have been introduced to the West from China by Marco Polo; certainly they have been a staple since the Middle Ages, and especially in Marco's Italy. The Fascists (who believed pasta unhealthy) were unable to discourage its consumption, though they called it the creation of the barbaric Ostrogoths who boiled it "with onions, garlic, and turnips and licked their fingers and their faces."

4 eggs
¼ cup water

Salt
4 to 5 cups flour, or as needed

Beat eggs with water and salt until well mixed. Place flour in a bowl, make a well, pour in eggs, and gradually stir until mixture can be kneaded. Knead into a soft dough. Place dough on a lightly floured board, cover with a damp cloth, and let stand for about 20 minutes. Knead again until smooth and elastic. Cut dough into thirds and roll out each section to paper thinness on a floured board. Let dry for 20 minutes. Roll jelly roll fashion and cut crosswise slices to desired width. Unroll slices, spread on cloth, and dry 5 to 6 hours before cooking. Dry noodles may be stored in a tightly covered jar. Before serving, boil in salted water for 8 to 10 minutes. Drain and serve in soup or as an entree. Serves 6.

TARHONYA
(Hungarian Egg Barley)

1 recipe Noodle Dough (above)
¾ cup butter

1 teaspoon paprika
Beef or chicken broth, to cover

Prepare the noodle dough and shape into 2 balls. Let dry for 30 minutes. Grate on coarse side of a grater over a clean cloth. Move grater so that dough does not pile up; there should be 1 thin layer spread over the cloth. Let dry for 5 to 6 hours. Dough may also be spread on cookie sheets and dried in a preheated 170° oven. Cool and store tarhonya until needed. To cook, sauté tarhonya in *one-half cup butter* until golden, stirring to brown evenly. Add paprika, sauté for 1 to 2 minutes, and cover with broth. Cover and simmer for 40 minutes or until soft. Toss with *remaining butter*, season with salt and pepper. Serves 8 to 10.

566

VARENIKI

The Russian boiled dumpling, like its Italian kin, ravioli, may be made with a variety of fillings. In Russia the contents change with the seasons. There is mushroom stuffing in autumn, sauerkraut at Christmas, and berry-filled dessert dumplings throughout the summer. Cottage or pot cheese Vareniki, the national favorite, is served all year round.

1 cup dry cottage cheese	$\frac{1}{8}$ teaspoon nutmeg (optional)
1 egg	1 recipe Noodle Dough (opposite)
Salt to taste	Melted butter
$\frac{1}{4}$ teaspoon white pepper	Sour cream

Mix cheese, egg, salt and pepper, and nutmeg. Roll out noodle dough to $\frac{1}{8}$-inch thickness and cut into 2-inch squares. Place 1 heaping teaspoon cottage cheese filling in the corner of each square. Bring over corner of dough to make a triangle and seal securely. Drop into boiling salted water and simmer for 10 to 12 minutes or until vareniki float. Drain well. Serve with melted butter and sour cream. Makes about 32 vareniki.

VARIATIONS: *Dessert Vareniki*: Cover $1\frac{1}{2}$ pounds berries, pitted plums, or cherries with $\frac{3}{4}$ cup sugar and let stand a few hours. Drain juice and boil to a thick syrup. Roll out dough. Fill with drained fruit and seal as above. Boil in slightly salted water and serve with fruit syrup and sour cream. *Pelmeni*: Roll noodle dough as described above. Fill with mixture of 1 pound lean ground beef, 1 tablespoon grated onion, 2 tablespoons fresh chopped dill, and salt and pepper to taste. Fill and cook as for vareniki.

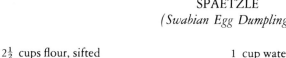

SPAETZLE
(Swabian Egg Dumplings)

$2\frac{1}{2}$ cups flour, sifted	1 cup water, or as needed
1 teaspoon salt	1 cup butter
$\frac{3}{4}$ teaspoon baking powder (optional)	$\frac{1}{2}$ cup bread crumbs
4 eggs, slightly beaten	

Resift flour with salt and baking powder into a large bowl. Make a well in the flour. Place the eggs in the well and with a wire whisk work the flour with the eggs, gradually adding water until dough becomes moist and not too stiff. Fill a large saucepan half full of water and bring to a simmer. Place a colander over the water and dribble in a spoonful of the dough—if it is too stiff to go through the holes, add a little more water. Force dough through colander a little at a time and simmer for about 3 minutes—until spaetzle float. Remove with a slotted spoon to a warm serving dish. Melt the butter in a frying pan and gently brown the bread crumbs until golden, stirring often to prevent scorching. Pour over the spaetzle and serve immediately. Serves 4 to 6.

DIEN HSING

These translucent dumplings, stuffed with minced meats and other fillings, are so highly appreciated by the Chinese that they are named "heart touchers." They are served sometimes as appetizers, sometimes as whole meals in restaurants which specialize in their preparation. Steaming permits the frugal Chinese to cook a variety of Dien Hsing, vegetables, and other foods in several layers.

4 cups flour	1 recipe Spring Roll filling (opposite)
2 cups boiling water	with 1 tablespoon cornstarch added

Place flour in a bowl, pour in boiling water, and stir briskly with a wooden spoon until dough looks firm and translucent and does not adhere to the sides of the bowl. Add a little more water if needed. Cover with a damp cloth and let cool. Place dough on a lightly floured pastry board or cloth. Roll into a sausage about 1 inch in diameter. Cut into 1-inch pieces. Roll each piece into a ball and flatten with the hand, keeping remaining pieces covered until all are done. Roll or press out to a 3-inch circle and put 1 heaping teaspoon of filling in center of circle. Form into turnover, turning the edges upon themselves to secure firmly. Steam on a cloth-covered rack in a covered pot for about 25 minutes. Makes 48. Instead of steaming, dumplings may be fried in oil (360°) for 3 to 4 minutes or until golden. Drain and serve hot.

MI-KROB
(Siamese Fried Noodles)

1 pound Chinese vermicelli or Thai rice noodles	$\frac{1}{4}$ pound bean curd, diced
	1 cup bean sprouts (optional)
2 cups peanut or sesame oil	1 tablespoon soy sauce
3 cloves garlic, minced	1 tablespoon lime or lemon juice,
2 large shallots, minced	or to taste
1 thick pork chop, boned and cubed	1 teaspoon sugar
1 chicken breast, split, boned, and cubed	4 eggs
12 large shrimps, shelled, deveined, and diced	Garnishes: chopped chives, powdered coriander, chopped chili peppers,
1 7½-ounce can crabmeat	grated orange rind

Scald the vermicelli in boiling water. Drain and spread out to dry on a towel placed on a pastry board. Heat *enough of the oil* in a large frying pan to cover the vermicelli. Fry in batches, turning once or twice. When golden, drain on paper towels. Fry the garlic and shallots in *3 to 4 tablespoons of oil*. Add pork and chicken and cook for 8 to 10 minutes, add the shrimp, cook for 5 minutes, then add the crabmeat, bean curd, and bean sprouts. Stir constantly. Add the seasonings and *more oil* if needed. Add the eggs. Stir until set. Break up the fried vermicelli and stir in. Serve hot with garnishes. Serves 6 to 8.

SOBA
(Japanese Buckwheat Noodles)

1½ pounds buckwheat vermicelli
    (Japanese soba)
Salt
2½ cups Dashi (page 421)
⅓ cup sake or dry sherry

½ cup soy sauce
1 tablespoon sugar
Ice cubes or crushed ice
6 to 8 scallions, bulbs and green tops,
    thinly sliced

Cook the vermicelli in boiling salted water. When tender rinse in cold water, drain well, and chill for several hours. Combine the dashi, wine, soy sauce, and sugar in a saucepan and simmer for 3 to 4 minutes. Cool and chill. At serving time arrange noodles on cracked ice in individual bowls. Top with scallions. Serve sauce as dip on side. Serves 5 to 6.

SPRING ROLLS

Chinese greet visiting friends and relatives on the first day of spring (the New Year) with tea and these filled "skins," sometimes called egg rolls.

2 cups flour
1 teaspoon salt
2 eggs, beaten
Cornstarch for dredging
Peanut or corn oil for frying
Filling:
½ cup minced roast pork
½ cup minced smoked ham
¾ cup minced cooked shrimp
½ cup shredded bamboo shoots

¼ cup shredded water chestnuts
4 scallions, minced
½ cup finely sliced dried mushrooms
    (previously soaked and drained)
1 slice ginger root, minced, or
    ¼ teaspoon powdered ginger
½ teaspoon sugar
1 tablespoon soy sauce
Salt and pepper
3 tablespoons peanut or corn oil

Beat flour and salt into eggs. Add about 2 cups water gradually to make smooth, thin batter, the consistency of heavy cream. Beat well in 1 direction only. Lightly oil a 6-inch skillet. Heat slowly. Pour in a scant tablespoon of batter. Tip and rotate pan so bottom is evenly coated. Cook just long enough to set—about 1 minute. Skins should be dry but not brown. Repeat, beating batter each time and oiling pan lightly. Stack skins and keep covered with a cloth wrung out in cold water until ready to use.

To prepare the filling: Mix meats, shrimp, and vegetables. Season with ginger, sugar, soy sauce, and salt and pepper to taste. Heat the oil and toss the filling in the hot oil to heat through. Drain well and cool before using. Pork may be replaced by beef, shrimp by chicken. Also, 1 cup blanched Chinese cabbage or 1 cup bean sprouts may be added. Place a row of about ¼ cup of cold filling 1 inch from center of skin. Fold short sides in, then roll up, as for jelly roll. Dredge lightly with cornstarch. Heat 1-inch depth of oil to 375°. Fry rolls until golden brown on both sides and drain. Serve with Chinese mustard and duck sauce. Serves 6 to 8.

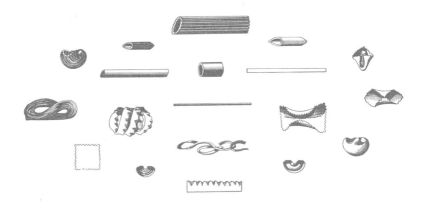

RAVIOLI FIORENTINA

The stuffed cases of pasta called Ravioli (from a word meaning "little turnips") have been relished by Italians since the thirteenth century. The recipe below, adapted from Bartolomeo Scappi's cookbook of 1570, is typical of Florence and consists, peculiarly, of a dumpling-like filling minus the dough cover. Its principal ingredient, spinach, was introduced to Europe by the Moors.

$\frac{1}{2}$ pound ricotta, cottage cheese, pot
  cheese, or farmer cheese
2 cups cooked chopped spinach
1 cup grated Parmesan cheese

2 eggs
Salt and nutmeg to taste
Flour for dredging
$\frac{3}{4}$ cup butter, melted

If using ricotta or cottage cheese, drain in refrigerator overnight in a strainer placed over a bowl. Press out excess whey before preparing. If using pot cheese or farmer cheese, rub through a fine sieve. Drain spinach, place in double thickness of cheesecloth, and wring out excess moisture. Mix cheese and spinach with *half the Parmesan cheese*, eggs, salt, and nutmeg. Shape mixture into balls about the size of walnuts. Dredge very lightly with flour, tapping off excess. Drop gently into lightly salted boiling water and simmer for 18 to 20 minutes. Remove with slotted spoon or strainer. Drain and serve with melted butter and *remaining Parmesan cheese* or serve in chicken or beef broth. Serves 4 to 6.

VARIATION: To use as pasta filling, prepare double recipe of Noodle Dough (page 566), adding 2 extra egg yolks, slightly beaten, and enough warm water to make a soft, pliable dough. Halve dough. Roll half into a $\frac{1}{8}$-inch-thick square. Place a teaspoon of filling at 2-inch intervals. Roll out remaining dough to same size. Cover the first strip and cut between the mounds with a pastry cutter. Poach in boiling salted water for 20 to 30 minutes or to desired softness. Remove and keep warm. Melt the butter, browning it lightly. Place a layer of ravioli in buttered casserole, pour over some butter, sprinkle with cheese, and repeat, ending with cheese. Bake in a preheated 400° oven for 20 to 30 minutes. Serves 6 to 8.

TIMBAL OF MACARONI ON CUSHIONS OF EGGPLANT

Sicilians consider pasta "blessed food," and dishes like the one below were often associated with miracles. Once when a fourteenth-century hermit, Guglielmo (beatified by Pope Paul III in 1537), dined at a neighbor's, the wife, who was in league with the devil, served pasta filled with chaff to mock the holy man. Unconcerned, the saint said grace and cut into his ziti, revealing to his astonished hostess a stuffing not of chaff but of ricotta. Ippolito Cavalcanti, Duke of Buonvicino, offered the following pasta dish in his *Cucina Teòrico-Pratica*, Naples (1839).

1 large eggplant, peeled and cut into
  $\frac{3}{4}$-inch-thick slices
Salt
Flour for dredging
$\frac{1}{2}$ cup olive oil

1 pound ziti macaroni
4 cups tomato or meat sauce
1 pound mozzarella cheese,
  diced or sliced
$\frac{1}{2}$ to $\frac{3}{4}$ cup grated Parmesan cheese

Sprinkle eggplant slices with salt; place in bowl and top with a plate to weight them down. After 20 minutes, remove slices and rinse and dry thoroughly. Dredge lightly on both sides with flour and fry in olive oil for about 10 minutes, turning once so both sides are golden brown. Drain and dice eggplant. Cook ziti in boiling water until tender. Drain thoroughly and mix with *one and one-half cups sauce*. Place half the ziti in the bottom of a rectangular baking dish, top with half the eggplant. Add remaining ziti and, finally, a layer of eggplant. Pour *remaining sauce* over eggplant. Cover with diced mozzarella cheese and sprinkle with grated Parmesan. Bake in preheated 375° oven for 15 minutes or until cheese is melted and golden brown on top. Serves 6.

NEAPOLITAN SPAGHETTI WITH FISH SAUCE

Not only has Naples long been renowned for its seafood, especially its small clams, but its chauvinistic citizens also boast making the best pasta in Italy. Even that eighteenth-century rogue Casanova, who was wont to limit praise to his own exploits, lavished it on this dish.

1 recipe Zuppa di Pesce (see Bouillabaisse, page 452)
3 to 4 tablespoons tomato paste

1 pound cooked spaghetti or linguine
1 cup minced parsley
Hot red pepper, crushed and dried

Prepare zuppa di pesce using any combination of fish and shellfish. Remove fish to heated platter. Spoon a little broth over fish and keep warm. Simmer fish soup until reduced by a third. Add tomato paste a little at a time, simmering between each addition until sauce is thick enough for spaghetti. Season to taste. Serve spaghetti topped with sauce and minced parsley. Pass hot peppers separately. Fish may be served separately or on spaghetti. Serves 6.

PLUM DUMPLINGS

Although the Chinese conceived and consumed dumplings thousands of years before anyone else, Western cooks, hearing about them from travelers, were quick to adapt them to native tastes. From the won ton prototype came stuffed dumplings ranging from ravioli to Hungarian plum dumplings. This lowly ball of dough, whose very name means "ill-shaped piece," has borne the brunt of endless unkind remarks but has suffered no loss of popularity.

1 pound small blue Italian plums (or apricots)	1 recipe Gnocchi di Patate dough (below)
12 to 15 sugar cubes	

Cut washed fruit just enough so that pits can be removed. Press 1 cube of sugar into the hollow of each piece of fruit and press fruit closed around it. Roll out kneaded dough and cut into pieces large enough to wrap around each piece of fruit. Enclose each piece completely. Cook in rapidly boiling salted water for about 15 minutes or until dumplings float. Reduce heat and simmer for 5 minutes longer. Remove and drain. Serve with melted butter or bread crumbs browned in butter or with sugar. Serves 4 to 6.

GNOCCHI DI PATATE

Since northern Italy became part of the Holy Roman Empire in 962, its cookery has reflected a certain Germanic gestalt. The Piedmontese Gnocchi (dumplings) below contain potatoes and closely resemble the Bavarian *Knödel*. The Tuscans, however, make theirs from spinach and dub the dumplings *strozzapreti* (choke the priest), in reference to a cleric who strangled from euphoria while eating them.

6 baking potatoes	2 teaspoons salt
3 egg yolks	2 to $2\frac{1}{2}$ cups flour

Boil or, preferably, bake potatoes until tender. Peel, mash, and chill overnight. Mix mashed potatoes with egg yolks and salt. Turn mixture onto a lightly floured board, make a well in the center, and add *1 cup flour*. Knead flour into the potato mixture, adding *more flour* as needed, until dough is smooth and resilient and is neither sticky nor too dry and crumbly. Roll dough into long sausages 1 inch in diameter. Slice into 1- to $1\frac{1}{2}$-inch pieces. Press finger along each slice so that dough curls over toward center. Bring 3 to 4 quarts of lightly salted water to a rolling boil and add gnocchi. Reduce heat and simmer uncovered until gnocchi float to the surface—about 3 to 5 minutes. Cook for 3 to 5 minutes longer or until done. Remove with a slotted spoon and serve with marinara sauce, melted butter, and grated Parmesan cheese, or with Pesto alla Genovese (page 627). Serves 6.

DAMPFNUDELN
(German Steamed Dumplings)

1 envelope dry yeast
$\frac{1}{4}$ cup warm water
$\frac{3}{4}$ cup sugar
$\frac{1}{2}$ cup butter
Salt
4 eggs, lightly beaten
4 to 5 cups flour, or as needed

Cooking liquid:
3 cups milk
1 cup water
3 tablespoons butter
2 tablespoons sugar
2 teaspoons vanilla extract

Combine yeast with warm water and *2 teaspoons sugar*. Stir until yeast becomes pasty. Let stand in a warm place for 10 minutes. Cream butter with *remaining sugar* and $\frac{1}{2}$ teaspoon salt until light and fluffy; then beat in eggs. Stir yeast into egg mixture and gradually add enough flour to make a smooth, soft ball. Knead well on a floured board. Gather dough into a ball and let rise for 1 hour or until doubled in bulk. Punch dough down, and with floured hands, shape into balls about 1 inch in diameter. Place in floured bowl, cover lightly, and let rise for 30 minutes. Combine remaining ingredients and put half the mixture in each of 2 large skillets and bring to a boil. Place equal number of dumplings in each skillet. Cover tightly, reduce heat, and simmer slowly for $\frac{1}{2}$ hour without lifting covers. If properly cooked, dumplings should be puffed up and done when liquid has evaporated and there is a sizzling sound. Serve with gravy as accompaniment to meat. For dessert, serve with stewed fruit or Custard Sauce (page 703) or make a small hole in the top of each dumpling and fill with 2 teaspoons prune jam melted in a little butter. Serves 8 to 10.

BOHEMIAN BREAD DUMPLINGS

3 tablespoons butter or rendered bacon
  fat
$\frac{1}{4}$ cup minced onion
2 tablespoons minced parsley
4 white rolls or 8 slices white or rye
  bread, with crusts, diced

2 to $2\frac{1}{2}$ cups flour, or as needed
2 large eggs
$1\frac{1}{4}$ cups milk
1 teaspoon salt

Heat the butter and sauté onions and parsley until soft. Add diced bread and continue sautéing until onions and bread begin to turn golden brown. Cool. Combine flour, eggs, milk, and salt and beat vigorously for 5 minutes until batter is bubbly. Mix bread through batter and let stand for 30 minutes. If batter is too thin to mold, add more flour as needed. Boil 8 to 10 cups of lightly salted water in a deep pot. With wet hands, shape mixture into large balls about $2\frac{1}{2}$ inches in diameter. Drop gently into boiling water and cook for about 15 minutes or until dumplings float. Reduce heat and simmer for 5 minutes longer. Remove dumplings with a slotted spoon. Drain and serve with meat and gravy or topped with onions and bread crumbs browned in butter. Serves 4 to 6.

PANCAKES

Pancakes predated leavened bread, and in their primitive form consisted of pounded grain mixed with water and fried in oil. Hebrew priests instructed the Israelites that "if thy oblation *be* [meal] *baken* in the frying-pan, it shall be made *of* fine flour with oil. . . . And every oblation . . . shalt thou season with salt." The Romans, however, preferred a sweet flavoring, and in Apicius' pancake recipe below, a syrup of pepper and honey was called for.

2 eggs	Pinch of salt
$\frac{1}{2}$ cup milk	7 or 8 tablespoons flour, or as needed
$\frac{1}{2}$ cup water	Melted butter for frying

Beat eggs with milk, water, and salt, using a rotary beater or wire whisk. Gradually add flour, a tablespoonful at a time, beating constantly until batter is about the consistency of heavy cream. Let stand for 30 minutes. Heat a 5-inch skillet and brush lightly with melted butter. Pour 2 or 3 tablespoons of batter into pan; tip and rotate pan quickly so that batter covers bottom. Pour excess back into batter bowl. Fry for about 1 minute, turn, and fry another 30 seconds to a minute. Add butter as needed. Fill pancakes with creamed seafood or chicken, use for Cheese Blintzes (opposite), or serve with honey. Makes 16 to 18 pancakes.

BLINI

During the Russian Maslyanitsa, or pre-Lenten "butter festival," street vendors sold these yeast-raised pancakes from makeshift stands. At home freshly made Blini were served at every meal, and a diner with a hearty appetite would devour two or three dozen at a sitting, along with the traditional spreads of melted butter, herring, caviar, and sour cream. The pancakes were also associated with more somber occasions. In pre-revolutionary days the lower and middle classes ate Blini after praying for the dead—a ritual performed three times a year. Blini, accompanied by *kootia* (boiled wheat) and vodka, were eaten at the gravesite, and the remains of this little meal were then dropped into the grave "to wet the dry lips of the dead."

1 envelope dry yeast	1 teaspoon salt
$\frac{1}{4}$ cup warm water	4 eggs, separated
1 teaspoon sugar	2 cups Clarified Butter (page 630)
2 cups milk, scalded and cooled to lukewarm	$\frac{1}{2}$ cup heavy cream, whipped (optional)
	1 pound caviar (salmon roe, pressed fresh caviar, or fresh beluga)
1 cup buckwheat flour, sifted	
1 cup white flour, sifted	2 cups sour cream

Soak yeast in warm water with sugar in a large warm bowl. Add *1 cup milk*. Sift flours together. Resift flours and salt and stir 1 cup of the mixture into yeast. Cover, let rise for $\frac{1}{2}$ hour. Add *remaining milk* and flour and slightly beaten yolks. Beat smooth. Let rise until doubled in bulk—about 1 hour. Add 3 *tablespoons clarified butter* and fold in stiffly beaten whites. Fold in whipped cream. Let rise for $\frac{1}{2}$ hour. Make pancakes either in 5-inch skillet, blini pan, or in Swedish pancake pan. Heat pan, add *1 teaspoon clarified butter*. Pour in 1 tablespoon batter, cook for 1 minute. Pour a little *butter* over pancake, turn and cook for about $\frac{1}{2}$ minute. Keep warm in a low oven. To serve: Place half the pancakes on a heated platter. Put a teaspoon of caviar on each pancake. Cover with remaining pancakes. Pour over some of the *remaining clarified butter* from a sauceboat and top with sour cream or whipped cream. Makes 24. Blini may also be served with smoked salmon or herring in sour cream instead of caviar.

CHEESE BLINTZES

1 pound pot cheese, farmer cheese, or
    well-drained cottage cheese
1 egg
Pinch of salt
1 to 2 tablespoons sugar, or to taste
Pinch of cinnamon

$\frac{1}{2}$ teaspoon vanilla extract
$\frac{3}{4}$ cup raisins (optional)
1 recipe Pancake batter (opposite)
Butter for frying
Sour cream

Mix cheese with egg, salt, sugar, cinnamon, vanilla, and raisins. Fry pancakes on one side only. Place brown side up and put 1 tablespoon of filling on edge of each pancake. Fold over once, turn sides in, and fold over once or twice more to form a small rectangular envelope. Fry slowly in hot butter until brown and serve topped with sour cream. Serves 6 to 8.

EGGS, CHEESE,
AND
FRITTERS

OMELETTE

Grimod de la Reynière, Paris' leading gastronome in the decades surrounding the Revolution, estimated that "they know in France 685 different ways of dressing eggs . . ." but for most Frenchmen the basic omelette was supreme. The oft-quoted advice that "omelettes are not made
without breaking eggs" comes from his contemporary, Robespierre.

3 eggs

¼ teaspoon salt

Freshly ground pepper

2 tablespoons butter

Blend eggs, salt, pepper, and 1 teaspoon cold water with a fork. Do not overbeat. Heat
the omelette pan. Add the butter; when it foams and starts to brown, pour in the eggs. Start
immediately shaking the pan back and forth, holding the handle with one hand. At the same
time, scramble the eggs with a fork for a few seconds or until they start to set. Draw cooked
edges toward center and tip pan so uncooked egg runs onto pan. Fold far edge of omelette to
the center of the omelette and turn onto plate, making another fold. Serves 1.

VARIATION: *Omelette aux Fines Herbes*: Mix 1 tablespoon chopped fresh herbs (such as chives,
parsley, chervil, or sorrel) with the eggs. Omelettes may be mixed or filled with cooked
vegetables and meats of any kind. Any mixture with a sauce or juice, such as tomato, should
be used as filling and not mixed with the eggs.

OMELETTE A LA MERE POULARD

This omelette was invented in 1877 by the enterprising wife of a restaurateur on the French island of Mont-St-Michel, after the famous abbey
there had been reopened to pilgrims. Shortly, the omelette seemed to
attract as many people as the shrine. King Oscar II of Sweden was so
intrigued he tried to reproduce it in Mère Poulard's kitchen.

4 whole eggs

2 egg yolks

4 tablespoons heavy cream

½ teaspoon salt

Freshly ground pepper

3 tablespoons butter

Beat the eggs, the egg yolks, *2 tablespoons cream*, salt, and some freshly ground pepper until well mixed. Let stand for 10 to 15 minutes. Melt the butter in an omelette pan until just turning golden and tilt the pan to coat it evenly. Pour in the eggs and stir briskly until omelette begins to set. Shake the pan continually. When omelette is set but still creamy in the center, pour in *remaining cream*, fold over and invert on a heated platter. Serves 2.

CHINESE SCRAMBLED EGGS WITH CRABMEAT

1 cup cooked crabmeat
2 tablespoons dry sherry
1 slice ginger root, minced, or
  $\frac{1}{4}$ teaspoon powdered ginger
$\frac{1}{3}$ cup peanut oil
1 scallion, minced

3 fresh mushrooms, sliced, or 3 dried
  Chinese mushrooms, presoaked
$\frac{1}{2}$ cup shredded bamboo shoots
6 eggs, well beaten
1 teaspoon salt
Pinch of pepper
Chopped parsley

Pick over crabmeat and mix with sherry and ginger. Heat the oil in a large frying pan and stir-fry scallion for 1 minute, add mushrooms and bamboo shoots and cook for 2 minutes. Add crabmeat and cook, stirring constantly; add eggs and salt and pepper and let set a little, then scramble. Eggs should have a creamy consistency. Sprinkle with chopped parsley. Serves 4 to 6.

VARIATION: Crabmeat may be replaced by lobster or fish fillets; diced vegetables such as string beans or bean sprouts may be stir-fried before adding eggs.

MARBELIZED TEA EGGS

Mr. Waller, Sir Kenelm Digby's informant on matters Oriental, reported that the Chinese occasionally doctored their eggs with tea. "This presently discusseth and satisfieth all rawness and indigence of the stomach, flieth suddenly over the whole body, and into the veins, and strengthneth exceedingly. . . ."

6 eggs	1 tablespoon black pepper
3 tablespoons black tea	$\frac{1}{2}$ teaspoon powdered aniseed
2 tablespoons salt	3 tablespoons soy sauce

Cover the eggs with cold water, bring to a boil, and simmer for 10 minutes. Remove eggs and cool slightly. Tap gently and roll between hands to crack shells all over. Do not peel. Return eggs to water, adding more water to cover if needed. Add remaining ingredients and simmer for 20 to 30 minutes or until egg shells are a deep brown. Cool and peel. Serve whole or cut into quarters. Serves 6.

VARIATION: *German Soleier*: Instead of using tea, boil the yellow outside peel of 3 onions in 3 cups water until water turns deep yellow-brown. Add $\frac{1}{4}$ cup salt and cool the brine. Crackle shells of hard-boiled eggs. Place eggs in jar and cover with the brine. Cover and refrigerate for at least 24 hours. Serve, shelled or unshelled, with cold beer.

HUEVOS RANCHEROS

Mexicans have always attached special significance to eggs. At the Mayan ceremony of *hetzmek*, babies were fed an egg that was supposed to endow them with the faculty of understanding. After the Conquest eggs became a sign of plenty, and impoverished pilgrims to Guadalupe Hidalgo would offer them as gifts to the Virgin. Still considered delicacies, eggs are rarely eaten unembellished but are typically accompanied by a spicy sauce as in the dish below.

3 tablespoons bacon fat or lard	1 small clove garlic, minced
8 tortillas (canned)	1 small can tomato sauce
1 medium onion, minced	Salt and pepper
4 small hot red peppers, minced, or $\frac{1}{2}$ teaspoon crushed dried red peppers	8 eggs
	2 to 3 tablespoons butter

Heat fat and fry tortillas until golden. Keep them warm. Fry the onion, peppers, and garlic in the same oil until soft but not brown. Add tomato sauce, season to taste. Fry the eggs in butter, season to taste. Place an egg on each tortilla and cover with tomato sauce. For a milder sauce, use less red pepper. Serves 4.

NARGIS KOFTA
(Indian Eggs with Ground Lamb)

1 recipe Shami Kabob mixture
  (page 521)
6 hard-boiled eggs, shelled and cut in
  half lengthwise
6 to 8 tablespoons butter

1 onion, chopped
1 clove garlic, minced
1 teaspoon curry powder
1 lime (optional)

Prepare lamb mixture. Divide into 12 parts and pack 1 part around each egg half. Heat butter in a skillet and sauté onion and garlic until they just begin to turn golden brown. Add curry powder and sauté for 1 minute. Add meat-covered eggs and sauté slowly for 8 to 10 minutes, turning gently with a wooden spoon or spatula until all sides are golden brown. Serve with butter and onions from pan and a liberal sprinkling of lime juice. Serves 6 as an appetizer.

AN EGG SALLET

The first edition of Massialot's *Le Cuisinier Roial et Bourgeois* appeared in 1691 and enjoyed immense popularity for a hundred years. This recipe comes from *Court and Country Cook*, the English translation.

1 head Boston lettuce
8 hard-boiled eggs, cut into quarters
  lengthwise
1 head fennel, thinly sliced
4 large cooked beets, chopped
8 anchovy fillets
2 teaspoons chopped parsley

$\frac{1}{2}$ teaspoon dried chervil
1 teaspoon fresh tarragon or
  $\frac{1}{2}$ teaspoon dried tarragon
1 teaspoon chopped chives
1 teaspoon chopped capers
$\frac{1}{3}$ to $\frac{1}{2}$ cup Vinaigrette Dressing
  (page 637)

Wash and separate the lettuce leaves. Dry thoroughly and make a bed of the lettuce in a salad bowl. Arrange eggs on lettuce, add the thinly sliced fennel. Sprinkle with the chopped beets. Criss-cross the anchovies over the salad. Add the herbs and capers to the vinaigrette dressing and put in a small pitcher. Toss together at the table. Serves 4.

SCOTCH WOODCOCK

The parsimonious Scots dote on this dish which (like the hareless Welsh "Rabbit") is no less delectable for want of a genuine woodcock.

$\frac{1}{3}$ cup butter
$\frac{1}{2}$ cup heavy cream
7 egg yolks, slightly beaten

Salt and pepper
4 to 6 rounds of fried bread, spread
   with Anchovy Butter (page 630)

Melt the butter in a frying pan. Beat cream and yolks, pour into hot butter, and stir until thick and creamy. Season to taste and pour over toast. Serves 2 or 3.

SPIEDINI ALLA ROMANO

Unlike many Romans of the first century A.D., Martial was partial to simple fare and would offer his guests hearty appetizers of cheese and eggs. As he explained in an epigram, "I'd rather have my food appeal to hungry feasters than to cooks." Today, Roman *rosticcerias* carry on his tradition and grill snacks like the one below on *spiedini* (skewers).

1 long loaf Italian bread
1 pound mozzarella cheese
1 cup milk
Flour
2 eggs, lightly beaten with
   1 tablespoon water
4 tablespoons butter

4 tablespoons olive oil
Sauce:
$\frac{3}{4}$ cup butter
1 small can anchovy fillets
2 tablespoons capers (optional)
Juice of $\frac{1}{2}$ lemon
Minced parsley

Cut bread into slices $\frac{1}{2}$ to $\frac{3}{4}$ inch thick. Trim off crusts to form squares. Cut cheese in $\frac{1}{4}$-inch-thick slices to match bread pieces. Run alternate slices of bread and cheese on 8-inch skewers, beginning and ending with bread. There should be about 6 slices of bread and 5 slices of cheese on each skewer. Push slices together so they are compact. Dip each skewer into milk so that bread is moistened but not soggy. Dredge with flour on all sides. Dip into beaten egg and let excess drip off. Dredge lightly again with flour. Heat butter and oil in a deep skillet at least 10 inches in diameter. Fry skewered bread and cheese slowly, turning frequently so all sides become golden brown. Keep finished spiedini in a preheated 250° oven until all are fried.

To make the sauce: Melt butter. Mince anchovies and add to butter with capers, lemon juice, and parsley. Heat but do not let butter brown. Spoon over spiedini. Serves 6.

AJOQUESO
(Mexican Rarebit)

3 sweet red peppers
1 large onion, finely chopped
1 clove garlic, minced
¼ cup olive oil
1½ cups grated sharp cheddar cheese
Salt and pepper

Dash of hot pepper sauce
1 tablespoon butter
2 teaspoons flour
1 cup heavy cream
Fried tortillas or
    toasted English muffins

Roast the peppers over a flame. Peel and remove seeds. Fry onions and garlic in the oil. Purée peppers, onion, garlic, and oil in blender. Return to a saucepan and heat with the cheese. Season to taste with salt, pepper, and hot pepper sauce. Blend butter with flour, add little by little to simmering sauce, and stir until smooth. Add cream and stir until very hot. Pour over tortillas or toasted muffins. Serves 4 to 6.

MOZZARELLA IN CARROZZA

Ancient Romans attributed dubious salubrious properties to cheese: in 36 B.C. Varro wrote that soft new varieties were "more nutritious and less constipating" than aged ones; and, more than a century later, Pliny commented that "Zoroaster lived thirty years . . . upon cheese, prepared in such a peculiar manner that he was insensible to the advances of old age." Both naturalists would doubtless approve of the modern mozzarella, a pliable, mild cheese made from buffalo milk in Naples, and customarily served fresh, dripping with whey, or melted in a "carriage" of bread as in the Neapolitan specialty below.

12 slices white bread, crusts removed
6 thick slices mozzarella cheese
Salt and pepper
1 cup half-and-half (milk and cream)
Flour for dredging
3 eggs, lightly beaten
Olive oil for frying

Sauce:
3 to 4 tablespoons butter
1 can drained anchovy fillets, minced
Lemon juice to taste
1 to 2 tablespoons well-drained capers
  (optional)

Form 6 sandwiches with bread and cheese, sprinkling a little salt and pepper on cheese. Sandwiches may be left whole or cut into quarters or halves. Dip each sandwich into half-and-half, dredge lightly with flour, then dip into eggs, letting excess drip off. Fry in hot oil, turning once so both sides become golden brown. Drain on paper towels. Serve plain or with sauce of melted butter, minced anchovies, lemon juice, and capers. Serves 6.

VARIATION: *Croque Monsieur*: Substitute ¾ pound diced Gruyère cheese for mozzarella. Place on bread with 6 slices of ham and fry in butter.

FONDUE BRILLAT-SAVARIN

The noted eighteenth-century gourmet appended this recipe to a little essay on fondue, in which he remarked that "it originated in Switzerland. . . . It is a wholesome, savory, and appetising dish, and being quickly cooked, is always useful when guests arrive unexpectedly."

½ pound Gruyère or fontina cheese, grated
1 cup milk
4 tablespoons butter

4 egg yolks or 2 whole eggs, lightly beaten
1 3½-ounce can white truffles, finely sliced (optional)
Freshly ground black pepper

Soak the cheese in the milk for ½ hour. Melt the butter in an earthenware casserole or chafing dish. Add the cheese, milk, and eggs. Stir with a wooden spoon over low heat until the cheese is melted and the mixture is creamy and smooth. Cover with a topping of thinly sliced white truffles and pepper. Serve over toast. Serves 3 or 4.

SOUFFLES

Several pages of Louis Eustache Ude's *The French Cook* (1813) are devoted to soufflés. He obviously felt they helped fulfill his subtitle's promise to reveal a "new method of giving good and extremely cheap fashionable suppers at routs and soirées." His advice on serving soufflés will never go flat: "If sent up in proper time they are very good eating, if not they are no better than other puddings."

3 tablespoons butter
3 tablespoons flour
1 cup hot milk
Salt and cayenne pepper
¼ teaspoon powdered nutmeg
4 eggs, separated

1 cup cooked finely ground meat, flaked fish, puréed vegetables, or grated Gruyère, Parmesan, or cheddar cheese
2 egg whites
Grated cheese or fine dry bread crumbs (optional)

Melt the butter. When hot and bubbly, add the flour, stir smooth and cook for 3 to 4 minutes. Do not brown. Add hot milk, stirring briskly. Season with salt, cayenne pepper, and nutmeg. Cool slightly and beat in yolks one at a time. Pour into a large bowl. Add meat, fish, vegetables, or cheese. Season to taste. Beat the 6 egg whites stiff and stir 2 to 3 tablespoons of egg white into mixture. Fold in remaining whites, gently but thoroughly, using a rubber spatula. Butter a 6-cup soufflé mold. The mold may be lined with bread crumbs for fish and meat and with cheese for vegetable or cheese soufflés. Pour in soufflé mixture. Bake in a preheated 350° oven for 35 to 40 minutes. To be slightly runny, cheese soufflés may be baked at 400° for 20 to 25 minutes. Serve immediately. Serves 4.

FRITTER BATTER

½ cup flat beer
⅔ cup flour, sifted
1 whole egg

⅛ teaspoon salt
1 egg white

Beat the beer, flour, and whole egg until smooth. Let stand for 30 minutes. Add salt to egg white and beat until stiff. Fold into batter. For desserts, white wine may be substituted for beer and 2 teaspoons of sugar added along with flour.

SIRNIKI
(Russian Cheese Fritters)

4 cups dry cottage cheese, pot
   cheese, or farmer cheese
⅔ cup sifted flour
4 egg yolks

¼ teaspoon salt
2 tablespoons sugar
Sour cream

Squeeze any moisture from cheese. Rub through sieve. Mix with flour, egg yolks, salt, and sugar. Roll into 3- to 4-inch-thick sausages. Chill for ½ hour. Cut into 1-inch cakes and fry in melted butter until golden on both sides. Serve hot with sour cream. Makes 18 to 20.

BOURREK
(Greek Spinach and Cheese Pastry)

1 cup feta cheese
1 cup finely chopped cooked spinach
   or 1 cup chopped parsley
Cream or milk as needed
Pepper

1 box filo pastry or 1 recipe
   Puff Pastry (page 684) made
   with only 4 turns
1 egg yolk

Soak cheese in water for 30 minutes. Drain and crumble. Mix cheese, spinach, and enough cream to soften the cheese. Add pepper to taste. Roll out the pastry to $\frac{1}{4}$-inch thickness on a floured wooden board and cut into 2-inch squares. Place a teaspoon of filling in one corner of square and fold pastry into a triangle. Seal edges with fork tines. Arrange on buttered cookie sheet. Mix egg yolk with 2 to 3 teaspoons water and brush bourreks. Bake in preheated 425° oven for 10 minutes. Lower oven to 350° and continue baking for 15 to 20 minutes or until golden brown. May be reheated. Makes about 24.

LIPTAUER CHEESE

The art of making pot and cream cheeses from sheep's milk was known even to Polyphemus, the one-eyed monster in the *Odyssey* who "milked his bleating ewes . . . thickened the milk, then, into curds and whey, [and] sieved out the curds to drip in withy baskets." However, the Hungarians went a step further, making their Liptauer cheese with such typically Slavic seasonings as caraway seeds and paprika.

$\frac{1}{2}$ pound cottage cheese
$\frac{1}{2}$ pound butter
$\frac{1}{2}$ teaspoon anchovy paste
2 tablespoons chopped capers
$1\frac{1}{2}$ tablespoons caraway seeds

2 tablespoons minced chives
$1\frac{1}{2}$ tablespoons prepared mustard
$1\frac{1}{2}$ tablespoons paprika
Salt to taste
1 clove garlic, halved

Cream the cheese and butter together until smooth and well blended. Work in all other ingredients except salt and garlic. Add a little salt after mixing, if needed. Rub a 4-cup crock or serving bowl with the cut clove of garlic and firmly pack cheese into it. Chill overnight or for at least 5 hours before serving. Spread on squares of thin caraway rye bread or Westphalian pumpernickel. Serves 10 to 12 as an appetizer.

TALMOUSE BIEN DELICATE

Cheese pasties, made in the shape of a *talmouse*, or tricornered hat, were already a very old French food when Nicolas de Bonnefons, valet to Louis XIV, proposed the recipe below. It appeared in his *Délices de la Campagne* (1654), a book which promised to give instruction in preparing "all that grows on the earth and in the waters."

1 cup thick Béchamel Sauce (page 618), heated	1 cup finely diced Gruyère cheese
2 eggs	1 recipe Puff Pastry (page 684)
½ teaspoon powdered nutmeg	2 egg yolks
	⅓ cup grated Parmesan cheese

Remove béchamel sauce from heat, beat in eggs, nutmeg, and cheese; reserve. Roll out puff pastry ⅛ inch thick and cut with a 3-inch cookie cutter. Put 2 teaspoons of filling in the center of each round. Dampen edges of pastry, pinch sides of it together to form a tricorn, and seal securely. Mix egg yolks with 2 tablespoons water and brush the pastry. Sprinkle with Parmesan cheese. Place 2 inches apart on greased cookie sheets. Bake in a preheated 350° oven for 30 minutes or until puffed and golden. Serve warm as an appetizer. Makes about 40.

TARTE BOURBONNAISE

The *quiche*, which Frenchmen claim originated in Lorraine, and Germans in Alsace, was preceded in culinary evolution by such cheese tarts as the one in this 600-year-old recipe, prepared by Taillevent for Charles VI.

½ recipe Short Pastry (page 682)	½ teaspoon salt, or to taste
2 cups light cream	Cayenne pepper
1 egg yolk	½ teaspoon powdered nutmeg
1 tablespoon flour	2 cups grated Gruyère cheese
4 whole eggs	2 tablespoons butter

Roll out the pastry and line a pie plate or a 9-inch flan ring placed on a cookie sheet. Prick with a fork, chill thoroughly. Line with foil and fill with rice or dried beans to keep shell from puffing. Bake for 10 minutes in preheated 425° oven. Discard foil and rice and cool. Scald cream and cool. Beat egg yolk with flour, beat in eggs, add cream, and beat until smooth. Season to taste with salt, pepper, and nutmeg. Sprinkle tart shell with cheese, pour in custard, dot with butter, and bake in a preheated 375° oven on bottom shelf for about 40 minutes. If custard puffs too much, prick top gently. Serve warm. Serves 6 to 8.

VARIATIONS: *Quiche Lorraine*: Add ½ pound thinly sliced bacon or ham cut into ½-inch pieces and cooked. Cheese may be omitted. If so, add 1 cup cream and 2 eggs to custard mixture. Use 8-inch tart shell. *Quiche Alsacienne*: Replace cheese with 4 large sliced onions that have been cooked slowly in butter for about 30 minutes.

VEGETABLES

Vegetables were slow to gain a respectable place on the European menu. Most people ate them at the behest of the family herbalist, whose list of panaceas was likely to be long and imaginative, prompting one writer to warn Elizabethans that "their stomacks be made a verie Apotecarie shoppe." The first of many European vegetarian societies was begun in 1847, based on the notion that "meat-eating begets ferocious dispositions, a callousness...but a vegetarian diet develops the gentler affections."

GHIVETCH
(Rumanian Mixed Vegetables)

4 onions, sliced
1½ cups olive oil
5 medium-size potatoes, peeled
    and cubed
5 carrots, sliced
1 unpeeled eggplant, cubed
¼ pound string beans, cut into
    julienne strips
1 green pepper, seeded and
    cut into strips
1 small head cabbage, shredded
1 small cauliflower, broken
    into flowerlets
1 pound lima beans, shelled

2 parsley roots or 1 parsnip, diced
1 large knob celery root, diced
1 turnip, cubed
2 zucchini, cubed
3 leeks, sliced
¼ pound okra, cut into thick slices
8 tomatoes, peeled, seeded, and
    coarsely chopped
½ cup minced parsley
1 bulb garlic, cloves separated
1 cup sour grapes or 2 greengage or
    sour plums
Salt and pepper
Yoghurt or sour cream (optional)

Fry sliced onions in *one-half cup olive oil* in 5-quart Dutch oven or casserole until golden brown. Add all vegetables (or selection of vegetables in season), herbs, and fruits and mix gently, sprinkling with salt and pepper. Bring *remaining oil* to a boil and pour over vegetables. Cover tightly and place over moderate heat until liquid begins to collect and boil. Place in preheated 350° oven for 1 to 1½ hours or until all vegetables are cooked and liquid has almost evaporated. Add more liquid if needed. Stir gently once or twice during cooking. Season to taste and serve hot with yoghurt or sour cream. Ghivetch may also be served at room temperature or slightly chilled. Serves 12 to 15.

VARIATION: *Ratatouille*: Use onions, eggplant, zucchini, green pepper, tomato, garlic, parsley, salt, pepper, and olive oil. Simmer together over low heat for 45 minutes. Serves 6 to 8.

LOCRO DE CHOCLO
(South American Succotash)

6 ears corn	1 tablespoon paprika
1 green pepper	1 yellow squash, 1 cup cubed pumpkin,
2 tomatoes (optional)	or 1 cup cubed zucchini
1 medium onion, minced	1 pound fresh lima beans or 1 package
3 tablespoons minced parsley	frozen lima beans
1 clove garlic, minced	$\frac{1}{3}$ cup water
$\frac{1}{3}$ cup olive oil or 3 slices bacon, diced	Salt and pepper to taste

Cut kernels from corn cobs and scrape all pulp and milk from cob. Grill pepper over flame and when it blisters, peel, seed, and cut into strips. Do the same with the tomatoes, chopping them after they are seeded. Fry onion, *one and one-half tablespoons parsley*, and garlic in olive oil or with bacon until golden brown. Add paprika, sauté for 1 to 2 minutes. Add tomato, pepper, corn, squash, and shelled lima beans and toss. Add about $\frac{1}{3}$ cup of water—just enough to moisten the vegetables slightly. Season to taste and cover tightly. Simmer for 30 minutes or until all vegetables are tender. Uncover and simmer rapidly for 5 to 10 minutes to reduce liquid. Check seasoning and sprinkle with *remaining parsley*. Serves 8.

VARIATION: Cook 3 sliced chorizo sausages with the vegetables.

FOOD FOR THE SAINTS

The Buddhists have always been staunch vegetarians, and they have studied the nutritional properties of vegetables, learning along the way how to turn them into attractive dishes with many tastes.

6 tablespoons peanut or sesame oil	3 sticks dried bean curd, soaked for 24
$\frac{1}{2}$ cup thinly sliced mushrooms	hours and cut into 2-inch lengths
$\frac{1}{2}$ cup thinly sliced Chinese cabbage	$\frac{1}{2}$ cup hair seaweed, soaked (optional)
$\frac{1}{2}$ cup thinly sliced onion	2 pieces dried lotus root, soaked in
$\frac{1}{2}$ cup thinly sliced snow peas	hot water
$\frac{1}{2}$ cup thinly sliced bean sprouts	$\frac{1}{4}$ cup soy sauce
1 cup thinly sliced winter melon	1 tablespoon sherry
1 cup thinly sliced zucchini	$\frac{1}{2}$ teaspoon salt
$\frac{1}{4}$ cup dried chestnuts, soaked	1 tablespoon cornstarch
	$\frac{1}{2}$ teaspoon sugar

Heat 5 *tablespoons oil* in a large frying pan. Add vegetables and stir-fry for 5 minutes. (Vegetables may be cooked in batches and then combined.) Mix 2 cups water with soy sauce, sherry, and salt. Add to vegetables. Bring to a boil, cover, and simmer until tender—about 15 minutes. Mix cornstarch, sugar, and 3 tablespoons water; add and stir until thickened. Stir in *remaining tablespoon oil* and serve. May be reheated. Serves 8.

TO MAKE FRENCH PUFFS WITH GREENE HEARBES

John Murrel touted his *Booke of Cookerie* (1631) as giving "a most perfect direction to furnish an extraordinary, or ordinary feast, either in Summer or Winter. Also a bill of Fare for Fish-daies, Fasting daies, Ember-weekes or Lent." He further guaranteed that dishes like the one below would "beautifie either Noblemans or Gentlemans Table. . . . All set forth according to the now new English and French fashion."

2 cups minced raw spinach, well dried and tightly packed	$\frac{1}{8}$ teaspoon powdered ginger
$\frac{1}{4}$ cup minced parsley	1 teaspoon sugar
1 cup minced endive or chicory, tightly packed	2 eggs, slightly beaten
	1 or 2 lemons, peeled and sliced paper thin
Salt and pepper	Flour for dredging
$\frac{1}{2}$ teaspoon dried summer savory	Double recipe Fritter Batter (page 583)
$\frac{1}{4}$ teaspoon powdered nutmeg	Vegetable shortening for deep frying

Mix the spinach, parsley, and endive with salt and pepper to taste, summer savory, nutmeg, and ginger. Add the sugar and the slightly beaten eggs. Mix well. Cut lemon slices into quarters. Form herb mixture into 1-inch balls around lemon pieces. Sprinkle with flour, dip in the batter, and deep fry in vegetable shortening heated to 360°, a few at a time until golden brown. Makes 24 to 30 puffs.

SPINAGE

Giles Rose, "one of the Master Cooks in his Majesties Kitchen," included this recipe in his 1682 book, *A Perfect School of Instructions for Officers of the Mouth.* Charles II's chef immodestly claimed it to be "a Work of singular Use for Ladies and Gentlewomen. . . . The like never before extant in any Language," though Mr. Rose knew all the while that it was from a book published in France twenty years earlier.

2 pounds spinach	1 cup heavy cream
4 tablespoons butter	2 drops almond extract (optional)
1 onion, minced	Salt and pepper
1 tablespoon flour	Fried bread triangles
1 cup puréed cooked green peas	

Wash the spinach. Steam it in its own moisture until it wilts—1 to 2 minutes. Press out the water and chop fine. Melt the butter and sauté the onion. Add the flour and cook for 3 minutes. Add the spinach, puréed peas, and cream. Bring to a simmer, stirring. Add almond extract and season to taste. Serve surrounded by triangles of fried bread. Serves 4 to 6.

CELERY FRITTERS

This method of preparing celery appeared in a cookbook bearing the provocative title: *Adam's Luxury, and Eve's Cookery; or the Kitchen-Garden display'd* . . . published anonymously in 1744.

1 bunch celery, cut into 2-inch pieces	1 cup flour
2 eggs, separated	Vegetable shortening for frying
¼ cup milk	1½ cups Sauce Espagnole (page 622)
Salt and pepper	

Cook the celery in boiling salted water until tender but still firm, about 10 minutes. Drain well. Beat the egg yolks with the milk, season with salt and pepper, and whisk into the flour. Beat the whites stiff and fold into the milk and flour. Dip the celery in the batter and fry, a few pieces at a time, in the fat heated to 360°—about 5 minutes or until puffed and golden. Serve very hot with the sauce passed separately. Serves 4.

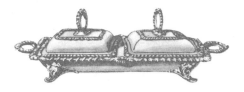

INDIAN PAKORAS FRITTERS

1 cup split pea or wheat flour, sifted	1½ cups water
¼ teaspoon baking powder	2 tablespoons grated onion
1 teaspoon curry powder	Corn or peanut oil for frying

Resift flour with baking powder and curry powder into a bowl. Add water gradually, beating with a wire whisk to make a thick, smooth batter. Add onion and let stand for 30 minutes. Heat oil to 360°. Stir batter and drop it by the tablespoonful into hot oil. Cook until puffed and golden, turning so both sides brown. Makes about 36. Various pieces of vegetables may be dipped into the batter and fried: thin slices of potatoes, chunks of eggplant, cauliflower-lets, crisp young spinach leaves, asparagus tips, zucchini slices, or onion slices.

CHOU-FLEUR DU BARRY

The Comtesse Du Barry, mistress of Louis XV, had as elevated a taste in food as in lovers, and she knew how to show her appreciation for each. As far as food was concerned, she once used her connections to have her cook decorated with the Cordon Bleu. Not surprisingly, chefs were more than happy to do and dare for her; this is one of the many dishes that bear her name.

1 head cauliflower	Salt and pepper
1 cup mashed potatoes	$\frac{1}{3}$ cup hot Beurre Meunière (see Beurre
$\frac{1}{4}$ cup heavy cream	Noir, page 630)
2 tablespoons butter	1 tablespoon chopped parsley

Cut cauliflower in pieces and cook in boiling salted water until tender—about 15 to 20 minutes. Drain well and purée. Mix the potatoes and cauliflower, add cream, butter, and salt and pepper to taste. Dome on a platter and pour on beurre meunière. Sprinkle with chopped parsley. Serves 6.

MUSHROOMS THE ITALIAN WAY

The ancients believed that mushrooms sprang from bolts of lightning. Though many epicures, particularly the Romans, admired their taste, few among them were sophisticated in the art of distinguishing the edible from the lethal, and mushrooms eventually fell out of culinary fashion. As late as the seventeenth century Edmund Gayton advised his fellow Englishmen that "Pepper and oyl and salt, nay all cook's art, Can no way wholesomeness to them impart"; but thanks to a newly enlightened generation of gourmets at the court of Louis XIV, edible fungi were beginning to make a comeback at the best-kept tables of Europe. The recipe below, by Vincent La Chapelle, is of north Italian origin, the addition of anchovies being characteristic of Genoa.

$1\frac{1}{2}$ pounds tiny button mushrooms	$\frac{1}{2}$ teaspoon each dried rosemary,
1 cup dry white wine	tarragon, and oregano
$\frac{1}{2}$ cup olive oil	$\frac{1}{2}$ small bay leaf
1 clove garlic, stuck with a toothpick	Salt and freshly ground pepper
Juice of 1 lemon	Anchovy fillets or chopped parsley
	as garnish (optional)

The smallest, freshest mushrooms should be used. Cut stems level with cap and reserve for other uses. Put remaining ingredients except garnishes in a saucepan. Bring to a boil and simmer for 8 to 10 minutes. Cool, discard garlic, and chill slightly but not long enough for oil to congeal. Serve garnished with anchovies or with chopped parsley. Serves 6.

MUSHROOMS IN SOUR CREAM

1½ pounds mushrooms, sliced or
    quartered, or whole button
    mushrooms
1 medium onion, finely chopped
⅓ cup butter

Salt and freshly ground pepper
1 cup heavy sweet cream, heated
2 cups sour cream, heated
2 tablespoons dry sherry (optional)
2 to 3 tablespoons chopped fresh dill

Wash mushrooms. Peel if necessary and remove woody part of stems. Slice or quarter. Brown mushrooms with the onion in hot melted butter in a large, heavy frying pan. Season with salt and pepper after liquid from mushrooms appears in pan. Add the sweet and the sour cream and simmer very gently, stirring constantly until very hot and smooth. Add sherry and dill. Serve immediately. Serves 6.

PETITS POIS A LA CREME

John Gerard, writing of the cultivation of this vegetable in England, said, "Pease, which by their great encrease did such good to the poore [during a famine in 1555] without doubt grew there for many yeares before, but were not observed till hunger made them take notice of them, and quickened their invention, which commonly in our people is very dull." Englishmen eventually learned to improve on their humble "pease" porridges, following the example of the French, who had been tutored by the Italians. The rage for Petits Pois which struck western Europe toward the end of the seventeenth century is described by one of the ladies of Louis XIV's court, who burbled, "the impatience to eat them, the pleasure of having eaten them, the joy of eating them again, are the three questions which have occupied our princes for the last four days. There are ladies who, having supped, and well supped, with the King, go home and there eat a dish of green peas before going to bed. It is both a fashion and a madness." The recipe following is by the eighteenth century French-English chef William Verral.

2 pounds young green peas
2 slices smoked bacon or ham
Bouquet garni (1 clove, 4 sprigs
    parsley, 1 small onion,
    cut up, tied in cheesecloth)
1 cup beef broth

½ cup heavy cream
Salt and pepper
1 tablespoon butter, softened
1 teaspoon flour
Pinch of sugar (optional)
Juice of ½ orange (optional)

Shell the peas and put in a saucepan along with bacon, bouquet garni, and broth and simmer for 10 minutes or until peas are tender and broth has almost evaporated. Remove bacon and bouquet garni. Add cream, and salt and pepper if needed. Mix the butter and flour and add to peas. Stir until sauce is thickened and very hot. Add sugar and orange juice. Serves 4.

CAROTTES A LA FLAMANDE

To the fourteenth-century author of *Le Ménagier de Paris* carrots were among life's basic necessities. The vegetable was one of the few which could be stored throughout the winter; its vivid color enlivened otherwise drab Lenten fare; and it was considered a cure for a variety of ills. The casserole below is adapted from a cookbook of 1825 by Archambault, who noted that during January carrots "arrive from Flanders which are very good to eat" and serve the Parisians until their own varieties ripen in June.

12 young carrots, sliced
Salt
4 tablespoons butter
1 cup beef broth

Pinch of sugar
2 tablespoons chopped parsley
Fried bread triangles

Parboil the carrots in salted water for 5 minutes. Drain well. Melt *2 tablespoons butter* in a saucepan; add the carrots, beef broth, and sugar. Cover and simmer until well cooked. Reduce the broth to practically nothing and add the *remaining butter* and parsley. Correct seasoning. Serve surrounded by little triangles of fried bread. Serves 6.

TZIMMES

Tzimmes is the traditional dish of the Jewish Sabbath, but it has been adapted over the years as fare for other Jewish holidays. On these occasions the ingredients are given symbolic significance. At Rosh Hashana, the Jewish New Year, a carrot and honey Tzimmes is served. The round pieces of carrot are interpreted as golden coins, suggesting future prosperity; the honey stands for sweetness of life throughout the coming year. The Succoth, or Festival of Thanksgiving, is celebrated with a Tzimmes containing sweet potatoes and fruit to symbolize the bounty of the harvest.

2 cups sliced cooked carrots
4 cups sliced cooked sweet potatoes
  or yams
3 tart apples, peeled, cored,
  and sliced

$\frac{1}{2}$ cup honey
$\frac{1}{4}$ cup vegetable oil
1 teaspoon grated lemon rind
Salt and pepper

Oil an 8-cup casserole and arrange alternating layers of carrots, sweet potatoes, and apples. Sprinkle each layer with some honey, oil, grated lemon rind, and salt and pepper. Cover, bake in a preheated 375° oven for 30 minutes, uncover, and bake until top is golden brown. Serves 6 to 8. Apples may be replaced by pitted prunes.

CAROTTES VICHY

The waters of Vichy are famed for soothing ailing livers. Carrots have a similar reputation. Combined in this recipe, they are a specialty of the French health resort and spa.

1 bunch carrots, sliced or cut into
  julienne strips
1 bottle Vichy water
$\frac{1}{2}$ teaspoon salt

3 tablespoons butter
1 tablespoon chopped parsley
Pepper

Place carrots, Vichy water, and salt in a saucepan. Bring to a boil, cover closely, and simmer on low heat until water is absorbed or until carrots are tender, about 20 to 25 minutes. Drain if needed. Toss with butter and parsley and season to taste. Serves 4.

TORTA DI SPARAGI

Though the spice trade was no longer an Italian monopoly in the seventeenth century, its legacy was apparent in the baroque medleys of seasonings used in recipes like the one below, adapted from Bartolomeo Stefani's *L'Arte di ben cucinare* of 1662; in the original, rose water, cinnamon, and Parmesan cheese all lent flavor to the asparagus. Stefani may have introduced the *sfoglia* (flaky) pastry crust, a specialty of his native Bologna, to the ducal court at Mantua where he served as chef.

$2\frac{1}{2}$ pounds fresh asparagus or 2
  packages frozen asparagus spears
Salt, pepper, and nutmeg or
  cinnamon to taste
3 tablespoons butter

$\frac{1}{4}$ cup grated Gruyère cheese
$\frac{3}{4}$ cup shredded prosciutto ham
  (optional)
3 eggs, beaten
3 tablespoons grated Parmesan cheese

Cook asparagus in boiling salted water until just tender; drain. Cut off tough ends and discard. Cut green portions and tips into 1- to $1\frac{1}{2}$-inch pieces, and return to pan. Sprinkle with salt, pepper, and nutmeg to taste and add butter. When butter has melted, turn into a buttered 9- or 10-inch pie plate. Sprinkle with Gruyère cheese, cover with prosciutto, and pour on beaten eggs. Top with Parmesan cheese and bake in preheated 350° oven for 30 to 40 minutes or until eggs are set and golden crust forms on top. Serves 4 to 6.

VARIATION: Asparagus may be placed in half-baked pie crust as indicated for Tarte Bourbonnaise (page 585). Top with cheese, eggs, and Parmesan mixture and bake as above.

BROCCOLI ROMANI AL PROSCIUTTO

According to Alexis Soyer, Apicius was so adept at boiling broccoli that "this dish alone would have been enough to establish his reputation." Tiberius' son developed such a fondness for Apician broccoli that the emperor admonished the boy to curb his appetite.

1 bunch broccoli	2 cloves garlic
Salt	6 thin slices prosciutto ham, cut into
4 tablespoons butter	julienne strips
2 tablespoons olive oil	¾ cup dry bread crumbs

Wash the broccoli and remove woody part of the stems. Cut through remaining thick stems for even cooking. Parboil in salted water for 5 to 8 minutes. Drain and reserve broccoli. Heat *2 tablespoons butter* and *1 tablespoon olive oil* and fry the garlic. When golden, remove and discard it. Sauté the ham. Add the broccoli and cook covered until stems are tender, turning occasionally. Add butter if necessary. Remove broccoli and ham to a heated platter. Heat *remaining butter and oil* and fry bread crumbs until golden. Sprinkle over broccoli. Serves 4.

GERMAN RED CABBAGE

The Egyptians ate cabbage to stave off drunkenness, and belief in that power persisted over the ages. John Gerard in his *Herball* (1636) explains the phenomena: "there is a natural enmitie betweene it and the [grape] . . . if it grow neere unto it, forthwith the vine perisheth. . . ."

1 3-pound head red cabbage	4 tablespoons wine vinegar
2 tablespoons butter	Salt
2 slices bacon, diced	1½ cups water, or as needed
1 tablespoon sugar, or to taste	Beurre Manie (page 630) or 1 small
1 large sour apple, peeled, cored,	potato, grated
and chopped	¼ cup red currant jelly (optional)
1 onion, minced	

Trim cabbage and shred, discarding core and heavy ribs. Heat butter and fry the bacon in it until it is rendered but not brown. Add sugar and sauté over low heat, stirring frequently until sugar turns golden brown. Add apple and onion, sauté for 2 to 3 minutes. Add the cabbage and toss with apple and onion. Pour in vinegar and braise in covered pot for 10 minutes, or until cabbage is bright purple, stirring occasionally to prevent scorching. Sprinkle with a little salt and add water to barely cover. Simmer covered for about 2 hours or until cabbage is tender. Add water as needed. Thicken sauce with beurre manie or by adding grated potato and simmering for 10 minutes more. Stir in jelly and heat until dissolved. This cabbage is best when reheated, so prepare it a day in advance. Serves 6 to 8.

SAUERKRAUT

3 pounds fresh or canned sauerkraut, well drained
5 tablespoons butter, finely minced bacon, or chicken fat
2 sour apples, peeled, cored, and chopped
1 large onion, chopped

3 to 4 cups water, or as needed
8 to 10 juniper berries or 1½ tablespoons caraway seeds
1 to 2 tablespoons flour or 1 small potato, grated
Salt and pepper to taste

If sauerkraut is very sour, rinse in a colander under cold running water and drain thoroughly, pressing out as much water as possible. Heat fat in an enameled Dutch oven and sauté apple and onion for 10 minutes or until golden brown. Add sauerkraut, stir with apple and onion. Cover and braise slowly for 8 to 10 minutes. Add water to half cover, along with juniper berries or caraway seeds. Cover and simmer slowly for about 1½ hours or until sauerkraut is soft. Add water if needed during cooking. To thicken juices, dissolve flour in 1 or 2 tablespoons water, stir in, and simmer gently for 5 minutes; or add grated raw potato, stir, and simmer for 10 minutes. Season to taste. Serves 6 to 8.

VARIATION: *Weinkraut (Wine or Champagne Kraut)*: Substitute dry white wine, apple wine, or champagne for the water.

JAPANESE STUFFED SQUASH

4 acorn squash, about 1 pound each
½ cake fresh bean curd, about ½ cup
⅔ cup ground cooked chicken
1 small carrot, shredded
6 dried Chinese mushrooms, soaked and cut into thin strips

1½ teaspoons salt
2 teaspoons sugar
½ teaspoon monosodium glutamate
1 cup chicken broth
2 teaspoons cornstarch

Cut a thin slice from base of each squash so they will stand level. Remove a 1-inch slice from top for cover. Scoop out seeds and filaments. Squeeze out moisture from bean curd and mash smooth. Mix with ground chicken, carrot, and mushrooms. Season with *1 teaspoon salt*, the sugar, and *one-quarter teaspoon monosodium glutamate*. Stuff squash with mixture. Place the squash side by side on a trivet or rack in a heavy pot with a lid. Pour in 1 inch boiling water. Place slices of squash for covers alongside the squash, not on top. Cover pot and steam for 1 hour or until squash is tender, adding water as needed. Mix *one-third cup cold chicken broth* with cornstarch and add to *remaining chicken broth, salt, and monosodium glutamate* in a saucepan. Heat, stirring, until hot and thickened. Remove squash to serving platter and top with squash covers. Pass thickened broth in a sauceboat. Serves 4.

SICILIAN ARTICHOKES

Pliny thought of artichokes as the "monstrous productions of the earth," and wondered how other Romans could eat them "when the very four-footed beasts instinctively refuse to touch them." It was only after the fifteenth century that the prickly plant became a staple of the Italian diet, and friendly vendettas were waged as to which region produced the best varieties. Advocating those from the vicinity of Rome, the French writer Stendhal remarked in 1832, "Everything falls like manna. Twelve hundred artichokes cost twenty-one sous"; however, in the next century, D. H. Lawrence rhapsodized over "great sheaves of young, purplish, seadust-colored artichokes" sold in the market at Palermo, Sicily, whence comes the recipe below.

4 large artichokes	$1\frac{1}{2}$ tablespoons dried basil
Juice of 1 lemon	4 anchovy fillets, chopped
$\frac{1}{4}$ cup chopped capers	Freshly ground pepper
1 cup chopped green olives	1 cup olive oil
1 cup fresh bread crumbs	4 cups chicken broth or water

Remove tough outer leaves from artichokes. Cut stems and snip off points of leaves. Press down hard on artichoke top to spread leaves. Remove choke or not, as desired. Parboil in unsalted water with lemon juice for 20 minutes. Mix capers, olives, bread crumbs, basil, and anchovies. Add a little pepper and *half the olive oil*. Stuff mixture into artichoke centers and some of the outer leaves. Place in a shallow baking pan with the broth. Pour *remaining olive oil* over artichokes and bake in a preheated 350° oven for 30 minutes. Serve in soup plates with some of the broth to dip leaves in. Serves 4.

STUFFED ARTICHOKE BOTTOMS

Introduced to Florence from Naples about fifty years before Catherine de' Medici's birth in 1519, the artichoke became one of her favorite foods, especially stuffed as in Scappi's recipe, adapted below. She stuffed herself with so many on one occasion that, according to one chronicler, she nearly burst.

10 large artichokes or canned
   artichoke bottoms
Lemon juice
$\frac{1}{4}$ pound mushrooms, coarsely chopped
1 clove garlic, minced
1 small onion, minced
3 tablespoons butter, olive oil, or
   combination

2 tablespoons minced parsley
2 tablespoons minced lean prosciutto
   ham (optional)
6 tablespoons grated Parmesan cheese
1 cup bread crumbs
Salt and pepper to taste
$\frac{1}{3}$ cup finely diced mozzarella cheese
   (optional)

If using fresh artichokes, cut off stems so they stand level. Rub cut ends with lemon juice to prevent blackening and cook until tender in boiling salted water—about 30 minutes. Discard all leaves and the fuzzy chokes and trim undersides. Sauté mushrooms, garlic, and onion in hot butter or oil until golden brown and dry. Mix with parsley, ham, *4 tablespoons cheese*, bread crumbs, salt, and pepper. Pack mixture firmly in mounds on each artichoke bottom. Top each with a little mozzarella if you are using it, then *sprinkle with Parmesan*. Pour a thin layer of olive oil into a shallow baking pan and arrange artichoke bottoms, stuffed side up, in a single layer. Bake in a preheated 375° oven for about 20 minutes or until top is golden brown. Serve as garnish for meat entree or as a hot appetizer. Serves 5 to 10.

VARIATION: Substitute large mushroom caps for artichoke bottoms.

BAGNA CAUDA COLLA CRUDITA

Raw vegetables in ancient Rome were often eaten for dessert, but by the first century A.D. they were recommended only as crisp preludes to a meal. Still a popular antipasto in Italy, they are dipped in the Piedmontese sauce below, literally "a hot bath."

3 tablespoons olive oil
$\frac{2}{3}$ cup butter

4 large cloves garlic, minced
6 to 8 anchovy fillets, minced

Gently heat oil and butter. Mash minced garlic and add. Cook slowly so neither butter nor garlic browns. Remove from heat and let stand for 15 minutes. Add anchovies and stir over low heat until anchovies "melt" into sauce. Serve in a small chafing dish as a dip for raw vegetables such as carrot sticks, celery sticks, scallions, cucumber slices, raw flowerlets of cauliflower or broccoli, zucchini, green or red sweet pepper slices. Makes about $2\frac{1}{4}$ cups.

IMAM BAYALDI

It seems that a well-known Turkish Imam, or priest, was as taken with his meals as with his mosque. One day his wife outdid herself in preparing his favorite vegetable, eggplant. When the Imam sampled the creation, he passed out with pure pleasure, hence Imam Bayaldi—the priest has fainted. Exercising a little poetic license, Englishmen have translated the name as the "Sultan's Swoon."

3 medium eggplants	Salt and pepper
$\frac{1}{2}$ cup olive oil	$\frac{1}{2}$ cup fresh bread crumbs, without crusts
2 cloves garlic, minced	1 tablespoon tomato paste
4 large onions	1 tablespoon chopped parsley
4 large tomatoes, peeled, seeded, and chopped	3 tablespoons chopped pine nuts (optional)
1 teaspoon sugar	3 tablespoons dried bread crumbs

Poach the eggplants in boiling salted water for 10 to 15 minutes, depending on their size. Cool immediately in cold water. Cut them in half lengthwise. Carefully scoop out the pulp without tearing the skin. Reserve the pulp. Oil the skins and the interior lightly. Arrange the eggplant shells in a well-oiled baking dish, skin side down. Heat $\frac{1}{2}$ cup olive oil in a large skillet and gently stew the garlic and onions until soft. Add the tomato and eggplant pulp, sugar, salt, and pepper. Simmer slowly over low flame for 20 minutes. Add fresh bread crumbs and tomato paste; cook, stirring for 2 to 3 minutes. Mix with parsley and pine nuts. Fill shells, top with dry bread crumbs, and bake in a preheated 350° oven for 20 minutes, covered; uncover, bake for 10 minutes longer. Serve hot or at room temperature. Serves 6.

RED BEANS WITH PLUM SAUCE

Many of Europe's most favored fruits had their origins in the Transcaucasus. Georgia, one of the Soviet republics located on the western edge of that huge region, is noted for its plums, which, in addition to making a powerful native brandy, are often used in cooking.

1 can (1 pound, 4 ounces) red kidney beans or 2 cups cooked red kidney beans	teaspoon crushed, dried chili peppers
	$\frac{1}{2}$ teaspoon dried basil
$\frac{1}{2}$ clove garlic	1 teaspoon minced coriander leaves or 2 teaspoons minced Italian parsley
Salt	$\frac{1}{2}$ cup damson plum jam
1 1-inch piece red chili pepper or $\frac{1}{2}$	2 tablespoons wine vinegar, or to taste

If beans are canned, turn into a strainer and rinse lightly under cold running water. Drain beans thoroughly and turn into serving bowl. Crush garlic with a pinch of salt, chili peppers, basil, and coriander or parsley in a mortar. Work to a smooth paste. Rub jam through a fine sieve and mix into herb paste, thinning with a few drops of vinegar at a time, to taste. Season sauce with salt, spices, and herbs, as needed, and fold into beans gently with a wooden spoon. Let stand at room temperature for 2 to 3 hours before serving, or in refrigerator overnight. Warm to room temperature before serving. Serves 4 to 6.

TAMIA

Some version of these bean cakes probably constituted an important part of the diet of the common people of ancient Egypt. The mighty Pharaohs may even have deigned to nibble on one now and then.

1 pound pea beans
2½ teaspoons salt
2 tablespoons minced onion
¼ cup minced parsley

2 cloves garlic, minced and mashed
2 tablespoons flour
2 eggs, beaten
Corn or olive oil for frying

Soak beans overnight. Drain, cover with cold water, add salt, and simmer for about 45 to 60 minutes. Keep beans firm. Drain, reserving water. Mix beans with onion, parsley, and garlic. Purée through a strainer or, in small quantities, in a blender, adding just enough reserved water to prevent sticking. Mix in flour blended with eggs. Heat about 1 inch of oil. Drop in mixture by heaping tablespoonfuls, and fry on both sides until crusty and golden. Drain on paper towels and keep hot in a preheated 300° oven until ready to serve. Makes 36 to 40.

FRIJOLES REFRITOS
(Mexican Refried Beans)

2 cups cooked red kidney beans
Salt and pepper
Cayenne pepper or chili powder

1 clove garlic, minced (optional)
⅔ cup lard, olive oil, or bacon fat

Drain beans well and mash. Season with salt and pepper, and cayenne or chili powder to taste. Fry garlic in *one-half cup fat*, discarding garlic when brown. Add bean purée to fat and fry, stirring until fat is absorbed. Cool. To refry, melt *remaining fat* and stir bean purée in the fat until it is all absorbed. Serves 4 to 6.

VARIATION: Purée half the beans and mix with remaining whole beans; fry until crisp.

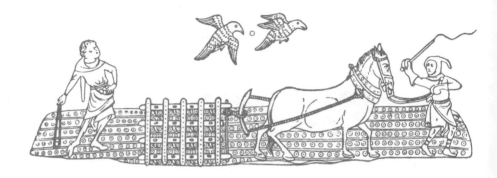

POTATOES PROVENÇAL

$\frac{1}{3}$ cup olive oil
$\frac{1}{2}$ clove garlic, minced
1 teaspoon grated lemon rind
1 tablespoon minced parsley
1 tablespoon minced chives

$\frac{1}{4}$ teaspoon powdered nutmeg
6 potatoes, peeled and
   very thinly sliced
Salt and freshly ground pepper
Juice of $\frac{1}{2}$ lemon

Heat the oil and add the next six ingredients. Simmer gently, covered, for 20 to 25 minutes or until tender, turning potatoes occasionally. Season to taste and squeeze lemon juice over potatoes. Serves 6.

POMMES DE TERRE DAUPHINOISE

"Dauphinoise" indicates, as is the case with this dish, food prepared with Swiss cheese and butter and browned. The method was perfected in Dauphiné, a French region bordering on Switzerland.

1 clove garlic
$\frac{1}{3}$ cup butter
6 large potatoes, peeled and
   thinly sliced
Salt and pepper

1 cup grated Gruyère cheese
2 eggs
2 cups heavy cream
$\frac{1}{4}$ teaspoon nutmeg

Rub an ovenproof dish thoroughly with garlic. Grease with *2 tablespoons butter*. Arrange the potatoes in layers in the dish. Sprinkle with salt, pepper, and cheese. Beat the eggs into the cream and add nutmeg. Pour over the potatoes. Dot with *2 tablespoons butter* and bake in a preheated 325° oven for 1$\frac{1}{2}$ hours. Dot with *remaining butter* and raise oven to 425°, bake until golden, or put under the broiler until slightly browned. Serves 8 to 10.

POMMES DE TERRE ANNA

Who was the mysterious Anna? Was it her beauty, her wit, or perhaps her healthy appetite that inspired the creator of this golden potato pie to name it for her? Adolphe Duglére, the discreet chef of Paris' Café Anglais in the mid-nineteenth century, never told.

6 large baking potatoes
Salt and freshly ground pepper

$\frac{2}{3}$ cup butter, melted

Peel the potatoes and slice them very evenly, about $\frac{1}{8}$ inch thick. Soak in ice water for $\frac{1}{2}$ hour. Drain and dry thoroughly. Generously butter a 10- or 11-inch pie plate. Arrange a layer of sliced potatoes at the bottom of the dish. Arrange slices around the sides of the dish, over-lapping slightly. Sprinkle with a little salt and a generous amount of pepper. Pour on some melted butter. Repeat in layers until dish is full. Bake in a preheated 425° oven for 40 to 45 minutes or until potatoes are tender when tested with a sharp knife. Place platter over pie plate and invert. Cut like a pie. Serves 6.

ROESTI
(Swiss Potato Cake)

8 large, very firm potatoes,
   boiled in their skins
$\frac{1}{3}$ cup butter

Salt
2 tablespoons water or milk

If possible, boil potatoes a day in advance. Peel, slice, and cut into julienne strips. Heat the butter in a large frying pan. Add the potatoes, season with salt, and toss them with a spatula until they have absorbed the butter. Spread potatoes in a round cake pan, sprinkle with water or milk. Cover with a flat lid or plate that fits inside the pan, and cook over low heat for 15 to 20 minutes to form a golden crust on the bottom. Shake the pan occasionally so the potato cake does not stick. When done, invert the pan onto the lid crusty side up. Slide onto a heated platter and cut like a pie. Serves 6 to 8.

POMMES DE TERRE LYONNAISE

3 large onions, sliced
$\frac{1}{2}$ cup butter

6 firm medium potatoes, boiled, peeled,
   and sliced
Salt and freshly ground pepper

Separate onions into rings and sauté in the hot butter until golden. Gently toss potatoes with onions until they are lightly browned. Season to taste. Serves 6. The cooked potatoes may be sautéed along with the onions.

STELK

Potatoes, the principal ingredient of Stelk, came to Ireland in the late sixteenth century. The first crop was reportedly raised by no less a personage than Sir Walter Raleigh at his country estate in Youghal. Soon after, and except during the tragic famine of 1845–46, potatoes were thriving so well that one alarmist warned that "the lazy root" was encouraging "slovenly and beastly habits amongst the labouring classes." Dire predictions not withstanding, Irishmen continued to eat potatoes at least twice a day—Stelk and a variation, Colcannon (traditional at Halloween), among them.

6 scallions with green tops, finely chopped
$\frac{1}{2}$ cup butter, heated
8 large potatoes, boiled and mashed

$\frac{1}{2}$ cup heavy cream, heated
$\frac{1}{2}$ cup potato cooking-water
Salt and pepper

Gently sauté the scallions in *2 tablespoons butter* until cooked but still green, about 5 minutes. Place the potatoes in a large saucepan, add the scallions, *3 tablespoons butter*, and the cream. Whip on very low heat until light and fluffy, adding a little potato water if needed. Season to taste with salt and pepper. Mound on a heated platter. Make a well in the mound and pour in *remaining butter*. Serves 6 to 8.

VARIATIONS: *Colcannon*: Use 4 cups hot mashed potatoes, 2 cups boiled, finely chopped, green cabbage or kale, 6 scallions, 4 tablespoons butter, 1 tablespoon minced parsley, $\frac{3}{4}$ cup scalded milk, salt, and pepper. Whip as above and season to taste with salt and pepper. *Dutch Stampot*: Combine 8 potatoes, cooked, peeled, and quartered, with 4 cups boiled, finely chopped, kale and simmer for a few minutes. Add 5 tablespoons butter, salt and pepper to taste, and 1 pound cut-up boiled frankfurters or knockwurst.

BUBBLE AND SQUEAK

The substance and sustenance in this onomatopoetically dubbed dish are leftover vegetables which first boil (bubble) and then fry (squeak).

4 cups well-drained, cooked, chopped cabbage
$\frac{1}{3}$ cup butter

1 small onion, minced
2 cups diced boiled potatoes
Salt and freshly ground pepper

Put the cabbage in a colander and press out as much water as possible. Melt butter in a 10-inch skillet and brown onion. Add the cabbage and potatoes and toss until they start browning; season with salt and freshly ground pepper, smooth mixture and cook until crusty and brown on the bottom. Invert on a heated platter and cut like a pie. Leftover diced or ground meat may be browned along with cabbage and potatoes. Serves 4 to 6.

POTATOES O'BRIEN

The essence of things Irish is this dish named for patriot William O'Brien, who served the Rebellion as both journalist and jailbird.

4 large baking potatoes
$\frac{1}{2}$ cup butter

1 small jar pimentos, minced
Salt and pepper

Boil the scrubbed potatoes in their jackets in salted water until just tender. Drain and cool enough to handle. Peel and dice them. Melt the butter in a large skillet and fry the potatoes until nicely browned. Add pimento, salt, and pepper and toss until well heated. Serves 4.

IRISH BOXTY

Boxty on the griddle
Boxty in the pan
If ye can't make Boxty
Ye'll never get a man.

6 to 8 baking potatoes
$3\frac{1}{2}$ cups flour
1 teaspoon baking soda
2 teaspoons salt

1 cup buttermilk, or as needed
Bacon rind or butter for frying
Garnishes: melted butter and sugar, jam
   or fruit preserves, or gravy

Boil *half the potatoes*, unpeeled, in salted water in covered saucepan until tender. Peel when cool enough to handle and mash while hot. Peel *remaining potatoes* and place in a bowl of cold water. Line a strainer with a double thickness of cheesecloth and suspend it over a bowl. Grate potatoes into strainer. Gather grated potatoes in cloth and wring out all excess water into bowl. Let water stand until clear. Combine mashed and grated potatoes. Pour clear water from bowl and scrape starchy sediment that has settled in bowl into potato mixture. Sift flour with baking soda and salt and mix into potatoes. Make a well in the center of the potatoes and slowly stir in just enough buttermilk to make a thick batter soft enough to drop from a spoon. Beat vigorously for 3 to 4 minutes or until mixture is bubbly. Let stand for 10 minutes. Heat a large heavy skillet and grease it lightly with bacon or butter. Drop batter a tablespoonful at a time to form small pancakes. Fry slowly until top is dry and bubbling and underside is golden brown—about 10 minutes. Turn and fry until puffed up and second side is brown— about 8 to 10 minutes. Serve hot with one of the suggested garnishes. Serves 8.

VARIATION: *Boxty on the Griddle*: Prepare raw grated and cooked mashed potatoes as in basic recipe. Add flour, soda, and salt, but eliminate buttermilk. Add 2 tablespoons caraway seeds. Knead on lightly floured board until dough is smooth and workable. Divide into quarters; press or roll each quarter into a round about $\frac{1}{4}$ to $\frac{1}{2}$ inch thick. Cut into quarters and fry slowly on hot greased skillet for about 15 to 20 minutes, turning once during that time so both sides are golden brown. Serve as a hot bread, spread with butter. Serves 8.

POMMES DE TERRE SOUFFLEES

One of the many legends that have grown up around the creation of this dish has to do with the French railroad. At the opening ceremonies of a new line, the train carrying the guests of honor to a celebration dinner was inauspiciously late in arriving at its destination. The waiting chef was forced to set aside potatoes that he had already started frying. When he put them back in the deep fat after the diners had finally arrived, pommes soufflées were born.

8 large even-size Idaho potatoes	Salt to taste
Vegetable shortening for frying	

Peel and trim potatoes so they are smooth. Cut into rectangular shape. Slice the potatoes lengthwise into uniform, $\frac{1}{8}$-inch-thick rectangles. Soak slices in ice water for 1 hour. Heat fat in deep fryer to 250°, immerse potatoes in fat in a wire basket. Cook, shaking often, until potatoes are pale gold. Remove and cool a little. Heat fat to 375° and return potatoes to fat, a few at a time. When puffed and a deep gold, remove, salt, and keep hot until all potatoes are cooked. Serve immediately wrapped in a napkin. Serves 6.

RATZELACH
(Polish Potato Pancakes)

8 medium-size old potatoes, peeled	2 teaspoons salt
1 large onion	$\frac{1}{2}$ teaspoon white pepper
1 large apple, peeled (optional)	2 tablespoons minced parsley (optional)
2 eggs, separated	Lard, corn oil, or vegetable shortening
2 to 3 tablespoons flour, potato flour,	
or cracker or matzo meal	

Grate peeled potatoes alternately with onion and apple into large strainer or colander set over a bowl. Press out as much water as possible and reserve liquid. Mix grated potato mixture with egg yolks and enough flour or meal to thicken to consistency of cooked cereal. Add salt and pepper. Pour off reserved liquid carefully and add starch that has settled on bottom of bowl to potato mixture. Fold in stiffly beaten egg whites and parsley. Drop from tablespoon into 1-inch depth of hot fat. Fry slowly for 5 to 8 minutes. Turn and brown other side. Drain on paper towel, sprinkle with salt, and serve with apple sauce. Serves 6 to 8.

VARIATIONS: Potato batter may be divided into fifths or sixths and poured as single pancakes into a 10-inch skillet. This will make 5 or 6 large, thin pancakes. Turn once so both sides are golden brown. Drain and serve topped with crisply fried bacon slices as an entree. *Kartoffel-kuchen (German Potato Cake)*: Heat 4 tablespoons fat in 8-inch square cake pan and add potato mixture. Bake in preheated 425° oven for 30 to 45 minutes or until top is crisp and brown and cake is thoroughly cooked. Invert onto serving platter and cut into squares.

CEYLON DUTCH POTATO PANCAKES

To the basic diet of Ceylon, the Portuguese, Dutch, and English settlers have made numerous additions. Potatoes, and the pancakes made from them, came with the seventeenth-century Dutch traders. Coconut flavoring, however, makes these *Aardappeln Koek* unmistakably Singhalese.

2 large baking potatoes
½ cup sifted flour
1 teaspoon baking powder
⅛ teaspoon salt

2 eggs, beaten
1½ cups Coconut Cream (page 632)
1 tablespoon sugar (optional)
½ cup Clarified Butter (page 630)

Boil the potatoes in their jackets, cool slightly, and peel. Mash the warm potatoes. Resift flour with baking powder and salt. Beat into potatoes alternately with eggs. Add coconut cream. Beat in sugar. Pour batter onto a hot, well-buttered griddle, turning pancakes when golden on one side—about 3 minutes. Serve with the clarified butter on the side. Serves 4.

DUM ALOO
(Indian Stuffed Potatoes)

6 baking potatoes
2 small onions, chopped
½ green pepper, seeded and diced
¼ cup green peas
Salt and pepper
Juice of 1 lime

½ cup butter
½ teaspoon powdered turmeric
¼ teaspoon chili powder
4 tomatoes, peeled, seeded, and chopped
1½ cups beef broth

Scrub the potatoes and halve them lengthwise. Scoop out pulp, leaving ½-inch-thick shells. Chop the pulp finely, mix with *half the onion*, the pepper, and the peas. Season with salt and pepper and *half the lime juice*. Stuff the potato halves with the mixture, rejoin the halves to make whole potatoes, and secure with 2 toothpicks on either side. Melt *half the butter* in a large frying pan and fry the potatoes on all sides until golden. Remove potatoes and reserve. Melt *remaining butter* in the frying pan and fry the *remaining onion*. Add the turmeric and chili powder and cook, stirring for 2 minutes; add tomatoes and simmer for 3 minutes on low heat. Add the broth, salt and pepper, and *remaining lime juice* to taste. Return potatoes to the pan, cover and steam over low heat until tender, about 35 to 40 minutes, turning them over halfway through steaming. Serves 6.

SALADS

SALAT

From the oldest known treatise on cooking in the English language comes this recipe for salad. The manuscript, *The Forme of Cury*, was compiled c. 1390 "by assent & avyssement of [the] maisters of phisik & of philosophie" in Richard II's court, and contains some 196 examples of medieval "cury," or cookery.

1 bunch watercress
1 bunch fennel, thinly sliced
1 clove garlic, minced
6 to 8 scallions, minced
4 shallots, minced
2 leeks, thinly sliced

$\frac{1}{2}$ teaspoon each dried sage and borage, or a few fresh leaves
1 sprig rosemary
2 tablespoons minced parsley
Vinaigrette Dressing (page 637)

Put all ingredients except dressing in a bowl. Toss with dressing. Serves 4.

FRENCH POTATO SALAD

10 medium potatoes, boiled
   in their jackets
1 clove garlic
$\frac{1}{4}$ cup dry white wine or
   dry vermouth, heated
$\frac{1}{4}$ cup beef broth, heated
3 tablespoons tarragon or wine vinegar
$1\frac{1}{2}$ teaspoons Dijon-style mustard

$\frac{1}{2}$ teaspoon salt
$\frac{1}{4}$ teaspoon pepper
$\frac{1}{2}$ cup olive oil
2 shallots, minced
3 tablespoons mixed chopped parsley,
   chervil, chives, and tarragon
Bibb lettuce or heart of romaine lettuce
1 to 2 tablespoons capers (optional)

Peel potatoes and slice thin. Put in a bowl well rubbed with cut clove of garlic. Pour in wine and broth and let marinate for 1 hour. Pour off any excess liquid. Meanwhile, beat vinegar into mustard, salt, and pepper. Gradually add oil in slow stream, beating constantly. Add shallots and herbs to potatoes. Pour on dressing, toss gently with 2 wooden forks. Garnish with lettuce and capers. Serves 6.

VARIATION: Tomato wedges, diced or sliced sausage, julienne strips of boiled beef, or quartered hard-boiled eggs may be added.

PARSLEY OF MACEDONIA

Long before vitamins were a consideration, Bancke's *Herbal* recommended that Englishmen take regular doses of parsley, which "multiplieth greatly a man's blood . . . [and] comforteth the heart and the stomach." A liberal serving of the garden herb goes into this recipe from Massialot's *Court and Country Cook* (1702). Such medleys of vegetables —or fruits—were often called Macedonias or Macedoines, possibly because of the mixture of races that inhabited that ancient land.

½ cup Aspic (page 635)
½ cup finely chopped parsley
½ cup each: cooked diced carrots, green beans, and potatoes; whole green peas and baby lima beans
½ cup Vinaigrette Dressing (page 637)
Salt and pepper

1 envelope gelatin
¼ cup water
2 cups mayonnaise
½ cup cooked lobster meat (optional)
1 black truffle, minced (optional)
Sprigs of watercress

Coat a 5- to 6-cup mold with aspic. Chill and repeat 2 or 3 times. Mix the parsley and vegetables with vinaigrette dressing. Season to taste. Soak gelatin in ¼ cup cold water and melt over boiling water. Cool to tepid and mix with mayonnaise. Mix vegetables, lobster, and truffle with mayonnaise mixture. Pour into prepared mold. Chill several hours. Unmold on a serving platter. Garnish with watercress. Serves 6.

GUACAMOLE

The avocado was well known to the inhabitants of Mexico centuries before the arrival of the Spanish conquistadors in the sixteenth century. The fruit was so much prized that native potters molded ceramic jars in its pear-like shape. From this indigenous plant the Mayans first prepared Guacamole, seasoning the puréed avocado with another native plant, the hot red pepper.

2 large ripe avocados
1 small onion, grated
1 large tomato, peeled, seeded, and chopped (optional)

3 tablespoons lime or lemon juice
Olive oil
Salt
Tabasco or chopped chili peppers

Mash the avocados to a purée, stir in the onion and tomato. Add lime juice to taste and just enough olive oil to thin to dipping consistency. Season with salt and Tabasco or chili peppers to taste. To prevent blackening, bury avocado pit in guacamole and refrigerate until serving. Serve as a dip with packaged corn chips. Makes about 2½ cups. A small grated cucumber, crisp bits of bacon, minced herbs, or a crushed garlic clove may be added.

SALADE NIÇOISE

1 small head Boston or romaine lettuce
  or 2 heads bibb lettuce
2 7-ounce cans white tuna fish in oil
3 hard-boiled eggs, quartered
2 or 3 large tomatoes, peeled and
  quartered
12 black olives, pitted

1 large green pepper, seeded and
  cut into eighths
12 anchovy fillets in oil
½ to ¾ cup Vinaigrette Dressing
  (page 637)
1 to 2 tablespoons capers (optional)

Arrange lettuce leaves in a salad bowl. Divide tuna into chunks and place on lettuce. Add the eggs, tomato sections, olives, and peppers. Crisscross with the anchovy and pour vinaigrette dressing over salad. Sprinkle with capers. Serves 4 to 6.

VARIATIONS: Cold cooked string beans or fennel root or pieces of cucumber may be added to salad. A blend of chopped herbs (parsley, tarragon, chervil, chives) may be added to dressing.

VEGETABLE PICKLES

Long before the days of Peter Piper, the Persians pickled not only peppers, but also eggplants, onions, cucumbers, and cauliflowers in a solution of vinegar and spices. Doctors prescribed pickles as the best remedy for obesity because their sour juices supposedly neutralized the effect of fatty foods. Another Persian myth, today upheld throughout the world, was that a craving for the preserves was sure proof that a woman was pregnant. Modern Iranians still serve pickles at every meal, maintaining, as the saying goes, their loyalty "to the friend who, though sour in form, is sweet in meaning."

6 white turnips
1 large or 2 small beets, halved
2½ cups water

1½ cups white vinegar
2½ teaspoons salt
4 cloves garlic

Slice a thin slice from top and bottom of each turnip. Cut turnips in finger-length strips, or, more traditionally, slice to within ¼ inch of the bottom and do not separate slices. Soak in water to cover overnight. Rinse thoroughly and drain. Place in glass jar with beets. Add remaining ingredients, cover, and let stand at room temperature for 3 days. Serve chilled.

VARIATIONS: Blanched flowerlets of cauliflower, sliced celery, slices or strips of carrot, blanched, peeled, and sliced eggplant, or strips of cucumber may all be pickled this way, alone or in any combination. Cucumbers and turnips will be dyed pink by beets. Chili peppers may be added to taste. *Indian Pickles*: The same vegetables or sliced lemons or limes are pickled as above, with the addition of 1 teaspoon crushed mustard seed, 1 tablespoon curry powder, 1 or 2 teaspoons chili powder, a pinch of powdered ginger, and ½ cup brown sugar.

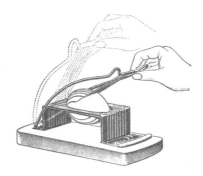

SALADE OLIVIER

For an hour or so before sitting down to dine, Russians whet their appetites with vodka and a great spread of assorted hors d'oeuvres called *zakuski*. A specialty of the table is the Salade Olivier named for a French chef in the service of Czar Nicholas II. Monsieur Olivier's creation was pronounced a triumph by his royal patron, and it quickly became the vogue. The chef fortunately escaped the fate of his employer and lived out his life as a prosperous restaurateur in Berlin.

1 3-pound roasted chicken	$\frac{1}{2}$ cup sour cream
4 boiled potatoes, peeled and sliced	Salt and pepper
4 hard-boiled eggs, cut in eighths	Hearts of lettuce
2 dill pickles, thinly sliced	Garnishes: 2 tablespoons capers,
$\frac{3}{4}$ cup mayonnaise	olives, tomato wedges

Cube chicken meat and mix with potatoes, eggs, pickles, mayonnaise, and sour cream. Season to taste. Serve on a bed of lettuce hearts, garnished with capers, olives, and tomatoes. Serves 6.

TABBOULEH
(Middle Eastern Salad)

1 cup cracked wheat (burghul)	3 tomatoes
3 cups chopped Italian parsley	Juice of 2 lemons, or to taste
2 tablespoons chopped fresh mint leaves	$\frac{1}{2}$ cup olive oil
5 scallions, bulbs and green tops chopped together	Salt

Soak burghul in warm water to cover for 1 hour. Drain and squeeze out as much water as possible. Combine with parsley, mint, scallions, *2 chopped tomatoes*, lemon juice, olive oil, and salt to taste. Chill and serve garnished with *remaining tomato* cut into wedges. Serves 6 to 8.

SALLAD MAGUNDY

Patrick Lambe, as master cook in His Majesty's Kitchen, managed to please a succession of British monarchs from Charles II through Queen Anne. His vast repertoire, including this recipe for Sallad Magundy, was published in *Royal Cookery or the Compleat Court-Book* (1710). The salad's peculiar name—Solomon Grundy and Salmagundy are other variations—derives from the Old French word for a mixture, *salmigondis*.

1 3-pound roasted or broiled chicken	1 cup seedless grapes
2 lettuce hearts	12 small boiled white onions
10 anchovy fillets in olive oil	2 tablespoons chopped parsley
4 hard-boiled eggs, chopped	$\frac{1}{2}$ cup Vinaigrette Dressing (page 637)

Cut the white meat of the chicken into very fine julienne strips. Dice the dark meat rather finely. Shred lettuce and place in a 1-inch-thick layer in a salad bowl. Place the white meat in a circle on the outer edge of the lettuce, alternating with *8 anchovy fillets*. Mix the diced dark meat with the eggs and *remaining anchovies*, chopped. Dome in the center of the salad. Mix grapes, onions, and parsley and put around the salad. At serving time, pour over the well-mixed vinaigrette dressing. Serves 4.

LEEKS IN POOR MAN'S SAUCE

Leeks, which Nero thought made him more eloquent, came to Britain with Julius Caesar's armies. In time the vegetable became the national emblem of Wales, for, as legend has it, Saint David told Welshmen to wear a leek in their cap when they went to war against the invading Saxons lest they mistake friends for enemies. Leeks also played a part in the *cymmortha*, the annual spring plowing cooperative, when each Welsh farmer contributed a leek to the communal stew as a symbol of his participation in togetherness.

12 medium even-size leeks	$\frac{1}{2}$ teaspoon dried basil
1 cup Sauce for a Poor Man (page 636)	2 tablespoons chopped parsley
2 hard-boiled eggs, riced	1 tablespoon chopped capers
$\frac{1}{2}$ teaspoon dried tarragon	

Trim leeks, cut in half lengthwise. Wash thoroughly. Bring to a boil in a little salted water. Simmer for 10 minutes, drain, and cool. Mix sauce with hard-boiled eggs, herbs, and capers. Pour over leeks. Serves 4.

COLD ASPARAGUS WITH WALNUTS

Asparagus, native to the eastern Mediterranean area, was cultivated by the ancient Greeks, despite warnings from a fourth-century B.C. writer that it caused blindness. Judging from a remark of the emperor Augustus —that a certain task should "be done quicker than you would cook asparagus"—the Romans liked their asparagus barely blanched. The vegetable's vogue in western Europe began when Louis XIV's gardener grew it for the royal table, and it was first popularized in England by Samuel Pepys. In China, where meat eating was prohibited by Buddhist law on certain days, many cooks favored such substitutes as the cooked asparagus and crunchy walnut salad below.

1½ pounds fresh tender asparagus tips	¼ cup soy sauce
1 cup finely chopped walnuts	⅓ cup sugar
1 to 2 tablespoons walnut or sesame oil	Pepper
¼ cup cider vinegar	

Cook asparagus in boiling water, covered, for 6 to 7 minutes or until just tender. Drain well and arrange in a serving dish. Mix remaining ingredients and pour over asparagus, lifting it so dressing penetrates. Sprinkle with pepper. Serve slightly chilled. Serves 6.

SALADE BAGRATION

In 1807 Prince Peter Bagration claimed victory at Eylau over the Napoleonic army, a costly battle but one which endeared the general to his countrymen. From the round of dinners in his honor, one of which Tolstoy described in *War and Peace*, came Bagration soup, a velouté garnished with macaroni, and this combination salad.

1 cup celery, cut into julienne strips	3 tablespoons chili sauce
1 cup cooked artichoke bottoms, cut into thin strips	4 hard-boiled eggs, whites and yolks riced separately
½ cup Vinaigrette Dressing (page 637)	¾ cup minced cooked smoked tongue or ham
2 cups julienned cooked breast of chicken	½ cup minced parsley
2 cups cooked elbow macaroni	¾ cup minced black olives or truffles
1½ cups mayonnaise	

Marinate the celery and artichoke bottoms in the vinaigrette dressing for 20 minutes. Mix with chicken and macaroni. Mix mayonnaise and chili sauce and toss with chicken mixture. Put in a bowl and smooth the top. Arrange riced whites of eggs, minced tongue, parsley, riced yolks, and olives in five pie-shaped wedges. Toss at the table. Serves 6.

AGURKESALAT
(Danish Cucumber Salad)

3 large cucumbers
2 tablespoons salt
$\frac{1}{3}$ to $\frac{1}{2}$ cup water
5 tablespoons vinegar

1 tablespoon sugar
$\frac{1}{2}$ teaspoon white pepper
2 tablespoons minced dill or parsley

Peel cucumbers, wash well, and slice very thin. Sprinkle with salt, cover, weight down, and let stand overnight or for several hours. Drain very well, pressing lightly on the cucumbers. Combine with all the ingredients except dill. Let marinate in refrigerator for 1 to 2 hours. Sprinkle with dill before serving. Serves 6 to 8.

CUCUMBER BORANI

Cucumbers, native to northwest India, had been so plentiful and cheap in ancient Egypt that the Jews, after fleeing to the desert, sorely missed one of the few amenities of their servitude: "We remember the [cucumbers], which we did eat in Egypt freely. . . . But now our soul *is* dried away; *there is* nothing at all, beside this manna, *before* our eyes." Cultivated in virtually every Near Eastern country today, the gourd is typically combined with yoghurt as in this Persian salad.

2 cups yoghurt
1 large cucumber, peeled and chopped
   or sliced paper thin
1 tablespoon minced onion or
   1 small clove garlic, minced

3 sprigs fresh mint leaves, chopped, or
   $\frac{1}{2}$ teaspoon dried mint
1 tablespoon lemon juice or
   white wine vinegar
Salt and pepper to taste

Beat the yoghurt smooth and mix with remaining ingredients. Season to taste with salt and pepper. Serves 3 to 4. Optional additions: 3 tablespoons each chopped walnuts and golden raisins; or $\frac{1}{4}$ teaspoon each marjoram and sweet basil.

TURKISH PEA BEAN SALAD

1 cup cooked white pea beans
1 tomato, peeled, seeded, and chopped
1 each small green pepper and sweet
   red pepper, seeded and diced

$\frac{1}{2}$ cup pitted and chopped black olives
$\frac{1}{2}$ cup Vinaigrette Dressing (page 637)
1 small red onion, thinly sliced
2 tablespoons chopped parsley

Mix beans with tomato, green and red peppers, black olives, and vinaigrette dressing. Arrange in a salad bowl, cover with onion rings, and sprinkle with parsley. Chill slightly. Serves 4.

HUMMUS BI TAHEENI

Cultivated since early times in eastern Mediterranean countries, the wrinkled beans known as chick-peas once served as the equivalent of popcorn at Roman circuses. In the Lebanese recipe below they are mixed with a paste made from sesame seeds which likewise have played an important role in Near Eastern cooking and lore.

2 cups cooked chick-peas (garbanzos or ceci)	$\frac{1}{2}$ cup taheeni (sesame seed paste)
Salt	$\frac{1}{3}$ to $\frac{1}{2}$ cup lemon juice, or to taste
2 cloves garlic	Olive or sesame oil
	Chopped parsley

Set aside *8 chick-peas* for garnish. Drain and purée *remaining chick-peas*. Pound 1 teaspoon salt and garlic together to a smooth paste. Add to the peas. Mix chick-peas with taheeni; add lemon juice and salt to taste. Place in a serving dish and sprinkle lightly with oil. Garnish with reserved whole chick-peas and chopped parsley. Use as a dip with crackers, pieces of Middle Eastern flat bread, or raw vegetables. Makes 2 cups.

BABA GANNOUJH

This traditional Lebanese salad is named "spoiled old daddy" because its inventor reputedly mashed the eggplant to a pulp to pamper his aged, toothless father.

1 large eggplant	$\frac{1}{3}$ cup sesame or olive oil
2 cloves garlic	Parsley sprigs
Salt	Pomegranate seeds (if available)
$\frac{1}{3}$ cup lemon juice, or to taste	

Eggplant should be cooked under open flame for characteristic smoky taste. Cut in half and broil skin side up until skin is black and crackling. Cool. Peel skin off and mash pulp well. Pound garlic with 1 teaspoon salt and mix smooth with *1 teaspoon lemon juice*; add to eggplant. Beat in *remaining lemon juice* and oil alternately. This may be done in a blender or mixing bowl. Add additional lemon juice and salt to taste. Pour into serving dish and chill. At serving time sprinkle with a little oil and garnish with parsley sprigs and pomegranate seeds. Serve as a dip with Middle Eastern flat bread, broken in small pieces, crackers, or raw vegetables. Makes about 2 cups.

KIMCH'I

Koreans, who like their food very highly spiced, consider these pickled raw vegetables an indispensable feature of almost every meal. Their preparation is generally entrusted to the oldest woman of the household on the assumption that only the judgment that comes with age can produce the fiery blending of ingredients that Koreans prize.

6 cups cut-up vegetables (such as cucumbers, Chinese cabbage, cauliflower, celery, onions, turnips, or carrots), alone or in any combination
3 tablespoons salt
4 scallions, bulbs and green tops, finely chopped

2 cloves garlic, minced
$\frac{1}{4}$ teaspoon crushed, dried chili peppers
1 $1\frac{1}{2}$-inch piece ginger root, chopped, or $\frac{1}{4}$ teaspoon powdered ginger
1 cup water

Sprinkle vegetables with *half the salt* and let stand for 15 minutes. Rinse and drain. Combine with *remaining salt*, scallions, garlic, chili peppers, ginger, and water. Marinate at room temperature for 2 days in summer, 4 days in winter unless kitchen is very warm. Cover bowl well as the pickling produces a very strong odor. Chill before serving. Serves 6 to 8.

CHINESE SMASHED RADISH SALAD

36 small red radishes
1 teaspoon salt
2 teaspoons sesame or peanut oil

2 tablespoons vinegar
5 teaspoons soy sauce
1 teaspoon sugar

Wash the radishes and dry them. Trim off tops and roots and crush radishes slightly with the flat side of a knife but not enough to break them apart. Sprinkle with salt and let stand for 10 minutes. Add remaining ingredients, toss, and chill for $\frac{1}{2}$ hour. Serves 6 to 8.

AEMONO
(Japanese Spinach with Sesame Seeds)

$1\frac{1}{2}$ pounds fresh spinach, washed and drained, or 2 packages frozen leaf spinach
$\frac{1}{4}$ cup sesame seeds

$\frac{1}{4}$ cup soy sauce
2 teaspoons sugar
$\frac{1}{4}$ teaspoon monosodium glutamate
2 tablespoons peanut oil

Cook spinach until barely tender in 1 cup boiling water. Drain and chill. Toast sesame seeds in a frying pan, stirring until they are golden and start to pop. Crush sesame seeds, mix with remaining ingredients, and pour over spinach. Serves 6.

SYDNEY SMITH'S SALAD DRESSING

The English clergyman Sydney Smith (1771–1845), in addition to being an essayist, wit, and decryer of all things American, was a poet laureate of a dressing for salad. He conveys, in the most heroic of couplets, here excerpted, the means to concoct his specialty:

> *Of mordant mustard add a single spoon,*
> *Distrust the condiment that bites too soon*
> *Yet deem it not thou man of taste, a fault*
> *To add a double quantity of salt —*
> *Four times the spoon with oil of Lucca crown*
> *And twice with vinegar procured from Town.*

1 small boiled potato, mashed	3 tablespoons white wine vinegar
2 teaspoons Dijon-style mustard	2 hard-boiled egg yolks
$\frac{1}{2}$ teaspoon salt	1 small onion, minced
$\frac{1}{8}$ teaspoon white pepper	$\frac{1}{8}$ teaspoon anchovy paste
$\frac{1}{2}$ cup olive oil	

Whip the hot potato with the mustard, salt, pepper, and oil. Work the vinegar and egg yolks into a smooth paste and add to the potato. Combine with the onion and anchovy paste. Serve over lettuce or vegetable salad. Makes about $1\frac{3}{4}$ cups.

TAPENADE

This purée of typical Provençal salad ingredients was put together and named (after the Provençal word for capers) by a Marseilles chef in the late nineteenth century.

30 small black olives, pitted	3 to 4 tablespoons lemon juice, or to taste
10 anchovy fillets, drained	
2 tablespoons capers	1 tablespoon powdered mustard
1 $3\frac{1}{2}$-ounce can tuna fish	2 teaspoons brandy, or to taste
$\frac{1}{2}$ to $\frac{3}{4}$ cup olive oil	10 hard-boiled eggs (optional)

Using an electric blender at low speed, or a stone mortar and pestle, work the olives, anchovies, capers, and tuna fish to a purée. Slowly add olive oil and lemon juice, alternately, beating constantly as for mayonnaise. Add enough oil to give a smooth, thick, spreadable paste. Beat in mustard and brandy. Spoon over and around 10 hard-boiled eggs that have been cut in half lengthwise or use as dip with vegetables. This mixture keeps well in the refrigerator for two weeks. Pack it into a crock and add a 1-inch layer of olive oil. Cover and store. Remove oil before serving. Makes 1 cup.

SAUCES

When a Neapolitan emissary, Prince Francesco Caraccioli, reported back that England had fifty different religions but only one sauce—and that, melted butter—his eighteenth-century readers must indeed have been astonished. Since the fourteenth or fifteenth century, any Continental cook worth his salt could conjure up a variety of sauces, commencing with the *sauces mères*, or the basic brown and white sauces, and elaborating with numerous subtly compounded variations. Carême, probably the greatest *saucier* in culinary history, claimed that "no foreign sauce is comparable to those of our great [nineteenth-century] cuisine"; and he was doubtless correct, for the vast majority of celebrated sauces today can be traced, if not to French origins, at least to French perfection. Grimod de La Reynière, who always had something to say about sauces when the opportunity was presented, declared, "It is the duty of a good sauce to insinuate itself all round and about the maxillary glands, and imperceptibly awaken into activity each ramification of the organs of taste; if not sufficiently savoury, it cannot produce this effect, and if too piquant, it will paralyze, instead of exciting, those delicious titillations of tongue and vibrations of the palate that only the most accomplished philosophers of the mouth can produce on the highly-educated palates of thrice happy *grands gourmets!*"

VELOUTE

4 tablespoons butter
1 tablespoon minced onion (optional)

4 tablespoons flour
5 cups hot veal, chicken, or fish broth

Melt the butter in a saucepan. Add the minced onion and cook without browning for 2 to 3 minutes. Add the flour and cook for 3 to 4 minutes until barely golden. Add the hot broth and stir well until smooth and thickened. Lower heat and simmer very slowly for about 1 to 1½ hours, skimming occasionally. Strain carefully. If not used immediately, brush surface with melted butter, cool, and store covered. Use as base for sauces. Makes about 2½ cups.

SAUCE SUPREME

1 recipe chicken Velouté (page 616)
1 cup strong chicken broth
3 mushrooms, minced

½ cup heavy cream
Salt and white pepper
2 to 3 tablespoons butter

Combine chicken velouté, chicken broth, mushrooms, and cream in a saucepan. Simmer very slowly, uncovered, for 15 to 20 minutes; skim carefully. Strain through a fine strainer. Season to taste and beat in the butter. If sauce is not to be used immediately, brush surface with melted butter, cool, and store covered in refrigerator. Reheat in top of double boiler before using. Serve with poultry. Makes about 3½ cups.

SAUCE BERCY

1 recipe Velouté (page 616) made with
fish broth and ¼ cup dry white wine
½ cup heavy cream

1 tablespoon minced parsley
1 tablespoon cold butter

To the velouté add heavy cream and minced parsley. Remove from heat and swirl in butter. Serve with fish. Makes 3 cups.

SAUCE ALLEMANDE

The French designation *allemande* is applied to any food prepared in a German fashion. This sauce, a variation of velouté, is so named because it is enriched with the eggs and cream prized by German cooks. The recipe is from Archambault's *Le Cuisinier Econome* (1825).

1 recipe chicken, veal, or fish Velouté
(page 616)
3 large mushrooms, minced
1 cup strong chicken, veal, or fish broth
Salt and white pepper
⅛ teaspoon powdered nutmeg

2 egg yolks
⅓ cup heavy cream
1 tablespoon lemon juice, or to taste
(optional)
1 tablespoon cold butter

Simmer velouté, mushrooms, and stock for 30 minutes, skimming occasionally. Season to taste with salt and pepper. Add nutmeg. Beat egg yolks into cream. Pour some hot sauce slowly into egg mixture, beating briskly; pour eggs back into sauce slowly and simmer over very low heat, stirring constantly, until hot and thickened. Do not boil. Put through a fine strainer. Add lemon juice; beat in butter until glossy. If sauce is not to be used immediately, brush surface of the sauce with melted butter and store, covered, in refrigerator. Reheat in double boiler before using, stirring in butter. Serve with poultry or fish. Makes 3½ cups.

BECHAMEL SAUCE

It was probably an ambitious cook in Louis XIV's household who belatedly affixed to this basic white sauce the name of Louis de Béchamiel, lord steward of the royal kitchens. Béchamiel, who had earned his sinecure as a financier, doubtless appreciated the culinary compliment.

Thick sauce:
3 to 4 tablespoons butter
3 to 4 tablespoons flour
1 cup milk
Medium sauce:
2 tablespoons butter
2 tablespoons flour
1 cup milk

Thin sauce:
1 tablespoon butter
1 tablespoon flour
1 cup milk
Plus:
1 small onion, minced (optional)
Salt and cayenne or white pepper

Melt the butter and, if using onion, stew until soft but not brown. Add the flour and cook, stirring for 3 minutes. Heat the milk and add, stirring until thick and smooth. Season to taste. Cook gently for 5 minutes. Strain before using. Makes 1 cup.

SAUCE BEARNAISE

For Baron Brisse, Béarnaise was the quintessential sauce, inspiring his somewhat Pavlovian prose: "It frightens me! With it one might never stop eating. Merely reading the recipe arouses my hunger." Created in 1835 at the Pavillon Henri IV, a restaurant outside Paris, the sauce was named in honor of the *grand gourmet's* native province, Béarn.

2 shallots, minced
3 teaspoons chopped fresh tarragon, or
    1½ teaspoons dried tarragon
½ teaspoon dried chervil or parsley
Pinch of salt

⅓ cup tarragon wine vinegar
6 egg yolks
2 dashes cayenne pepper
1 cup butter, at room temperature,
    cut into small pieces

Put shallots, *1 teaspoon fresh tarragon (or one-half teaspoon dried)*, chervil, salt, and vinegar in an enameled saucepan. Simmer until liquid is reduced to about 2 tablespoons. Add 1 tablespoon cold water, egg yolks, and pepper. Beat until thick with a wire whisk or rotary beater. Put over low heat or in a double boiler over hot, not boiling, water and add the butter piece by piece, beating after each addition, until butter is absorbed. Beat until thickened and hot. Strain or not. Add the *remaining tarragon* and serve. Serve with broiled meats. Makes 2 cups.

VARIATION: *Blender Béarnaise:* Put cooked vinegar mixture and yolks into the blender. Flick blender on and off to mix. Turn on low speed and pour in hot melted butter in a steady, thin stream. Turn on high a few seconds. Remove from blender and add remaining tarragon.

MORNAY SAUCE

During the Second Empire, leading figures in French society and government looked with especial favor upon the Restaurant Durand, where the latest gossip and this excellent new sauce could both be found.

2 cups medium Béchamel Sauce
  (page 618)

$\frac{1}{3}$ cup grated Gruyère cheese
$\frac{1}{3}$ cup grated Parmesan cheese

To the heated medium béchamel sauce add the grated Gruyère cheese and grated Parmesan cheese. Stir together until cheese has melted. Coat fish, poultry, or vegetables with sauce and glaze in oven.

HUMMER SAO
(Norwegian Lobster Sauce)

2 cups Sauce Allemande (page 617)
  made with fish stock
1 cup diced lobster meat

2 tablespoons butter
Salt and pepper
3 tablespoons cognac or sherry

Heat the sauce allemande. Sauté the lobster in the butter. Add to sauce and heat, stirring over very low heat. Season to taste. Do not let the sauce boil. Add cognac and serve, or keep warm over hot water. Makes about 3 cups.

SAUCE NANTUA
(French Lobster Sauce)

$1\frac{1}{2}$ cups medium Béchamel Sauce
  (page 618) made with half milk and
  half fish stock
$\frac{3}{4}$ cup heavy cream, scalded

$\frac{1}{4}$ cup Lobster Butter (page 629)
Salt and pepper
$\frac{1}{2}$ cup finely diced lobster
  or shrimp meat

Combine béchamel sauce with *one-half cup cream* and reduce by a third, stirring occasionally. Strain through a fine sieve, add *remaining cream* and shellfish butter. Season to taste and garnish with diced shellfish. Serve with fish. Makes about $2\frac{3}{4}$ cups.

BROWN SAUCE

2 tablespoons butter
2 tablespoons flour
2 cups beef broth or brown stock

1 tablespoon tomato purée (optional)
Salt and pepper

Heat the butter until it is hot and bubbling; then stir in flour until smooth. Fry slowly until mixture turns medium brown. Slowly stir in broth and bring to a boil; reduce heat and simmer for 20 to 25 minutes or until smooth and thickened. Stir in tomato purée, salt and pepper to taste, and simmer for 5 to 10 minutes longer. Makes 2 cups.

VARIATION: For a richer flavored sauce, brown 2 tablespoons minced onion, 1 tablespoon minced carrot, and 1 tablespoon minced celery in 3 tablespoons butter before adding flour. Follow basic recipe and strain finished sauce, puréeing vegetables through a strainer.

SAUCE IN RAGOUT THE CITIZEN'S WAY

$\frac{1}{4}$ cup minced parsley
1 teaspoon each minced fresh mint
  leaves, tarragon, basil, and chervil, or
  $\frac{1}{2}$ teaspoon each dried herbs
2 shallots, finely chopped
2 tablespoons butter or olive oil

1 anchovy, minced
1 cup Brown Sauce (above)
$\frac{1}{2}$ cup beef broth
1 truffle, minced (optional)
1 tablespoon lemon juice
Salt and pepper

Put the herbs and shallots into the hot melted butter and stew gently until the shallots are transparent. Add the anchovy, brown sauce, and broth, and simmer gently for 10 to 15 minutes, skimming as needed. If sauce becomes too thick, add more broth. Add the truffle, lemon juice, and salt and pepper to taste. Serve with lamb or beef. Makes $1\frac{1}{2}$ cups.

CHINESE SWEET AND SOUR SAUCE

$\frac{1}{4}$ cup corn or peanut oil
1 clove garlic, minced
4 scallions, bulbs and green tops,
  chopped
4 dried mushrooms, soaked
  and finely sliced
$\frac{1}{2}$ small carrot, finely sliced

2 tablespoons shredded bamboo shoots
$\frac{1}{3}$ cup sugar
4 slices ginger root, minced
2 tablespoons vinegar
3 tablespoons soy sauce
1 tablespoon cornstarch
$1\frac{1}{2}$ cups chicken broth

Heat the oil and fry the garlic for 1 minute. Add the scallions and other vegetables and fry for 2 to 3 minutes, stirring. Add sugar, ginger, vinegar, and soy sauce. Stir and simmer for 1 to 2 minutes. Mix cornstarch with *a little broth* and add to vegetable mixture along with *remaining broth.* Simmer, stirring until thickened. Serve with fish or meats. Sliced water chestnuts may be added or substituted for bamboo shoots. Serves 4 to 6.

RAISIN SAUCE

¾ cup red wine vinegar
Bouquet garni (1 bay leaf, ½ teaspoon
   dried thyme, 8 sprigs parsley,
   6 peppercorns, 2 cloves, 1 shallot,
   tied in cheesecloth)
2 cups strong beef broth
2 tablespoons currant jelly

½ cup seedless white or black raisins,
   soaked and drained
1 teaspoon brown sugar
Salt
1 tablespoon cornstarch
2 tablespoons Madeira, or to taste
   (optional)

Simmer vinegar with the bouquet garni until vinegar is reduced by half. Add broth and simmer for 5 to 6 minutes. Remove the bouquet garni. Add the currant jelly, raisins, brown sugar, and a pinch of salt. Dissolve cornstarch in 1 or 2 tablespoons cold water and add to broth. Stir and simmer until the jelly is melted and the sauce thickened. Stir in Madeira. Serve with tongue or smoked ham. Makes about 3 cups.

A THICK SAUCE WITH PEPPER

The black pepper that fires this old English sauce, a variation on the French poivrade, was a luxury commodity until the seventeenth century when permanent missions opened India's Malabar Coast to European trade. Before then the spice—or "specie" as it was first called—was considered legal tender, with rents often negotiated in peppercorns.

2 tablespoons olive oil
1 onion, sliced
1 carrot, diced
1 bay leaf
4 sprigs parsley
¼ teaspoon each fresh thyme and basil,
   or ⅛ teaspoon each dried herbs
1 clove garlic, halved

3 slices lemon
2 cups Brown Sauce (page 620)
1 tablespoon tomato paste
½ cup red wine vinegar
½ cup beef broth or as needed
Salt to taste
1 teaspoon cracked pepper
2 tablespoons butter

Heat the oil and simmer the onion and carrot for about 5 minutes. Add all ingredients except pepper and butter and simmer for 25 to 30 minutes. Add the pepper and cook for about 8 minutes, adding beef broth if the sauce is too thick. Strain through a fine sieve, pressing on the vegetables. Correct the seasoning. Return to a saucepan and reheat. Remove from heat and swirl in the butter. Serve immediately with broiled meats. Makes about 2 cups.

SAUCE ESPAGNOLE

This basic brown sauce has doubtless been in the French repertoire since the fourteenth century when sauces and their makers first received the blessings of Louis XII. The version below is from one of the most influential cookbooks of the eighteenth century, Menon's *La Cuisinière Bourgeoise* (1746), but the popular designation "espagnol" was applied sometime later by Carême, who thought the sauce's color very like the Spanish complexion.

2 tablespoons butter	$\frac{1}{2}$ cup dry white wine
1 onion, finely chopped	3 cups Brown Sauce (page 620)
1 small carrot, diced	2 cups beef broth
Bouquet garni (1 bay leaf, $\frac{1}{2}$ teaspoon	2 tablespoons tomato paste
dried thyme, 4 peppercorns, parsley	Salt and pepper
sprigs, tied in cheesecloth)	

Melt the butter in a saucepan and cook the onion and carrot until soft and browned. Add the bouquet garni, wine, brown sauce, and *1 cup broth*. Simmer for 1 hour, skimming with care. Strain into a clean saucepan, add tomato paste and *remaining broth*, and stir well. Simmer for $\frac{3}{4}$ hour, skimming as before. Season to taste and strain again. Use as directed or cool and store in refrigerator. Makes about 4 cups.

SAUCE MARCHAND DE VIN

During the fourteenth century Bordeaux began to export its wines in large quantity to England. Nevertheless, local wine merchants often found themselves with an unsalable surplus or a poor vintage "so sour that it would corrode a horse's hoof"; to salvage it they would use it in sauces like the one below.

$\frac{1}{2}$ cup dry red wine	Salt and pepper to taste
4 shallots, minced	1 tablespoon chopped parsley
$1\frac{1}{2}$ cups Sauce Espagnole (above)	2 to 3 teaspoons lemon juice
1 teaspoon meat glaze (available in jars)	1 tablespoon butter

Reduce wine with shallots by half. Add sauce espagnole and simmer. Add meat glaze, salt and pepper, parsley, and lemon juice. Remove from fire and swirl in the butter. Serve with roast meats. Makes about 2 cups.

VARIATIONS: *Marchand de Vin Butter*: Reduce wine and shallots. Cool and add meat glaze, parsley, lemon, and $\frac{1}{2}$ cup butter. Season to taste. *Bordelaise Sauce*: Add $\frac{1}{2}$ bay leaf and $\frac{1}{4}$ teaspoon dried thyme to wine and shallots, and 1 ounce sliced marrow along with meat glaze.

SAUCE ROBERT

In Rabelais' day the onion was judged excellent for exorcizing ghosts, warding off baldness, and curing dog bites, hence his remark that this old French sauce is "so salubrious and so essential."

2 tablespoons butter
1 medium onion, finely diced
$\frac{1}{2}$ cup dry white wine
$1\frac{1}{2}$ cups Sauce Espagnole (page 622)

$\frac{1}{4}$ teaspoon sugar
1 tablespoon Dijon-style mustard
Salt and pepper

Melt the butter in a saucepan and stew the onion without browning it. When soft, add the wine and boil to reduce by a third. Add sauce espagnole and simmer 10 minutes. Add sugar. Remove from heat, add the mustard, and season to taste. Do not let sauce boil after mustard has been added as it will curdle. Sauce may be strained before adding mustard. Serve with grilled meats. Makes about $1\frac{1}{2}$ cups.

DEMI-GLACE SAUCE

2 cups Sauce Espagnole (page 622)
2 teaspoons meat glaze (available in jars)

$\frac{1}{3}$ cup Madeira wine or tawny port

Reduce the sauce espagnole by a quarter. Add the meat glaze and the wine. Strain. Do not cook further. Serve with meat. Makes 2 cups.

SAUCE DUXELLES

$\frac{1}{4}$ pound mushrooms
2 shallots, minced
$\frac{1}{2}$ small onion, finely chopped
2 tablespoons butter
1 tablespoon olive oil

Salt and pepper
$\frac{1}{2}$ cup dry white wine
$1\frac{1}{2}$ cups Sauce Espagnole (page 622)
1 tablespoon tomato purée
1 tablespoon minced parsley

Peel the mushrooms and reserve peels; remove woody stems and reserve. Mince mushroom caps and sauté with shallot and onion in heated butter and oil in a large skillet. Season with salt and pepper and simmer rapidly until all moisture has evaporated; reserve. Combine wine and mushroom peelings and stems with $\frac{1}{2}$ cup water, simmer until liquid is reduced by half. Add the sauce espagnole and tomato purée and simmer for 10 minutes, skimming carefully. Strain, add the reserved mushrooms and minced parsley, and season to taste. Serve with meat or Squab à la Duxelles (page 470). Makes about $1\frac{1}{2}$ cups.

VARIATION: *Sauce Italienne*: Add $\frac{1}{4}$ cup minced ham to above with the cooked mushrooms.

623

ZITRONEN KOMPOTT
(German Fresh Lemon Compote)

6 large lemons
¾ cup superfine sugar
½ cup slivered pistachio nuts or
  almonds

6 tablespoons Grand Marnier or
  maraschino liqueur

Peel lemons and slice as thinly as possible. Arrange slices in glass or ceramic serving bowl. Sprinkle both sides with sugar. Top with nuts and sprinkle with liqueur. Marinate in refrigerator for 2 hours. Serve with pork, duck, goose, ham, or fish. Serves 6 to 8.

AVGOLEMONO SAUCE
(Greek Egg-Lemon Sauce)

4 egg yolks
Juice of 1 lemon

1 cup hot lamb, chicken, or
  vegetable broth
Salt and white pepper

Beat egg yolks and gradually add lemon juice. Pour hot broth slowly into eggs, beating constantly. Pour into top of double boiler and set over hot, not boiling, water. Cook for 5 to 8 minutes, stirring continually until sauce is thick enough to coat a wooden spoon. Season with salt and pepper. Pour over Dolmates (page 522) or serve with lamb dishes, artichoke hearts, or asparagus. Makes 1 cup.

SAUCE SOUBISE

Charles de Rohan, the last Prince de Soubise, knew greater success in the kitchen than on the battlefield. His name graces several onion-based recipes, including this sauce which appears in *The Modern Cook*, by the eighteenth-century chef Vincent La Chapelle.

2 large onions, chopped
¼ cup butter
1½ cups medium Béchamel Sauce
  (page 618)

Salt and pepper
Nutmeg
Pinch of sugar
¼ cup heavy cream

Pour boiling water over the onions and simmer for 5 minutes, drain well, and dry. Heat the butter and stew the onions, covered, without browning, for about 10 minutes. Purée through a fine strainer. Combine with béchamel sauce. Season to taste, add cream, and heat well before using. Serve with meats. Makes about 2½ cups.

HOLLANDAISE SAUCE

Although Hollandaise was a French creation, its name was not totally inaccurate. The Dutch cities of Leyden and Delft exported so much of their renowned butter (the sauce's principal ingredient) in the seventeenth century, that they were forced to import cheaper butter from England and Ireland. The following Sauce Bâtarde, the illegitimate child of Hollandaise, contains flour.

4 egg yolks	$\frac{1}{4}$ teaspoon salt
1 tablespoon cold water	2 dashes cayenne pepper
$\frac{2}{3}$ cup butter, at room temperature, cut into small pieces	1 tablespoon warm lemon juice, or to taste

Place egg yolks and water in the top of a double boiler. Beat well with a wire whisk to mix. Place over 1 inch of hot (not boiling) water over low heat. Beat yolks until foamy and light. Add butter, piece by piece, whisking well between each addition. Keep beating until all the butter has been added and sauce is thick. Add salt, cayenne pepper, and lemon juice to taste. If sauce separates, add 1 tablespoon boiling water, beat until smooth. Serve with fish, eggs, or vegetables. Makes 2 cups.

VARIATION: *Sauce Mousseline*: Fold in $\frac{1}{2}$ cup heavy cream, whipped, to finished hollandaise. *Sauce Maltaise*: Substitute 2 tablespoons orange juice for lemon juice.

SAUCE BATARDE

$\frac{1}{2}$ cup butter	2 tablespoons heavy cream
3 tablespoons flour	Salt and pepper
2 cups boiling water	1 to 2 tablespoons lemon juice
3 egg yolks	

Melt *3 tablespoons butter* in a saucepan, add the flour, and stir and cook without browning for 3 minutes. Add the boiling water and stir briskly with wire whisk until thickened and smooth. Cook for 10 minutes. Beat the egg yolks with the cream and gradually add some hot sauce to them, beating constantly. Return to the saucepan. Heat, but do not boil. Stir until thickened. Season to taste with salt, pepper, and lemon juice. Strain through a sieve. Remove from heat, whisk in the *remaining butter* bit by bit. Keep warm in a double boiler over hot water. Serve with vegetables and fish. Makes about 3 cups.

SAUCE POMME D'AMOUR

The plump, sanguine tomato, a gift conveyed by Spaniards from the New World to the Old, was thought to be a favorite of Venus and was credited with aphrodisiac powers. Archambault, whose *Cuisinier Econome* (1825) supplies this recipe, says that the love apple's beautiful color and taste made it useful in many ragouts and entremets.

4 tablespoons olive oil
1 .large onion, chopped
8 large fresh tomatoes or
  6 canned tomatoes
Bouquet garni (4 sprigs parsley, 3 celery
  tops with leaves, 3 peppercorns, 1 large
  bay leaf, $\frac{1}{4}$ teaspoon dried thyme, tied
  in cheesecloth)

2 teaspoons wine vinegar
1 clove garlic (optional)
6 leaves fresh basil or
  $\frac{1}{2}$ teaspoon dried basil
1 teaspoon sugar
1 teaspoon salt
$\frac{1}{4}$ teaspoon pepper
2 tablespoons butter (optional)

Heat the oil and simmer the onion until transparent. Meanwhile, halve the tomatoes. If very juicy, squeeze them lightly to remove excess water. Add to the onion, along with all remaining ingredients except butter. Simmer on very low heat for 45 minutes, stirring so sauce does not stick or scorch. Purée through a fine strainer. Season to taste. Remove any excess oil. Add butter. If the sauce is thin, it may be cooked longer, with care, to reduce it. Use on pasta or seafood. Makes about $3\frac{1}{2}$ cups.

SAUCE VERTE

Troubadours had long glorified green sauce in song when Taillevent, in his *Le Viandier* of the late fourteenth century, gave its first written recipe. He began: "Take some white bread and boil it in vinegar . . ." for at that time *roux* (flour and butter mixtures) were unknown and sauces were thickened with *panades* of bread crumbs. In a later work, Rabelais wrote of a captive king's piquant punishment: "he shall mix ginger and verjuice into a sauce and hawk it through the streets—a green sauce crier."

1 cup fresh white bread crumbs
$\frac{1}{4}$ cup dry white wine (approximately)
$\frac{1}{2}$ pound sorrel or young spinach
6 parsley sprigs
2 sprigs fresh tarragon or

$\frac{1}{2}$ teaspoon dried tarragon
1 sage leaf or $\frac{1}{4}$ teaspoon dried sage
$\frac{1}{2}$ cup heavy cream
Salt and pepper
$\frac{1}{8}$ teaspoon powdered ginger

Soak the bread in enough wine to moisten well. Stir on low heat until bread is a smooth paste. Blanch sorrel and herbs for 1 minute, drain well. Put bread and greens in blender for 1 minute, pour back into saucepan; add cream, salt, pepper, and ginger. Heat, stirring. Serve with veal or lamb. Makes about $1\frac{1}{2}$ cups.

PESTO ALLA GENOVESE

Basil, once so rare that only the *basileus*, or sovereign, might cut it, and then only with a golden sickle, became popular in Italy during the Middle Ages, flavoring such foods as this Genovese pasta sauce. The herb is a variety of mint and is indigenous to India, where it is considered an omen of happiness.

2 cups fresh basil leaves or ½ cup
  dried basil, moistened with olive oil
3 cloves garlic
½ cup pine nuts

Pinch of salt
1 cup grated Parmesan cheese
1 cup olive oil

Pound in a mortar the basil, garlic, pine nuts, and salt. Work in cheese. When the mixture is a smooth, thick paste, trickle in the olive oil. Work in until sauce is the consistency of a very thick cream. Makes 1½ cups.

SALSA VERDE
(*Italian Green Sauce*)

¾ to 1 cup minced parsley
1 or 2 cloves garlic, crushed
1 teaspoon salt
Pinch of black pepper

2 tablespoons coarsely chopped capers
2 cups olive oil
⅓ to ½ cup lemon juice

Combine parsley, garlic, salt, pepper, and capers and beat into olive oil. Add lemon juice gradually, to taste. Sauce should be thick with parsley, so add as needed. Serve with Bollito Misto (page 555) or any boiled meats or poultry or use as salad dressing with half the amount of parsley. Makes about 3 cups.

JALAPENA
(*Mexican Hot Sauce*)

¼ cup olive oil
1 small onion, minced
1 clove garlic, minced
1 large can plum tomatoes, drained
½ teaspoon sugar

1½ cups beef broth
1 can Jalapeña chili peppers
Hot pepper, minced, to taste
½ teaspoon dried thyme

Heat the oil and fry the onion and garlic. Add the tomatoes and sugar and simmer for 10 to 15 minutes; add the broth and simmer briskly for 5 to 6 minutes. Add chopped chili peppers, hot pepper, and the thyme. Serve with Enchiladas (page 554). Makes about 4 cups.

FLAVORED BUTTERS

The use of butter in cooking predates the Old Testament, and the practice of mixing it with various condiments and spices undoubtedly is almost as old as the basic ingredient itself. The French, whose enthusiasm for butter is proverbial, are credited with inventing many of the most subtle blendings.

BERCY BUTTER

2 shallots, minced
½ cup dry white wine
½ cup butter, softened
1½ cups diced, poached beef marrow
    (optional)

Salt and freshly ground pepper
1 to 2 tablespoons lemon juice
1 tablespoon chopped parsley

Put the shallots and the wine in an enameled saucepan and reduce wine by half. Cool completely. Cream with butter and marrow. Season to taste with salt, pepper, and lemon juice. Mix with the parsley. Serve with fish. Makes about 2 cups.

CHIVRY BUTTER

2 tablespoons minced parsley
2 teaspoons minced fresh chervil
1 teaspoon minced fresh tarragon or
    ½ teaspoon dried tarragon

1 teaspoon chopped chives
2 shallots, minced
½ cup butter, softened

Blanch herbs for 1 minute in boiling water to bring out green color. Put all ingredients in blender. Blend for 1 minute at low speed and chill. Serve with fish or meat. Makes about 1 cup.

SNAIL BUTTER

1 cup butter, softened
4 shallots, finely minced,
    sautéed in butter
3 cloves garlic, crushed
¼ cup finely chopped parsley

Salt to taste
Freshly ground pepper to taste
Dash of powdered nutmeg
Dash of dried thyme

Cream all the ingredients until very smooth and well blended. Use for Escargots à la Bourguignonne (page 450) or serve over broiled fish. Makes about 1 cup.

LOBSTER BUTTER

½ pound cooked lobster or shrimp shells   Lobster roe, stomach, and any small
½ cup butter, softened   pieces of cooked lobster flesh

Put the well-broken-up lobster shells and butter in a bowl and pound together. Put through a fine strainer, pressing and mashing to push butter through. Mix with roe, stomach, and any lobster meat and strain again. Chill before using. Serve with fish. Makes ¾ cup.

MAITRE D'HOTEL BUTTER

½ cup butter, softened   1 tablespoon lemon juice
2 tablespoons minced parsley   Salt and pepper to taste
1 teaspoon chopped fresh tarragon   1 to 2 teaspoons prepared mustard
  (optional)

Mix all the ingredients and chill. Serve with broiled meats and fish. Makes ¾ cup.

MOST DAINTIE BUTTER

Sir Hugh Plat, author of *Delightes for Ladies, to Adorne their Persons, Tables, Closets and Distillatories: With Bewties, Bouquets, Parfumes, and Waters* (1602), was obviously concerned with the well-being of the whole woman. A prefatory ode graciously proclaimed, "Of Sweetes the Sweetest I will now commend, To Sweetest creatures that the earth doth beare"; and he called upon his "wearied Muse [to] Repose her selfe in Ladies laps awhile." In the pages that followed, gentle Elizabethans discovered advice not only on preparing such table delicacies as spicy butters, but also instructions on curing freckles, brushing teeth, coloring the hair, and constructing "a delicate stove to sweat in."

½ cup butter, softened
1 tablespoon powdered cinnamon or
  paprika, or 1 teaspoon powdered
  nutmeg or mace

Cream butter with spice, pack into crock, and chill. Serve as spread on canapés or with hot pancakes or waffles. Makes ½ cup.

VARIATION: *Russian Nutmeg Butter*: Add 2 teaspoons minced chives and a dash each lemon juice and white pepper to softened butter, along with the nutmeg. Chill and serve as spread on canapés or with hot pancakes or waffles.

CLARIFIED BUTTER OR INDIAN GHEE

Melt required amount of butter very slowly to separate the oil from the white residue. Let stand for a few minutes and strain very carefully, not letting residue or water pour back into butter. Use as directed in recipe.

GARLIC BUTTER

2 to 4 cloves garlic $\frac{1}{2}$ cup butter, softened

Blanch the garlic in boiling water. Drain well, mince, and mash to a fine pulp. Cream butter and garlic. Serve with meat or fish or use to make garlic bread.

BEURRE NOIR

> Browned butter was in such wide use in sixteenth-century France that Rabelais could describe a fellow with a black eye as having an eye "au beurre noir" without losing a reader.

$\frac{2}{3}$ cup Clarified Butter (above) $1\frac{1}{2}$ tablespoons red wine vinegar
1 tablespoon chopped parsley   1 tablespoon capers (optional)

Brown the butter in a heavy saucepan until it is rich brown and gives off a nutty aroma. Remove from heat. Add parsley and pour into sauceboat. Rinse out butter pan with the vinegar and add to browned butter. Capers may be stirred in with the parsley. Serve with brains, fish, vegetables, and eggs. Makes about 1 cup.

VARIATION: *Beurre Meunière*: Omit parsley and capers and replace vinegar with lemon juice.

ANCHOVY BUTTER

6 anchovy fillets or 1 teaspoon $\frac{1}{2}$ cup butter, softened
  anchovy paste

Purée anchovies and mix with the butter. Serve on crackers as appetizer or with fish.

BEURRE MANIE

Take equal parts of soft butter and flour and cream together until very smooth. Use as needed to thicken hot liquids. One tablespoon beurre manié added to 1 cup of liquid will make a thin sauce; for a thicker sauce use 2 tablespoons of beurre manié. Add beurre manié to liquid gradually, stirring between additions until liquid has thickened to desired consistency.

FRUIT CHUTNEY

Many Westerners traveling in the East have been grateful to this pungent sauce for sparing them precise knowledge of what they were eating. The name comes from the Hindi *catnī*, to lick.

3 pounds peeled, pitted, and cubed raw fruit (pineapple, plums, cherries, apricots, peaches, apples, or pears)
3 cups cider vinegar
½ teaspoon crushed dried red chili peppers or 3 fresh chili peppers, minced
1 strip lemon peel

½ cup minced ginger root or 1 teaspoon powdered ginger
1½ cups brown sugar
1 clove garlic, crushed
1 teaspoon salt
1 cup golden raisins
½ pound almonds, shelled, blanched, and slivered (optional)

Prepare fruit as necessary. Bring vinegar to boil in enameled saucepan; add chili peppers, lemon peel, ginger root, sugar, garlic, salt, raisins, nuts, and fruit. Cover and simmer slowly for about 1 hour, stirring frequently with a wooden spoon, until mixture is thick and syrupy. Chill thoroughly, preferably overnight, before serving. Serve with curries and meats. Makes 4 cups. May be stored in sterilized, sealed jars.

MINT CHUTNEY

1 cup fresh mint leaves
6 scallions, bulbs and green tops, or 1 small onion, minced
3 tablespoons minced parsley
1 teaspoon salt

1 tablespoon sugar, or to taste
½ teaspoon chili powder or ¼ teaspoon cayenne pepper
½ teaspoon curry powder
1 tablespoon lemon juice

Purée in a blender or pound in a mortar the mint leaves, scallions, parsley, salt, sugar, chili, and curry. Add lemon juice and blend in well. Season to taste and chill in refrigerator for several hours before serving. Serve with curries or roast or broiled lamb. Makes ⅓ to ½ cup.

CURRIES

From the Hindi *turcarri*, meaning sauce, comes the English word curry, applied to any kind of Indian stew in which poultry, meats, eggs, cheese, or vegetables are simmered with spices. The selection and proportions of the many spices (commercial curry powders are seldom used) and the condiments which accompany the curry have made for an almost infinite number of regional variations. Thai curries are heavily seasoned with red or green chili peppers and are the hottest of their kind. Ceylon curries almost always contain coconut milk or cream. The south of India specializes in Vindaloos, made with vinegar and mustard oil, the latter an especially effective preservative in the hot climate. Koorma curries are typical of northern India and usually include yoghurt in their preparation. Pickles, chopped nuts, shredded coconut, chutneys, and crisp breads are traditional side dishes. The recipes below are adapted from *The Indian Domestic Economy and Receipt Book*, published in 1853 by the Christian Knowledge Society, Madras, for British Colonials.

COCONUT CREAM OR MILK

White meat of 2 fresh coconuts or
  2 cups packaged unsweetened
  coconut, shredded or grated

2 cups scalded milk

Steep coconut meat in hot milk for 20 minutes. Strain through a sieve lined with double cheesecloth, pressing all liquid out of coconut meat. To make a very thick cream, place coconut cream in the top of a double boiler and cook over simmering water for 1 hour. Chill thoroughly and lift off cream from surface. To make coconut milk, resteep coconut meat in additional fresh milk. Makes 2 cups.

VINDALOO CURRY

1 large onion, minced
2 to 3 cloves garlic, minced
3 tablespoons Ghee (page 630)
  or mustard oil
1 tablespoon powdered coriander
2 teaspoons powdered turmeric
1 teaspoon each: cumin, crushed dried

chili peppers, powdered ginger or
  minced ginger root, and dry mustard
$\frac{1}{2}$ teaspoon dried fennel
$\frac{1}{2}$ teaspoon black pepper
$\frac{1}{2}$ cup vinegar, or as needed
$2\frac{1}{2}$ pounds stewing beef or pork or 1
  chicken, cut into 1-inch cubes

Sauté the onion and garlic in hot butter until golden. Stir in spices and herbs and enough vinegar to make a smooth, thick paste. Add meat or poultry and turn through spice mixture until well coated. Cover and simmer for 1 to 1½ hours, adding water only if necessary to prevent scorching. Correct seasonings and serve. Serves 6.

VARIATION: To make a hotter sauce, combine spices and vinegar into a paste, mix through meat, and marinate overnight. Brown in fat with onions and garlic and cook as above.

KOORMA CURRY

2 3-pound frying chickens, or 2½ pounds stewing lamb or beef, cut into 1-inch cubes, or
12 hard-boiled eggs, cut in half, or
2½ pounds any cooked or raw vegetable, cut for serving, or
3 pounds shrimps, shelled and deveined, or
3 small lobsters, shelled and cut up
2 onions, chopped
3 cloves garlic, minced

1 inch ginger root or ¼ teaspoon powdered ginger
1 teaspoon each: black pepper, powdered cumin, and mustard powder
¼ teaspoon each (optional): powdered cloves, cinnamon, and coriander
2 teaspoons poppy seeds
¼ cup Ghee (page 630)
3 cups yoghurt
Salt
1 tablespoon dried, unsweetened coconut (optional)

Marinate meat, eggs, vegetables, or shellfish in mixture of onion, garlic, and remaining spices for ½ hour. Heat butter and fry curried pieces for 5 minutes, stirring frequently. Add yoghurt, cover, and simmer gently until mixture is done. Do not add liquid during cooking; shake pan to prevent scorching. Season with salt and sprinkle with coconut. Serves 6.

VARIATION: Chopped cashew nuts or almonds and 1 to 2 tablespoonfuls of lemon or lime juice may be added to the finished curry.

DAL
(Indian Lentil Purée)

3 tablespoons butter
1 large onion, chopped
1 hot green chili pepper, minced, or ½ teaspoon dried crushed red chili pepper
2 cups washed uncooked lentils

or yellow split peas
4½ cups boiling water or light beef broth
1 teaspoon turmeric or curry powder
1 tablespoon crushed mustard seed
1 tablespoon chopped fresh coriander
1½ teaspoons salt, or to taste

Melt the butter in a large saucepan and sauté onion and pepper. Add lentils and water. Simmer until tender—about 45 to 60 minutes. Add remaining ingredients and mix well. Serves 6 to 8. Dal is served as a condiment or as a thickening agent in many Indian dishes. To thicken sauces, cook dal as dry as possible without scorching. Stir into sauce in place of a roux.

CHAUD-FROID SAUCE

Summoned to an audience with Louis XV, the Maréchal de Luxembourg had to leave his château just as dinner was about to be served. When he returned the chicken was cold, the sauce had jelled, and the serendipitous *chaud-froid* (hot-cold) glaze was born.

$2\frac{1}{2}$ cups chicken broth
1 medium onion, sliced
1 small carrot, diced
1 stalk celery, chopped
Bouquet garni (4 sprigs parsley,
  1 parsley root, $\frac{1}{2}$ bay leaf, pinch
  dried thyme, tied in cheesecloth)
$\frac{1}{4}$ cup butter

$\frac{1}{4}$ cup flour
$\frac{3}{4}$ cup heavy cream
2 egg yolks
Salt and pepper
2 envelopes unflavored gelatin
$\frac{1}{2}$ cup dry white port wine
Fresh tarragon leaves
Aspic (page 635)

Put chicken broth, vegetables, and bouquet garni in a saucepan and simmer for 15 minutes. Strain and reserve broth. Melt butter, add flour, and cook, stirring, for 2 to 3 minutes. Add strained hot broth and stir until thick and smooth. Add *one-half cup cream* and simmer gently for 10 minutes, skimming as needed. Beat *remaining cream* with egg yolks. Slowly pour some hot sauce into eggs and cream, stirring briskly, and return slowly to remaining sauce, still stirring constantly. Cook over very low heat, but do not boil. Continue stirring until very hot and thick; correct seasoning. Meanwhile soak gelatin in the port wine for 5 minutes. Add port and gelatin to sauce. Remove from heat and stir until gelatin is completely melted. Set saucepan in a bowl of ice and stir until just cool but not jellied. Remove from ice. Makes enough to coat a galantine or large roast chicken.

To coat a Galantine (page 490): Place galantine on a cake rack over a platter. Spoon sauce over meat. Chill until set. Repeat 4 or 5 times, chilling between coatings. If sauce becomes too thick, reheat and cool again to coating consistency. Blanch the tarragon leaves for 30 seconds in boiling water. Arrange in a pattern on the galantine before chilling fifth coat of sauce. Put 2 or 3 coats of clear aspic over tarragon leaves and chill. Place remainder of aspic, cubed, around galantine. Garnish platter with watercress. Cutouts of pimento or truffles or hard-boiled egg daisies may be combined with tarragon leaves as decorations.

BROWN CHAUD-FROID SAUCE

$2\frac{1}{2}$ cups Demi-glace Sauce (page 623)
2 envelopes unflavored gelatin
1 cup beef broth

Salt and pepper
3 tablespoons Madeira wine

Reduce demi-glace sauce to 2 cups. Soak gelatin in the broth, add to the hot demi-glace sauce, and stir until melted. Season to taste. Strain carefully, add the wine, and cool, stirring back and forth with a wooden spatula until thickened enough to coat meats. Place meat to be coated on a cake rack over a platter. Spoon sauce smoothly over meat. Chill until set; repeat coating with sauce until desired degree of coating has been obtained. Reheat sauce if it becomes too thick or set and cool again to coating consistency. Makes about 3 cups.

VARIATION: For duck replace beef broth with broth from neck, giblets, and carcass of the duck.

ASPIC

4 cups strong, clear chicken, beef, veal, or fish stock

2 envelopes unflavored gelatin

Heat *three and one-half cups stock*. Soak gelatin in *remaining cold stock* for 5 minutes; stir into hot stock until dissolved. Cool and use as directed. Any remaining aspic may be chilled in a shallow dish, then chopped or cut into shapes and used as garnish. Unused aspic will keep and may be reheated and rechilled.

CUMBERLAND SAUCE

Several eighteenth-century dishes were named for William Augustus, Duke of Cumberland, the third son of King George II. Currants appear in many Cumberland recipes, including this one for a game sauce.

Rind and juice of 1 orange
Rind and juice of $\frac{1}{2}$ lemon
4 shallots, minced
$\frac{1}{3}$ cup currant jelly, melted

1 cup port wine
1 teaspoon prepared mustard
$\frac{1}{4}$ to $\frac{1}{2}$ teaspoon powdered ginger
Cayenne pepper

Cut rinds in julienne strips and simmer in water for 15 minutes. Drain well. Simmer the shallots in water separately until tender. Drain and press out any moisture. Add orange and lemon rind and shallots to currant jelly. Add wine and strained orange and lemon juice. Dilute mustard with a little sauce and stir in. Season with ginger and cayenne pepper to taste. Serve cold with game. Makes about 2 cups.

SAUCE FOR A POOR MAN

Though Vincent La Chapelle's career was entirely devoted to pleasing the palates of lords and ladies, some of his recipe titles suggest stirrings of a social conscience. The "poor man" might disguise leftovers with the sauce recipe below: the better-fed "citizen" would improve "all sorts of fowls and fish" with Sauce in Ragout the Citizen's Way (page 620), which calls for such luxury ingredients as anchovy and a truffle.

4 scallions, minced	3 tablespoons wine vinegar
2 tablespoons minced parsley	½ cup olive oil
2 shallots, minced	Salt and freshly ground pepper

Mix all these ingredients and serve over cold vegetables. Chopped hard-boiled eggs and any desired herbs may be added. Makes about 1½ cups.

SAUCE RAVIGOTE

1 recipe Vinaigrette Dressing (page 637)	1 teaspoon chopped fresh chervil or ½ teaspoon dried chervil
2 tablespoons minced shallots or onions	2 tablespoons chopped parsley
2 tablespoons minced capers	1 teaspoon chopped fresh tarragon or ½ teaspoon dried tarragon
1 tablespoon chopped chives	

Mix all the ingredients together and serve with salads or cold vegetables or cold boiled poultry or meats. Makes 1¼ cups.

FROSSEN FLØDEPEBERROD
(Danish Frozen Horseradish Cream)

2 cups heavy cream	4 tablespoons freshly grated horseradish root
1 to 2 teaspoons sugar, or to taste	Salt and white pepper
1 tablespoon lemon juice or vinegar, or to taste	

Whip cream until it begins to thicken, then add sugar. When stiff, fold in lemon juice or vinegar, horseradish, salt, and pepper. Pour into mold or small tray and freeze to sherbet consistency. Serve spooned over hot boiled beef or chicken, herring or salmon, or with hot boiled codfish. Makes about 2½ cups.

VARIATION: If fresh horseradish is unavailable, substitute 2 tablespoons well-drained bottled horseradish and eliminate lemon juice or vinegar. Adjust sugar to taste.

HOT HORSERADISH SAUCE

$1\frac{1}{2}$ cups medium Béchamel Sauce   2 tablespoons prepared horseradish
  (page 618), heated

Combine béchamel and horseradish. Serve with fish and boiled beef. Makes about $1\frac{2}{3}$ cups.

VINAIGRETTE DRESSING

The French borrowed from the Greek and Roman custom of dipping
bread in oil and vinegar to create their classic, tart dressing.

$1\frac{1}{2}$ teaspoons Dijon-style mustard   3 tablespoons red or white wine vinegar
$\frac{1}{4}$ to $\frac{1}{2}$ teaspoon salt, or to taste   9 tablespoons olive oil
$\frac{1}{4}$ teaspoon black pepper

Blend mustard, salt, and pepper in the vinegar, stirring well with a fork. Trickle in the oil
while stirring. Makes $\frac{3}{4}$ cup.

VARIATION: Lemon juice may replace vinegar or be used in a half-and-half combination.
One teaspoon chopped fresh tarragon leaves or $\frac{1}{2}$ teaspoon dried tarragon, or 2 tablespoons
chopped parsley, dill, or chives may be added.

637

AIOLI

Garlic mixed with oil, the forerunner of mayonnaise, probably sauced the food of ancient Egypt. Romans brought *alium oleum* to Europe, and, improved with egg yolks, it became a favorite throughout the Mediterranean. In Provence Aioli is used almost as lavishly as butter is in northern France—at the fast night meal on Christmas Eve it is traditionally served over a whole succession of dishes. Ali-oli is the Spanish version, known there since at least the eleventh century when it was listed in a manuscript on sauces. Skordalia is of Greek origin.

6 cloves garlic, crushed
4 egg yolks
2 cups olive oil, at room temperature

Lemon juice to taste
Salt to taste

To prepare in a blender, combine garlic and egg yolks and mix at low speed. Gradually add oil in a very slow stream until mixture is the consistency of mayonnaise. Season with lemon juice and salt. To prepare by hand, work crushed garlic, salt, and egg yolks together in a bowl, using a wooden spoon. Add oil in a slow stream, beating constantly as for mayonnaise. Season with lemon juice and salt. Serve with fish. Makes about $2\frac{1}{2}$ cups.

VARIATIONS: *Greek Skordalia*: Follow above recipe. When sauce is right consistency, season with lemon juice and salt and stir in 2 tablespoons blanched, ground almonds, walnuts, or pine nuts, and 2 tablespoons fine bread crumbs. *Spanish Ali-oli*: This sauce is similar to the above but is made without egg yolks. Crush the cloves of a whole bulb of garlic in a mortar with a generous pinch of salt to act as an abrasive. Gradually and slowly pour in 2 cups olive oil, beating constantly as for mayonnaise. When mixture is the consistency of mayonnaise, work in lemon juice. For a milder garlic flavor, use half amount of garlic and add 2 slices of crustless white bread, crumbled, working it into the oil with the crushed garlic.

ROUILLE DE MARSEILLE

1 4-ounce jar pimentos
1 hot red chili pepper or hot
   pepper sauce to taste
5 cloves garlic, mashed

1 egg yolk
$\frac{2}{3}$ cup olive oil
$\frac{1}{3}$ cup hot fish broth

Mince and mash the drained pimentos with the hot chili pepper. (If the chili is raw it should be simmered in boiling water for 5 minutes.) Add the garlic and mash into a smooth paste or purée in blender. Add egg yolk and dribble in the oil very slowly, stirring briskly or blending on medium speed as for mayonnaise. Leave at room temperature until ready to serve. At serving time gradually beat in the hot fish broth. Pass in a sauceboat, to be added to Bouillabaisse (page 452) or Bourride (page 453). Makes 2 cups.

MAYONNAISE

One of the many men credited with introducing Mayonnaise to France is the Duc de Richelieu; he is said to have discovered it in 1757 when the French captured Mahon on the island of Minorca. The sauce was permeated with garlic but the duc cleverly discerned its true character, separated it from the gross flavor, and brought it thus to France.

3 egg yolks
$\frac{1}{2}$ teaspoon salt
$\frac{1}{2}$ teaspoon dry mustard
Cayenne pepper

$1\frac{1}{2}$ cups olive oil, or half olive oil and
   half salad oil
1 teaspoon lemon juice or wine vinegar

Have all the ingredients at room temperature. Beat the egg yolks, salt, mustard, and a dash or 2 of cayenne pepper until well mixed and thickened. Add oil, drop by drop, beating constantly. When mayonnaise starts to blend, oil may be added a little faster. Add lemon juice or vinegar to taste. Chill before serving. Makes 2 cups.

TARTARE SAUCE

1 teaspoon Dijon-style mustard
$1\frac{1}{2}$ cups mayonnaise
2 tablespoons minced scallions
2 teaspoons chopped chives

1 tablespoon chopped sweet gherkins
   (optional)
1 tablespoon chopped olives (optional)
2 tablespoons chopped capers

Mix mustard with mayonnaise. Add remaining ingredients and chill slightly. Serve with fish. Makes about 2 cups.

BEURRE MONTPELLIER

$\frac{1}{4}$ bunch watercress sprigs
2 tablespoons parsley
1 teaspoon fresh tarragon or
   $\frac{1}{2}$ teaspoon dried tarragon
1 tablespoon chopped chives
1 teaspoon fresh chervil or
   $\frac{1}{2}$ teaspoon dried chervil
2 shallots, minced

1 sour gherkin, minced
1 small clove garlic, minced
2 anchovy fillets, minced
Yolks of 2 hard-boiled eggs
1 cup butter, softened
$\frac{1}{2}$ cup mayonnaise
Salt and cayenne pepper

Mince all the herbs, put them in blender along with the shallots, gherkin, garlic, anchovy, hard-boiled egg yolks, and butter and blend at low speed. Work in mayonnaise gradually, season to taste, and chill. Serve with cold fish. Makes about 3 cups.

TO MAKE WINE VINEGAR

Ever since biblical times when Ruth was ordered to "come thou hither . . . and dip thy morsel [of bread] in vinegar," the acid made from fermented wines has puckered ancient palates. The Romans served rare Egyptian vinegar in finely wrought gold and silver cruets, and they used more plebeian varieties to marinate perishable fruits and vegetables, tenderize meat, heal wounds, and prevent scurvy. By the seventeenth century, Europeans were adding seasonings like pepper, mustard, garlic, tarragon, or saffron to vinegar, and the English had even invented a powdered version to be carried in travelers' pockets. In eighteenth-century France mademoiselles habitually drank the liquid to reduce (as it purportedly shrank the stomach), though Brillat-Savarin condemned the practice with an acerbic tale of a friend who died after drinking a glass of vinegar every day for a month.

Pour $\frac{1}{2}$ cup red wine vinegar into an empty, unrinsed quart-size red wine bottle. Add any leftover red table wine whenever you have some. Keep the bottle tightly corked. Let stand at room temperature for 2 to 3 months before using the first of the vinegar. To make white wine vinegar, follow the same steps, using white wine vinegar as a starter in an empty quart-size white wine bottle and adding leftover white table wine.

RED WINE MARINADE

The doctor who watched over Governor Panza's eating in *Don Quixote* listed among taboo items marinated meat "because it was too hot and contained too many spices." As any good Spaniard would, Sancho fired him. Even in the time of Apicius, whose recipe appears below, marinades were more prized for the flavor they imparted than for their preservative qualities.

2 large onions, chopped
1 large carrot, sliced
3 shallots, chopped
2 celery stalks, chopped
2 cloves garlic, minced
2 whole cloves
$\frac{1}{2}$ teaspoon each fresh rosemary, thyme, and oregano, or $\frac{1}{4}$ teaspoon each dried herbs

2 crushed bay leaves
12 juniper berries
10 peppercorns
2 tablespoons chopped parsley
1 teaspoon salt
Cayenne pepper to taste
1 bottle red wine
$\frac{1}{2}$ cup red wine vinegar
1 cup olive oil

Combine all ingredients. Simmer for 10 minutes and cool. Pour over meat. Let marinate for 24 to 48 hours in refrigerator, turning occasionally, before cooking as directed in recipes.

SAUCE REMOULADE

The name of this sauce derives possibly from *rémouleur* (knife grinder) in recognition of its cutting flavor. Mustard, a contributor, is a specialty of Dijon, where since the fifteenth century *moutardiers* have mixed the seeds with verjus to achieve that particular French twist.

$1\frac{1}{2}$ cups mayonnaise
2 tablespoons drained minced capers
$\frac{1}{3}$ cup drained minced sour pickles
2 teaspoons grated onion
2 teaspoons Dijon-style mustard

2 teaspoons each chopped fresh parsley, tarragon, chives, and chervil, or
1 teaspoon each dried herbs
Dab of anchovy paste

Mix all the ingredients. Serve cold with shellfish. Makes about 2 cups.

HOT SAUCE REMOULADE

2 tablespoons olive oil
1 small onion, finely chopped
1 clove of garlic, crushed or minced
1 cup Brown Sauce (page 620)
$\frac{1}{2}$ cup dry white wine
$\frac{1}{2}$ teaspoon each fresh tarragon, chervil, basil, or $\frac{1}{4}$ teaspoon each dried herbs

2 tablespoons minced parsley
$\frac{1}{2}$ lemon, cut into slices
2 cloves
2 teaspoons chopped capers
Salt and pepper to taste
2 teaspoons Dijon-style mustard

Heat the oil; brown the onion and garlic. Add remaining ingredients, with the exception of the mustard. Stir until smooth and simmer for 10 minutes. Add the mustard; heat through; strain and serve with roasted or boiled meats. Makes about $1\frac{1}{2}$ cups.

MUSTARD DILL SAUCE

$\frac{1}{3}$ cup hot yellow Dijon-style mustard
$\frac{1}{3}$ cup sweet brown German- or Swedish-style mustard
1 tablespoon sugar, or to taste
2 to 3 tablespoons olive oil

2 tablespoons white or cider vinegar, or to taste
Salt and white pepper
1 to 2 tablespoons minced fresh dill

Combine the 2 mustards and stir in sugar. Gradually add olive oil in a slow stream, beating constantly as for mayonnaise. Sauce should be the consistency of thick sour cream. Add vinegar slowly to thin sauce slightly. Season with salt, pepper, and more sugar and/or vinegar to taste. Stir in dill. Serve with maatjes herring, smoked salmon, or Gravad Lox (page 467). Makes about 1 cup.

BREADS
AND
ROLLS

When Omar Khayyám assembled a loaf of bread, a jug of wine, and his favorite lady for an evening's pleasures, he was repeating a ritual—however more poetically—that was as old as Egyptian civilization. It was in Egypt that bakers first learned to leaven bread with fermenting agents, using the soured dough of one batch to "start" the fresh dough of the next. First-century Gauls improved on this method by using yeast from the scum in wine barrels to make their dough rise. Though leavened loaves rapidly became popular, they have never entirely supplanted flat breads. Pliny's opinion that "people who live on fermented bread have weaker bodies" may have had something to do with the decision to feed only flat breads to Rome's armies. In medieval France the prejudice was more specific: brewers' yeast was considered unhealthful, and people leavened their bread with sour dough or baked unleavened trenchers. A recipe for "white trencher plates which may be eaten" was offered in Hannah Woolley's *Queen-like Closet* (1684).

> *"Take two eggs beaten very well, yolks and whites, two spoonsful of sack, one spoonful of rosewater, as much flour as will make it a stiff paste, then roul it thin and then lay it upon the outsides of plates well buttered. Cut them to fit the plates and bake them upon them, then take them forth and when they are cold take a pound of double refined sugar beaten and searced with a little ambergreece, the white of an egg and rosewater. Beat these well together and line your plates all over with it and set them into the oven again till they be dry."*

White bread has been a status symbol in Europe ever since wealthy Romans took to serving guests wheaten loaves instead of their daily dark breads. It continued to be a rarity through the Middle Ages, coarse flours—made even of peas, chestnuts, and acorns—going into the peasants' common fare. In England it was not until 1440 that a London guild of white-bread makers was licensed to produce "all maner of whyte brede . . . in Chepe for Pore men." By the end of the eighteenth century few Britons would eat anything else, and, according to Tobias Smollett, bakers were becoming adept at turning a nice profit with flours made into "a deleterious paste, mixed up with chalk, alum, and bone-ashes."

WHITE BREAD

1 envelope dry yeast	$2\frac{1}{2}$ teaspoons salt
1 cup milk	3 tablespoons butter
1 tablespoon sugar	6 cups flour, sifted

Dissolve yeast in $\frac{1}{4}$ cup warm water in a large mixing bowl. Scald milk and add 1 cup water. Dissolve sugar, salt, and butter in milk and water mixture. When it is lukewarm stir into yeast in mixing bowl. Add *three cups sifted flour* and mix well. Add *remaining flour*. Mix until dough leaves sides of bowl. Turn onto a floured board. Knead with both hands by folding dough on itself and pushing it away with the heel of the hand. Repeat, adding sifted flour to board as needed. Continue until dough has bubbles under its surface, is elastic, and no longer sticks to the hands (about 10 minutes). Place it in a buttered bowl. Roll it around until all surfaces are buttered. Put in a warm place. Cover with a dry towel and allow it to rise until doubled in bulk, about 1 hour. Punch down, knead for 2 minutes, and shape into 2 loaves. Place in buttered loaf pans. Allow to stand for about $1\frac{1}{2}$ hours or until doubled in bulk. Bake in a preheated 400° oven for 15 minutes. Lower heat to 350°; bake for 55 minutes or until bread shrinks from sides of pan. Cool on racks. For a soft crust, butter surface and cover with a towel after removing bread from oven. For a crisp crust, place a dish of boiling water on lower rack of oven for first 20 minutes of baking.

PRETZELS

Just when a baker knotted the first pretzel is unknown. Perhaps it dates back to the Roman Era whence its name, meaning bracelet, is descended. Flemish painters, imagining pretzels to be as old as the Bible, often used them as props in scenes of the Last Supper. Because the dough contains no shortening, eggs, or milk, pretzels keep extremely well, and their saltiness has made them a favorite accompaniment to alcoholic drinks throughout northern Europe. Two basic varieties are made from the same dough: the thin, hard type are baked; the thicker, bagel-like pretzels below are boiled before baking and are often eaten, split and buttered, as a midmorning snack.

1 envelope dry yeast	Butter as needed
Pinch of sugar	4 teaspoons bicarbonate of soda
2 teaspoons salt	Coarse salt for sprinkling
$1\frac{1}{2}$ tablespoons caraway seeds (optional)	Caraway seeds for sprinkling (optional)
4 to 5 cups flour, sifted	

Dissolve yeast in $\frac{1}{4}$ cup warm water, then stir in 1 cup warm water and sugar. Set in a warm place for 45 minutes to 1 hour. Pour yeast mixture into a bowl and stir in salt and caraway seeds. Gradually beat in enough flour to make a stiff dough. Turn out onto a floured board and knead vigorously for 8 to 10 minutes or until dough is smooth and elastic. Place in buttered bowl and spread a little butter over the top of the dough. Cover lightly with a towel and set in a warm place to rise for 45 minutes or until doubled in bulk. Shape pretzels into sticks or twists, rolling pieces of dough between hands. Roll to half the thickness desired for finished pretzels. Bring 4 cups of water to a boil with bicarbonate of soda. Drop 2 or 3 shaped pretzels at a time into water and boil for 1 minute after they float to the surface. Remove carefully with a slotted spoon, drain, and place on buttered cookie sheet. When all pretzels are on the sheet, sprinkle with salt and caraway seeds. Bake in preheated 475° oven until golden brown—about 12 minutes. Remove from baking sheet and cool on a rack. Pretzels will keep for weeks in an airtight container. Makes 12 large twisted pretzels or 36 8-inch pretzel sticks. Serve plain, or split and sandwich together with butter.

VARIATION: *Crisp Pretzels*: Prepare and shape dough into very thin sticks or twists as described above, but do not boil. Place on buttered cookie sheet, brush with 1 egg yolk beaten with 2 tablespoons milk, and sprinkle with salt and caraway seeds. Let rise until almost doubled in bulk—about 25 minutes. Bake as directed above.

PAIN ORDINAIRE

Strange statutes had long regulated the French baking profession. One thirteenth-century law forbade Parisian millers to grind grain on a certain bridge on Sundays because a nearby church needed the river waters for holy purposes. Another stated that to become a master baker an apprentice must throw a pot of walnuts at the mayor's wall. By the seventeenth century the rules were more reasonable, establishing standard prices and weights for such breads as Pain Ordinaire.

2 envelopes dry yeast
2 teaspoons sugar

$1\frac{1}{2}$ teaspoons salt
6 cups flour, sifted

Dissolve yeast and sugar in $\frac{1}{2}$ cup warm water for 10 minutes in a large, warm bowl. Add salt to $1\frac{1}{2}$ cups of warm water and add the water to the yeast. Work in the flour. Turn out the dough on a floured board and knead for 10 minutes or until smooth and elastic. Butter surface of dough. Place in buttered bowl, cover, and let rise for $1\frac{1}{2}$ hours or until doubled in bulk. Knead 2 or 3 times and divide into 4 small sections or 2 large pieces. Shape and stretch these into long French loaves tapering at the ends. Place loaves well apart on greased cookie sheets. Cover and let rise for 30 minutes. Cut diagonal slashes on the loaves. Brush with plain or salted water (1 teaspoon salt to $\frac{1}{2}$ cup water) and bake in a preheated 400° oven for 15 minutes. Place a pan with 1 inch of boiling water on lower rack of oven. Lower heat to 350° and bake about 20 minutes or until bread is golden and sounds hollow when tapped on bottom.

ARABIC BREAD

Ever since Allah reputedly gave man grain by sending it from heaven securely wrapped in seven handkerchiefs, the Arabs have regarded bread, or *El Aish* (literally meaning "life"), as sacrosanct. At one time bread could not even be sold but was given away or exchanged. Today bakers throughout the Near East hawk their flat round loaves, which serve as plates as well as food, and shout, "Allah Karim!" (God is merciful); if an Egyptian finds a piece on the street he touches it to his lips and forehead and feeds it to a stray dog. In Iraq bread is stuffed with meat and given to the poor as an offering of thanks.

1 recipe Pain Ordinaire dough (above)

Prepare dough. Knead for 10 minutes until smooth. Divide into 10 to 12 balls of dough. Roll balls out on floured board into 5- to 6-inch pancakes. Place on greased cookie sheets and bake in a preheated 475° oven for 10 to 12 minutes. Do not open oven door during baking. Bread should be golden brown and puffy. For softer bread, brush surface with melted butter as soon as it is removed from the oven and cover with a cloth to cool.

645

BARMBRACK

Perhaps because currant-studded Barmbrack is authentically Irish, it was used by Lady Gregory, one of the founders of Dublin's famous Abbey Theater, to revive flagging spirits and waning Irish genius backstage. Having done its job, Barmbrack was passed around again to celebrate the success of plays like *Juno and the Paycock*.

2 envelopes dry yeast
$\frac{1}{3}$ cup sugar
$\frac{1}{3}$ cup each golden raisins, currants, and chopped candied rinds
4 cups sifted flour, or as needed
2 teaspoons powdered cinnamon

1 cup milk
4 tablespoons butter
$\frac{1}{2}$ teaspoon salt
1 whole egg, beaten
1 egg white, beaten

Dissolve the yeast in $\frac{1}{3}$ cup warm water with *one teaspoon sugar*. Mix the fruits with *two table-spoons flour* and reserve. Resift the *remaining flour* with cinnamon. Heat the milk and add *one-quarter cup sugar*, butter, and salt. Put flour-cinnamon mixture in a warm bowl. Make a well in the center of the flour, add reserved fruits, and pour in dissolved yeast, milk, and beaten egg. Work into a dough. Place dough on a floured board and knead well for 10 minutes, adding sifted flour to the board if needed until dough is smooth and elastic and no longer sticky. Place in a warm, greased bowl and butter surface of the dough. Cover with a cloth and let rise until doubled in bulk, about 45 minutes. Punch dough down and knead for about 2 minutes or until the dough is elastic again. Divide in 2 parts. Fill 2 well-greased loaf pans two-thirds full. Let rise again for 20 minutes and bake in a preheated 425° oven for 10 minutes. Lower heat to 350° and bake for 20 minutes. Brush the loaves with egg white. Sprinkle surface with *remaining sugar* and bake for 10 minutes. Raise the heat to 400° and bake 10 minutes longer. Loaves will shrink from the sides of the pans when done. Remove from pans and place loaves on their sides on cake racks to cool. For softer crusts, cool covered with a cloth. If desired, substitute 1 cup whole wheat flour (sifted twice) for 1 cup white flour.

SWEDISH LIMPA BREAD

$\frac{3}{4}$ cup ale
$2\frac{1}{2}$ cups rye flour, sifted
1 envelope dry yeast
1 teaspoon sugar
1 cup warm milk
$\frac{1}{3}$ cup butter, melted

$\frac{1}{2}$ cup molasses
6 to 7 cups white flour, sifted
1 tablespoon salt
1 tablespoon fennel seeds
1 tablespoon caraway seeds
$\frac{1}{2}$ cup diced candied orange rind

Heat the ale and work with the rye flour into a stiff dough, kneading in a bowl for 10 to 15 minutes. Butter the bowl and the dough and let stand overnight in a warm place. Dissolve the yeast in $\frac{1}{4}$ cup warm water; add the sugar and let stand for 20 minutes. Put the warm milk in a large, warm bowl and add the melted butter, yeast, and molasses. Resift white flour with the salt. Reserve a little of it for the kneading board. Gradually add the rest of the flour to yeast mixture. Add the rye dough and mix well. Put on a floured board and knead for 10 to 15 minutes. Dust fennel, caraway, and candied rind with a little flour, and work into dough. Replace in a buttered bowl, butter the surface of the dough, and let rise for $1\frac{1}{2}$ to 2 hours or until doubled in bulk. Knead again and divide into 2 oval loaves. Put them on buttered cookie sheets. Cover and let rise for $\frac{1}{2}$ hour. Brush with cold water and bake in a preheated 400° oven for 15 minutes; reduce heat to 350°. Brush twice more with cold water and bake for another 40 to 60 minutes or until loaves sound hollow when tapped.

CHALLAH

In ancient times twelve loaves of unleavened bread were placed every Sabbath on the high altar of the Temple at Jerusalem. Each loaf represented one of the twelve tribes of Israel. After the destruction of the Temple and the dispersion of the Jews, the day was marked with a commemorative service performed on the Sabbath eve in the home. The Challah represented the ritual loaves; instead of black bread, the daily fare of most Jews, it was a much-prized, pure white loaf. It was known affectionately in eastern Europe as "a warm twist" because the dough was usually braided before baking and then served fresh from the oven.

1 tablespoon sugar	1 tablespoon salt
$\frac{1}{4}$ teaspoon powdered saffron	2 eggs, slightly beaten
$\frac{1}{4}$ cup vegetable oil	1 egg yolk for glazing
2 envelopes dry yeast	$\frac{1}{2}$ cup poppy seeds
6 to 7 cups flour, sifted	

Add sugar, saffron, and oil to 2 cups warm water. When slightly cooled, pour $\frac{1}{2}$ cup of mixture into a large, warm mixing bowl, adding the yeast. Resift flour with the salt. Add about $\frac{1}{2}$ cup flour to the yeast mixture to make a sponge, and let it rise for 30 minutes. Add remaining sugar-water mixture. Beat in the eggs lightly and add 6 cups flour. Turn onto a floured board and knead for 10 minutes. Place it in a greased bowl, grease surface of dough, cover, and let it rise until doubled in bulk—$1\frac{1}{2}$ to 2 hours. Knead again for 10 minutes on floured board, then cut in half. Cut each half into 3 pieces and roll these to make long sausages. Braid 3 rolls out from center toward each end to form oval loaves. Secure ends of strips. Place on greased cookie sheets, cover lightly, and let rise for 30 minutes more. Brush with egg yolk mixed with 2 tablespoons water, sprinkle with poppy seeds, and bake in a preheated 400° oven for 15 minutes. Lower the heat to 375° and bake for 45 minutes more or until golden and hollow-sounding when tapped. Makes 2 loaves.

HOLIDAY BREADS

The spices used in the holiday breads below and their symbolic shapes and meanings vary. However, they are all based on the same type coffee-cake dough, and each is an integral part of some festivity in its native country. German Dreikönigsbrot and Mexican Rosca de Reyes are served on Twelfth Night (January 6), traditionally the day when the Magi came to Jesus in the manger. A figure of the Christ child is implanted in the Mexican version and the lucky—or unlucky—recipient is expected to give a party four weeks later on Candlemas Day. Greek Basilópitta is eaten on Saint Basil's Day (January 1). A trinket representing jewelry and other valuables is implanted in the bread to signify the saint's rescue of Caesarea from Roman looters. The Russian Koulitch and the Polish Babka are Easter breads. The latter takes its name from the wide-skirted, grandmotherly shape of the deep pan in which it is baked. Italian Panettone was supposedly invented when Tonio, a baker's apprentice, fancied up the standard Milanese Christmas Eve *pane* (bread) in order to impress his boss and so to win the daughter's hand. The Dresdener Stollen recipe below is the most famous of many regional variations of Germany's Christmas bread.

Coffeecake dough:
2 envelopes dry yeast
$\frac{1}{2}$ cup sugar
1 cup milk, scalded
1 teaspoon salt
$\frac{1}{2}$ cup butter
3 whole eggs or 6 egg yolks, well beaten

1 teaspoon grated lemon rind (optional)
1 teaspoon vanilla extract
4 to 5 cups flour, sifted
Rich coffeecake dough:
1 recipe coffeecake dough plus
  3 whole eggs or 6 egg yolks and
  $\frac{1}{2}$ cup butter, softened

Dissolve the yeast in $\frac{1}{4}$ cup warm water with *one teaspoon sugar* until it bubbles. Put hot scalded milk, salt, butter, and *remaining sugar* in a large, warm bowl. When milk has cooled to tepid add yeast, beaten eggs, lemon rind, vanilla, and enough flour to make a soft but not sticky dough. Mix well with the hands. Invert on a floured pastry board and knead for 10 minutes or until smooth and elastic. Place in a buttered bowl and roll the dough around to butter the surface; cover lightly and let rise in a warm place until doubled in bulk—about 1 to $1\frac{1}{2}$ hours. Punch dough down and knead for 2 to 3 minutes. Shape dough and bake as directed for the breads below. To make a rich coffeecake dough, work in the extra butter with the flour; add the additional eggs to the dough and proceed as above.

Dreikönigsbrot: Prepare coffeecake dough. After dough has risen, punch down and knead 3 or 4 times. Insert 1 whole blanched almond and form into a round loaf, place on a greased cookie sheet. Brush with $\frac{1}{4}$ cup melted butter. Crush 12 cubes of sugar and mix with 1 teaspoon cinnamon and $\frac{1}{3}$ cup chopped nuts; sprinkle mixture on dough. Let rise for 20 minutes and bake in a preheated 400° oven for 10 minutes. Reduce heat to 350° and bake for 50 to 60 minutes longer or until loaf sounds hollow when tapped. Cool on a rack.

Rosca de Reyes: Dust 2 cups chopped mixed candied fruit with flour and knead into coffeecake dough. Let rise covered in a buttered bowl for about 1 hour. Knead again 3 or 4 times, and insert 1 lima bean or a very small china figure representing the Christ child. Roll dough into a thick sausage; bring ends together to form a ring. Let rise for 20 minutes and bake in a preheated 375° oven for about 35 to 40 minutes or until ring sounds hollow when tapped. Cool on a rack. Ice with thin Sugar Icing (page 702) and decorate with halved candied red and green cherries and angelica.

Basilópitta: Prepare coffeecake dough, adding ½ teaspoon each cinnamon and nutmeg, 1 teaspoon powdered anise, and 1 teaspoon grated orange or lemon rind along with the flour. Knead dough on a floured board until smooth and satiny—about 10 minutes. Place dough in a buttered bowl, cover, and let rise until doubled in bulk—about 1 hour. Punch down, and knead again for 2 to 3 minutes. With two-thirds of dough make 2 round flat loaves about 1 inch thick. Insert a small trinket in each loaf. Place on buttered cookie sheets. Roll half the remaining dough into 2 thin sausages. Place in a circle on top of loaves, near the edge. With the last of the dough make numerals of the new year in thin strings, and place in center of loaves. Let rise for 20 minutes. Brush with egg yolk mixed with 2 teaspoons cold water. Bake in a preheated 450° oven for 15 minutes. Lower heat to 350° and bake for another 30 to 40 minutes or until golden brown and loaf is hollow sounding when tapped.

Koulitch: Soak ⅛ teaspoon saffron strands in ¼ cup rum and soak ½ cup golden raisins in ⅓ cup dry white wine while preparing coffeecake dough. Strain rum into dough, discarding saffron; add raisins and wine, ½ cup lightly floured candied fruits, and ½ cup toasted slivered almonds; knead well on a lightly floured board, adding flour if necessary so dough is not sticky. Place in a buttered bowl and let rise, covered, until doubled in bulk—about 1 hour. Knead once or twice and put into 2 tall, well-buttered and floured cylindrical molds (46-ounce fruit juice cans may be substituted). Let rise until two-thirds full. Bake in a preheated 400° oven for 20 minutes. Lower heat to 350° and continue baking for about 1 hour or until a tester inserted in the center comes out clean. Remove bread from molds and cool on racks. Decorate with thin Sugar Icing (page 702). Slice from top into round slices. Koulitch is traditionally served with Paska (page 718).

Babka: Add 1 teaspoon powdered cardamom and ¾ cup golden raisins dredged with flour to rich coffeecake dough. Knead well on a floured board. Let rise, covered, in a buttered bowl until doubled in bulk, about 1 hour. Punch down, and place dough in a 9-inch buttered tube mold, filling pan half full. Let rise until dough nearly reaches the top of the pan. Bake in a preheated 350° oven for 40 to 50 minutes. Remove from pan and cool on a rack. Mix 4 tablespoons rum with ¾ cup warm thin Sugar Icing (page 702) and pour over babka.

Panettone: Prepare rich coffeecake dough. Knead on a well-floured board, adding a little extra flour to make a firmer dough. Sprinkle with flour, $\frac{1}{2}$ cup each golden and black raisins, and diced candied citron. Knead into dough until well distributed. Brush dough with 2 tablespoons melted butter and let rise in a buttered bowl until doubled in bulk—about $1\frac{1}{2}$ to 2 hours. Butter a tall 3-quart casserole, add dough, brush with 2 tablespoons melted butter, and let rise for 40 to 60 minutes or until doubled in bulk. Cut a deep cross in the dough with kitchen shears. Bake in a preheated 400° oven for 10 minutes, lower heat to 350°, and bake until well risen and brown, about 50 to 60 minutes. Sprinkle with sugar when cool.

Stollen: Add $\frac{1}{2}$ teaspoon almond extract and 2 teaspoons grated lemon rind to rich coffeecake dough. Knead 4 minutes. Mix 2 cups raisins with 2 or 3 tablespoons flour and knead into the dough for about 3 minutes. Set in a warm, buttered bowl and brush surface of dough with 2 tablespoons melted butter; cover and let rise until doubled in bulk—about 1 hour. Put back on floured board, punch down and flatten into a wide oval, $\frac{1}{2}$ inch thick. Brush with 2 tablespoons butter, fold over three-quarters of the oval, lengthwise, leaving an uncovered edge. Set on buttered cookie sheet and brush with 2 tablespoons melted butter. Let rise for 20 minutes or until doubled in bulk and bake in a preheated 375° oven for 1 hour. Brush with 2 tablespoons melted butter; cool before serving. Dust with confectioners' sugar.

GOUGERE
(*Burgundian Cheese Puffs*)

$1\frac{1}{2}$ cups diced Gruyère cheese   1 recipe Cream Puff Paste (page 725)

Add *one cup diced cheese* to hot cream puff paste and beat until well mixed. Butter a cookie sheet and spoon out a ring of mounds of the dough so the mounds touch, or drop individual teaspoonfuls to form small puffs. Top with *remaining diced cheese*. Bake in a preheated 375° oven for 40 minutes, lower the heat, then prick each puff to let steam escape. Bake 5 minutes longer. Serve hot or warm as a light entree or appetizer. Serves 6.

SALLY LUNN

At least one tradition insists that there was indeed a Sally Lunn, an eighteenth-century lass who hustled heavenly hot breads in the streets of Bath. An enterprising baker named Dalmer, impressed with Sally's success, bought her out but continued to call the fine product after the girl who had popularized it.

1½ envelopes dry yeast	½ teaspoon salt
⅓ cup sugar	4 eggs, separated
1 cup milk, scalded	3½ cups flour, sifted
¼ cup butter, melted	

Dissolve the yeast in ½ cup warm water with *one tablespoon sugar*. Pour the scalded milk into a large, warm bowl, add *remaining sugar*, butter, and salt. When lukewarm, beat in the egg yolks. Add the yeast, then gradually add the flour, beating well with a wooden spoon. Cover and let rise in a warm spot for about 1 hour or until doubled in bulk. Beat the egg whites stiff and fold in. Pour into 2 well-buttered 1-pound loaf pans, half filling them. Cover again and let rise for 30 minutes. Bake in a preheated 350° oven for 40 to 60 minutes or until well puffed and golden. Cool a few minutes in the pan, then on a cake rack. Serves 8.

GUGELHUPF

Gugelhupf, a turban-shaped cake found in Germany, Austria, and Alsace, originated in Vienna in the seventeenth century. Modeled after a sultan's headdress, it was introduced by some inventive Viennese bakers to celebrate the defeat of the Turks at the city gates in 1683.

2 envelopes dry yeast	¾ cup warm milk
½ cup sugar	½ cup raisins
4 cups flour, sifted	1 teaspoon grated lemon rind
¼ teaspoon salt	1 teaspoon vanilla extract
1 cup butter, softened	⅓ cup slivered blanched almonds
4 eggs, slightly beaten	Confectioners' sugar for dusting

Place the yeast and *one teaspoon sugar* in a warm bowl; add ½ cup warm water and *one-half cup flour*. Mix lightly and let rise for 30 minutes. Resift *remaining flour* and the salt into the dough. Beat in butter and eggs alternately with the milk. Beat the mixture well. Add raisins, lemon rind, vanilla, almonds, and *remaining sugar*. Beat well with a wooden spoon until batter is elastic and no longer clings to the spoon. Butter the surface of the dough and let it rise, covered, for 1 hour. Place dough in buttered and floured Gugelhupf mold or tube pan. Let the dough rise again for 30 minutes. Bake in a preheated 350° oven for about 1 hour or until cake is well risen and tester comes out clean. Dust with confectioners' sugar.

CROISSANTS

Croissants supposedly take their name and shape from the crescent which adorned the banners of Islam. In 1686 the Turks besieging Budapest built underground tunnels to gain access to the city. Bakers, who were up all night working, overheard the attackers and warned the city in time for a successful defense. In recognition of their service, the city gave the bakers a patent to make this commemorative pastry.

2 envelopes dry yeast
1 tablespoon sugar
3½ cups flour, sifted
1 teaspoon salt

1 cup butter, softened
1 cup scalded milk, slightly cooled
1 egg yolk for glazing

Soak yeast in ½ cup warm water with 1 tablespoon sugar until bubbly, about 8 to 10 minutes. Resift flour with salt into a large, warm bowl. Make a well in the flour. Pour in the yeast, add *four tablespoons butter*, and gradually add enough milk to make a soft but not sticky dough. Put dough on a pastry board sprinkled generously with flour and knead for 2 to 3 minutes. Place dough in a buttered bowl. Butter surface of dough and cover lightly. Let rise in a warm place for about 1 hour or until doubled in bulk. Roll out dough on floured board to a rectangle about 16 by 18 inches, rolling forward only. Spread *three tablespoons butter* to within ½ inch of edges over center third of dough. Fold one end over butter. Spread this dough with *three more tablespoons butter*. Bring over the other end of dough. Press edges together. Give the dough a quarter turn, as for puff pastry, and roll out again to a rectangle 24 by 10 inches. Spread with *three tablespoons butter* and fold, applying *remaining 3 tablespoons butter* and folding as above. Wrap in buttered wax paper and chill for 30 minutes. Roll out dough to a rectangle 24 by 10 inches. Bring edges to the center of dough and close like a book. Chill for 30 minutes, give dough a quarter turn, roll out and fold again. Chill for 2 hours. Cut dough in half so folds face edge of board. Keep one half chilled in buttered paper. Roll out other half on board to 15- by 10-inch square, then cut into 5-inch squares. Cut these into triangles. Roll up into cylinders, starting with wide end. Place on buttered cookie sheet with tip of triangle underneath. Curve ends toward the middle to form crescents and press ends together. Let rise covered with a cloth for 20 minutes. Brush croissants with egg yolk mixed with 1 tablespoon water. Separate tips of croissants and bake in a preheated 475° oven for 18 minutes; lower heat to 400° and bake for about 8 to 10 minutes or until golden brown. Repeat with second half of dough. Makes 24. To reheat day-old croissants, moisten with a very little water and heat for 6 to 8 minutes in a preheated 400° oven or reheat in a double boiler.

BRIOCHE

Louis Eustache Ude's appetite for the *petit pain* of his native land must surely have exceeded that of his English readers, when he included in *The Art of Cookery* (1815) a recipe for "a *brioche* with twelve pounds of butter . . . a bushel of flour . . . sixty eggs . . . a quarter pound of salt, the same quantity of sugar, and half a pound of yeast, etc." As an afterthought Ude counseled, "It is not always requisite to make the *brioche* so fine." Reduced to more reasonable proportions, the Frenchman's pastry may be made as follows.

1 envelope dry yeast	1 teaspoon salt
1 teaspoon sugar	1 cup butter, softened
$\frac{3}{4}$ cup warm milk	6 eggs
4 cups flour, sifted	1 egg yolk for glazing

In a large warm bowl dissolve the yeast and the sugar in $\frac{1}{4}$ cup warm water. Add the warm milk, *half the flour* resifted with the salt, and beat well with a wooden spatula or spoon. Cover and let rise for 45 to 60 minutes or until doubled in bulk. Add butter, eggs, and *remaining flour*. Beat well. Turn out on a floured board and knead and pound dough until it does not stick to the hands. Return to well-buttered bowl, butter surface of the dough, cover, and let rise until doubled in bulk—about 1 to $1\frac{1}{2}$ hours, or in refrigerator overnight. Butter individual fluted brioche molds or muffin tins. Make $2\frac{1}{2}$-inch balls of dough, place in mold, cut a 1- by $1\frac{1}{2}$-inch cross in the dough with kitchen scissors, and insert a small, pear-shaped lump of dough into it. Brush with egg yolk, let rise for 15 minutes, and bake in a preheated 400° oven for 25 to 30 minutes or until dark golden brown and well puffed. Makes 12 to 14.

VARIATION: Brioche dough may also be made in 2 1-pound loaf pans or in a tubular mold. Brush as above, let rise for 30 minutes, and bake in preheated 400° oven for 45 to 50 minutes or until golden brown.

CHESTER CAKES

1 cup butter, softened	*Filling:*
8 ounces sharp cheddar cheese, grated	$1\frac{1}{2}$ cups grated sharp cheddar cheese
2 cups flour, sifted	$\frac{1}{2}$ cup butter, softened
Cayenne pepper	1 tablespoon dry sherry (optional)
	Salt and cayenne pepper to taste

Cream the butter and combine with the cheese. Work in the flour and a few dashes cayenne pepper. Wrap in foil and chill for 1 hour. Roll out $\frac{1}{4}$ inch thick and cut into $1\frac{1}{2}$-inch rounds. Bake on a buttered cookie sheet in a preheated 350° oven for 15 minutes or until golden. Combine filling ingredients and mix until smooth and creamy. When cakes are cool spread half of them with filling; top with remaining cakes. Keep in an airtight box. Makes 30 to 36.

BATH BUNS

Yeast, sweeteners, and fine white flour are the basic ingredients of the Englishman's bun, a kind of bread which probably originated as a "boon" offered on holy days; it has long since been a favorite accompaniment to afternoon tea. Bath Buns are the invention of some forgotten baker of that celebrated eighteenth-century health resort, Bath. Chelsea Buns were first prepared in the early 1700's at the Old Original Bun House, London, where trade occasionally reached near-riot proportions. (One Good Friday the proprietress was forced to post a notice that there would be "Chelsea Buns, as usual [but] no Cross Buns [for] to encourage or countenance a tumultuous assembly at this particular period might be attended with consequences more serious than have hitherto been apprehended." Pope Ladies were a New Year's Day specialty of Hertfordshire. Their curious name recalls an old English legend about a ninth-century damsel named Joan whose unrequited love for a Benedictine monk led her (disguised) into the priesthood and eventually to the Papacy. For reasons lost to culinary history, she is always made with arms but no legs. Saint Catherine's Wigs are a Dorset tradition, part of the November 25th celebration for the patron saint of maiden ladies.

2 envelopes dry yeast	1½ cups milk, scalded
½ cup sugar	3 eggs, beaten
6 cups flour, sifted	1 cup chopped candied rinds
1 teaspoon salt	1 egg yolk for glazing
¾ cup butter	¼ cup crushed lump sugar

Dissolve the yeast in ¼ cup warm water with *one teaspoon sugar*. Resift the flour with the salt into a warm bowl. Using 2 knives or a pastry blender, cut in the butter until mixture resembles fine meal. Add the *remaining sugar* to the hot milk; cool until lukewarm. Combine with yeast mixture and add to the flour. Add eggs; beat the mixture well (this is a soft and sticky dough). Knead on a well-floured board until smooth and elastic. If necessary, add more flour. Dust peels with flour and knead into dough. Return dough to a buttered bowl. Cover and let rise until doubled in bulk (about 1½ hours). Shape into 24 round buns. Set on buttered cookie sheets. Brush with egg yolk mixed with a little cold water and sprinkle with crushed sugar. Let rise for 30 minutes, then bake in a preheated 375° oven for about 25 minutes.

VARIATIONS: *Chelsea Buns*: Eliminate candied rinds. After dough has doubled in bulk, roll into a square on a floured board. Brush with melted butter and sprinkle with currants and sugar. Roll as for jelly roll and cut into slices 1½ inch thick. Lay slices down side by side on a greased baking pan. Let rise for 30 minutes and bake as directed above. *Pope Ladies*: Sift 1 teaspoon nutmeg with the flour; eliminate candied rinds. After dough has doubled in bulk, form "bodies" by dividing dough into 5-inch oval pieces tapering to a point. Attach smaller pieces of dough to form head and arms. Use currants for eyes, and a tiny piece of dough for the nose. Place on greased cookie sheet. Brush with egg and water mixture. Cover lightly and let rise for 30 minutes. Bake as directed above. *Saint Catherine's Wigs*: Sift the following spices with the flour: $\frac{1}{2}$ teaspoon each powdered nutmeg, ginger, and cinnamon and $\frac{1}{8}$ teaspoon each powdered cloves and mace. Substitute 3 tablespoons caraway seeds for candied rinds. After dough has doubled in bulk, form into 6-inch buns. Cut a deep cross in each, so buns may be divided into 4 triangular pieces after baking. Proceed as directed above. *Hot Cross Buns*: Sift $\frac{1}{2}$ teaspoon cinnamon and $\frac{1}{4}$ teaspoon nutmeg with flour. Substitute currants for candied rinds. Proceed as directed above. Instead of sprinkling with crushed sugar, glaze with thin Sugar Icing (page 702) in the form of a cross.

PAIN PERDU

Pain perdu, or "lost bread," is reclaimed from staleness in Robert May's old English recipe for a kind of French toast. The Germans have a similar recipe, *Arme Ritter* (Poor Knights), and a wine-soaked variation humorously called Drunken Maidens.

4 eggs	1 tablespoon dry sherry
1 cup milk	1 small loaf French bread
$\frac{1}{8}$ teaspoon salt	$\frac{1}{2}$ cup butter
1 tablespoon sugar	Sugar or honey

Beat the eggs, milk, salt, sugar, and sherry until just mixed. Pour into a shallow oblong pan. Slice the loaf of bread into 1-inch-thick slices, slightly on the slant, discarding the ends. Soak the bread in the egg mixture for 15 minutes on each side. Fry the bread slices in very hot butter until golden on both sides, adding butter as needed. Serve very hot, sprinkled with sugar. Pour on honey if desired. French toast may also be made with stale loaf brioche, pound cake, or ordinary white bread.

CINNAMON TOAST

Cinnamon, one of the principal flavorings in old English cookery, was used in many of the "Kickshaws . . . and A La Mode Curiosities" of Robert May's seventeenth-century recipe book. Along with sugar and other spices, cinnamon was sold by the Freemen of the Mistery of Grocers, a trade guild licensed to sell "gross" weights or "groceries."

4 slices white bread, crusts removed	1 tablespoon powdered cinnamon
$\frac{1}{2}$ cup sugar	$\frac{3}{4}$ cup butter, melted

Cut the bread into sticks 4 inches long, 1 inch wide. Mix the sugar and cinnamon. Dip the bread in the melted butter, roll in the sugar-cinnamon mixture, and bake in a preheated 350° oven until hot and bubbly. Serve immediately. Serves 4.

WIENERBRØD

Danish bakers many years ago adapted Viennese yeast puff pastries. These became popular snacks with coffee, a favorite beverage of the Danes since the eighteenth century. When imported to America they were called Danish pastry, but in Denmark they are *Wienerbrød*, or Viennese bread, in deference to their ancestry.

2 envelopes dry yeast
$\frac{1}{3}$ cup sugar
1 cup milk, scalded
1 egg, beaten
4 cups flour, sifted
1 teaspoon powdered cardamom
$\frac{1}{4}$ teaspoon salt
$1\frac{1}{2}$ cups butter, softened
1 egg yolk for glazing

Thin Sugar Icing (page 702)
Fillings:
1 recipe Almond Paste (page 703), or
1 recipe Pastry Cream (page 702), or
$1\frac{1}{2}$ cups thick fruit purée mixed
with 2 tablespoons butter and $\frac{1}{2}$
teaspoon grated lemon rind, or
$1\frac{1}{2}$ cups jam or jelly

Dissolve the yeast in $\frac{1}{2}$ cup warm water with *one teaspoon sugar* in a large, warm bowl. Add *remaining sugar* to scalded milk and cool to lukewarm. Add to the yeast. Add the beaten egg, *half the flour*, the cardamom, and salt. Beat well with a wooden spoon. Add enough *remaining flour* to make a soft dough. Turn out on a lightly floured pastry board and knead for 10 minutes. Put dough in a well-buttered bowl, roll it around to butter all the surface. Cover and let rise in a warm place until doubled in bulk, about 1 hour. Punch down and knead again on a floured board for 2 to 3 minutes. Roll out to a rectangle about $\frac{1}{4}$ inch thick. Spread with *three-quarters cup butter* to within $\frac{1}{2}$ inch of edges. Fold a third of the dough over onto the pastry. Bring opposite third on top of first folded third. Seal the edges by rolling lightly with the rolling pin. Give the dough a quarter turn, as for puff pastry. Roll out again. Spread with *remaining butter*. Fold again in the same manner. Chill for 15 minutes. Put indentations in the dough with 2 fingers to remember the position of the dough. Give the dough a quarter turn. Roll out, fold, and turn again. Roll out and fold again and chill for 15 minutes. Shape into forms as described below, using desired fillings. Place shaped pastries on greased cookie sheet. Let rise for 20 minutes; brush with egg yolk mixed with a little water. Bake in a preheated 400° oven for 15 minutes, turn oven to 350° and bake for an additional 10 to 15 minutes. When cool, frost with thin sugar icing. Makes 12 to 18 depending on size.

To shape envelopes: Roll out dough $\frac{1}{4}$ inch thick. Cut into 4-inch squares. Spread with 1 tablespoon filling. Bring corners to center, pressing edges firmly into pastry.

To shape cockscombs: Roll out dough $\frac{1}{8}$ inch thick. Cut into 5-inch-wide strips. Place filling along center of strips. Fold ends over filling so they overlap in the center. Sprinkle with sugar and chopped nuts. Cut into 4-inch pieces, then gash 5 times on 1 side. Bend slightly to spread the cuts.

To shape crescents: Roll out dough $\frac{1}{8}$ inch thick. Cut into 5-inch squares. Divide squares into triangles. Place filling on wide part and roll up into a crescent. Bend tips to shape crescent.

LUSSEKATTER

Luciadagen, or Saint Lucia's Day, announces the opening of the Yuletide season in Sweden. The day is named after a Christian martyr of Sicily who became a symbol of generosity to the Swedish people. The story evolved that Lucia, wearing a white gown and a halo of fire, crossed the icebound lakes of Sweden to bring refreshments to the village poor. Every December 13th morning a young lady of the household appointed to represent the saint dresses in a flowing white robe and a crown of green leaves and lighted candles. She then carries a tray of buns and coffee to the members of the family. Lussekatter, or Lucia cats (a reference to the catlike raisin eyes at the top of the buns), are a favorite food of this bedside repast.

$\frac{1}{2}$ teaspoon dried saffron	1 egg
2 envelopes dry yeast	$\frac{1}{2}$ cup currants
$\frac{1}{4}$ cup sugar	$\frac{1}{2}$ cup diced candied fruit rinds
$\frac{1}{3}$ cup butter	4 cups flour, sifted
1 teaspoon salt	$\frac{1}{2}$ cup raisins, or as needed
1 cup milk, scalded	1 egg yolk for glazing

Soak the saffron in 3 tablespoons boiling water for 2 hours. In a large, warm bowl dissolve the yeast in $\frac{1}{4}$ cup warm water with *one teaspoon sugar*. Put *remaining sugar*, butter, and salt into the scalded milk and stir until sugar and butter are melted. Add strained saffron water. Cool milk to lukewarm and pour into yeast bowl. Beat egg into milk. Coat the currants and rinds with *two tablespoons flour*. Gradually work the *remaining flour* into the yeast. Add fruits; turn out onto a floured board and knead for 10 minutes or until smooth and no longer sticky, adding flour as needed. Place dough in a buttered bowl and roll it around to grease it well. Cover with a cloth and let rise in a warm place until doubled in bulk (about $1\frac{1}{2}$ hours). Punch the dough down and put on pastry board. Knead 2 or 3 times and divide into round buns. Press 2 raisins into top of each bun. Place on buttered cookie sheets. Brush tops with egg yolk beaten with a little water. Let rise $\frac{1}{2}$ hour. Bake in a preheated 400° oven for 15 minutes. Lower the heat to 350° and bake another 20 minutes. Makes about 24 buns.

IRISH SODA BREAD

The making of this traditional Gaelic bread may date from the Middle Ages. Owing to the shortage of wood fuel in the land, it is often baked in a shallow-hearth oven over a smoldering peat fire.

2 cups flour	$\frac{1}{4}$ teaspoon salt
2 teaspoons baking powder	2 tablespoons lard or olive oil
$\frac{1}{2}$ teaspoon baking soda	1 cup buttermilk, or as needed

Sift flour with dry ingredients. Cut lard into flour. Add buttermilk to make a soft dough. Turn out on a lightly floured board and knead lightly to blend, for 1 to 2 minutes. Shape into a round, high loaf and place on a greased cookie sheet. Cut a deep cross in the dough with wet kitchen shears. Bake in a preheated 450° oven for 40 to 45 minutes or until golden brown. If desired, $\frac{1}{2}$ cup raisins dusted with flour may be worked into dough after kneading.

CRUMPETS

Ralph Nickleby, the capitalistic uncle in Charles Dickens' *Nicholas Nickleby*, concluded that the surest way to an Englishman's purse was through his stomach, and so devised the "United Metropolitan Improved Hot Muffin and Crumpet Baking and Punctual Delivery Company" to prove his point.

1 small potato, peeled and quartered	1 teaspoon salt
2 envelopes dry yeast	$2\frac{1}{2}$ cups sifted flour, or as needed
1 teaspoon sugar	Soft butter for griddle and spreading

Boil the potato in $1\frac{1}{2}$ cups salted water for 15 minutes or until very soft. Drain and reserve the water. Mash the potato. Dissolve yeast and sugar in $\frac{1}{2}$ cup warm potato water; let stand for 10 minutes or until bubbly. Add remaining potato water and salt. Work in mashed potato and enough flour to make a heavy batter. Cover and let rise for 30 minutes in a warm place. Beat rapidly for 5 minutes with a wooden spoon. Cover and let rise again for 30 minutes. Repeat beating and rising twice more at $\frac{1}{2}$-hour intervals. Grease the insides of 4 muffin rings (well washed small fish cans with tops and bottoms removed may be substituted for rings). Heat a griddle, grease it lightly, and keep griddle at low, even heat. Place muffin rings around sides of griddle, half fill with batter, and bake for about 15 minutes on one side. Batter will rise as it bakes. Turn and bake for about 5 minutes on the other side. At serving time spread the rough side (the side with holes) generously with butter and toast under the broiler. Serve immediately with preserves. Makes about 12 crumpets.

SINGING HINNIES

Scones, popular throughout Scotland, Ireland, and northern England, are a particular teatime favorite. Scottish literature is full of encomiums to "souple scones," and one writer goes so far as to recommend such cakes for "beauty to the skin and sweetness to the temper." The Singing Hinnies below are an English variety that take their name from the way they are supposed to have sizzled when cooked over an open fire.

$\frac{1}{2}$ cup currants or raisins
2$\frac{1}{2}$ cups flour, sifted
$\frac{1}{2}$ teaspoon salt
$\frac{1}{2}$ cup sugar
2 teaspoons baking powder

1 teaspoon baking soda
$\frac{1}{3}$ cup butter
1 egg, beaten
1 cup sour cream
Rind of $\frac{1}{2}$ lemon, grated

Dredge the currants in *two tablespoons flour*. Resift *remaining flour* with dry ingredients. Cut in butter until mixture looks like coarse meal. Mix egg with 1 tablespoon water and add to flour along with the sour cream, currants, and lemon rind. Mix well. Divide dough into 24 balls. Flatten to $\frac{1}{2}$-inch-thick round cakes. Bake on a greased cookie sheet in a preheated 425° oven for about 12 to 15 minutes or until golden brown. Makes 24.

VARIATION: *Orange Scones:* Replace $\frac{1}{4}$ cup sour cream with 3 tablespoons orange juice and 1 teaspoon grated orange rind. Proceed as above.

BANNOCKS

British legend has it that King Alfred, when pursued by the Danes, took refuge in an old woman's cottage but kept his identity secret. She agreed to let the stranger stay so long as he watched the Bannocks on her fire. Preoccupied with his own safety, he let the pancakes burn, and the irate lady delivered Alfred a lesson—a barrage of burnt Bannocks—that Englishmen still remember. Scotsmen also cook Bannocks, taking care to beat them sunwise (clockwise), an old Druid practice.

1 cup oatmeal
1 cup flour, sifted
$\frac{1}{2}$ teaspoon salt
1 teaspoon baking soda

$\frac{1}{2}$ teaspoon cream of tartar
2 tablespoons corn syrup
2 eggs, beaten
1 cup buttermilk, or as needed

Mix dry ingredients in a bowl. Add syrup and eggs and pour in enough buttermilk to make a thin batter. Beat well, until bubbles appear. Heat a well-greased griddle and drop batter from pitcher or tablespoon to form 3-inch circles. Bake until golden brown, turning only once. Serve warm with butter and honey. Makes 12 pancakes.

PURI
(Indian Fried Bread)

3½ cups flour, sifted
1 teaspoon salt
¼ cup butter, melted

1 cup yoghurt, or as needed
Fat for frying

Resift the flour with the salt. Add the melted butter and enough yoghurt to make a stiff dough. Knead well and let stand, covered with a damp cloth, for 30 minutes. Divide into 1½-inch balls, then roll out into paper-thin pancakes. Heat fat to smoking (375°) and fry the puri a few at a time until they become puffed and take on a golden color. Drain them on paper towels. Serve immediately. Makes about 24.

CHAPATIS

These unleavened whole wheat breads are eaten primarily in northern India where wheat is grown. Both the Chapati and the Paratha are made on griddles and served with curries, lentils, and pellãos. Parathis are often stacked in several layers and filled with grated vegetables such as potatoes and onions.

2½ cups whole wheat or white flour
1 teaspoon salt

½ cup water, or as needed

Put the flour and salt in a bowl. Add water gradually until dough is soft but not too wet. Sprinkle board with a little sifted white flour mixed with whole wheat flour and knead dough for 10 to 15 minutes. Cover with a damp cloth and let rest for 45 to 60 minutes. Heat a pancake griddle, grease lightly. Take small balls of dough (about 1½ inches), flatten with the hand, and roll out into 5-inch circles about ⅛ inch thick. Test griddle to determine right heat so chapatis will not burn. Cook slowly on both sides. Chapatis turn a greyish-brown when cooked and should have toasted spots. Keep hot in a preheated 300° oven until all dough has been cooked. Serve hot. Makes 36 to 40.

VARIATION: *Parathis*: Rub ½ cup butter into 2½ cups whole wheat flour. Then add enough water for a soft, manageable dough. Proceed as for chapatis. Spread each rolled-out circle with ¼ teaspoon softened butter and fold over into a half moon. Repeat spreading with butter and folding into a triangle. Roll out to enlarge triangle and toast on a lightly greased griddle. Instead of spreading with softened butter, parathis may be made with a potato filling: Mix 3 boiled and mashed potatoes with 2 chopped and fried onions, 4 teaspoons of mixed parsley, finely chopped chives, and mint leaves, ½ teaspoon chili powder, ¼ teaspoon powdered ginger, and salt and pepper to taste. Place 1 tablespoon of filling on each rolled-out circle of dough, fold over, seal edges, and roll out again about ⅓ inch thick. Toast on both sides on a lightly greased griddle.

660

PIZZA

The parent of Pizza (the Italian word for pie) originated in Naples and in Augustan Rome was described in the *Moretum*, a poetic work attributed to Virgil, as a half-baked disc of unleavened dough sprinkled with herbs. When the popes ruled from Avignon during the Middle Ages, the pastry was one Italian intrusion to which the French were not diplomatically immune, and they added onions and anchovies to create the Provence specialty, Pissaladière, also below.

Crust:
1 recipe Pain Ordinaire dough
  (page 645) plus ¼ cup olive oil
  or 4 tablespoons lard
Pizzaiola sauce:
3 tablespoons olive oil
3 cloves garlic, sliced
1 1-pound 13-ounce can Italian plum
  tomatoes, drained and chopped

2 tablespoons dried oregano, or to taste
1 teaspoon dried basil
2 tablespoons Italian tomato paste
Salt and pepper
Topping:
1 pound well-drained mozzarella cheese,
  diced or coarsely grated
½ cup grated Parmesan cheese

Prepare bread dough, working in oil or lard. Let rise until doubled in bulk. Divide in half. Roll and stretch each piece of dough to cover a well-oiled 12-inch pie plate.

To make the sauce: Heat olive oil and fry sliced garlic in it until golden brown. Add tomatoes, oregano, and basil and simmer gently, covered, for 15 minutes. Gradually add tomato paste, simmering between additions until sauce is thick. Season with salt and pepper and simmer slowly, uncovered, for 5 minutes. Divide over each round of dough and top with mozzarella cheese. Sprinkle with Parmesan cheese and a few drops of olive oil. Set pie plates on cookie sheets and bake in a preheated 425° oven for 20 to 30 minutes or until dough is crisp and brown and topping is melted and bubbling. Makes 2 12-inch pizzas. Two packages of refrigerator yeast crescent rolls may be substituted for the homemade yeast dough. Open packages and knead dough together for a few minutes. Roll out to fit pie plates and top as described.

VARIATIONS: For additional pizza toppings, use ½ pound sliced, fried sausage, 2 cans of well-drained anchovy fillets, or 8 or 10 sliced cooked meatballs, with or without mozzarella cheese. *Pissaladière*: Slice 4 pounds of peeled onions into very thin rings. Sauté slowly in ½ cup olive oil for about 40 minutes or until onions are soft but not brown. Add 8 seeded and chopped peeled tomatoes to the onion along with a pinch of dried basil. Simmer rapidly until tomatoes are cooked and mixture is dry—about 5 minutes. Divide in half and spread over rolled-out yeast dough. Arrange 1 can well-drained anchovy fillets in a lattice pattern over each pie. Dot with halved black olives and set on cookie sheets. Bake as above.

CAKES, TARTS
AND
COOKIES

TORTEN

Nineteenth-century Danubian nations under the spell of three-quarter time and *Gemütlichkeit* created the richest and creamiest layer cakes, or *torten*, in Europe. Vienna was the undisputed capital of the confectioner's art. There the Sachertorte was born, a progeny of the confectioner, Franz Sacher. Herr Sacher made enough money from his business to found the famed Hotel Sacher where the crowned heads of Europe came to pay homage to the rich chocolate-glazed torte. From Budapest came the Dobos Torta, which bears the name of a well-known *konditorei* proprietor. The Linzertorte, whose descent is obscure, could well be the contribution of Linz, the capital of upper Austria which like Vienna and Budapest is located on the banks of the Danube. Their Prussian kinsmen claim the Sandtorte, whose name refers to its sandy texture, the result of generous amounts of cornstarch.

LINZERTORTE

1½ cups ground almonds
1 teaspoon powdered cinnamon
Pinch of powdered cloves

1 recipe Rich Tart Pastry (page 681)
2 cups raspberry jam, or as needed

Blend almonds and spices into flour before combining ingredients. Butter and flour a 9-inch round cake pan. Roll two-thirds of dough to a circle slightly larger than pan. Fit on bottom and sides. Spread with *one cup raspberry jam*. Roll out remainder of dough, cut into thin strips and form a lattice over the jam, pressing strips to sides of the cake. Bake in a preheated 325° oven for 50 to 60 minutes or until toothpick comes out clean. Use *remaining jam* to fill in spaces between lattice strips.

YUGOSLAVIAN WALNUT TORTE

8 eggs, separated
1½ cups sugar
1 teaspoon vanilla extract or
   1 tablespoon rum
Pinch of salt

1½ cups coarsely ground walnuts
1 cup heavy cream, whipped, sweetened,
   and flavored with rum or vanilla or
   coffee Butter Cream (page 700)

Beat yolks with *all but one tablespoon sugar* until thick and pale yellow. Reserve *remaining sugar*. Stir in vanilla. Beat egg whites with salt until they begin to stiffen. Add *reserved sugar* and continue beating until whites are stiff and glossy. Stir ½ cup egg white into yolks. Add remaining egg white and nuts and fold together, gently but thoroughly, with a rubber spatula. Butter 2 9-inch round cake pans or a 9-inch spring form pan and sprinkle lightly with flour. Pour batter into pan and bake in preheated 350° oven for about 1 hour or until cake springs back when lightly pressed. Cool in pan until cake shrinks away from sides. Fill layers with *half the whipped cream* and top with *remaining cream*.

VARIATION: *Nut Roll:* Cover an 11- by 16-inch jelly roll pan with buttered wax paper. Pour prepared batter into pan and spread evenly with a spatula. Bake as above and cool in pan. Sprinkle with 2 tablespoons rum, cover with a damp towel, and chill for several hours or overnight. Turn cake onto 2 overlapping large sheets of wax paper sprinkled with confectioners' sugar. Peel off paper and spread cake with 2 cups flavored whipped cream or coffee butter cream. Roll cake, using paper to help lift and roll. Wrap in wax paper and chill for 1 hour before serving. Sprinkle with confectioners' sugar before serving. Hazelnuts or blanched almonds may be substituted for walnuts.

DOBOS TORTA

1 recipe Génoise batter (page 667)
1 recipe chocolate Butter Cream
   (page 700)

1 cup sugar
1 cup coarsely chopped blanched
   almonds or hazelnuts

To prepare the 8 thin layers of cake used to make the torte, butter 7- or 8-inch round cake pans and line with wax paper. Butter and flour the lined pans and pour in batter to ¼-inch depth. Bake in a preheated 350° oven for 15 minutes. Remove very carefully from pans and gently peel off paper. Return to warm pans so that layers will cool without becoming hard. When all cake layers are baked, place first layer on a cake platter, spread with a thin layer of chocolate butter cream, top with second layer, and repeat, spreading 7 layers of cake with butter cream. Refrigerate the cake. Put the sugar in a saucepan and cook without stirring until sugar is a light caramel color. Pour it into a well-oiled 7- or 8-inch round cake pan. As soon as it begins to harden, mark out thin lines in the caramel to facilitate cutting portions at serving time. When caramel has set, lift out of pan and place on remaining cake layer. Top cake with caramel layer. Fill in sides of cake with chocolate butter cream and cover the sides with chopped nuts. Chill overnight. Serves 8 or more.

SACHERTORTE

¾ cup sweet butter, softened
¾ cup sugar
6 ounces semisweet chocolate, melted
8 egg yolks
¼ teaspoon salt
10 egg whites

1 teaspoon vanilla extract
1¼ cups flour, sifted
½ cup apricot preserves
1 cup chocolate Fondant Icing
   (page 701)

Cream the butter, gradually add the sugar, and beat until light and fluffy. Add the melted chocolate and mix well. Beat in the egg yolks one by one, mixing well with each addition. Add salt to egg whites and beat until they stand in stiff peaks but are still moist. Fold a third of the egg whites into batter with the vanilla. Resift flour and fold into batter alternately with remaining egg whites. Pour into a 10-inch buttered spring form pan. Bake in a preheated 350° oven for 35 to 45 minutes or until a toothpick inserted in center comes out clean. Cool in the pan for 10 minutes. Remove ring and set bottom of pan on a cake rack. Let cool for several hours, or preferably overnight, before icing. When cold, spread with puréed apricot preserves. Cover preserves with chocolate fondant icing, pouring it on cake and turning the cake so icing runs over it. Spread on sides as necessary.

SANDTORTE

1 pound sweet butter
2 cups sugar
5 whole eggs
4 eggs, separated
Rind of 1 lemon, grated
4 tablespoons rum or brandy

2 teaspoons vanilla extract
Pinch of salt
2¼ cups cornstarch or flour, or a
   combination of both
Vanilla Sugar (page 705)

Melt butter and chill until solid again. Reserve *1 tablespoon sugar*; cream *remaining sugar* with butter until light and fluffy. Gradually add 5 whole eggs and 4 yolks, beating thoroughly between additions. Add lemon rind, rum, and vanilla and beat until mixture is thick and nearly white. Beat egg whites with salt and, as they begin to stiffen, add *reserved sugar* and continue beating until egg whites are stiff and glossy. Stir 3 tablespoons egg white into batter. Place remaining egg white on top of batter. Sift cornstarch onto whites and fold together into batter, gently but thoroughly, with a rubber spatula. (The more cornstarch used, the drier and "sandier" the cake will be. For a smooth, moist cake, use more flour or all flour. Proportions may be varied to suit individual taste as long as the total amount of flour and/or cornstarch equals 2¼ cups.) Butter a 9-inch fluted pan or 1 large loaf pan and sprinkle lightly with flour. Turn batter into pan and bake in preheated 350° oven for about 1 hour and 15 minutes or until toothpick comes out clean. Cool in pan for 10 minutes. Turn out of pan onto rack and cool. For improved flavor allow the cake to stand for 24 hours before being cut. Sprinkle the sandtorte with vanilla sugar.

SIMNEL CAKE

The English mid-Lent custom of "going a-mothering" evolved from the ancient practice of giving gifts to the Mother Church. Subsequently mothers of all sorts became the beneficiaries, with their children, theoretically, doing the buying or baking of these "mothering cakes."

$\frac{3}{4}$ cup butter
$1\frac{3}{4}$ cups sugar
4 eggs
2 cups flour, sifted
1 teaspoon salt
1 cup currants

$\frac{1}{3}$ cup thinly sliced candied lemon rind
$\frac{1}{3}$ cup thinly sliced candied orange rind
$2\frac{1}{2}$ cups Almond Paste (page 703)
1 recipe almond Butter Cream
   (page 700)

In a large bowl cream butter and sugar until light and fluffy. Beat in eggs, one at a time. Resift flour with salt and add gradually to mixture. Fold in currants and rind, dredged in a little flour. Butter an 8-inch spring form pan and line with buttered wax paper. Pour in half the batter. Spread almond paste filling over batter and fill with remaining batter. (May be made in 3 layers with 2 layers of almond paste.) Bake in a preheated 350° oven for 1 hour or until cake is golden and springs back when touched. Cool in pan. Ice with almond butter cream.

GATEAU TROIS FRERES

Service à la russe, introduced to France in the mid-nineteenth century, effected a sort of bloodless coup on long-established eating habits. The panoply of meats simultaneously displayed on a table was replaced by individual portions served directly from the kitchen; and the tiered rococo cakes, which people could only feast their eyes on, literally came down off their pedestals, to be superseded by more palatable creations. Among the first "modern" cakes was Trois Frères, invented about 1844 by the Julien brothers, operators of a Paris *pâtisserie*.

5 eggs, at room temperature
$\frac{3}{4}$ cup sugar
$\frac{1}{8}$ teaspoon salt
$1\frac{1}{4}$ cups rice flour, sifted

$\frac{1}{2}$ cup butter, melted and slightly cooled
$\frac{1}{4}$ cup maraschino liqueur
1 cup apricot jam, or to taste
Angelica for decoration

Place eggs, sugar, and salt in the top of an enamel or pyrex double boiler. Set over 1 inch of barely simmering water and beat until tripled in bulk and slightly warm (about 15 minutes with an electric mixer, 25 with hand beater). Fold in the flour, butter, and *one tablespoon liqueur*. Do not overmix. Pour into a buttered and floured 6-cup fluted ring mold. Bake in a preheated 350° oven for 25 to 30 minutes or until toothpick comes out clean. Cool on a rack. Purée apricot jam in a strainer and mix with *remaining liqueur*. Coat cake and decorate with angelica.

REGENT CAKE

Charles Elmé Francatelli, a pupil of the great Carême, was *maître d'hôtel* in Queen Victoria's kitchens. In this role he was chief architect of those masterpieces of culinary Victoriana—presentation cakes, featured at almost every palace affair. This recipe for a cake honoring Prince Albert appeared in Francatelli's *The Modern Cook*.

1 recipe Génoise batter (opposite)	$\frac{1}{2}$ cup butter, softened
$\frac{3}{4}$ cup strained apricot preserves	$\frac{1}{2}$ cup Pastry Cream (page 702)
1 tablespoon rum, or as needed	8 blanched almonds, halved
$\frac{2}{3}$ cup chestnut purée	$\frac{3}{4}$ cup thin Sugar Icing (page 702)

Divide the génoise batter among 3 buttered 8-inch round cake pans lined with buttered wax paper and bake for 15 to 20 minutes in a preheated 350° oven. Unmold and cool on cake racks. Thin apricot preserves with rum to spreading consistency. Mix the chestnut purée with the butter and pastry cream. Beat smooth. Spread 2 of the cake layers with a thin layer of apricot preserves and cover each layer with half the chestnut filling. Top with third cake layer, spread with jam. Place a circle of the almonds on the jam. Ice with thin sugar icing so almonds show through. Serves 8 to 10.

SPANISH CAKE

Explicit directions for baking this cake—but no explanation of the name —appear in Johan Winberg's eighteenth-century Swedish cookbook.

Double recipe Puff Pastry (page 684)	blackberry jam, and raspberry jam
$\frac{3}{4}$ cup each: prune jam (lekvar) or	6 egg whites
Damson plum jam, black cherry	$\frac{1}{2}$ teaspoon cream of tartar
preserves, applesauce, red currant	$\frac{3}{4}$ cup sugar
jam, gooseberry preserves, strawberry	2 teaspoons lemon juice
preserves, orange marmalade,	2 tablespoons diced candied fruit rind

Prepare dough for puff pastry and make only the first four turns. Roll it about $\frac{1}{8}$ inch thick and cut into 10 9-inch circles. Prick all over with a fork and chill for 30 minutes. Place circles on unbuttered baking sheets. Bake in a preheated 350° oven for about 35 minutes or until pale golden brown. Cool. Rub each fruit jam through a strainer, washing strainer between each change. Spread 1 side of each of 9 layers with a different fruit jam. Pile layers on top of each other, ending with the tenth, plain layer. Beat egg whites and as they begin to foam add cream of tartar and sugar, $\frac{1}{2}$ tablespoonful at a time, beating thoroughly between each addition. Add lemon juice toward end of beating. Beat until meringue is very stiff and thick, but not dry. Place layer cake on a baking sheet and spread top and sides with a thick layer of meringue, decorating it with elaborate swirls. Sprinkle with candied fruits and place in 250° oven for about 20 to 30 minutes or until meringue is dry but has not taken on color. Serves 10 to 12.

GALICIEN

The pistachio nuts that flavor this cake's icing were first brought from the Levant to Europe by the Roman Emperor Vitellius in the first century A.D. The Galicien itself was the creation of the Pâtisserie Frascati, a famous old Parisian pastry shop.

2 Génoise cake layers (below)   1 recipe Boiled Icing (page 700)
1 recipe pistachio Butter Cream (page 700)   ½ cup chopped pistachio nuts

Spread layers with butter cream and frost with boiled icing colored with green food coloring. Sprinkle with chopped pistachio nuts.

GENOISE
(French Layer Cake)

6 eggs, at room temperature   ⅓ cup sweet butter, melted and
1 cup sugar   slightly cooled
1 cup flour, sifted   1 teaspoon vanilla extract

Place eggs and sugar in the top part of a large enamel or pyrex double boiler. Stir just enough to mix. Set pan over 1 inch of barely simmering water (it should never boil) and beat mixture until nearly tripled in bulk and slightly warm (about 25 to 30 minutes with a hand beater or 15 minutes at high speed with an electric beater). Scrape the sides with a rubber spatula. Remove from heat; gradually and gently fold in flour, butter, and vanilla. Do not overmix. Pour into 2 9-inch well-buttered and floured cake pans or an 11- by 16-inch jelly roll pan. Bake in a preheated 350° oven for 30 minutes or until springy to the touch. Turn cakes onto rack to cool. Use for filled and frosted layer cakes and petits fours.

667

SPONGE SHEET

6 eggs, separated	1 teaspoon vanilla extract
$\frac{1}{4}$ teaspoon salt	$\frac{1}{2}$ cup flour
$\frac{1}{2}$ cup sugar	

Beat egg whites and salt until mixture stands in soft peaks. Add *4 tablespoons sugar*, 1 table-spoon at a time, beating until meringue is stiff. Beat egg yolks in a separate bowl with *remaining sugar* until thick. Add vanilla. Fold some meringue into yolks and pour back into remaining meringue. Sprinkle with *2 tablespoons flour* and gently fold together. Repeat in *three more portions* and fold until well blended. Do not overmix. Pour into a buttered 11- by 16-inch jelly roll pan lined with buttered and floured wax paper. Bake in a preheated 400° oven for 10 to 12 minutes or until cake is golden. Remove cake from pan immediately and cool on rack. Use for Buche de Noël (opposite), Igel (below), and jelly rolls.

VARIATION: *Chocolate Roll:* Replace 3 tablespoons of the flour with 3 tablespoons unsweetened cocoa. Roll cake while still warm, cool, unroll, and fill with 2 cups sweetened whipped cream flavored with 1 teaspoon vanilla extract and sprinkle with confectioners' sugar. Chocolate roll may be iced with chocolate icing. *Walnut Roll*: Replace 5 tablespoons of the flour with 5 table-spoons ground walnuts. Add 1 tablespoon unsweetened cocoa or 2 teaspoons instant coffee diluted in 1 tablespoon boiling water and cooled. Fill with 2 cups sweetened whipped cream flavored with vanilla or coffee-rum flavoring. Sprinkle with sugar and chopped walnuts.

IGEL

European desserts often take a delightfully playful turn, as with the Igel, a cake made to resemble the hedgehog, with raisins for eyes and split almonds for quills. An English variation on German Igel also follows.

$\frac{1}{2}$ pound ladyfingers or 1 recipe Sponge Sheet (above)	$\frac{1}{4}$ pound toasted or sugar-glazed split, blanched almonds or Chocolate Curls (page 705)
1 recipe chocolate or mocha Butter Cream (page 700)	2 seedless raisins or chocolate bits

Mound ladyfingers on top of each other to form an oval, half-domed "body," using butter cream to stick them together, or cut three graduated slices of sponge sheet, spreading butter cream between layers to make the body form. Spread tops and sides with butter cream. Stick almonds into body for quills, use an almond for the mouth and raisins for eyes. Serves 6.

VARIATION: English Hedgehogs are shaped from cake as above. Sprinkle each layer with sherry and spread with Frangipane Cream (page 702). Coat with mocha butter cream and spike with almonds, using currants or raisins for eyes and forming the head from small bits of cake stuck together with frangipane cream. Pour sherry-flavored Custard Sauce (page 703) around hedgehog on serving platter.

NUNS' CAKE

One of the few entertainments permitted the sisterhood of a nunnery in medieval England was the baking of these caraway cakes. By Elizabethan times, however, the confection had been secularized, becoming something of a harvest treat. Farmer-poet Thomas Tusser enjoined his spouse, "Wife, sometime this weeke if that all thing go cleare, An ende of wheate sowing we make for this yeare, Remember you therefore though I do it not The Seede Cake. . . ."

1 cup butter	3 teaspoons baking powder
1½ cups sugar	¾ cup milk
6 egg yolks	1 tablespoon caraway seeds
3 egg whites	1½ teaspoons vanilla extract
3½ cups flour, sifted	or rose water
¼ teaspoon salt	Confectioners' sugar for dusting

Cream butter and sugar until light and fluffy. Add the egg yolks, beating well. Stir egg whites, breaking up just slightly, and add to mixture. Beat well for 1 minute. Resift flour, salt, and baking powder 3 times and fold into mixture gradually, alternating with the milk. Fold in caraway seeds and vanilla. Pour batter into buttered and floured 9-inch tube pan. Bake in a preheated 350° oven for 50 to 55 minutes or until toothpick comes out clean. Cool for 2 to 3 minutes, unmold, and invert to cool on a cake rack. Serve sprinkled with powdered sugar or iced with vanilla-flavored Boiled Icing (page 700) or vanilla Fondant Icing (page 701).

BUCHE DE NOËL
(French Christmas Log)

½ cup confectioners' sugar, or as needed	Optional garnish: ¼ cup Marzipan
1 recipe Sponge Sheet (opposite)	(page 703) tinted pale green, and
1 recipe mocha Butter Cream (page 700)	2 tablespoons sugar

Sprinkle the sugar on a tea towel. As soon as the sponge sheet is baked invert it out of the pan onto the sugar so the wax paper is on top. With the aid of the towel, roll cake tightly, lengthwise. Do not remove wax paper. Cool, unroll, and peel off the wax paper. Trim away any crusty edges. Spread with *one-third of the mocha butter cream* and roll, without the aid of the towel. Chill for 30 minutes. Cut 2 to 3 inches off each end, diagonally. Place these "branches" on either side of the main "log," with the diagonal edge against the log. Spread *remaining butter cream* all over the cake and on cut edges. Use a fork to make rough streaks resembling bark all over log and branches. Decorate with green marzipan to resemble moss. Sprinkle with sugar for sparkle. Chill well. Serves 8.

SAVARIN

The centuries-old Polish Gugelhupf is the supposed ancestor of this kirsch-soaked Savarin and its predecessor, Baba au Rhum. Legend has it that King Stanislas Leszczynski, who maintained his eighteenth century Polish court in French exile and occasionally dabbled in the kitchen, was the man responsible. He is supposed to have been the first to douse a cake in spirits, naming his invention Baba after one of the heroes of *The Arabian Nights*. The Savarin, a Parisian variation that dates from the 1850's, is named after a French hero—Jean Anthelme Brillat-Savarin.

1 cup milk, scalded
1 envelope dry yeast
$\frac{1}{4}$ cup warm water
$\frac{1}{2}$ cup sugar
$\frac{1}{2}$ teaspoon salt
4 eggs
$\frac{2}{3}$ cup butter, melted and
 slightly cooled

$\frac{3}{4}$ cup raisins
$3\frac{1}{2}$ cups sifted flour, or as needed
Syrup:
$1\frac{1}{2}$ cups sugar
2 cups water
$\frac{1}{3}$ cup kirsch, rum, or cognac,
 or as needed
Juice of $\frac{1}{2}$ lemon

Scald the milk. Dissolve yeast in warm water with *one tablespoon sugar*. Pour milk into a large, warm bowl, and when lukewarm, add yeast and salt. Beat the eggs and *remaining sugar*, add butter, and add to the yeast and milk. Add the raisins rolled in *some flour*, and *enough flour* to make a heavy, thick batter. Beat for 5 minutes with a wooden spoon. Cover with a cloth and set in a warm place to rise until doubled in bulk, about $1\frac{1}{2}$ hours. Punch dough down. Butter an 11-inch ring mold and fill the ring a little less than half full. Cover and let dough rise until doubled in bulk. Bake in preheated 350° oven for 35 minutes and cool in the ring. Prepare syrup: simmer sugar and water for 10 minutes. Cool; add liquor and lemon juice. Remove cake from mold, pour $\frac{1}{4}$ cup syrup over cake, and return cake to mold. With a skewer make deep holes in the cake and pour in remaining syrup until well soaked. Let soak for several hours. Serve with a bowl of sweetened whipped cream flavored with the same liquor as syrup. Fill center with fresh or brandied fruit or guava shells.

VARIATION: *Baba au Rhum*: Fill 12 well-greased baba molds or small custard cups two thirds full of savarin dough. Let rise, uncovered, in a warm place until dough reaches top of mold. Set molds on a cookie sheet and bake in a preheated 350° oven for about 20 minutes or until a toothpick inserted in center comes out clean. Remove from molds and cool. Prick all over with a fork and pour on syrup made with rum. Let stand in syrup, basting frequently. Serve cold or reheat in syrup and flambé with $\frac{1}{4}$ cup heated dark rum.

GATEAU A LA STANLEY

Of the many honors heaped upon the famous nineteenth-century explorer Sir Henry Stanley none was sweeter than this cake recipe bearing his name. It appears in Francatelli's *The Modern Cook*, a compilation of recipes from the Victorian era.

1 2-inch piece vanilla bean or 1 teaspoon vanilla extract
1½ cups sugar
1 cup water
12 greengage plums, fresh or canned in heavy syrup

1 recipe Savarin dough (opposite), baked in a fluted mold
1 recipe Glace Plombières (page 732) or vanilla ice cream
2 tablespoons kirsch (optional)

If using fresh plums, place vanilla bean, sugar, and water in a saucepan and simmer, covered, for 5 minutes. Add the washed plums (halved and pitted if very large) and simmer very gently so as not to break the skins of the fruit—about 10 minutes or until tender. Cool. One drop of green coloring may be added to intensify the color. If using canned plums, drain and reserve syrup (eliminating need for first 3 recipe ingredients). At serving time fill the cake with ice cream. Top with drained plums. Add kirsch to plum syrup and pour over cake. Serves 8.

BLITZKUCHEN

Coffee was regarded by nineteenth-century Germans as a ladies' drink. Middleclass housewives, after they completed their daily chores, would gather at friends' houses and enjoy a "kaffeeklatch"; the coffee was spiced with local gossip and accompanied by pastries. *Blitzkuchen*, which literally translated means lightning cake, is a quickly made coffeecake—an ideal complement for the favorite beverage of the burghers' wives.

1½ cups flour, sifted
Pinch of salt
2 teaspoons baking powder
⅓ cup sugar
4 tablespoons butter, melted
1 egg

⅔ cup milk
Rind of ½ lemon, grated, or ½ teaspoon vanilla or almond extract
Crumb Topping (page 680) or butter, cinnamon, and sugar to cover

Resift flour with salt, baking powder, and sugar. Beat together melted butter, egg, milk, and flavoring. Add dry ingredients to batter and beat thoroughly until smooth. Pour into a lightly buttered 8- or 9-inch square pan and cover with crumb topping or dot with butter and sprinkle with cinnamon and sugar. Bake in preheated 375° oven for 25 to 30 minutes or until golden brown. As an alternate, ½ teaspoon cinnamon, sifted with the dry ingredients, may be used as a flavoring instead of lemon rind or vanilla.

CHEESECAKE

Xanthippe, whose ill temper and shrewishness have provided an example to nagging wives ever since, knew that the way to a man's ire was through his stomach. She once snatched from the embattled Socrates a cheesecake that one of his admirers had sent, threw it to the ground, and trampled on it for good measure. Her husband, bearing this early martyrdom with rare grace, found some consolation in the fact that his wife would not have any either. Cheesecake was a favorite food of the ancients, the subject of numerous philosophical treatises, and a ritual offering to the deities. It was also a reward, given in a pan-Hellenic contest, to the Greek who could stay awake the longest. Cheesecake migrated to Italy with the rise of the Roman Empire, and was adapted from Athenaeus as described below. Its baroque descendant, the ricotta cheesecake following, appeared in Bartolomeo Stefani's *L'Arte di ben cucinare*, c. 1662.

SESAME HONEY CHEESE TART

$\frac{1}{2}$ recipe Short Pastry (page 682)
1 pound cream cheese, at room
    temperature
$\frac{1}{2}$ cup heavy cream
$\frac{1}{2}$ cup honey
$\frac{1}{3}$ cup sugar

$\frac{1}{2}$ teaspoon powdered nutmeg
3 egg yolks, well beaten
2 tablespoons toasted ground
    sesame seeds
3 egg whites, stiffly beaten

Roll out pastry $\frac{1}{8}$ inch thick. Line a 10-inch buttered pie plate and make a standing $\frac{1}{2}$-inch fluted edge. Chill while preparing filling. Beat cream cheese until smooth. Mix with the cream. Add the honey and sugar mixed with the nutmeg. Add egg yolks, beating well. Add sesame seeds and fold in egg whites. Pour into prepared pie shell. Bake in preheated 350° oven for 45 minutes.

TORTA DI RICOTTA

$1\frac{1}{2}$ pounds ricotta cheese, well drained
3 tablespoons flour
5 tablespoons sugar
4 egg yolks
Rind of $\frac{1}{2}$ orange, grated
Rind of 1 lemon, grated

1 tablespoon rum or brandy or
    $1\frac{1}{2}$ teaspoons vanilla extract
2 tablespoons currants
4 tablespoons lightly toasted pine nuts
3 egg whites, stiffly beaten
3 tablespoons confectioners' sugar
    mixed with $1\frac{1}{2}$ teaspoons cinnamon

Combine cheese, flour, sugar, egg yolks, rind, and rum and beat thoroughly for 7 to 8 minutes. Add currants and nuts and mix well. Fold in stiffly beaten whites, gently but thoroughly, using a rubber spatula. Butter a 9-inch spring form pan and dust inside lightly with flour, tapping out excess. Turn batter into pan and bake in a preheated 375° oven for about 45 minutes or until firm and golden brown on top. Do not open oven door before 40 minutes. Cool cake in pan, remove rim, and sprinkle top of cake with cinnamon sugar.

GERMAN CHOCOLATE POTATO TORTE

4 medium-size baking potatoes
¾ cup butter, softened
1¾ cups sugar
4 eggs, separated
2 ounces bitter chocolate, melted

1 tablespoon strong black coffee
2½ cups flour, sifted
1 teaspoon baking powder
1 cup ground almonds

Boil, peel, and mash potatoes a day in advance. Rub through a strainer and measure off 2 cups. Cream butter with *all but 2 tablespoons sugar*. Beat in egg yolks, one at a time, beating well between additions. Fold in chocolate, coffee, and potatoes. Beat egg whites with *remaining sugar* until stiff and glossy. Turn into egg yolk batter. Resift flour with baking powder over whites; add nuts. Fold all together gently but thoroughly, using a rubber spatula. Turn into 2 unbuttered 9-inch round cake pans or an 8-inch spring form pan. Bake in a preheated 350° oven for about 30 minutes (45 minutes for spring form pan) or until cake springs back to touch. Cool in pan. Fill with chocolate Butter Cream (page 700) or whipped cream.

SCHWARZWÄLDER KIRSCHTORTE
(Black Forest Cherry Cake)

1 recipe German Chocolate Potato
  Torte (above) or 2 9-inch
  chocolate cake layers
¼ cup kirsch, or to taste
1 recipe chocolate Butter Cream
  (page 700)

2 cups pitted, halved black cherries,
  fresh or canned
2 cups heavy cream
1 tablespoon sugar, or to taste
Chocolate Curls (page 705) or ¾ cup
  grated semisweet chocolate

Prepare cake batter and bake in 2 unbuttered 9-inch round cake pans. Cool slightly. Slice off crown of cakes to level the layers and sprinkle each layer with *one tablespoon kirsch*. Cool completely. Spread bottom layer with chocolate butter cream. Place *one and one-half cups cherries* on butter cream and press lightly into cream. Top with second layer. Whip cream, sweetening it with sugar and adding *remaining kirsch* to taste. Spread cream over top and around sides of cake. Decorate with chocolate curls or grated chocolate and *remaining cherries*. Chill for several hours before serving.

CHRISTMAS MEDIVNYK

The Ukraine was a great honey producing center in the days before sugar became the universal sweetener. Through the years honey has remained a popular ingredient in Ukrainian cakes and pastries, especially those served during the Christmas and New Year's season. The Medivnyk, which takes its name from the Ukrainian word *med*, meaning honey, is the traditional Christmas honey cake.

1 cup honey	4 cups flour, sifted
1 teaspoon powdered cinnamon	$\frac{1}{2}$ teaspoon salt
$\frac{1}{2}$ teaspoon powdered cloves	$1\frac{1}{2}$ teaspoons baking powder
$\frac{1}{2}$ teaspoon powdered nutmeg	1 cup raisins
2 teaspoons baking soda	$\frac{1}{2}$ cup currants
$\frac{1}{2}$ cup butter, softened	$\frac{1}{2}$ cup chopped pitted dates
1 cup brown sugar	1 cup chopped walnuts
4 eggs, separated	

Heat honey to boiling and add spices and baking soda. Allow mixture to cool. Cream butter with brown sugar and beat in egg yolks one at a time until mixture is light. Add honey mixture and mix well. Resift *three and three-quarters cups flour* with salt and baking powder. Mix into honey. Mix fruits and nuts with *remaining flour* and add to batter. Beat egg whites until stiff and fold into batter. Pour into 2 loaf pans lined with buttered brown paper. Bake in a preheated 300° oven for about 2 hours or until toothpick comes out clean. Cool on rack. Age cakes a few days before serving.

PLUM CAKE

Isabella Beeton, at a youthful 24, produced *The Book of Household Management*, a formidable tome that established her as unchallenged dean of Victorian domestic matters. In her effort to relieve English cookery of its unfortunate reputation, she set an invaluable precedent, including precise measurements and cooking times in her recipes. More than a cookbook, Mrs. Beeton's "bible" ranged from medical advice to manners and morals. The 1107-page text, containing this recipe, is still in print, more than a century after its publication.

$1\frac{2}{3}$ cups diced, mixed, glazed fruits	1 cup butter, softened
2 teaspoons grated lemon rind	$\frac{1}{2}$ cup sugar
$\frac{3}{4}$ cup dark raisins	6 eggs
$\frac{1}{2}$ cup dark rum, cognac, or bourbon	$1\frac{1}{2}$ teaspoons baking powder
$\frac{1}{2}$ cup slivered blanched almonds	$\frac{1}{8}$ teaspoon salt
$1\frac{3}{4}$ cups flour, sifted	$1\frac{1}{2}$ teaspoons vanilla extract

Butter a 10-inch tube pan and line with buttered wax paper on bottom and sides. Flour well, shaking out excess. Soak fruit, rinds, and raisins in the rum for 3 to 4 hours. Drain well and mix fruit and almonds with *three-quarters cup flour*. Reserve. Cream butter and sugar until light and fluffy. Beat eggs until very light and whip gradually into butter and sugar. Fold in fruits and almonds. Resift *remaining flour*, baking powder, and salt and fold into butter and eggs, along with vanilla. Pour batter into prepared pan and bake in a preheated 350° oven for 60 to 65 minutes or until cake is golden and shrinks from the sides of the pan. Cool on a rack.

PARKIN FINGERS

Parkin is an English ginger cake traditionally associated with Guy Fawkes' Day, November 5. All over England these cakes are served to commemorate the failure of Guy Fawkes to blow up the Houses of Parliament on November 5, 1605. Every year the hapless conspirator is denounced anew with bell-ringing, bonfires, and parades. Parkin is served everywhere, and in parts of Yorkshire, where the cake is especially popular, November 5 is called Parkin Day.

$\frac{1}{2}$ cup molasses
6 tablespoons butter
$\frac{1}{2}$ cup brown sugar
$\frac{1}{2}$ teaspoon baking soda
1 egg, beaten
2 cups flour, sifted
1 teaspoon baking powder

$\frac{1}{2}$ teaspoon salt
2 teaspoons powdered ginger
$\frac{3}{4}$ cup sour cream
1 teaspoon grated lemon rind
1 recipe Sugar Icing (page 702) made with lemon juice instead of water

Heat molasses. Add butter, sugar, and baking soda and cool. Beat in the egg. Resift flour with baking powder, salt, and ginger into a large bowl. Make a well and pour in molasses and sour cream. Work flour into molasses mixture until smooth. Add lemon rind and beat well. Butter and flour a 7- by 11-inch pan and pour in batter. Bake in a preheated 350° oven for 15 to 20 minutes or until cake springs back when touched. Cool for about 10 minutes and remove. Ice with sugar icing. Cut into "fingers." Makes 24.

THE MANNER OF MAKING SAVOY BISCUIT

6 eggs, separated
1 cup sugar
2 teaspoons vanilla extract

$\frac{3}{4}$ cup potato flour or
cornstarch, sifted
$\frac{3}{4}$ cup flour, sifted
1 teaspoon baking powder

Beat egg yolks and sugar for about 15 minutes or until mixture is very light and forms a ribbon when beater is lifted. Add the vanilla. Mix the flours and baking powder and beat egg whites very stiff. Fold flour carefully into yolks; then fold in whites. Pour into a buttered and floured 8-inch spring form pan. Bake in a preheated 350° oven for 45 to 50 minutes. Grated lime or lemon rind may be added as flavoring.

AEBLEKAGE
(Danish Apple Cake)

2 pounds cooking apples, peeled,
quartered, and cored
Sugar to taste
1 teaspoon vanilla extract
2 to 3 cups bread or cake crumbs

1 cup butter, melted
1 cup red currant jelly, or to taste
1 cup heavy cream, whipped, sweetened,
and flavored with vanilla extract

Cook the apples in very little water until soft and most liquid has evaporated. Sweeten to taste and flavor with vanilla. Butter 9- by 9-inch baking dish. Place in layers crumbs, apples, butter, and jelly, ending with crumbs and butter. Bake in a preheated 400° oven for 30 minutes or until golden. Serve warm with whipped cream.

SAINT FANOUREO CAKE

Whenever Greeks wished to recover wayward possessions, they pledged a fruit cake to Saint Fanoureo, the patron saint of the "lost and found." Upon the article's return, its owner took the cake to church for a blessing and gave it to the poor.

1 cup orange juice
$\frac{1}{2}$ cup brandy
2 tablespoons butter
2 cups golden raisins
$\frac{3}{4}$ cup sugar
$\frac{1}{2}$ cup honey
Pinch of salt

1 tablespoon powdered cinnamon
$\frac{1}{4}$ teaspoon powdered cloves
2 cups flour, sifted
2 teaspoons baking powder
$\frac{1}{2}$ teaspoon baking soda
2 tablespoons grated orange rind
$\frac{1}{2}$ cup sesame seeds (optional)

676

Combine orange juice, brandy, butter, raisins, sugar, honey, salt, cinnamon, and cloves in a large, heavy-bottomed saucepan. Bring to a boil, reduce heat, and simmer for 10 minutes or until thick and syrupy. Set pot in cold water to cool mixture completely. Resift flour, baking powder, and baking soda into cooled syrup. Beat vigorously for 8 to 10 minutes or until batter is smooth and bubbly. Stir in grated rind. Turn into a well-buttered 7-inch fluted tube pan or an 8-inch loaf pan. Sprinkle with sesame seeds. Bake in a preheated 325° oven for 1 to $1\frac{1}{2}$ hours or until cake tests done. Sprinkle with a little brandy and cool cake in pan.

PUMPERNICKEL SPICE TORTE

2 cups dry pumpernickel crumbs
$\frac{1}{4}$ cup brandy or rum
$\frac{1}{3}$ cup finely ground walnuts, pecans, or hazelnuts
$1\frac{1}{2}$ squares semisweet chocolate, finely grated
6 eggs, separated
1 tablespoon finely minced candied orange rind
1 tablespoon finely minced candied lemon rind

1 tablespoon orange juice
2 teaspoons lemon juice
$\frac{1}{8}$ teaspoon each powdered clove and nutmeg
$\frac{1}{4}$ teaspoon powdered cinnamon
Pinch of salt
1 cup sugar
$1\frac{1}{2}$ cups heavy cream, whipped, sweetened, and flavored with rum, brandy, or vanilla, or 1 recipe rum-flavored Butter Cream (page 700)

Soak crumbs in brandy. Combine soaked crumbs with nuts and chocolate and set aside. Beat egg yolks lightly and stir in rinds, fruit juices, and spices. Beat egg whites with salt until they begin to stiffen. Add sugar gradually, 2 or 3 tablespoons at a time, beating thoroughly between additions, until whites are stiff and glossy. Stir one cup egg whites into yolk mixture; then add remaining egg whites and crumb mixture and fold gently but thoroughly with a rubber spatula. Grease the bottom of a 9-inch fluted or plain tube pan and pour in batter. Bake in a preheated 350° oven for about 1 hour or until cake is high, golden brown, and springs back when lightly pressed. Cool thoroughly in pan. Remove from pan and serve with whipped cream or butter cream and decorate with additional candied fruit rind. For more flavor allow cake to mellow in refrigerator for 24 hours before being cut.

DUNDEE WEDDING CAKE

The many-tiered frosted wedding cake is a relatively modern culinary concoction. As late as the Middle Ages an English bride entered upon her new estate with nothing more than a shower of grain, symbolizing fertility, to sweeten her marriage vows. (The custom of throwing rice was borrowed later from the Orient.) Eventually this ritual was refined, the grain becoming the flour for biscuits which were broken over the bride's head. From the custom of stacking the edible ammunition in a great pile came the next stage of wedding cake—a pyramidal mound of sweet, soft cakes glazed over with an icing of hardened white sugar—as devised by the cooks of Restoration England. By the eighteenth century when Tobias Smollett described the following scene, the single cake, replete with modern superstitions, was an important feature of a proper wedding: "A cake being broken over the head of Mrs. Tabitha Lismahago, the fragments were distributed among the bystanders . . . on the supposition that every person who ate the hallowed cake should that night have a vision of the man or woman whom Heaven designed should be his or her wedded mate." Whether the bride too had a vision after the blow struck by the bridal cake the author neglected to tell. The fruity Dundee Cake below is often served at traditional Scottish weddings.

$1\frac{1}{2}$ cups each: currants, black raisins, white raisins, and chopped candied rind

4 cups flour

$2\frac{2}{3}$ cups butter, softened

2 cups sugar

12 eggs

$\frac{1}{4}$ teaspoon salt

2 teaspoons baking powder

1 teaspoon powdered cinnamon

$\frac{1}{4}$ teaspoon powdered nutmeg

1 cup ground blanched almonds

1 tablespoon grated lemon rind

$\frac{1}{2}$ cup cognac (optional)

1 cup slivered blanched almonds

Double recipe Marzipan (page 703)

Double recipe vanilla Fondant Icing (page 701)

Dredge the fruits and rinds with *4 to 6 tablespoons flour* and reserve. Beat the butter until creamy. Add the sugar and beat until fluffy. Beat in the eggs one at a time, beating well after each addition. Resift *remaining flour*, salt, baking powder, and spices and fold a third at a time into sugar-egg batter. Fold in dredged fruit, ground almonds, lemon rind, and cognac. Beat well to mix. Pour into 8-inch and 6-inch spring form pans, buttered and lined with buttered brown paper. Smooth over tops with the back of a spoon and sprinkle with slivered almonds. Bake in a preheated 325° oven for $1\frac{1}{2}$ to 2 hours or until cakes shrink at the sides. Cool on a rack. Spread each cake with marzipan and fondant icing. Place smaller cake on top and cover with Fondant Icing. Decorate as desired. Serves 20.

KASUTERA

Japan's repertory of native cakes was greatly augmented by the country's westernization. This sponge cake was the first European import, and remains the favorite. Kasutera is at its best in the port city of Nagasaki, where the Spanish or Portuguese were believed to have introduced it.

6 eggs	1 cup flour, sifted
$\frac{3}{4}$ cup sugar	1 teaspoon baking powder
$\frac{1}{3}$ cup honey	Confectioners' sugar for dusting

Beat eggs until light. Beat in sugar and honey. Resift flour and baking powder and fold into eggs. Pour into a 9-inch square cake pan lined with wax paper on bottom only. Bake in a preheated 350° oven for about 45 minutes or until toothpick comes out clean. Invert on a cake rack and cool. Turn right side up on a cake plate and sprinkle with confectioners' sugar.

GATEAU SAINT-HONORE

The bakers of Paris named this, one of their prettiest cakes, after Honoré, Bishop of Amiens c. 660 and patron saint of pastry cooks.

$1\frac{1}{2}$ envelopes unflavored gelatin	1 cup sugar
Double recipe Pastry Cream (page 702)	$\frac{1}{4}$ teaspoon cream of tartar
1 recipe Cream Puff Paste (page 725)	6 egg whites
$\frac{1}{2}$ recipe Short Pastry (page 682)	

Dissolve gelatin in $\frac{1}{3}$ cup cold water. Prepare pastry cream and chill two-thirds of a cup. Add gelatin to remaining hot pastry cream and stir until melted. Cool. Prepare cream puff paste and cool. Mix short pastry and roll it out to a 9-inch round. Place on a buttered cookie sheet and chill for 10 minutes. Put half the cream puff paste in a pastry bag with a plain, wide tube and pipe an even roll (about 1 inch thick) of cream puff paste around the edge of the short pastry. Prick short pastry with a fork and bake in a preheated 425° oven for 25 to 30 minutes. Cool on a cake rack. Make about 16 to 18 walnut-size cream puffs with remaining cream puff paste. Bake in a preheated 425° oven for 15 minutes. Lower heat to 350° and bake 10 to 15 minutes longer. Prick with the tip of a sharp knife. Turn heat off and let puffs stand in warm oven for 8 to 10 minutes to dry. Cool on cake rack. Open puffs partially on the bottom and fill each with about 1 teaspoon of the reserved two-thirds cup cold pastry cream. Place the sugar, $\frac{1}{2}$ cup water, and cream of tartar in a saucepan. Stir once and simmer until golden brown. Holding puffs between tongs, dip them in the caramel. Set them side by side on the raised rim of the prepared shell to make a high wall. As the caramel cools they will stick securely. If caramel hardens in the pan, reheat until it softens. Beat egg whites until stiff and fold into remaining cool pastry cream and gelatin. Chill until set. Pile in uneven mounds with a large kitchen spoon into prepared shell. Keep chilled until ready to serve. Serves 6 to 8.

SIR KENELM DIGBY'S CREAM CHEESE PASTRY

$\frac{1}{2}$ pound cream cheese
1 cup butter, softened
2 egg yolks (optional)

2 cups flour, sifted
$\frac{1}{2}$ teaspoon salt

Soften the cream cheese in a bowl and add the soft butter. For a richer pastry add egg yolks to the cheese and butter. Sift the flour with the salt and work into cheese mixture. Refrigerate for 30 minutes before using. Roll between sheets of wax paper. Use as directed for meat and fish pastries or desserts. Makes enough for both crusts of 1 9-inch pie or 16 tartlets.

HOT WATER DOUGH

$\frac{2}{3}$ cup lard
$2\frac{1}{2}$ cups flour, sifted

1 teaspoon salt
1 egg yolk for glazing

Melt lard in $\frac{1}{2}$ cup boiling water in a large saucepan. Add the flour and salt and stir until well mixed. Turn out on a lightly floured board; when cool enough to handle knead until smooth. Cover and leave in a warm place for 30 minutes. While still warm roll out to desired thickness for topping for meat pies. Mix egg yolk with 2 teaspoons water and brush on the dough before baking. Makes enough for top and bottom crusts of an 8-inch round deep dish meat pie.

CRUMB CRUST

$1\frac{1}{2}$ cups finely crushed gingersnaps,
    graham crackers, vanilla wafers,
    or zwieback

$\frac{1}{3}$ cup sugar
$\frac{1}{3}$ cup butter, melted

Mix crumbs, sugar, and melted butter. Press firmly into a 9- or 10-inch pie plate, covering the sides to the rim. (Reserve $\frac{1}{4}$ cup of crumbs as topping for filled pie, if desired.) Bake in a preheated 400° oven for 5 minutes and cool.

CRUMB TOPPING

$\frac{1}{4}$ cup butter
$\frac{1}{4}$ cup sugar
1 teaspoon powdered cinnamon

$\frac{1}{2}$ cup coarsely chopped walnuts
    or pecans (optional)
$\frac{1}{2}$ to $\frac{3}{4}$ cup flour

Cream butter with sugar and cinnamon; mix in nuts. Add flour gradually, stirring until mixture is crumbly. Use for topping cakes or pies. Makes about $1\frac{1}{2}$ cups.

RICH TART PASTRY

2 cups flour, sifted
Pinch of salt
$\frac{1}{3}$ cup sugar
$\frac{3}{4}$ cup butter, cut into small pieces
2 eggs

Rind of 1 lemon, grated
$\frac{1}{3}$ cup finely ground almonds or other
    nuts or sesame seeds (optional)
1 to 2 tablespoons rum or brandy

Resift flour, together with salt and sugar, into a wide mixing bowl. Make a well in the center and into this place the butter, the lightly beaten eggs, the lemon rind, and nuts if desired. Gradually blend ingredients together with fingertips or a fork, working quickly and lightly until dough sticks together in a ball. Sprinkle with a little rum or brandy as you work and add more flour if dough is sticky. Wrap in wax paper and chill for 1 hour or until firm and smooth enough to roll. Cut dough in half and roll out to desired thickness between sheets of wax paper. This makes enough for 1 9-inch pie crust with lattice strip topping.

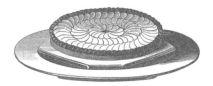

FRUIT TART

> Massialot's *Le Cuisinier Roial et Bourgeois*, the source of this recipe, first appeared in the reign of Louis XIV and remained in vogue for more than a century, going into numerous French and foreign editions.

1 recipe Rich Tart Pastry (above)
4 cups fresh or canned purple plums,
    peaches, or apricots, drained
$\frac{1}{4}$ cup sugar
$\frac{1}{2}$ teaspoon grated lemon rind

$\frac{1}{2}$ teaspoon grated orange rind
2 tablespoons butter
$\frac{1}{2}$ teaspoon vanilla extract
$\frac{1}{4}$ cup currant jelly, melted

Butter a 9-inch flan ring placed on a buttered cookie sheet or use a 9-inch pie plate. Line with the pastry dough rolled out to $\frac{1}{4}$-inch thickness. Flute edges of dough. Line with wax paper and fill with rice or dried beans to retain shape. Bake in a preheated 400° oven for 6 to 7 minutes and cool without removing from ring. Meanwhile, carefully remove the pits from *2 cups fruit*, halve the fruit, and reserve. Remove pits from *remaining fruit*, drain well, and purée. Mix with sugar, lemon and orange rind, and butter, and cook over low heat to evaporate liquid—about 8 to 10 minutes. Add vanilla and spread fruit purée in the bottom of pastry shell. Arrange fruit halves over purée, cut side down. Bake in a preheated 400° oven for 20 minutes. Remove from oven and brush with melted currant jelly. Cool completely. Serves 6. The purée may be replaced by Pastry Cream (page 702).

SHORT PASTRY

2½ cups flour, sifted
1 teaspoon salt
½ cup butter

¼ cup vegetable fat or lard
5 tablespoons ice water, or as needed

Resift flour and salt into a bowl. Using knives or a pastry blender, cut in butter and fat until it looks like coarse meal. Add ice water by the tablespoon until pastry just holds together. Roll out ⅛ inch thick. Makes enough for top and bottom crusts of 1 9-inch pie or 16 tartlets.

DARIOLES

Darioles, a variety of cream-filled tart, have been a popular dessert on both sides of the English Channel since the Middle Ages. Taillevent prepared them in the 1300's for his royal employers, and a recipe for "Daryoles" beginning, "Take wyne and Fressche brothe, Clowes, Maces, & Marow, & pouder of Gyngere, & Safroun, & let al boyle to-gedrys . . ." appeared in an English manuscript on cookery of about the same time.

½ recipe Puff Pastry (page 684) or
   1 recipe Short Pastry (above)

1 recipe Frangipane Cream (page 702)

Line 12 baba molds with pastry rolled very thin. Push upward gently with the fingers so pastry extends ⅛ inch above molds. Fill with cream and bake in a preheated 350° oven until pastry is golden and cream is set, about 25 minutes. Tartlet pans may be substituted.

CONGRESS TART

The particular congress for which this tart was named occurred in 1647 when the Peace of Westphalia leading to the end of the Thirty Years' War was negotiated in German Osnabrück. An almond macaroon tart marked with a pastry cross was presented to the assembled dignitaries.

Double recipe Short Pastry (above)
1 recipe Macaroon batter (page 698)

2 teaspoons cream

Roll out *half the pastry dough* to ¼-inch thickness and line 16 buttered 3-inch tartlet pans. Flute the edges. Fill the pastry shells with macaroon batter. Roll out *remaining pastry dough* and cut strips of it to make a cross on each tartlet. Attach by moistening with a very little water, if needed. Brush pastry with cream and bake in a preheated 400° oven for 10 minutes, lower heat to 350°, and bake for about 15 to 25 minutes longer.

TARTELETTES AMANDINES

Ragueneau, a character in Rostand's *Cyrano de Bergerac*, was a pastry cook of such exquisite sensibilities that he traded tarts for triolets and made his shop a meeting place for hungry poets. Occasionally, he set his own recipes to rhyme, as in the following:

> *Beat your eggs, the yolk and white,*
> *   Very light;*
> *Mingle with their creamy fluff*
> *   Drops of lime-juice, cool and green;*
> *   Then pour in*
> *Milk of almonds, just enough.*
> *Dainty patty-pans, embraced*
> *   In puff-paste—*
> *Have these ready within reach;*
> *   With your thumb and finger, pinch*
> *   Half an inch*
> *Up around the edge of each—*
> *Into these, a score or more,*
> *   Slowly pour*
> *All your store of custard; so*
> *   Take them, bake them golden-brown—*
> *   Now sit down! . . .*
> *Almond tartlets, Ragueneau!*

1 envelope unflavored gelatin	2 teaspoons grated lime rind
$\frac{1}{4}$ cup lime juice	$\frac{1}{2}$ teaspoon almond extract
5 eggs	1 cup heavy cream, whipped
$\frac{1}{2}$ cup sugar	16 baked tartlet or patty shells
Pinch of salt	

Soak the gelatin in the lime juice and melt over hot water. Place the eggs, sugar, and salt in the top of a 12-cup double boiler over 1 inch barely simmering water. Beat with a rotary or electric beater until the eggs have practically filled the pan. Add the cooled gelatin and beat for a few seconds longer. Remove from heat, cool, and fold in lime rind, almond extract, and whipped cream. Pour into tartlet shells and chill before serving.

VARIATION: *Cold Lime Soufflé*: Line the bottom and sides of a buttered 6-cup soufflé dish with ladyfingers. Sprinkle $\frac{1}{3}$ cup sherry over the ladyfingers on the bottom of the dish. Tie a collar of doubled wax paper around the dish to extend $2\frac{1}{2}$ inches above rim. Butter the inside of the wax paper. Pour in lime filling. The mixture should come above the rim of the dish. Chill for several hours. At serving time carefully remove wax paper collar. Serve with sweetened whipped cream or Apricot-Orange Sauce (page 704).

PITHIVIERS

The citizens of Pithiviers, France, can be grateful that this puff pastry was named, hundreds of years ago, after its birthplace rather than its creator, for it is now the town's main claim to fame.

½ recipe Puff Pastry (below)   1 egg yolk for glazing
Frangipane Cream (page 702)   Confectioners' sugar for dusting

Roll out the pastry to about ⅛-inch thickness. Cut 2 8-inch circles with a scalloped cutter. Place 1 circle on a cookie sheet, spread with frangipane cream to within ½ inch of edge. Moisten the edge with cold water and cover cake with second circle. Seal well but do not damage scalloping. With a sharp knife make arcs from center of cake to edge without cutting through the pastry. Brush the cake with egg yolk beaten with 2 teaspoons cold water and chill for 30 minutes. Bake in a preheated 350° oven for 40 minutes. Sprinkle with confectioners' sugar and bake about 20 minutes longer or until golden brown and shiny. Cool.

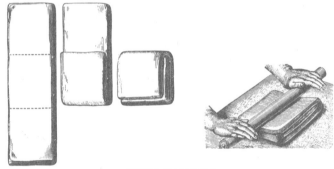

PUFF PASTRY

Culinary historians conjecture that ancient Persians first made *feuilletage* (flaky or puff pastry), passing the recipe along with their empire to the Greeks. In medieval France *gâteaux feuilletés* were so popular that Robert, Bishop of Amiens, mentioned them in a charter of 1311, but it was not until the seventeenth century that the arduous process of making puff pastries was simplified, probably by Claude Lorrain, an erstwhile *pâtissier* before becoming a landscape painter.

2 cups sweet butter   1 teaspoon salt
4 cups flour

Knead the butter until waxy. Shape into a flat, square cake, wrap in foil, and refrigerate. Sift the flour with the salt into a bowl. Gradually add about 1½ cups water (all may not be needed) and knead on a lightly floured board until dough is smooth and elastic—about 20 to 30 minutes. Wrap the dough in foil or in a cloth well wrung out in cold water; chill for 30 minutes. Roll it out on a well-floured board into a $\frac{1}{2}$-inch-thick square. Roll edges a little thinner than center. Lightly flour the square of butter and place in the center of the dough. Fold the 4 edges of the dough to completely cover the butter, sealing edges. Roll out with a floured rolling pin, rolling forward only, until a long rectangle is obtained. Should dough tear, take a little dough from the edges and mend immediately to entrap air. Strip should be about 8 inches wide and 16 inches long. Fold a third of the strip over and bring opposite end over this so as to have 3 layers of dough. Pass rolling pin lightly over edges to seal. Turn the pastry a quarter turn and repeat rolling and folding. Wrap, chill for 30 minutes, unwrap, and repeat rolling, folding, and chilling 4 times more, always keeping edges of dough facing you when rolling out. The last 2 "turns" should be made just before pastry is used.

VARIATION: *Vol-au-vents*: Roll out puff pastry $\frac{1}{4}$ inch thick. Using a fluted cutter, cut 6 3-inch rounds. Moisten edges with water. Cut 6 additional 3-inch rounds and remove a 2-inch circle from center. Place these on top of first 6 rounds. Replace little center cutouts. Mix 1 egg yolk with 2 teaspoons cold water and brush vol-au-vents. Place on buttered cookie sheet and bake in a preheated 425° oven for 20 minutes or until golden and very puffed. When vol-au-vents are done, cool for 10 minutes. Lift off centers, remove loose dough inside, fill with desired filling and replace the centers, or lids.

MILLE-FEUILLES

The original cream-filled Mille-feuille or "thousand leaf" puff pastry was the probable creation of Carême, who may have used it as a *grosse pièce d'entremets* to adorn a banquet table. It often goes by the name Napoleon, not out of respect for the corpulent corporal but as a corruption of Napolitain, referring to the Neapolitan manner of making sweets and ices in layers of alternating texture and color.

1 recipe Puff Pastry (opposite)
1 recipe Pastry Cream (page 702)
1 envelope unflavored gelatin
1 cup heavy cream, whipped

2 tablespoons dark rum or
  cognac (optional)
Confectioners' sugar for dusting

Roll out puff pastry into $\frac{1}{8}$-inch-thick wide square. Cut and trim into 3 strips, 5 by 15 inches, and place on an ungreased cookie sheet. Chill for 30 minutes. Prick strips all over with a fork and bake in a preheated 400° oven for 10 minutes. Lower heat to 350° and bake for 30 minutes longer or until golden and puffed. Cool. While cake is baking, prepare filling. Make pastry cream; then dissolve gelatin in $\frac{1}{4}$ cup water, melt over hot water, and add to pastry cream. When cool, fold in whipped cream and rum. Chill. Place strip of pastry on a cookie sheet and cover with half the cream. Add another strip of pastry, more cream, and last strip of pastry. Fill in with pastry cream from the side and smooth. Chill for at least 1 hour. Sprinkle with confectioners' sugar before serving. Cake may also be filled with $1\frac{1}{2}$ cups heavy cream, whipped, flavored with vanilla or cognac, and sweetened. Serves 8.

HARRY VIII'S SHOESTRINGS

Charles Elmé Francatelli promised "in addition to English cookery, the most approved and *recherché* systems of French, Italian, and German cookery" in his *Modern Cook* (1895). The author was a pupil of the incomparable Carême and Queen Victoria's head chef. The flair he acquired is evidenced in this recipe for a suitably colorful remembrance of the jaunty sixteenth-century monarch.

$\frac{1}{2}$ recipe Puff Pastry (page 684)
1 egg yolk for glazing
Sugar for sprinkling

$\frac{1}{2}$ cup currant jelly, or as needed
$\frac{1}{3}$ cup strained greengage plum
  or apricot jam

Roll the pastry dough $\frac{1}{4}$ inch thick, cut into 3-inch squares. Wet the centers of the squares. Bring corners of the squares to meet in the center and secure by lightly pressing down on them. Cut out a small section between the folds to form 2 bows. Wet the centers lightly again, and place a small ring of dough (made from bits of pastry) in the center of each. Mix the egg yolk with 2 teaspoons cold water and brush the pastries. Bake on buttered cookie sheets in a preheated 350° oven for 15 minutes, sprinkle with sugar, and bake 15 minutes longer. Cool. Have 2 pastry bags ready, one containing currant jelly, the other jam. Draw 2 currant jelly lines on the circle part of bows and around center. Fill center and between the currant lines with jam. Makes 30 to 36 pastries.

BAKEWELL TARTS

The Derbyshire market town of Bakewell is better known for its tarts or "puddings" than for its considerable industry. Although there is no firm rule for making them, they commonly consist of a tart shell lined with jam and filled with lemon curd.

$\frac{1}{2}$ recipe Puff Pastry (page 684)
1 cup apricot, strawberry, or black
  raspberry jam
Lemon curd:
4 egg yolks

1 cup sugar
1 cup butter, melted and cooled
Rind of $\frac{1}{2}$ lemon, grated
Juice of 3 lemons
3 egg whites, stiffly beaten

Remove pastry from refrigerator $\frac{1}{2}$ hour before using. Roll out $\frac{1}{8}$ inch thick. Cut into rounds large enough to line small tart pans. Line 20 buttered fluted tartlet pans with rounds of pastry. With the fingers work the pastry up so bottoms are very thin and sides extend over pans. Prick the bottoms well with a fork. Put in a $\frac{1}{2}$-inch layer of jam and chill. Beat the egg yolks, then beat them with the sugar until very light. Add the butter, lemon rind, and juice. Fold in egg whites. Pour over jam filling. Bake for 25 to 30 minutes in a preheated 350° oven until curd is set. Serve warm or cold.

GALETTE DES ROIS

When Jean des Lyons published an *Ecclesiastical Discourse against the Paganism of Bean Kings* in 1664, he raised a storm of protests all over France, for he was attempting no less than the supression of Twelfth Night. It was, as Des Lyons knew, a celebration that had more in common with ancient Roman rites than Christian Epiphany, and the spectacle of French citizens plucking beans from cakes and pronouncing themselves mock kings for a night was in his view an affront both to Church and Crown. Fortunately for posterity, Louis XIV did not feel at all threatened. Indeed, some of the gayest Twelfth Night parties were given at his court, where, according to the gossipy *Mercure galant* for January 1684, the following scene took place at Versailles: "The salon had five tables; one for the Princes and Seigneurs, and four for the ladies of the court. . . . At each [a Galette was served and] a bean discovered inside. At the men's table it fell to the Chief Equerry, who was proclaimed King; at the four other tables it went to a lady of the court. Then the New King and the several New Queens, each in their own little State, chose Ministers, and named Ambassadresses or Ambassadors to make friendly overtures to neighboring Powers, and propose alliances and treaties." Twelfth Night Gâteaux and Galettes (the first a yeast cake typically prepared in southern France, the second a flaky pastry popular in Paris) were once again *causes célèbres* in the eighteenth century when the Pâtissiers prevailed upon the government to forbid the rival guild of Bakers from making the holiday specialty. Still later, in the wake of the French Revolution, the cakes were forbidden altogether, the Jacobins imagining them to be dangerous holdovers from the aristocratic *ancien régime*. Cooks who continued to make them, said one government watchdog, "should be unmasked and suspended and an end should be put to the orgies at which they dare to fete the shadow of the tyrant."

$\frac{1}{2}$ recipe Puff Pastry (page 684)   1 egg yolk
1 blanched almond

Roll out the pastry $\frac{1}{2}$-inch thick and cut about an 8-inch round. Insert the almond into a small cut made on the underside of the dough and place on a buttered cookie sheet. Score it with the back of a knife into a design without cutting the pastry. Cut the edges of the galette with a small sharp knife to make a design. Brush with egg yolk mixed with 1 teaspoon cold water. Chill for 30 to 40 minutes. Bake in a preheated 400° oven for 30 to 35 minutes or until well puffed and golden brown. Serves 6 to 8.

MINCE PIE

Long before Francis Bacon wrote that "Mincing of meat in pies saveth the grinding of the teeth," mixtures of spices and liquor had been used to preserve perishable meats and fruits. By the seventeenth century Mince Pie had politico-religious connotations: at Christmastide, Cavaliers would bake rectangular "coffins," or crusts, for the spicy filling and often created monstrous affairs weighing over a hundred pounds; Puritans, however, thought they detected in the pie's design overt allusions to Christ's manger and the Magi's gifts. When they tried to prohibit pastors from eating them, Sir Richard Steele countered on the clergy's behalf: "The Christmas-pie is . . . a kind of consecrated cake and a badge of distinction. And yet, it is often forbidden the Druid [preacher] of the family. Strange that a surloin of beef . . . when entire, is exposed to the utmost depredations . . . but if minced into small pieces, and tossed up with plumbs and sugar, it changes its property, and forsooth is meat for his master."

1½ pounds boiled beef	2 teaspoons powdered cinnamon
½ pound suet	1 teaspoon each: powdered mace,
4 cups beef broth	cloves, and nutmeg
1½ teaspoons salt	2 cups finely chopped candied rinds
2 pounds apples, peeled, cored,	2 lemons with rind, ground up
and chopped	3 oranges with rind, ground up
3 cups brown sugar, tightly packed	1½ cups cider
2 cups raisins	1 cup cognac
1½ cups currants	1 cup dark rum

Grind the meat with the suet. Combine with the broth and all but the last 2 ingredients. Simmer for 3 hours, stirring frequently. Cool. Add cognac and rum. Pack in sterilized quart jars, seal with paraffin, and age for at least 2 to 3 months. Makes 4 quarts.

To make mince pie: Roll out Short Pastry (page 682), fit into pie plates or tart pans, fill with mincemeat, cover with pastry, and seal edges with cold water and crimp with the fingers or the tines of a fork. Brush with cream. Bake in a preheated 400° oven for 30 to 35 minutes for large pies, or 20 minutes at 425° for small pies and tarts. Lower heat if they brown too much. A quart of filling makes 1 large pie or 16 tartlets.

COVENTRY GODCAKES

On New Year's Day in Coventry it was once customary for children to visit their godparents, who would bless them and give them Godcakes. These rich currant tarts are triangular in shape, the three corners possibly representing spires of Coventry churches. They were sold by fancy bakers and street peddlers at prices running from a halfpenny to a pound.

2 tablespoons butter
3 tablespoons brown sugar
6 tablespoons currants
3 tablespoons each finely chopped candied lemon and orange rind

$\frac{1}{2}$ teaspoon each: powdered cinnamon, nutmeg, and allspice
1 recipe Puff Pastry (page 684)
1 egg for glazing

Cream butter and sugar, add currants, rinds, and spices. Divide pastry into 4 pieces. Roll out each piece to 8- by 8-inch square, about $\frac{1}{4}$ inch thick, and cut each square into 4 squares. Divide filling among squares, placing filling on a corner of each piece of pastry. Fold over to make triangles, moistening the edges with water to seal. Press down with the tines of a fork and prick surface of pastry to let steam escape. Mix egg with 2 tablespoons cold water and brush pastries. Bake in a preheated 425° oven for 12 to 15 minutes or until puffed.

MAIDS OF HONOUR

One legend has it that a penny-wise pastry maker from sixteenth-century Richmond, capitalizing on the snob appeal of the town's renowned palace, named his confections Maids of Honour after the women at court, and eventually sold the recipe for a royal £1000. Another asserts that Anne Boleyn invented the tiny tarts to win Henry VIII's heart, and succeeded in elevating herself from maid of honor to queen.

$\frac{1}{3}$ cup soft bread crumbs
Pinch of salt
1$\frac{1}{4}$ cups milk, scalded
$\frac{1}{2}$ cup butter
2 tablespoons sugar

Rind of 1 lemon, grated
2 eggs, well beaten
$\frac{3}{4}$ cup ground blanched almonds
1 recipe Short Pastry (page 682)

Add the bread crumbs and salt to the hot milk. Stir and let stand for 10 minutes. Add the butter, sugar, lemon rind, and eggs, mixing all together thoroughly. Fold in almonds. Roll out pastry $\frac{1}{8}$ inch thick and line 16 large or 24 small buttered tart tins, leaving a rim of pastry above the shells. Prick well with a fork, line with wax paper filled with rice to retain shape. Bake in a preheated 450° oven until set, about 5 to 6 minutes. Remove paper and rice. Cool and fill two-thirds full with custard. Place on cookie sheets and bake in preheated 300° oven until custard is set, about 20 minutes.

APPLE FLORENTINE

Whole apples go into the deep-dish pie that warms many an English-man, especially in Bedfordshire, at Christmas. As the name suggests, Apple Florentine has Italian origins, though the Renaissance pope for whom it was occasionally prepared never knew the special savor of well-spiced ale that English cooks consider an indispensable part of the recipe.

6 large apples
½ cup sugar
2 teaspoons grated lemon rind
½ recipe Short Pastry (page 682)
1 egg yolk for glazing

2 cups ale
½ teaspoon powdered nutmeg
1 stick cinnamon
2 cloves

Peel and core the apples. Put close together in a deep 10-inch pie dish and sprinkle with *six tablespoons sugar* mixed with the lemon rind. Pour in 3 tablespoons water. Roll out pastry ¼ inch thick and cover apples. Make a 1-inch-wide hole in center of pastry and put a small collar of pastry around it, wetting it slightly with cold water to join. Brush pie with egg yolk beaten with 2 teaspoons cold water. Bake in a preheated 400° oven for 30 to 35 minutes. Meanwhile, bring ale, *remaining sugar*, and spices slowly to the boiling point, but do not boil; let spices steep in hot ale. When apple pie is done, pour hot ale into center hole through a funnel and serve immediately.

BAKLAVA

Persians, renowned *pâtissiers* since antiquity, invented the diamond-shaped Baklava which contained a nut stuffing perfumed with jasmine or pussy willow blossoms. In the sixth century the sweetmeat was intro-duced to the Byzantine court of Justinian I at Constantinople, where the Greeks discovered *phyllo* (thin pastry) and adopted the dessert which they serve today on New Year's and other joyous occasions.

1¾ cups sugar
Juice of ½ lemon
2 tablespoons rose water
⅔ cup butter, melted, or peanut oil

3 cups coarsely ground walnuts or
   slivered blanched almonds
1 recipe Puff Pastry (page 684)
   or 1 package frozen filo pastry, thawed

Bring *one and one-half cups sugar* and ½ cup water to a boil and simmer until very thick and sugar spins a thread (215° on a candy thermometer). Add the lemon juice, simmer for 5 min-utes, skimming carefully. Flavor with *one tablespoon rose water* and cool. Add *half the melted butter*, cooled, to the nuts and mix to a paste with *remaining sugar* and *remaining rose water*. If using puff pastry, roll out to a large square 16 by 16 inches, $\frac{1}{8}$ inch thick. Cut the pastry into 4 8- by 8-inch pieces. Butter or oil an 8- by 8-inch cake pan. Line cake pan with 1 piece of pastry. Spread with a layer of nut mixture. Repeat layers, ending with pastry. If using the filo pastry, brush each leaf with melted butter or oil. Use 10 leaves for each layer; spread with nuts and make as above on an oiled cookie sheet or in a 12- by 8-inch buttered pan. Cut into squares or diamonds with a very sharp knife. Pour on *remaining butter* and bake in a preheated 425° oven for 10 minutes. Lower heat to 375° and bake for 35 to 40 minutes or until well puffed and golden. Remove and pour on the syrup. Cool before serving.

VARIATION: *Bourma*: Substitute 6 cakes of coarsely crumbled shredded wheat for puff paste. Place 1 layer of shredded wheat in bottom of pan, top with half the nut filling. Repeat, ending with third layer of shredded wheat. Pour on remaining butter and bake as above, but remove from oven 25 minutes after oven heat has been lowered. Pour syrup over bourma and cool.

BOLO FOLHADO

Portuguese settlers were so impressed by the fertility of sixteenth century Ceylon that the historian João de Barros wrote, "it seems as if nature had made it a watered orchard." The coconut (from *coco*, Portuguese for grimace, after the fruit's "shriveled smile") palm was a veritable tree of life for the natives who ate its fruit, drank wine from its sap, and thatched their homes and hats with its leaves. As culinary mentors, the Portuguese taught the islanders to further exploit this wealth in such *bolos*, or pastries, as the following.

3 cups flour, sifted	$\frac{1}{2}$ cup butter, softened
1 teaspoon baking powder	$\frac{1}{4}$ cup thick Coconut Cream (page 632)
$\frac{1}{2}$ teaspoon salt	2 cups ground, unsalted cashew nuts
$1\frac{1}{2}$ cups sugar	4 teaspoons rose water
3 egg yolks	Cream for glazing

Resift flour with baking powder, salt, and *two tablespoons sugar*. Make a well and put in the egg yolks, *half the butter*, and the coconut cream. Work quickly into a dough and knead for 1 to 2 minutes on a floured board. Roll out into a $\frac{1}{4}$-inch-thick rectangle and spread with *remaining butter*. Fold over, bringing one end to center and other end over it. Roll into a ball and chill for 30 minutes. Divide into 4 portions, one slightly larger than the others. Roll the 3 smaller pieces into 7- or 8-inch rounds and the larger piece into about a $9\frac{1}{2}$-inch round. Combine *remaining sugar* and $\frac{3}{4}$ cup water. Boil until syrupy, about 5 minutes. Mix with the nuts and flavor with rose water. Cool completely. Place one small round of pastry on a buttered cookie sheet, put a layer of nut mixture on it, cover with another small round and repeat, ending with large round of dough which should cover the top and sides of the mound. Seal to edge of bottom dough layer and flute. Brush with cream and bake in a preheated 400° oven until golden, about 45 to 60 minutes. Allow to cool. Serve sliced. Serves 6.

MADELEINES

Ever since a consciousness-expanding bite of Madeleine provided Marcel Proust with sufficient recall to write his seven volume *Remembrance of Things Past*, the little scallop-shaped cake, according to A. J. Liebling, has been "as firmly established in folklore as Newton's apple." Originating in Lorraine, Madeleines were in vogue at Versailles c. 1730. To Proust, who had eaten them in his childhood, they bore "in the tiny and almost impalpable drop of their essence, the vast structure of recollection." However, Liebling lamented, "In the light of what Proust wrote with so mild a stimulus, it is the world's loss that he did not have a heartier appetite"; with a full meal "he might have written a masterpiece."

¾ cup sugar

5 eggs

1 cup flour, sifted

⅛ teaspoon salt

½ cup butter, melted and slightly cooled

1 teaspoon vanilla extract

Place sugar and eggs in a bowl and beat until lemon colored and thick and mixture sticks to beater. Resift flour with salt and fold into mixture quickly and carefully, along with the butter and vanilla. Vanilla may be replaced by 1 teaspoon grated lemon peel, or both may be used. Pour into buttered and floured madeleine molds. Bake in a preheated 350° oven for 15 to 17 minutes or until golden. Makes 40 cakes.

OUBLIES

Although *oublie* is actually a corruption of *oblaye*, referring to a type of nonconsecrated wafer, it is an amusing coincidence that the wafers were first made from "forgotten" pastry. It was the custom in French bakeries since medieval times to give the day's leftovers to the lowest ranking apprentices in the bakery shop, to be put to whatever profitable use they could devise. Oublies were thus sold on the streets at the end of the working day, the bakery boys capturing their customers with the engaging cry, "Voila le plaisir!" or "Here is pleasure!"

1 cup flour, sifted

1 cup sugar

1 egg

3 tablespoons butter, melted

2 teaspoons orange flower water

1 cup milk

1 teaspoon grated lemon rind

Mix together the flour, sugar, egg, melted butter, and orange flower water. Work until smooth and shiny. Gradually add milk, stirring until smooth. Stir in the lemon rind and let stand for 1 hour. Heat 1 or more wafer irons (a Scandinavian wafer iron may be used) until a drop of water sizzles on outside. Grease the iron, pour in 1 tablespoon batter, and cook over high heat, turning to cook evenly, 3 to 4 minutes on each side or until light golden color. Remove wafer and roll into a cylinder while still hot or leave unrolled. Makes 32 wafers.

BIRNENWECKEN

From prehistoric times, man has found sun- and fire-drying excellent ways to preserve surplus food. The Swiss use these methods to keep fruits, enjoying them through the winter as supplements to their daily breads. This pear cake is a specialty of the Berne district.

2 pounds dried pears
½ pound prunes
¼ pound figs
1 cup dry red wine
1 tablespoon butter
1½ cups chopped walnuts
1 cup coarsely chopped raisins
2 tablespoons each: minced candied orange peel, lemon peel, and citron
1 cup sugar

3 tablespoons powdered cinnamon
1 tablespoon powdered cloves
⅓ cup kirsch
3 tablespoons rose water or lemon juice, or to taste
Quadruple recipe Short Pastry (page 682) or double recipe Pain Ordinaire (page 645)
1 egg yolk for glazing
Vanilla Sugar (page 705)

Soak pears, prunes, and figs overnight in a mixture of wine and enough water to cover. Add butter and simmer in the wine for 40 minutes or until liquid evaporates and fruit is soft. Drain and cool. Remove pits from prunes and chop fruit coarsely. Add all remaining ingredients except pastry dough, egg yolk, and vanilla sugar, and mix thoroughly. This filling improves in flavor if it is left to ripen for 2 to 5 days in the refrigerator. Prepare dough as directed and roll out to 4 to 6 rectangles, each about 5 inches wide and 9 to 10 inches long. Spoon a ½-inch-thick strip of filling down the center of each dough rectangle, leaving 1½-inch band of dough on each side. Wrap dough around filling and gently turn over onto lightly buttered and floured cookie sheet so the seam side of the dough is down. Pinch ends closed with a little cold water and flatten rolls slightly. Prick the dough in several places with the tines of a fork. Cut a few diagonal slashes on each roll with a knife. If using yeast dough, let rise for 30 minutes. Brush dough with 1 egg yolk beaten with 2 tablespoons milk and bake in 375° oven for 30 to 45 minutes or until golden brown. Cut into 1- to 2-inch slices and serve warm or cold, sprinkled with vanilla sugar. Makes 30 to 40 slices.

VARIATION: If dried pears are unavailable, substitute peeled and cored fresh pears. Simmer for 5 minutes, drain, and add to cooked prune and fig mixture.

HAMENTASCHEN

Purim, the noisiest and merriest holiday in the Jewish calendar, celebrates the triumph of the beautiful Jewess, Queen Esther, over the wicked councilman, Haman. Envious of the exalted position of the Jews in Persia, Haman connived to destroy them. At a great banquet which Esther prepared for her husband, King Ahasuerus, she successfully pleaded the cause of the Jews and exposed Haman's treachery. Haman was sent to the gallows on the very day that the decree against the Jews was to be promulgated. Thenceforth, on the eve of Purim Jews have gone to the synagogue to hear the *Megillah*, the "Book of Esther," and rejoice in their deliverance. The children of the congregation are supplied with noisemakers which they rattle furiously at each mention of Haman's name—a symbolic "Bronx cheer" for the evil minister. The traditional food of this holiday is Hamentaschen, a tricornered poppy- or prune-filled bun meant to represent Haman's hat, his pockets (purse), or perhaps his donkey-shaped ears.

$1\frac{1}{2}$ recipes Rich Tart Pastry (page 681)
    made with 2 teaspoons baking powder
2 cups prune jam (lekvar)
2 teaspoons flour
Rind of 1 lemon, grated

Rind of $\frac{1}{2}$ orange, grated
$\frac{1}{3}$ cup finely ground walnuts
2 teaspoons powdered cinnamon
$\frac{1}{4}$ cup sugar, or to taste

Prepare pastry, sifting baking powder in with flour before cutting in butter. Blend prune jam with remaining ingredients, adding sugar to taste. Roll dough out to a $\frac{1}{4}$-inch thickness and cut into 20 to 24 3- to 4-inch circles. Place a heaping tablespoonful of filling in the center of each circle, then pinch edges of circle up around filling to form tricorn hats or pockets. Place $1\frac{1}{2}$ inches apart on a buttered cookie sheet. Bake in a preheated 350° oven 20 minutes.

CHINESE ALMOND COOKIES

$2\frac{1}{2}$ cups flour, sifted
$\frac{1}{2}$ cup ground blanched almonds
$\frac{1}{4}$ teaspoon salt
$1\frac{1}{2}$ teaspoons baking powder
$\frac{3}{4}$ cup vegetable shortening or butter

$1\frac{1}{2}$ teaspoons almond extract
$\frac{1}{2}$ cup sugar
2 egg yolks for glazing
20 to 24 whole blanched almonds

Mix all ingredients except egg yolks and whole almonds. Knead until smooth and divide into 20 to 24 balls. Flatten into round cakes and place 2 inches apart on ungreased cookie sheet. Brush with egg yolks mixed with a little water and press a whole almond in center of each cookie. Bake in a preheated 375° oven for 12 to 14 minutes or until golden. Makes about 24.

KOURABIEDES

According to Alexis, an ancient Greek dramatist, "He was a clever man who first invented the use of sweetmeats; for he added thus a pleasant lengthening to the feast, and saved men from unfill'd mouths and idle jaws unoccupied." Though such sweets as the crescent-shaped sugar cookie, Kourabiedes, may do little to inhibit gossip mongers in modern Greece, they are, nevertheless, served at virtually every festive occasion.

2 cups butter, softened
½ cup sugar
1 egg yolk
2 tablespoons cognac
1 teaspoon vanilla extract
4 cups flour, sifted

2 teaspoons baking powder (optional)
½ teaspoon powdered cloves
¼ teaspoon salt
½ cup toasted and finely chopped
    blanched almonds
Confectioners' sugar for dusting

In a bowl cream the butter and sugar until fluffy and light. Beat in the yolk until mixture is lemon colored. Add cognac and vanilla. Resift flour, baking powder, cloves, and salt. Work in the flour and the toasted almonds. Knead well. The dough will be stiff. Chill for 30 minutes. Roll into a long sausage, ½ inch thick. Cut into 2-inch pieces. Set on buttered cookie sheets and curve into crescents. Bake in a preheated 350° oven for 20 to 25 minutes or until barely golden. Cool and dust generously with confectioners' sugar. Makes about 40 cookies.

MA'AMOUL

John Keats' allusions to "lucent syrups" and "spiced dainties, every one, From silken Samarcand to cedared Lebanon" may have been inspired by cookies like the Lebanese Ma'Amoul. These Easter delicacies contained aromatic conserves and were traditionally molded in the bowls of ornately carved wooden spoons.

2 cups semolina or farina
1 cup butter
2 teaspoons orange flower water
2 teaspoons rose water

¾ cup sugar
1¼ cups finely chopped walnuts
Confectioners' sugar for dusting

Put semolina in a bowl, pour in 1½ cups boiling water, and stir briskly until thickened. Add the butter and mix well. Let stand well covered in a cool place overnight. Knead the mixture for 10 minutes. Form into 2-inch balls. Push a hollow into the center of each. Mix flavorings, sugar, and nuts and fill the cookies. Close cookie dough over filling. Arrange on buttered cookie sheets; flatten slightly with the hand. Crisscross with the tines of a fork. Bake in a preheated 350° oven until golden, about 20 to 25 minutes. Dust liberally with confectioners' sugar while still hot. Makes about 18 cookies.

SPRINGERLE

Springerle, southern German dialect for "little horse," is a traditional German cookie with roots in ancient pagan rites. The cookies originally were animal shaped, for in pre-Christian times it was the custom among Germanic tribes to celebrate the Winter Solstice, Julfest, with the sacrifice of real animals or tokens baked in dough. Springerle and literally hundreds of other cookies, many of them cut out or imprinted with wonderfully carved molds, have long since become associated with the Yule festivities. A sampling from a number of European countries is offered below.

4 eggs	$\frac{1}{2}$ teaspoon salt
2 cups sugar	1 teaspoon baking powder
Rind of 2 lemons, grated	$\frac{1}{4}$ cup whole aniseeds
$3\frac{1}{2}$ cups sifted flour, or as needed	

Beat eggs until light. Gradually beat in sugar, beating well with each addition, until mixture is very pale and thick. Stir in lemon rind. Resift *three cups flour* with salt and baking powder and add to egg mixture, adding *enough remaining flour* so that dough is smooth and not sticky. Chill dough for 1 hour. Sprinkle pastry board with sugar. Roll dough $\frac{1}{3}$ inch thick and cut with springerle molds or press with springerle roller. Butter cookie sheets and sprinkle with aniseeds. Separate cookies and place on sheets; let rest for 24 hours. Bake in a preheated 325° oven for 15 to 20 minutes or until cookies are barely golden on the edges. Do not brown. Cool and store in an airtight container for 10 days before using. Makes about 75 cookies.

GERMAN PFEFFERNUSSE

2 eggs	1 teaspoon baking powder
$1\frac{1}{2}$ cups sugar	$\frac{1}{8}$ teaspoon salt
3 cups flour, sifted	$1\frac{1}{2}$ ounces blanched almonds, ground
1 teaspoon powdered cinnamon	$1\frac{1}{2}$ ounces candied citron, minced
$\frac{1}{2}$ teaspoon each powdered allspice	1 teaspoon grated lemon rind
and cloves	$\frac{1}{2}$ cup rum
$\frac{1}{4}$ teaspoon black pepper	Confectioners' sugar for dusting
$\frac{1}{4}$ teaspoon powdered cardamom	

Beat eggs and sugar until light and fluffy. Resift flour with spices, baking powder, and salt. Add almonds, citron, and lemon rind to the sugar and eggs. Work in the flour. Chill dough. Form long rolls 1 inch in diameter and cut into $\frac{1}{2}$-inch-thick slices. Dry on cookie sheet overnight. Place on greased cookie sheet and bake in a preheated 300° oven for 15 to 20 minutes. Sprinkle with rum while warm and roll in confectioners' sugar. Store in airtight jar. Sprinkle with confectioners' sugar again before serving. Makes about 100 cookies.

DUTCH SPECULAAS

4 cups flour, sifted
4 teaspoons baking powder
½ teaspoon salt
1 tablespoon powdered cinnamon
1 teaspoon powdered cloves
1 teaspoon powdered nutmeg
½ teaspoon white pepper

½ teaspoon powdered aniseed
1 cup butter, softened
1 cup brown sugar
1 teaspoon grated lemon rind
⅓ to ½ cup milk
½ cup slivered blanched almonds

Resift the flour with all the dry ingredients. Cream butter and sugar until light and fluffy. Mix with seasoned flour and lemon rind. Add enough milk to make a soft dough. Roll out on a lightly floured board into a square about ½-inch thick; cut into 3-inch squares. Place on buttered cookie sheets and sprinkle with almonds, pressing them in lightly. Bake in a preheated 350° oven for 15 to 20 minutes or until light brown. Makes about 40 cookies.

BASLER LECKERLI
(Swiss Honey Cookies)

1⅓ cups honey
⅓ cup kirsch
1 cup sugar
¼ cup each finely chopped candied
    lemon and orange rind
Rind of 1 lemon, grated
1 cup coarsely ground almonds

1 tablespoon powdered cinnamon
1 teaspoon each powdered cloves
    and nutmeg
⅛ teaspoon salt
1 teaspoon baking soda
4 cups sifted flour, or as needed
1 recipe Sugar Icing (page 702)

Bring the honey to a boil in a large saucepan. Remove from heat and stir in the kirsch and sugar. Put back on low heat and cook until sugar is dissolved. Stir in the rinds and almonds. Remove from heat and cool to tepid. Resift the spices, salt, and baking soda with *three and one-half cups flour* and work into honey mixture gradually, stirring in *more flour* as needed so dough leaves the sides of the pan and is not sticky. This may take as long as 15 minutes. Put dough on a lightly floured board and roll out to ¼-inch thickness. Cut with special leckerli or springerle cookie cutters or into about 2- by 3-inch bars. Set closely side by side on generously buttered and floured cookie sheets. Cover with cloth and let stand at room temperature overnight. Bake in a preheated 350° oven for 20 to 25 minutes or until golden brown. Remove from heat and brush with icing while hot. Let cookies ripen in airtight containers for about 1 month before using. Makes about 45 cookies.

INDIAN BARFI

¾ cup sugar
1 tablespoon rose water
1 cup powdered milk, sifted

1 teaspoon powdered cardamom
½ cup chopped pistachio nuts

Boil sugar and 1¼ cups water until it spins a thread. Add rose water and powdered milk. Stir until thickened. Cook on low heat, stirring occasionally, for about 3 minutes or until very thick. Stir in cardamom powder and pistachios. Pour into a 9- by 9-inch well-buttered pan and let cool. Cut into diamonds and serve as cookies. Makes about 24 cookies.

PETTICOAT TAILS

Ladies' petticoats c. 1700 inspired the bell shape of these buttery Scottish shortbreads, a favorite accompaniment at teatime.

1 cup butter, softened
½ cup granulated or brown sugar
3 cups flour, sifted

½ teaspoon baking powder
1 teaspoon vanilla extract

Cream butter with sugar. Resift flour with baking powder and add to butter. Add vanilla. Press into 4 7-inch round pans and prick well all over with a fork. Press a small juice glass into the center of each pan to form a circular mark; then mark off eight wedges from circle to edge of each pan. Bake in a preheated 350° oven for about 20 minutes or until golden. Cool in pan. Gently cut markings and lift off. Almond extract or grated orange or lemon rind may be substituted for vanilla. Shortbreads may be decorated with multicolored sugar before baking or iced with thin Sugar Icing (page 702). Store in airtight box. Makes 32 shortbreads.

MACAROONS

Like macaroni, Macaroons were probably an Italian invention, both of them named for the process of mashing the ingredients—in this case almonds—to a pulp. They are one of the most popular of French *gâteaux*, or little oven cakes, and a specialty of the city of Nancy.

½ pound almonds, ground
¾ cup sugar
Pinch of salt

3 egg whites, unbeaten
½ teaspoon almond extract

Pound the ground almonds in a mortar, adding alternately the sugar, salt, egg whites, and almond extract. Line cookie sheets with brown paper and force small mounds of dough through a pastry bag fitted with a plain tube, or drop from a teaspoon. Space 2 inches apart.

Smooth tops with a pastry brush moistened with water. Bake in a preheated 400° oven for 15 to 20 minutes or until golden and puffed. Makes about 40. Keep in an airtight box. Instead of almonds ½ pound canned almond paste may be used; almond extract should then be omitted.

BISCOTTI ALL'ANICE

Italian Biscotti, French Biscuits, and German Zweibacken are all types of hard, dry cakes which have been twice cooked, as their names imply. First baked in loaf form, they are then sliced and toasted to a golden turn to make them crisp and long lasting. Europeans taste their first bracing biscuits as teething babies and, for the rest of their lives, are seldom without some plain or flavored variation to accompany wines, liquors, or cheese. The Biscotti with anise are an Italian specialty.

1⅓ cups sugar
4 eggs
2½ cups flour, sifted

1 tablespoon lightly crushed aniseed
Anisette liqueur (optional)

Beat sugar and eggs together until mixture is thick and almost white—about 10 minutes by hand, 5 minutes at medium speed in an electric mixer. Gradually resift flour into batter, stirring between additions. Stir in aniseed and turn batter into 2 8-inch buttered and floured loaf pans. Level batter with a spatula and bake in a preheated 375° oven for 20 to 25 minutes or until top is dry and pale golden brown. Turn cakes out of pans and cut into slices ¾ inch thick. Arrange slices on a lightly buttered cookie sheet and return to 375° oven for about 10 minutes, turning once so both sides of slices become golden brown. Sprinkle lightly with anisette, cool, and let dry. Stored in airtight container, these will last several weeks. Makes about 35 biscuits.

ENGLISH BRANDY SNAPS

1½ cups flour, sifted
¼ teaspoon salt
2 teaspoons powdered ginger
¼ teaspoon powdered nutmeg

¾ cup butter, melted
1 cup brown sugar
½ cup molasses
¼ cup brandy

Resift flour with dry ingredients. Mix hot melted butter, sugar, and molasses and add flour and brandy. Drop batter by heaping teaspoonfuls onto lightly buttered cookie sheets. Leave 2½-inch space between cookies. Bake in preheated 300° oven for 12 minutes. Cool until cookies can be easily picked up with the fingers. Roll loosely around the handle of a wooden spoon to form curls. If cookies harden before rolling, reheat slightly. Store in an airtight container. Cookies may be shaped into cones and filled with sweetened whipped cream mixed with finely chopped ginger preserves. Makes about 48 cookies.

ICINGS AND DESSERT SAUCES

Throughout the ages the justification for many a cake has resided in its icing, a term traced to the fact that the sugary coating hardened shortly after being applied. According to one nineteenth-century compendium, "There is no other class of culinary goods in which the ingenuity and skill of the cook . . . finds more scope for practice than in making and decorating Cakes." The writer went on to explain that expertise in the art of sugar-piping or ornamentation requires "persevering practice," a "thorough appreciation of the laws of design," and "manual dexterity" in forcing icing from paper or silk bags through variously shaped tubes. Carême, the consummate sugar-piper of his day, dabbed minute motifs on individual Napolitains and emblazoned enormous set pieces with such rich culinary paints as Butter Cream, Fondant (literally "melting"), and the other icings listed below.

BUTTER CREAM

$\frac{1}{2}$ cup sweet butter, softened
$3\frac{1}{2}$ cups confectioners' sugar
$\frac{1}{8}$ teaspoon salt
1 egg yolk
1 tablespoon milk, if needed

Flavorings:
1 teaspoon vanilla or almond extract; or
2 teaspoons strong coffee, rum, or
cognac; or 4 ounces bitter chocolate
melted in 2 tablespoons water and
cooled; or 3 tablespoons crushed
Pralin (page 705) or pistachio nuts

Cream the butter until fluffy. Beat in the sugar, salt, and egg yolk until thick and creamy. Add milk, if needed for consistency. Flavor with one or a combination of flavorings and tint with food coloring as desired. Makes about $2\frac{1}{2}$ cups.

BOILED ICING

2 egg whites
$\frac{1}{8}$ teaspoon salt

1 cup hot Sugar Syrup (page 704)
1 teaspoon vanilla extract

Beat the egg whites and salt until they stand in moist, glossy peaks. Pour in the hot syrup very gradually, beating hard until frosting is thick and of a good spreading consistency. Flavor with vanilla. Makes about 2 cups, enough to fill and frost a 9-inch layer cake. Icing may be flavored with almond extract or lemon juice tinted with 1 or 2 drops food coloring. Water in syrup may be replaced by fruit juice, such as strawberry, raspberry, orange, or pineapple juice. Add 1 teaspoon lemon juice to fruit flavorings.

DARK CHOCOLATE ICING

6 ounces semisweet chocolate
2 tablespoons butter
1 teaspoon vanilla extract

$\frac{1}{8}$ teaspoon salt
2 cups confectioners' sugar, sifted
$\frac{1}{3}$ cup milk, or as needed

Melt the chocolate in top of a double boiler over simmering water until completely melted. Add butter, vanilla, and salt. Mix with the sugar, beat hard with a wooden spoon, adding milk until icing becomes thick and is of a good spreading consistency. Makes about $1\frac{3}{4}$ cups, enough to ice a 9-inch layer cake.

FONDANT ICING

4 cups sugar
2 tablespoons corn syrup

$1\frac{1}{3}$ cups cold water

To prepare fondant: Put sugar, corn syrup, and water in a heavy saucepan and stir constantly over low heat until sugar is completely melted (this is a very important step in the making of fondant as any unmelted sugar will cause crystallization of the syrup). Cover the saucepan and cook on low heat for 5 minutes so steam will melt crystals on sides of the pan. Remove cover and with a pastry brush dipped in warm water wash off from the sides of the saucepan any sugar crystals. Boil uncovered for 5 minutes or until sugar reaches 238° (or can form a soft ball in cold water). Remove from heat being careful not to jar the pan, and let stand until bubbles have disappeared. Pour with care onto a marble slab wiped off with a damp cloth or to the depth of 1 inch in a pyrex dish rinsed with cold water. Do not scrape saucepan. When fondant is cool enough to handle, work it with a spatula with a scraping and folding motion. As it thickens, it will become opaque and eventually will make a thick white crumbly mass. Knead this mass a little at a time until soft and no sugary lumps remain. Allow to stand at room temperature for 24 hours or longer covered with a damp cloth or in a covered container. It may then be stored in the refrigerator for several weeks. Use for coating candies or icing cakes. Makes 3 cups.

To prepare fondant icing: Warm 1 cup fondant in the top of a double boiler over 1 inch of barely simmering water, making sure water does not touch upper saucepan. Thin the fondant with about 1 tablespoon boiling water to a pouring consistency. Pour fondant on the cake and tilt and rotate the cake to spread icing. Do not spread with knife or it will spoil glossy finish of icing. Rewarm fondant icing as needed if it hardens. Makes enough to ice top of 9-inch layer cake.

VARIATIONS: *Chocolate Fondant Icing*: Soften 1 cup fondant in a double boiler. Add 2 ounces melted semisweet chocolate and about 1 tablespoon boiling water (or rum, cognac, or any liqueur) as needed to thin the fondant. *Coffee Fondant Icing*: Thin fondant with 1 to 2 tablespoons strong coffee. *Orange Fondant Icing*: Thin fondant with 1 to 2 tablespoons orange liqueur (such as triple-sec, cointreau, or curaçao).

SUGAR ICING

3 to 4 cups confectioners' sugar   Vanilla extract

Gradually add 2 to 4 tablespoons boiling water to sugar until icing is of a thick, spreading consistency. Flavor with a few drops of vanilla. For a thin icing, add additional boiling water very slowly until icing is of desired consistency. Makes about 2 cups.

PASTRY CREAM

Rich fillings had embellished cakes, pies, and other desserts for centuries before Louis Eustache Ude observed that "all crèmes are made in the like manner; the taste and colour only vary." Medieval French cooks, attempting to copy renowned English custards, renamed them *crèmes* (from the Latin *cremare*, to burn) after pitfalls presumably encountered. However, the French soon surpassed their mentors, and by the nineteenth century few were immune to the delicate confections, except perhaps Alexandre Dumas' fictional Porthos, who was more musketeer than gastronome. When offered some creams, he declined thus: "with regard to sweet dishes, I recognize only pastry, and even that should be rather solid; all those frothy substances swell my stomach, and occupy a space which seems to me to be too precious to be so badly tenanted." Among the cream fillings which have made culinary history are such pastry creams as Saint-Honoré, named for the patron of pastry cooks, and Frangipane, the macaroon-flavored creation of Count Cesare Frangipani, a suitor of Catherine de' Medici; and the whipped cream Chantilly, commemorating the Prince of Condé's château.

6 egg yolks
Pinch of salt
$\frac{3}{4}$ cup sugar
4 tablespoons flour

$1\frac{1}{2}$ cups milk or light cream
1 2-inch piece vanilla bean or
    2 teaspoons vanilla extract

Beat the egg yolks with the salt and sugar until thick and very light. Add the flour and beat until smooth. Meanwhile, scald the milk with the vanilla bean and pour into the eggs, stirring briskly. Return to the saucepan, place on low heat, and stir until the mixture is thickened. Keep stirring until the custard is very smooth. Remove from the heat and strain. If not using the vanilla bean, add the vanilla extract. Cool, covered with a piece of buttered wax paper. Stir well before using. Makes about 3 cups.

VARIATIONS: *Frangipane Cream*: Add 1 cup crumbled macaroons, $\frac{1}{2}$ cup toasted ground almonds, and $\frac{1}{3}$ cup butter. After pastry cream has been cooked and slightly cooled, $\frac{1}{2}$ cup heavy cream, whipped, may be folded in. *Crème Saint-Honoré*: Add $\frac{1}{2}$ envelope unflavored gelatin to pastry cream while still hot. Cool and fold in 4 stiffly beaten egg whites.

ALMOND PASTE

Since antiquity, almond paste has been the basis of innumerable confectioneries, among them the Marzipan which Crusaders first tasted in the lands of Islam. It was shaped like the *mawthabān*, a medieval coin of the realm. The candy gradually became standard holiday fare throughout Europe; the gifts given to Queen Elizabeth one New Year included a chessboard, Saint Paul's Cathedral, and Saint George, all modeled in Marzipan. Shaped into battlements, the candy also inspired a parlor game of the period, as described by the poet John Taylor, in which "Castles for ladies and for carpet knights [were] Unmercifully spoiled at feasting fights" by volleys of sugarplums from the assembled.

$1\frac{1}{2}$ cups finely ground blanched almonds
1 cup sugar
2 egg whites
$\frac{1}{4}$ teaspoon almond extract

Pound the almonds, sugar, and egg whites until they are smooth; flavor with almond extract. Keep in an airtight container. Use in baking as directed in recipes. Makes about $2\frac{1}{4}$ cups. Almond paste may also be purchased in cans.

VARIATION: *Marzipan*: Add 1 cup confectioners' sugar, a few drops of any desired flavoring, and a drop or two of food coloring to 1 cup of almond paste. Place on a cold surface and knead 15 to 20 minutes. Mold into desired candy shapes or spread over cakes before icing.

CREME CHANTILLY

$1\frac{1}{2}$ cups heavy cream
3 to 4 tablespoons sugar
1 to 2 teaspoons vanilla extract

Whip the cream until it begins to stiffen; add sugar and vanilla to taste. Continue beating until stiff. Makes 2 to $2\frac{1}{2}$ cups.

CUSTARD SAUCE

3 egg yolks
$\frac{1}{4}$ cup sugar
Pinch of salt
$1\frac{1}{2}$ cups light cream
1 teaspoon rose water (optional)
1 teaspoon vanilla or almond extract
or 1 tablespoon rum, brandy,
sherry, or dry white wine

Beat the yolk of egg, sugar, and salt until very light in color. Scald the cream and pour into the eggs, stirring briskly. Pour into the top of a double boiler placed over 1-inch barely simmering water. Cook, stirring until mixture coats the spoon—about 7 to 8 minutes. Cool, stirring occasionally; flavor with rose water and vanilla extract and chill. Makes $2\frac{1}{2}$ cups.

APRICOT-ORANGE SAUCE

$\frac{1}{2}$ cup canned apricot nectar
$\frac{1}{2}$ cup orange marmalade
Juice of 1 orange

1 tablespoon lemon juice, or to taste
$\frac{1}{4}$ cup slivered blanched almonds
2 tablespoons orange liqueur (optional)

Mix apricot nectar with marmalade and set over very low heat until marmalade melts. Remove from heat; stir in orange and lemon juice. At serving time, add almonds and orange liqueur. Serve at room temperature with puddings and soufflés. Makes about $1\frac{1}{2}$ cups.

HOT CHOCOLATE SAUCE

2 cups milk
2 egg yolks
$\frac{1}{4}$ cup sugar
2 teaspoons cornstarch

3 ounces semisweet chocolate, grated
1 teaspoon vanilla extract or 2 teaspoons
   rum, brandy, or strong coffee
2 egg whites, stiffly beaten (optional)

Scald milk in top of double boiler and cool slightly. Beat egg yolks with sugar and cornstarch until frothy. Pour milk into yolk mixture slowly, beating constantly. Pour back into top of double boiler and add grated chocolate. Set over hot, not boiling water and cook slowly, stirring constantly until sauce becomes thick enough to coat a spoon. Stir in flavoring. To make a foamy sauce, fold in stiffly beaten egg whites after adding flavoring and whip until frothy. Serve hot or cold. Makes $2\frac{1}{2}$ cups.

HARD SAUCE

$\frac{1}{2}$ cup sweet butter, softened
$1\frac{1}{4}$ cups confectioners' sugar
1 egg white, slightly beaten

1 teaspoon vanilla extract or
   1 tablespoon cognac or rum

Cream the butter with the sugar and egg white until thick and fluffy. Flavor with vanilla, cognac, or rum. Chill well before using. Serve with steamed puddings. Makes $1\frac{1}{4}$ cups.

SUGAR SYRUP

4 cups sugar
2 cups water

$\frac{1}{4}$ cup white corn syrup

Boil all ingredients together until syrup reaches 240° on a candy thermometer. Stored at room temperature in an airtight container it keeps indefinitely. Makes 2 to 3 cups. Use as directed in icings or as a base for candies.

PRALIN

1 cup sugar

$\frac{1}{8}$ teaspoon cream of tartar

$\frac{1}{2}$ cup water

1 cup slivered blanched almonds

Bring the sugar, cream of tartar, and water to a boil. Cook, stirring until sugar is dissolved. Add the almonds and cook without stirring until syrup and almonds have turned a golden brown. Pour into a well-buttered pan and cool. Remove almonds and place on a board, cover with a cloth, and using a rolling pin crush into small pieces or a powder, depending on use. Store in a closed jar. Makes 1 cup pralin pieces or $\frac{1}{2}$ cup powder. Use on cakes, as a topping for ice cream, or in puddings.

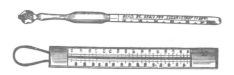

VANILLA SUGAR

Produced by a variety of orchid, vanilla was first cultivated in Mexico, where Spanish conquistadors tasted it in the chocolate drink of the Aztecs. Cortes carried it back to Europe, along with cacao beans, in the 1520's; but it was several decades before anyone thought to use it independently as a flavoring. Queen Elizabeth's apothecary is cited for that sapient discovery.

2 cups sugar

1 vanilla bean

Put sugar in a jar with vanilla bean; close tightly. Let stand for at least 2 days before using. Use for flavoring desserts according to directions in recipes.

CHOCOLATE CURLS

3 ounces semisweet chocolate

Melt chocolate in top of double boiler set over boiling water. When completely melted, stir with a wooden spoon until smooth and pour onto a flat plate or marble slab. Spread to a 6-inch circle. Cool until chocolate is firm but not brittle. Draw the blade of a paring knife across top of chocolate, holding blade parallel to the plate, so that chocolate is peeled off in curls. For chocolate shavings, let squares of semisweet chocolate soften slightly at room temperature and draw a knife across the back.

DESSERTS
AND
SWEETS

MILK AND EGG SWEET CUSTARD

Such delicacies as custards were suitable only for women and children, so the ancient Greeks thought. The Roman philosopher Seneca agreed, charging that Apicius in recipes like the one below softened Roman fiber and "through his teachings corrupted the era."

1 quart milk
1 2-inch piece vanilla bean or
   2 teaspoons vanilla extract
$\frac{1}{2}$ cup honey with 2 tablespoons sugar

$\frac{1}{4}$ teaspoon salt
4 whole eggs
2 egg yolks
$\frac{1}{2}$ teaspoon grated lemon rind

Scald the milk with the vanilla bean or extract, honey mixture, and salt; then cool. Beat eggs and egg yolks together. Add milk mixture to eggs. Beat until smooth. Add the grated lemon rind. Pour into a 6-cup mold or individual custard cups. Bake in a pan of water in a preheated 350° oven for 45 minutes or until a knife comes out clean when inserted 1 inch from edge of custard. Chill and, if desired, unmold. Serves 6 to 8.

BLANC-MANGER

To cooks of medieval England, Blanc-manger or "white food," meant a smooth mixture of almond milk, rice, honey, and poultry which had been put through a "sarse" (sieve). By the late 1600's however, Blanc-manger specified a delicate dessert cream which often took such imaginative shapes as fish set afloat in quivering ponds of wine jelly. At the outset of the Victorian era, Grimod de la Reynière mourned that "only two or three cooks of the old school were reputed to know how to make it and we are very much afraid that the secret may have been lost since the Revolution."

1 cup finely ground blanched almonds
$2\frac{1}{2}$ cups heavy cream
$\frac{3}{4}$ cup sugar
2 envelopes unflavored gelatin

1 teaspoon rose water (optional)
1 teaspoon almond extract
3 egg whites, stiffly beaten
$\frac{1}{8}$ teaspoon salt

Pour 1½ cups cold water over almonds and let them stand for 2 to 3 hours. Strain through a cloth, pressing hard on almonds to extract all possible liquid. Reserve almond "milk," discard the nuts. Scald the cream with the sugar, stirring until sugar is melted. Soak the gelatin in ½ cup cold water, dissolve in the hot cream, then cool. Flavor with rose water and almond extract and combine with the almond milk. When the mixture begins to set, fold in the egg whites with the salt. Pour into a 2-quart buttered ring mold and chill until set. Unmold. Fill with berries, serve with almond-flavored Custard Sauce (page 703). Serves 6.

BAVARIAN CREAM

Although the Victorians pretended not to brook much that was overtly sensuous, they were enthralled by the glistening quiver of this penultimate pudding. The mid-to-late-nineteenth century was the heyday of molded desserts, and the Bavarian reigned supreme, being spectacular in both taste and appearance. Its origin is dubious, perhaps the creation of a French chef employed in Bavaria.

2 envelopes unflavored gelatin	¾ cup sugar
2 cups milk	7 egg yolks
1 2-inch piece vanilla bean or	Pinch of salt
2 teaspoons vanilla extract	2 cups heavy cream, stiffly whipped

Soak the gelatin in ½ cup cold water. Scald the milk, with the vanilla bean and sugar, in the top of a large double boiler. Beat the egg yolks and salt until thick and lemon colored. Gradually beat into the hot milk. Cook over 1 inch barely simmering water, stirring with a wooden spoon until custard coats the spoon—about 10 minutes. Strain into a large bowl, add gelatin, and stir until dissolved and cool. When custard starts to thicken, fold in the cream. Pour into an 8-cup mold rinsed out in cold water. When using vanilla extract, add at same time as gelatin. Chill for several hours. Unmold. Serves 8 to 10.

VARIATIONS: *Coffee Bavarian Cream*: Replace ½ cup of the milk with ½ cup very strong coffee. *Chocolate Bavarian Cream*: Use ¼ cup sweet cocoa in place of ¼ cup of the sugar, and 1 tablespoon dark rum instead of vanilla. *Raspberry Bavarian Cream*: Add 1 extra egg yolk and use 1 cup brown sugar instead of the granulated sugar. Fold in 1 cup of puréed raspberries along with the whipped cream. Other puréed fruits may replace raspberries.

KAERNEMAELKS FROMAGE
(Danish Buttermilk Mousse)

2 envelopes unflavored gelatin
2 cups buttermilk
½ cup sugar

¾ cup chopped blanched almonds
1 teaspoon grated lemon rind
2 cups heavy cream, whipped

Soak the gelatin in ½ cup water. Mix the buttermilk, sugar, almonds, and lemon rind. Melt the gelatin over boiling water. Cool and add to the buttermilk mixture, stirring it in well. When the buttermilk mixture begins to stiffen, fold in the whipped cream. Pour into a glass bowl or an 8-cup mold, first rinsed in cold water. Chill well until set. Unmold. Serve with fresh or thawed frozen strawberries or other fruit. Serves 8.

APPLE CREAM

For Sir Theodore de Mayerne the compiling of the *Archimagirus Anglo-Gallicus* (1658), from which this recipe was taken, was just a side line. Professionally he held the influential post of physician to Charles I and directed the Company of London Distillers in making "strong Waters." His name was so widely esteemed that even sixty-five years after his death an enterprising quack could successfully tout "Sir Theodore de Mayerne's . . . Opiate for the teeth; viz makes them clean and white as Ivory, although black and rotten, fasteneth and preserveth them."

6 apples, quartered
1½ cups sugar
2 cups rosé wine
Rind of 1 lemon
Pinch of dried rosemary

Pinch of dried thyme
1 envelope unflavored gelatin
½ cup sweet sherry
1 cup heavy cream, whipped

Place the apples in a pan with the sugar, rosé wine, lemon rind, rosemary, and thyme. Simmer until apples are very soft. Strain and reserve wine. Purée the apples through a fine strainer into a bowl, add reserved wine. Soak gelatin in sherry for 5 minutes. Melt over hot water and add to apples. Stir well and cool. When the apple mixture begins to stiffen, fold in the cream. Pour into a mold that has been rinsed in cold water and chill in the refrigerator until firm. Unmold. Serve plain or with a Custard Sauce (page 703). Serves 6 to 8.

MOUSSE AU CHOCOLAT

In nineteenth-century France a recipe writer did well to watch both his pots and his politicians. The cookbook in which the next two recipes appeared was first published in 1806 under the title *Le Cuisinier Impérial*; subsequent editions—thirty-two in all—were renamed *Le Cuisinier Royal* and *Le Cuisinier National* to suit the government in power. The author, Monsieur Viard, evidently had a patrician audience in mind, for he provided instructions for serving sit-down dinners for twenty to sixty guests.

$\frac{1}{2}$ pound semisweet chocolate
$\frac{1}{2}$ cup water or strong coffee
6 eggs, separated
$\frac{1}{2}$ cup sugar

3 tablespoons dark rum or cognac, or
  2 teaspoons vanilla extract
Pinch of salt
1 cup heavy cream, whipped

Melt the chocolate in the water over low heat. Cool slightly. Beat the egg yolks with the sugar until thick and very pale. Mix in the chocolate and flavoring. Whip the egg whites with the salt until stiff. Fold the whipped cream into the chocolate and then fold in the egg whites. Pour into a 10-cup serving dish. Chill for at least 6 hours before serving. Serves 8 to 10.

PETITS POTS DE CREME

2 cups heavy cream
$\frac{1}{2}$ cup sugar

1 tablespoon orange flower water or
  1 teaspoon vanilla extract
6 egg yolks

Scald the cream, add the sugar and orange flower water. Beat the egg yolks until thick and very pale. Gradually pour in the cream, stirring briskly. Pour into 8 individual custard cups. Put the cups into a pan containing 1 inch of hot water and bake in a preheated 350° oven until a knife inserted into custard comes out clean—about 15 minutes. Chill. Serves 8.

VARIATIONS: *Chocolate Pots de Crème*: Use only $\frac{1}{4}$ cup sugar and 4 egg yolks. Melt 4 squares semisweet chocolate with $\frac{1}{4}$ cup water or coffee. Beat into egg yolks. Add 1 teaspoon vanilla. Proceed as above. *Caramel Pots de Crème*: First caramelize the sugar with 2 tablespoons water. Proceed as above. *Pistachio Pots de Crème*: Scald the cream with $\frac{1}{2}$ cup finely chopped pistachios. Beat 1 whole egg and 4 yolks and proceed as above. Add a little green coloring before pouring into custard cups.

ZUPPA INGLESE

A dukedom, a country palace, and this rich dessert were among the many tributes bestowed on Lord Nelson by the grateful Neapolitans after his victory over Napoleon in the Nile in 1798. "English Soup," as it was called, was the creation of an anonymous pastry cook smitten with the admiral, the English, and their spirit-soaked Trifles.

2 8-inch spongecake layers	$\frac{1}{2}$ cup blanched slivered almonds
1 cup dark rum	$1\frac{1}{2}$ cups heavy cream, whipped,
1 recipe Pastry Cream (page 702)	sweetened, and flavored with
$\frac{1}{4}$ cup minced candied fruit	vanilla extract

Cut the spongecake into 4 layers. Put 1 layer of cake on a serving platter and sprinkle with *four tablespoons rum*. Mix the pastry cream with the candied fruit and the almonds. Put one-third of the pastry cream mixture on first cake layer. Put second layer of cake on cream and repeat, sprinkling with *four tablespoons rum* and adding half the remaining pastry cream. Add third layer of cake, spread with remaining pastry cream, and sprinkle on remaining rum. Top with last cake layer. Chill for several hours. Cover with whipped cream. Serves 8.

VARIATION: *Trifle*: Cut 2 spongecake layers into strips and place in large, deep glass bowl. Sprinkle with $\frac{1}{2}$ cup sherry or Madeira and let wine soak in. Spread with strawberry or raspberry jam and cover with pastry cream; top with whipped cream and crystallized violets. *German Plettenpudding*: Place a layer of ladyfingers in a bowl. Sprinkle with sweet sherry, then cover with a layer of thawed frozen raspberries and juice, and then cover with a layer of pastry cream. Sprinkle with crumbled macaroons and repeat, ending with pastry cream. Sprinkle with toasted, slivered blanched almonds. Chill well before serving.

ZABAGLIONE

Catherine de' Medici, bride of Henry II in 1533, is often credited with bringing the culinary enlightenment to France. As part of her considerable dowry, she imported a small staff of Florentine cooks equipped to produce the finest in Renaissance cuisine. Zabaglione, a hot, foamy custard steeped in the sweet, fortified Marsala wine of Sicily, was one of her most appreciated gifts. The recipe below is from *L'Arte di ben cucinare* (1662) by Bartolomeo Stefani.

6 egg yolks	6 tablespoons Marsala wine
3 tablespoons sugar	or sweet sherry

Place egg yolks in the top of a double boiler and beat with a rotary or electric beater. Gradually add the sugar and beat until foamy. Place over 1 inch of simmering water. Add wine (traditionally, half an eggshellful of wine per yolk). Beat until mixture triples and is very thick and hot. Serve hot as a dessert in parfait or wine glasses or as a sauce for beignets or poached fruit. Serves 6.

VARIATION: *Cold Zabaglione*: Pour hot zabaglione into a bowl. Set in a larger bowl of ice and beat vigorously until cold and thick. Chill until ready to serve.

APPLE CHARLOTTE

No sooner had Carême created Charlotte Russe to please Czar Alexander I, than many culinary historians began to credit him with Apple Charlotte. In fact, the apple dessert is much older (although the version below comes from the English edition of Beauvillier's *Art of French Cooking*, 1824) and shares nothing in common with Carême's confection except a shadowy lady's name, a special mold in which both are made, and a delicious result.

5 pounds apples, peeled, cored, and sliced	$\frac{1}{4}$ cup applejack, Calvados, or dark rum
1 cup sugar	$\frac{2}{3}$ cup apricot preserves, strained
Rind of 1 lemon	2 teaspoons vanilla extract
16 thin slices white bread	1 cup heavy cream, whipped, sweetened, and flavored
1 cup butter, melted	

Put apples, sugar, and lemon rind in a saucepan with $\frac{1}{3}$ cup water. Cover and cook on low heat, occasionally stirring with a wooden spoon, for about 10 minutes or until just tender. Uncover and continue cooking and stirring until the juice has evaporated and mixture is very thick. If purée is thin, add 1 cup crumbled stale cake, ladyfingers, or macaroon crumbs. Cut *four bread slices* into rectangles to cover the bottom of an 8-cup charlotte mold. Cut *eight slices bread* into sticks $1\frac{1}{2}$ inches wide to stand overlapping around sides of mold. Butter mold, dip bread into melted butter, and line bottom and sides of mold. Discard lemon rind and add applejack, apricot preserves, and vanilla to apples. Pour mixture into mold. Cut *remaining bread slices* into rectangles, dip in butter, and cover apples. Bake in a preheated 375° oven for 45 minutes or until bread is golden brown. Let cool for 30 minutes, invert quickly onto a serving platter, and cool 20 to 30 minutes longer before removing mold. Serve with sweetened whipped cream flavored with applejack. Serves 6 to 8. Other fruit purées may be substituted for apples.

711

CABINET PUDDING

After shrewdly serving as chef to both Louis XVI and a Bonaparte, Louis Eustache Ude moved across the Channel, where in 1813 he published *The French Cook; or The Art of Cookery*. Stating in the preface that "This work, not withstanding the utility it might be of in Paris, is more particularly intended for England," he included such solid fare as Cabinet Pudding, also called Poudin à la Chancelière, to honor either a Parliamentarian or a Chancellor's wife. In this recipe the abstemious Ude remarked, "some people will add a little brandy, but I disapprove."

2 cups milk	1 cup raisins
1 2-inch piece vanilla bean or	3 tablespoons cognac or rum
1 teaspoon vanilla extract	24 ladyfingers
3 eggs	2 cups Custard Sauce (page 703)
⅔ cup sugar	flavored with cognac or rum

Scald the milk with the vanilla bean. Beat the eggs with *one-half cup sugar* and pour in the hot milk, stirring briskly. Soak the raisins in the cognac. Butter a deep 8-cup mold, such as a charlotte mold, and sugar it with *remaining sugar*. Arrange a layer of ladyfingers, cut to fit, on bottom of mold and pour over some strained custard to soak the cake, sprinkle with raisins. Repeat layers, ending with ladyfingers and custard. Set in a pan half full of hot water and bake in a preheated 350° oven until an inserted knife comes out clean, about 50 to 60 minutes. Remove pan from water and let set for 8 to 10 minutes. Unmold and pour on the custard sauce. Serve hot. Serves 8. Raisins may be replaced by 1 cup diced preserved fruit.

SANKHAYA
(Thai Coconut Custard)

8 small coconuts	2 cups Coconut Cream (page 632)
1 cup palm sugar or brown sugar	8 eggs, lightly beaten

Scrape coconut shells until smooth and free of fibers. Saw off tops a third of the way down to form lids. Pour out liquid and dry inside of coconuts. If fresh coconuts are not available, custard may be baked in individual custard cups. Dissolve sugar in the coconut cream, add eggs, and beat thoroughly. Strain through fine sieve into coconuts or baking dishes. Cover with lids. Set on rack or trivet in large pot with enough boiling water to come to the bottom of the coconuts. Cover pot and steam for about 30 minutes or until custard is firm. (Lift lids of coconuts during cooking to check.) If using custard cups, make a tight lid with a triple thickness of aluminum foil. Add more boiling water as needed. Serve hot or cold. Serves 8.

SOUFFLE

Patrons of La Grande Taverne de Londres, which opened in Paris in the 1780's, were perhaps the first to enjoy this dessert soufflé. It comes from the repertoire of Beauvilliers, who, wrote Brillat-Savarin, "was for more than fifteen years the most famous restaurateur in Paris. . . . Vehicles of all nations were constantly at his door; he knew all the heads of foreign contingents, and learned to speak all their languages as well as was necessary for his business. . . . When he became aware that a party of wealthy folk had sat down at one of his tables, he would approach them with a very zealous air, bow to the ground, and flatter his guests with the most marked attention. . . . But this amphitryonic rôle lasted but a moment; having fulfilled it, he withdrew from the scene; and ere long the swollen bill . . . amply established the difference between a host and a restaurateur." Beauvilliers' *L'Art du Cuisinier*, written toward the end of his notable career, "bears the seal of enlightened practice," Brillat-Savarin noted, "and still commands the same respect with which it was received on first appearance."

3 tablespoons butter	1 2-inch piece vanilla bean or
3 tablespoons flour	2 teaspoons vanilla extract
1 cup milk	4 egg yolks
$\frac{1}{3}$ cup sugar	6 egg whites
	$\frac{1}{4}$ teaspoon salt

Melt the butter in a large saucepan. Add flour and cook for 3 minutes without browning. Scald milk with sugar and vanilla bean. Pour into flour and butter, stirring briskly. Simmer for 4 to 5 minutes and cool. Remove vanilla bean. Beat in the egg yolks, one by one. Beat egg whites with salt until stiff but moist and fold into yolk mixture. If using vanilla extract, fold in with egg whites. Pour into a 6-cup buttered and sugared soufflé mold. Bake in a preheated 400° oven for 20 minutes. Sprinkle with sugar and bake for 5 minutes more for a runny soufflé, 10 minutes for a firm soufflé. Serve immediately. Serves 4. Serve plain or with fruit sauce or Apricot-Orange Sauce (page 704).

VARIATIONS: *Apricot or Prune Soufflé*: Add 1 cup puréed cooked apricots or prunes to soufflé mixture before adding egg yolks. Add 2 tablespoons of kirsch before folding in egg whites; omit vanilla. *Coffee Pralin Soufflé*: Replace $\frac{1}{4}$ cup milk with $\frac{1}{4}$ cup strong coffee. Add $\frac{1}{3}$ cup crumbled Pralin (page 705) before adding egg whites. *Strawberry Soufflé*: Marinate 2 cups sliced strawberries in $\frac{1}{2}$ cup triple-sec or cointreau, $\frac{1}{2}$ cup orange juice, and 1 tablespoon lemon juice for 1 hour. Drain $\frac{1}{2}$ cup strawberry juice and add to $\frac{1}{2}$ cup milk to prepare soufflé. Place berries in bottom of soufflé dish with remaining juice, cover with soufflé mixture, and bake as above. *Chocolate Soufflé*: Use only 3 egg yolks. Melt 2 squares unsweetened chocolate in 2 tablespoons water or strong coffee. Add to soufflé mixture before adding egg yolks. Reduce vanilla flavoring to 1 teaspoon. Serve immediately with whipped cream sweetened to taste or with Custard Sauce (page 703) flavored with rum or brandy.

OMELETTE SOUFFLE

Grimod de la Reynière, *doyen* of French gastronomes in the decades following the French Revolution, awarded this sweet omelette his certificate of *"légitimation"* concluding with the opinion that "this dainty, as is immediately apparent, is nutritive, salubrious, and of excellent taste; it cannot fail to be adopted wherever it is known."

8 eggs, separated

4 tablespoons sugar

2 teaspoons orange flower water or
   1 teaspoon vanilla extract

Salt

$\frac{1}{4}$ cup butter

Beat the egg yolks with *three tablespoons sugar* and the orange flower water until thick and very light. Beat the egg whites with a little salt until stiff. Fold into the yolks. Heat the butter until it froths in a 10-inch skillet that has an ovenproof handle. Add the eggs and cook gently for 5 minutes. Put the frying pan into a preheated 400° oven for 10 minutes. Fold in half and sprinkle with the *remaining tablespoon sugar*. Put under the broiler for 1 minute to glaze. Slide onto a heated platter and serve immediately. Serves 4. A little grated lemon rind may be added to the yolks. The omelette may be spread with cherry, strawberry, or apricot jam before folding.

OEUFS A LA NEIGE

5 eggs, separated

$\frac{1}{4}$ teaspoon cream of tartar

$\frac{1}{4}$ teaspoon salt

$1\frac{1}{4}$ cups sugar

2 cups milk

1 2-inch piece vanilla bean or
   2 teaspoons vanilla extract

2 tablespoons cognac or rum (optional)

Beat egg whites with cream of tartar and salt until they stand in soft peaks. Beat in *three-quarters cup sugar*, 2 tablespoons at a time, until meringue is very thick and stiff. Scald milk, *3 tablespoons sugar*, and vanilla bean in a wide, deep saucepan. Shape the meringues with a large tablespoon and poach in the milk over a very low heat for about 3 minutes. Turn gently with two forks to cook them on the other side. Remove with a slotted spoon to a serving dish. Beat the egg yolks until very thick and pour into the hot milk in a thin stream, beating constantly. Open the vanilla bean and scrape seeds into custard. (If using vanilla extract, add to the hot milk.) Cook custard in the top of a double boiler over 1 inch of barely simmering water, stirring with wooden spoon until mixture coats spoon. Cool. Add cognac and pour around meringues. Caramelize *remaining sugar* and dribble over meringues. Serves 5 to 6.

FRANKFORT CHOCOLATE PUDDING

½ cup butter
¾ cup sugar
5 eggs, separated
3 ounces semisweet chocolate, melted
1 tablespoon rum or brandy

1½ cups grated almonds
3 tablespoons dry bread or
zwieback crumbs
Whipped cream or Hot Chocolate Sauce
(page 704)

Cream the butter and *two-thirds cup sugar* together until light and fluffy. Add egg yolks, one at a time, beating between each addition. Add chocolate, rum, nuts, and crumbs and stir in thoroughly. Beat egg whites with *one tablespoon sugar* until they stand in stiff, glossy peaks. Fold into chocolate mixture gently but thoroughly, using a rubber spatula. Spread the inside of a melon mold or other pudding mold with butter. Sprinkle with *remaining sugar* and tap out excess. Pour filling into mold, cover tightly, and place in larger pan with enough water to come a little more than half way up the sides of the mold. Cover larger pot and steam pudding for about 1¼ hours or until completely set. Remove from hot water and let stand for 5 minutes before removing cover. Invert onto serving plate and serve with whipped cream or chocolate sauce. Serves 6 to 8.

SNOW SPONGE WITH MANDARIN ORANGES

Thick clusters of mandarin orange groves surround Japan's resort city of Atami where this dish is a specialty. The golden fruit is thought to be named for the richly colored robes of the Chinese mandarins.

1½ envelopes unflavored gelatin
1 can mandarin oranges
2 cups sugar

2 egg whites
1 teaspoon almond extract

Soak the gelatin in ½ cup cold water. Drain the syrup from the mandarin oranges. Add enough water to this syrup to make 1½ cups. Add the sugar and boil for 5 minutes. Melt gelatin in the hot syrup and cool to lukewarm. Beat the egg whites until stiff and dry. Slowly pour the syrup over the egg whites, beating constantly, using an electric mixer or rotary beater. Stir in the almond extract. Pour into an 8- by 8-inch pan, first rinsed in cold water. Add mandarin oranges, pushing them below the surface. Chill until set. Cut into squares to serve. Serves 6 to 8.

LASAGNE WITH CHEESE AND NUTS

Francesco di Marco Datini, a fourteenth-century fabric merchant and Renaissance Prato's leading citizen, left detailed records of almost every aspect of his life—even to the desserts served in his household during Lent. Virtually identical to his sweetened lasagne is the noodle kugel still prepared by eastern Europeans.

1 pound lasagne noodles, broken into bite-size pieces	3 egg yolks
	2 tablespoons sugar
2 cups ricotta or cottage cheese, well drained	$\frac{1}{4}$ cup currants (optional)
	Pinch of salt
1 cup heavy cream	Crumb Topping with nuts (page 680)

Cook broken lasagne noodles in lightly salted water until tender. Drain well. Mix cheese with cream, egg yolks, sugar, currants, and salt. Butter an 8-cup soufflé dish. Turn noodles into dish and mix thoroughly with cheese. Sprinkle crumb topping over noodles. Bake in pre-heated 425° oven for 40 minutes or until cheese is set and top is golden. Serves 8.

CLIPPING TIME PUDDING

English rice pudding recipes have remained basically unchanged since the Middle Ages, when the following instructions were given: "Nym ye ris, whes hem clene, seethe hem fort til hit breke, let it kele, do thereto almand mylke, and of Kyne [cow's milk] colour yt salt, and gif yt forth." The hearty version below was a sheepshearing-time specialty when, in Thomas Tusser's words, "neighbours none other things crave, But good cheere and welcome like neighbours to have."

$\frac{1}{2}$ cup rice	1 teaspoon powdered cinnamon
$\frac{1}{4}$ teaspoon salt	$\frac{1}{2}$ cup currants
3 cups milk	$\frac{1}{2}$ cup raisins
1 1-inch piece vanilla bean or 1 teaspoon vanilla extract	3 whole eggs, beaten
	3 egg yolks, beaten
$\frac{1}{2}$ cup sugar	Marrow from 2 bones

Boil the rice and salt in 2 cups water for 5 minutes. Drain well. Scald the milk with the vanilla bean; remove bean. If vanilla bean is not available, add vanilla extract. Add the rice, sugar, and cinnamon to 2 cups of the milk. Simmer gently until soft and creamy, about 20 minutes. Meanwhile, soak the currants and raisins in a little boiling water. Mix the beaten eggs and egg yolks and remaining milk. Strain into rice with the drained currants and raisins. Stir in the marrow, cut up small, and pour into a shallow 8-cup oven dish. Bake in a preheated 350° oven until custard is set—about 35 to 40 minutes. Cool and chill. Serves 6 to 8.

GURIEV KASHA

This hearty Russian pudding, a holiday favorite, was named after high-living Minister of Finance Count Guriev, who for nearly a dozen years managed the state funds of Czar Alexander II.

4 cups milk
$\frac{1}{2}$ cup sugar
$\frac{3}{4}$ cup semolina or farina
1 cup finely ground walnuts or pecans
1 cup finely ground blanched almonds

$\frac{1}{2}$ teaspoon almond extract
1 cup chopped mixed candied fruits
1 cup cherry or apricot preserves
$\frac{1}{2}$ cup vanilla wafer crumbs

Pour milk into a saucepan, add sugar, and bring to a boil. Trickle in the semolina and stir until thickened. Lower heat to simmer and cook for 5 minutes. Add nuts and almond extract to the cooked semolina. Put a layer of semolina in a buttered 10-cup pudding or deep pie dish. Cover with a sprinkling of the candied fruit; then a layer of jam. Repeat until dish is filled, ending with semolina. Cover with vanilla wafer crumbs. Bake in preheated 350° oven for 30 minutes. Put under the broiler to brown top. Cool and serve cold. Serves 10.

EIGHT PRECIOUS PUDDING

Confucius' pronouncement about the perfection of the number eight is recalled in this rice pudding sweetened with eight fruits. It is one of the few desserts considered fit to end a Chinese banquet.

2 cups rice
$\frac{1}{2}$ cup sugar
2 tablespoons lard
$1\frac{1}{2}$ cups preserved fruits in any
    combination: red and green plums;

cooked pitted prunes, raisins, or
dates; 1 small can whole chestnuts;
or candied lotus seeds
$\frac{1}{2}$ cup honey
1 cup blanched almonds or walnuts

Cook the rice in 4 cups water for 30 minutes. Drain and add sugar and lard. While rice is cooking, oil a heatproof dish, 7 to 8 inches wide with an 8- to 9-cup capacity. Mix fruit with honey. Arrange half the fruit to make a decorative pattern around bottom and up sides of dish. Spoon half the rice over the fruit. Arrange remaining fruit over the rice. Top with remaining rice and cover with foil. Place heatproof dish on a rack inside a large pot. Pour in boiling water to come three-quarters of the way up the rice pudding dish, cover dish, and steam for 45 minutes. Remove cover and let steam evaporate before removing inner bowl. Remove foil, place serving platter over rice, and invert bowl in one swift motion so fruits will be on top of rice pudding. Serve hot or cold. Serves 8.

717

PASKA

Orthodox Russians greet Easter with the preparation of this molded cheese dessert. Paska is commonly decorated with the letters XB, meaning "Christ is Risen," or with a simple cross.

2 pounds cottage or pot cheese,
 well drained
½ cup butter
1 cup heavy cream
1 cup sugar

4 egg yolks
½ cup diced candied fruit and rinds
½ cup slivered blanched almonds
2 teaspoons vanilla extract

Cream the cheese and butter together. Scald the cream and add the sugar. Beat the egg yolks until thick and light and slowly add the hot cream, beating constantly. Pour back into top of double boiler and cook over hot but not boiling water, stirring until custard coats a spoon. Cool, stirring occasionally, and add to the cheese mixture. Add fruit, almonds, and vanilla extract. If wooden paska molds are not available, line an 8-cup flower pot (one with a hole in the bottom) with cheesecloth and press in the mixture. Fold over the cheesecloth and put a weight on top of cheese and a dish under pot. Refrigerate overnight so liquid may drain out of cheese. Unmold and decorate with whole almonds. Write the letters XB on one side with colored icing. Serve with Koulitch (page 649). Paska is also delicious served with berries. For a richer dessert substitute cream cheese for cottage cheese. Serves 14 to 16.

PEKING DUST

With the annual approach of autumn in the ancient walled capital of Peking, a swirling wind envelopes the summer-dried city in a cloak of silken dust. It is that peculiar phenomenon which gives this soft, buff-colored chestnut dessert its name. Mont-Blanc, following, is the Gallic equivalent. A mound of puréed *marrons*, or chestnuts, topped with Crème Chantilly, it looks very like France's grandest mountain peak.

2 pounds chestnuts (may be canned
 in water and drained)
1½ cups milk
½ cup sugar

1 2-inch piece vanilla bean or
 2 teaspoons vanilla extract
1 recipe Crème Chantilly (page 703)

If using fresh chestnuts, cut a cross on the flat side with a sharp knife. Put in cold water and boil for 15 minutes. Peel while still warm, removing chestnuts from the water one by one. Scald the milk and sugar with the vanilla bean (if using vanilla extract add later with chestnuts). Add the chestnuts, fresh or canned, to the milk and boil on low heat until chestnuts are very soft—about 25 to 30 minutes. Drain well. The milk may be reserved for use in other desserts. Purée the chestnuts. Cool and chill for 1 hour. Oil the ring portion of a 9-inch spring form pan. Set the ring on a serving platter. Put the chestnut purée in a colander; push through with a wooden spoon onto the platter, piling gently like vermicelli, and doming slightly. Refrigerate for 20 to 25 minutes and remove ring mold. Dome crème chantilly onto the chestnuts. Decorate with Glacéed Fruits (page 738). Serves 8 to 10.

VARIATION: *Mont-Blanc*: Proceed as above, adding $\frac{1}{4}$ cup butter and 3 tablespoons cognac to the puréed chestnuts. Omit the glacéed fruits.

ZOLOBIYA

When a certain Abu al-Hasan in *The Arabian Nights* tried to cozzen his caliph out of some gold and found instead that the plot had backfired, he bemoaned, "Verily, all that is sticky is not a pancake they cook," comparing his messy situation to Zolobiya, a confection as old as the venerable tale. Today the loop-shaped fritters are typically eaten at evening gatherings during Ramadan, the month in the Moslem calendar when food is forbidden between dawn and dusk.

$\frac{1}{2}$ cup yoghurt

2 cups cornstarch, sifted

1 tablespoon peanut oil

1 teaspoon baking soda

$3\frac{1}{2}$ cups sugar

2 to 3 tablespoons honey

Vegetable shortening for deep frying

Slowly mix the yoghurt, cornstarch, oil, and baking soda until smooth and free from lumps. Add $\frac{1}{2}$ cup water or enough to make a batter thin enough to pour through a large funnel. Meanwhile, bring sugar and 2 cups water to a boil in a saucepan. Boil for about 5 minutes or until syrup spins a thread. Add honey and simmer for 3 to 4 minutes. Keep warm. Pour 1 inch of shortening into a large skillet and heat to 360°. Hold finger on tip of a large funnel and fill with batter. Open funnel halfway and release batter into hot fat, making 2 or 3 circles on top of each other for one fritter, about 3 inches in diameter. Fry until golden. Remove with a slotted spoon and drain on paper towel for a few seconds. Dip in the warm syrup and place on a cake rack over a platter to drain. Cool and store in airtight containers. Makes 48.

JALEBI

When the Moslems began to build their Indian empire, c. 1000 A.D., they brought with them this Middle Eastern version of the doughnut.

1 envelope dry yeast
1 teaspoon saffron threads
$2\frac{2}{3}$ cups flour, sifted
2 cups corn syrup

Vegetable oil for frying
$1\frac{1}{2}$ teaspoons powdered nutmeg or mace
1 tablespoon lime juice

Dissolve the yeast in $\frac{1}{4}$ cup warm water. Soak the saffron in $\frac{1}{4}$ cup boiling water for 15 minutes. Put the flour in a bowl and add $1\frac{1}{2}$ cups warm water and the dissolved yeast. Add the strained saffron water and beat well. Warm the corn syrup in the top of a double boiler over hot water. Pour 2 inches oil into a heavy pan and heat to 360°. Put the batter in a large funnel and move funnel in circles to make batter rings in the fat. Hold finger on tip of funnel when not using. Make only a few at a time so fat remains at constant temperature. When golden, turn, and fry until golden on second side. Remove and drain on paper towels. Add nutmeg and lime juice to the warm corn syrup. Dip jalebis into syrup and put on wax paper or a buttered platter. Serve warm or cold. Makes 8 to 10 doughnuts.

BISMARCKS

Kuchenmeisterei in Nürnberg, a fifteenth-century treatise on mastering the art of cakemaking, introduced this recipe for jelly doughnuts, traditional fare in Germany on *Fastnacht*, or Shrove Tuesday. In Berlin the doughnuts are known as Bismarcks after the illustrious Prussian statesman of whom Berliners are particularly fond. However, there is no historical evidence that Bismarck was partial to jelly doughnuts.

2 envelopes dry yeast
5 tablespoons sugar
$\frac{1}{3}$ cup butter, softened
1 teaspoon salt
Rind of 1 lemon, grated
1 cup milk, scalded
3 egg yolks

1 tablespoon rum
3 to 4 cups flour
1 teaspoon powdered nutmeg
2 cups apricot or raspberry jam
Vegetable fat or oil for deep frying
Vanilla Sugar (page 705)

Dissolve yeast in $\frac{1}{2}$ cup water with *two teaspoons sugar*. Cream butter with *remaining sugar*, salt, and lemon rind. When thoroughly blended stir in hot milk and mix until butter melts.

Cool until barely tepid and beat in egg yolks, rum, *one cup flour*, nutmeg, and yeast mixture. Gradually stir in *remaining flour* or enough flour to make dough soft and pliable but not sticky. Knead on a floured board until smooth and elastic. Place in bowl, cover lightly, and let rise until doubled in bulk, about 1 hour. Punch down on a floured board and roll to $\frac{1}{4}$-inch thickness. Cut into 3-inch rounds. Place a generous teaspoonful of jam on top of half of the dough circles. Top with remaining halves, pinching edges closed and sealing with water or egg white. Cover lightly and let rise for 40 minutes or until doubled in bulk. Deep fry in 365° fat, a few at a time. Fry for 3 to 5 minutes on each side and turn so both sides become golden brown. Remove with a slotted spoon and drain on paper towel. Sprinkle with vanilla sugar and serve warm. Makes about 30 doughnuts.

VARIATION: *Bohemian Crullers*: Shape dough into long sausage-like rolls, about 5 or 6 inches in length. Let rise, deep fry, and dust with sugar.

WELSH SAUCER BATTERS

> Parsimonious fruit pickers along the Welsh-English border sandwich windfall apples and other soft fruits between two saucer-size batter cakes to make this quick and delicious teatime snack.

6 peaches, nectarines, or apples, or	$1\frac{1}{2}$ cups milk
12 plums or apricots, or 5 cups	$1\frac{1}{2}$ cups flour, or as needed
blueberries or raspberries	Rind of $\frac{1}{2}$ lemon, grated
4 tablespoons sugar	Lemon juice (optional)
6 eggs, separated	Sugar for sprinkling

Preheat oven to 375°. Place 12 5-inch individual pie tins or small ovenproof fruit saucers in oven to heat. Peel, pit, and slice fruit as necessary; leave berries whole. Place fruit in small ovenproof casserole that has a lid, sprinkle with sugar, and mix gently; set aside. Drop egg yolks into a wide mixing bowl and egg whites into a bowl for beating. Stir milk into yolks, beating until well blended. Gradually add flour to yolk mixture, beating smooth between additions. Add enough flour for a thick, heavy batter, but one that can still be stirred. Beat egg whites to stiff but shiny peaks. Turn onto yolk batter, sprinkle with grated lemon rind, and fold together gently but thoroughly using a rubber spatula. Remove tart pans or saucers from oven and rub insides well with butter. Pour batter into pans until pans are three-quarters full. Place covered casserole of fruit and filled tart pans in the oven. Bake for 10 minutes or until tarts are puffed up and golden brown and fruit takes on a rich color and its liquid is syrupy. Slide 6 tarts into deep dish saucers or onto individual cake plates. Divide fruit and a little syrup over the top of each tart and sprinkle lightly with lemon juice. Remove remaining tarts from pans and invert over fruit to cover. Sprinkle with sugar and serve hot. Serves 6.

VARIATIONS: Frozen fruit may be substituted for fresh. Thaw fruit, drain off most of the liquid, and heat on the stove, adding a little sugar if needed during the cooking. Spoon onto baked tarts as described above.

BEIGNETS EN LACS D'AMOUR

These fritters in syrupy "lakes of love" were the unlikely progeny of Augustinian monks, who first peddled them door to door in the six-teenth century. The recipe below is from Le Sieur Menon's popular *La Nouvelle Cuisine*, a three-volume cookbook that first appeared in the mid-eighteenth century.

Rind of 1 lime, grated
4 dry macaroons, crumbled
1 tablespoon orange flower water,
  cognac, or rum

1 recipe Cream Puff Paste (page 725)
Vegetable fat for deep frying
Sugar for sprinkling
Custard Sauce (page 703)

Add grated lime rind, macaroons, and orange flower water to cream puff paste while still warm. Heat fat to 360° and drop in the dough from a teaspoon in walnut-size amounts. Fry a few at a time. Raise the heat to 375°. The beignets turn of their own accord and take about 10 minutes to cook, turning deep gold. Remove beignets with a slotted spoon and drain on paper towel. Cool the fat to 360° before frying the next batch; add fat as needed. Sprinkle beignets generously with sugar and keep warm in a preheated 300° oven. Pile on a heated platter and serve with Custard Sauce (page 703) flavored with rum or cognac or with whipped cream sweetened to taste. Makes 40 to 45 beignets.

CAMOTE Y PINA

Long after Spanish colonial rule in Mexico had ended, the traditions of Old World cookery were kept alive in the convents of the Church. Most especially the nuns were noted for their desserts and candies, sold in towns and cities as a means of support for the sisterhood. This sweet potato and pineapple confection combines two principal ingredients in-digenous to the Americas but is prepared in a manner recalling the rich, heavy sweets brought to Spain by the Moors.

2 cups mashed cooked sweet potatoes,
  fresh or canned
$1\frac{1}{2}$ cups brown sugar
1 cup grated fresh pineapple or
  well-drained canned crushed pineapple

$\frac{1}{2}$ teaspoon cinnamon, or to taste
1 cup coarsely chopped nuts (optional)

Purée sweet potatoes through a sieve or food mill. Cook sugar and $\frac{3}{4}$ cup water in heavy-bottomed saucepan until mixture reaches thread stage. Add potatoes to syrup and simmer over low heat for 10 minutes, stirring constantly. Add pineapple and cinnamon and simmer 3 to 4 minutes more. Stir in nuts, spoon into sherbet glasses, and let cool at room temperature or chill for 20 minutes in refrigerator. Serve plain or topped with whipped cream. Serves 6 to 8.

VACHERIN

Marie Antoinette, who played at being a dairymaid in a rustic cottage at Versailles, also liked to amuse herself occasionally with cooking. One of her most successful efforts was this decorative meringue "bowl."

2 recipes Swiss Meringue (below)	$\frac{1}{4}$ cup sugar
3 cups strawberries or other fruit	$2\frac{1}{2}$ cups heavy cream
2 tablespoons kirsch	$1\frac{1}{2}$ teaspoons vanilla extract

Trace 5 8-inch circles on 2 or 3 large buttered and floured cookie sheets. Spread 1 circle with *one-quarter-inch layer of the meringue*. Place *remaining meringue* in a pastry bag with a number 8 tube and outline remaining 4 circles with rings of meringue. Butter and flour a small cookie sheet and press out 20 little rosettes or other small decorative shapes. Reserve remaining meringue. Bake shaped meringues in a preheated 200° oven for 40 minutes. Cool. Gently loosen meringues from cookie sheets. Set meringue layer on small buttered and floured cookie sheet, spread a film of reserved meringue on edge, and place first ring on base layer. Repeat until all rings are in place, forming a shell. Attach rosettes on top with unbaked meringue. Spread remaining unbaked meringue to conceal rings. Replace in preheated 200° oven and bake until dry, about 15 minutes. Do not let meringue color. Turn off oven and let vacherin dry for several hours. Mix fruit with kirsch and *two tablespoons sugar*. Whip cream with *remaining sugar* and vanilla. Fold fruit and cream together and fill the vacherin. Serves 8 to 10.

VARIATION: Half a cup of grated sweet chocolate and $1\frac{1}{2}$ cups marron pieces soaked in cognac may replace fruit. Fold into whipped cream and fill shell.

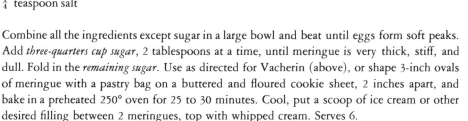

SWISS MERINGUE

5 egg whites	2 teaspoons vanilla extract
$1\frac{1}{4}$ teaspoons cream of tartar	$1\frac{1}{4}$ cups sugar
$\frac{1}{4}$ teaspoon salt	

Combine all the ingredients except sugar in a large bowl and beat until eggs form soft peaks. Add *three-quarters cup sugar*, 2 tablespoons at a time, until meringue is very thick, stiff, and dull. Fold in the *remaining sugar*. Use as directed for Vacherin (above), or shape 3-inch ovals of meringue with a pastry bag on a buttered and floured cookie sheet, 2 inches apart, and bake in a preheated 250° oven for 25 to 30 minutes. Cool, put a scoop of ice cream or other desired filling between 2 meringues, top with whipped cream. Serves 6.

CROQUEMBOUCHE

Croquembouche or *croque-en-bouche* is defined as any pastry which crumbles in the mouth. Recipes for Croquembouches made of everything from meringues to chou paste, as this one is, appear in many old cookbooks. This version is from Urbain Dubois' *Artistic Cookery* (1870).

1 recipe Cream Puff Paste (page 725)	1 cup sugar
1 recipe Pastry Cream (page 702)	¼ teaspoon cream of tartar

Spoon out cream puff paste in 1-inch mounds to make about 3 dozen puffs. Bake as directed, cool, and fill from underneath with a teaspoonful of pastry cream. Prepare caramel by putting sugar, cream of tartar, and ⅓ cup water in the top of a double boiler and boil without stirring until golden brown. Keep warm over hot water. Spear puffs with a fork, dip in caramel, and arrange in a layer on a round serving platter with caramel on top. Continue piling in a pyramid, ending with one puff. Pour over any remaining caramel. (Reheat caramel if it has hardened.) Serve with a fork and spoon to separate puffs. Serves 6 to 8.

SFINGI DI SAN GIUSEPPE

An old Italian festival, still celebrated *con brio* in Sicily, is the March 19 anniversary of Saint Joseph, when waifs, widows, and beggars are given a slight respite from daily hardship. On that day each citizen contributes according to his means flowers, food, candles, or cash to a community banquet held outdoors in the piazza. One elaborately set table is reserved for the three guests of honor—an aged carpenter, the village virgin, and an orphan—representing the Holy Family. After the *bambino's* blessing and shouts of "Viva la tavola di San Giuseppe," eager recipients stuff their stomachs with all they can eat, including the cream puffs, below.

	Filling:
1 recipe Cream Puff Paste (page 725)	2 cups ricotta cheese, well drained
1 tablespoon sugar	3 tablespoons sugar
½ teaspoon grated orange rind	3 tablespoons chopped chocolate bits
½ teaspoon grated lemon rind	3 tablespoons rum or liqueur
½ teaspoon vanilla extract	

When making the cream puff paste, add 1 tablespoon sugar to the water, butter, and salt called for in the recipe; after beating the eggs into dough, beat in the above quantities of orange and lemon rinds and vanilla. Drop by the tablespoon 3 inches apart on buttered cookie sheets. Bake in a preheated 400° oven for 10 minutes, reduce heat to 350°, and bake for 20 to 25 minutes or until well puffed and dry. Cool and slit each puff from the side. Fill with ricotta filling made by puréing drained cheese through a strainer until very smooth and beating with remaining ingredients. Makes 16 to 18 puffs.

724

CREAM PUFF PASTE

Cream Puff Paste, or *pâté chou*, is distinguished by its versatility. Baked, it may be used for a variety of filled puffs and éclairs. Deep fried, it becomes *beignets*, or fritters, such as Pets de Nonne.

1 cup water
½ cup butter
¼ teaspoon salt

1 tablespoon sugar (optional)
1 cup flour
4 eggs

Place water, butter, salt, and sugar in a 4-cup saucepan and bring to a rolling boil. Lower the fire and add flour all at once. Beat with a wooden spoon until the dough forms a ball and does not stick to sides of pan. Remove from the heat and beat in the eggs, one by one, until smooth and glossy. Use as directed to prepare cream puffs or beignets.

To make cream puffs: Drop dough by the tablespoon 3 inches apart on buttered cookie sheets. Bake in a preheated 400° oven for 10 minutes, reduce heat to 350° and bake for 20 to 25 minutes or until well puffed and dry. Cool, slit, and fill with flavored Pastry Cream (page 702), whipped cream, or ice cream. Makes 16 to 18 puffs. Smaller-size puffs may be filled with cheese, chopped hard-boiled eggs, or seafood mixed with mayonnaise, for cocktails. Omit sugar when preparing dough for unsweetened fillings.

To make pets de nonne: Drop dough by the tablespoon into vegetable shortening heated to 360°; fry until puffed and golden. Serve with brandy-flavored Custard Sauce (page 703).

CLOUTED CREAM

Andrew Boorde stated in his *Dyetary of Helthe* of 1542 that "Clowtyd crayme and nawe crayme put together, is eaten more for a sensuall appetyte than for any good nouryshement." However, the "Physycke doctour's" words meant little to dairy maids in southwest England, who continued to transform fresh cow's milk into this thick cream.

2 cups heavy cream

Place cream in the top of a double boiler over barely simmering water. Cook uncovered for 3 to 4 hours, replenishing water as needed. Let cool completely. Lift off heavy crust on surface with care and discard. Chill cream and serve with berries, Raspberry Fool (page 737), or Fruit Tart (page 681). Makes about 1½ cups.

CREPES

After weeks of carnivorous activity, Europeans on Shrove Tuesday ex-
piated their sins and expedited the Lenten period of penance by cooking
crêpes with any remaining lard or animal fat. French pancakes were
folded and then drenched in liqueurs; the Irish variety contained charms
to indicate the finder's future; English crêpes were filled with fruit and
spices, and though denigrated by one puritanical polemicist as "sweet
bait which ignorant people devore very greedily," another seventeenth-
century writer rhapsodized. "Hark I hear the pancake bell, And fritters
make a gallant smell."

1½ cups flour, sifted	1 egg yolk
⅛ teaspoon salt	1 to 1½ cups milk
1 tablespoon sugar (optional)	3 tablespoons butter, melted
2 whole eggs	Butter for frying

Make a well in the flour and add salt, sugar, eggs, and egg yolk. Start whisking in the flour
from the sides, gradually alternating with milk to make a batter the consistency of light
cream. Add cool melted butter. Let stand for 30 minutes. Place about 1 teaspoon of butter in
a 5-inch heated frying or pancake pan. Add a rounded tablespoon of batter and rotate pan in
all directions to spread batter evenly. Fry for 1 minute, add a little butter, and turn pancake.
Fry for 30 seconds. Stack and reserve. Makes about 18 crêpes.

VARIATIONS: *Hungarian Palatschinken*: Prepare crêpe batter with 4 tablespoons of sugar. Mix
½ cup apricot preserves with 2 tablespoons rum, cognac, or kirsch. Heat an 8-inch frying pan
and brush the bottom with butter. Pour in a very thin layer of batter, swirling it around to
spread evenly. Cook gently until browned, turn and cook for a few seconds. Fill immediately
with apricot preserves and roll up. Repeat until all pancakes are made. Arrange pancakes side
by side. Keep warm in a low oven. Sprinkle with Vanilla Sugar (page 705) and serve immediately. Makes about 12 pancakes. *German Kaiserschmarren ("The Emperor's Nonsense")*: Soak
½ cup raisins in a little rum. Fry pancakes on both sides; reserve on heated platter until all
are done. Using 2 forks, tear pancakes into small strips or pieces. Melt ⅔ cup butter in a large
skillet. Add pancakes, raisins, 1 teaspoon powdered cinnamon, and 1 cup sugar and toss over
low heat for 2 to 3 minutes or until ingredients are well mixed and sugar begins to melt. Sugar
should retain some of its graininess. Serve immediately. Serves 8. *Russian Karavai*: Put 1½
pounds large pitted prunes in a bowl and pour in 1 cup boiling water. Let steep for 30 minutes.
Mash or purée. Add ½ cup raisins, ¼ cup chopped walnuts, ¼ cup honey or brown sugar,
1 apple, peeled, cored, and chopped, 1 teaspoon powdered cinnamon, and 2 tablespoons softened butter. Mix ingredients well and spread between the pancakes, ending with a pancake.
Cover thickly with meringue (see Spanish Cake, page 666) and bake in a preheated 350° oven
for 10 to 15 minutes or until meringue is golden.

CREPES SUZETTE

When still just a lowly assistant waiter at the Café de Paris in Monte Carlo, Henri Charpentier created for Edward, Prince of Wales, this classic sweet pancake, "one taste of which would reform a cannibal into a civilized gentleman," as he later recalled. The crêpes were promptly named for a young lady in the Prince's party and the future chef's career launched.

1 2-inch-square piece of lemon rind	1 recipe Crêpes (page 726)
1 2-inch-square piece of orange rind	$\frac{1}{2}$ cup butter
$2\frac{1}{2}$ tablespoons Vanilla Sugar	$\frac{1}{2}$ cup each maraschino, curaçao,
(page 705)	and kirsch liqueurs, combined

Cut rind from fruit without taking any of the white pith. Cut each square of rind into thin strips. Place in jar with Vanilla Sugar, close tightly, and let stand for at least 1 or 2 days. Cook pancakes according to recipe and fold each in quarters, handkerchief style. At serving time, place chafing-dish pan directly over burner. Add butter, and when it has melted pour in *two-thirds of combined liqueurs*. When liqueurs are warm, ignite. When flame has died out, add the √anilla Sugar and strips of rind to pan and let sugar melt to a syrup. Add crêpes and spoon sauce over them, turning each crêpe once. Add *remaining liqueur* and when warm, ignite. Serve crêpes when flames burn out. Serves 6 to 8.

STRAWBERRIES ROMANOFF

The thoughtful individual who first combined strawberries and cream is sadly anonymous, but mention was made as early as 1560 by Henri II's physician that ladies enjoyed this delicacy as an evening dessert. Thomas Venner, "Doctor of Physic," concurred a hundred years later: "Verily with strawberries and sugar, Creame is, for them for whom it is convenient, a very delicate and wholesome dish. And whosoever he be that delighteth to eat a dish of Creame, let him not be parsimonious of sugar." The Russian version below bears the name of the family which dominated that country's history for some three centuries.

3 pints fresh strawberries or	$\frac{1}{3}$ cup kirsch or rum
2 packages frozen strawberries	2 cups heavy cream
$\frac{1}{2}$ cup sugar	Vanilla extract

If using fresh berries, hull, cut in half, and sprinkle with *one-third cup sugar* and the kirsch. For frozen berries, eliminate the sugar. Marinate in the refrigerator for 1 hour. Whip the cream, sweeten with *remaining sugar*, and flavor with a few drops of vanilla extract. Fold the marinated strawberries into the whipped cream. Serve very cold. Serves 6. If desired, strawberries may be replaced by raspberries or thinly sliced fresh or frozen peaches.

PLUM PUDDING

The flaming Plum Pudding, now synonymous with English Christmas, began in the Middle Ages as a first-course porridge, served with meats. As its thicker form evolved, it migrated to the end of the meal, with no sign of meat but the vestigial suet. The first published recipe for the pudding as we know it appeared in 1675. Its change in form is partially due to its having been disguised when the Puritans outlawed the dish as sinfully rich. Surely the most spectacular pudding ever produced was a Brobdingnagian 900-pounder, created by Devon villagers in 1819. The version below is slightly less ambitious.

1 cup flour, sifted	5 eggs
1 teaspoon baking powder	$\frac{3}{4}$ cup milk
$\frac{1}{2}$ teaspoon salt	Juice and grated rind of 1 lemon
$\frac{1}{2}$ teaspoon powdered nutmeg	$\frac{1}{2}$ pound suet, finely chopped
1 teaspoon powdered cinnamon	2 cups raisins
$\frac{1}{4}$ teaspoon each: powdered cloves	$\frac{3}{4}$ cup chopped mixed candied rind
and allspice	$\frac{1}{2}$ cup slivered blanched almonds
1 cup packed brown sugar	1 cup currants
1 cup fresh fine bread crumbs	$\frac{1}{2}$ cup cognac or dark rum

Resift *three-quarters cup flour*, baking powder, salt, and spices. Mix with brown sugar and bread crumbs. Beat eggs until light and frothy and add to dry ingredients alternately with milk. Add lemon juice, grated rind, and the suet. Mix raisins, candied rind, nuts, and currants with *remaining flour* and add to pudding along with cognac, folding in well. Pour pudding into a 12-cup mold or bowl. Cover with double foil and set on a trivet in a pot containing 1 inch of water. Cover and steam for $4\frac{1}{2}$ to 5 hours, adding water to pot as needed. Serve with Hard Sauce (page 704). Serves 12 to 14.

SIR KENELM DIGBY'S BREAD PUDDING

8 slices bread

6 eggs, separated

½ cup plus 2 tablespoons sugar

4 cups half-and-half
  (milk and cream)

1 tablespoon vanilla extract

¼ teaspoon salt

1 to 2 cups cherry preserves or
  preferred flavor

Cut bread slices in half. Beat 6 egg yolks and *two egg whites* together until well mixed, then gently beat in the *half cup sugar* and the half-and-half. Add vanilla. Butter a 9-inch square ovenproof dish. Arrange bread slices side by side in 2 layers. Pour on the custard. Let stand for 30 minutes, then bake the pudding in a pan of hot water in a preheated 350° oven for 50 minutes. Remove from water, bake 10 minutes longer. Cool. Beat *remaining egg whites* with salt and the *two tablespoons sugar* until stiff and glossy. Spread jam thickly over pudding and cover with meringue. Bake for about 15 minutes in preheated 350° oven or until golden. Cool. Serves 6.

FIG PUDDING

The fig tree, like the grape vine, was invested with divinity by the ancients. The Greeks believed it to be Ceres' gift to Athens and consequently planted a grove of fig trees in the public square of the city, appointing *sykophantēs*, literally, fig-informants, to report any illegal picking of the sacred fruit. The Romans also rendered the tree great honors, for legend had it that their founding princes, Romulus and Remus, had been born beneath its sheltering limbs. A sacrifice was offered every year in the grove which grew in the Forum. Twenty centuries later, many Englishmen mark Palm Sunday with the eating of fig puddings perhaps in recollection of Christ's triumphal entry into Jerusalem and his encounter with a barren fig tree.

1 cup flour, sifted

1 teaspoon baking powder

1 pound dried figs, finely chopped

½ pound suet, ground

1 cup fresh bread crumbs

½ cup brown sugar

1 cup milk

2 eggs

¼ teaspoon salt

½ teaspoon powdered nutmeg

½ teaspoon powdered ginger

Resift flour with baking powder in a bowl. Mix with figs, suet, bread crumbs, and sugar. Beat milk and eggs, add salt, nutmeg, and ginger and mix with fig mixture. Pour into a mold with a tight-fitting cover. Place in a pot with enough boiling water to come two-thirds of the way up the sides of the mold. Cover and steam for 3½ to 4 hours, adding water as needed. Serve hot with Custard Sauce (page 703) or Hard Sauce (page 704). Serves 8 to 10.

SHARBATEE GULAB

Sherbet (from *sharbah*, Arabic for drink), originating as a cold fruit beverage in ancient Persia, was subsequently adopted by nontippling Turks. A popular refreshment for sultans and their harems, it was eaten, according to Thomas Bailey Aldrich, as a prelude to amatory pursuits:

> . . . *The pet of the harem, Rose-bloom,*
> *Orders a feast for his favorite room.*
> *Glittering square of colored ice,*
> *Sweetened with syrup, tinctured with spice.* . . .

Also designating a dessert ice today, sherbet in liquid form still symbolizes Middle Eastern hospitality; it is customarily served to guests in *gulabi*—pearwood bowls—and sipped from slender-handled spoons.

5 cups fresh rose petals	3 cups shredded fresh or frozen pineapple
$2\frac{1}{2}$ cups sugar	1 tablespoon rose water
$\frac{1}{4}$ cup lemon juice	Crystallized rose petals for garnish

Soak rose petals in 1 quart cold water overnight in refrigerator. Drain well and discard petals. Make a syrup of the rose water and sugar by boiling them together for 5 to 7 minutes. Cool, then add lemon juice, pineapple, and rose liquid. Freeze in chilled ice trays covered with foil until thick. Stir well and refreeze to sherbet consistency, or freeze in an ice cream freezer. Serve garnished with crystallized rose petals. Makes about $2\frac{1}{2}$ quarts. As alternative, use $\frac{3}{4}$ cup rose petal jam instead of the rose petals, water, and sugar. Heat and strain the jam and dilute with 3 cups water; proceed as above.

WALDMEISTEREIS
(German Woodruff Ice)

$1\frac{1}{4}$ cups sugar	Juice of $1\frac{1}{2}$ oranges
3 cups white Rhine wine	Juice of 2 lemons
1 bunch fresh or $\frac{1}{4}$ cup dried woodruff	

Combine sugar with 1 cup water and cook slowly for about 7 minutes or until they form a light syrup. Cool. Stir in wine. Pour over woodruff in large glass or ceramic bowl. Marinate for 30 minutes for fresh woodruff, $1\frac{1}{2}$ hours for the dried. Remove woodruff, add fruit juices, and strain into ice cream freezer or refrigerator trays. Freeze for 1 hour, whip, refreeze. Whip and refreeze every 30 minutes until sherbet is completely frozen. Makes 1 quart.

BISCUIT TORTONI

Opened in 1798, the Café Tortoni was for almost a century Paris' most fashionable rendezvous, with Talleyrand, Prince Metternich, and the Duc de Morny among its brilliant habitués. The establishment was operated by a Neapolitan ice-cream maker, who had come to France to make his fortune. When Louis XVIII tried to buy the establishment as a reward for one of his subjects who had played a leading role in capturing a political enemy, Tortoni demanded so high a price that the offer was dropped. The café closed in the 1880's, leaving only this famous frozen cream dessert to posterity.

1 cup crumbled macaroons
$2\frac{1}{2}$ cups heavy cream
$\frac{1}{3}$ cup confectioners' sugar

Pinch of salt
$1\frac{1}{2}$ teaspoons vanilla extract

Soak the macaroons in *one and one-quarter cups cream* with the sugar and salt until thoroughly soaked and soft. Whip *remaining cream* until thick but not stiff. Fold in macaroon mixture and flavor with vanilla. Fill 10 to 12 $\frac{1}{2}$-cup pleated paper cups almost to the top. Freeze. When frozen sprinkle with crumbled Pralin (page 705), candied cherry halves, or toasted chopped almonds. Serves 6 to 8.

CINNAMON SHERBET

Though cinnamon, native to southwest China and Ceylon, has imparted flavor to Chinese cuisine since 2500 B.C., it was all but unobtainable in ancient Greece. Herodotus rationalized that the evergreen shrub which produced the aromatic bark grew on mountain tops reached only by the legendary phoenix. The Romans valued the spice as an aphrodisiac as well as a digestant. In Renaissance Italy cinnamon, combined with *granite*, or sherbet, as given below, reputedly stimulated jaded appetites and enabled overstuffed stomachs to carry on.

2 cups sugar
8 cups water

$\frac{1}{4}$ teaspoon oil of cinnamon
$1\frac{1}{4}$ cups toasted chopped pine nuts

Boil sugar and water together for 5 minutes or until they form a light syrup. Chill until cool. Stir in oil of cinnamon and pour into covered 1-quart mold or refrigerator trays covered with double thickness of aluminum foil. As sherbet sets and becomes slushy, beat with rotary mixer to break up ice particles. Do this every $\frac{1}{2}$ hour for 3 to 4 hours or until sherbet is hard. Fold in nuts with last beating. Makes 1 quart.

VARIATION: For colored sherbet, stir in 3 or 4 drops red food coloring with last beating.

GLACE PLOMBIERES

Ice cream, the successor to water ices and sherbets, was born in sixteenth-century Tuscany and made its French debut at the wedding of Catherine de' Medici when her Florentine cooks prepared a different flavor for every day of the festivities. It was not until the 1670's, however, that the Sicilian Francesco Procopio opened his Café Procope and introduced the rest of Paris to the royal addiction; by the middle of the nineteenth century there were dozens of shops catering to idle rich and aspiring middle class alike. About this time ice cream had also become *de rigueur* at banquets, with *bombes glacés* only the first of a succession of ice creams such as Glace Plombières, named for a French town.

1 quart light cream or half-and-half (milk and cream)	8 egg yolks
$\frac{1}{4}$ teaspoon salt	$\frac{3}{4}$ cup sugar
1 2-inch piece vanilla bean or 2 teaspoons vanilla extract	1 teaspoon almond extract

Scald the cream with the salt and vanilla bean; remove vanilla bean and reserve. Beat the egg yolks and sugar until light. Gradually strain the hot cream into the egg yolks, stirring briskly. Squeeze vanilla seeds into custard. Put into the top of a double boiler and cook for about 10 minutes, stirring over 1 inch of barely simmering water until mixture coats the spoon. Add almond extract (and vanilla extract, if vanilla bean is not available). Cool, stirring occasionally. Pour into chilled ice tray and cover with foil. Freeze for 1 hour, then stir thoroughly. Freeze 30 minutes and stir again. Repeat for third time within 30 minutes. It may now be packed into a 2-quart melon or ring mold and frozen until needed. Mixture may also be frozen in an ice cream freezer. Makes about 2 quarts.

VARIATIONS: *Butter, Rum, and Pralin Ice Cream*: As ice cream begins to thicken, add 3 tablespoons butter mixed with 3 tablespoons rum and $\frac{1}{4}$ cup finely chopped Pralin (page 705) and proceed as directed. *Marron Ice Cream*: Add 1 cup chopped marron pieces in brandied syrup to the partially frozen ice cream. *Peach Ice Cream*: Add 2 cups peeled, stoned, and crushed peaches to the partially frozen ice cream.

PRINCE PÜCKLER'S BOMBE

A very versatile Prussian, Hermann von Pückler-Muskau by name, was a hero on the battlefield, a prolific writer, and a noted cook and gourmet. For his service to the Crown the King of Prussia bestowed upon him in 1822 the title of prince. The prince in turn attached his name to this spherical three-layered ice cream dessert.

1½ cups coarsely crushed macaroons
3 tablespoons rum
1 pint chocolate ice cream
1 pint vanilla ice cream
1 pint strawberry ice cream or
    raspberry sherbet

1 cup heavy cream, whipped, sweetened,
    and flavored with vanilla extract
Fresh strawberries or shaved chocolate
    (optional)

Chill a 6-cup fluted bombe mold for 1 hour. Sprinkle macaroon crumbs with rum and let stand until well moistened. Remove chocolate ice cream from freezer and let soften until it can be packed into the mold, but do not let it melt to a liquid. Pack firmly into bottom of mold, pressing well into sides. Sprinkle with a layer of one third of the crumbs, cover mold and freeze until crumbs and ice cream are hard. Let vanilla ice cream soften, pack into mold, top with half the remaining crumbs, cover and freeze. Repeat with strawberry ice cream and top with remaining crumbs. Cover mold and freeze for 6 to 8 hours or until ice cream is very hard. Unmold and slice in long wedges to serve. Serve plain or garnish bombe with whipped cream and fresh whole strawberries or shaved chocolate. Serves 8.

RØDGRØD MED FLØDE

Red fruit jelly with cream, served almost daily in some Danish households, is made with all manner of red fruits or berries. It is sometimes splashed with Cherry Heering, a liqueur that has been warming Danes since Peter Heering made his first batch in 1818.

1½ cups red raspberries
1½ cups red currants
1 cup sugar, or to taste

½ cup cornstarch
1 teaspoon vanilla extract

Wash berries and currants and cover with cold water, about 4 cups. Bring to a boil and simmer for 10 minutes. Put through a sieve, add sugar, and return to heat. Bring to a boil, stirring constantly. Dissolve cornstarch in a little cold water and add to fruit. Simmer for about 2 minutes (do not boil), stirring until thickened. Add vanilla. Pour into a glass bowl rinsed in cold water. Chill for several hours until set. Serve with sugar and cold milk or cream. Serves 6. One quart of red fruit juice flavored with cherry liqueur may replace berries and currants.

VARIATION: *Russian Kissel*: Replace raspberries and currants with 3 cups cranberries.

PECHE MELBA

Auguste Escoffier set down for his admirers and for posterity the following account of the creation of his most revered dessert. "Madame Nellie Melba, the *grande cantrice* of Australia, sang at Covent Garden . . . in 1894. She stayed at the Savoy Hotel . . . at which time I was directing the kitchens of that important establishment. One evening, when Lohingrin (*sic*) was to be performed, Madame Melba gave me two seats in the orchestra. As you know, in that opera a swan appears. The following evening Madame Melba gave a *petit souper* for several friends, among them Monseigneur le Duc d'Orléans, and to show her that I had profited agreeably from the seats that she had graciously offered me, I sculpted in a block of ice a superb swan, and between the two wings I buried a silver bowl. I covered the bottom of the bowl with vanilla ice cream and on this bed of ice cream I placed peaches . . . soaked for several minutes in a syrup of vanilla. . . . A puree of fresh raspberries covered the peaches completely. Thus deliciously completed, this dessert was to become world famous. . . ."

1 package frozen raspberries, thawed
$\frac{1}{2}$ cup currant jelly, melted
6 scoops vanilla ice cream

6 peach halves, poached in vanilla
   syrup or canned
Slivered almonds (optional)

Purée raspberries and heat with the currant jelly. Cool. Place a scoop of ice cream in each dish. Top with peach half, cover with raspberry sauce. Sprinkle with almonds. Serves 6.

PEACHES IN WINE

As the name reveals, the *persica*, or peach, came to the West by way of Persia some 2,000 years ago. The fruit tree found a particularly salubrious climate in the region around Paris, where in the seventeenth century Louis XIV took a special interest in its cultivation. Peaches did not fare so well in England. William Lawson's influential *A New Orchard and Garden* (1618) advised husbandmen that they "meddle not with Apricoekes nor Peaches . . . which will not like our cold parts unlesse they be helped with some reflex of Sunne." The peaches that did get to market were considered so fragile that they were promptly plunged into a preservative of wine, as in the recipe below from William Verral's *Complete System of Cookery* (1759).

6 large fresh peaches
$1\frac{1}{2}$ cups Rhine wine
1 cup sugar

$\frac{1}{2}$ teaspoon powdered cinnamon
Rind of 1 lemon, cut into thin slices
$\frac{1}{4}$ cup Clarified Butter (page 630)

Peel and halve the peaches. Remove and reserve stones. Marinate peaches in wine, sugar, cinnamon, and sliced lemon rind for several hours, turning fruit often. Wrap stones in cheesecloth and crack with a hammer. Remove kernels and blanch, split, and reserve. Drain and dry the peach halves on paper towel. Heat the wine marinade and cook without stirring until caramelized. Meanwhile, heat the butter and gently sauté the peaches. Put the peaches in a serving dish with the peach kernels. Pour on the carmelized wine and serve. Serves 4 to 6.

CHARTREUSE OF FRUIT IN WINE JELLY

The French owe a double debt of gratitude to the monks of La Grande Chartreuse, a monastery near Grenoble. The first is for their famed green and yellow cordials, whose original recipe was compounded in the reign of Henry IV. The second is for their method of preparing dishes *à la chartreuse*, a form of culinary subterfuge in which the Carthusians disguised foods forbidden them on fast days as something else. Chartreuses originally described certain meat dishes but have long since come to denote elaborate vegetable and dessert dishes, too. Since the Victorian era, they have been served with a decorative coating of aspic.

2 envelopes unflavored gelatin
1 bottle rosé or port wine
1 cup sugar
Rind of 1 lemon
$\frac{1}{2}$ cup halved pitted cherries

1 can mandarin orange sections
1 large ripe banana, sliced
1 cup halved pitted grapes
1 cup heavy cream, whipped, sweetened, and flavored with vanilla extract

Soak the gelatin in $\frac{1}{2}$ cup cold water. Bring the wine to a boil with *one-half cup sugar* and lemon rind. Simmer for 5 minutes and add gelatin. Stir until dissolved. Discard lemon rind and pour $\frac{1}{2}$ inch of the wine jelly into an 8-cup ring mold first rinsed in cold water. Chill to set. Arrange halved cherries on jellied wine cut side up, sprinkled with *sugar*. Pour in $\frac{1}{2}$ inch more cool wine jelly and let set. Continue layers of fruit, *sugar*, and wine jelly, ending with jelly. Heat wine jelly slightly if it sets before being used. When mold is full chill until set. Unmold and serve with center filled with whipped cream. Serves 8 to 10. Any choice of fruit may be substituted for those listed above.

735

PERIS IN SYRIPPE

The original recipe for these pears, probably from the twelfth century, directed the cook to "Take Wardons (pears) and pare hem and caste hem in a potte and boile hem til thei ben tendre." The desired flavor was "poynante and also doucet." Today, wine replaces the vinegar to give this dish its sweet-and-sour flavor.

6 very hard pears	6 to 8 whole cloves
⅔ cup sugar	3 or 4 pieces cracked ginger or
½ to 1 bottle dry red wine	pinch of powdered ginger
Strip of dried orange rind	4 or 5 threads saffron (optional)
1 stick cinnamon	

Peel whole pears, leaving stem on if possible. Stand pears upright in a narrow earthenware or enameled cast iron casserole. Add sugar and enough wine to cover the pears half way. Add remaining ingredients and enough water to completely cover the pears. Cover casserole and bake in a preheated 250° oven for 5 to 7 hours, turning pears occasionally as liquid cooks down. Bake until pears are completely tender but not falling apart and liquid becomes a rich syrup. Cool in syrup. Remove cinnamon, cloves, orange peel, and cracked ginger, and serve with whipped cream or Custard Sauce (page 703).

VARIATION: *Elizabethan Pears and Vine Leaves*: If fresh grape leaves are available, place alternate layers of washed leaves and peeled, halved hard pears in the casserole until it is full. Add spices and seasonings listed above and fill casserole with apple cider. Bake as directed; discard leaves before serving.

HONEYED APPLES

It is only with the advent of Western influence that desserts have taken their place as a last course in the Chinese meal. China's cuisine has always possessed sweet dishes, but traditionally they have appeared throughout the meal to afford contrast with the main dishes. This sweet, also made with bananas, is served during the meal or at its conclusion.

2 egg whites	⅔ cup sugar
2 tablespoons cornstarch	3 tablespoons peanut oil
2 tablespoons flour	¼ cup corn syrup
2 firm juicy apples	2 tablespoons sesame seeds
Vegetable shortening for deep frying	

Make a batter of the unbeaten egg whites, cornstarch, and flour, mixing until smooth. Peel and core the apples and cut into ½-inch slices. Dip in the batter and deep fry in hot oil (360°) until golden. Drain on paper towels. Mix sugar with peanut oil and stir until sugar melts; add corn syrup. Add apples and sesame seeds and stir until apples are well coated with syrup. Cook until syrup caramelizes, about 3 to 5 minutes. Remove apples and place on a heated and oiled platter so they will not stick. Serve with a bowl of ice water. Hot apples are to be held with chopsticks or a fork and dipped into ice water to harden syrup. Serves 4.

RASPBERRY FOOL

Though Jerusalem-bound Crusaders complained that the going was "very hard and stoney and maketh pilgrims very bony," one also noted that "raspberries grow by the way, with pleasure you may assay." In Elizabethan times raspberries were often "layde to the inflammation . . . in the eyes" to "quencheth such hoate burninges," but they were more commonly served in desserts easy enough for even a fool to make.

2 cups puréed raspberries,   1 tablespoon kirsch or rum
  sweetened to taste   1 cup heavy cream, whipped

Combine fruit and kirsch and fold into the whipped cream. Chill well. Serves 4. Other berries or fruits may be substituted for raspberries.

FRUITS BLANCHIS

The directions for these sugar-whitened fruits come from Archambault's *Le Cuisinier Econome*, published in Paris in 1825. The author commends his book as "indispensable to the most sumptuous households, as well as the simplest tables, in both city and country."

1 egg white   1 pound seedless grapes
1 cup sugar   (in small bunches)

Beat the egg white with $\frac{1}{2}$ teaspoon water until very frothy. Place sugar in a flat dish. Dip washed and drained bunches of grapes in the egg white; roll in the sugar. Set on sugared plate, allow to dry; chill. Use as garnish. Any small fruits may be treated the same way.

GLACEED FRUITS AND NUTS

The Renaissance ladies loved sweetmeats, and no gentleman would have stepped out of his chambers without his *bonbonnière* at the ready. Often it was filled with these candies which had the advantage of being un-meltable in the hand while they melted the heart.

Sugar Syrup (page 704) as needed
Choice of the following:
Dates, pitted and filled with
   green-tinted marzipan
Prunes, pitted and filled with white
   marzipan, topped with an almond

Pineapple chunks
Cherries, pitted
Pears, peeled, cored, and halved
Nut meats

Cook syrup to light caramel. Keep syrup hot over simmering water and dip fruits or nuts quickly one at a time into syrup and set on an oiled cookie sheet to dry. Serve as candy or use to decorate cakes.

KOREAN DATE BALLS

36 dates, pitted
3 tablespoons sugar

1 teaspoon powdered cinnamon
$\frac{1}{4}$ cup finely crushed pine nuts

Steam dates for 20 minutes, mash or put through a strainer. Add sugar and cinnamon. Roll into small, bite-size balls. Roll in pine nuts. Serve as dessert or candy. Makes about 18 balls.

DONCASTER BUTTERSCOTCH

In Britain, according to an old cookbook, "candy-making is a regular adjunct to courting. . . . It draws together all the lads and lasses . . . and the fun and the daffing that go on during the boiling, pulling, clip-ping, cooling, are . . . worth the money." Visitors to the annual fair in Doncaster, a coal town in Yorkshire, could treat themselves to this chewy butterscotch specialty.

$2\frac{1}{4}$ cups sugar
2 cups milk
$\frac{1}{3}$ cup butter

$\frac{1}{8}$ teaspoon cream of tartar
2 teaspoons vanilla extract

Melt the sugar in a saucepan with the milk. Add the butter and cream of tartar. Bring to a boil and simmer until mixture hardens when a small amount is dropped into cold water. Add vanilla. Pour a $\frac{1}{2}$-inch layer into a shallow 7- by 12-inch buttered dish. Let cool slightly, mark out into small squares and let set for 2 to 3 hours. Makes 60 pieces.

MOTHER-IN-LAW'S EYES

This witty name is applied by Brazilians to one of their favorite party sweetmeats: wrinkled prunes stuffed with pale marzipan.

30 large prunes or dates, pitted
2 cups Marzipan (see Almond Paste, page 703)

1 cup sugar or ground Brazil nuts

Stuff fruit with balls of marzipan and roll in sugar or nuts.

PASTILLES OF FRUIT

The quince tree, indigenous to western Asia, has been cultivated for its tart, pear-shaped fruit for more than four thousand years. Persians, who had a propensity for poisoning each other, considered the quince an effective antidote, and later, Greek suitors gave quinces in lieu of engagement rings to their betrothed. Pragmatic Romans not only manufactured perfumes and hair dyes from the versatile quince, but used it in wines and sauces and even made a kind of marmalade by steeping the fruit, with its branches and leaves, in containers filled with honey and wine syrup. In Elizabethan times it was fashionable for "ladyes of high degree" to exhibit their culinary skills by concocting quince pies, preserves, and the candies called Pastilles, below.

3 pounds quinces or apples
2 pounds sugar
1 cup grated almonds, hazelnuts,
  walnuts, or pistachio nuts (optional)

Rind of $1\frac{1}{2}$ lemons or 1 orange, grated
$\frac{1}{2}$ teaspoon powdered cinnamon
Confectioners' sugar for sprinkling

Peel and core quinces or apples and cut into eight parts. Steam for about 30 minutes in very little water until soft. Cool completely in a covered pot. Purée through a strainer or in a food mill and combine with sugar in heavy-bottomed saucepan. Simmer gently over low heat, stirring frequently until mixture becomes very thick. It should crackle when a little is dropped into ice water. This will take from 30 minutes to 1 hour, depending on the moisture in the fruit. Stir in the next 3 ingredients. Pour a $\frac{1}{2}$-inch-thick layer on a baking sheet, platter, or pan and chill thoroughly. Cut into squares or into fancy shapes with cookie cutters. Leftover scraps may be rolled between sheets of waxed paper and cut. Sprinkle both sides with confectioners' sugar and store between sheets of waxed paper in an airtight container. Makes about 60 1-inch squares.

VARIATIONS: *Apricot or Raspberry Pastilles*: Substitute 3 pounds unpeeled, stoned apricots or 4 pounds raspberries. Cook, cool, and purée. Combine with 3 pounds sugar and cook slowly until mixture comes away from sides of pan. Proceed as above.

TURKISH DELIGHT

Few of Mohammed's precepts have been honored as assiduously as the one which went, "The love of sweetmeats comes from the faith." The Turks not only became skilled confectioners—one nineteenth-century Englishwoman gushing that the candy makers were "the finest race of men in Constantinople"—but they also regarded the corpulence of their women, whose intake of treats was prodigious, as a beauty asset. The recipe for Lokum, or Turkish Delight, invented by Hadji Bekir, was a long-guarded secret. In modern Istanbul his descendants still monopolize the trade.

3 envelopes unflavored gelatin
½ cup lemon juice, or to taste
¾ cup cornstarch
1¾ cups hot Sugar Syrup (page 704)

5 teaspoons rose water
½ cup coarsely chopped pistachio nuts
3 drops red food coloring (optional)
Confectioners' sugar

Soak gelatin in lemon juice. Mix cornstarch with ½ cup cold water and add to syrup. Cook until very thick. Remove from heat; add gelatin and lemon juice. Stir until melted. Add rose water, pistachios, and coloring. Put a layer of confectioners' sugar in an 8-inch square pan, pour in candy, and let set for several hours. Sprinkle with confectioners' sugar and cut into 1-inch squares. Roll in more sugar and keep in an airtight container. Makes 64 pieces.

VARIATION: *Apricot Turkish Delight*: Decrease rose water to 2 teaspoons and add 1 cup puréed apricots along with pistachios.

CANDIED FRUIT PEEL

Hieroglyphics document that candy (from the Arabic *qandi*) sweetened the diet of ancient Egyptians. From those early combinations of herbs, spices, and honey colored with vegetable dyes the Persians later refined the art of confectionery, employing scents of flower petals and cardamom seeds to flavor fruits like citrons which had been crystallized in sugar. By Elizabethan times anything edible was candied, including such exotica as eringoes (roots of sea-holly)—which Falstaff used to invoke the elements: "Let it snow eringoes"—as well as more plebeian fruits like orange and lemon peels.

3 large grapefruits or
5 large navel oranges

2¾ cups sugar
1½ teaspoons powdered ginger

Cut fruit in half crosswise and remove fruit pulp. Scrape out all membranes and remains of fruit pulp but leave white pith under skin. Cut peels into long strips ¼ to ½ inch wide. Cover with boiling water, simmer for 5 minutes, and drain well. Repeat 4 more times, using fresh boiling water each time and draining well between blanchings. This will remove bitter oils from the peels. Combine 1 cup water with *2 cups sugar* in a heavy-bottomed saucepan, add ginger, and simmer until sugar dissolves. Add peels and mix with syrup. Cook slowly, partially covered, for 30 to 45 minutes, or until all syrup is absorbed and peels are soft. Turn onto a large sheet of foil or waxed paper, spreading peels in a single layer. Cool thoroughly and sprinkle liberally with *remaining sugar*. Let stand uncovered until completely dry, about 5 to 7 hours or overnight. Stored in a tightly closed jar, peels keep almost indefinitely and may be used diced in baking or served as a confection. Makes about 8 to 10 cups. Orange and grapefruit peels should not be combined as the distinctive flavor of each would be spoiled.

SAVORY OF WILD CHERRIES

Laurentius, the long-suffering Roman host of the marathon banquet described in *The Deipnosophists*, all but lost his temper when the subject turned to cherries. "You, O Greeks, lay claim to a good many things, as either having given the names to them, or having been the original discoverers of them. But you do not know that Lucullus, the Roman general . . . was the first man who introduced this plant into Italy from Cerasus [in Asia Minor]; and he it was who gave the fruit the Latin name of *cerasus*, cherry, after the name of the city. . . ." Laurentius' guests remained unconvinced and so do most historians, for there is evidence that cherries, though native to Asia Minor, were known in central Europe even in the prehistoric era; mounds of cherry pits, the remnants of paleolithic parties, have been uncovered in caves. Cherries have been a favorite fruit in Italy for at least two thousand years, and Bartolomeo Stefani, the seventeenth-century author of the recipe below, wisely recommends readers not to add all sorts of extra flavorings as cherries are delicious enough as they are.

4 pounds dark, ripe bing cherries   1 pound sugar

Wash cherries, remove stems, cut in half, and remove pits. Wrap 8 or 10 pits in a double thickness of cheesecloth and hit with a hammer to crack pits. Combine kernels of pits with cherries and sugar. Cook slowly in a heavy-bottomed saucepan without adding water for 1 to 1½ hours or until mixture is thick and syrupy. Stir with a wooden spoon every 15 minutes. Pack in sterilized jars, seal, and store. Serve over ice cream or as a condiment with meats. Makes 1½ quarts.

VARIATION: This may be made with all wild or sour cherries, or with a combination of sour and bing cherries. For sour cherries, use 1 pound sugar for each pound of cherries. For a mixture of sour and bing cherries, use ¾ pound sugar to each pound of fruit.

741

DRINKS

MULLED WINE

The making of mulled wine, or hippocras as it was known in earlier times, was not a matter to be left to chance. Dr. Andrew Boorde, author of the influential fifteenth-century *Dyetary of Helthe*, cautioned his readers "to make Ypocras, hit were get lernynge and for to take the spice thereto aftur the proportionyne." Nor should anyone in low spirits drink the potent brew. "Melancholy is colde and drye; wherefore melancholy men must refrayne from . . . immoderate thurste, and from drynkyng of hot wynes and grosse wyn."

$\frac{1}{2}$ teaspoon black peppercorns
$\frac{1}{2}$ teaspoon cloves
2 sticks cinnamon

$\frac{1}{4}$ cup sugar
2 bottles red Burgundy wine
1 cup kirsch or cognac

Tie spices in cheesecloth. Simmer spices, sugar, and wine for 4 to 5 minutes to blend flavors. Add kirsch, heat through, and pour into heated mugs. Makes about 12 drinks.

BISHOP

Dutch sailors introduced their English mates to this hot spiced wine. The name may have come from its rich garnet color, reminiscent of a high churchman's robes. It was sometimes served in a fancy bowl shaped like a bishop's miter. Bishop has been enjoyed since the Middle Ages; the ecclesiastical variations were contrived later in England.

2 oranges, each studded with
   10 to 12 cloves
12 cubes sugar

1 lemon
3 bottles ruby port
Freshly grated nutmeg

Roast oranges in a preheated 400° oven for 30 minutes. Rub sugar cubes into skin of lemon. Quarter the oranges, put in a saucepan with the sugar and the juice of the lemon. Add the wine and heat to boiling point, stirring to melt the sugar. Simmer for 1 to 2 minutes. Serve in heated mugs with a sprinkling of nutmeg. Makes 12 drinks. An Archbishop is made as above with Bordeaux wine, a Cardinal with champagne, and a Pope with Burgundy.

742

RUMFUSTIAN

To Englishmen in past centuries, the prefix "rum" might signify any drink that was strong and delicious. This concoction, which works its spell without any West Indian spirits, meant simply "knaves brew."

1 bottle medium dry sherry	Rind of 1 lemon
$\frac{1}{2}$ cup sugar	12 egg yolks
1 teaspoon powdered nutmeg	1 quart beer
$\frac{1}{2}$ teaspoon powdered mace	1 pint gin
1 stick cinnamon	

Heat together the sherry, sugar, spices, and lemon rind. Beat the egg yolks until very foamy. Beat in the beer and gin. Slowly pour hot strained sherry into eggs, beating constantly so eggs will not curdle. Heat, stirring, until nearly boiling. Serve immediately in heated mugs. Makes 15 to 20 drinks.

GLÖGG

For Scandinavians, Yuletide festivities include vestiges of such ancient Viking rites as decking halls with evergreens, slapping people with twigs to stir up the blood, and taking care not to clank kettles brewing Christmas beverages—a noise indicating the presence of death. Glögg, containing aquavit (literally, "water of life"), a spirit distilled from grain or potatoes, is traditionally quaffed with this toast: "Skål! Min skål, din skål, alla vackra flickors skål!" meaning health to all, but particularly to pretty girls.

2 bottles red Bordeaux wine	8 dried figs
1 large orange, studded with	2 bottles aquavit
10 cloves	1 pound cube sugar
15 cardamom seeds	2 cups raisins
1 2-inch cinnamon stick	2 cups blanched whole almonds

Heat wine in an enameled saucepan with orange, cardamom, cinnamon, and figs. Pour into silver punch bowl or bottom pan of a chafing dish. Heat aquavit in an enameled saucepan. Place cubes of sugar on a grill set over the punch bowl. Pour some hot aquavit over sugar and ignite sugar. Continue pouring aquavit over sugar to keep it burning. When all sugar has melted, ladle glögg into mugs and garnish each serving with a few raisins and almonds. Makes 32 punch cups.

VARIATION: Place sugar directly into empty silver bowl, moisten with hot aquavit and ignite. Keep pouring aquavit until all is flaming. Pour in wine that has been heated with remaining ingredients to put out flame. Serve as above.

HOPPEL POPPEL

On visiting the Low Countries in the seventeenth century, the French poet Théophile de Viau observed: "All these gentlemen of the Netherlands have so many rules and ceremonies for getting drunk that I am repelled as much by the discipline as by the excess." Even the ladies liked to tipple, especially at birthday parties at which they earnestly and invariably became "cupshoten" on drinks like the one below.

4 egg yolks	1 quart hot milk
7 tablespoons sugar	1 cup rum or cognac
1 teaspoon vanilla extract	

Beat egg yolks with sugar until frothy and pale yellow. Stir in vanilla and slowly pour in very hot milk, beating constantly. Mix with rum and pour into heated mugs or punch cups. Dust with nutmeg and serve. Makes 6 to 8 drinks.

WASSAIL BOWL

"Be well" is what Wassail originally meant when Anglo-Saxons drank to each other's health. Later associated with the Christmas season, Wassailing came to connote caroling and revelry, too. Garnished with savory, hissing "roasted crabs," Wassail was served on each of the twelve days of Christmas from an outsize bowl. Poorer folk, toting a large wooden bowl with them, sang from door to door in exchange for refills, and in some parts of England ended their tour with a carol to the fruit trees: "Wassaile the trees, that they may beare You many a plum and many a peare. . . ." A great treat of the Wassail Bowl was the toast that swam in the ale. Consumed with expressions of good wishes, it gave rise to the custom of "drinking a toast."

18 crab apples, cored	1 teaspoon nutmeg
2½ cups brown sugar	½ teaspoon powdered cloves
3 quarts ale	6 eggs, separated
1 bottle sweet sherry	1 cup cognac, heated
5 slices fresh ginger root or 1 teaspoon powdered ginger	10 slices buttered toast, cut in quarters

Sprinkle apples with *one-half cup brown sugar*; bake in a preheated 400° oven for about 30 minutes. Heat ale, sherry, and spices in a large saucepan. Beat egg yolks until thick. Beat egg whites until very stiff and fold thoroughly into the yolks. Pour the ale mixture into the eggs in a thin stream, beating hard. Put the hot apples in a heated bowl, add ale-egg mixture and cognac. Serve immediately in mugs. Pass toast to dip or float in mugs. Makes 18 drinks.

SYLLABUB

Hannah Glasse, the dauntless authoress of *The Art of Cookery* (1747), gave recipes for several Syllabubs, including this "whipt" drink. It takes its name from Sillery (a wine of the Champagne district) and "bub" (Elizabethan slang for a bubbling drink). Syllabubs are wine and milk concoctions, which distinguish them from the myriad milk drinks made with spirits. They were occasionally made by placing a bowl of wine under the cow and milking directly into it. Since new milk is naturally very foamy, the usual chore of beating was thus avoided.

Rind and juice of 2 oranges
4 cups light cream or half-and-half
  (half milk, half cream)
$\frac{1}{2}$ cup sugar

1 teaspoon orange flower water
1 cup semidry sherry or Madeira
$\frac{1}{4}$ cup cognac

Put all ingredients in a bowl and beat by hand, or at low speed with an electric beater, until very bubbly. Makes 12 drinks.

GOSSIP'S CUP

The Englishman's devotion to his native ale has over the centuries prompted fierce defenses. John Coke in his 1549 *Debate between the Heralds of England and France* argued, "we have good-ale . . . beyng [among the] more holsome beverages for us than your wynes, which maketh your people dronken, also prone and apte to all fylthy pleasures and lustes." A century later John Taylor feared subversion from Dutch beer, "a boorish Liquor, a thing not knowne in *England*, till of late dayes an Alien to our Nation, till such times as Hops and Heresies came amongst us, it is a sawcy intruder in this Land." Gossip's Cup, dating from Elizabeth's reign or earlier, was so named for its ability to loosen the celebrant's tongue.

1 12-ounce bottle ale
2 tablespoons cognac
1 teaspoon brown sugar

Rind of 1 lemon
Pinch each powdered ginger and nutmeg

Heat all ingredients until just hot but not boiling. Serve in a heated mug. Makes 2 drinks.

ATHOLE BROSE

One of Scotland's most ancient drinks is this "brose," or brew, named for the mountainous region of Athole. Originally it consisted of hot whiskey and oatmeal, the latter since replaced by honey. Besides being a New Year's Eve specialty, it is regarded as a first-rate cold remedy.

Drambuie   Heavy cream
Honey

Mix in equal portions, warm slightly, and stir until smooth. Cool and serve cold.

POSSET

Sir Fleetwood Fletcher, a gastronomic versifier of the English Enlightenment, set down this recipe for sack Posset.

> *From fam'd Barbadoes on the western Main*
> *Fetch sugar, ounces four—fetch Sack from Spain,*
> *A pint,—and from the Eastern Indian coast*
> *Nutmeg, the glory of our northern Toast;*
> *O'er flaming Coals let them together heat*
> *Till the all-conquering Sack dissolve the sweet;*
> *O'er such another Fire put Eggs, just ten,*
> *New-Born from Tread of Cock and Rump of Hen:*
> *Stir them with steady hand and conscience Pricking*
> *To see the untimely end of ten fine Chicken;*
> *From shining shelf take down the brazen skillet,—*
> *A quart of milk from gentle cow will fill it.*
> *When boiled and cold, put milk and Sack to Egg;*
> *Unite them firmly like the Triple League,*
> *And on the fire let them together dwell*
> *Till Miss sing twice—You must not kiss and Tell,—*
> *Each Lad and Lass take up a silver spoon,*
> *And fall on fiercely like a Starved Dragoon.*

10 eggs, well beaten   1 teaspoon powdered or freshly grated
$1\frac{1}{2}$ cups sweet sherry, Madeira, or   nutmeg
   tawny port   Pinch salt
$\frac{1}{2}$ cup sugar, or to taste   4 cups hot milk

Beat eggs until frothy. Beat in wine. Sift sugar, nutmeg, and salt. Add to the hot milk and pour into the eggs, beating briskly. Serve in heated mugs. Makes 8 to 10 drinks.

CAUDLE

When medieval travelers took one for the road, it was often a Caudle, a warming liquid combination of cereal and spirits that sustained them until solid food was available. Recipes for Caudles may be found in a number of medieval manuscripts, most notably the *Forme of Cury*, prepared c. 1400 by officers in Richard II's court. Caudles remain popular among rural working people where they still fulfill a definite need that beer or straight whiskey cannot match.

4 cups boiling water
$\frac{1}{4}$ cup oatmeal (may be quick or instant)
Pinch of salt
$\frac{1}{2}$ teaspoon powdered mace

$\frac{1}{4}$ teaspoon powdered ginger
1 teaspoon grated lemon rind
2 tablespoons brown sugar
4 cups ale or stout

Cook all ingredients except ale until oatmeal is tender—about 10 minutes. Heat ale and mix. Makes 6 to 8 drinks.

SPANISH SANGRIA

1 orange, sliced
1 lemon, sliced
4 or 5 strips cucumber peel
1 bottle dry red or white wine

2 to 3 tablespoons cognac
8 ounces iced soda water
Ice cubes

Combine all ingredients, except soda and ice, in a pitcher. Chill well. At serving time, add soda and ice cubes to pitcher. Serve in large wine glasses. Makes 4 to 6 drinks.

747

CRITERION SWIZZLE

As an antidote to the "villainous compounds" which commonly passed for cocktails in Victorian England, Leo Engel of London's Criterion Hotel set down the best of his repertoire in a bar guide published in 1878. Criterion Swizzle, he said, came from India, adding that "tastes differ. An Indian likes a cocktail swizzled [i.e. frothed with a stick]; a North American, within the last few years, will not take one unless it is stirred with a spoon; a South American will have it shaken; an Englishman, who has travelled in America, is more particular than any one of the others until you find out his taste, and is most difficult to please." Three other Engel concoctions follow: Badminton is named for the country seat of the Duke of Bedford; the provocative-sounding Alabazam and Bosom Caresser must go undeciphered.

2 dashes orange bitters
4 tablespoons cognac

½ tablespoon noyau liqueur
or white crème de cacao

Pour ingredients over shaved ice in an old-fashioned glass. Stir with a swizzle stick. Drink through short straws. Makes 1 drink.

BADMINTON

1 small unpeeled cucumber, very thinly
  sliced
¼ cup sugar

¼ teaspoon powdered nutmeg
1 bottle red Bordeaux wine
1 split soda water

Place all ingredients in a large silver pitcher half full of cracked ice. Let stand for 20 minutes and serve. Makes 4 drinks.

ALABAZAM

1 teaspoon sugar
2 dashes orange bitters
1 tablespoon curaçao

1 teaspoon lemon juice
¼ cup cognac

Put ingredients into a cocktail shaker with some cracked ice. Shake well and strain the mixture into a whisky sour glass. Makes 1 drink.

BOSOM CARESSER

1 egg $\frac{1}{2}$ cup cognac
$1\frac{1}{2}$ tablespoons strawberry syrup

Shake all together with cracked ice and strain into old-fashioned glasses. Makes 2 drinks.

PLANTER'S PUNCH

After Britannia established her West Indian possessions in the seventeenth century, buccaneering gave way to pursuits like slave trading, sugar producing, and rum manufacturing. Initially, Puritanical colonists complained that "people drink much of it, indeed, too much, for it often lays them asleep on the ground . . . a very unwholesome lodging." Gradually, however, rum's soporific properties and economic importance were appreciated, and planters swigged drinks like the one below.

2 teaspoons sugar $\frac{1}{3}$ cup dark rum
2 dashes orange bitters   1 slice orange
$\frac{1}{4}$ teaspoon grenadine syrup (optional)   1 pineapple stick
1 tablespoon water or soda water   1 maraschino cherry, with stem

Dissolve sugar, bitters, and grenadine in the water in a tall stem glass or highball glass. Add rum, fill with crushed ice, and decorate with fruit. Makes 1 drink.

ROMAN PUNCH

As Grimod de La Reynière explained, the purpose of a spiritous drink taken between courses was to brace "the fibres of the stomach and to accelerate the peristaltic movement which produces digestion." By the 1860's the English upper classes had adopted this custom at formal dinners and served drinks like Roman Punch, whose only connection with Rome was its connotation of orgies.

1 quart lemon or orange ice   2 quarts champagne, well chilled
8 tablespoons arrack, or maraschino
   or orange liqueur

Put $\frac{1}{2}$ cup fruit ice in each of 8 highball glasses or tulip-shaped champagne goblets. Add 1 tablespoon arrack or liqueur to each, mixing it gently into ice. Slowly pour champagne into each glass, stirring with a long-handled spoon or cocktail stirrer. Serve at once with straws and long-handled spoons. Serves 8.

GIN PUNCH

Abraham Hayward, in *The Art of Dining* (1899), took great pains to set the record straight on the origins of this popular Victorian libation. Theodore Hook, an English satirist of the day, was often and incorrectly credited with having devised the punch because of his "frequent and liberal application of the discovery." It was, however, Mr. Stephen Price who on "one hot evening in July [when Hook] strolled into the Garrick [Club] in that equivocal state of thirstiness which it requires something more than common to quench" came to his rescue with this intoxicating remedy—a half dozen cups of it.

1 cup gin	$\frac{1}{2}$ teaspoon grated lemon rind
$\frac{1}{2}$ cup maraschino liqueur	$\frac{1}{4}$ cup Sugar Syrup (page 704)
$\frac{1}{4}$ cup lemon juice	1 quart soda water or ginger ale

Mix ingredients and pour over a block of ice in a punch bowl. Makes about 16 punch cups.

 WINE PUNCH

Like sailors everywhere, British salts on shore leave in sixteenth-century India quickly discovered the native brew with the most wallop—Punch (from the Hindustani word for five), compounded of a sweet, sour, bitter, weak, and spirited ingredient. Soon their landlubbing compatriots adopted the drink, varied it as in the recipe below, and coined the adage that "Punch cures the Gout, the Cholic, and the Phthisic [consumption], and it is to all men the very best of Physic." One spectacular brew concocted in 1599 by the Commander of the Fleet contained eighty casks of brandy, 1,300 pounds of sugar, and 25,000 limes and was served by boys in boats, adrift on the sea of punch, to some 6,000 guests.

1 medium pineapple, peeled and diced, or 1 quart hulled, slightly crushed strawberries, or 12 peeled and sliced peaches	$\frac{1}{2}$ to 1 cup sugar, as needed
	2 bottles white Rhine or Moselle wine or 2 bottles dry red wine
	1 bottle dry champagne, well chilled

Place fruit in glass punch bowl with the sugar. Vary amount of sugar depending on tartness of fruit. Crush fruit lightly and let stand until sugar dissolves. Add Rhine wine and chill for 4 hours. Just before serving, add champagne. Ladle into punch cups, adding some fruit to each. Ice should not be necessary as it will dilute wine, but if punch is to stand for a while during serving, add a large block of ice before adding champagne. Makes 24 punch cups. Red wine usually requires $\frac{1}{2}$ cup more sugar than white wine.

KALTE ENTE

"Cold Duck" is a German punch that relies on the *spritz*, or tingling quality, of Moselle wine for its special character. Its curious name refers to the appearance of the punch bowl, decked with a spiraling lemon peel artfully arranged to look like the head and body of a duck.

2 tablespoons lemon juice
4 tablespoons sugar
1 large lemon

2 bottles Moselle wine, well chilled
1 bottle dry champagne, well chilled

Combine lemon juice and sugar in a large glass punch bowl and stir until sugar dissolves. To make the "duck" cut the rind partially off the lemon in a long spiral "neck," starting with 1 slice about 1-inch down from the top to form a cap or "head." Place the cap over the side of the bowl and the whole lemon in the bottom, so that the spiral forms a connecting "neck." Pour Moselle wine into bowl and chill for 30 to 40 minutes or until serving time. Just before serving, pour in chilled champagne. Place 1 ice cube in each punch cup and add punch. Makes 24 punch cups.

CRIMEAN CUP A LA MARMORA

In 1855 Alexis Soyer took his pots and pans to the Crimean battle front, where, according to Florence Nightingale, he cooked "large quantities of food in the most nutritious manner for great numbers of men." In between military engagements, the irrepressible inventor treated the officers to drinks, like the one below, utilizing the local *champanskoe*.

Juice and grated rind of 4 lemons
$\frac{1}{3}$ cup sugar
2 quarts soda water
4 cups syrup of orgeat (bottled), or
  Sugar Syrup (page 704) flavored with

2 teaspoons almond extract
2 cups cognac
1 cup maraschino liqueur
1 cup dark rum
2 quarts champagne, iced

Mix lemon rind with sugar in a punch bowl, crushing together to impregnate sugar with lemon flavor. Pour in the strained lemon juice and the soda water. Stir to dissolve the sugar. Add the orgeat syrup and beat with a whisk. Add cognac, maraschino, and rum and let marinate. At serving time add a block of ice and pour in champagne. Makes 40 punch cups.

MAY WINE BOWL

Woodruff, a woodland herb which had imparted bouquet to Mediterranean wines since pre-Christian times, was given a host of other uses by the Germans. During the Middle Ages it not only was "good for healing all sicknesses that come from heat," but when steeped in the first of the spring wines, as below, purportedly purged the blood.

1 large bunch fresh woodruff or ½ cup
  dried woodruff
½ cup sugar

3 bottles Moselle wine, well chilled
24 strawberries or 12 unpeeled orange
  slices, halved

Wash fresh woodruff and pick off dead leaves. Marinate woodruff with sugar and *one bottle of wine* in refrigerator—1 hour for fresh woodruff, 2 hours for dried woodruff. Pour into a glass punch bowl. Add *remaining wine* just before serving. Ladle into punch cups and garnish each with fruit. Makes 24 punch cups.

VARIATION: To make a sparkling May wine bowl, substitute 1 bottle well-chilled dry champagne for 1 bottle of Moselle.

ELIZABETHAN MULLED CIDER

Apple cider came to England by way of Normandy, where it had been the chief drink since the twelfth century. How much the Elizabethans fancied it may be judged by the account in John Evelyn's *Sylva*, a 1664 book on arboriculture: "It was by the plain Industry of one Harris, (a fruiterer to King Henry the Eighth) that the Fields, and Environs of about thirty Towns, in Kent onely, were planted with Fruit, to the universal benefit and general Improvement of that County to this day." Evelyn went on to predict that "the preference for Cider, wholesome, and more natural Drinks, do quite vanquish Hopps, and banish all other Droges of that nature [for when] honest countrymen shall come to drink it . . . they will find it marvelously conducive to health; and labouring People, where it is so drank, affirm that they are more strengthen'd for hard work by Cider than by the very best beer."

12 cups apple cider
1½ teaspoons whole cloves
1½ teaspoons whole allspice

6 sticks cinnamon
1½ cups brown sugar
1 bottle Calvados or applejack

Put the cider in a large saucepan, add the spices tied in cheesecloth and the brown sugar. Bring to a boil, stirring gently to dissolve sugar. Simmer for 10 minutes to blend flavors. Add Calvados. Simmer for 1 minute; discard spices. Serve in heated mugs. Makes 18 drinks.

KVASS

Kvass, a low potency brew beloved in Old Russia, inspired England's George Thurberville to write this doggerel description in 1568.

Drink is their whole desire, the pot is all their pride;
The soberest head doth once a day stand needful of a guide.
If he to banquet bid his friends, he will not shrink
On them at dinner to bestow a dozen kinds of drink,
Such liquor as they have, and as the country gives;
But chiefly two, one called kwas, *whereby the Moujike lives,*
Small ware and water-like, but somewhat tart in taste;
The rest is mead, of honey made, wherewith their lips they baste.

10 slices dark sour pumpernickel   2 to 3 tablespoons honey or sugar
1 tablespoon malt

Crumble bread and put it in a large bowl or crock. Pour in 4 cups boiling water, add malt, cover and let steep at room temperature for 24 hours or until bubbly and fermented. Sweeten with honey and pour into a bottle. Chill. Makes 1 quart. Serve as a drink or use in sour soups such as Russian Okroshka (page 436).

MEAD

The very name Mead smacks of the legendary Saxon age when Teutonic tribes prescribed the fermented honey drink for their gods. No small part of the action in *Beowulf* took place in the mead hall, where the hero eventually hailed his dispatch of the monster Grendel with several honeyed snorts. The stimulating brew was also given throughout the Middle Ages to inordinately young couples politically spliced by their parents. To spur on these children who were not yet amorously inclined, mead was served for the first month of marriage, which came to be called the honeymoon.

2 cups honey   2 pinches each: powdered mace, cloves,
½ cup brown sugar   nutmeg, ginger, and cinnamon,
Grated rind and juice of 1 lemon   pepper, and dried rosemary
2 egg whites or 1 egg, lightly beaten   1 envelope dry yeast

Place all ingredients except yeast in a large kettle with 4 quarts water and simmer gently for 1 hour, skimming the surface as needed. Cool to lukewarm. Dissolve yeast in ¼ cup of the mixture and add to remaining brew. Pour into a sterilized crock or jars. Let age for 3 months. Strain and bottle. Serve well chilled. Makes 4 quarts.

TURKISH COFFEE

6 tablespoons finely pulverized coffee   2 tablespoons sugar

Put 1½ cups water in a saucepan and stir in coffee and sugar. Place over high heat until coffee comes to a boil. Remove from heat until water is no longer boiling. Return to heat until water comes to a boil again, then remove as before. Repeat process until coffee has come to a boil 3 times. Pour into demitasse cups and serve while still frothy. Do not stir before drinking. Makes 6 demitasse cups. Coffee may also be made as above in individual, long handled Turkish coffee pots.

CAFE DIABLE

6 cubes sugar   2 sticks cinnamon
Rind of 1 orange, cut in slices   ¾ cup cognac, warmed
Rind of 1 lemon, cut in slices   4 cups freshly brewed
15 cloves   strong coffee, hot

Combine sugar, rinds, and spices in a chafing dish or a large silver or heatproof bowl. Add *all but two tablespoons cognac.* Heat *remaining cognac* in a silver ladle or serving spoon and ignite it. Pour flaming into bowl to ignite cognac and let it burn until all sugar has melted. Add coffee, stir, and serve in demitasse cups. A teaspoonful of flaming cognac may be spooned into each cup as it is served. Makes 8 demitasse cups.

MOROCCAN MINT TEA

Moroccans take their tea with much ceremony, sugar, and a strong flavoring of mint. When guests are present the infusion is prepared before them in brass or silver vessels, often in two batches; the glasses are then filled from both pots so that the subtle flavor differences of each tea will find their complements in the other.

1½ tablespoons tea leaves (black or   10 sprigs mint
    green tea)   ½ to ⅔ cup sugar

Rinse a 1-quart silver or porcelain teapot with boiling water. Place tea in pot and pour over it ½ cup boiling water. Swish pot around and carefully pour off water (this removes bitter taste from the tea leaves). Put mint sprigs (leaves and stalks) in pot with tea and add ½ cup sugar. Fill with 4 cups boiling water and steep for 7 to 8 minutes, pushing mint down so it does not float above water level. Add sugar to taste. Makes 4 cups.

SCHOKOLADENSUPPE

Germans were at first reluctant to adopt the thick chocolate drinks which were the rage in other fashionable centers of Europe. However, they were eventually won over by reports of chocolate's restorative properties, summed up in Brillat-Savarin's prescription: "Let any man . . . who shall find the accustomed polish of his wit turned to dullness, feel damp oppression in the air and time hanging heavily, or be tortured by a fixed idea which robs him of all liberty of thought . . . let all such . . . administer to themselves . . . chocolate . . . and they will see marvels."

4 cups milk	1 teaspoon vanilla extract
Pinch of salt	2 ounces semisweet chocolate, melted
1 tablespoon sugar, or to taste	2 egg yolks

Combine milk, salt, sugar, and vanilla. Scald without boiling. Beat melted chocolate into scalded milk. Beat egg yolks with 1 tablespoon cold water. Remove chocolate milk from heat and gradually pour a small amount of it into egg yolks, beating constantly. Pour egg mixture back into remaining chocolate, beating constantly. Heat but do not boil. Makes 4 cups.

CHOCOLATL DE MOLINILLO

In old Mexico, beans of the cacao tree served as currency, and only the rich could afford to literally drink up their wealth in chocolate beverages. Most Indians bartered the seeds for merchandise of the kind recorded by one missionary: "He who wants a Mayan public woman for his lustful uses can have one for eight to ten cacao beans." The Aztec emperor, Montezuma, received some sixteen million beans annually from one city alone, more than sufficient to feast his honored guests on golden goblets of *chocolatl* beaten to a froth by a wooden *molinillo*.

4 ounces sweet baking chocolate	1 to 2 tablespoons sugar, to taste
2 ounces unsweetened chocolate	$\frac{1}{4}$ to $\frac{1}{2}$ teaspoon vanilla extract,
4 cups milk	to taste (optional)
1 large stick cinnamon	1 or 2 egg whites (optional)

Combine chocolates in top of double boiler and melt over boiling water. Meanwhile, heat milk with cinnamon stick until very hot but not scalded or boiling. Pour into chocolate with cinnamon stick and stir well to blend milk and chocolate. Add sugar and vanilla to taste. For thick foam, add 1 or 2 lightly beaten egg whites. With chocolate over simmering water, place a Mexican wooden mill (*molinillo*) or a wire whisk upright in the hot chocolate and roll handle between hands to twirl it or beat with a rotary beater until chocolate foams. Remove cinnamon stick and pour chocolate into heated cups. Makes 4 to 6 cups.

ACKNOWLEDGMENTS

In the following list of picture credits, page numbers appear in boldface type.

Audot, Louis, *La cuisinière de la campagne* . . ., 1889, **605, 621, 726**. Bettmann Archive, New York, **575, 728**. Bibliographisches Institut, pub., *Meyers Konversations-Lexikon*, 1890, **719**. Bibliothèque Nationale, Paris; Service Photographique, **637**. Cassell and Company, pub., *Cassell's Dictionary of Cookery*, 1888, **610**. Cervio, *Il trinciante* . . ., 1593, N.Y. Public Library, Rare Book Division, **556, 557**. *Le confiturier royal*, 1791, **675**. De Bry, *East Indies*, Part III, 1598, N.Y. Public Library, Rare Book Division, **479**. Descourtilz, Theodore, *Flore médicale des Antilles*, 1821–28, **599**. *Dialogues of Creatures* . . ., 1530, **462**. Doolittle, Justus, *Social Life of the Chinese*, 1865, **561**. Dubois, Urbain, *Artistic Cookery*, 1870, **459, 495, 496, 534, 537, 634, 735**. Du Maurier, George, *English Society*, 1897, N.Y. Public Library, Prints Division, **408**. F[ella], T[homas], *A Book of Diverse Devices*, 1585–1622, Folger Shakespeare Library, Washington, D.C., **650**. Ferrario, Giulio, *Il costume antico e moderno*, 1823–38, **402**. Funk and Wagnalls, pub., *Jewish Encyclopedia*, 1905, Vol. X, **394**. Garrett, Theodore F., ed., *The Encyclopaedia of Practical Cookery*, 1898, **464, 507, 508** (right), **511, 584, 619, 657, 658, 682, 694, 729**. Gerard, *The herball* . . ., 1636, N.Y. Public Library, Rare Book Division, **437, 565**. Germanisches Nationalmuseum, Nuremberg, **553**. Gouffé, Jules, *Le livre de pâtisserie*, 1873, **693, 701, 725**. Hagdahl, *Kok-Konsten*, 1896, **393, 439, 474, 490, 498, 503, 504, 523, 525, 530, 532, 569, 580, 596, 629, 638, 664, 670, 681, 684, 711, 714, 723** (right), **730, 732, 737**. Kircher, Athanasius, *China monumentis* . . ., 1667, **631**. Knox, Thomas W., *The Boy Travellers in the Far East*, 1880–1905, **513**. Marshall, A. B., *Fancy Ices*, 1894, **708**. Marshall, A.B., *Larger Cookery Book*, 1891, **546, 579,**

662. N.Y. Public Library, Prints Division, **386, 412, 421, 484, 519, 539, 667, 717, 750, 752**. Nylander, Margareta, *Kokbok för husmödrar*, 1886, **398**. *Les plantes potagères*, 1904, **427, 563, 614**. Scappi, *Dell'arte del cucinare*, 1643, N.Y. Public Library, Rare Book Division, **388, 424, 432, 542, 661**. Yates, Lucy H., *The Model Kitchen*, 1905, **611, 712**.

Grateful acknowledgment is made for permission to quote from the following works:

Apicius, *The Roman Cookery Book*, translated by Barbara Flower and Elisabeth Rosenbaum, copyright © 1958 by George G. Harrap and Company Ltd., London.

Brillat-Savarin, Anthelme, *The Physiology of Taste*, published 1960 by Dover Publications, Inc., New York.

David, Elizabeth, *Italian Food*, copyright © 1958 by Elizabeth David. Published by Alfred A. Knopf, Inc., New York.

Dumas, Alexandre, *Dictionary of Cuisine*, copyright © 1958 by Louis Colman. Published by Simon and Schuster, Inc., New York.

Hartley, Dorothy, *Food in England*, published 1962 by Macdonald & Co. Ltd., London.

The editors wish to express their deep gratitude to the institutions and individuals mentioned below for their invaluable assistance and advice.

Booknoll Farm, Hopewell, New Jersey
    Miss Elisabeth Woodburn
Corner Book Shop, New York
    Miss Eleanor Lowenstein
La Fonda del Sol, New York
    Mr. and Mrs. Luidj Hassan, Otis, Massachusetts

INDEX

758